*A Reader in the Methodology
of Social Research*

The Language of

SOCIAL RESEARCH

Concepts and Indices

Multivariate Analysis

The Analysis of Change Through Time

Formal Aspects of Research on Human Groups

The Empirical Analysis of Action

General Problems in the Philosophy of Social Science

Edited by PAUL F. LAZARSFELD
and MORRIS ROSENBERG

THE LANGUAGE OF SOCIAL RESEARCH

THE LANGUAGE

OF

SOCIAL RESEARCH

A READER IN THE METHODOLOGY

OF SOCIAL RESEARCH

EDITED BY *Paul F. Lazarsfeld* COLUMBIA UNIVERSITY

AND *Morris Rosenberg* CORNELL UNIVERSITY

THE FREE PRESS, *New York*
COLLIER-MACMILLAN LIMITED, *London*

For information, address:

THE FREE PRESS
A DIVISION OF THE MACMILLAN COMPANY
60 Fifth Avenue, New York, N.Y. 10011

Collier-Macmillan Canada, Ltd., Toronto, Ontario

DESIGNED BY SIDNEY SOLOMON

FIRST FREE PRESS PAPERBACK EDITION 1965

To Charles Y. Glock and his "Young Turks"

at Columbia University's Bureau of Applied Social Research

Socrates. Shall I propose that we look for examples of art and want of art, according to our notion of them, in the speech of Lysias which you have in your hand, and in my own speech?

Phaedrus. Nothing could be better; and indeed I think that our previous argument has been too abstract and wanting in illustration.

(Plato. *Phaedrus*)

Contents—An Overview

Contents

SECTION II — MULTIVARIATE ANALYSIS

SECTION III — THE ANALYSIS OF CHANGE THROUGH TIME

SECTION IV —

FORMAL ASPECTS OF RESEARCH ON HUMAN GROUPS

SECTION V — THE EMPIRICAL ANALYSIS OF ACTION

General Introduction

THERE IS a well-known story about the centipede who lost his ability to walk when he was asked in which order he moved his feet. But other details of the story are buried in conspiratorial silence. First of all, there is no mention of the fact that the inquiry came from a methodologist who wanted to improve the walking efficiency of the centipede community. Then, little attention is paid to the other centipedes who participated in the investigation. Not all of them reacted with such disastrous effects. Some were able to give rather reasonable answers; from these the investigator worked diligently to arrive at general principles of walking behavior.

When the methodologist finally published his findings, there was a general outcry that he had only reported facts which everyone already knew. Nevertheless, by formulating this knowledge clearly, and by adding hitherto unobserved facts at various points, the average centipede in the community was eventually able to walk better. After a generation or so, this knowledge was incorporated into textbooks, and so filtered down to students on a lower level of scholarship. In retrospect this was the outstanding result. Of course, the great centipede ballet dancer and other creative walking artists continued to depend on hereditary endowments, and could not be produced by the school system. But the general level of walking, characteristic of the centipede in the street, was improved. In this way, individuals endowed with great personal gifts started out at a higher level, and achieved creative performances unparalleled in the past.

Fables of this kind are often told when there does not seem to be any satisfactory way of providing a precise statement of what we have in mind. The burden of definition is shifted to the reader. He is invited to draw the implications from the fable, and to form from them his own picture of whatever is being described. It is indeed tempting to rest the definition of a methodologist upon something like this centipede story. Just as it would be difficult to elaborate a definition of an historian, so it is difficult to catalogue the interests of a methodologist or to specify his functions in any detail. But the present book is a Reader on methodology in the social sciences. It is therefore incumbent on us, as the editors, to make a serious attempt to circumscribe what is meant by methodology and to consider what role it does or should play in the development of modern social research. We can facilitate our task somewhat by first recalling closely related efforts which are usually subsumed under the heading of "philosophy of science."

EXPLICATION AND CRITIQUE

As a result of modern positivism, interest in clarifying the meaning of concepts and statements has become quite general. A recent monograph by Hempel has been welcomed for its contributions to such clarification.* He indicates what role *explication* plays in modern logic. It does not develop strict rules of thinking. Rather, it tries to narrow the gap between everyday language and scientific language, without ever claiming that this gap can be bridged completely.

Explication aims at reducing the limitations, ambiguities, and inconsistencies of ordinary usage of language by propounding a reinterpretation intended *to enhance the clarity and precision of their meanings* as well as their ability to function in the processes and theories with explanatory and predictive force.†

When we transfer terms like "personality" or "law" or "cause" from everyday language into scientific usage, we must always make decisions for which we ourselves take the responsibility. We give up certain connotations which these terms have in order to make the remainder more precise and more easily amenable to verification and proof. In this sense, as Hempel points out, an explication cannot be qualified simply as true or false; but it may be judged as more or less adequate according to the extent to which it attains its objectives.

Social scientists who are interested in methodology can easily find occasion for such explication. It is instructive to examine the work of a classical writer, say, one in the field of public opinion research, and to see how his statements might be translated into the language of modern research procedures. It will be found, on the one hand, that such writings contain a great richness of ideas which could be profitably infused into current empirical work; on the other hand, it will be found that such a writer tolerates great ambiguity of expression. By proper explication, we can bring out the more precise meanings which might be imputed to him; and we would be especially interested to see which of his statements permit verification. The task of such explication is not to criticize the work, but rather to bridge a gap, in this case between an older humanistic tradition and a newer one which is more empirically oriented.

As a matter of fact, the need for such explication is particularly urgent in the social sciences. When the natural scientist makes a discovery, it usually turns out to be so different from everyday experiences that the very nature of the phenomenon forces him to develop precise and sharp terminology; the extreme example of this, of course, is mathematics. But in speaking about human affairs we are accustomed to common sense, everyday language, and we cannot avoid transferring these colloquialisms to the classroom and to the debating halls where we discuss social matters. Everyday language is notoriously vague, however, and therefore clarification and purification of discourse are very important for the social scientist. We must make deliberate efforts toward semantic analysis.

Another and related line of intellectual activity is that which has been called the *"critique of theory."* The word critique has been taken over

---

* Carl Hempel, *Fundamentals of Concept Formation in Empirical Science* (Chicago: University of Chicago Press, 1952). International Encyclopedia of Unified Science, Vol. 11, No. 7.
† *Ibid.*, p. 12.

from German philosophy, and can be easily misunderstood. When Kant wrote his *Critique of Pure Reason,* he obviously did not mean to be critical of rational thinking; by "critique" he meant an analysis of the conditions under which such thinking is possible. The same meaning is found also in the field of literary and artistic criticism; here, too, the idea is not that the critic necessarily disapproves of a piece of art, but that he analyzes its structure. In the same way, criticism of theoretical systems implies only that their foundations and tacit assumptions are clearly brought to light.

The main American representative of critical analysis is Bridgman, and a short essay of his provides what is perhaps the best introduction to critiques of this kind.* In his introductory statement, Bridgman puts the task quite clearly:

The attempt to understand why it is that certain types of theory work and others do not is *the concern of the physicist as critic, as contrasted with the physicist as theorist.* The material for the physicist as critic is the body of physical theory, just as the material of the physicist as theorist is the body of empirical knowledge.

The distinction between "theory" and "critique" is important. The critic deals with empirical material—but once removed. By bringing out clearly what the theorist (or analyst) does with his primary data he contributes in his way to the progress of research. In the introduction and conclusion of his essay, Bridgman brings to the American reader an understanding of the general intellectual influences which emanated, at the turn of the century, from writers like Poincaré in France and Mach in Germany. If one were to write the intellectual history of the generation of European students who grew up during the first decades of the twentieth century, one would probably rank this kind of critique, along with psychoanalysis and Marxism, as the main intellectual influences which shaped the climate of thinking in the period.

It is interesting that Bridgman places great emphasis on the educational value of such critiques. He points out that the difficulty of assimilating the creative ideas of others is one which is greatly underrated in modern education. And he feels that if more stress were put on the development of critical faculties, the creativeness and inventiveness of the young natural scientist would be considerably enhanced.

In light of all this it was very tempting for the editors of this Reader to feature it as a contribution to the philosophy of the social sciences. But a more modest terminology seemed more appropriate to the present state of the social sciences. They have a long past but a very recent history only. Yesterday's concepts are forgotten for the sake of today's notion. Who remembers Tarde's laws of imitation when he writes about reference groups? Who wonders in what respect they are different answers to the same concern, or whether they tell the same story in different words? And where is there real continuity in the formulation of theories? Has Comte's hope to understand the development of society anything to do with Parsons' efforts to analyze social systems? The danger is that we shall end up with a few logical commonplaces if we try to bring out what is common

---

* *The Nature of Physical Theory* (Princeton: Princeton University Press, 1936), p. 2.

to the various ways in which scholars, say in the last century, have tried to make a science out of the more general and much older attempts to understand human society.

The term methodology seemed more appropriate. It implies that concrete studies are being scrutinized as to the procedures they use, the underlying assumptions they make, the modes of explanation they consider as satisfactory. Methodological analysis in this sense provides the elements from which a future philosophy of the social sciences may be built. If our linguistic feeling is adequate, the term should convey a sense of tentativeness; the methodologist codifies ongoing research practices to bring out what is consistent about them and deserves to be taken into account the next time. Methodology and the related activities of explication and critical analysis have developed as a bent of mind rather than as a system of organized principles and procedures. The methodologist is a scholar who is above all *analytical* in his approach to his subject matter. He tells other scholars what they have done, or might do, rather than what they should do. He tells them what order of finding has emerged from their research, not what kind of result is or is not preferable.

This kind of analytical interest requires self-awareness, on the one hand, and tolerance, on the other. The methodologist knows that the same goal can be reached by alternative roads, and he realizes that instruments should be adapted to their function, and not be uselessly sharp. Thus, a reminder is needed on the ways in which methodology can *not* be defined. For example, it is probably less rigorous and more general than formal logic; on the other hand, it has less substantive content and is more formal than what has been called the psychology or sociology of knowledge. Similarly, the methodologist is not a technician; he does not tell research workers *how* to proceed, what steps to follow in the actual conduct of an investigation. And neither is it his task to indicate what problems should be selected for study. But once the topic for investigation has been chosen, he might suggest the procedures which, in the light of the stated objectives, seem most appropriate.

Enough of generalities. Further understanding will best be served by describing how and why the material in this Reader has been selected.

THE ORGANIZATION OF THIS READER

Originally, we had intended to divide the Reader into two sections of roughly equal length. One of these sections, it was planned, would contain methodological papers concerned with specific aspects of social research. The second section would then offer examples of superior work which could be used to illustrate the general principles developed in the first part. It turned out, however, that the number of studies making use of sophisticated research practices is far greater than the number of papers which articulate or codify or discuss the procedures themselves. As a result, the largest part of the Reader is given over to examples of research. For the teacher who has himself reflected on the nature of methodology, this should be welcome; we provide him with specimens of good work with which he can illustrate his own ideas. But for the teacher who would like to find an elaborate discussion of what methodology involves, our Reader has an unavoidable shortcoming; he will be forced to develop for himself the systematic discussions of which the concrete research examples are illustrative.

We have tried to overcome this shortcoming somewhat in brief introductions to each of the specific sections. In these we have tried to point out the most useful aspects of each study, and especially those which deserve to be generalized. But, in spite of these introductions, our Reader cannot take the place of a systematic presentation; it can only emphasize the need for it and is at best a first step.

Before considering how our selections were organized, it is important to explain what was eliminated from the Reader and what was finally included in it. The eliminations were of three major kinds. First of all, we eliminated those topics for which there is already a standardized literature. Included in this category are problems of sampling, problems of questionnaire construction, and experimental techniques. It is interesting to note that all of these comprise techniques of data collection. It might almost be said that *the Reader emphasizes the analysis of material which has been properly collected.* At the other extreme, we also excluded topics of research whose methodological implications have not yet been codified adequately at all. Thus, our Reader does not contain examples of the following kinds of research: sociological studies of formal organizations, political institutions, etc.; the rationale of participant-observation in community studies; anthropological field work; or the tradition of mass observation. Occasionally, we found very enlightening articles on these topics; and we also knew of excellent studies in these fields. But in none of these cases could we find systematic analyses of the methodological problems involved. The third principle of elimination applied to works which required mathematical knowledge beyond that which the average social scientist is likely to have. Thus, our Reader does not contain any examples from modern work on scaling and measurement, or from recent efforts to develop specific mathematical models for social behavior.

It is quite possible that we were too selective at times. As a matter of fact, it would be a good thing if the publication of this Reader were to bring opposition from scholars who feel either that they have adequately codified the kind of procedures which we excluded, or that we have been provincial and that it is possible to develop a good organization of additional studies along different lines than those about which we have felt confident. This would represent an excellent example of continuity in methodological work, to which we hope the present Reader will contribute. Then, a future edition of this volume, or the work of another colleague, will make up for the deficiencies of our own experiences or reading. The positive principles which guided our selection and organization of materials for this Reader are as follows:

We started with basic questions of *how units and variables are formed in the social sciences.* Such problems range from simple matters of classification to subtle questions of quantification and measurement. As mentioned above, we have explicitly excluded mathematical discussions from the present Reader; consequently, this first substantive section cannot consider the full range of problems in concept formation. But the examples which we have included do raise the following sorts of questions: Are there any general principles of classification, and, if so, can these be stated with precision? How does one go about establishing categories for materials collected by the social researcher? What is meant by "multi-dimensional classification," and how does the concept of "property space" relate to such classification? What are some of the major principles in index formation, and what is the mutual relationship between indices and concepts? What is meant by the "interchangeability of indices," and what implications does this have for social research? The introduction to this section, like that to all others, will offer a more detailed description of how the individual items were selected and how they were organized (Section I).

Once the matter of these basic units or variables has been dealt with, the next major problem is obviously *the interrelationship of such variables in a coherent analysis*. This problem might have been formulated in any of a variety of ways. We might have focused our attention on techniques of survey analysis, for it is in modern survey work that problems of dealing simultaneously with many variables have become especially apparent. But it was decided that a limited focus of this kind might be misleading. There are other modes of social research, notably those which use published statistical materials for the investigation of some specific topic, which also face the task of organizing vast amounts of data into understandable intellectual structures and of isolating probable causal relationships in these data. Thus, the studies which we selected are drawn from a number of different fields. They exemplify ways of analyzing economic data and population statistics, as well as survey materials. But common to all of these examples is the need to manipulate several variables at the same time in order to arrive at inferences regarding social phenomena. Once more we have explicitly avoided any discussion of specific statistical techniques, such as those of multiple correlation, that might be used in this kind of analysis. Instead, we have confined ourselves to the basic methodological problems, indicating the kinds of assumptions which are made when large masses of data are used in order to develop generalizations about human behavior (Section II).

Then the *time dimension* has been added. The dynamics of social change is so broad a topic that a special Reader could be devoted to it alone. We have selected studies which show the problem in its most elementary form, but which at the same time permit us to carve out its methodological elements. Perhaps the oldest empirical studies of social change are those which examine the interrelationship between two variables, let us say, the economic system and the political ideology of a society, at different periods. More recently, the same type of problem has been studied over shorter intervals of time, making use of data specifically collected for this purpose. These so-called "panel studies," that is, successive observations of the same individuals, make it possible to relate the behavior or attitudes of a person at one time to his behavior or attitudes some weeks or months later. A third kind of study included in this section of the Reader are those which have been labelled "prediction studies." The objectives of these investigations is generally to determine which characteristics permit an accurate prediction of subsequent behavior, performance, or attitude (Section III).

The formation of variables, the study of their interrelation, and the analysis of their change through time form the backbone of all social research. However, the kind of variables that we treat is obviously also a relevant consideration. And here there enters an arbitrary element. Thus, it is meaningful to differentiate between variables which refer to behavior and others which refer to attitudes; it also makes good sense to distinguish between variables which describe the state of an individual or a social system at a particular moment of time, and those which describe the same states over longer periods of time. But neither of these distinctions were considered essential in the preparation of this volume. The one which seems most important for a Reader in the social sciences is that which differentiates between variables pertaining to an individual and other *variables which refer to a collective,* viz., a group, or organization, or institution. Therefore, a section is dedicated to what we call the "formal analysis of group behavior." This phrase has all the ambiguities found in a newly developed field. We have concentrated primarily on those variables and those research procedures in which groups of people form the unit of analysis. The examples selected for inclusion here deal, for instance, with the different dimensions by which groups may be described, with the correlations among different characteristics of a group, and with various patterns of relationship within a group. This particular focus has meant a lack of attention to organizational and institutional analysis; but as we mentioned in an earlier connection, the methodological problems of such studies have not yet been systematically codified anyhow (Section IV).

There is a danger that "methodology" may be identified with "quantification." This would be a blatant misunderstanding. The historian, the clinical psychologist, the linguist, need their own codification of procedures. The editors of this Reader wished to include one area which covered elements of the kind usually called qualitative; at the same time they did not want to move too far into uncharted seas. They finally decided upon a group of investigations concerned with the *empirical study of actions,* in the sense of choice among a number of alternatives in situations where a decision is required. There exist a considerable number of investigations as to why people vote, buy, migrate, etc. They all require that the investigator make causal imputations on the basis of reports he elicits from the actors themselves. The methodology of these studies is controversial. Some authors claim that it is altogether impossible to find out why people act the way they do. Others collect cases and report them without much critical self-awareness. This therefore seemed a good topic on which to show the contributions which methodology can make in the organization of research material, which is of obvious practical importance but which, so far, has been left mainly to the discretion of common sense (Section V).

The five sections just sketched conclude the analysis of specific research operations selected for this Reader. Still it seemed desirable to include a section on *general methodology.* There certainly exists the beginning of a philosophy of the social sciences. The editors were decided to stay away from general discussion of whether there is a difference between natural and social science, whether introspection is a legitimate source of data, whether society precedes the individual, and similar general topics. But they did not want to keep away from this Reader the fruit of recent progress in logical analysis as it does or might apply to social inquiry. Attention was focused on four topics of this kind: the specification of problems, the clarification of meaning, the logical structure of larger chains of propositions, and the nature of evidence (Section VI).

Two problems of organization which confronted the editors of this Reader deserve mention. In classifying and placing the specific items selected for inclusion in this volume, it was almost inevitable that we encountered an overlapping between the different sections. It turned out that this overlap was of two essentially different kinds. The simpler kind is that brought about by the richness of an article or study. It sometimes happens that a single paper deals with a variety of methodological problems, and, if it is a particularly good paper, it can serve to exemplify two or more methodological principles. In the introductions to the different sections, where each of the papers is discussed briefly, we shall point out where such productive overlapping is most likely to appear. A more complicated problem is that, in certain respects, the sections themselves are overlapping. It is obvious, for example, that certain general principles of index formation apply to individuals as well as to groups. Therefore, some problems which are at present treated separately in Section I and in Section IV might, under another mode of organization, have been considered together. Similarly, all problems involving a time dimension are reserved for Section III; but many of them consist really of multivariate analysis which was considered generally in Section II. It is probably impossible to avoid such inconsistencies, and no further effort will be made to excuse them. If the person who uses our Reader is aware of the organization of the main sections, he will not have great difficulty tracing a particular idea through its different phases.

Our second problem centered around the dilemma of extension vs. intensity. There are two ways of looking at a collection of papers such as the present one. On the one hand, it can be viewed as a sampling of the best articles in the field; if this view is adopted, the volume might be entitled an anthology, comparable to anthologies of best short stories, of best poems, or of best plays. But the same kind of collection can also be viewed as an opportunity to bring together items which articulate and illustrate a particular intellectual position. Then different criteria of selection are employed. Articles are included, not only because they are considered to represent a high standard of work, but also because they are relevant to or consistent with a specific set of concerns and interests. It is this latter position which we have adopted. *The items included in the present Reader were chosen because we felt that they were particularly good examples of a point of view which we, the editors, wanted to express and exemplify.* The same kind of decision was made with regard to the number of methodological problems to be covered in the Reader. It was our feeling that the value to be gained by comparing several papers on the same topic—examining the different aspects emphasized, the different methods of investigation employed, and the different kinds of assumptions made—justified focusing on a limited number of problems and illustrating each of these with a set of related articles. The alternative possibility, that of covering a broad range of problems, but in less detail, would make it difficult, we felt, to articulate whatever principles of organization and systematization we have been able to achieve.

Our general scheme is the outgrowth of more than a decade of methodological work carried on at Columbia University. It is not surprising, therefore, that the source for a considerable number of selections are colleagues and junior associates of the senior editor. As a matter of fact, at a number of points in this Reader, it was necessary to commission the writing of special papers because no other selections were available to fill an indispensable place in the whole structure. Inversely, the Reader, as a whole, can be considered a programmatic statement of a working team supported by Rockefeller and Ford Foundation funds. It is the plan of the *Columbia Project for Advanced Training in Social Research* to provide more detailed methodological documentations in the areas covered by the present volume, and to slowly cover additional areas until something like a series on principles of social research is available.

It now remains to discuss in some detail the contribution which such methodological work is likely to make to the advancement of the social sciences.

THE ROLE OF METHODOLOGY IN DEVELOPMENT OF THE SOCIAL SCIENCES

One function of methodology is to provide formal training for young social scientists which will enable them to do better research. Every field of intellectual activity has its own ways of developing disciplined thinking among its young scholars. The natural scientist gets this training by studying mathematics and by learning the precise operations implied in experimentation. The humanist obtains formal training through intensive study of classical languages. But the kinds of formal training appropriate for the natural scientist, on the one hand, and for the humanist, on the other, are not especially suited to the needs of the modern social scientist. While mathematical models and experimental studies are coming to play an increasingly important role in the investigation of human behavior, they are not likely to become dominant modes of inquiry in the near future. And, although the social scientist might benefit from the study of Latin and Greek, his interest in contemporary materials largely limits the usefulness of these classical languages. He must therefore develop discipline of thinking in some other way. The kind of analytics called for in methodological studies *provide the required formal training*.

Methodology also increases the social scientist's ability *to cope with new and unfamiliar developments in his field*. Perhaps the best way of clarifying this idea is to elaborate the difference between technology and methodology mentioned in an earlier connection. The individual who learns how to develop certain indices or tests, or who becomes adept in the application of particular statistical techniques, masters the skills only which are available at the moment. When, in the future, new skills are proposed, he can probably learn them as well. However, will he be able to decide which of these skills are useful and which are not? Will he understand the assumptions underlying various techniques? Will he have criteria by which to appraise whether or not certain procedures are appropriate to certain problems? Obviously, the ability to make judgments of this kind is not developed merely by learning the techniques of the present or of the past. What is needed is a training which will enable the student to meet the research situations, ten or twenty years hence, which cannot possibly be foreseen now. A well-trained methodologist will be able, many years after the completion of his formal education, to confront new developments in his science. He will be equipped to judge their merits, to relate them to past trends, and to make a reasoned choice as to what he wants to integrate into his own thinking, thus furthering the self-education which every responsible scholar continues most of his life.

A third way in which methodology can aid in the advancement of the social sciences is through its *contributions to interdisciplinary work*. In recent years, many scholars have expressed the hope that developments in the different social sciences could be more closely coordinated; but where such efforts at integration have been made, they have often resulted in disappointment. There are certainly many reasons to account for this. But one source is undoubtedly the fact that various disciplines put different emphases on where they place thorough scholarship and where they are satisfied with a procedural dilettantism.

—Economists who study business cycles have developed sophisticated ways of analyzing social processes; sociologists, on the other hand, often talk loosely— and with excessive complexity—about similar problems in their own field.

—Sociologists and social psychologists have become skilled in the art of questionnaire construction; economists, when they make use of such schedules, do so with little understanding of well-tested principles.

—Historians use quotations from newspapers and other documents haphazardly, without any apparent awareness of modern techniques of content analysis.

—Anthropologists, in accepting vague information and incorporating it into their work, do not seem to recognize how far historians have advanced techniques for checking and appraising evidence.

—For the past 50 years economists have given careful attention to the logic of index formation; sociometrists often put together any index which happens to come to their minds.

Such discrepancies mean that the results obtained by the several social sciences are often lacking in comparability. This, in turn, obviously interferes with interdisciplinary endeavors. Methodological analysis can help to overcome these barriers. Careful study of the basic assumptions underlying particular procedures may reveal their applicability to a broad range of problems, and may cut across the traditional lines separating different disciplines. Of course, there is no guarantee that what the economist means by the measurement of utility and what the sociologist and social psychologist mean by attitude measurement will turn out to be fundamentally similar. But whatever points of convergence exist certainly cannot be uncovered until the two areas are minutely and intensively compared. Equally detailed analysis of the way in which different disciplines formulate their problems—the explanatory models which they set up—should also give impetus to productive interdisciplinary work. By showing that two or more branches of the social sciences are concerned with the same kinds of problems however different the terminology they may use, such analysis may lead to important integrations of existing knowledge, and to significant prescriptions for future interdisciplinary efforts.

Our fourth point is derivative from the preceding ones. Methodology can make a direct contribution to the advancement of our knowledge of human affairs, inasmuch as it provides organizing *principles by which such knowledge can be integrated and codified.* Which parts of an existing body of data are worthwhile; where does there seem to be overlapping of knowledge; what is the most fruitful line of further development? These are questions whose answers are facilitated by the kinds of methodological analysis described earlier. In this connection we might consider what has sometimes appeared to be a controversy over the proper role of methodology. It is an undisputed historical fact that methodological self-criticism has served a very important function at crucial phases in the development of the natural sciences. The only question is at what point in the history of a science such methodological analysis becomes most significant. In the physical sciences it came at a rather late stage. It was only after many centuries of observation and experiment that the resulting knowledge could be systematically organized. The natural sciences thus had a long past of discovery before methodological work was introduced and was recognized as important.

If he reasons by analogy only, one might say that methodological analysis in the social sciences should wait until systematic study of human behavior has achieved a longer history. Actually, however, the position of the social sciences is quite different. Although rigorous investigation of human affairs, comparable to precise study of natural phenomena, is only quite recent, we have been accumulating knowledge about social behavior for many centuries. Interest in, and speculations about, the nature of social life have as long a history as does such life itself. Thus, before we even begin the systematic study of human behavior, we have an almost limitless store of proverbial wisdom, of introspective accounts, and of general observations about the way in which human beings behave in their societies. Indeed, this store is so vast that it is especially important to sift out the true from the untrue, and to study the conditions under which particular common sense generalizations hold. At one time or another, almost every social scientist has played a game by arraying against each other the contradictory statements about social behavior which can be found in our fund of proverbial knowledge.* It is at this point that methodology becomes useful. We must sort out this knowledge and organize it in some manageable form; we must reformulate common sense statements so that they can be subjected to empirical test; we must locate the gaps so that further investigations are oriented in useful directions. In other words, the embarrassment of riches with which modern social sciences start forces them to develop organizing principles at an early stage.

Emphasis on the roles which methodology can play should not lead us to overestimate its importance or to underestimate the importance of concrete substantive work. It is sometimes said that scholars who are creative do research, while those who are uncreative only talk about it. In the last analysis, it is the creative, substantive worker who really advances a science; certainly we do not want to imply otherwise. Our position is

---

* See, for example, Robert S. Lynd, *Knowledge for What?* (Princeton: Princeton University Press, 1939), pp. 60-62, and H. A. Simon, "Some Further Requirements of Bureaucratic Theory" in *Reader in Bureaucracy*, R. K. Merton, A. P. Gray, B. Hockey, and H. C. Selvin, eds. (Glencoe, Ill.: The Free Press, 1952), pp. 51-58.

rather a sociological one. Once the creative scholar has matured and has begun his work, there is perhaps very little which he can gain from methodological reflection. At this point it is probably best to leave him to his own devices. But during the period of his training, during the time when he tries to acquire the knowledge and modes of thinking which he might use later—during this formative period a thorough grounding in methodology will be valuable. An analogy might serve to make this point clearer. It is sometimes hard to understand how it happens that sports records, like those of the Olympic Games, are continually bettered—runners run faster miles, pole vaulters clear greater heights, and so on. It is unlikely that, over the last fifty years, the capacities of *homo athleticus* have improved in any Darwinian sense. But training techniques, styles of running, and athletic equipment have steadily been refined. Great athletic stars are born; but good coaches can so raise the level of the average participant that when a star appears he starts from a higher level than did the star of a generation ago. He therefore is able to reach greater peaks of achievement, even though his individual capacities need not be superior to those of his predecessors. In the same sense, methodology, self-awareness of the field, provides a better starting background for the individual creative scholar.

Concepts and Indices

Introduction

No SCIENCE deals with its objects of study in their full concreteness. It selects certain of their properties and attempts to establish relations among them. The finding of such laws is the ultimate goal of all scientific inquiries. But in the social sciences the singling out of relevant properties is in itself a major problem. No standard terminology has yet been developed for this task. The properties are sometimes called aspects or attributes, and often the term "variable" is borrowed from mathematics as the most general category. The attribution of properties is interchangeably called description, classification, or measurement, using this last term in a very broad sense. The present section centers around this theme: how do we in social research establish devices by which we characterize the objects of empirical social investigations? The best way of carving out this problem area is to follow the typical process by which social research establishes its "variables" when we deal with complex objects. Using once more rather arbitrary language, the main purpose of this section is to exemplify how concepts are translated into empirical indices.

The first step seems to be the creation of a rather vague image or construct that results from the author's immersion in all the detail of a theoretical problem. The creative act may begin with the perception of many disparate phenomena as having some underlying characteristic in common. Or the author may have observed certain regularities and is trying to account for them. In any case, the concept, when first created, is some vaguely conceived entity that makes the observed relations meaningful. Next comes a stage in which the concept is specified by elaborate discussion of the phenomena out of which it emerged. We develop "aspects," "components," "dimensions," or similar specifications. They are sometimes derived logically from the overall concept, or one aspect is deduced from another, or empirically observed correlations between them are reported. The concept is shown to consist of a complex combination of phenomena, rather than a simple and directly observable item. In order to incorporate the concept into a research design, observable indicators of it must be selected. At least two questions concerning this process have to be raised:

(a) How does one "think up" a number of indicators to be used in empirical research?

(b) Once a battery of indicators has been drawn up, how does one select those that will be used as measures of the concept in contrast to the indicators that are used in validating, correlating, or making predictions from the concept? In other words, which indicators are considered "part of" the concept, and which are considered independent of or external to it?

The last phase in the process is the construction of an index to summarize the observations made on the indicators.

The central tool developed for handling and clarifying index problems is that of property space. This means that we think of each indicator as a dimension in geometrical space. Each "element" is a point in this space. An index then is a rule according to which various points will be considered equivalent. If the index is given by a formula, the latter describes surfaces or lines of equivalent elements. If the indicators are all dichotomous attributes, then certain typological problems can be formalized usefully by translating them into the geometrical language of attribute spaces. This will be discussed in greater detail later.

Our main selections attempt to follow this line of procedure.

A. *Conceptualization and empirical research.* Selection (1) is a typical example of the first analytical phase of the whole process. Landecker takes the notion of "integration" and shows that the term really covers a variety of meanings, which must be distinguished before the concept can be translated into empirical research procedures. This speculative phase of the task does not come up only when we deal with rather complex concepts. Even such a simple notion as, for example, whether a person is unemployed requires a considerable amount of pre-analysis before an unemployment census can be taken. In Selection (2) Jaffe and Stewart show that various concepts of unemployment lead to different census-taking devices and finally to different numerical results.

B. *Selection of appropriate indicators.* The choice of appropriate indicators is very much a matter of ingenuity, to be exercised anew in every empirical study. In Selection (3) Rice reports how he was able to develop an indicator of radicalism when he could not collect first-hand information but was restricted to the use of available voting statistics. Kendall, in Selection (4) has culled from *The American Soldier* all the examples in which the authors had to invent devices by means of which they tapped attitudes, although the soldiers themselves were hardly aware of these attitudes or might not have revealed them if they had been confronted with a direct question. To avoid misunderstanding it should be stressed that in this section we use the word "indicator" when we refer to one specific observation, we use the word "index" when we are confronted with a combination of several indicators into one measurement. In the literature the word index is sometimes used in the way just mentioned and sometimes it is synonymous with indicator. We have not changed the terminology of the original authors, because once the distinction is kept in mind the special use of words is of no importance.

C. *The notion of property space.* The notion of property space is quite basic in the theory of index formation. The basic idea is quite simple and is an extension of the Cartesian coordinate system known to all high school students from plane analytic geometry. The only difference is that on a given dimension we do not need to have quantitative measurements. Rank orders and even arbitrary classifications can locate a person on each axis and, consequently, in the property space as a whole. In Selection (5), Barton shows how well this notion organizes quite a number of empirical research operations. We may begin with a property space and "reduce" it to fewer dimensions. In this way we may either arrive at typologies or end up with a single dimension. In the latter situation, we might obtain a new way of ordering cases. For example, if we divide people according to their vote intentions and their attitudes on various political issues, we might then classify them in terms of their degree of party orthodoxy, irrespective of which party and which issues were involved. Conversely, we might start with a typology which some author proposes, and perform a "substruction," by which is meant the developing of an attribute space which permits us to test the logical consistency of a typology. Most of all, the algebra of index formation turns out to be greatly clarified by thinking of it as a partition of a property space into "equivalent sub-spaces."

While it is important all through this Reader to keep in mind the abstract notion of a property space, it is equally useful to realize how it corresponds to well-known research procedures. An IBM card is, after all, nothing else than such a space, and locating a point in it is equivalent to the multi-dimensional classification of a given set of materials. Selection (6) has the purpose of showing the idea of multi-dimensional classification in a somewhat unusual context. Jacob takes atrocity stories, which were used in war propaganda, and shows how they can be classified in a variety of dimensions. The degree of atrocity can vary according to the object against which it is committed, according to the distance between object and perpetrator, and so forth. Obviously, this kind of multi-dimensional classification is closely related to the idea of conceptual analysis. The paper by Angell [Selection (7)] is particularly useful as material for student exercises. It is possible to trace what considerations lead the author to use certain dimensions and to reject others. The formulas he develops show what points in his property space he considers as equivalent for the purpose at hand.

D. *Comparison and evaluation of indices.* Very often an analyst will have to make a choice between a variety of indicators. The examples in this group show various ways in which he can proceed. In Selection (8) Stouffer compares two ways in which neurotic dispositions of soldiers can be measured. The total distribution of scores makes much more sense with one of two measures. Instead of comparing aggregate distributions, we might want to compare how various variables locate each respondent separately. This is done in Selection (9), in which Lundberg and Friedman compare three indices of socio-economic status. In Selection (10), Horwitz and Smith carry the procedure one step further. They not only compare the indices with each other; they relate each variable to an outside criterion and thus compare the indices according to the results they lead to in an empirical investigation. In Selection (11) the problem is not to compare different variables, but to see what happens if the same material is combined in a variety of ways. Hovland and his associates deal here with the measurement of "improvement," which is a vexing one in many empirical studies.

E. *Problems of classification.* Our final three selections do not quite fit into the main theme of this section, but they are closely related to it and are of great practical importance in social research. Sometimes it happens that the investigator does not start with a general concept. He has before him a diffuse amount of empirical material—for example, answers to an open-ended question in a questionnaire—and he now wants to organize his material in the most useful way. While his solution is arbitrary to a certain degree, he is usually guided by some general principles, whether he knows it or not. Selection (12) explains some of the more formal considerations which should enter into the establishment of empirical classifications.

The purpose of such rules is, of course, to end up with meaningful statistical findings. Sometimes, however, the procedure is reversed and we use numerical findings as guides to classification. In Selection (13), Speier had available the answers to attitude questions as they were given by privates and noncommissioned officers. He classified the questionnaire items according to whether the answers were numerically affected by rank differences. Then he looked at the various groups of questions thus obtained and asked himself what their content had in common. An interesting combination of the two procedures is given in Selection (14) where Radermacher cross-tabulates, for students in adult education courses, the occupation of the students and the courses they are attending. A rough classification of occupations and courses permits a first orientation. But then she is guided by numerical results and focuses on those combinations of occupation and course which show special affinity. As a result Radermacher is able to combine a large number of detailed results into a revealing pattern of findings.

This section is best utilized by having students apply the main ideas to new material. As far as the analysis of concepts is concerned, any discursive writing can be taken as a starting point. For indicators one might cull special groups of studies, such as those which use a basic concept like frustration or cohesion. For the formation of indices one might take a census volume, where the tracts are described in terms of housing conditions, rental, number of unemployed, and so on; various indices of "economic conditions" can be compared in terms of the property space idea. For classification exercises, the students can be asked to answer themselves a somewhat complex question, e.g., why they are enrolled in a specific course. There is also hardly an issue of any social science journal where some article does not introduce a "measure" for a concept. The reasoning given by the authors should be traced in the light of the general principles around which this section is organized.

$$A. \left\{ \begin{array}{l} \textbf{CONCEPTUALIZATION AND} \\ \\ \textbf{EMPIRICAL RESEARCH} \end{array} \right.$$

1. TYPES OF INTEGRATION AND THEIR MEASUREMENT

by Werner S. Landecker[1]

EVER SINCE the days of Comte and Spencer, sociologists have been concerned with the integration of smaller units into social wholes. The literature has dealt with such questions as these: What constitutes the difference between a group and a mere sum total of individuals? In what sense is it one single entity? What is the nature of its unity?

From the modern empirical point of view the problem of social integration is as challenging as it was from the older, more speculative point of view. However, a change has occurred as to the kind of question asked about integration. Nowadays it seems less pertinent to ask: What *is* integration? If this question is asked at all, then it is only in preparation for the more fruitful question: How can integration be measured? And, again this latter question is not of interest in itself but merely a preliminary step, which leads to genuine problems of research such as these: Under what conditions does social integration increase? Under what conditions does it decrease? What are the consequences of a high degree of integration? What are the consequences of a low degree of integration? Sociology is in need of basic research oriented toward this kind of problem.

Early in the exploration of a type of phenomena it seems advisable to break it up into as many subtypes as one can distinguish and to use each subdivision as a variable for research. This appears to be a more fruitful procedure than to attempt immediately to generalize about the generic type as a whole. The main advantage of subclassification in an initial phase of research is that it leads to problems of relationship among subtypes which would evade the attention of the investigator if he were to deal with the broader type from the very beginning. Generalizations on the higher level of abstraction will suggest themselves as a matter of course, once regularities common to several subtypes are discovered.

We do not know enough about social integration to postulate any one set of data as the index of integration as such. Thus in this paper problems will be formulated with reference to social integration in particular respects. No general definition of social integration will be offered, but several types of integration will be stated and defined. Each type will refer to one particular respect in which some degree of integration may exist in a group. To determine relationships among the types is a problem for research.

Reprinted from the *American Journal of Sociology*, Vol. 56, 1950-51, pp. 332-340, by permission of the author and the publisher. (Copyright, 1951, by the University of Chicago.)

Research may show a correlation between some of these types sufficiently high to suggest that one can be used as an index of the other in further investigations. It may also be discovered that one particular type is basic to all others and therefore can be designated as a measure of social integration in general. Or research may lead to the construction of a composite index, with several types of integration as units. Even the types themselves must be considered as entirely provisional. They may turn out to be useful, or, on the other hand, research may show the necessity of modifying the very typology from which it proceeds.

In order to distinguish among the different ways in which a group may be integrated, it is necessary to assume the existence of different types of group elements. A typology of integration can be developed on the premise that for sociological purposes the smallest units of group life are cultural standards, on the one hand, and persons and their behavior, on the other. If one uses this premise as a criterion of types of integration, three varieties suggest themselves: integration among cultural standards, integration between cultural standards and the behavior of persons, and integration among persons.

The first of these, which we will call "cultural integration," varies along a continuum ranging from extreme consistency to a high degree of inconsistency among standards within the same culture. Integration between cultural standards and the behavior of persons will be called "normative integration," since it measures the degree to which the standards of the group constitute effective norms for the behavior of the members. It varies from an extremely high frequency of conformity to cultural standards to a high frequency of violation. The manner in which persons are integrated in relation to one another will be employed as an additional criterion in classification. There is integration among persons in the sense of an exchange of meanings, or communication; and there is integration among persons in the sense of an exchange of services, or division of labor. Integration with respect to an exchange of meanings will be called "communicative integration." It ranges from communication throughout the group to the prevalance of barriers to communication within the group. Integration with respect to an exchange of services will be called "functional integration," in that it measures the degree to which the functions exercised by the members of the group constitute mutual services. Functional integration varies from extreme interdependence to a high degree of self-sufficiency.

In place of the initial threefold distinction, four types of integration have emerged in the preceding sketchy analysis: cultural, normative, communicative, and functional integration. Each varies along a continuum of its own, ranging from one theoretical extreme to the other. Each raises its own problems of index construction, with which the remainder of the paper will be concerned.

1. Cultural Integration. The work of anthropologists like Linton and Benedict has made it apparent that cultures are configurations which vary in internal consistency or integration.[2] But, while the concept of cultural integration is familiar, it has not received a sufficiently specific and quantifiable definition for purposes of research. Linton's conception of cultural integration can probably be represented most adequately in terms of a proportion among types of culture traits which he calls "universals," "specialties," and "alternatives." His theory is that, "while the universals and specialties within any culture normally form a fairly consistent and well-integrated unit, the alternatives necessarily lack such consistency and integration."[3] Thus cultural integration can be measured by determining the proportion of alternatives in relation to universals and specialties. The lower the proportion of alternatives, the higher the degree of cultural integration.

The accuracy of Linton's assessment of two of his types, alternatives and specialties, in their significance for cultural integration is not beyond question. If "alternatives" are taken to mean traits which a culture offers to the person as a matter of choice, then one may wonder whether alternatives seriously affect the internal consistency of a culture. As long as freedom of choice exists and a clash of moral pressures is lacking, it is doubtful whether the person is faced with a real dilemma. Nor is it apparent that the function of a culture as a universe of discourse is impaired among persons faced with the same cultural alternatives, even though they do not make the same choice at one time. Therefore, it is possible to restrict the concept of cultural integration to a relationship among traits which constitute cultural standards in the sense that they require adherence.

Inconsistency among cultural standards can exist in two forms. It may occur, first, in the form of contradictory demands made by universals. For example, the same culture may demand altruistic behavior and competitive behavior, without necessarily limiting each to a particular group or situation. The more inconsistencies of this kind exist in a culture, the lower the degree of its integration. Therefore, it seems possible to measure cultural integration in terms of the frequency of inconsistency among universals. The criterion of inconsistency should not be sought in logic but in experience. Durkheim suggests that the idea of contradiction depends upon social conditions.[4] What may appear to an outsider as a logical contradiction is not necessarily felt as such by those who live under these standards. Therefore the earmark of inconsistency among standards should be an *experienced* difficulty.

A second form of inconsistency among standards exists in the area of cultural specialties, although not all standards of specialty character are relevant to cultural integration. The situations to which some of these standards refer exist only among the specialists themselves. Many standards which have evolved in an occupational category refer to situations which do not exist outside that category. For example, the medical profession has a code of ethics, and so have realtors. Obviously, professional standards for physicians and for realtors are not and cannot be the same. Nevertheless, the two sets of standards do not clash because each refers to situations which do not exist in the other profession. Therefore, differences among standards which vary from one another not only with respect to the persons who uphold them but also with respect to their situational reference do not interfere with cultural integration.

In distinction to the preceding type of standard, which might be called "specialty with specialist reference," there is another type which might be called "specialty with societal reference." The latter is the kind of standard which is shared mainly by members of a particular group or category but which establishes norms for situations which are society-wide in their scope. If several "specialties with societal reference" are at variance with one another, cultural inconsistencies exist. For example, if labor and management differ in their standards as to the proper place of labor and of management in the business enterprise, two sets of specialties are in conflict with each other. The same is true if different segments of the population disagree in their standards as to whether divorce is right or wrong, whether the government should own the big industries, or as to what is right and wrong in race relations. The larger the number of inconsistent specialties with societal reference in a culture, the lower the degree of its integration.

Thus indices of cultural integration can be developed in several ways, each apparently measuring a somewhat different phase. Following Linton, one might use the proportion of alternatives in a culture as a negative index of its integration. On the other hand, from the point of view suggested in the preceding paragraphs, an index would be constructed on the premise that the fewer the inconsistencies among universals and among specialties with societal reference among all standards in a culture, the higher the degree of integration of that culture.[5] Possibly, research might show a high correlation among these indices, since one may expect that an increase in alternatives and an increase in inconsistency among universals and specialties would occur under the same conditions.

II. Normative Integration. Cultural standards can be viewed not only in relation to one another but also in relation to the persons for whom they establish norms. Integration in relation between standards and persons is called "normative integration," and it varies with the degree to which conduct is in accord with such norms. The importance of integration in this sense has received particular attention in the work of R. C. Angell. He considers obedience to societal norms as the difference between a mere society and one that possesses elements of moral community.[6] It is symptomatic of what he assumes to be the basis of societal integration, i.e., the orientation of persons by common values.

In recent studies of American cities, Angell has devised an index of social integration as shown by conformity to social standards.[7] His index of integration is composed of two, more specific, indices—a crime index, which measures integration negatively, and a welfare effort index, which measures it positively. The crime index is made up of rates for those crimes which are most reliably reported, i.e., murder and nonnegligent homicide, burglary, and robbery. The welfare effort index is based on the assumption that social standards demand that the citizen contribute a share of his resources to the welfare of the community as a whole. The index consists of the amount raised by the Community Chest in proportion to the quota established, the number of pledgers in proportion to the number of families in the community, and the proportion of the amount raised to other family expenditures as expressed in the volume of retail sales in the community. The welfare effort index and the inverted crime index are combined into the integration index in such a manner that the crime index receives greater weight because it correlates more highly with variables which accompany community integration than does the welfare effort index.

If the accuracy of crime reporting increases, as is likely, further gains in the development of this index can be expected. The selection of reliably reported crimes for the purpose of index construction has been accomplished at a price; most crimes selected are acts of violence. Conceivably, crimes of this character are expressive of nonconformity in a relatively limited segment of the total population. If it should become possible to include offenses which involve at least some amount of white-collar criminality, such as fraud and embezzlement, a more significant measure of normative integration could be obtained. However, the need for further contributions to the measurement of normative integration is greatest with regard to social groups other than the community as such. The local community is a unit for the tabulation of crimes and of contributions to welfare chests. An index based on such data cannot be used, and is not intended, as a measure of the normative integration of groups like the family, the labor union, the service club, the church congregation, the congeniality group, or the juvenile gang. Not only are the data required for the index not available for such groups, but also in many instances such data would not be indicative of the behavior of the group relative to its own norms, which may be concerned primarily with other than civic responsibilities. It is particularly with respect to this phase of normative integration that future efforts at index construction are required.

III. Communicative Integration. The extent to which communicative contacts permeate a group, the degree of its communicative integration, will bear some relation to the integration among its cultural standards and the integration of conduct with these standards. The precise statement of these relationships awaits research; and as prerequisites for such research, ways are needed to determine the degree to which the members of a group are linked to one another through communication.

The degree to which communication constitutes a connection throughout the group has not yet entered into the focus of the sociologist as a variable for research. Therefore, in the absence of experience with the problem, what will be suggested here as a guide in measuring communicative integration is not a master-index but a number of more or less tentative indices, each of limited applicability. In fact, it will be seen that several of the potential indices rest on assumptions which themselves need to be tested further by research.

The more comprehensive the network of interpersonal communication, the smaller the number of socially isolated persons. It would appear, therefore, that the percentage of group members who display symptoms of social isolation can be used as a negative index of communicative integration. It was one of Durkheim's hypotheses that social isolation of the individual is one of several situations in which suicide is relatively frequent.[8] "Egoistic suicide," as Durkheim calls it, is committed by the person who is detached from social contacts beyond the point of toleration. This involves, as its most crucial element, a lack of, or at least relatively little participation in, communication with others. If it were possible to develop definite criteria by which "egoistic suicide" could be distinguished from other types of suicide that do not involve social isolation, rates of "egoistic suicide" in different groups could be used as a measure of their relative degree of communicative integration.

Some mental disorders constitute another, very similar symptom of isolation. To explain delusions of grandeur or of persecution as the result of restrictions in communication was one of the fruitful implications of Cooley's theory of the "self."[9] More recently, the hypothesis, in this or another form, has received support among psychiatrists[10] and social psychologists.[11] The relationship between mental disorders and isolation from communication needs to be explored further. Presumably, certain disorders lack this particular functional basis. As the etiology of mental disorders advances, it will become possible to distinguish disorders symptomatic of lack of communication from those which are not. Once this is accomplished, it could be assumed that a high incidence of the disorder in question expresses a high frequency of socially isolated persons and, in this sense, a low degree of communicative integration of the group. Perhaps a more accurate index could be obtained by combining the rate for the relevant types of mental disorder and that for suicide.

Indices consisting of rates of suicide or personality disorders would determine the frequency of isolation through the observation of its symptoms. A more direct approach could be taken by attempting to discover the proportion of persons in a group who lack intimate social contacts. Communicative integration would vary inversely with the proportion of such persons. Research techniques which have been developed in studies of patterns of social visiting in the community[12] and of the frequency of personal contacts in the neighborhood[13] could be utilized for the purpose of determining the local number of isolated persons. Another useful technique would be that which has been employed in so-called "social participation" studies. These deal mostly with the participation of the individual in organized groups.[14] As their scope is being extended to include the analysis of membership not only in formally organized but also in informal associations,[15] they yield information as to the frequency of persons who are not in close communication with others.

T. M. Newcomb has stressed the function of barriers to communication in the maintenance of antagonistic relationships.[16] It would follow that the degree to which interpersonal relations in a group, on the average, are antagonistic would be indicative of the degree to which its members fail to communicate with one another. On this premise, sociometric techniques of measuring the volume of attraction and rejection in a group as a whole would seem to be a device by which the adequacy of communication in the group can be indirectly measured. Among the several forms which sociometric research has taken, perhaps the one most relevant to the task of measuring the communicative integration of the small group is the technique of measuring "group morale" designed by L. D. Zeleny.[17] In its simplest form the technique consists in determining the number of attractions or "likes" that are found in a group and expressing it as a ratio of the total number of attractions which would be theoretically possible in that group, i.e., if each member were attracted to each other member. Allowance is made for the intensity of the attraction measured. This ratio Zeleny calls the "morale quotient." If one assumes with Newcomb that, in general, hostility is indicative of disturbances in communication, Zeleny's "morale quotient" would seem to constitute a useful measure of the communicative integration of a group.

One way in which barriers to communication may interfere with the communicative integration of the group is by isolating the person. Indices discussed up to this point are concerned with this phase of communicative integration. Another manner, also pointed out by Newcomb,[18] in which barriers to communication may be drawn can be described by a line which divides several major subdivisions of a group from one another without necessarily creating isolated persons. Within each of these subdivisions communicative links may be strong. However, in relations between them, misunderstandings and distortions restrict communication and, on their part, are augmented by the very barriers to communication which they themselves foster. Thus prejudice bears a close relation to communicative integration. It flourishes where the communicative links among the subdivisions of a population are weak. Groups which lack much give-and-take of ideas develop unrealistic, prejudiced notions of one another. This conclusion is supported by studies which show that prejudice is acquired in contacts with those who share it rather than with those who are its objects.[19]

Thus the volume of communication among the subgroups of a society constitutes a distinct aspect of this type of integration. There seem to be several ways in which it can be measured. One may, first of all, focus on barriers to communication, in the residential distribution of minorities; spatial contacts provide opportunities for communication, and residential segregation is a barrier to it.[20] Elaborate techniques to measure residential segregation have been devised[21] and can be employed as a negative measure of integration.

Since weaknesses in communicative integration are highly interdependent with prejudice, the problem of measurement can also be approached on the premise that prejudice is symptomatic of barriers to communication. In fact, it would seem that measures of prejudice can be used as negative measures of the degree to which the subgroups of a population are linked by communication. A number of techniques to measure prejudice have been developed[22] which would serve as useful tools for integration research.

IV. Functional Integration. Functional integration is the degree to which there is mutual interdependence among the units of a system of division of labor. This type of integration is of prime concern from the modern ecological point of view as formulated by A. H. Hawley.[23] Although division of labor is a strictly behavioral and observable phase of integration, not all obstacles to its measurement have been overcome. Measurement is difficult because interdependence is a phenomenon with several dimensions. First of all, it involves specialization, a characteristic which may exist in a number of degrees and for which no generally applicable index has been devised. However, to demonstrate specialization does not mean to show division of labor among the specialists, because a given number of persons specialized in different ways are not necessarily interdependent. Some may be organized into one, and others into a different, system of division of labor. Thus we need to ask: Who exchanges functions with whom? in addition to asking how specialized these functions are.

So far, only limited aspects of functional integration have been subjected to direct measurement. The Bureau of the Census has defined a metropolitan district as a territory with a specified minimum of population density, surrounding a metropolitan center. Thus the area is measured over which a presumably high degree of functional interdependence ex-

tends, but the degree of that interdependence is not determined. Other indications of the extent of metropolitan districts are newspaper circulation,
the distance over which commuting takes place, the area over which metropolitan stores provide free delivery, and the volume of telephone calls.[24]
D. J. Bogue has measured the degree to which a population is concentrated
in each of four types of economic activity: retail trade, wholesale trade,
services, and manufacturing. As indices of specialization he uses the proportion of the population employed in any of these activities, the number
of establishments of any of these types per population, and the value in
dollars of business done in the kind of establishment concerned. Thereby
he is able to determine not only the degree to which a local population is
functionally concentrated in each of these fields of activity but also its
corresponding interdependence with other local units of the larger area
dominated by the same metropolitan center.[25]

For more indirect devices to measure functional integration no other
writer is as suggestive as Durkheim. His best-known idea on the subject
is to use, as an index of what he calls "organic solidarity," the proportion
of legal norms with merely restitutive sanctions among all norms in a legal
system. His basic assumption is that, as division of labor increases, legal
norms with punitive sanctions diminish and those with restitutive sanctions
increase proportionately. The validity of this assumption is dubious, especially in view of the relative paucity of punitive sanctions in societies
with very little division of labor. Nevertheless, his hypothesis suggests the
need for research to determine whether and to what degree the frequency
of a particular type of legal sanction correlates with other measures of
functional integration.

Less well known but also relevant is his theory that, with increasing
division of labor, it becomes more and more difficult for the member of a
group to break away.[26] He applies this idea to the family by suggesting
that the more division of labor there is in the family, the more difficult it
is for the individual to live outside the family relationship. One would
expect that Durkheim might have proceeded to propose that the functional
integration of the family be measured negatively by certain rates of separation of individuals from the family, possibly by a combination of rates
of divorce and of desertion. The reason why Durkheim did not actually
pursue this idea is presumably the fact that a low separation rate may be
indicative not only of a high degree of functional integration but also of
a high degree of cohesion due to other causes. Nevertheless, the frequency of separation from the group could be used as a measure of its
functional integration if research techniques were employed to hold other
types of integration constant.

For the purpose of measuring the functional integration of a community,
variables could be employed which distinguish urban, highly differentiated
populations from rural, much less differentiated populations. Care would
have to be taken to limit the index, as much as possible, to variables which
are symptomatic of the difference in division of labor rather than of other
urban-rural differences. For example, the proportion of the nonfarm population in an area might be a useful measure. The larger the proportion of
the nonfarm population is, the higher the degree of functional differentiation will be. The fact that reproduction rates are lower in urban than in

rural areas suggests another possible index of functional integration. These and similar measures are limited, however, in that they do not apply to all kinds of groups. For example, they would be useless as measures of functional integration in comparison among groups within the urban community. Such groups, being in an urban environment, can be expected to be made up of people in nonfarm occupations and with low reproduction rates. And yet such groups within the urban community may differ considerably in functional integration. At present, it seems we are better equipped to measure functional integration by different indices for different types of groups than by employing one single index of functional integration for all types of groups.

Four types of integration were described in this paper: cultural, or consistency among the standards of a culture; normative, or conformity of conduct in the group to cultural standards; communicative, or exchange of meanings throughout the group; and functional, or interdependence in the group through exchange of services. In each of these four respects, integration may range from high to low.

The immediate problems suggested by this analysis are methodological. In order to promote substantive research involving different aspects of integration, more effort must be spent in developing techniques of measuring integration in its several forms. With respect to the measurement of all four types, unmet problems of basic importance were pointed out. But, while the area as such is, by and large, underdeveloped, the present status of the component types is not identical. Future work on normative integration should be facilitated by research experience already gained with a measuring device. In so far as communicative integration is concerned, index construction has not yet been attempted, but a considerable amount of relevant theory and research, especially in social psychology, may prove instrumental in this task. With respect to functional integration, indices have been developed which measure the spatial area within which functional interdependence exists, and a promising beginning has been made in measuring the degree of interdependence among spatially defined units. For groups other than local communities, however, no practicable measure of functional integration has as yet been provided. Finally, in the area of cultural integration the first step from preliminary theoretical considerations to the actual development of measuring devices is still to be taken.

2. THE RATIONALE OF THE CURRENT

LABOR FORCE MEASUREMENT

by A. J. Jaffe and Charles D. Stewart

ENUMERATION OF THE POPULATION as *employed, unemployed,* or *not in the labor force* is not so simple as may appear on the surface. Indeed, even where the general technical procedure adopted can be made appropriate for the ends desired, a large number of important decisions affecting the details of the procedures must be made at every stage of the measurement process. These decisions must be made on the basis of some general principle if a systematic, consistent, and meaningful classification of the population is to be obtained. At the present time, for example, there is little if any disagreement as to the superiority of the labor force over the gainful worker approach* of measurement for our purposes. However, there is considerable controversy over the adequacy of the resulting estimates, particularly estimates of unemployment.[1] The criticisms center around the decisions made with respect to the classification of certain persons or groups as employed, unemployed, or out of the labor force. What is the underlying criterion for determining these basic questions of classification?

No official statement of the rationale underlying the Census Bureau's Monthly Report on the Labor Force exists in published form.[2] That a definite rationale was explicit in the thinking of the economists and statisticians who formulated the labor force measurement and designed the structure of definitions and classification, in light of practical problems of enumeration, is known through oral accounts. Essentially it is a principle of labor market relationships which provide the criteria for all decisions with respect to classification. Recognition of this, however, has been clouded by overemphasis on the behavioristic or the current activity features of the new approach. By testing the whole structure of definitions and classification of the Monthly Report on the Labor Force for internal consistency, it becomes apparent that reconciliation is possible only in terms of a particular theory of labor market relationships.

The notion of labor market attachment is implicit, of course, in the gainful worker approach to measurement. What is new in the labor force measurement is the consistent application, to each decision with respect to

---

Reprinted from *Manpower Resources and Utilization*, pp. 62-73, by permission of the authors and the publisher. (Copyright, 1951, by John Wiley and Sons, Inc.)

* [At an earlier point (pp. 19-20) the authors note:

"The gainful worker definition of the working force is distinguished by its emphasis on occupational status and experience. It aims to provide a measurement of the numbers of persons, classified by occupational experience, who generally pursue such occupational activities to obtain money income for the support of themselves and others. This certainly is one significant approach to working force measurement, and it is a useful one where the intent is to provide an inventory and information on labor resources.

"In contrast, the emphasis that is placed explicitly upon current activity of the individual, in terms of his relationship to the labor market, is the distinguishing feature of the monthly measurement of the labor force in the United States. It was introduced for measurement of short-run changes to serve needs not met by the gainful worker measure of the working force. The two approaches can be carried on simultaneously, as alternative approaches to the measurement of the working force, to serve different needs for data."—ED. NOTE.]

classification, of a principle of labor market relationships conceived in terms of the competition of individuals for available jobs.

Thus the labor market relationships of the individuals in the population are viewed as a continuum arranged in order of degree of attachment. Those with jobs exert a pressure on the labor market by virtue of the fact that they occupy one of the jobs afforded by the economy. It may be noted that those with jobs may likewise be seeking other jobs than the ones they have, but for purposes of census enumeration, which requires the classification of each individual in one category or the other, this complicating factor is ignored. Those without a claim to a specific job but seeking one—the unemployed—are competing for the remaining unfilled job openings. They, of course, exert a pressure on the entire structure of the labor market, especially on wage levels; in numbers they may exceed the available unfilled positions.

It can hardly be denied that in some real sense many persons who are excluded from the labor force, within the time reference of the enumeration, exercise an influence on the labor market. This includes particularly persons who are occasionally in the labor force or may potentially be drawn into the labor market.

The concept of the labor market implied by the classification according to degrees of job attachment, or pressures on the labor market in terms of competition for jobs, is admittedly crude and mechanistic in nature. It serves here only as a basis for systematic and consistent classification.

In the following sections we shall examine the rationale of the particular definitions of employment and unemployment that provide the basis for labor force enumeration in the Monthly Report on the Labor Force. Whether the resulting series of data represents the kind of working force statistics intended to serve the needs for information with respect to the crucial problem of unemployment depends (as we will observe) on the adequacy of the general criteria of labor market relationships in providing a consistent and meaningful basis for classification of the employed and unemployed.

Definition and Classification of the Employed[3]

EMPLOYMENT DEFINED IN TERMS OF THE MARKET

Employment is defined in terms of the market; only persons who have jobs that contribute directly or indirectly to production for the market qualify as *employed* under the census definition. This restrictive definition of work, which excludes a very substantial part of all work performed in human society, is not accidental nor completely arbitrary. What are excluded are essentially home-produced services—the everyday duties of the homemaker and the chores and ministrations of family life. The definition is based upon the use, in social analysis, for which the data are intended. As in economics generally, the significant problems for analysis are held to be those that center in the market economy. There are many interrelations between the home and market sectors of the economy, and the distinction between home and market activities, both in labor force and national income statistics, is not without certain arbitrary features. Yet it can hardly be denied that the significant fluctuations in total production or employment, particularly in a modern industrialized nation, are those that occur in production for the market, whatever line may be drawn between home and market production. Labor force statistics and analysis focus attention on the distinction between the economic and other activities of the population, and they necessarily require a clear-cut definition of what is work.

Any activity that contributes or is intended to contribute to the national product, in the now familiar sense of national income accounting, qualifies as *work* in the census definition.[4] This embraces any activity for pay or profit, whether of the wage or salary workers in private or public employment, or of self-employed persons, including unpaid family workers in farm or business enterprises. The only serious difficulty arises in the enumeration of unpaid family workers. Conceptually the matter is simple: If family work on a farm or in a store, for example, contributes to an effort to earn money income from the sale of goods or services on the market, then the family worker so engaged qualifies as employed. Procedurally the matter is more complicated, because complete enumeration of such workers depends upon careful census practices. Since incidental household chores in farm families are so difficult to separate from work which contributes to production for the market (including home-consumed produce), the solution adopted is an arbitrary one. In enumerating farm households, persons reporting less than 15 hours in the week are automatically excluded as workers, on the theory that they are engaged only in household chores unrelated (or at most but very slightly related) to market activities of the family.

THE INACTIVE EMPLOYED

The critical problem in a three-way classification of the population as employed, unemployed, or out of the labor force—so far as the employed category is concerned—is with respect to the so-called "inactive employed."[5] These are persons who are reported as with a job but not at work for a variety of specified reasons. It has been proposed that the problem could be avoided by classifying the labor force in three categories: "at work," "with a job but not at work," and "unemployed." It is quite properly assumed that the public demands a single total figure of the employed and the unemployed. As a matter of fact, the data are now published in sufficient detail to permit analysts to recombine and analyze them in any way they wish.[6] In any case, the originators of the American labor force survey set themselves the ambitious task of classifying all persons with significant labor market attachments into meaningful groupings of *employed* and *unemployed,* and this they did according to what we have referred to as a theory of labor market pressure involving the relation of labor supply to available jobs.

The *inactive employed* in this view comprise those persons who, while not at work, have certain job attachments which place them in a significantly different position with respect to competition for available jobs than others who are seeking work (including the so-called "inactively unemployed").

Inactively Employed for Personal Reasons. There has been little question of the propriety of classification of three of the fringe categories as employed. These include persons who report they have a job but were not at work during the enumeration week because of (*a*) temporary illness, (*b*) paid or unpaid vacations, or (*c*) attending to personal affairs. Such persons exert no pressure on the labor market. They do not regard themselves as unemployed.[7] Only on some criteria of labor input[8] rather than labor market attachment could they be regarded as nonworkers and classified as out of the labor force.

Inactively Employed for Economic Reasons or Because of Weather Conditions. The degree to which labor market attachment, rather than current activity as such, is the touchstone for definition and classification of the employed is shown by the agreement in the handling of the three fringe groups above. More difficulty, however, arises when we consider four other groups which involve elements of involuntary idleness related to other than purely personal factors.

When a person is idle because of a labor dispute at his own place of employment,[9] the loss of work opportunity may be beyond the individual's control, or there may be a question (legal or otherwise) whether the individual has a job to return to, or when. The question is complicated by the fact that the worker may be regarded as unemployed under state unemployment compensation laws, even though according to census procedures he is "with a job but not at work." Perhaps because the numbers involved in any one month are relatively small, there now appears to be little controversy about the handling of this group in census enumeration. But the only valid ground for classification as employed is that such workers have a job attachment. If they do not feel that they have, they are of course counted as unemployed whenever they report they are seeking work.

Persons involuntarily idle because of bad weather in the enumeration week are also classified as employed. The correctness of this classification depends, again, upon the guiding principle of labor market relationships. It was proposed, at one time, to distinguish between agricultural and nonagricultural workers and to classify the latter as unemployed on the grounds of involuntary idleness. Generally, however, such workers consider themselves as with a job, even though they may be eligible for unemployment compensation under their state law. Irregular employment because of weather conditions is a recognized concomitant of certain occupations, as in the construction industry, and to some degree it may be compensated for by the wage rates. In any case, the rationale of the classification is the worker's appraisal of his relationship to the job—whether, all things considered, he is or is not seeking another job. The classification implies a rejection of involuntary idleness as the determining criteria of employment or unemployment status.

A distinction may properly be drawn between involuntary idleness resulting from economic factors and that resulting from weather or personal factors. This is the basis for the very considerable criticism that is leveled against the classification of persons on temporary layoff as employed: i.e., with a job but not at work.[10] The argument put forward is that the person is involuntarily without work because the economy has not functioned in such a fashion as to provide him a job during the census week.[11] This argument is a frontal attack on the theory of labor market relationships as the determining criterion for all questions of definition and classification. For it is urged that, regardless of the fact that the respondent may consider that he has a job and is not seeking another job, he ought to be classified as unemployed.[12] It may be noted that persons on temporary layoff are not subject to referral to jobs in connection with unemployment compensation. In effect, the view is that labor force statistics should primarily provide a measure of the economy's utilization of the currently available labor force. Whether the emphasis on what may appear to be largely subjective factors, which determine, on a theory of labor market attachments, how this group of fringe workers are classified, should be abandoned, in order to obtain statistics that better reflect the functioning of the economy from month to month in terms of jobs, is again the question of what kinds of data are desired.[13]

Inactively Employed Because of Expectation of a Job in the Future. Perhaps the most tenuous of the labor market attachments that qualify a person for inclusion as an *inactive employed* is expectation of a future job. Where the respondent reports he "has obtained a job at which he is scheduled to report to work at some specific date," he is counted as with a job but not at work. The presumption is that he behaves with respect to the labor market differently from a person seeking work and also that an employer has committed a job position to him—a position that is not open to others. Where the job in question is currently held by another, problems arise with respect to the adequacy of the mechanistic notion of "pressures" for available jobs. In short, we count two persons as employed and exerting no pressure on the labor market where (by assumption) only one job exists. But the assumption probably is not realistic; generally the new hire will not involve a layoff. More likely the job is a vacancy or a position not immediately intended to be filled.[14]

Obviously a person expecting to start work next Monday or the 25th of the month has a significant labor market attachment. If he is not to be excluded from the labor force count, he must be classified in one of two ways: (1) with a job not yet started, or (2) seeking work. It is argued[15] that it is more precise and realistic to count him as unemployed until he reports to work. On the other hand, while we do not know for certain whether the individual regards himself as unemployed or with a job, we are perhaps justified in assuming that he is not seeking work. Unlike those classified as unemployed, he has found a job. Again, if he reports he is seeking work, despite his prospective job, he is counted as unemployed.

The choice between the two alternatives, as in the handling of temporary layoffs, must ultimately be on the basis of the kind of labor force statistics we believe will best serve purposes of social policy. Our purpose in this section is to suggest the basic principle (now utilized in the collection of current labor force statistics in the United States) which permits classifying as *employed* persons who have different degrees of attachment to the labor market.

Definition and Classification of the Unemployed[16]

THE UNEMPLOYED ARE LOOKING FOR WORK

The *unemployed* are defined also in terms of the market economy—more specifically in terms of labor market behavior or relationships. By assumption, the work sought by them must be such as to contribute to the national product in a national income accounting sense. The activity *seeking work,* which aims to provide as objective and verifiable a basis for enumeration as possible, is viewed as a competition for available jobs at, presumably, prevailing but unspecified wage rates.[17]

Subjective, or attitudinal, factors are considerably more important in determining *unemployment* than employment status. Thus the opinion-polling aspect of labor force surveys is more clearly evident, and the criticism is easily made that unemployment inquiries of this kind rest too largely on subjective factors. It is precisely for this reason that *seeking work,* which is in its nature more objective and verifiable, although subject to difficulties, has been made the basis for classifying respondents as unemployed.

The problems that arise from the subjective character of *job wanting* refer largely to those population groups, particularly among students, women, and older persons, who are not—or ordinarily are not regarded to be—regularly in the labor market. But job wanting is necessarily a personal judgment, shaped by all the factors impinging upon the individual, and can only be determined by him. For adult men with family responsibilities there is probably no question, in the public mind or in their own minds, of their status as unemployed. For others, except possibly those persons obviously unable to work, there is no readily applied test of the genuineness of their looking-for-work status. The individual's own expression of desire, backed up by some evidence of actual looking for work, is the only assurance of the intensity and reality of this desire.

Although no special tests have been made, there is little evidence that the unemployment totals are inflated by any appreciable number of persons whose desire to find work is simply frivolous. On the contrary, there is considerable evidence that many persons who might be considered as strongly motivated to report themselves unemployed actually reported themselves as not in the labor force. During the months immediately following the end of World War II, for example, a very considerable number of persons protected their legal rights to unemployment compensation by remaining technically available for referral to a "suitable" job (at least up to the moment of referral), but reported withdrawal from the labor market in the current labor force survey.[18] Also, tests made to check whether procedures are adequate to provide a full count of the unemployed show that large numbers of the persons who are not now enumerated as unemployed have at best rather indefinite attitudes about wanting a job. Nevertheless, significant numbers of persons who were not in the labor force at the times of these tests reported behavior that could have permitted classifying them as unemployed.

THE INACTIVE UNEMPLOYED

Jobless Persons, Temporarily Ill, or Who Believe No Work Is Available. The intention is to include as unemployed all those without jobs at any time during the survey week who are looking for work, and to exclude generally all those who are not. However, an effort is made to count two groups of persons who for special reasons do not engage in any overt act of looking. They are regarded as unemployed on the basis of the principle of labor market relationships, although they cannot be so identified by any act of looking. These two groups of the so-called *inactive unemployed* are persons not looking for work: (1) because they are temporarily ill, and (2) because they believe no work is available in their community or line of work.

Apparently there is little question of the propriety of including these two groups as unemployed.[19] The justification is that they would be looking

for work except for one of these two reasons. The person temporarily ill
in this category is one who is immediately desirous of work and presumably available to report to work shortly. The person who is not looking
because of a belief that no job is available is assumed to be familiar
enough with the condition of the local labor market (as in a one-industry
town) to know that no purpose is to be served immediately by actively
looking. This is such a common situation and such a common-sense attitude that no serious question has been raised of the legitimacy of the
unemployment status of persons in this category. The experimental work
of the Works Progress Administration demonstrated the need for attention
to the enumeration of such persons who would not be included under a
literal application of the *actively seeking work* rule, particularly during
periods of depression. In terms of the pressure they exert on the labor
market, they are more than latent or potential job seekers who come into
the labor market when suitable job openings appear.[20] Here there can be
no question but that they are real competitors for the type of jobs that
usually exist and for which they will compete as soon as industry opens up.

The typical case is the one-industry town. However, the principle is broad
enough to apply to instances where there are no job opportunities in a particular line of work. Factors of labor immobility—both occupational and
geographic—are thus recognized as real factors determining unemployment status, which set objective limits to excluding persons from the labor
force for their failure to search for work. It should be noted that this rule
is applied only to *regular* and not to occasional workers. The lack of job
opportunity may be the result of any fluctuation in activity, seasonal or
cyclical, and is not restricted to chronic or extremely depressed area or
industry situations. In effect, the situation referred to is industrial rather
than agricultural in character, for unpaid family workers who move in and
out of the labor force in response to seasonal peak requirements are excluded from the operation of the rule. This, again, is explicable only in
terms of the difference in the nature of the labor market status of wage
earners and of unpaid family workers in the typical case.

Indefinite Layoff. Persons on indefinite layoff (or layoff of more than
30 days in duration) are treated as a special case and are frequently considered a third group of the inactive unemployed. Although there is no
question generally concerning their unemployed status, the technical handling of this group under present survey procedures has led to the conclusion that there is an inconsistency in differentiating temporary layoffs as
being "with a job but not at work" from indefinite layoffs as being "unemployed."

Whether Census Bureau procedure imputes looking for work to persons
on indefinite layoff, as some claim, or simply defines those on indefinite
layoff as unemployed, as seems to be the case, is irrelevant so far as any
question of principle is concerned. The argument often made is that it is
frequently as reasonable to impute "looking for work" to persons in the
definite-layoff group as to those in the indefinite-layoff group. The difficulty would be avoided if census procedures required enumerators to
determine whether persons on indefinite layoff are actually seeking work.
If they are not actually seeking work, they would be out of the labor force,
under the general approach, except that, if they believed no work was
available, they would come under the rule of inactive job seekers.

3. OBJECTIVE INDICATORS OF SUBJECTIVE VARIABLES

by Stuart A. Rice

MENTAL STATES have been discussed in a manner very much as if they were objective realities which could be defined and measured. Now attitudes and motives in themselves offer a valid subject of scientific inquiry, but they are not susceptible of measurement. It is only when they find expression in behavior that they yield to quantitative analysis. One of the main tasks of a quantitative science of politics, therefore, is a search for behavioristic materials representative of the intangible subjective elements of political activity. Thus in experiments by Allport and Hartman, each student was asked to select and check a previously prepared statement which most nearly approximated his own opinion. The investigators could not determine how competently their subjects could appraise their own opinions. Nor were they able to guard against deliberate error in the appraisals. More than one would-be wag may have falsified his statement with some humorous intent.[1] The investigators were dependent upon the behavior of their subjects for inferences concerning its source. They were forced to *assume* that the former bore some close and direct relationship to the latter.

There are numerous forms of political behavior which might be measured, at least in theory. There is one, however, that seems most easily obtainable, that is characteristically associated with American politics, and that is clearly related to the underlying attitudes. This is the *vote*. Votes are by no means certain or universal indicators of political attitudes or political activity. There is overlapping both ways. Many political activities neither consist in nor lead to voting. On the other hand, there are many votes which have no connection with agencies of organized government. There are beauty contests, for example, elections to scientific societies, and the choice between oranges and grapefruit in a cooperative boarding house. Professor Catlin[2] would possibly regard all of the latter as political questions. Without agreeing or disagreeing with his theoretical position, I wish to accept it as a methodological convenience at this point. Since I find it difficult to distinguish between political and other questions, it is likewise difficult to distinguish between political and other votes. And there is no need for the distinction. The voting process has the same general form and the same general value as an indicator of attitude wherever it is employed.

Votes are useful indexes of political attitudes, then, because they are

Reprinted in part from *Quantitative Methods in Politics*, pp. 92-97, by permission of the author and the publishers. (Copyright, 1928, by Alfred A. Knopf, Inc. Current copyright holder is Appleton-Century-Crofts, Inc.)

the most tangible and measurable units of political behavior. They are tangible because simple and precise. They are measurable, for although each is really a *gross* measure of attitude, the value of which may differ widely in different individuals, they are nevertheless assumed to have equal value and are counted and recorded officially. They provide the closest analogy within the field of politics to the monetary unit in the quantitative analyses of economic statisticians. Just as one of the major tasks of the latter is to convert the raw indexes in terms of dollars into refined indexes of economic conditions, in the same way the political statistician must manipulate and combine his raw indexes, the votes, into expressions which are indicative of the political situation in which he is really interested.

Like a newly invented tool in the physical sciences or the mechanical arts, an index may permit of observations or may facilitate the determination of relationships which have hitherto been obscured. My purpose is to emphasize the necessity, if one is to engage in quantitative political research, of being constantly on the alert to devise indexes *suited to the purpose at hand*. General or advance instructions as to procedure can no more replace ingenuity in this respect than can the legendary manual upon ways of killing a cat. I shall therefore give no rules for devising indexes, but shall instead cite here an illustration of the manner in which one required index was fashioned. This may serve not as a pattern for identical use in other inquiries, but as suggestive of ingenious possibilities.

In making my study *Farmers and Workers in American Politics*,[3] I desired to secure an index by means of which the varying degrees of "progressivism" to be found in various parts of the state of Nebraska might be determined. No vote for a single candidate or upon a single issue in a state election seemed available for the purpose, especially since the aggregate vote for a recognized old-party candidate at a general election always contains the unknown effect of "straight party voting." A peculiar situation in the election of 1922 provided the basis for devising the index desired.

In the primary election of 1922, R. B. Howell, a "Progressive Republican" won the Republican nomination for United States senator in the State of Nebraska. C. W. Bryan, a "Progressive Democrat" won the Democratic Party nomination for governor. As a result, a "progressive" and "composite slate," headed by Howell and Bryan, and containing candidates nominated by the Progressive Party as well as by the old parties, was "officially endorsed by the Nonpartisan League, the local labor organizations and the Committee of 48."[4] Both Howell and Bryan were elected, the former receiving 59.8 per cent of the combined vote of the Republican and Democratic candidates for senator, the latter 56.6 per cent of the combined Republican and Democratic vote for governor.[5]

A measure of the extent to which voters of any group *split their votes* on behalf of the "progressive slate" will serve as an index by which the progressivism of the group may be gauged. It is obvious that if every Republican and Democrat had voted a "straight party ticket" the percentage of the total Republican and Democratic vote received by Howell would have varied inversely as the percentage of the vote received by Bryan, and *vice versa*. Each percentage would be the reciprocal of the other, for added together they would equal 100 per cent, i.e., all of the Republican and

Democratic votes. Where Howell, Republican, was strongest, Bryan, Democrat, would be weakest, and so on. Hence the correlation between the percentage of Bryan votes and the percentage of Howell votes in the various counties would in such a case be negative and perfect; i.e., r would $= -1.0$.

On the other hand, if every Republican supporter of Howell voted likewise for Bryan, and if every Democratic supporter of Bryan voted likewise for Howell, the correlation between the percentages of the vote received by each would be positive and perfect; i.e., r would $= 1.0$. In this case Bryan and Howell would each receive 100 per cent of the combined Republican and Democratic votes.

A simple measure of progressivism is thus obtained by averaging the percentage of the senatorial vote received by Howell with the percentage of the gubernatorial vote received by Bryan. If the average is 100 per cent, then it is clear that *all* Republican and Democrats *split their votes in support of both progressive candidates.* If the average is 50 per cent it is clear that all Republicans and Democrats cast *straight party ballots.*[6] If the average is 0 per cent it is clear that all Republicans and Democrats split their votes *by the rejection of both progressive candidates.* Thus an average above 50 per cent indicates a tendency for voters to split ballots in behalf of the progressive candidates; the higher the average the greater the tendency. Conversely, an average of less than 50 per cent indicates a tendency for voters to split ballots in behalf of the conservative candidates on both tickets.

While in fact both Howell and Bryan were elected, it is nevertheless probable that each received a comparatively poor vote in the counties in which the other received a comparatively good vote. This is suggested when the percentages of the vote received by each in the various counties are correlated. The coefficient of correlation is found to be

$$r = -.228 \pm .038$$

Of 93 counties in Nebraska, Howell carried all but 6, while Bryan carried all but 10. There were no duplications among the 16 counties. Two counties only showed an average percentage of votes for Bryan and Howell of less than 50 per cent. Thus the state as a whole was quite uniformly progressive in its vote, although some sectional variations were discovered.

4. A REVIEW OF INDICATORS USED IN "THE AMERICAN SOLDIER"

by Patricia L. Kendall

[The publication of the first two volumes of *The American Soldier,* by Samuel A. Stouffer and his associates, stimulated an interest among methodologists to analyze and codify certain of the research procedures employed in that work.

Reprinted from "Problems of Survey Analysis," pp. 183-186, in *Continuities in Social Research: Studies in the Scope and Method of "The American Soldier,"* edited by Robert K. Merton and Paul F. Lazarsfeld, by permission of the author, the editors, and the publisher. (Copyright, 1950, by The Free Press.)

In an article entitled "Problems of Survey Analysis," Kendall and Lazarsfeld sought to make explicit certain of the research techniques, both qualitative and quantitative in nature, employed by the analysts of The Research Branch of the Information and Education Division of the Army. In the selection which follows, Kendall points out the ingenuity exercised by the authors of *The American Soldier* in selecting appropriate items as indicators in survey research.—ED. NOTE.]

ON SOME OCCASIONS a single item in a survey seems sufficient to indicate the existence of a fairly complex set of attitudes. Prior to our active entrance into the war, Research Branch analysts were interested in determining the extent to which men inducted into the Army through the Selective Service system maintained a feeling of identification with civilian life. The notion of identifying with a group suggests a complicated phenomenon for which one might want numerous and varied indices. Actually, only one question was used in the Research Branch study, but it seems to have accomplished its objective. The question, asked of both regular Army men and the selectees, read as follows: "Which do you prefer to wear on furlough, uniform or civilian clothes?" The difference in the expressed preferences of the two groups was large: 30 per cent of the selectees, as contrasted with 62 per cent of the regulars, said that they preferred to wear their uniforms.[1] (I, 64, Chart III)* The choice of what kind of clothes to wear when not on active duty symbolizes so directly one's sense of identification with either the Army or with civilian life that no other index seems needed.

In other instances the index for the concept may be found in the contrasting answers given by one group to a pair of questions. Toward the end of the war, the Research Branch found that 81 per cent of a sample of enlisted men believed that *civilians* would consider a Private or a Pfc "not good enough to get a rating," while only 25 per cent felt that *other soldiers* would have this attitude. (I, 231)[2] This simple comparison of the attitudes imputed to civilians and those imputed to other soldiers might be considered an index for "in-group" versus "out-group" experiences. First of all, the finding suggests that soldiers look on other soldiers, co-members of their in-group, with sympathy and understanding; they seem to maintain a kind of solidarity which prevents criticism of those in a low status. Secondly, the fact that these same soldiers attribute very different attitudes to civilians seems to indicate that they do not consider civilians members of the group to which they belong. And, since the attitudes attributed to civilians are critical ones, it appears that soldiers think of individuals on the home front as constituting a "hostile" out-group.

It is not always possible, however, to find quantitative indices for the concepts being considered. It might happen, for example, that the researcher has failed to ask any questions appropriate to the study of in-group attitudes. This is particularly likely to be the case in secondary analyses which make use of data collected primarily for other purposes. But even where there are no quantitative indices, the researcher can sometimes call on *qualitative* evidence for the concepts or relationships in which he is interested. The qualitative material is generally the observation of symbolic acts or incidents. A few characteristic illustrations may help to clarify the nature and use of these indices.

---

* References to the first and second volumes of *The American Soldier* are referred to as I and II respectively. Page numbers are indicated by Arabic numerals.

At one point in their analysis, Stouffer and his associates wanted to indicate that certain features of Army life bore a resemblance to the situation one would find in a *caste system*. Had this concern been a major one, the analysts might have proceeded in a number of different ways. First of all, they might have carried out a survey among officers and enlisted men, noting the numbers and kinds of contacts which took place between them. From such a survey, quantitative indices of caste structure might have been developed. Or, a second type of study, an "institutional analysis," might have been undertaken. Here the researchers would have examined all the formal rules and regulations of the Army, studied lines of command, and so on. From such an analysis, they would have decided the extent to which the Army exhibited features typical in a caste structure. Neither type of data was immediately available, and since the point was of incidental rather than primary importance, no attempt was made to collect the data in precisely the form we have suggested.

The index which actually was used by the Research Branch was the existence of a ritualistic tradition which would not have been maintained had the Army not had certain elements of a caste system. The authors note that while it was possible for enlisted men to become officers, there was no direct promotion:

"Enlisted men selected for officer candidate school were first discharged from the Army and then readmitted in their new and very different status." (I, 56, fn. 2)

Just as it is impossible to move from one caste to another, in an ethnic caste situation, so an enlisted man about to become an officer must leave the Army system before reentering in his new status.

The index of caste features in the Army was a custom sanctioned and maintained by formal rules of Army procedure. Another custom, this time one which grew up spontaneously among combat personnel in the Air Corps, is cited by Research Branch authors as an index of the importance of a fixed tour of combat. A result from *The American Soldier* referred to earlier in this paper suggested the importance of that tour, and other findings pointing to the same conclusion are reported in other sections of the volumes. But as the authors themselves state:

"The sharp focus among men in the heavy bombers upon completion of the tour of duty would be almost sufficiently documented by a single fact, namely the widespread existence of the 'Lucky Bastard' clubs. By the spring of 1944 it was common for bomber groups to award 'Lucky Bastard' certificates to crew members after the completion of their thirtieth mission. This practice appears to have developed spontaneously among the men themselves and was not explicitly sanctioned by the high command." (II, 383)

In other words, the fact that men who had completed their missions were made members of a special club, and the fact that they were called the "lucky bastards," is a qualitative index of the psychological importance of a stated tour of combat.

Along somewhat similar lines, the Research Branch analysts noted the importance which returnees placed on being allowed to wear the insignia of their overseas units when serving in new units in the United States. (II, 508) This observation was used to indicate the ambivalence experienced by these soldiers.

5. THE CONCEPT OF PROPERTY-SPACE*
IN SOCIAL RESEARCH

by Allen H. Barton

THE IDEA OF PROPERTY-SPACE

EVERYONE IS FAMILIAR with the idea of indicating location in space by means of coordinates. Every point on this page can be described by two numbers: its distance from the left-hand side and its distance from the bottom (or from any other pair of axes we choose). The location of any point on the earth's surface can be indicated by giving its latitude and longitude, using as base lines the equator and the Greenwich meridian.

Other properties besides location in physical space can likewise be indicated by coordinates. A man can be characterized by his scores on tests of mathematical and linguistic ability, just as by his latitude and longitude. These two scores locate him in a "property-space" with the two dimensions of mathematical ability and linguistic ability. We can chart this property-space on paper by using mathematics score as one axis and linguistic score for the other, just as we can chart the earth's surface. Of course in the latter case we are making a spatial representation of actual spatial dimensions, only on a smaller scale. In the former our distances on paper represent the numbers of correct answers to questions given by people taking tests, or in a larger sense, the ability of their minds to perform certain tasks.

The dimensions on which we "locate" people in property-space can be of different kinds. Most psychological test scores are for all practical purposes *continuous variables,* but they usually do not have equal intervals or a meaningful zero point. They provide only a relative ordering of people. Once we have located a representative sample of the United States population in our mathematical-linguistic property-space, we can say that a man is in the fifth percentile of the population in mathematical ability and in the fortieth in linguistic ability. Sometimes social scientists do work with continuous variables which do have a zero-point and equal intervals, at least formally: age, income, size of community, number of hours spent watching television.

---

* The concept of property-space has been developed in several papers by Paul F. Lazarsfeld. This paper is an outgrowth of a seminar on concepts and indices in social science, sponsored jointly by the Columbia University Planning Project for Advanced Training in Social Research and the Ford Center for Advanced Study in the Behavioral Sciences, and directed by Paul F. Lazarsfeld. It summarizes a collection of examples of the application of the concept of property-space to social research operations which was presented at the seminar.

More often, probably, the dimensions will be qualitative properties, which locate cases in one of a number of classes, like "State of birth," "military rank," or "occupation." State of birth locates everyone born in the continental U. S. in one of 49 *unordered classes* (counting District of Columbia). Military rank locates members of the armed forces in what is by definition a set of *rank-ordered classes,* ranging from buck private up to five-star general. Occupations in themselves do not necessarily form a set of ranked classes, although some of them are specifically defined in terms of degree of "skill." We might simply list them arbitrarily, as in alphabetical order. Or we might draw upon outside information about them—for example average income, as known from census data, or prestige status, as discovered through surveys—to arrange them in one or another rank-order.

The simplest type of property by which an object can be characterized is a *dichotomous attribute,* such as voter/non-voter, white/non-white, male/female, or Democrat/Republican. It is always possible to simplify a more complex property by reducing the number of classes which are distinguished. A continuous variable can be cut up to form a set of ranked classes, like income brackets or age levels. A set of ranked classes, in turn, can be simplified by combining all those above a certain point into one class and all those below into a second class, forming a dichotomy. This is done when we reduce the military hierarchy to the distinction between officers and enlisted men, or the income brackets to above or below a certain amount. By picking out one aspect of a set of unordered classes we can sometimes order them into a dichotomy, as when we classify states as east or west of the Mississippi, or occupations as manual or non-manual.

When we chart the property-space formed by two qualitative characteristics the result is not, of course, a continuous plane, but an array of cells each representing one combination of values on two properties. For example, a study of the 1952 election described people's "political position" in October 1952, in terms of the two dimensions of "usual party affiliation" and "degree of political interest." If one asks Americans what their usual party affiliation is, almost everyone falls into three categories: Republicans, Democrats, and independents. These are natural divisions. Degree of interest on the other hand can be divided into any number of ranked categories we please, depending on the alternatives we offer the respondent. In the present case they could rate themselves as having high, medium, or

Table 1—A Qualitative Property-Space of Political Position

		USUAL PARTY AFFILIATION		
		Republican	Democratic	Independent
DEGREE OF POLITICAL INTEREST	High			
	Medium			
	Low			

low interest. These two trichotomous dimensions then define a nine-fold property-space as shown in Table 1.

We can locate a person within this property-space by giving as co-ordinates his usual party affiliation and his degree of political interest.

There is no reason why we cannot characterize objects by as many properties as we want. We can add a test in historical knowledge to tests in mathematics and language, and characterize our subjects by three coordinates. These can still be presented in the form of a physical model, by using a box in which everyone is located by distance from the left-hand side, from the front, and from the bottom. If we add a fourth test, for instance, of reading speed, we can give our subjects four coordinates and locate them in a four-dimensional property-space. Thus we can say that someone is in the fifth percentile of the U. S. population in mathematics, the fortieth in language skill, the sixtieth in historical knowledge, and the twenty-ninth in reading speed. We can no longer represent this by a physical model, but we can perform mathematical operations on the four coordinates just as well as on two or three.

In dealing with qualitative property-spaces which have limited numbers of categories on each dimension, we can still chart the property-space on paper even though it is three-dimensional or even higher-dimensional. Let us take the two dimensions of occupation, dichotomized as manual/non-manual, and political preference, dichotomized as Democratic/Republican. These give us a fourfold table. If we add the dimension of father's occupation, again dichotomized as manual/non-manual, we now have a "two-story" fourfold table: occupation and party of sons of manual workers and occupation and party of sons of non-manually employed people. This can be physically represented by a cube with eight cells, with the original fourfold table repeated on both the "first floor" and the "second floor." If

Table 2—A Three-Dimensional Attribute-Space Laid Out in Two Dimensions

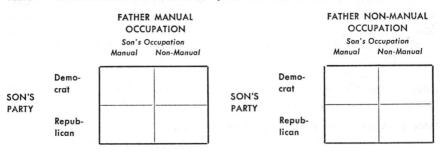

we want to represent this cube on a flat piece of paper, all we have to do is to lay the two "stories" side by side, as an architect would two floor plans (Table 2).

Now suppose that we ask a fourth question, for example, the father's usual party, again dichotomized as Democratic/Republican. Our property-space then becomes a four-dimensional "cube." But we can still lay out each level on this fourth dimension on paper just as we did those on the third (Table 3).

The combination of dichotomous attributes produces a type of property-space which may be labeled "dichotomous attribute-space."[1] Position in a

Table 3—A Four-Dimensional Attribute-Space Laid Out In Two Dimensions

		FATHER MANUAL OCCUPATION			FATHER NON-MANUAL OCCUPATION	
		Son's Occupation			Son's Occupation	
		Manual	Non-Manual		Manual	Non-Manual
FATHER DEMO-CRAT	Son Demo-crat			Son Demo-crat		
	Repub-lican			Repub-lican		

		Son's Occupation			Son's Occupation	
		Manual	Non-Manual		Manual	Non-Manual
FATHER REPUB-LICAN	Son Demo-crat			Son Demo-crat		
	Repub-lican			Repub-lican		

dichotomous attribute-space can be indicated as a response-pattern of plus and minus signs, where we have assigned these values (arbitrarily or otherwise) to the two sides of each dichotomy and arranged the dimensions in some order. Thus a Democratic manual worker, whose father was a Democratic manual worker, might be indicated by the coordinates $(++++)$. A Republican non-manually employed person, whose father was a Democratic manual worker, would have the coordinates $(--++)$, and so on. (This system of notation is often used in "political score-sheets" which show how Congressmen voted on a series of bills, a plus sign showing a "correct" vote and a minus sign a "wrong" vote, in terms of a given political viewpoint or economic interest.)

If we are particularly interested in one of the dimensions as a criterion or dependent variable, we may present a dichotomous attribute-space in abbreviated form by showing only the "background" factors as dimensions in the chart, and filling in each cell with a figure showing the per cent who are "positive" on the criterion behavior. No information is lost since the attribute is a dichotomy, and all those not positive are classified as "negative" on the attribute. It is as if we had raised three-dimensional bars from the two-dimensional chart of background characteristics with a height proportional to the positive answers on the criterion behavior, and then replaced them with figures indicating their height just as altitudes are shown on a flat map. Thus Table 3 could be presented as an eight-fold table showing the dimensions of father's occupation, father's party, and son's occupation; the cells would be filled in with figures showing "per cent Democrat" (or vice versa).

Such tables are particularly useful in permitting the effects of the various background variables to be compared, holding the others constant in each case.[2]

To suggest how far the use of very high-dimension property-spaces has actually developed in social research, we need only note that the results of each interview in a survey are normally punched on an IBM card containing 80 columns, each with twelve rows. Such a card provides for an 80-dimensional property-space, with each property having twelve classes. In practice one never uses all eighty dimensions simultaneously to characterize a respondent; however they are all available to use in whatever smaller combinations we select. If we consider each position in the 80 by 12 matrix as representing a dichotomous attribute (each can either be punched or not punched), we have the possibility of locating each respondent in a dichotomous attribute-space of 960 dimensions.

An interesting application of a high-dimensioned property-space is found in W. J. Goode's *Religion Among the Primitives*.[3] He first picks out five elements which he considers basic to the description of primitive religious systems: (1) personnel; (2) societal matrix; (3) sacred entities; (4) ritual; and (5) belief. These are not all single dimensions; each is what might be termed an "attribute-area." "Personnel" is thus described in two dimen-

Table 4—Abbreviated Presentation of a Four-Dimensional Attribute-Space

FATHER'S OCCUPATION

		Manual		Non-manual	
		SON'S OCCUPATION		SON'S OCCUPATION	
		Manual	Non-manual	Manual	Non-manual
	Democratic				
		_____%	_____%	_____%	_____%
FATHER'S PARTY		Dem.	Dem.	Dem.	Dem.
	Republican				
		_____%	_____%	_____%	_____%
		Dem.	Dem.	Dem.	Dem.

sions: (a) extent of formal religious training (both leaders and followers trained, leaders only, or neither); and (b) extent of identification of the sacred with the secular leadership of the community. The "societal matrix" is described initially by five dimensions: rationality/traditionalism, self-interest/other-interest, universalism/particularism, specificity of relationships/diffuseness, and impersonality/emotional involvement in daily interaction. These are reduced to form two polar types labelled "basic-rural" and "basic-urban," and societies located along a range between the two poles. The "sacred entities" are described as ranging from a highly abstract and distant entity, through broad natural forces like the sun and the rain, various anthropomorphic entities such as ancestral spirits, to the concrete and prosaic entities of animals, plants, and other natural objects. "Ritual" is described by the degree of elaboration and symbolism. "Belief" turns out to be highly complex, involving, among others, beliefs about the soul, beliefs relating to the ritual, beliefs about punishment for violation of norms, and beliefs about the origin of gods, men, and the world.

In his final classification, five particular societies are described by their position on these dimensions, omitting that of "belief" which was apparently too complex to permit a simple set of categories. The use of the property-space makes clear that these five prolonged and intensive studies of different cultures only fill in a very small portion of the whole range of possible types.

THE REDUCTION OF PROPERTY-SPACE

One of the uses to which the concept of property-space can be applied is to clarify the operation of reduction. By reduction we mean the combining of classes in order to obtain a smaller number of categories. This is often done for purely practical purposes in order to keep the number of groups compared small enough so that each will have enough cases in a limited sample. It may also be done for theoretical reasons. We will discuss the types of reduction which occur rather frequently in social research, although their methodological characteristics often are not recognized.

a. Reduction through Simplification of the Dimensions. One obvious type of reduction occurs if we simplify continuous variables to ranked classes, or a set of classes to a dichotomy. Let us return to the two-dimensional property-space of "political position" represented in Table 1. It was considered that for some purposes the major distinction on the dimension of party affiliation was between those who identified with either party on the one hand and the independent voters on the other. It was also believed that the most important distinction on the interest dimension was between the highly interested and those with medium or low interest. With each dimension reduced to a dichotomy, the property-space as a whole was reduced to the four cells of a fourfold table (Table 5).

Table 5—Reduction of a Property-Space by Simplifying the Dimensions

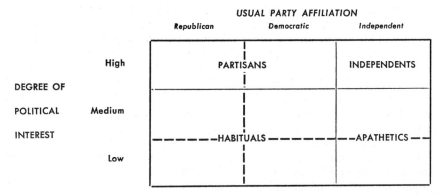

Those who have some party identification and high interest were labeled "partisans"; those who were independent and had high interest were labeled "independents." Those who identified with a party but had only medium or low interest were called "habitual party voters," and those who identified with no party and had only medium or low interest were called "apathetics." What has been gained by this is the elimination of distinctions which were considered less relevant for certain purposes, to make it easier—especially with a limited number of cases in the sample—to examine the separate and joint effects of the two dichotomies of "party identification/non-identification" and "high interest/less than high interest." It was expected that each of the four groups might show distinctive behavior on certain attributes. There was no question at least in the first instance of achieving a single rank-ordering for the four classes; the two-dimensional form was preserved.

b. Numerical Indices and the Reduction of Qualitative Property-Space. We are often faced with situations in which we have two measures which we believe express essentially the same underlying characteristic or have their effects in the same direction, so that we would like to combine them to form a single dimension for analysis. A technique often employed because of its simplicity is to give each category on each dimension a certain weight, and add these together to get index scores for the cells. Thus a study of mass communication habits might rate reading, radio listening, and movie attendance each as "high," "medium," and "low" according to certain cultural standards. This creates a three-dimensional property-space of twenty-seven cells. By weighting each communication channel equally, and scoring the low, medium, and high positions 0, 1, and 2 respectively, respondents could be classified into seven ranked groups with scores 0-6. This may be termed arbitrary numerical reduction. Table 6 illustrates the scoring.

Table 6—Arbitrary Numerical Reduction of a Three-Dimensional Property-Space of Levels of Taste

		HIGH IN READING (2)			MEDIUM IN READING (1)			LOW IN READING (0)		
		Radio listening			Radio listening			Radio listening		
		H(2)	M(1)	L(0)	H(2)	M(1)	L(0)	H(2)	M(1)	L(0)
MOVIE	H (2)	6	5	4	5	4	3	4	3	2
PREFER-ENCE	M (1)	5	4	3	4	3	2	3	2	1
	L (0)	4	3	2	3	2	1	2	1	0

Such a reduction necessarily assumes that for the purpose at hand all combinations with the same index score are equivalent and can be grouped together. This means among other things that a score of 3 can be obtained in two quite different ways: by being "medium" on all three dimensions, or by being high on one, low on another, and medium on the third. Likewise scores of 4 and of 2 represent mixtures of patterns. One can score 2 by being high on one communications channel and low on the other two, or by being medium on two and low on one. If we are trying to rate people in terms of "cultural level," it might seem absurd to group together people whose taste was "middlebrow" on two communications channels and "lowbrow" on one with people who were "highbrow" on one and "lowbrow" on two. If we don't like to do such things, we must use some other, more pragmatic method of combining categories than an arbitrary numerical reduction. Another way out would appear if such anomalous combinations rarely appeared at all, thus presenting us with a "functional reduction."

Another problem is the matter of weighting. We might argue that reading has a deeper impact on people than the other media, or that it provides for a freer expression of their tastes as contrasted with movies and radio where you may have less opportunity to select just what you want. On either basis a case could be made for giving reading taste a higher weight than preferences in movies and radio—say twice as much. In this case the highbrow reader with lowbrow radio and movie preferences—if he exists—would rate above the pure middlebrow.

c. Numerical Indices and the Reduction of Continuous Property-Space. While we are mainly concerned here with qualitative properties which form sets of classes, it should be noted that the process of reduction through index formulas is also applied to continuous variables. If we return to our example of mathematics and language scores, we might want to combine them equally to measure a more general area of intellectual ability. This means that all points in the property-space whose coordinates add up to a given sum are considered to be equivalent. If the weights are equal, all points on any line at a 45 degree angle to the axes and a negative slope must have the same index score (Table 7).

Table 7—Reduction of a Continuous Property-Space by Means of Numerical Index-Lines

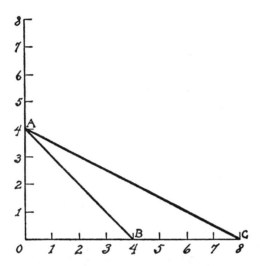

The index line AB, for instance, links all points having a score of 4 on an equally weighted index; these include the configurations (4,0), (3,1), (2,2), (1,3), and (0,4) as well as all intermediate points. The index line in a continuous property-space is analogous to a row of cells which are given the same value in a qualitative property-space (see Table 6, where diagonal rows of cells have equal index scores.)

If someone maintains that language score is a good deal more important than mathematics score, either in terms of a valuation of language ability as more important to some ideal of human development, or in terms of some particular job for which it is a more important means to achieving given goals, he will give language score relatively more weight. At twice the weight for mathematics score, we would obtain index lines with a much flatter slope like AC. AC links all points having a score of 8 on the new index; we now see that it equates such configurations as (4,0), (3,2), (2,4), (1,6), and (0,8). This expresses the fact that the formula applies a coefficient of 2 to the first (language) coordinate.

d. Pragmatic Reductions of Property-Space. We have discussed one method of adjusting numerical reductions so that they will more closely approximate our values or our experience—through weighting the various properties differently. Yet for some purposes any system of weighted indicators works too rigidly, and groups categories together too arbitrarily. There may be interactions among the different properties such that each combination must be considered in its own right before it can be properly classified.

If we return to our example of mass-communication habits, we can observe three "pure types" which present no difficulty: those who are high in all three communications habits, those who are medium in all, and those who are low in all. We now have the problem of classifying the remaining combinations. We might add to the "pure highbrows" those three groups which were high on two and medium on only one communications channel. Likewise we might add to the middlebrows all those who make two middlebrow choices, with the other choice either high or low. To the lowbrows we could add those who were low on two and middle on one.

But what should be done with those groups with two preferences at one extreme and one at the other? These may constitute special types which should be kept separate. Those with two highs and one low might be labelled, somewhat unkindly, "slummers." They might include people who find a "primitive" beauty in certain low-brow material, like New Orleans jazz or sporting prints, as well as those who abandon themselves to soap opera or Mickey Spillane. If we feel that in spite of these lapses they are still essentially highbrows, we would put them along with all the others making two or more highbrow choices. The people with two low preferences and one high may be a still more significant group. They might be a distinctive type, perhaps like the old ideal of the self-educated working man who skipped standardized middle-class popular culture to enjoy the classics. We might call them, somewhat awkwardly, "looking-up brows." There remain, finally, six groups with one high, one middle, and one low preference. From the given data we cannot tell whether they are broad-minded, or indiscriminate, or what might be the reason for such a peculiar set of choices. We might call these the "broadbrows." The results of this reduction are shown in Table 8.

Table 8—Pragmatic Reduction of a Three-Dimensional Property-Space of Levels of Taste

		HIGH IN READING			MEDIUM IN READING			LOW IN READING		
		Radio listening			Radio listening			Radio listening		
		H	M	L	H	M	L	H	M	L
MOVIE	H	High	High	Slum.	High	Mid.	Broad	Slum.	Broad	L.U.
PREFER-	M	High	Mid.	Broad	Mid.	Mid.	Mid.	Broad	Mid.	Low
ENCE	L	Slum.	Broad	L.U.	Broad	Mid.	Low	L.U.	Low	Low

This pragmatic reduction of the twenty-seven possible patterns gives us a set of six types, which do not by any means fall along a single dimension. It appears that we are classifying on the one hand by the predominate level preferred, and on the other according to the amount of "spread" of a person's choices. The three pure types run diagonally through a cube which has been cut into thirds on each side to give twenty-seven smaller cubes, from the "high-high-high" corner to the "low-low-low" corner. Adjacent to them are the groups which deviate only one step from a pure type, who have also been classified with the highs, middles, and lows. The other three types deviate still further from the main axis of the cube as marked by the three pure types. The "slummers" and the "looking-uppers" are the purest deviants.

Another form of pragmatic reduction is exemplified in the analysis of panel studies. Suppose we ask people which party they intend to vote for at the beginning of the campaign, and repeat the question at the end of the campaign. By using their political positions at those two points in time as our two dimensions, we obtain a nine-fold table (assuming that they can answer either Democratic, Republican, or don't know—or in the second wave, that they did not vote.) If, for some purposes, we are not interested in distinguishing Democrats from Republicans as such, but only in the question of the modes of constancy and change which people have displayed, we can reduce the table to five categories: party constants, party changers, those who crystallized, those who withdrew from a party choice, and those who never crystallized (Table 9).

Table 9—Pragmatic Reduction of a Property-Space of Political Position at Two Points in Time

		VOTE INTENTION AT BEGINNING		
		Democratic	*Don't know*	*Republican*
VOTE ON ELEC- TION DAY	Demo- cratic	Party constant	Crystal- lized	Party changer
	Non- voter	Withdrew	Uncrystal- lized constant	Withdrew
	Repub- lican	Party changer	Crystal- lized	Party constant

Reductions of this sort are of great importance in survey research. If we want to relate "types of constancy" or "change of vote intention" to other variables, it is a good deal easier to work with a set of five categories than with nine; the results we are interested in stand out more clearly and the number of cases is more likely to permit significant results. This is particularly true when both variables we want to relate are initially quite complicated. If we wanted to relate the nine-fold classification presented in Table 1 (usual party affiliation by degree of political interest) to the nine-fold classification of types of change during the campaign which was presented in Table 9 we would have an 81-fold table which would be extremely difficult to work with and demand an enormous sample. By reducing the first to four types—Independents, Partisans, Habituals, and Apathetics—and the second to the five types of change—Party constants, Crystallizers, Withdrawers, Uncrystallized constants, and Party changers—we obtain a manageable number of categories in the form of a four-by-five table.

e. Functional Reductions of Property-Space. Whenever we attempt to reduce sets of scores or combinations of qualitative attributes to a one-dimensional order, we run into the problems of arbitrary weighting or of making decisions in a pragmatic reduction. One method of avoiding these problems and still achieving the reduction of a multidimensional property space to a one-dimensional ranking, is to deliberately seek out items such that many of the cells will have few or no actual cases in them, and most cases will fall into easily ranked categories. A well-known case of such a naturally-occurring, or functional, reduction is the social distance scale, now generalized by Guttman. Such a scale is found whenever properties have the cumulative relationship, so that as one goes up the scale one continues to be positive on the previous-level questions. Thus anyone who consents to having a certain nationality marry into his family should also consent to having them as friends and as fellow workers. The "non-scale types" simply do not occur with any great frequency, and the cases order themselves.

The notion of a Thurstone scale also implies a certain functional reduction of a property-space. Here people who answer questions too far apart on the scale should not occur; with an eleven-question scale we should find the great bulk of the cases falling close to the diagonal of an eleven-dimensional dichotomous attribute-space, answering only closely adjacent questions in terms of their predetermined scale values. The rating of judges which determines the scale value is also used to rule out questions which do fall too far out of line, in that they would be agreed with by considerable numbers at opposite ends. This is likewise the general principle of item analysis, although less rigorously enforced by that method.

SUBSTRUCTION OF THE PROPERTY-SPACE OF A TYPOLOGY

In discussing reduction, we have employed the concept of property-space to clarify the operations by which initially complex classifications are simplified and in some cases formed into rank-ordered categories. We will now apply the property-space concept to another problem: the clarification of typologies.

It is a common practice for both intuitive analysts and empirical researchers to think in terms of a few outstanding "types" of people, situations, or institutions. A study of community leadership is based on the distinction between the "cosmopolitan" versus the "locally-oriented" type of leader. Analysts of social norms traditionally classify them as "folkways," "mores," and "law." Psychologists speak of extroverted and introverted personalities; anthropologists of folk and urban communities.

These types when examined in detail turn out to be defined as clusters of many different attributes. The cosmopolitan leader is distinguished from the local leader by his geographical mobility, his education, his channels of becoming a leader, his interests, his communications behavior. Folkways, mores, and law are distinguished in terms of how they originated, how they are enforced, how deeply they are felt, and so on for each set of types. It appears that the types must represent a reduction or a selection of categories from a fairly complex property-space. The understanding of such types will often be assisted if we reconstruct the entire property-space and see how they were derived from it. The procedure of finding, for a given set of types, the property-space in which they are located and the reduction which has implicitly been used in their formation, has been termed "substruction."

It is not claimed that this formal analysis will necessarily help in the initial creation of sets of types which are fruitful in disclosing new relationships. Neither is it claimed that it describes the actual mental processes of those who create typologies. It is rather intended to assist us in understanding and working with the typologies which are created by someone's fruitful insight. If a typology leads us toward understanding of whole networks of related variables, as for instance the "cosmopolitan/local" typology helped to meaningfully organize a wide range of data,[4] it should be worthwhile to break it down into its components, to study the part played by each. In this process we may also find combinations of properties which were overlooked in constructing the initial typology, and bring to light the assumptions which led to the bypassing of certain combinations or the ignoring of certain distinctions.

For an example we may turn to Kingsley Davis' presentation of the traditional typology of social norms.[5] Among the types which have been distinguished are the following: *Folkways, Mores, Law, Customary law, Enacted law, Customs.*

Folkways are defined as norms which are considered obligatory in the proper situation, but which are not tremendously important or supported by very strong social sanctions. They are enforced by informal social controls rather than formal control agencies, and originate through the gradual growth of tradition rather than by deliberate enactment.

Mores are norms which are believed to be extremely important for the welfare of the society and are therefore very strongly sanctioned. Folkways and mores are similar, however, in originating in tradition rather than in deliberate enactment, and in being enforced by informal sanctions, depending on the spontaneous reactions of the group rather than on the reactions of officials acting in some official capacity.

Law arises when some formal machinery of enforcement is present. If the norms which are enforced in this way have originated in an unplanned manner through tradition, and there is no legislative agency to enact new rules or change old ones, we may speak of a system of *customary law*. On the other hand, what we regard as fully-developed law is the product of thought and planning, of deliberate formulation, and subject to change through regular institutional procedures. This may be called *enacted law*.

Custom is a broad term embracing all the norms classified as folkways and mores. It connotes long-established usage—practices repeated by generation after generation, and enforced by spontaneous community pressures.

In his discussion, Davis suggests a great many attributes of the various types of norms. Some of these, however, seem to be more basic, in that others are expressly stated to be derivative from them. Others seem to be so closely related that there is little need to distinguish them—strength of sanctions, for example, seems to vary closely with strength of group feeling about the norm; changeability seems to vary with the mechanism by which the norm originates. This represents in itself a form of functional reduction. The types listed here seem to have been defined basically in terms of the three dimensions: *how originated* (tradition vs. organized enactment); *how enforced* (informal vs. formal sanctions); and *strength of group feeling* (stronger or milder). The property-space which is formed when we put together these three dimensions is shown in Table 10.

Table 10—A Property-Space Substructed for a Typology of Norms

		HOW ENFORCED			
		Informal Enforcement GROUP FEELING		Formal enforcement GROUP FEELING	
		Strong	Mild	Strong	Mild
	Tradition	Customs		Laws	
HOW ORIG-INATED		MORES	FOLKWAYS	CUSTOMARY LAW	
	Enactment	XX	XX	ENACTED LAW	

It will be noted that some of the types embrace more than one cell—that is, they leave one or ~~more dimensions~~ unspecified. "Customs" is thus

a generic term for informally-enforced, traditional norms, regardless of the group feeling; if we want to distinguish the latter dimension, we talk of "mores" or "folkways." "Laws" cover four cells, while the notions of customary and enacted law make no distinction as to the actual strength of the group feeling regarding the content of the law. This is of course an important distinction in the sociology of law and of crime.

It also appears that certain combinations have been left out—those involving formal enactment with only informal enforcement. Perhaps this omission is based on a certain evolutionary assumption, whereby a society first develops formal enforcement machinery for its traditional norms and only then develops institutions for the enactment of new norms or the change of old ones. It might be, however, that certain types of norms are enacted in a modern society without any provision for formal enforcement; this is possibly true of some "laws" against ethnic and religious discrimination in employment and public service, which affirm the principle but provide no enforcement. We might want to formulate a new term for such legislation, since it is not exactly "law" in the sociological sense.

Another example of the substruction of a property-space for a typology can be based on a study of the structure of authority in the family, which was conducted by the Institute of Social Research in Germany in the early 1930's.[6] Erich Fromm, the director of the study, suggested as a theoretical basis for classifying the questionnaire data the following four

Table 11—A Property-Space Substructed for a Typology of Family Relationships

		CHILDREN'S ACCEPTANCE		
		High	Medium	Low
	Strong	1	2	3
		I	I	IV
PARENTS' EXERCISE	Moderate	4	5	6
		II	II	IV
	Weak	7	8	9
			III	

The above scheme can be related to Fromm's four types, which were, of course, originally conceived by a quite different procedure (Table 12).

Table 12—Relation of the Substructed Property-Space to the Original Typology

Fromm's type	Attribute Combination	Exercise	Acceptance
I Complete authority	1 and 2	Strong	High or Medium
II Simple authority	4 and 5	Moderate	High or Medium
III Lack of authority	8	Weak	Medium
IV Rebellion	3 and 6	Strong or Moderate	Low

types of authority relationships: *Complete authority, Simple authority, Lack of authority, Rebellion.*

By using the procedure of substruction and reduction, it is possible to attain a thorough research procedure and at the same time to exhaust the possible significance of Fromm's types. The authority relationship in a family is determined by the way in which the parents exercise their authority, and by the way in which the children accept it. Through questionnaires, the parental exercise of authority was rated as either strong, moderate, or weak; likewise the children's acceptance of authority was rated as high, medium, or low.[7] This makes logically possible nine combinations (Table 11).

Combinations 7 and 9 are not covered. Apparently it was assumed that neither very high nor very low acceptance was possible for an authority which was scarcely exercised at all. The substruction, however, may be used as a tool for discovery. It points out the logical possibility that there might be children who want an authority which is not actually exercised over them—combination 7. These discovered combinations suggest further research.

The reader may disagree with the above substruction, and may think that other combinations should be matched with Fromm's types; or he may feel that there are certain contradictions between the combinations and the types. Then he may try to improve the types on the basis of the general scheme suggested above. He will see for himself that the procedure of substruction may very probably lead to improvements in typologies which have been constructed on the basis of theoretical considerations or intuitions. The proof of the success of the procedure lies, of course, in concrete applications which lie beyond the scope of the present exemplification.

The problem comes up whether, to every given system of types, only one attribute space and the corresponding reduction can be substructed. The answer is probably "no." The typological classifications used in current social research are often somewhat vague and therefore more than one logical substruction can usually be provided for them. The different attribute spaces originating this way can be transformed one into another, however. The procedure of transformation is very important because it is the logical background of what is in general understood as an interpretation of a statistical result. It could be shown that such an interpretation is often nothing else than transforming a system of types from one attribute space into another with different coordinates, and therewith changing simultaneously one reduction into another. There is no opportunity here to discuss this question.

The operations of reduction, substruction and transformation could be called "typological operations" because their application links any system of types with an attribute space. The logic of these typological operations has not been given enough attention so far, and its careful study could improve considerably the use of types in practical research. These remarks were mainly concerned with illustrating these typological operations. The main one is the reduction of an attribute space to a system of types. Four kinds of reduction were distinguished: the simplification of dimensions, the functional, the arbitrary numerical and the pragmatic. The last one is the most frequent and most important in empirical research; its inversion is called substruction. Substruction consists in matching a given system of types with that attribute space and that reduction from which it could have originated logically. This substruction of an attribute combination to a given system of types permits one to check the omissions or overlappings in this system and points the way to its practical applications.

6. A MULTI-DIMENSIONAL CLASSIFICATION
OF ATROCITY STORIES

by Philip E. Jacob

[Between November 1939 and June 1941, the Princeton Listening Center
recorded short-wave broadcasts of news reports and topical talks disseminated
chiefly from Berlin, London, Rome, and Paris. Philip E. Jacob analyzed the
strategy of atrocity propaganda utilized in these broadcasts. In the selection
below, one of the basic "techniques of intensifying an appeal" is discussed.—ED.
NOTE.]

THE ATROCITY STORY, trusted servant of Allied propaganda in World War I,
has enjoyed an adverturesome career in the radio broadcasts of the present
belligerents, with the Germans, even more than the British or French, finding the weapon to their liking. Radio atrocity campaigns have in effect become vital strategies of conflict. Broadcasters rarely present instances of
brutality haphazardly or as isolated news items. They weave them into
themes which are used in various patterns depending upon the military, diplo-
matic or propaganda activity of the opponent, the attitudes of the particular
audience in mind, and the immediate and long-run objectives of the belligerent. Atrocity stories thus serve as a sensitive barometer of the war. In
addition they illustrate vividly the techniques employed by the propagandists
to intensify emotional appeal and establish credibility, for these techniques
were exploited to the fullest in order to assure the success of the atrocity
campaigns in the face of indifference and skepticism.

What Is an "Atrocity"? An "atrocity" is an abnormal occurrence; i.e.,
behavior which departs from the accustomed patterns of human activity.
It is, however, behavior which so violates the deep-seated standards of social
conduct, the ethic of those witnessing or hearing about the incident, as to
shock them, cause acute nervous discomfort, and arouse the emotion of
horror. It may or may not involve material injury to persons or property. It
must, however, if it is to be considered an atrocity, injure some institution,
convention, practice, attitude or value which a particular audience considers
basic to its whole way of life.

Social standards or norms are not fixed entities and furnish no absolute
criterion by which to judge what constitutes an atrocity. They change as
new forms of behavior establish themselves as normal and normal forms of
behavior become out-of-date. Social standards also vary with the circumstances surrounding the act. What is gangsterism in peace, becomes heroism
if carried out against the enemy in wartime. They vary further with the
cultural background of the audience. The social standards invoked in a

Reprinted in part from "Atrocity Propaganda," pp. 211-212, 239-240, 243-246, in *Propaganda by Short Wave*, edited by Harwood L. Childs and John B. Whitton, by permission of
the author, the editors, and the publisher. (Copyright, 1942, by the Princeton University
Press.)

given incident depend, finally, upon the relationship between the participants and the audience. If the enemy executes civilians it is "brutal murder."
If one's own side does likewise, the state is "protecting its citizens against
criminals."

Considering these variations in social standards, an atrocity must be defined as an act which horrifies a particular audience at a particular time, and
under a given set of circumstances. The reaction may be either an unex-
pressed attitude or overt action. Within limits, an opinion poll helps to
uncover the former. With regard to the latter, one can conceive of a "conscience level" in an audience, a point at which the emotional tension aroused
by an event breaks out into public expressions of horror, oral or written;
into pressure group activity; and ultimately, into government action. An
atrocity, then, is an event which crosses the conscience level of an audience
to a greater or less degree and elicits various forms of overt response. As
the public's view of atrocities changes, the conscience level shifts up or
down. If the conscience level declines, acts formerly considered atrocities,
occur without affecting the audience's conscience significantly enough to
produce overt reaction on its part. If the conscience level rises, some acts
which formerly occurred without a flurry of comment now occasion an out-
burst of public indignation.

The post-World War period witnessed a definite lowering of the conscience level in every part of the world. This was reflected in the general
breakdown of international morality and a lowering of standards of humanity
in warfare. National policies, whether democratic or totalitarian, hardened
a widespread conviction that in the face of alleged national necessity, there
was no "law," and the human conscience, brutalized by two decades of
war and violence, grew numb to horror. In particular, a deep-seated skepticism arose with respect to all atrocity stories—a legacy of World War
propaganda and of the post-war muckraking which followed.

Though the public's conception of an "atrocity" has steadily become
more limited since the World War, the propagandists of the present war
have adopted, virtually unchanged, the definition of their predecessors in
1914-1918. The belligerents, furthermore, whatever their differences in
ideology or conduct, have agreed almost completely with one another as
to what constitutes an atrocity. At least by implication they have accepted
certain "laws" as criteria of human conduct in wartime. This does not
mean that they feel obliged to obey these laws. They merely use them in
judging atrocities committeed by the other side.

Techniques of Presentation. Two problems have chiefly concerned the
belligerent broadcasters in the presentation of atrocities to their audience—
intensity and credibility. Intensity is the excitement value which attaches
to an item, the capacity to produce "stirredness" in an audience. Intensity
enables the appeal to win a place in the audience's focus of attention in
competition with other events and to arouse not only interest but active
concern. Credibility is the impression of truth. It appeals to the rational
faculty of the audience, satisfying its "canons of critical veracity."[1] Actual
truth, or validity, is irrelevant to credibility, except in so far as it may
help to induce belief.

The standards, both in intensity and of credibility, which an atrocity
propagandist must meet to make his appeal effective have risen since the

first World War. Because people now expect war to be horrible, it is not so easy to shock their sensibilities. An incident must be much more intense than before to qualify as an effective "atrocity." On the other hand, in the face of widespread consciousness and of resistance to propaganda, and a heightened skepticism of atrocity propaganda in particular, the task of establishing belief is also much harder. Many of the requirements of credibility, furthermore, conflict with those of intensity, creating an added dilemma. The more intense the news, the greater are the efforts required to induce belief. Yet incidents which are easily believed, are not likely to meet the tests of intensity.

British broadcasters in this war have usually resolved the conflict of credibility and intensity in favor of credibility. Research into English propaganda methods in the first World War has put the British on the defensive, especially in regard to the reliability of atrocity stories, and provided German propagandists with excellent material for effective counterattack. Consequently, the British have discussed atrocities with great caution and little emotion.

The Nazis have had an even greater reputation for unreliability. Their strategy, however, aimed at confusing attitudes rather than rousing strong emotions, has enabled them to place less emphasis on the attainment of belief. While they have by no means neglected the use of devices to establish credibility, they have also reached high levels of intensity, comparable in many cases to British standards of the first World War. Lord Haw-haw and Fred Kaltenbach in particular have become atrocity specialists of the first order.

A detailed quantitative analysis has been made of the techniques used to enhance propaganda for the period between January and April 1940. The German techniques differ but little from those of the other belligerents.

[The author discusses, in general terms, the following techniques: actuality, emphasis (in terms of time devoted to the story), variety, abnormality, individuality (in terms of specificity of details), and integration with the audience's frame of reference. For the present purpose the most interesting aspect is *abnormality*, because for it the author develops specific criteria along a number of dimensions. The description of his coding procedure follows.—ED. NOTE.]

Techniques of Intensifying an Appeal. In the case of an atrocity, the degree of abnormality is a fundamental determinant of intensity. Abnormality can only be determined in reference to the particular social norms or standards of conduct prevailing at a given time, in a given place and under given circumstances. In Table I an attempt has been made to erect a rough scale of abnormality by which to judge "atrociousness." This has as its point of reference the standards of conduct which now appear prevalent under conditions of war in what might be called Western civilization, particularly in England, Germany and the United States. The attempt is necessarily in part subjective in that it is based on *a priori* estimates of the extent of overt audience responses which different types of atrocities will arouse. On the other hand, an objective quality is present in that the opinions of the belligerent broadcasters as to degrees of atrociousness have been scrutinized.

The scale rates the victim of the atrocity, the effect of the act, the weapons or procedure used and the intent of the perpetrator. The victim is measured according to its proximity to the human level of life, the degree of "innocence," defenselessness and expected risk of injury as indicated by its military significance and use, and finally, according to its symbolic significance. The effect of the atrocity is measured by the number of victims involved, the extent of damage to property, and the character of the injury sustained by persons. The weapons used are rated according to the extent of direct contact involved between perpetrator and victim. This is based on the assumption that civilization has depersonalized human intercourse and that the personal, or face-to-face weapon or procedure, has become the primitive, hence the abnormal. The intent of the perpetrator is graded according to its deliberateness.

Table I—Scale of Atrociousness (Based on Degree of Abnormality)

I. VICTIM

A. Proximity to human level of life
1. Inanimate
2. Nonhuman
3. Human
B. Military significance or use (degree of "innocence," defenselessness and expected risk of harm)
1. Of inanimate objects
   a. permanent and direct military use
   b. temporary but direct military use
   c. indirect military use
   d. no military use—in vicinity of military objectives
   e. no military use—not in vicinity of military objectives
   f. no military use—objects belonging to neutrals
2. Of animate objects
   a. the armed forces
   b. hostile civilians (armed)
   c. occupation or residence near military objectives
   d. prisoners
   e. civilians generally (enemy)
   f.   "   "   (neutrals)
   g.   "   "   (perpetrator's own side)
   h. workers
   i. women, children, aged
C. Symbolic significance
1. National
2. Humanitarian
3. Religious

II. EFFECT

A. Number of victims
1. One object
2. Several objects
3. Many objects
4. The whole of a class of objects

B. Extent of damage (property)
1. Partial destruction
2. Total destruction
C. Character of the injury (persons)
1. Civic disability, robbery, etc., causing social or mental discomfort
2. Physical discomfort, indirect injury to life and limb
3. Death or normal wounding
4. Mutilation
5. Sexual mutilation

III. WEAPONS OR PROCEDURE
(degree of impersonality)

A. Impersonal (perpetrator and victim not face-to-face)
1. Policies
2. Projectiles
   a. long-range artillery, bombs
   b. torpedos (directed at specific object)
   c. machine guns (increasingly specific object of attack)
B. Personal (perpetrator and victim)
1. Formal procedures
2. Nonformalized procedures
   a. general
   b. indirect attack (without use of perpetrator's hand)
   c. weapons used against victim at a distance
   d. weapons used directly on victim
   e. body of the perpetrator used

IV. INTENT OF PERPETRATOR

A. Accidental
B. Uncontrolled
C. Indiscriminate
D. Deliberate
1. Deliberateness alleged or implied
2. Deliberateness inheres in the act

7. THE COMPUTATION OF INDEXES
OF MORAL INTEGRATION

by Robert C. Angell

[In his study of "The Moral Integration of American Cities," Robert C. Angell undertook to investigate the degree to which cities held common ends and values. In his first study, a "welfare effort index" was established, based on the assumption that in a morally integrated city the people would have a sense of responsibility for the well-being of their neighbors, and a "crime index" was set up, based on the assumption that "the more the people of a community are knit together in a real moral order, the less they will violate one another's persons or property." The relationship between these indexes was examined, and their relationship to some of the items of Thorndike's "goodness of cities" index was noted.

Some time later a second study was undertaken with a different sample of cities. The "crime index" was computed as in the first study, but a new "welfare effort index" had to be developed because the original type of data was not available for the new sample of cities. By a rather elaborate calculation, the two indexes were combined into a "Moral Integration Index." The methods employed to arrive at these indexes are described below. In addition, a survey research was conducted in four cities; Angell describes how scores were assigned to the replies of the respondents.

In order to obtain a more complete understanding of the writer's intention, it is necessary to consult some of the author's more detailed papers.[1] The selection presented here gives the main ideas and sufficient illustrative data to serve as a first introduction to a rather elaborate research program.—ED. NOTE.]

A. The Welfare Effort Index (First Study). This index was based upon the data available in two tables in the United States Children's Bureau publication, *The Community Welfare Picture as Reflected in Health and Welfare Statistics in 29 Urban Areas, 1938.* From Table 8, "Percentage Distribution of Expenditures by Sources of Funds and Urban Areas," I obtained for each city a figure that I termed the "Percentage Local." This was a summation of percentages derived from local public funds, private contributions, and income from endowments. From Table 9, "Per Capita Expenditures by Sources of Funds and by Urban Areas," I obtained the "Per Capita Local" figure for each city. It sums the percentages from the same three sources. The Percentage Local and Per Capita Local scores for each of the twenty-eight cities are given in Table I. (Washington, D.C., had to be omitted because local public funds could not be separated from federal funds.)

The scores on the Welfare Effort Index, also shown in Table I, were computed in the following manner: First, the Per Capita Local expenditure

Reprinted from "The Moral Integration of American Cities," *American Journal of Sociology,* Vol. LVII, No. 1, Part 2, July, 1951, pp. 123-126, by permission of the author and the publisher. (Copyright, 1951, by the University of Chicago.)

was corrected for level of living by using as a divisor an index worked out by the Children's Bureau for each of the urban areas. Second, the Per Capita Local figure as corrected was multiplied by a fraction whose numerator was the average of the percentages of expenditures that derived from nonlocal sources for all areas and whose denominator was the percentage of expenditures deriving from nonlocal sources for the particular area. Finally, all products were multiplied by 10.

Table I—Per Capita Local Expenditures for Welfare, Percentage Local, and Welfare Effort Scores for Twenty-eight Urban Areas, 1938

Area	Per Capita Local	Percentage Local	Welfare Effort Index
Buffalo	18.95	41.8	266.7
Syracuse	18.81	39.4	235.6
Springfield (Mass.)	19.19	39.9	233.5
Milwaukee	18.75	33.2	199.5
Cincinnati	16.91	36.5	191.5
Baltimore	11.12	40.1	166.1
Richmond (Va.)	11.41	46.4	153.6
Providence	13.56	29.1	148.2
Hartford	15.02	32.7	139.0
Indianapolis	12.44	25.9	132.0
Cleveland	13.68	20.2	131.2
Los Angeles	14.05	31.1	115.5
Louisville	8.14	31.9	111.6
Canton	9.12	21.9	105.0
San Francisco	15.24	26.2	101.7
Bridgeport	10.45	27.6	101.4
Dayton	9.46	20.2	93.2
St. Louis	9.24	21.9	89.9
Kansas City (Mo.)	9.94	24.1	83.3
Columbus (Ohio)	8.01	18.1	72.2
New Orleans	5.41	12.9	71.7
Grand Rapids	6.37	13.2	65.7
Wichita	7.34	24.0	65.2
Atlanta	6.73	18.6	63.5
Houston	6.21	28.3	63.5
Birmingham	3.45	14.1	62.8
Dallas	5.84	23.6	50.7
Wilkes-Barre	4.13	6.7	50.6
Mean, 28 areas	11.04	26.8	114.6

B. The Crime Index (First and Second Studies). In the two statistical studies the Crime Index was computed in almost the same manner. The chief difference was that in the first a five-year summation of crimes was taken, and in the second a three-year *average*. The data were drawn from the *Uniform Crime Reports* published by the Federal Bureau of Investigation. Consultation with criminologists and a study of the Bureau's own *Ten Years of Uniform Crime Reporting,* 1930-1939 convinced me that murder and nonnegligent manslaughter, robbery, and burglary were the three most reliable categories for my purpose. The five-year totals for each of the twenty-eight cities in the first study for each of these types of crime are given in Table II.

The crime scores were computed as follows: First, standard yearly frequencies per 100,000 population were established for cities between 100,000 and 1,000,0000. These proved to be 6.51 for murder and nonnegligent manslaughter, 65.58 for robbery, and 390.90 for burglary. Second, the standard burglary frequency was then divided by each of the other two and the square roots of the two quotients taken. These square roots, 7.75 and 2.44, respectively, were used as factors by which to multiply the number of homicides and robberies for each city before combining them with the burglaries by addition. The effect of this complicated operation was to give the crimes in the three categories weights proportional to the square roots of their frequencies. One homicide equals, not one burglary, but 7.75 burglaries. This seemed a justifiable procedure, since it appeared to be better than weighting one homicide as equal to one burglary or than weighting all homicides as equal to all burglaries. Finally, the sums of the three categories as thus manipulated were divided by the 1940 population of each city in thousands to give the crime scores that are recorded in the last column of Table II. In the second study the procedure was the same except that a yearly average was obtained and this average was divided, not by the total population, but by the population over fifteen years of age. Few crimes are committed by those younger than fifteen.

   C. *The Welfare Effort Index* (*Second Study*). This index was computed from data kindly supplied by Community Chests and Councils, Inc. In the second statistical study the data for 1940 were used. When I wished to check the rating of the four cities in which survey research was carried on

Table II—Number of Crimes in Specified Categories January 1, 1936, to December 31, 1940, and Crime Scores for Twenty-eight Cities

City	Murder and Non-negligent Man-slaughter	Robbery	Burglary	Crime Index
Milwaukee	47	252	2,670	6.22
Buffalo	70	453	3,371	9.14
Providence	16	85	2,259	10.20
Syracuse	10	118	2,105	11.99
Wilkes-Barre	4	111	918	14.18
Springfield (Mass.)	6	63	2,019	14.79
New Orleans	366	678	2,968	15.07
Bridgeport	27	129	2,026	17.35
Wichita	17	95	1,861	19.34
St. Louis	321	2,420	7,483	19.46
Grand Rapids	10	190	3,022	21.73
Baltimore	347	3,127	10,663	24.43
Dayton	95	558	3,419	26.15
Hartford	17	106	4,122	27.18
San Francisco	115	2,813	11,174	29.81
Canton	16	533	2,130	32.91
Cleveland	348	5,684	13,106	33.79
Kansas City (Mo.)	199	2,495	6,462	35.32
Houston	340	1,486	9,865	41.89
Cincinnati	257	2,687	10,711	42.23
Los Angeles	393	8,169	42,229	43.36
Dallas	347	902	8,638	45.86
Indianapolis	178	2,379	11,353	47.90
Birmingham	363	835	8,158	48.54
Richmond (Va.)	181	1,026	6,565	54.25
Columbus (Ohio)	80	2,075	11,311	55.54
Louisville	202	2,017	12,600	59.83
Atlanta	524	2,442	13,373	77.46

after the war, I obtained the 1947 figures and computed the index in the same manner as before.

The cards of Community Chests and Councils, Inc., show the population covered by the campaign in each city, the quota assigned, the amount raised, and the number of persons making pledges. From these data the following formula was constructed to give a welfare effort score:

$$\frac{\text{Amount raised}}{\text{Quota}} + \frac{\text{Pledgers}}{\text{No. of families in the area}} + \frac{\text{Amount raised}}{.0033 \times \text{Yearly retail sales}}$$

Each of the three ratios fluctuated around unity, so that the scores fluctuated around 3.0. It was thought that each of the three ratios measures one aspect of welfare effort—degree of achievement of goal, proportion of families giving, and economic sacrifice involved.

D. The Integration Index. The Integration Index used in the second statistical study was computed by using the Crime Index and the Welfare Effort Index of that study. To determine whether they should be weighted equally or in some other manner, each of these two was correlated with the two causal factors which had already emerged as important—mobility and heterogeneity. The coefficients of correlation were: crime with mobility +.45; crime with heterogeneity +.58; welfare effort with mobility —.57; and welfare effort with heterogeneity —.20. The average correlation of crime with these two factors was +.51 and of welfare effort —.38. Since the real significance of a correlation coefficient is revealed by its square, and since the squares in this case were .26 and .14, I decided to weight crime twice as much as welfare effort in computing the Integration Index.

The Crime Index and the Welfare Effort Index were combined in the following manner: The crime scores were reversed by subtracting them from 20 (they ran originally from 1.6 for Milwaukee to 17.5 for Atlanta). This was done in order to make the high values indicate strong integration. The varieties of the Welfare Effort Index were then translated into a distribution having the same mean and standard deviation as the crime series by the formula

$$x_1 = M_1 + \frac{\sigma_1}{\sigma_1}(x_2 - M_2)$$

given by Karl Holzinger in *Statistical Methods for Students of Education,* page 121; the crime variates were multiplied by 2 in order to give them double weight in the final integration score; the two scores for each city were added; and the sums were divided by 3 to bring the integration scores back to a series having the same mean and standard deviation as the constituent series.

E. Indexes in the Survey Research. In the tables dealing with the survey research some of the figures are percentages, but most of them are indexes. The great majority of these indexes are derived from three- or five-step codes. In the former case the number of respondents falling in the high or "good" category was multiplied by 5, in the middle category by 3, and in the low category by 1. In the five-step case the numbers in the various categories were multiplied, respectively, by 5, 4, 3, 2, or 1. In both cases these moments were then added and the sum was divided by the total number of respondents. Thus, these indexes are weighted averages.

Occasionally the term "special index" appears in the tables. The need for this type of index arises from the fact that several of the questions in both cross-section and leader interviews resulted in multiple answers. The question asked of the leaders, "How did you first get started in taking an active part in community affairs?" will serve as an example. Respondents often gave more than one answer. For instance, a leader might lay great stress on the fact that community leadership was a tradition in his family, but he might also mention that friends influenced him and that business reasons played a part. In such a case the coder recorded the reasons in the order of their importance. According to the general run of the answers to specific questions, it was decided how many answers for any one respondent would be coded. Sometimes the maximum was two, usually it was three, and once or twice it was four. The usual situation was that the number of answers dropped away very rapidly after the first one. For instance, if in one of the cross-sections 100 respondents gave a first reason why they liked their city, perhaps only 50 would give a second, and only 10 a third. This raises a difficulty for computing an index. In such a case it would obviously be inappropriate to give equal weights to first and third answers, since, if this were done, an individual who gave three answers would have three times the weight of an individual who gave only one. On the other hand, to deal only with the first answers would also be a distortion, because some reason of importance might appear hardly at all as a first answer but frequently as a second.

This problem was met in the following manner: The percentage of all respondents giving a specified first answer was computed and multiplied by 4. For instance, if 33 persons among 100 respondents gave as their primary reason for liking the city that it was friendly, then 132 points were scored for this fact. If 15 more gave this as a second reason, this was multiplied by 2 and 30 points was added to the 132. If 8 gave it as a third reason, this was multiplied by 1 and the 8 points were added. Finally, if fourth reasons were being used, and 4 gave friendliness as their fourth reason for liking the city, this was multiplied by ½ and the 2 points added. Thus, an index figure of 172 would be reached. The maximum score on any such special index item is 400—the result if all the respondents gave the same answer as the most important reason for them. The maximum possible sum of all the scores assigned on such a question to different reasons varies with the number of answers by any one respondent that are coded: if two, the maximum sum is 600; if three, 700; if four, 750.

8. INDICES OF PSYCHOLOGICAL ILLNESS

by Samuel A. Stouffer

ONE OF THE OBJECTIVES of social science is to develop techniques for prediction which will enable the user to predict more efficiently than if these techniques did not exist. By more efficiently we mean that the percentage of correct predictions is higher, on the average, than would otherwise be obtained for the same expenditure of effort.

The Research Branch* frequently in its surveys was in the position of having to make informal or implicit predictions. For example, the interpretation of any observed relationship between two variables usually carries with it the implication that the association found at a given time and place will be found at some future time and place. In some cases, especially when controlled experiments have been used, the results carry the additional implication that if one manipulates X, one can expect a change in Y —in other words, that X can be regarded now and in the future, as a "cause of Y." All too often to satisfy the scientific consciences of members of the Research Branch, predictions forced by military exigencies had to be made when the data were quite inadequate.

As is so often the case with problems of prediction, the major difficulty lay in the lack of clarity as to the criterion situation. If one is using a poll to predict a presidential election, one has a simple and definite criterion in the number of votes actually cast for each candidate at the presidential election. If one is predicting, however, on the basis of test scores, which men psychiatrists will reject for the Army after a psychiatric examination at induction stations, it turns out that the criteria are variable indeed.

A study is reported of over 100,000 men constituting the entire population examined at all the induction stations in the United States in August 1945. For each man we have data on his score on the Neuropsychiatric Screening Adjunct (NSA), i.e., the screening test developed by the Research Branch for the Surgeon General, and on the disposition made by the examining physicians. There we see a rather astonishing fact—that, although the test scores had much the same frequency distribution throughout the United States, the proportions of men rejected on psychiatric grounds varied all the way from 0.5 per cent at one induction station to 50.6 per cent at another.

Reprinted in part from *Measurement and Prediction*, Studies in Social Psychology in World War II, Vol. IV, pp. 473-477, by permission of the author and the publisher. (Copyright, 1950, by the Princeton University Press.)

* Research Branch of the Information and Education Division, U. S. Army, World War II.

Not only did the psychiatric rejection rate fluctuate from one induction station to another, but so also did the reasons for psychiatric rejections. If, for each station with fifty or more psychiatric rejects, we set *all* psychiatric rejects equal to 100 per cent, we find that the proportions among these psychiatric rejects classified as *psychoneurotic* varied from 2.7 per cent to 90.2 per cent, while the proportions classified as *psychopathic* varied from nothing up to 81.3 per cent. Such variations may seem almost fantastic, but, of course, one must remember that psychiatry is still far from an exact science, that the number of competent psychiatrists is not too large, and that the time which physicians could devote to the examination of any one man was extremely limited.

Variations were especially large in the South, as might be expected due to lack of trained psychiatrists. Thus at the induction station in New Orleans, 74.6 per cent of the psychiatric rejects were found to be psychoneurotic, but only 22.7 per cent were at Oklahoma City. Only 2.2 per cent of the psychiatric rejects in New Orleans were found to be psychopathic, as compared with 70.9 per cent in Oklahoma City. But such variations were not confined to the South. In Boston, 57.9 per cent of the psychiatric rejects were found to be psychoneurotics; in New Haven only 25.0 per cent. In Chicago the figure was 71.8 per cent; in Detroit, 31.5 per cent. In San Francisco the figure was 69.1 per cent; in Seattle-Portland the figure was 22.9 per cent.

The scoring of the screening test was so designed that about a third of American young men, on the average, would manifest signs indicative of the need of very careful psychiatric examination. This does not mean that all these men should have been rejected. Rather, the cutting point was set high enough to include among the one third practically all of the psychiatric cases, as well as some who, upon careful examination, should be accepted by the Army. Part of the prediction problem was to find whether or not this one third did include most of the eventual psychiatric rejects.

Actually, this one third screened by the test included 80.8 per cent of the psychoneurotic rejects, 68.2 per cent of the psychopathic rejects, 70.8 per cent of the psychotic rejects, and 56.4 per cent of all other psychiatric rejects. All told, it screened 69.5 per cent of all psychiatric rejects. At the same time, it screened, as cases also worth examining, 21.8 per cent of the men eventually admitted and 30.3 per cent of the men rejected by the physicians on other than psychiatric grounds.

In spite of the very great variability from one induction station to another in psychiatric diagnosis, there was no station with as many as fifty psychiatric rejects in which the test did not screen at least half of those eventually rejected for psychiatric grounds, and in all but four of these stations the proportions screened were between 60 per cent and 96 per cent.

The variability of psychiatric diagnosis is not exactly news to psychiatrists, but until this study was made there was no uniform scoring device against which the variability throughout the United States could be compared. Hence, if there was three times as high a psychiatric rejection rate in one city as in another, there was no answer if somebody chose to argue that maybe one city did have three times as many psychiatric cases in proportion to its population as another.

How the Research Branch data throw light on such discrepancies may be illustrated in detail by a comparison of data from the Chicago and Detroit induction stations:

	Chicago	Detroit	Number of Cases
Proportion rejected on psychiatric grounds among all men examined	7.6%	21.6%	4,523
Proportion screened by NSA as worth careful examination	24.1	26.9	4,235

We see that, *in spite of the fact* that the test scores showed about the same proportion in the two populations as needing careful examination (24.1 per cent in Chicago and 26.9 per cent in Detroit), the Chicago psychiatric examination rejected only 7.6 per cent while the Detroit examination rejected nearly three times as many. Let us continue:

	Chicago	Detroit
Psychiatric diagnosis of all psychiatric rejects:		
Psychoneurotic	71.8%	31.5%
Psychopathic	10.7	39.0
Psychotic	1.2	——
All others	16.3	29.5
	100.0%	100.0%
Total number of rejects	344	915

Not only did Detroit reject three times as many as Chicago, but also among the rejects the "causes" of rejection were very different.

Because the distribution of test scores at the two stations was about the same, yet the psychiatric diagnoses were so different, one cannot expect to find the test very efficient in predicting psychiatrists' behavior. We have the following findings:

	Chicago	Detroit
Proportion screened by NSA as worth careful examination, among:		
Men later accepted for military service	19.5%	15.3%
All psychiatric rejects	64.6	60.9
Psychoneurotic rejects	69.0	88.8
Psychopathic rejects	62.2	58.2
Psychotic rejects	75.0	..
All other rejects	42.9	35.3

There can be no doubt that the test tended to screen a much larger proportion at each induction station among those subsequently rejected on psychiatric grounds than among those accepted. That the discriminating power of the test was as effective as these data show is all the more noteworthy in view of the widely divergent standards of psychiatric diagnosis, acceptance, and rejection which it seems probable were applied at the two stations.

The same kind of discrepancies, as between Chicago and Detroit, are also seen all over the United States. In general, the relationship of the NSA test scores to the psychiatric diagnosis was about the same elsewhere as at these two stations; on the average, somewhat more discriminating but not much more.

Thus we have illustrated a central problem of prediction in social science —namely, the difficulties of making predictions when the behavior to be predicted (in this case, actually, the behavior of psychiatrists with respect to the individual tested) is itself unstandardized and subject to great variation.

9. A COMPARISON OF THREE MEASURES
OF SOCIOECONOMIC STATUS

by George A. Lundberg and Pearl Friedman

DEFINITION OF CONCEPTS and testing of hypotheses are carried out in the mature sciences through the use of appropriate instruments of observation and measurement. The perfecting of such instruments must proceed in the social as in the other sciences by extensive testing of tentative scales, through comparison of the results shown by different types of instruments and through the correlation of such results with accepted criteria of validity. The necessary data for the improvement of the scales and the interpretation of their results can be secured only from careful analysis of the results of many applications of the scales to actual and varied samples of phenomena.

The present paper reports the results achieved in a Vermont rural township from scoring 232 homes with three measures of socioeconomic status, namely: (1) the Chapin *Social Status Scale 1933, Revised 1936;*[1] (2) the Guttman-Chapin Scale, 1942 (same as (1) but with differently weighted items);[2] and (3) the Sewell Scale, 1940.[3]

The population scored lives in a rural area including an unincorporated village in southwestern Vermont. The population of the entire township in 1940 according to the Federal census was 1577; the number of families, 418. A comparison of the occupational distribution for the whole township according to a contemporary directory[4] and for the sample scored is shown in Table I.

Table I—Occupational Distribution of the Population of Shaftsbury Township, Vermont, 1941

	Survey Sample %	Manning's Directory %
Farmers	30.1	26.2
Skilled	13.2	8.4
Semi-skilled	21.5	20.8
Unskilled	7.3	13.5
White collar	8.2	10.6
Business	4.3	4.1
Professional	4.7	4.1
None	10.7	12.3
	100.0	100.0
Number of cases	(233)	(370)

It will be seen that the occupational distribution of our sample approaches very closely the occupational distribution of the township as a whole. Only in one instance, namely, the proportion of unskilled, does our sample differ from the whole population by as much as 6.2%. There is strong reason to

Reprinted from *Rural Sociology*, Vol. 8, 1943, pp. 227-236, by permission of the authors and the publisher. (Copyright, 1943, by the Rural Sociological Society.)

believe that our sample is highly representative not only of this township but of a much larger area of rural New England. However, the present paper is primarily concerned with the comparison of three different measures of socioeconomic status rather than with the representativeness of the scores and other findings, which will be reported in a later paper.

Chart I and Tables II and III show the distribution of scores for each of the three instruments. The difference in position of the curves on the horizontal scale indicates, of course, merely the difference in the basis of standardization, i.e., the absolute values assigned to different items constituting the scale. This basis for the Chapin scale, both in its original and its revised form, is considerably lower than for the Sewell scale, as is indicated by their respective means. (See Table IV.) Of greater interest is (1) the distribution of scores around their respective means (Table IV) and (2) the reasons for the occurrence of radically different *relative* scores for the same home, according to the three scales (Table VI). The latter point will be considered below.

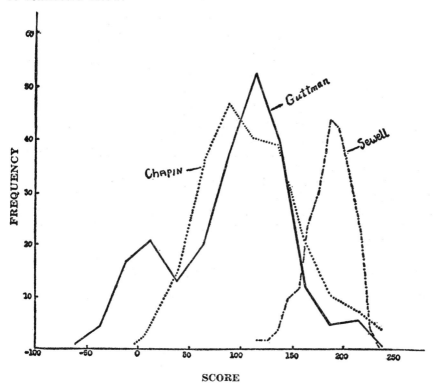

SCORE

Chart 1. The Distribution of Scores of Socioeconomic Status of 233 Families of a Rural Vermont Township According to the Chapin, Chapin-Guttman, and Sewell Scales, 1941.

As will be seen from Chart I, the chief effect of the Guttman revision of the Chapin scale is to decrease certain low scores to a degree which distorts the normality of the distribution as compared with both the unrevised Chapin scores and the Sewell scores. The correlation between the scores of the Sewell and the Guttman-Chapin scale is also lower than when the unrevised Chapin scores are used. (Guttman-Chapin and Sewell, $r = + .73$

± .031; unrevised Chapin and Sewell, r = +.76 ± .028.) The reason for
the sharp increase in the frequency of the lower scores of the Guttman-
Chapin scale is the relatively heavy increase in weights which the revision

Table II—Frequency Distribution of Chapin Social Status Scores (Shaftsbury
Township, Vermont, 1941)

Score	F
0- 24	11
25- 49	15
50- 74	36
75- 99	47
100-124	40
125-149	39
150-174	22
175-199	10
200-224	8
225 and over	4
	232

assigned to negative answers to the subjective items of the original Chapin
scale. Thus, a "spotted or stained" condition of the living room and fur-
nishings was weighted —4 in the Chapin scale (1936) as compared with
—19 in the Guttman revision. The corresponding weights on the item
"articles strewn about in disorder" are —2 (Chapin) as against —20 (Guttman). Negative weights of other items of this type are also heavily increased
in the Guttman revision. Altogether, the negative weights in Part II of the
Chapin Scale are increased by Guttman a total of 61 points whereas the
increase in positive weights on the corresponding items total only 33.[5] This
accounts for the asymmetrical distribution of the low scores in the Guttman
revision (Chart I).

Whether the results shown by the revised scale or by the original shall
be regarded as more valid for the cases here under consideration depends,
of course, upon what criteria of validity we adopt. If the "common sense"
criterion of the field workers in this survey is adopted, the feeling was that
the Guttman revision assigned too much weight to the subjective items in
the Chapin scale. Not only are these items objectionable in themselves because they are relatively subjective, but they are also highly dependent on

Table III—Frequency Distribution of Sewell Socioeconomic Status Scores
(Shaftsbury Township, Vermont, 1941)

Score	F
110-119	2
120-129	2
130-139	3
140-149	10
150-159	12
160-169	24
170-179	32
180-189	44
190-199	42
200-209	32
210-219	23
220-229	4
230-239	1
	231

chance factors such as the particular time of the interview (e.g., "house cleaning" time, soon after moving into a house, etc.). Assuming a random sample, which was certainly approached in the present case, and assuming that in a random sample socioeconomic status is normally distributed, the distortion of the normality of the distribution by the Guttman revision of the Chapin scale suggests the presence of spurious factors in the considerations on which the revision is based. In any event, the Guttman revision results in a higher coefficient of variation for the distribution as a whole (Table IV).

Table IV—Comparison of Distribution of Scores According to Three Scales

| Measures | SCALES | | |
	Chapin	Guttman-Chapin	Sewell
Mean	108.2	92.2	184.8
Median	104.1	100.8	186.9
Mode	90.1	101.9	188.5
Standard Deviation	50.2	59.5	22.0
Coefficient of Variation	46.3%	64.5%	11.9%

The distribution of scores obtained from the Sewell scale for this sample is conspicuously homogeneous and symmetrical. A coefficient of variation of only 11.9% as compared with 46.3% (Chapin scale) and 64.5% (Guttman Revision) characterizes in a summary fashion one of the results of the application of the three measures.

It will be recalled that the Sewell scale was standardized for farm families in Oklahoma whereas the Chapin scale was standardized for urban working class families in Minneapolis.[6] This fact and certain details of its construction suggest that the Sewell scale should be the more valid instrument for the sample here under consideration. In order to observe, however, the operation of each of the three instruments in particular cases, we consider below a selected group of actual cases in which the discrepancies between the three scales were largest.

Table VI indicates the relative decile positions of ten cases on which scores secuied from the Chapin scale and from the Sewell scale showed the greatest discrepancy. The table also shows the position of these cases on the Guttman-Chapin scale. To make the scores comparable their decile position in their respective distributions is given in the last three columns of the table.

These are, of course, extreme cases. The correlation noted above (r = +.76) between the scores of the Chapin and the Sewell scales for this sample indicates that, on the whole, there is good agreement in their results. A careful scrutiny of the cases of maximum disagreement is valuable, however, in revealing the peculiarities of either or both scales. Accordingly, we consider below the particular conditions surrounding these cases which resulted in the gross disagreement of the two principal scales in the relative socioeconomic rating of these families and the effect of the Guttman revision in each case (Table VI).

The low Chapin score of Case 217 is due chiefly to the absence of fireplace with utensils, desk, and periodicals, especially the last item, which in this scale receives a weight of 8 points for each periodical taken. On the other hand, the Sewell scale credits this family with 14 points for high school education of both husband and wife and gives them a total of 38 points for church membership, church and Sunday School attendance, and the wife's membership in the P.T.A. Thus the Sewell scale assigns a total of 52 points to aspects of the family's social status for which they receive no points on the Chapin scale. The Sewell scale further takes into consideration the relatively spacious and comfortable house (room-person ratio, 7 points) with running water (8 points), kitchen sink (7 points) and separate kitchen, dining room, and living room (18 points). The items enumerated above altogether account for about half of the points in the total score on the Sewell scale. The Chapin scale assigns no credit to these features. The Guttman revision places this case in the same decile of its distribution as does the Chapin scale, namely, the fourth. The Sewell scale places the family in the ninth decile. There is no doubt that by the standards existing in this community this family belongs above the mode as the Sewell scale places it, rather than at the mode as the Chapin scale has it. On a self-rating scale of "very comfortable," "comfortable," "not so comfortable," this family further confirmed the validity of the Sewell rating by estimating itself as "very comfortable."

Table VI*—Extreme Cases of Disagreement in Socioeconomic Scores According to the Chapin Scale, the Gutman-Chapin Scale, and the Sewell Scale

Case (Serial Number)	SCALE SCORES			DECILES		
	Chapin Score	Guttman-Chapin Score	Sewell Score	Chapin	Guttman-Chapin	Sewell
3	62	99	192	2	5	6
5	242	127	186	9	8	5
34	102	67	207	5	4	9
41	96	123	211	5	7	9
79	36	13	188	1	2	6
111	70	7	200	3	2	8
176	156	8	160	9	2	2
205	74	64	193	3	3	7
217	82	78	208	4	4	9
226	105	130	210	5	8	9

* [Table V appears in footnote 6.—Ed.]

The same general factors in varying degrees also account for the discrepancy in the scores assigned by the two scales to Cases 3, 34, 41, 111, 205, and 226. In Cases 3 and 226 the Guttman revision agrees more nearly with the Sewell scale, by placing the case in an adjoining decile. In Cases 34 and 111 the discrepancy is increased slightly by the Guttman revision, but it agrees closely with the Chapin score. In Case 41 the Guttman revision places the case in an intermediate position as compared to the other two scales. Case 205 is placed in the same relative positions by the Chapin scale and the Guttman revision.

Another case of this type but with some differences in detail is Case 79. The Chapin scale places it in the first decile, whereas the Sewell scale places it slightly above the mean and exactly at the mode for this community. The Guttman revision agrees closely with the Chapin scale. Again the self-rating of "comfortable" agrees with the Sewell score. The low Chapin score is the result of no large rug, no window drapes, no fireplace, library table, armchairs, piano bench, desk, or periodicals. In addition, the general condition of the living room and furniture further reduces the score by almost the maximum possible. On the basis of the data taken into consideration in the Chapin scale, this seems to be a family legitimately classified as of low status. The Sewell scale in this case arrives at its total score by the accumulation of small credits for the more numerous items which it includes. The house and the room-person ratio receive minimum credit, except for a separate kitchen and finished floors and woodwork. On the other hand, the case receives maximum credit for piped water, kitchen sink, linoleum on the kitchen floor and power washer. Also the family receives maximum credit for education of both husband and wife and the latter's church membership and participation in the P.T.A., but very little credit for other social participation. The general picture is that of a large family of a skilled industrial worker which by common sense standards is perhaps regarded in the community as of average status.

In Case 5 a radically different set of circumstances accounts for the discrepancy in the scores on the Chapin and the Sewell scales, with the Guttman revision again agreeing closely with the Chapin rating. The high Chapin score (242) is accounted for almost entirely by the fact that the family takes 15 periodicals which on the Chapin scale receive 8 points each. This weight is reduced in the Guttman revision to 2, which accounts mainly for the lower Guttman score (126). The explanation of the surprisingly large number of periodicals was that "they just love to read." The wife also said "I'd like to write books" in answer to the question "If you could do whatever you liked, what would you most desire to do?" Since this literary urge does not receive specific recognition in the Sewell scale, the case receives only an average score on this scale although it receives the maximum credit for possession of books (8) and for the wife's education (8) and next to maximum credit for the husband's education (6). On the other hand, the family score on church and Sunday School attendance and membership in farm cooperatives and P.T.A. is the minimum. Also, there is no piped water in the house, and no rugs or carpets on the living room floor, no telephone and no life insurance. Clearly this is a case of neglect of the "physical" in favor of the "spiritual" life, and whether it is more properly rated in the ninth decile by the Chapin scale or the fifth decile on the Sewell scale is one of these questions which must be decided entirely on the basis of whatever criteria of validation are adopted. The family rates itself as comfortable, which is in agreement with the Sewell rating (fifth decile). Whichever way it is decided, the decision must be kept in mind as a fundamental one in the definition of the term *socioeconomic status* whenever that term as defined by a given scale is used. There is obviously no point in trying to settle the question by arguing about what socioeconomic status "really is."

A similar but even more aggravated case is 176, which falls in the second decile of the Sewell distribution and in the ninth decile of the Chapin distribution. (The self-rating was "comfortable"). The high Chapin score results chiefly from the fact that the family reports taking nine periodicals. The Sewell scale, on the other hand, credits the family with minimum or low scores on education, participation in church and community organizations, and records that there is no separate kitchen and dining room. The apparent incongruity of the large number of periodicals in this situation is partly explained by the fact that the list includes *Hunting and Fishing, Field and Stream, National Sportsman, Woman's Day, American Agricul-*

turist, and *New England Homestead.* The Guttman revision of the score of this case (8) brings it into the same decile on this scale as it is on the Sewell scale. This results from the reduced weight given to periodicals in the Guttman revision and from the heavy penalties assigned by this scale to poor and unkempt conditions of articles in the living room.

Thus, in three of the ten cases of extreme discrepancy, namely Cases 3, 176, and 226, the Guttman revision agrees more nearly with the Sewell rating. In six cases (5, 34, 79, 111, 205, 217) the Guttman and the Chapin scores agree more closely; and in one case (41) the Guttman revision takes an intermediate position. With the exception of one case (41), the self-rating of all of these ten families corresponded more closely to the Sewell score.

The self-rating consisted of asking the person interviewed, usually the wife, after the Sewell schedule had been completed, whether she would characterize the family situation as "very comfortable," "comfortable," or "not so comfortable." The question is, of course, somewhat ambiguous, and somewhat delicate under existing conventions. It was not intended to use the results as tests of validity of the scales but rather as an indication of the standards of individual cases and as a possible clue to maladjustment. The statistical results secured from the question were as follows:

On the whole, the population takes an optimistic view of their situation. Eighty-eight per cent of all answering the question rate themselves as "comfortable" or "very comfortable," including more than half (62%) of those in the lowest 23% of the Sewell distribution. (The proportion not answering is about the same in each socioeconomic group.) Of the middle 51% of the distribution, three times as many (18) regard themselves as "very comfortable" as compared to those who regard themselves as "not so comfortable" (6), although the overwhelming majority (70) in this middle group regard themselves as "comfortable." The upper 26% of the Sewell distribution are the most conservative in their self-estimate, since more of them (26) regard themselves as only "comfortable" rather than as "very comfortable" (23).

Table VII—Self-Rating of 230 Rural Families Compared to Their Socioeconomic Rating on the Sewell Scale (Shaftsbury, Vermont, 1941)

Sewell Scores	Not so Comfortable	Comfortable	Very Comfortable	No Answer	Total
Under 170 (Lower 23%)	15	26	1	11	53
170-199 (Middle 51%)	6	70	18	24	118
200 and up (Upper 26%)	0	26	23	10	59
TOTAL	21	122	42	45	230
Per Cent	9.	53.	18.	19.	99.

The recent notable growth in number and quality of scales of the type here under consideration is undoubtedly one of the most encouraging developments in recent social science. The significance of these instruments in the testing of hypotheses and the development of scientific theory far transcends their other "practical" values. The greatest weakness of the social sciences is not their paucity of generalizations but the lack of reliable techniques of determining *under what conditions* these generalizations are true and *to what extent* they are true under varying conditions. As P. W. Bridgman[7] has pointed out, in science a question is regarded as meaningless unless a set of operations can be specified and carried out which would yield a definitive answer. This fact is only beginning to be faced in the social sciences. Hitherto it has been customary to regard the development of instruments for the objective definition of the categories and testing of hypotheses in sociological theorizing as a somewhat pedantic side issue. Actually, this is a crucial matter without which social theorizing is meaningless in Bridgman's sense. The elaborate theories which today constitute the principal content of the social sciences, remain, in effect, merely hypotheses until they are more specifically defined and tested.

This end cannot be achieved until more specific definitions of the concepts used in sociological theory are formulated. It is not a matter of arriving at a single "true" definition of such words as "status," "prestige," "class," etc., but a matter of inventing instruments of whatever number or graduations are necessary meaningfully to discriminate with objectivity and precision the phenomena and the relationships we talk about in our theorizing. The development of scales and tests for the measurement of abilities, personality traits, attitudes, and other personal characteristics has greatly advanced psychology and sociology in the last two decades. There are some evidences that the necessities of the present war may impart a considerable impetus to this movement. It is to be hoped that a substantial part of future developments will be in the direction of defining more objectively the distinctively sociological concepts which figure so largely in the theorizing of all the social sciences.

10. THE INTERCHANGEABILITY OF SOCIO-ECONOMIC INDICES

by Hortense Horwitz and Elias Smith

IN A PREVIOUS PAPER[1] the following fact was reported. The proportion of Republican votes goes up with the socio-economic status of the voters; this does not vary substantially if different indices of status are used—even if these indices are not highly correlated among themselves. The present paper endeavors to present the additional information gained from the study of three surveys conducted by the National Opinion Research Center of the University of Denver: a nationwide poll made in May, 1942, covering about three thousand five hundred cases; a nationwide poll made in November, 1942, covering about three thousand four hundred cases; and a nation-

This is a previously unpublished paper.

wide poll made in January, 1944, covering about three thousand four hundred cases. These surveys will henceforth be referred to respectively as No. 112, No. 120, and No. 128.

The indices used are of two kinds: the intuitive ratings by the interviewers of the economic status of the respondent, set down in terms of A, B, C, or D levels; and indices indicative of economic levels based on the "economic characteristics" (home ownership, car ownership, etc.) of the respondent.

Since the intuitive ratings were in four steps, the index constructed was a four-step one, to make them as comparable as possible, made up of identical information available on each survey, namely, telephone ownership, car ownership, and college education. The respondent was classified according to his possession of all three, telephone and car and some or complete college education (very high), any two (high), any one (average), or none (low). The association between these two indices showed a correlation of .68 for Survey No. 112 (and approximately that for No. 120 and No. 128), a figure high but quite far from complete; *yet we shall see that their influence on a number of third variables was almost the same.*

To give an idea of the distribution of the two indices and their interrelation, Table 1 provides the actual figures from Survey 112, pertaining to large Northern cities and small rural places in the South.

Table 1—Interrelation of Two Measures of Socio-Economic Status

Itemized Index Score	URBAN NORTH					RURAL SOUTH				
	Intuitive Rating						Intuitive Rating			
	A	B	C	D	Total	A	B	C	D	Total
3	34	93	31	..	158	12	16	10	..	38
2	27	100	174	13	314	10	45	61	3	119
1	2	30	153	59	244	1	16	146	62	225
0	..	4	106	130	240	..	3	56	120	179
Total	63	227	464	202	956	23	80	273	185	561

The third variables were in all cases obtained from the answers to questions on cost of living, wage and salary limitation, government regulation of prices, and group participation in the war effort, questions on attitudes which would be sensitive to social differences.

The wording of the questions is given in the Appendix. The answers were dichotomized to give as even a break as possible.

For each question, then, two measures of association were computed, one with the ABCD rating and one for the itemized property rating. The original data were all in the form of 2 x 4 tables. For such tables Mosteller has suggested a formula which is a natural extension of the point correlation of a fourfold table. For each stratum i we compute the value $s_i t_i$, where s_i are the number of people who give a "positive" and t_i the number who give a "negative" answer to the question; n_i is the number of respondents in each stratum. For the whole sample the corresponding symbols will be S, T and N. The Mosteller measure of association between answer and social status then is given by the formula

$$r = \sqrt{1 - \frac{\sum_i \frac{s_i t_i}{n_i}}{\frac{ST}{N}}}$$

The distribution of property and the intuitive assessment of residents probably varies by region of the country and by size of community. Therefore, each sample was divided into six groups according to whether the interviews were made in the North or in the South, and whether the respondents lived in cities of more than 100,000 population, in places with less than 2,500 population, or in towns in between these size classes. With seventeen questions available this gave us 102 pairs of coefficients of associations to work with.

The main result is recorded in Table 2. Along the horizontal stub the associations with the itemized property index is divided into intervals of .05 points; along the vertical stub the intuitive A-B-C-D rating, as assigned by the interviewer, is treated the same way. In the diagonal of Table 2 the cases are entered where a question correlated with socio-economic status the same way, irrespective of what index of status was used. This happened in 51 of the cases, just half of all available. In 31 cases the rating showed a smaller association than the itemized index; in 20 cases the matter was reversed. In only 4 cases was there a discrepancy of .1 or more between the two indices. The reader will, of course, notice the basic difference between Table 1 and 2. In Table 1 the plain frequencies for the two indices are cross-tabulated; as a result, the *respondents* are classified according to their positions on the two measures. Table 2 has *questionnaire items* as the counting unit. It was preceded by the computation of 102 pairs of coefficients of association, and classifies each item according to how strongly it is associated with the two measures of socioeconomic status.

The importance of this result can best be shown by raising a substantive problem. Which type of question is most sensitive to social stratification?

Table 2—Coefficients of Association between Answers to Attitude Questions and Socio-Economic Status, the Latter Being Measured by Two Different Indices

		ITEMIZED INDEX							
		0—.05*	.05—.10	.10—.15	.15—.20	.20—.25	.25—.30	.30+	
	0 — .05	..	5	1	1	..	..	..	7
	.05 — .10	1	17	3	2	1	..	1	25
A B C D	.10 — .15	1	3	8	4	1	..	..	17
RATING	.15 — .20	..	1	4	8	4	1	..	18
	.20 — .25	..	..	3	4	10	4	3	24
	.25 — .30	..	..	..	1	1	4	..	6
	.30+	..	1	..	..	..	..	4	5
		2	27	19	20	17	9	8	102

* All intervals include their upper limits.

We cannot give the answer directly by inspecting Table 2. There each entry pertains to a question answered in one of the six sub-regions, each of which provided a sample of approximately 550 cases. The variations between regions, for the same index, is considerable and would obscure variations between indices. (While no analysis of variance was done, an inspection of the figures gives the impression that the regional differences are actually greater than the index differences.)

The final procedure taken was therefore as follows. The seventeen questions were ranked in the 6 sampling areas and the average rank computed for each of the two indices. The five with the highest and the five with the lowest average rank were then singled out for inspection. The result is not without interest. There were three questions which were most sensitive to social stratification, according to both measurement devices, the intuitive rating and the itemized index. The questions clearly dealt with labor matters.

"Do you feel that the labor leaders are doing all they could do right now to help win the war?"[2]

"Do you think the Government's attitude toward labor unions is too strict, about right, or not strict enough?"

One question, in the top group on the intuitive rating side, was number six according to the itemized index. Its wording is as follows:

"Do you think there is any danger of the cost of living going so high in the next year that you'll really have trouble getting along?"

While this does not deal with labor matters, it deals with the standard of living in a way which would obviously make a low-income person feel differently from a high-income respondent.

On the lower end the result is even clearer. Four questions were among the least sensitive, irrespective of what index was used. All of them dealt with matters which were clearly of a more "objective nature" and did not involve the class position of the respondents.

"Do you feel that as a whole the people in charge of factories—the executives —are doing all they could do right now to help win the war?"

"How do you feel about having the government regulate prices during the war—in general, are you for it or against it?"

"Do you think there should be any limit on how high wages and salaries should go during the war?"

"Are you living better now—that is, are you buying more things, or better things than you used to before the war?"

We thus have a two-fold result. We applied the idea of the interchangeability of indices to a substantive problem: the answers to questions which imply the economic position of the respondent are much more correlated with the status of respondents than questions which refer to general economic policy. And this finding would be the same, irrespective of which of our two indices are used to "measure" the socio-economic status of respondents.

APPENDIX 1

Questions from Surveys No. 112, 120, 128

Survey No. 112

"Do you feel that as a whole the people in charge of factories—the executives—are doing all they could do right now to help win the war?

"How about the workers in factories? (Are they doing all they could do right now to help win the war?)

"How about the labor leaders?

"Do you think the Government's attitude toward labor unions is too strict, about right, or not strict enough?

"From what you have heard, would you say there are any workers in war industries who are purposely holding back on the job?

"Do you think limiting incomes so no person can make more than $25,000 a year, after paying taxes, is a good idea, or not?"

Survey No. 120

"In general, do you feel that the people in this country are taking the war seriously enough?

"Do you feel that as a whole the people in charge of factories—the executives—are doing all they could do right now to help win the war?

"How about the workers in the factories? (Are they doing all they could do right now to help win the war?)

"How about the leaders of labor unions?

"How do you feel about having the government regulate prices during the war—in general, are you for or against it?

"Do you think there should be any limit on how high wages and salaries should go during the war?"

Survey No. 128

"In general, do you think food prices are about where they should be, too high, or too low?

"Are you living better now—that is, are you buying more things, or better things than you used to before the war?

"Do you think there is any danger of the cost of living going so high in the next year that you'll really have trouble getting along?

"Do you think there should be any limit on how high wages and salaries should go during the war?

"Would you be willing to have the government freeze your own income where it is now?"

11. A BASELINE FOR MEASUREMENT OF PERCENTAGE CHANGE

by Carl I. Hovland, Arthur A. Lumsdaine and Fred D. Sheffield

[During World War II, the Experimental Section of the Research Branch of the Army's Information and Education Division conducted a number of studies on the effectiveness of mass communications media. In the volume reporting some of the findings of the Experimental Section, detailed accounts of experimental studies on the effectiveness of certain films were presented. In the selection below, taken from a methodological appendix, the authors discuss certain numerical problems involved in evaluating indices of effectiveness of these films.—ED. NOTE.]

A COMMONLY USED METHOD of measuring effects of an experimental variable on qualitative responses is to show the percentage making the key

Reprinted from *Experiments on Mass Communication*, pp. 284-289, by permission of the authors and the publisher. (Coypright, 1949, by the Princeton University Press.)

response in the control group, the percentage making this response in the experimental group, and the difference between these two percentages. The "effect" is therefore indicated by the difference between the percentages.

However, this measure of effect is a function of the existing level of frequency of the key response prior to the experiment. If nearly all members of the population are unfamiliar with a particular fact prior to a film showing, a very effective film can yield a numerically large change when effects are expressed in this way. But if nearly everyone is already familiar with the fact, the effect is limited in size because only a small proportion did not know the fact initially and therefore only a small "effect" of the film can be obtained.

Thus the measure has serious disadvantages for determining the relative effectiveness of a film in teaching two different facts that are not equally well known initially. A different ceiling is imposed on the magnitude of effect for each different initial level, and the comparison is biased against items that are well known initially. Similarly, the measure introduces a bias if used for comparing the effects of a film on two or more groups that differ in initial level prior to the film. For example, if nearly all of the better educated know a particular fact, they can show little learning if effects are measured as the difference between control and film percentages, whereas the poorly educated, who are in general poorer learners, can show a large effect because they knew so little to begin with that there was considerable room for improvement.

This "ceiling" artifact is even further exaggerated if effects are measured as "percentage improvement," in which the baseline is the initial level and effect is expressed as the proportion of increase in this initial level. Thus a change from an initial level of 10 per cent to a final level of 20 per cent exhibits 100 per cent improvement, whereas a change from 80 per cent to 90 per cent—with the same 10 per cent difference in percentages— is only a 12 per cent improvement. Since the baseline and the ceiling are inversely correlated, the ceiling effect is exaggerated by the use of per cent improvement.

The "Effectiveness Index." Both of these measures of effects—the difference in percentage and the proportionate increase in the initial level—are inadequate in comparisons in which the baseline varies for the two things being compared. In many cases a more appropriate measure is the increase in number checking the correct response divided by the *maximum increase possible* as a baseline. Thus if the initial level is 10 per cent correct answers and the film increases the number to 20 per cent, the difference between the percentages is 10 per cent. But since the initial level was 10 per cent, the maximum change possible is 90 per cent. Therefore the increase, divided by the maximum increase possible is 10 per cent divided by 90 per cent, or 11 per cent. Similarly, if the initial level is 80 per cent and the film increases the level to 90 per cent, the increase is again 10 per cent; but 10 per cent out of a maximum possible increase of 20 per cent (i.e., 100 per cent minus 80 per cent), gives a film effect of 50 per cent of the total possible increase.

This measure of effect is termed the "effectiveness index." It is so named because it is a measure which indicates the extent to which the film achieves maximum effectiveness in the particular area involved and with the particular measuring instrument used. If P_1 is used to indicate the initial per cent and P_2 the final per cent, the effectiveness-index is expressed by the following formula:[1]

$$\text{Eff. index} = \frac{P_2 - P_1}{100 - P_1}$$

This measure of effect may be interpreted as the effect of the film in increasing the frequency of correct responses among those initially having the wrong response. The major argument in favor of the effectiveness index is that the relative value of a particular instructional technique is thus ascertained on the basis of those individuals who do not already know the content of the instruction; therefore, any comparisons that are made to determine relative effectiveness should be free of distortion due to lack of effects among those who already know the material.

The per cent who check wrong answers initially is of course not actually the per cent who did not *know* the right answer initially. An indeterminant number of individuals will check the correct answer initially because they merely guessed, and happened to guess correctly. However, the increase in per cent is also not the actual number who changed as a result of seeing the film, because the increase would be generally accompanied by a reduction in the number who get the answer right by guessing. Thus the number who actually learned the material is really greater than the increase in correct responses, depending on the initial amount of guessing. Provided the film does not change the proportion who guess correctly among those who do not know the correct answer, the two factors above exactly balance each other so that the increase in frequency of correct responses divided by the initial frequency of errors gives the proportion who were changed of those who initially did not know the correct answer. This may be shown as follows:

Let k_1 and k_2 represent the percentages of the sample that actually *know* the correct answer before and after the film respectively. Then $100 - k_1$ is the percentage who did not know initially and $100 - k_2$ is the percentage who still do not know after the film. Now if X is the proportion of those who do not know who will guess correctly, then the obtained percentages of correct responses before and after the film, P_1 and P_2, respectively, will be as follows:

$$P_1 = k_1 + X(100 - k_1)$$
$$P_2 = k_2 + X(100 - k_2)$$

The effect, as computed from the increase in correct responses divided by the initial number of wrong responses, is equal to $\frac{P_2 - P_1}{100 - P_1}$. Substituting from above,

$$\frac{P_2 - P_1}{100 - P_1} = \frac{[k_2 + X(100 - k_2)] - [k_1 + X(100 - k_1)]}{100 - [k_1 + X(100 - k_1)]}$$

$$= \frac{k_2(1 - X) - k_1(1 - X)}{100(1 - X) - k_1(1 - X)}$$

$$= \frac{k_2 - k_1}{100 - k_1}$$

It can be seen that this final expression is exactly the expression desired, namely, the increase in number *knowing* the correct response divided by the total who did not know it originally. In other words, it is the percentage who learned the answer among those who previously had not known it.

It will be noted that no assumption was made about the value for X, the proportion of correct guesses among those not knowing the correct answer. It was assumed, however, that X stays the same after the film, that is, that the correct choice is still just as attractive a guess among those who did not learn the correct answer.

In any case, the measure of effect obtained is unbiased by statistical ceiling effects. It always measures the increase as the proportion of the total increase possible.

Two illustrations from a study of [the film] "The Battle of Britain" are shown below, comparing "effects" as measured in the three different ways discussed above. The comparisons are made for the type of situation in which change as a function of maximum change possible appears to be the most appropriate measure. The examples illustrate how the conclusion is altered by using less appropriate measures that are biased by ceiling effects. In the first example the "effects" are compared for two different fact-quiz items with different initial levels; the second example compares "effects" at four different educational levels.

First Example

		PER CENT ANSWERING CORRECTLY	
		Reason British Navy could not be used	British military equipment after fall of France
	Control	36%	5%
	Film	55	18
Effect measured as difference between per cents		19	13
Effect measured as per cent improvement		53	260
Effect measured from base of maximum increase possible (effectiveness index)		30	14

In this example the effects are roughly the same for the second item as for the first if only the differences between per cents are considered, and the effect on the second item is about five times as great if "per cent improvement" is used, whereas the effect on the second item is about half as great as for the first item if the ceiling is equalized for the two groups by using the effectiveness index.

Second Example

		PER CENT ANSWERING CORRECTLY THE ITEM ABOUT THE BRITISH NAVY			
		Grade school men	Men with some high school	High school grads.	College men
	Control	31%	29%	38%	55%
	Film	32	57	60	78
Effect measured as difference between per cents		1	28	22	23
Effect measured as per cent improvement		3	97	58	42
Effect measured from base of maximum increase possible (effectiveness index)		1	39	35	51

In the above example the effect of the ceiling is to produce marked curvilinearity in the curve of effects expressed as differences, which is greatly exaggerated by the use of "per cent improvement," whereas the expected positive correlation between magnitude of effects and learning ability is found if the ceiling effect is equalized.

These examples were chosen to illustrate situations in which the appropriate base line is the maximum effect possible. In other types of situations the other base lines might be adequate. For example, in a comparison of two alternative presentation methods in teaching the same material, the same questions would be asked of samples from the same population, and the conclusion about relative effects from the comparison of the two presentations would be the same whichever of the three base lines is used. However, a distorted picture of the absolute magnitude of the effects might result from improper interpretation of the measure used. This is particularly true of the per cent improvement measure in which huge "improvements" may reflect only a small educational accomplishment merely because the starting level was very low.

The preceding considerations of base lines for measuring effects have been discussed from the standpoint of measuring instructional effects of a film on factual information. The same considerations apply, however, in the measurement of changes on opinion items. In this case the concept of "guessing" is not as appropriate as the more general concept of "unreliability," and the concept of "believe" is more appropriate than the concept of "know." Otherwise, the argument in the case of fact-quiz items may be directly transferred to the case of opinion items.

An important limitation to the utility of the effectiveness index as a measure for comparing changes lies in the fact that its sampling distribution has not been satisfactorily worked out, so that at present there is no adequate method available for determining whether two effectiveness indices *differ* reliably. Therefore, to the extent that the use of the index is desirable for this comparison of changes starting from different initial levels, the development of the sampling distribution of the measure becomes a problem for future statistical research.

Special complications arise if it is desired to extend the concept underlying the effectiveness index beyond the case of single qualitative measures such as percentages so as to cover *averages* of several responses. If one wishes to use the effectiveness index in representing a film's effect on the average number of correct or desired responses to a small (or at least finite) number of items, there are two alternative procedures possible. Either one may compute an effectiveness index separately for each item and average the obtained separate effectiveness indices, or an "effectiveness index" may be computed in terms of average change divided by "average change possible." The two procedures will in general lead to somewhat different numerical results unless the size of the effectiveness indices for individual items is uncorrelated with initial level of response over the range of items involved.

With the first procedure, experience indicated that obtained distributions permitted comparisons of means by the *t*-test, treating each effectiveness index as a raw "score." The main difficulty encountered with this procedure was that, with small samples, the value of a mean effectiveness index can be grossly influenced by a single deviant E.I. value such as is likely to occur with an initial level that leaves very little room for change and consequently gives a very unstable denominator in the E.I. formula.

Possible gross distortion of the average value by an aberrant and unstable component item is much less likely with the second procedure suggested above—i.e., computing a single effectiveness index based on the average obtained and "average change possible" for a set of several items. But this alternative introduces special difficulties of its own. In the first place, use of single effectiveness indices instead of averages over several observations leaves one without a measure of variability from item to item. Second, such an application of the logic of the effectiveness index necessitates defining E.I. in quite general terms as "obtained change divided by maximum change possible" rather than more specifically as "obtained number of individuals changing divided by maximum number who could change." This makes the unit of measurement a response rather than an individual, and consequently fails to differentiate changes in one or two items for a large number of persons from changes on more items by a small number of persons.

12. SOME GENERAL PRINCIPLES
OF QUESTIONNAIRE CLASSIFICATION

by Paul F. Lazarsfeld and Allen H. Barton

BEFORE WE CAN INVESTIGATE the presence or absence of some attribute in a person or a social situation, or before we can rank objects or measure them in terms of some variable, we must form the concept of that variable. Looking at the material before us in all its richness of sense-data, we must decide what attributes of the concrete items we wish to observe and measure: do we want to study "this-ness" or "that-ness," or some other "-ness"? The precise origin of our notion of this-ness or that-ness may be extremely varied, but it usually seems to involve combining many particular experiences into a category which promises greater understanding and control of events.

In this way we put together a great many behavior items and come up with concepts such as adjustment, authoritarian leadership, prestige, or bureaucracy. When we have formed some such category, we may then break it down into component elements upon which to base research instruments —instructions to coders, ranking scales, indicators; these in turn may be recombined in multi-dimensional patterns, typologies, or over-all indices. We are concerned with the question: How does one go about forming such categories in the first place? Why pick out certain elements of the situation and not others? Why combine them in just these categories?

It can properly be argued that one cannot lay down a set of handy instructions for the categorization of social phenomena: such instructions would be nothing less than a general program for the development of social theory. One cannot write a handbook on "how to form fruitful theoretical concepts" in the same way that one writes handbooks on how to sample or how to construct questionnaires.

The purpose of this section is not that ambitious. It happens that research does not always begin with general theoretical categories and theoretically prescribed relations among them. At the present stage of the social sciences a great deal of research must be of an *exploratory* nature, aiming at qualitative answers to such questions as the following: What goes on in a certain

Reprinted in part from "Qualitative Measurement in The Social Sciences: Classification, Typologies, and Indices," pp. 155-165, in *The Policy Sciences*, edited by Daniel Lerner and Harold D. Lasswell, by permission of the authors, the editors, and the publishers, Stanford University Press. (Copyright, 1951, by the Board of Trustees of Leland Stanford Junior University. One of the Hoover Institute Studies made possible by a Carnegie Corporation grant.)

situation? What do young people do when making up their minds about choosing a career? What kinds of reactions do people have to unemployment? What are the channels of information about public issues in an American community?

Where research contains exploratory elements, the researcher will be faced by an array of raw data for which ready-made theoretical categories will not exist. He must formulate categories before he can do anything else. Probably the best way to start is with fairly concrete categories—the sort of categories which experienced policy-makers or participants in the situation use, worked out in as clear and logical a form as possible. The job of figuring out what theoretical categories are applicable to the given field of behavior will be a long one, and will involve switching back and forth between concrete categories closely adapted to the data themselves and general categories able to tie in with other fields of experience, until both concrete applicability and generality are obtained. The immediate problem is to get the raw data classified in some reasonable preliminary way, so that it can be communicated, cross-tabulated, and thought about.[1]

We will therefore try to codify the procedure used by experienced researchers in forming such preliminary, concrete category systems for the raw materials turned up by exploratory research. Some of the rules are entirely general and formal, derived from textbooks of logic; others have grown out of practical experience. Most of the examples will be drawn from the classification of responses to open-ended questions, but it is hoped that the discussion will also be relevant to the analysis of communications content, of personal documents, and of systematic observations.

The requirements of a good classification system for free responses may be summed up in four points:

1. *Articulation:* The classification should proceed in steps from the general to the specific, so that the material can be examined either in terms of detailed categories or of broad groupings, whichever are more appropriate for a given purpose.

2. *Logical correctness:* In an articulated set of categories those on each step must be exhaustive and mutually exclusive. When an object is classified at the same time from more than one aspect, each aspect must have its own separate set of categories.

3. *Adaptation to the structure of the situation:* The classification should be based on a comprehensive outline of the situation as a whole—an outline containing the main elements and processes in the situation which it is important to distinguish for purposes of understanding, predicting, or policy-making.

4. *Adaptation to the respondent's frame of reference:* The classification should present as clearly as possible the respondent's own definition of the situation—his focus of attention, his categories of thought.

ARTICULATION

The basic purpose of classification is to simplify the handling of a great number of individual items by putting them into a smaller number of groups, each group consisting of items which act more or less alike in relation to the problem being studied. This raises the following problem:

If the classification is kept very simple, with only a few broad groupings, it will combine many elements which are not very similar. Important distinctions of a more detailed sort will be lost completely. On the other hand, if the classification preserves all distinctions which may be of any significance, it will contain too many groups to be surveyed and handled conveniently.

The solution of this dilemma is to use an "articulate" classification: a classification with several steps, starting with a few broad categories and breaking them down into many more detailed categories. In this way one can eat one's cake and have it too: when a few broad categories are sufficient, only the simple first step need be used; when a more detailed study is required, the finer distinctions can be found preserved in the later, finer steps of the classification system.

An example will make clear the advantages of articulation. In a study of young people which was made in New Jersey during the 1930's, two thousand boys were asked the question, "What can the community do for its youth?" The replies were so numerous and diversified that a classification in several steps was needed for their analysis. The categories used, with their percentages of response, are shown in Table I.

Table I (In Percentages)

Employment		24.5
More	18.7	
Better conditions	5.8	
Education		16.4
High school	3.9	
Free college	3.8	
Free vocational schools	2.0	
Free adult education	4.6	
Education in general	2.1	
Recreation		29.6
Community centers	9.8	
Outdoor activities	14.9	
Parks and playgrounds	6.2	
Swimming pools	5.3	
Other outdoor facilities	3.4	
Clubs	4.9	
Other suggestions		5.4
No suggestions given		24.1
Total		100.0

Results presented in this form are much easier to read—they "make more sense" than a long list of detailed categories presented in a completely unstructured way. Furthermore they can be handled statistically in ways which would otherwise be impossible. If the sample were divided into small subgroups in terms of other variables, for instance age and income, the results for the many detailed categories might become statistically unreliable. However, the few broad categories of the first step could still be used with statistical confidence.

It is not always easy to fit detailed categories together to form an articulated system. Where, in the system given above, should one put the response, "better library facilities?" Is it "education" or "recreation"? The trouble here is that the concrete categories in which the data were gathered were not adapted to the final classification scheme. The scheme is set up in terms of "functions"; the answer, "library facilities," is in terms of a concrete institution with several functions. If the answers are to be classified in the present scheme, the right questions must be asked in the first place. When someone suggests a concrete institution with multiple functions, a further question must be asked to discover which of these functions the respondent had in mind.

It should also be kept clearly in mind that there are usually several alternate ways in which a classification can be formed. The responses to the youth survey might have been classified in terms of the distinction between activities aiming at economic advancement, at gratification of cultural wants, and at physical recreation. Some education activities would then fall into the "economic advancement" category, while the remainder, along with some of the recreation items, would fall into the "cultural gratification" category.

LOGICAL CORRECTNESS

A classification meets the requirements of logic if it provides exhaustive and mutually exclusive categories at each step of the classification.

An example of lack of exhaustiveness would be the classification of persons influencing voters as "family," "friends," "fellow workers," and "neighbors." This would leave no place for contacts with party workers or with casually encountered strangers. Of course, any classification can be made exhaustive by including an "other" category. This meets the purely logical requirement, but it defeats the purpose of the classification which is to distinguish elements which behave differently in terms of the problem under study.

Mutual exclusiveness means that there should be one and only one place to put an item within a given classification system. There are two sources of violations of this rule: (1) the use of categories on one step of the classification which are wholly included in others; and (2) the mixing of different aspects of objects in a single-dimensioned classification scheme.

An illustration of the first error would be the classification of sources of information as "mass media," "personal contacts," and "newspapers." Newspapers are obviously a subclass of mass media. We should either revise the first category to read, "mass media" (excluding newspapers), or else relegate "newspapers" to a second step in the classification under "mass media," perhaps along with "radio," "magazines," "television," and so on.

Lack of mutual exclusiveness due to mixing different aspects can be illustrated by the following classification of the output of a radio station: "musical programs," "dramatic programs," "serious programs," "recorded programs," etc. These categories belong to various dimensions and they must not be lumped together. If one is interested in classifying programs in terms of all these aspects simultaneously, a multi-dimensional classification must be set up. The categories of such a system are all possible combinations of the varieties on each dimension, for instance: "popular recorded music," "serious recorded music," "popular live music," and so on. Each program will then appear in only one category. If one is not really interested in combining the different aspects, each should be set up as a separate classification system.

ADAPTATION TO THE STRUCTURE OF THE SITUATION

The codification of practices that make for good classification has been easy so far, since it has dealt with matters of form. But now one comes to the heart of the matter: how to set up those particular categories which will be best adapted to the material and the problem being studied? The purpose of categories is to organize a great many concrete items into a small number of classes, so that the situation studied can be more easily understood. In the long run this must involve relating the categories used in any particular situation to more general systems of concepts which cover wide areas of human behavior, so that social theories can be developed which will make each particular situation easier to understand and control.

In many cases the researcher simply uses the customary terms of everyday life. Channels of political influence easily divide themselves into "mass media" and "personal contacts." "Mass media" again subdivide into "radio," "newspapers," "magazines," etc., on the basis of obvious physical and organizational distinctions. In other cases the researcher may take culturally given categories. For example, political values might be categorized as "liberty," "equality," and "fraternity," following the French Revolutionary slogan, and perhaps "security" would have to be added to adapt the system to current materials. Organizations are self-classified as "educational," "recreational," "religious," and so on.

In most exploratory research, however, the investigator will have to develop his own categories. It is naturally not possible to give completely general rules for forming categories which will be best adapted to *any* problem under study. But there is one frequently occurring type of situation for which fairly clear procedures can be laid down. This arises when one is trying to classify "reasons" for certain kinds of action: why people vote for a certain candidate, why soldiers stand up or break down under fire, why people migrate from place to place, or why pogroms, lynchings, or revolutions break out. This case, where the researcher must set up a classification of factors influencing a certain kind of action, will be discussed in detail here.

One starts with a collection of observations of people in those situations, reports about their behavior, or interview material in which the participants themselves are asked to explain their behavior. It is usually not possible to arrive at a satisfactory classification system simply by grouping items which seem similar in content. Rather it is necessary to build up a concrete picture or model of the whole situation to which the reports refer, and then locate the particular report within this "structural scheme." This involves an interacting process. First it is necessary to visualize the concrete processes and activities implied by the responses, through introspection and an imaginative qualitative analysis of the data, to get a preliminary scheme. Then one tries to apply this scheme systematically to the data, returns to the structural scheme for refinement, reapplies the revised scheme to the data, and so on. One may thereby end up with a classification rather different from that with which one started.

We will give two examples of this procedure of formulating a structural scheme for the classification of interview material; one is drawn from market research, the other from *The American Soldier*.[2]

Suppose we want to classify the reasons why women buy a certain kind of cosmetics. Women have a great many comments on their reasons which are hard to group if one takes them at face value. But visualize a woman buying and using cosmetics. She gets advice from people she knows, from advertising, and from articles in mass media; in addition she has her own past experiences to go on. She has her own motives and requirements: she uses cosmetics in order to achieve various appearance values so as to impress others—one might even find out whom—and perhaps to impress herself. The cosmetics have various technical qualities which relate to these desired results. She may also worry about possible bad effects on health or appearance. There are the problems of applying the cosmetics. And finally there is the expense. All of the women's comments might be related to the following scheme: "channels of information," "desired appearance values," "prospective 'audience,'" "bad consequences," "technical qualities," "application problems," and "cost." The reason the comments would fit is that the scheme of classification matches the actual processes involved in buying and using cosmetics. These are the processes from which the respondent herself has derived her comments; the classification, so to speak, puts the comments back where they came from.

Suppose we are studying soldiers' behavior in combat. We ask certain general questions about their behavior, and get a great many responses which are hard to group. But let us, in the words of *The American Soldier,* "analyze the typical and general determinants of behavior in the immediate combat situation. A tired, cold, muddy rifleman goes forward with the bitter dryness of fear in his mouth into the mortar burst and machine-gun fire of a determined enemy."[3] What exactly is he up against? The authors list:[4]

1. Threats to life and limb and health
2. Physical discomfort
3. Deprivation of sexual and concomitant social satisfactions
4. Isolation from accustomed sources of affectional assurance
5. Loss of comrades, and sight and sound of wounded and dying men
6. Restriction of personal movement
7. Continual uncertainty, and lack of adequate cognitive orientation
8. Conflicts of values:
   a) Military duty vs. safety and comfort
   b) Military duty vs. family obligations
   c) Military duty vs. informal group loyalties
9. Being treated as a means rather than as an end in oneself
10. Lack of privacy
11. Long periods of enforced boredom, mingled with anxiety
12. Lack of terminal *individual* goals (short of end of war)

On the other hand there are factors which help to offset the stresses:[5]

1. Coercive formal authority
2. Leadership practices—example, encouragement
3. Informal group:
   a) Affectional support
   b) Code of behavior
   c) Provision of realistic security and power
4. Convictions about the war and the enemy
5. Desires to complete the job by winning war, to go home
6. Prayer and personal philosophies

With such an initial visualization of the situation, we can begin to classify free responses in interviews, statements in personal documents, in the mass media of communication, or reports by observers; and we can also reclassify the answers to a great many poll-type questions. Where the analyst has such intimate familiarity with the concrete material as well as the guidance of a certain amount of social theory, the set of categories which he creates is very likely to be useful for understanding the situation.

One brief example may be given of the role of social theory in improving the classification system. The authors of *The American Soldier* note that in many types of organization coercive formal sanctions are not as effective in themselves as they are through the informal group sanctions and the internal sanctions (guilt) which they call up.[6] It would therefore be advisable to get additional information from those respondents who mention formal sanctions as a factor in the combat situation, so that they can be further classified to show whether it is these sanctions *per se* or their effect *through informal and internal sanctions* which are actually affecting the respondent's behavior.

Conversely the authors warn that the mentioning only of informal and internal sanctions by no means implies that formal sanctions play no role. The formal sanctions may play an important part in establishing the norms of the informal group and of the individual conscience, which thereafter will direct the individual's activities along lines laid down by the formal authority. Of course there will exist some informal group and individual norms which run contrary to those derived from the formal authority. A more complete structural scheme on which we might thus base a classification of men's behavior in combat (or of statements relating to it) is given in Table II.

Table II—How Norms Bear on Individual Behavior in Combat

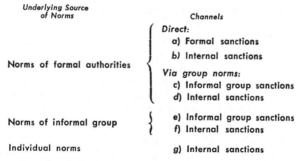

Examples of each of the categories in Table II would be:

a) I fight because I'll be punished if I quit.

b) I fight because it's my duty to my country, the Army, the government; it would be wrong for me to quit.

c) I fight because I'll lose the respect of my buddies if I quit.

d) I fight because it would be wrong to let my buddies down.

e) You have to look out for your buddies even if it means violating orders, or they won't look out for you.

f) You have to look out for your buddies even if it means violating orders because it would be wrong to leave them behind.

g) I am fighting because I believe in democracy and hate fascism.

One could go on to include other formal and informal groups outside the immediate army situation: churches, family, political groups, and so on, which are sources of norms important to behavior in battle.

To formulate once more the general procedure: the situation or process is visualized which serves as a frame of reference for the whole list of comments or behavior items to be classified, as required by the study. This situation or process is then divided into its different "natural parts" on the basis of experienced personal judgment or general theoretical directives. The thought moves in two directions, building up from the list of comments an organized model of the situation and concurrently dividing this whole into parts. Finally the two tendencies will have to meet. To put it another way: the line of progress is not directly from the single concrete piece of data to the group into which it might fit; it proceeds rather from the concrete answers to the over-all structure which seems to be involved; from this structure the thought turns to the component parts, and here are found the adequate groups for the classification. In this process both intimate knowledge of the concrete situation and the guidance of social theory are needed, both to formulate the initial structural scheme and to refine it as one goes on trying to fit the concrete material into it.

Besides true theoretical models there are certain types of fairly standard structural schemes which have been developed in applied research for use in standard situations. These are discussed in some detail in Zeisel's *Say It With Figures* (1947). We shall only list them here:[7]

1. *The push-pull scheme,* used in studies of reasons for migration from place *A* to place *B,* or for shifting one's preference from any item *X* to any other item *Y.* The elements in this scheme are: the attributes of *X* and the attributes of *Y.*

2. *The attributes-motives-influences scheme,* used in classification of reasons for choosing a given item *X.* The elements of this scheme are: the attributes of *X,* the motives of the respondent, the channels of influences concerning his choice.

3. *The technical-properties—resulting-gratification scheme* for studying "what is it about *X*" that the respondent likes. The elements of this scheme are: technical properties of *X,* resulting gratifications from *X* to the respondent. (For instance: I like *X* beer because it's made with more malt, and more malt means better flavor; I like *X* because he is honest, and an honest mayor means lower taxes; I like the New Deal because it uses Keynesian economic techniques, and that eliminates mass unemployment.)

4. *The where-is-it, what-barrier-keeps-it-there, who-is-to-blame scheme* for studying respondent's explanation of shortages of anything. (For instance: sugar is short because it comes from Java, and Java is occupied by the Japanese—so it's the Japs' fault. Or: there's plenty of sugar in the country; the government is keeping it back to create a war psychology, so the government—or the enemy who makes such action necessary to the government—is to blame.)

5. *The underlying-reasons—precipitating-cause scheme,* used in classifying answers to the questions "why did you do so and so?" and "why did you do it *just then?*" This just adds one or several stages to *any* of the elements in the attributes-motives-influences scheme. (For instance: I wanted a car, and when they came out with such nice models I went out and bought one; or, I wanted a car, but when I met my girl friend I just had to have one so I bought one; or, I wanted a car, and when the salesman came around and talked to me about it I bought one.)

ADAPTATION TO THE RESPONDENT'S FRAME OF REFERENCE

One of the first things one notices in applying a structural scheme to the analysis of interview material is that the responses of any given individual may be seriously incomplete in terms of the whole scheme. If this is simply the result of poor interviewing—for instance, of failing to follow up "why" questions with proper detailed probes—the ultimate remedy is good interviewing. But if the incompleteness and vagueness are inherent in the respondent's definition of the situation, they cannot be eliminated and one may not want to eliminate them.

For example, a survey of the Norwegian public asked about their explanations for the bad postwar living conditions and their ideas of what should be done about them.[8] The whole array of answers could be classified only in terms of an outline of all major elements of the Norwegian economy. Most individual answers, however, covered only a small part of that structure. Some people wanted less taxes, but did not know what expenses should be cut; others wanted more imports without explaining where the foreign exchange would come from; some people had specific proposals about particular industries, while others had only general suggestions for "more freedom" or "fairer distribution." This was natural, since the respondents who had not followed professional discussions of the economic situation could hardly obtain from their own experience a coherent picture of the whole economic structure.

However, the object of the survey was not to study the Norwegian economy itself, but rather to find out what the public's perceptions and attitudes regarding the economic situation were, and how these related to the respondents' socioeconomic position and political behavior. Therefore, the economic structural scheme was used only as a basis for a much looser and more "psychological" set of categories. Respondents were classified in terms of whether they focused on the production or the income-distribution side of the economy, what goals they seemed to look toward, and which policy measures they advocated. The result was not to find out what the respondent thought about all economic questions, but to find out what economic questions he thought about, and what his opinions were with regard to *those* questions. To classify the many respondents who gave partial or vague answers, special categories had to be introduced at each level of the classification scheme. A highly simplified version of the classification scheme is given in Table III to make clear what is involved in adapting a set of categories not only to the objective situation but also to the respondent's frame of reference.

This classification might not tell much about the state of the Norwegian economy, but it would tell a great deal about the state of mind of the Norwegian people. Of those giving relatively definite answers, we would know how many thought mainly of altering the income distribution and how many thought in terms of improving production. We would know how many desire change in each of various directions, and how many have unclear notions about what kind of change they want. We would know how many choose each of several major alternative policies as means to their goals, and we know how many have no idea how to achieve their desired goal. Among the remainder, Group III, we see the interesting phenomenon of

Table III—Classification of Responses to Questions on What Should Be Done About Economic Situation

I. Answer in terms of changing the income distribution:

Goal		Means
1. More equality	{	a) Taxes and controls
		b) Social welfare services
		c) Measures against private capital
		d) No means specified
2. Less equality	{	a) Less taxes and controls
		b) Less welfare services
3. Vague: "Better," "Fairer," etc.		a) Vague or no answers

II. Answer in terms of improving production:

1. Raise physical production	{	a) Raise wages
		b) Labor participation in management
		c) Less controls and taxes
		d) "Everyone work harder"
		e) No means specified
2. More rational production	{	a) Better central planning
		b) Less controls and taxes

III. Economic sector and goal not clearly specified:

a) More controls (purpose unspecified)
b) Less taxes and controls (reason unspecified)
c) Unspecified changes in tax system
d) "Continue government's policies" (unspecified)
e) Other suggestions of unspecified purpose

those who have policies to suggest, but who cannot say exactly what they are supposed to accomplish.

It is not implied that the responses classified above should be taken at face value. If it turned out that most businessmen wanted lower taxes and less controls "in order to encourage production," while workers wanted higher wages and more participation in management, also "to encourage production," one might suspect that in many cases self-interest was being rationalized. It is an interesting fact that the actual results found many poor people demanding greater equality, but practically no rich people overtly demanding greater inequality. It might be possible by intensive interviewing to obtain material for a classification in terms of "deeper" feelings and beliefs. A trained psychologist handling intensive interviews or case histories might be able to classify respondents in terms of hidden or unconscious motives, using cues and indicators which he is specially trained to notice and interpret.

Something of this kind was done by Roethlisberger and Dickson in their study of workers' complaints in the Western Electric Plant. A complaint was considered "not only in relation to its alleged object, but also in relation to the personal situation of the complainant. Only in this way is the richer significance of the complaint realized. The significance of B's grouch about piece rates is better grasped in relation to the increased financial obligations incurred by his wife's illness; C's attitude toward his boss is greatly illuminated by the experience he relates in connection with his father; D's complaint about smoke and fumes is more readily understood in relation to his fear of contracting pneumonia."[9]

Another way in which classification was adapted to the respondent's frame of reference was to distinguish two types of items in the work situation: "(1) topics which in general the worker takes for granted unless something goes wrong; (2) topics which he does not take for granted even if they are favorable. . . . Subjects such as tools, machines, lockers, washrooms . . . are not talked about unless there is some complaint to be made. This is particularly true of most items relating to plant conditions; therefore, topics with a high index of dissatisfaction in this area do not necessarily indicate poor working conditions."

Still another such distinction was made when three categories of objects of complaint were distinguished: those referring to objectively ascertainable facts ("the doorknob is broken"); those referring to more subjective sense experiences ("the work is dirty" or "the room is hot"); and those referring to social facts ("ability doesn't count") or to social norms ("unfairness") which are not sensory elements at all.

It should be noted that the kind of classification scheme given in the Norwegian example above can also serve a quite different purpose: the tabulation of incomplete data resulting from unsatisfactory data-gathering techniques. This problem arises when one must analyze superficially carried out open-ended questions, unsystematically gathered case materials, or documents originally written for other purposes. The meaning of the categories is rather different in this case: the "vague" and "unspecified" categories do not necessarily constitute real categories of people; they may largely measure deficiencies in the data-gathering procedure. By separating out the incomplete answers, one may observe the distribution of the remaining complete answers. However, one should always realize that if the people with incomplete data could be properly classified, they might upset the proportions observed. The type of classification suggested clarifies the situation as much as possible, but it also indicates the margin of possible error involved in basing one's conclusions only on the portion of respondents about whom full data is available.

13. THE EFFECT OF MILITARY RANK
ON VARIOUS TYPES OF ATTITUDES

by Hans Speier

[The following selection is drawn from a symposium on the scope and method of Vols. I-II of *The American Soldier*. These volumes were based on the analysis of data collected by the Research Branch, Information and Education Division, U. S. Army. In the article below, Speier indicates how he re-classified responses to

Reprinted in part from *"The American Soldier* and the Sociology of Military Organization" in *Continuities in Social Research: Studies in the Scope and Method of "The American Soldier,"* Robert K. Merton and Paul F. Lazarsfeld, editors, pp. 120-127, by permission of the author, the editors, and the publisher. (Copyright, 1950, by the Free Press.)

a wide variety of attitude questions within the framework of Mannheim's theory of "perspectivist" thought.—ED. NOTE.]

THE WAR-TIME FINDINGS of the Research Branch will contribute to a better understanding of many social relations in civilian peace-time life; the authors point out on several occasions that their data are of interest to current research. In this connection a word might be said about the usefulness of *The American Soldier* to students of the sociology of knowledge.

Karl Mannheim and some of his followers have speculated a great deal about "perspectivistic thinking" of various social classes. "Perspectivistic thinking," varying according to class position and interest, comprises a great variety of mental processes which Mannheim did not clearly distinguish, *e.g.,* explanations of social reality, policy preferences regarding the most desirable state of affairs, expectations as to the future course of events and demands upon oneself and others. Mannheim contended moreover that not only axiological but also methodological and epistemological aspects of thinking differ according to the "perspective" afforded by given class positions in society. Unfortunately, Mannheim never succeeded in defining social class in terms that would permit a test of his theory. Nor did he give a satisfactory account of the nature of the relationship between the individual who has an opinion about social or other phenomena and the social class to which he is presumed to "belong" or, as in the case of the "intelligentsia," not to belong. Finally, the "ideological" material which he imputed to various class positions was not analyzed according to specific content characteristics, his distinction between "ideology" and "utopia" being the only precarious effort in this respect.[1]

Advance in the sociology of opinion will depend on empirical studies, in which opinions are classified according to theoretically relevant content characteristics and examined as to the frequency of their association with various social roles and ranks. It should be possible to exploit the contribution to opinion research, which *The American Soldier* makes, along these lines.

There are many tables in *The American Soldier* showing that differences in attitude and opinion are associated with marital status, education, age, regional origin, combat experience, branch of service, *etc.* From the point of view of both the sociology of military organization and the sociology of opinion the association of opinions with race and rank are of particular interest.

For example, the well known social perspectivism associated with race can be illustrated by responses to the question, "Do you think that most (Negroes) (white people) are doing *more* than their share or *less* than their share to help win the war?" The percentage checking the response "they are doing more than their share" was considerably higher in both the Negro and the white sample of respondents with respect to the in-group than it was with respect to the out-group. (I, 511)*

The opinions in this case were concerned with both in-group and out-group behavior separately, but the hierarchical relationship of the two groups, which the respondents presumably felt to prevail in some more or

---

* References to *The American Soldier* are handled in the following way. The first and second volumes are referred to as I and II respectively. Page numbers are indicated by Arabic numerals.

less vague sense, was not involved in the question which they answered, unless one were to regard the words "their share" in the wording of the question as alluding to this relationship. Furthermore, the question did not call for judgments about the behavior of the out-group *toward* the in-group and of the in-group *toward* the out-group. If questions had been asked directly concerned with the status of whites and Negroes or with the treatment of Negroes by whites, *etc.,* even larger differences in group opinions might have resulted. It is entirely possible that the "social perspectivism" reflected in the cited instance does not hold generally, representing a constant perspective for each group, regardless of the subject matter on which opinions are expressed.

In other words, just as the two groups will not be expected to display any "social perspectivism" on, say, simple arithmetic (although they may well differ in arithmetical knowledge and skill), their views on other aspects may differ somewhat and on still other aspects may indeed be strikingly "perspectivistic." Instead of searching for an immutable perspective associated with social position, it might be more fruitful to assume a continuum of degree of opinion differences associated with social position and to determine the changing "perspectives" from a given social position with reference to specific subject matters.

In attempting to put these subject matters into a rank order of ascending importance to the social perspectivism of status groups, the following gross distinctions may be made:

I. Non-social subjects (*e.g.,* the weather)
II. Social subjects (*e.g.,* cooperation)
   1. not involving the hierarchy of which the groups are a part
   2. involving this hierarchy

Non-social subjects comprise both matters entering immediately and concretely into human experience and more remote or abstract matters. Since the experiences of groups differ according to their functions in society, their views of non-social subjects also differ widely; farmers as a group "know more" about rain than city people and "evaluate" it with reference to different needs. Similarly, the comprehension of abstract relations or remote causes, *e.g.,* meteorology, presupposes expert knowledge typically possessed by specialized groups of particular training and function in society. Such differences are here disregarded, as we are concerned with the dependence of the opinions of *status* groups upon the subject matter on which their views converge or differ. It is assumed that the unequal distribution of power, privilege and prestige among status groups does not in itself affect their views on non-social subjects, much as unequal education may do so. Of the many sub-categories which can be introduced in category II-1, it would seem especially pertinent to include subjects which involve the self as distinguished from subjects which do not do so. Similarly, an especially pertinent distinction within category II-2 would appear to be that between the hierarchy itself, including rules and practices associated with it, and the qualities and behavior of the component groups of that hierarchy. Thus:

II. *Social Subjects*
   1. which do not involve the hierarchy of which the groups are a part:
     (i) Subjects which do not involve the (collective) self, *i.e.* either the

individual who expresses an opinion or the status group to which he belongs. (Examples: the nature of a common enemy, the chances to defeat him, *etc.*)

   (ii) Subjects which involve the (collective) self, *i.e.* either the individual who expresses an opinion or the status group to which he belongs. (Example: my hatred of the enemy.)

   (iii) Subjects which indirectly throw light on the implications of the hierarchy merely by virtue of the fact that the opinions of one status group about a subject pertaining to itself can be compared with the opinions of another status group about the same subject. (Example: the enlisted men's working habits as viewed by both enlisted men and officers.)

  2. which involve the hierarchy of which the groups are a part:

   (i) Subjects which pertain to this hierarchy as a whole, its characteristics, merits, *etc.* (Example: rewards and punishments viewed as part of the system, not as given or received by other groups.)

   (ii) Subjects which pertain to the behavior, characteristics and merits of any status group in interaction or comparison with other status groups. (Example: confidence in leadership of superiors.)

We could propose the hypothesis that the difference between opinions on the same subject matter expressed by groups high or low in power, privilege or prestige will increase as the subject matter is more closely and directly related to the status characteristics and relations of the group.

It should now be noted, however, that this hypothesis rests on the assumption of latent or overt conflict between the groups within the hierarchy. Differences in opinion on social subject matters, and particularly on those involving hierarchy, may imply, even if this is not explicitly expressed, divergent opinions about the justice of the prevailing order or about the justice of social practices and rules. If a lower status group "accepts" the existing stratification, does not contest the distance separating it from the higher group, emulates its superiors or regards the existing order as divine, similarity rather than difference in opinion concerning the social system is likely to prevail. In this sense, difference in opinion may be a sign of social disorder. The more severe this disorder, the more diversified are the subjects on which opinions differ. Obviously, a particularly alarming sign of social disorder would be differences of opinion on social subjects *not* involving the hierarchy when these differences reflect conflicts about status.

Since the socially prevailing notions of justice enter into many moral judgments, it is to be expected that opinions involving moral values will be more susceptible to perspectivism than factual judgments. This distinction between factual and moral judgments can be introduced into any of the categories of class II, but it is difficult to say whether factual opinions on subject matter low in the rank order are more or less susceptible to perspectivism than a moral judgment on subjects of high rank. For example, officers and men may disagree more in their (factual) opinions about officers' privileges (II-2-ii) than in their (moral) views of fairness in the Army (II-2-i) or of enemy treachery. (II-1-i)

In Table I thirty-nine subject matters on which opinions were expressed by both officers and enlisted men have been selected from *The American Soldier* and arranged with the initial hypothesis in mind. The arrangement roughly approximates the rank order of subjects which has just been discussed. Six classes of opinions, A-F, have been distinguished and the average difference between the percentage of officers and that of enlisted men expressing each stated opinion has been computed for each class of opinions.

Table I—Differences in Opinions of Officers and Enlisted Men on Various Subject Matters[2]

A. Opinions about reality not involving Army as a whole, self or relations between officers and enlisted men

Item No.	Page Ref. Opinion	(Specific Subject)	DIFFERENCE Absolute	Ratio
	II, 198-9	The shell shocked should be treated as sick men		
1		Division B	− 3	1
2		Division C	5	1.2
3		Division D	5	1.1
4		Division E	7	1.1
5		Division F	− 4	1.1
	II, 147	It will be tough to beat the Japanese		
6		Pacific theater respondents	− 7	1.1
7		European theater respondents	− 5	1.1
		It will be tough to beat the Germans		
8		Pacific theater respondents	− 11	1.1
9		European theater respondents	− 9	1.1
	II, 146	All or most of our equipment better than		
10		that of Japanese	− 2	1
11		that of Germans	6	1.1
	II, 294	(Other) men in rear doing as much for front as could be expected in circumstances		
12		Division A (Pacific)	8	1.1
13		Division B (")	10	1.2
14		Division C (")	5	1.1
15		Division D (")	16	1.1
16		Division E (Europe)	28	2.2
		AVERAGE A	8.2	1.2

B. Opinions about the individual self, not involving hierarchical relations: feelings of officers and, respectively, enlisted men in combat

	II, 174-5	When the going was tough (Pacific theater)		
17		prayer helped a lot	8	1.1
18		it helped a lot to think that you couldn't let the other men down	− 24	1.4
19		it helped a lot to think that you had to finish the job in order to get home	11	1.3
20		I was helped a lot by thoughts of hatred for the enemy	− 8	1.2
21		it helped a lot to think of what we are fighting for	6	1.2
		AVERAGE B	11	1.2

C. Opinions, not involving moral judgment, about the behavior of enlisted men

22	I, 417	Main reason for soldiers' obedience is fear of punishment	21	1.7
23	I, 421	Most soldiers usually work hard enough to get by	4	1.1
24		Most soldiers usually put all they have got into their work	5	1.1
25	I, 418	An enlisted man is usually more concerned with what other enlisted men think than with what his officers think	11	1.1
		AVERAGE C	10.2	1.3

Table I (Continued)

Item No.	Page Ref.	Opinion (Specific Subject)	DIFFERENCE Absolute	Ratio
D. Opinions about the Army as a whole				
26	I, 423	Army mostly does not keep promises	35	1.9
27	I, 422	Promotion depends on whom, not what, you know	20	1.3
28	I, 419	Army places too much importance upon military courtesy	51	3.8
29		Army places too much importance upon spit and polish	34	1.9
30	I, 394	Military discipline is about right at this post	− 20	1.5
31		In most ways I have gotten a square deal from the Army	− 24	1.6
32	I, 422	Army does not try its best to praise and reward the exceptionally good soldier	20	1.4
33	I, 421	The harder a man works the better his chance of success	− 35	2.2
	I, 396	Soldiers have good reasons to gripe about:		
34		too strict discipline about petty things	28	2.2
35		not getting enough passes and furloughs	25	1.9
36		wrong men get the breaks	25	1.9
37		too much "chicken" to put up with	22	1.5
38		work too hard and hours too long	14	2.5
39		promotions frozen or too slow	1	1
40		wrong job assignment	5	1.1
		AVERAGE D	**24.9**	**1.8**
E. Opinions, involving moral judgments, about the behavior of enlisted men				
41	I, 420	It's all right for a man to goldbrick if he doesn't get caught	27	7.8
42		It's all right for a man to goldbrick if he doesn't make more work for the men	23	2.7
43	I, 419	Most soldiers lose respect for a man who is always trying to goldbrick	− 11	1.1
44	I, 420	Most soldiers lose respect for a man who is always bucking for promotion	12	1.2
45	I, 419	Most soldiers lose respect for a man who is too GI	30	1.6
		AVERAGE E	**20.6**	**2.9**
F. Opinions about relations between enlisted men and officers				
46	I, 394	Disagree that Army would be a lot better if officers and men were more friendly with each other	− 32	3.1
47		All or most officers would be willing to go through anything they ask their men to go through	− 55	2.5
48	I, 374	If enlisted men have to observe curfew, officers should too	49	2.4
49		Officers deserve extra privileges because of their responsibility	− 44	2.9
50	I, 398	Regular civilian reader of B-Bag would get untrue picture of the problems of most soldiers in European theater	− 42	3.6
		AVERAGE F	**44.4**	**2.9**

Class A includes items (No. 10 and 11) dealing with equipment, *i.e.* "non-social subjects" (rank order: I), and no item lower than II-1-i in the rank order.

Class B is composed of items belonging in category II-1-ii.

The items in class C, dealing with behavior of the enlisted men, fall into category II-1-iii and are factual rather than moral in quality.

Class D contains moral and factual opinions falling into category II-2-i.

Items No. 34-40 have been regarded as part of this class despite the reference to the "griping" of the enlisted men in the wording of the opinion, under the assumption that the distribution of opinions was predominantly dependent upon the specified content of each complaint, which clearly belongs in this class.

Class E comprises moral items of category II-1-iii.

Finally, class F contains only items falling into the last category of the rank order (II-2-ii).

The results of Table I as summarized in Table II show:

(1) There is no constant social perspective associated with social status; instead, there are various social perspectives associated with social status depending on the subject matter to which the opinion pertains.

(2) There is virtual agreement among the two status groups on matters not involving the hierarchy of which they are a part (opinion classes A-C) with the partial exception of category II-1-iii. (see (3) below)

Table II—Social Perspectivism According to Rank Order of Subject Matter

Class in Table I	Rank Order of Subject Matter	DIFFERENCE Ratio	DIFFERENCE Absolute
A	I to II-1-i	1.2	8.2
B	II-1-ii	1.2	11
C	II-1-iii (factual)	1.3	10.2
D	II-2-i	1.8	24.9
E	II-1-iii (moral)	2.9	20.6
F	II-2-ii	2.9	44.4

(3) When officers' and enlisted men's opinions about the enlisted men are compared, it appears of great importance whether these opinions are factual or moral in character (classes C and E). Such moral opinions appear to be subject to a high degree of perspectivism otherwise associated only with subject matters that involve hierarchical relations more directly, as is true of classes D and F.

(4) Opinions on hierarchical relations are particularly sensitive to perspectivistic "distortion." (Classes D and F)

(5) It should be stressed once more that the absence of social perspectivism for relatively wide areas of reality testifies to, and reflects the fact that the Army was a well functioning social organization, particularly in its dealings with the environment and the enemy.

Noticing that officers grossly overestimated the favorable attitudes of their men toward many aspects of military life, the Research Branch was led to suggest that "one of the elements in this habit of officers . . . was a product of the tendency to project one's own attitudes upon the men." (I, 393) It is not possible to explore on the basis of the available data whether or not the theory of projection is equally applicable to the views which the men held of the officers. Nor was it possible to decide whether or not this explanation held for the officers only in a situation in which the justice of privileges was subconsciously questioned by them or consciously considered to be in conflict with the principles of civilian society. Further peacetime research that would help to answer problems of this kind could proceed from the pertinent findings and interpretations in *The American Soldier* and add to our knowledge of social stratification as well as of the sociology of opinions. Continuous research on peacetime social organizations along the lines here sketched might in time develop an index of social integration which would have high diagnostic and predictive value.

14. THE AFFINITY OF OCCUPATION AND SUBJECT MATTER AMONG ADULT EDUCATION STUDENTS*

by Lotte Radermacher and Elias Smith

FOR A PERIOD between the two World Wars the city of Vienna, Austria, had an elaborate system of adult education. A considerable part of the budget for these courses came from the city government which was then controlled by the Social Democratic labor movement. This labor movement, in turn, placed heavy stress on the importance of education, and attendance of those courses was part of the tradition of organized workers. (Approximately two-thirds of the Viennese population as a whole, and the overwhelming majority of workers, voted at the time for the labor party.) Among intellectuals of liberal persuasion, it was considered obligatory to teach an occasional adult education course. As a result, the students in these courses included quite a number who had enrolled because they wanted to hear a prominent person to whom they would not otherwise have access. In general, however, the enrollees were of low formal education.

In Vienna, at this time, compulsory education ended at the age of fourteen. At the age of ten, however, a bifurcation took place. Middle-class children were likely to be enrolled in the so-called "middle schools." There they received an education which qualified them for entrance into the university at the age of eighteen, although a large number of them stopped there and went into business. It can be assumed that the sub-group of "students," as they are labelled in the subsequent analysis, came from these middle schools to attend courses not included in their regular curriculum. The large majority of the other enrollees in the adult education courses can be assumed to have stopped their formal education at the age of fourteen. There would, however, be a considerable difference in regard to the grade which each respondent ended up with. A large number of less gifted children have to repeat grades, and therefore would leave school, finally, with only five to seven grades completed.

The Basic Tabulation. The purpose of the present paper is to analyze Table 1 in detail. This represents a cross-tabulation of the occupation of each enrollee and the subject matter of the course he took.† At the beginning of the study it was obviously necessary to settle on two classifications, one applying to occupations and the other to courses. At these early phases of the inquiry, both of

---

* This is part of a study reported by the senior author in *Zeitschrift fuer angewandte Psychologie,* 43 (1932). The junior author has reanalyzed some of the data and put the main findings of the original study into a context more easily understandable to a contemporary American reader.

† The unit of this analysis is the enrollment card. A person who took more than one course would therefore appear more than once in the table. Such multiple enrollment, however, was not too frequent, because the adult education schools did not lead to any certificate. The present excerpt is restricted to men. The results pertaining to women, and reported in the original paper by the senior author, did not add to the substance of the discussion. Table 1, as given here, is thus a reproduction of half the original table with the stubs properly translated.

Table I—Cross-Tabulation of Subject Matter of Course, and Occupation of Enrollee (Chance Values in the Lower Right Hand Corner of Each Box)

	1. metal workers	2. printing	3. other skilled workers	4. unskilled	5. civil servants	6. sales personnel	7. office personnel	8. independent shopkeepers	9. semi-professionals	10. "students"	11. retired	12. others	13. Total	14. Coefficient of specificity
1. languages	294 / *405	125 / 126	454 / *535	21 / *39	156 / *214	412 / *556	579 / *697	56 / 59	57 / 57	*333 / 290	20 / *42	35 / 46	2782 / 2782	161
2. spelling and arithmetic	*274 / 210	46 / *67	*424 / 279	*61 / 20	*160 / 111	185 / *212	134 / *301	6 / 18	11 / 32	104 / *151	16 / 22	29 / 23	1450 / 1450	342
3. philosophy	223 / 241	89 / 77	295 / 320	2 / 23	83 / *127	278 / 246	*420 / 348	22 / 22	34 / 36	152 / 173	29 / 25	21 / 28	1667 / 1667	61
4. history	50 / 61	17 / 19	80 / 81	7 / 6	28 / 33	47 / 63	105 / 88	12 / 6	5 / 8	43 / 44	12 / 7	8 / 7	424 / 424	21
5. social science (incl. law and economics)	98 / *138	57 / 43	142 / *184	6 / 13	*98 / 72	166 / 142	238 / 199	25 / 12	10 / 22	68 / 98	20 / 16	28 / 18	956 / 956	86
6. literature and art	114 / *199	69 / 62	149 / *245	7 / 10	112 / 112	182 / 202	*385 / 285	24 / 18	56 / 30	*233 / 143	10 / 21	10 / 22	1376 / 1376	209
7. mathematics	*116 / 70	7 / *22	*134 / 93	8 / 7	*74 / 37	40 / *72	31 / *101	3 / 6	15 / 15	32 / 50	9 / 7	15 / 18	484 / 484	169
8. technical subjects and natural sciences	*276 / 102	30 / 36	123 / 153	4 / 11	45 / 61	58 / *118	116 / *165	12 / 10	11 / 17	98 / 83	7 / 12	15 / 13	795 / 795	365
9. geography and geology	92 / 73	24 / 23	107 / 96	7 / 7	36 / 38	70 / 74	75 / *109	4 / 6	15 / 11	48 / 52	13 / 8	10 / 8	501 / 501	23
10. biology	31 / 32	5 / 10	57 / 43	2 / 3	17 / 17	25 / 33	47 / 46	3 / 3	10 / 5	18 / 23	4 / 3	4 / 4	223 / 223	15
11. medicine	81 / 90	24 / 28	133 / 119	15 / 9	47 / 48	111 / 93	129 / 129	4 / 8	11 / 13	40 / 65	13 / 9	14 / 10	622 / 622	25
12. drawing	55 / 68	*42 / 21	*162 / 82	5 / 7	36 / 36	24 / *70	67 / *99	5 / 6	20 / 11	52 / 49	0 / 7	4 / 7	472 / 472	158
13. TOTAL	1704 / 1704	535 / 535	2260 / 2260	164 / 164	902 / 902	1742 / 1742	2444 / 2444	153 / 153	255 / 255	1221 / 1221	1781 / 1781	194 / 194	11752 / 11752	1642
14. Coefficient of specificity	436	49	246	125	104	148	261	34	61	109	42	22		

these "stubs" combined a mixture of common sense, statistical tradition, and vague expectations as to what classification might be relevant for the final interpretation. For example, among the male enrollees with manual occupations a distinction was made among

1. metal workers
2. typographers
3. other skilled workers
4. unskilled workers.

The justification for separating the first three groups will subsequently become evident. The number of unskilled workers, as can be seen from Table 1, is very small; this is explained by the fact that their level of education was so low that they did not have the equipment to follow any of the courses.

A special fifth group, civil servants, includes persons in such occupations as maintenance workers in city buildings, mail carriers, and streetcar conductors. They were combined in one group because it was considered likely that their position in a civil service hierarchy might direct their educational interest in special directions. White-collar workers were divided into

6. sales personnel
7. office personnel.

Representatives of two more groups were so rare in number that they will not receive special discussion. These groups were:

8. independent shopkeepers
9. semi-professionals, like nurses or
   grade school teachers.

The two final groups are best characterized by their age, either very young or very old:

10. "students" (see above)
11. retired.

The *courses* in which these various groups could enroll were first classified into two major groups:

I. *General utility courses*: (1) languages, and (2) elementary courses, covering essentially arithmetic and spelling.

The remaining courses can be called:

II. *General information courses*: their content is obvious from the stub of our main table.

These other courses will be further subdivided, according to more specific principles, which must now be explained.

The Statistical Procedures Used. The central problem was to study the affinity between occupation and subject matter. The statistical measure for this affinity was derived from a comparison of actual enrollment (E) and chance values (C). These chance values are those which would be expected if the various occupations were randomly distributed over the various courses, given the existing distributions of occupation and enrollment. In Table 1 we find two figures in each box. In the upper left-hand corner the actual enrollment is reported. In the lower right-hand corner the chance value appears. In each case, the chance value is computed by multiplying the marginal sums for each line and each column which meet in a specific box, and then dividing by the total size of the male sample.

When the chance value is smaller than the actual enrollment, we speak of a *positive* affinity. People in an occupational group then have a more than average interest in the subject matter taught. If the chance value is larger than the actual enrollment, we speak of a *negative* affinity. People in such an occupational group have a small likelihood of enrolling in such a course.

It is necessary to have a measure as to when such differences ought to be taken seriously. In a table of this size it is permissible to take the square root of the chance value as a measure of the probable error. Our critical ratio, therefore, is $S = \dfrac{E - C}{\sqrt{C}}$. Any affinity for which S was numerically larger than 2.5 was considered significant. The cells for which this is the case are marked with an asterisk. If the affinity is positive, then the asterisk has been put beside the figure on actual enrollment; for negative affinity, the asterisk has been put beside the chance value.

Finally, a measure of specificity was devised for every course and every occupation. There are courses which have a considerable affinity to many occupations, as indicated by a relatively large number of asterisks in a particular row. There are also some occupations which have affinities to many courses; this is seen by looking down the columns. In constructing this measure of specificity, it does not matter whether the affinity is positive or negative; therefore S^2 was used as the basic figure. The measure then is $\sum_i S_i^2$ taken either over columns, for occupations, or rows, for courses. This is, of course, nothing else than the traditional Chi-square; but it is used here only as a descriptive index. The specificity values are given in the marginal column and row.

The Core Pattern. It is now possible to subclassify the courses further, by grouping together the four which have the lowest specificity values. These happen to be history (4), geography and geology (9), biology (10), and medicine (11). It will turn out presently that this group, isolated on the basis of numerical results, can be interpreted in a meaningful substantive way. For the moment, it is enough to see that we thus arrive at three major types of courses:

      I General utility courses
      II (a) Information courses, with occupational specificity
      II (b) Information courses, without occupational specificity

Returning now to the occupations, we eliminate, for the moment, the last two, Nos. 10 and 11, as they are not occupations in the same sense that the others are. And we also eliminate Nos. 4, 8, and 9, because, as was mentioned before, there are so few persons in these groups that they cannot be studied in detail.

We are now in a position to turn to our main task. It would be impossible to see any implications of the basic table if we were forced to attend simultaneously to 144 measures of affinity. We therefore tried to isolate a core pattern which might be indicative of a general finding. After this has been brought out clearly, we can then consider details.

The core pattern has been derived by a combination, first, of a common-sense classification, and then a further refinement of categories, guided by the numerical results of Table 1. By this latter device, we have already achieved a subdivision of the so-called information courses. We can now utilize the same procedure to order further the relevant occupations. We note a rather interesting relation between columns 1 and 7 in Table 1. *In every row, that is, for every course, the metal workers and the office personnel have an exactly opposite affinity.* "Drawing" is the only exception; it includes artistic as well as technical courses. Obviously, the former represent best the interest pattern of a manual worker, and the latter the interest pattern of a white-collar worker. It would therefore make sense to order the other occupations according to whether the affinities they reveal in their courses of study are similar to one or the other of these extremes. This can be done fairly well for the remaining occupations, with the single exception of civil servants. In order not to be confused by the figures, we shall, for the moment, distinguish only three kinds of affinities: significant ones (designated by two positive or two negative signs), totally insignificant ones (with a critical ratio of practically 0, designated by zero), and finally, affinities which are pronounced but which do not meet our criteria of significance (designated by a single positive or negative sign).

Having rearranged the occupations along lines discussed in the preceding paragraph, and having replaced the numerical figures with symbols of three types of affinities, we obtain the following *core pattern*:

Core Pattern of Findings Extracted from Table I

	Metal Workers (1)	Other Skilled Workers (3)	Printers (2)	Sales Personnel (6)	Office Personnel (7)	Civil Servants (5)
I. Utility courses						
languages (1)	— —	— —	0	+ +	+ +	— —
spelling, arithmetic (2)	+ +	+ +	— —	— —	— —	+ +
II. (a) Information courses						
literature and art (6)	— —	— —	0	—	+ +	0
philosophy (3)	—	—	+	+	+ +	+
social sciences* (5)	— —	— —	+	+	+	+ +
drawing (12)	—	+ +	+ +	— —	— —	0
mathematics (7)	+ +	—	—	— —	— —	—
natural science (8)	+ +	+ +	— —	— —	— —	+ +

* Includes economics and law.

The Interpretation of the Core Pattern. What does this core pattern suggest? To gain further understanding, let us look first at the six bottom lines, embracing the information courses with occupational specificity. They are now arranged in such a way that they also order the occupations with fairly good consistency. Literature has a strong positive affinity for office personnel, and a strong negative affinity for manual workers. At the other end of the list, the natural sciences have a high affinity for metal workers, and a strong negative affinity for the white-collar employees. Printers occupy a middle position between the other manual workers and the white-collar people. "Other skilled workers" and "sales personnel" are less extreme than metal workers and office personnel, respectively.

The courses, in turn, divide into two clear groups. Literature, philosophy, and the social sciences have positive affinities for white-collar people and negative affinities for manual workers. Drawing, natural science and mathematics appear in a reverse position.

Turning now to the first two rows of the table, we note a very sharp difference between the two kinds of utility courses. Languages have a positive affinity for white-collar people, while the basic courses in arithmetic and spelling have strong affinity for the manual workers; the corresponding negative affinities are equally strong, in the reverse direction.

We can now go one step further and introduce a psychological interpretation. Those who enroll in these adult education courses can have two types of motivation. They either want to *make up for deficiencies* in their basic education, or they want to *increase their general knowledge*. These, in modern terminology, are the two *manifest* functions of the courses. The function of enlarging one's knowledge can be further subdivided: it can either be closely related to one's work, or it may be of a more general nature. These might be called the *latent* functions of this particular kind of motivation.

These latent functions now permit a sharp distinction between white-collar personnel and manual workers. According to the courses which they select, the latter want to acquire knowledge closely related to the technical nature of their work. For the white-collar people the courses seem more to serve the function of a general liberal education. Or to state it in still different terms, it is probably true that both groups enroll in these courses with the hope that this will lead to some kind of socioeconomic advancement. But advancement for the manual workers lies mainly along the lines of improved skills in the shop; for the white-collar people, on the other hand, advancement is more likely to come via the parlor, and by assimilation of the intellectual amenities of the middle class. All of these distinctions are seen most clearly for the metal workers and the office personnel. The three other occupational groups under consideration here fall in between, with the printers representing something of a transitional type.

We have placed the civil servants in a special column. They behave, in most respects, like the manual workers. This is understandable when it is recognized that they are usually in low-paid, manual jobs. They are different, however, in one interesting respect: unlike manual workers, they have a strong positive affinity to the social science courses. This is probably due to the fact that the civil servants were preparing for advancement examinations in which the knowledge of some law was likely to play a role.

This, in essence, is the core pattern of Table 1. We can still interpret some further details. We are now in a better position to understand, for example, why courses in biology and history have such a low occupational specificity. For the manual workers, these subjects are not sufficiently related to their work in the factory; for the white-collar workers, they do not have as much parlor-talk value as do art, philosophy, and the social sciences.

The group of "students" show only two positive affinities: with languages and with literature and art courses. This is understandable in view of the curriculum of the Austrian schools from which students went on to universities. Many of them concentrated on the classics, and therefore adolescents who wanted to learn modern languages had to receive their instruction elsewhere. Furthermore, these schools were the antithesis of the "progressive schools" in this country, and they paid little attention to self-expression through either literature or art.

Among the four course groups which lack occupational specificity, we find only one significant affinity, although 48 were possible: the office personnel show considerable interest in geography and geology, an exception for which no explanation is readily available. The retired people have only one strong negative affinity, to wit, languages. This can be explained easily in two ways: first of all, such persons do not ordinarily expect to travel, and, secondly, they would probably have some difficulty in learning new languages. The unskilled workers exhibit a pattern very similar to that for the working-class as a whole, but they are less specific, probably because they are a small and very unrepresentative group. The same would be true for the small group of semi-professionals who do not show any significant affinity one way or another.

In sum, it turns out that a large number of findings can be organized by a type of classification which weaves back and forth between general considerations and guidance provided by the statistical results themselves. As was indicated, the main finding represented in the core pattern contains a strong element of interpretation. But this could be checked to some extent. The manifest functions of the courses could be studied by direct interviews, in which a sub-sample of students might be asked what purpose they had in mind when they enrolled in the courses. It would be somewhat more difficult to obtain evidence for the latent functions. One would probably have to get retrospective interviews from alumni, in which they would be asked to report any changes in their lives which came about as a result of having availed themselves of this type of adult education.

Auxiliary Readings

A. CONCEPTUALIZATION AND EMPIRICAL RESEARCH

R. N. Sanford, T. W. Adorno, E. Frenkel-Brunswik, and D. J. Levinson, "The Measurement of Implicit Antidemocratic Trends," in T. W. Adorno, et al., *The Authoritarian Personality* (New York: Harper & Bros., 1950), Chapter VII.

> Explains in detail how the notion of an authoritarian personality was first conceptually analyzed into its component elements and then translated into a specific set of questionnaire items—the F-scale.

R. K. Merton and A. S. Kitt, "Contributions to the Theory of Reference Group Behavior," *Continuities in Social Research: Studies in the Scope and Method of "The American Soldier,"* R. K. Merton and P. F. Lazarsfeld, eds. (Glencoe, Ill.: The Free Press, 1950), Chapter II.

> Shows the various specifications which can be brought to bear on a concept which was originally introduced to interpret in a general way a large variety of empirical observations.

B. SELECTION OF APPROPRIATE INDICATORS

R. Barker, T. Dembo, and K. Lewin, "Frustration and Regression," in *Child Behavior and Development*, R. Barker, J. C. Kounin and H. F. Wright, eds. (New York: McGraw-Hill, 1943), pp. 441-458.
Children are rated by an observer on a scale called "constructiveness of play" reflecting the degree of maturity they demonstrate in playing with toys. The measure of *regression* is interpreted as the difference in the degree of constructiveness of play before and after the frustrating situation.

E. D. Chapple, "The Interaction Chronograph: Its Evaluation and Present Application," *Personnel*, Vol. 25, 1948-49, pp. 295-307.
Starting with the observation that certain statements of emotional intensity were associated with the length of time and frequency of contacts between people, the author developed an instrument to record, at the time people spoke to one another, who spoke first and for how long, who interrupted whom how often, etc. Develops measures of tempo, activity or energy, initiative, dominance, synchronization, ability to listen, flexibility, etc., on the basis of these relationships.

M. Rokeach, "Generalized Mental Rigidity as a Factor in Ethnocentrism," *Jour. Abn. and Soc. Psych.*, Vol. 43, 1948, pp. 259-277.
The author developed several devices to measure "mental rigidity." One of these involved exposing his subjects to a series of problems requiring a certain pattern of thought for solution; he then gave them slightly different problems involving a new way of thinking and observed those who failed to readjust rapidly. He found this mental rigidity related to questionnaire items on ethnocentrism.

L. S. Cottrell, Jr. and R. I. Dymond, "The Empathic Responses," *Psychiatry*, Vol. XII, 1949, pp. 335-359.
The "empathic ability" of people is measured by noting the frequency with which they are able to predict correctly the attitudes which other respondents express in a questionnaire. Empirical findings based on this index are summarized. The theoretical background for the entire approach is discussed in detail.

C. THE NOTION OF PROPERTY-SPACE

L. J. Cronbach and G. C. Gleser, "Assessing Similarity Between Profiles," *Psychological Bulletin*, Vol. 50, No. 6, 1953, pp. 456-473.
A profile can be considered as a point in a property-space, the dimensions of which are tests. Similarity then corresponds to "distance" between points, which can be measured by a variety of conventions.

S. A. Stouffer and L. C. DeVinney, "How Personal Adjustment Varied in the Army—Preliminary Considerations," *The American Soldier*, Vol. I. (Princeton: Princeton University Press, 1949), Chapter III.
"Morale" is described as a "point" in four dimensions: personal esprit; personal commitment; satisfaction with status and job; approval or criticism of the army. A movement of this point corresponds to a change in morale; and how to measure it is a matter of discussion.

F. J. Roethlisberger and W. J. Dickson, "The Urgency and Tone of Industrial Topics," *Management and the Worker* (Cambridge: Harvard University Press, 1939), Chapter XI.
When workers discuss work at the factory a specific aspect of the job situation might either be approved, criticized, or not mentioned at all. Call the frequency of the first two reactions x and y. Then $x + y$ indicates urgency and $\dfrac{x}{y}$ feeling tone. The two indices correspond to two different families of lines in a two-dimensional property-space.

D. COMPARISON AND EVALUATION OF INDICES

Hans Zeisel, "Coordinating the Measurement of Broadcasting Audiences," *Marketing Research* (Dubuque, Iowa: W. C. Brown Co., 1952), Chapter 2.
Shows that many audience measures are in use, but that they all are different ways of describing the distribution of time spent on listening.

S. P. Zobel, "On the Measurement of the Productivity of Labor," *Journal of American Statistical Association,* Vol. 45, 1950, pp. 218-224.

The usual method of measuring worker productivity by dividing output by man-hours is criticized. A whole host of factors, e.g., expensive machinery, are shown to be involved, and several formulae are suggested to give more appropriate weights to these various factors.

M. J. Ulmer, *The Economic Theory of Cost of Living Index Numbers* (New York: Columbia University Press, 1949).

Compares two indices currently in use and relates them to an "ideal" measure, based on the theory of indifference curves. The second chapter deals with "the problem of definition": how indices are related to an intended meaning if the latter can be derived from a theoretical context.

E. PROBLEMS OF CLASSIFICATION

F. J. Roethlisberger and W. J. Dickson, "The Analysis of Complaints; Fact vs. Sentiment," *Management and the Worker* (Cambridge: Harvard University Press, 1939), Chapter XII.

Discusses in detail the role of a conceptual scheme in the classification of workers' complaints. Distinguishes between their manifest and latent content.

B. Berelson, "The Categories of Content Analysis," *Content Analysis in Communications Research* (Glencoe, Ill.: The Free Press, 1951), Chapter V.

Shows how a system of classification can be derived from an analysis of the act of communication. The whole book contains many examples of classifications which permit the discussion of the relation between the purposes of studies and the "stubs" used in ordering the material.

D. P. Cartwright, "Analysis of Qualitative Material," *Research Methods in the Behavioral Sciences,* D. Katz and L. Festinger, eds. (New York: Dryden Press, 1953), Chapter 10.

Contains many concrete examples and gives good advice on problems of coding and classification.

B. Kass, "Overlapping Magazine Reading," *Communications Research, 1948-49,* P. F. Lazarsfeld and F. Stanton, eds. (New York: Harper and Bros., 1949), pp. 130-151.

In an effort to measure the "cultural propinquity" of magazines, the magazine readership habits of several thousand respondents were analyzed. For each pair of magazines, the proportion of joint readership was computed. Finally, the magazines were ordered in terms of the pattern of overlapping readership. The meaning of this order, as well as the reasons for "irregular" cases, is discussed.

C. G. Hempel, "Classification," *Fundamentals of Concept Formation in Empirical Science* (Chicago: University of Chicago Press, 1952), International Encyclopedia of Unified Science, Vol. II, No. 7, Chapter IX.

Gives a concise summary of the present doctrine of classification from the point of view of modern logic.

Multivariate Analysis

Introduction

THE FIRST SECTION dealt essentially with various ways in which we can characterize people, or any other objects which are of interest to the social scientist. Whether we speak of classification, the measurement of variables, or the formation of indices, the end result of this phase of research will always be the same: the investigator will have transferred a piece of social reality into a set of objects which are given a place in a variety of conceptual dimensions which the investigator considered pertinent to his purpose. The symbol and the complete formal equivalent of such a representation is the IBM card. To each dimension corresponds a column; the position along the dimension is given by the punched square.

A very important part of social research consists in studying and interpreting the relations among these variables. In a somewhat facetious way one could say that any subject matter under investigation has to be translated into IBM language. Wherever we have a set of variables available, anything knowable about the matter can be expressed in this language. It is necessary to understand clearly its scope and its limitations. Beginning with the latter it will become obvious from our selections that the interpretations of many findings go beyond the manipulation of variables; and the formation of the variables themselves requires a great deal of preceding theoretical thinking. On the other hand, one should not underestimate the range of subject matter which can be covered by this language. Attitudes, personality traits, interpersonal contacts, etc., are characteristics of people which can quite naturally be introduced as variables into a survey type of investigation. They provide the empirical base for interpretations which thus are lifted beyond the realm of mere speculation.

The term "IBM language" undoubtedly has a derogatory overtone and is therefore not recommended for further use. One could go to the other extreme and point out that there is a close affinity between it and what modern logicians call the Boolean calculus of classes. But the esoteric term "Boolean language" might be equally deterrent. As a compromise, the expression "multivariate analysis" has been chosen. While this term has a narrower meaning in mathematical statistics, it seems descriptive enough to serve our purpose. This purpose is to carve out as an important area of research skill *the study and interpretation of complex inter-relations among a multiplicity of characteristics*. In very concrete terms, the task most of the time boils down to the following type of situation.

A sample of people is characterized by a variable. They hold an opinion or have made a choice or have some other property in which we are interested. In addition, we have data on the respondents' backgrounds, previous experiences, collateral attitudes, social contacts, and so on. How, in the light of these data, can we explain variations in the dependent variable? The selections presented in this section and their organization are intended to answer this question.

A. *The general idea of multivariate analysis.* The first division tries to convey and to exemplify the general idea of multivariate analysis. The simplest case occurs when we start with the relation between two variables and introduce a third one for elaboration and elucidation. This procedure leads to a surprising number of "modes of explanation" and furnishes most of the logical elements entering into more complex cases. Selection (1) reviews the matter systematically. It shows how one may fruitfully distinguish the following: the "true" interpretation, the conditional relationship and the detecting of spurious factors. This selection was originally written for expository purposes and it is therefore not necessary to repeat here its basic theme.

The next two selections provide two coherent and concrete pieces of investigation; there the elements carved out in Selection (1) can be retraced in a realistic context. Lipset in Selection (2) analyzed the factors determining the position adopted by a sample of students in regard to the oath controversy at the University of California. The reader's attention should be directed particularly to the way in which he isolated the influence of the different newspapers which the students read. The tracing of such influences by multivariate analysis has often been attempted but rarely achieved. In Selection (3) Stouffer and DeVinney had as their object the study of attitudes of soldiers toward promotion opportunities in army units. They brought out clearly how, as each additional variable was introduced, increased understanding was achieved. (A further aspect of their analysis is taken up once again in Selection [1] of Section IV.)

B. *Some specific problems.* The number of problems one meets in multivariate analysis is very large indeed, but three topics of importance have been chosen for special exemplification. The first deals with the interplay of "sociological" and "psychological" var-

iables. Psychologists have at times expressed the belief that this form of analysis restricts the investigator to the use of characteristics like income, age, and so on, and prohibits a real understanding of the relations empirically found. This, however, is clearly a misunderstanding which is easily dispelled by examples like Selection (4). Suchman and Menzel start with data showing that the various minority groups vote more frequently for the Democratic party than the white Protestant majority in the community. This is the type of information which is sometimes, by critics, assailed as "external." But nothing keeps us from introducing more specific information. In addition to a man's religious affiliation we can find out whether it is of importance to him; if a person belongs to a civic organization we can find out how active he is there and whether it brings him in contact with people of other creeds or races. The authors give many examples where such specifying variables lead to an elucidation of "psychological connections" through the devices of multivariate analysis.

Next, we wish to emphasize the nature of conditional relations discussed in Selection (1). They are the aspect of multivariate analysis which is intellectually most productive and yet is very often misunderstood or at least overlooked. In Selection (5), we start with two findings. Women are less likely to go to the polls on election day than men; women are also less interested in politics than men. Is lack of interest therefore an explanation for the difference in voting habits? The answer can come only from a comparison of the sexes *within* different degrees of interest. At first sight this sounds like a partial correlation with "interest kept constant." But actually it is just the *separate* inspection of the different interest classes which gives the crucial result and which would be obliterated by a partial correlation approach. As a parallel, Selection (5) also carries out a comparison between educated people who vote more frequently and uneducated respondents who furnish more vote delinquents. Here multivariate analysis attributes to "political interest" a role different from the one it has in the case of the sex comparison. A similar procedure is followed by Rosenberg in Selection (6). His point of departure is a finding that students who want to get ahead in the world are also distrustful of other people. But this relation is again greatly modified by the sex of the respondent. Women are under less social pressure to get ahead; for them, therefore, the (conditional) relationship between the two psychological variables is much more pronounced.

Finally, an additional example seemed desirable to show how many precautions an investigator has to take if he wants to safeguard the interpretation of an initial result. In Selection (7), Havemann and West found that people who had graduated from an Ivy League college were subsequently more successful financially than people who came from small colleges. But the former also came from more well-to-do families. How can we be confident that it is the college and not the previous family background of students which accounts for the subsequent financial success? By introducing an additional variable into the analysis they are able to make their interpretation much more cogent.

C. *Deviant Case Analysis.* Any multivariate analysis reaches a barrier for one of two reasons. Either the available variables have been exhausted or so many cross-tabulations have been made that the number of cases in many cells have become too small. Still we may not have achieved closure. The investigator will be confronted by cases which cannot be accounted for in the terms of his own analysis. He will want to extend it at least in a speculative way and lay the ground for more extended and refined future multivariate analysis. At this point a clear insight into the logic of deviant case analysis is required. Three short selections serve this purpose. In Selection (8), Kendall and Wolf present the general idea. In Selection (9), Merton gives a specific example. Selection (10) by Horst shows

that deviant case analysis also appears in the area of prediction studies which form a part of Section III.

D. *The testing of hypotheses.* All the examples given so far started with a simple result and the purpose of a more refined analysis was to account for it. But the same procedures also come into play when the intellectual sequence is somewhat different. In some of the most valuable social research studies, the investigator starts with a hypothesis obtained from theoretical considerations or general insight and then uses empirical findings to test it. His data may either be available from conventional records or he might collect them anew for his special purpose. An example of such an analysis is Selection (11), in which Klineberg shows that there is no definitely established difference in the native intelligence of Negro and White children; the opposite opinion is due to an improper interpretation of data which Klineberg rectifies by an intricate multivariate analysis. In Selection (12), Katona starts with a thesis of the economist Keynes dealing with the relation between income and savings. From a large sample of respondents Katona collected information about these two variables, as well as data on a considerable number of additional ones. As a result he could show that the factors which determine savings are really much more complex than the Keynesian theory assumes. The bearing of such a finding on economic theory is a very interesting question which, however, goes beyond the scope of this Reader. In Selection (13), V. O. Key set out to prove that in many elections in the South, personal ties with a candidate play a very great role in voting behavior. Key analyzed a considerable number of elections which were held under quite varying conditions. By a device which is impressive in its ingenious simplicity, he proved his point and accounted well for deviant cases.

The utilization of this section by teacher and student can proceed in a variety of ways. It should be useful to take the concrete studies included and to locate their procedures in the general scheme presented in Selection (1). But, in addition, the formalism of multivariate analysis should be applied to examples of verbal reasoning. In any textbook of sociology, one can find discussions of the way various factors combine to determine human behavior. Such writing often is clarified and improved if it is translated into more abstract "modes of explanation." On the other hand, the student should become aware that any empirical result can be improved by the addition of further variables. In Selection (7), e.g., the question can be raised whether the Ivy League college improves the financial future of its initially poorer alumni by giving them good training *or* by useful social contacts. By what kind of further information and what kind of analysis could this question be settled? In Selection (5), the statement is made that some women do not vote because they feel that voting is not women's business. How does this part of the selection relate to the material on deviant case analysis? How could the hunch derived from the interviews be lifted to the level of solid evidence? The teacher will have no difficulty in spotting other possible connections between the various selections of this section.

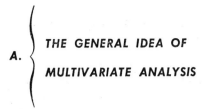

A. THE GENERAL IDEA OF MULTIVARIATE ANALYSIS

1. INTERPRETATION OF STATISTICAL RELATIONS AS A RESEARCH OPERATION*

by Paul F. Lazarsfeld

THE ROLE OF TEST FACTORS

THE STARTING POINT for the present discussion is a research procedure which is applied almost automatically in empirical research. Whenever an investigator finds himself faced with the relationship between two variables he immediately starts to "cross-tabulate," i.e., to consider the role of further variables. The procedure may be demonstrated by using data that represent in somewhat stylized form the results obtained in many studies of radio listening tastes. By relating age of respondent to the program to which he usually listens, it is found that older people listen more to religious programs and political discussions on the air than do younger people, while there is practically no age difference in listening to classical music.

Table 1—Proportion of Listeners in Two Age Groups

	YOUNG % Listen	OLD % Listen
Religious programs	17%	26%
Discussion programs	34	45
Classical music programs	30	29
(Total Cases)	(1000)	(1300)

Every research man knows that age is related to education; because of the recent extension of formal education, younger people in a community are usually better educated than the older ones. In the present sample the relation between age and education is as follows: (The education break is between those who completed high school and those who did not; the age break is at 40.)

Table 2—Relation Between Age and Education

	Young	Old	Total
High Education	600	400	1000
Low Education	400	900	1300
Total	1000	1300	2300

* This is an address given at the Cleveland meeting of the American Sociological Society in 1946 and has not been published before. The main points, however, have been incorporated into subsequent papers, some of which are mentioned in the auxiliary reading list to this section.

We thus deal with three variables: age, education, and type of listening. To simplify matters, we converted each variable into a dichotomy. Education, which is introduced here to elaborate and to clarify the original relationship, is called the *test variable* (t). Age is conventionally called the independent variable (x) and listening the dependent variable (y). Sometimes for brevity of expression we will use the symbols xyt, in the sense indicated in the previous sentence. But, otherwise, no mathematics will be used in this exposition.

Simple reflection will show that three relations can be drawn between three such variables. One relates age to listening: [xy], and the corresponding information has been given in Table 1, for each of the three program types. Then we have the relation between age and the test factor, education: [xt]. This is, of course, the same for all program types and the figures, rounded out but substantially correct, are reported in Table 2. Finally, we have [ty], the relation between education and listening. This again is different for all the programs, and the data will be given presently.

For better understanding, one should take into account at this point that the entire fourfold Table 2, and any one line in Table 1, give the same type of information. The content of Table 2 could be summarized by stating that 60% of the young people but only 31% of the old people are in the high education group. Inversely, we could convert any line of Table 1 into a fourfold table, giving for the two age classes the number of people who listen or do not listen to a certain type of program. We shall use both types of presentation, according to which is convenient.

Various coefficients have been developed to "measure" the relation between two such dichotomies. For our present purpose, the only distinction we will need is whether the two are unrelated or related in some substantial way. Therefore, the simplest index will be best and this is the so-called standardized cross-product. For Table 2, for example, it is

$$[xt] = \frac{600 \cdot 900 - 400 \cdot 400}{2300^2} = .08.$$ (The value of this cross-product,

incidentally, is about one-fourth of what the so-called point correlation would show.) There does exist a relation between education and age for, otherwise, the cross-product would vanish.

The research operation we are describing here thus starts out with an original relation [xy], then introduces a test variable, and thus creates two more relations [xt] and [ty]. But the most important results obtained with the help of the test variable are two *partial relations*. We can now raise the following question. If we study people in the high education and low education groups separately, what happens to the relation between age and listening? The answer is given in Table 3.

Table 3—Relation Between Age and Listening to Religious Programs, by Education

	HIGH EDUCATION				LOW EDUCATION		
	Young	Old			Young	Old	
Listen ·	55	45	100	Listen	115	285	400
Don't Listen	545	355	900	Don't Listen	285	615	900
	600	400	1000		400	900	1300

The figures pertain to religious programs. To make them more comparable with the first line of Table 1, we use the per cent presentation and then see that *within each educational group the relation between age and listening has practically disappeared*. (The first line of Table 4 repeats information presented in Table 1.)

Table 4—Proportion of Listeners to Religious Programs

Young	Old
17%	26%

HIGH EDUCATION		LOW EDUCATION	
Young	Old	Young	Old
9%	11%	29%	32%

We can now perform the same analysis for the other two program types listed in Table 1. The results are reported without discussing all the intermediate steps. The main point to note is how different the role of the test variable is from one example to the next. We begin with listening to discussion programs on the radio.*

Table 5—Proportion of Listeners to Discussion Programs

Young	Old
34%	45%

HIGH EDUCATION		LOW EDUCATION	
Young	Old	Young	Old
40%	55%	25%	40%

The data of Table 1 are repeated in the first line of Table 5, as they were in Table 4. Table 5 shows that, *within* educational groups, age makes an even larger difference than for the sample as a whole.

Now, how about listening to classical music? From Table 1 it might appear that age plays no role here. However, notice: the footnote shows that educated people listen more to this type of program, and we know that younger people are more highly educated.

Carrying out the full tabulation scheme reveals indeed a rather complex structure, exhibited in Table 6.

Table 6—Proportion of Listeners to Classical Music

Young	Old
30%	29%

HIGH EDUCATION		LOW EDUCATION	
Young	Old	Young	Old
32%	52%	28%	19%

Table 6 shows that age plays a different role for high and low educated respondents. In a more sophisticated environment, maturation leads to more attention to such cultural matters as good music. In a "culturally impoverished" environment, the peak of such interest seems to come near to the age when school influence still prevails; with increasing age, cultural interests decline.

---

* To complete our information we still need to know how education is related to listening; or, in other words, we need to know [ty]. The data are as follows:

LISTEN TO DISCUSSION PROGRAMS				LISTEN TO CLASSICAL MUSIC			
	Yes	*No*			*Yes*	*No*	
High Education	460	540	1000	Low Education	280	1020	1300
Low Education	460	840	1300	High Education	404	596	1000
TOTAL	920	1380	2300	TOTAL	684	1616	2300

It is the logic, not the substantive details, of these three examples, to which one should attend. The introduction of age had a different effect in each example cited in Table 1. With religious programs it decreased the original difference; with discussion programs it led to an increase; with classical music it brought to light two counter trends which were concealed in the original findings.

A GENERAL SCHEME FOR THE RELATION BETWEEN THREE DICHOTOMIES

The gist of the preceding examples can be put into a general formula. In order to understand its importance, we must first give more consideration to what was variously called partial associations, partial fourfold tables, or partial differences. There are always two of them, as can be seen from Table 3 and from the second lines in Tables 4 and 5. The original relation [xy] is split into two conditional relations for high and low education people separately, and an obvious symbolism to be used for the two of them is [xy;t]' [xy;t]". Their meaning is similar to the statistician's partial correlation; the latter, however, really corresponds to an average of our two partials. The very fact that we can separate them, and can have different relations on each side of the test factor is of the essence for our present purpose.

The whole structure consisting of the two original variables and the test variable can be formulated as follows:

Form 1) $[xy] = [xy;t]' \oplus [xy;t]'' \oplus [xt] \cdot [ty]$

This shows that the original relationship can be described as the sum of the two partial relationships and an additional factor which is the product of what are called the marginal relationships between the test factor and the two original variables. One remark as to the arithmetic of this formula. The plus signs are encircled because it is not really a straight sum: a weighted sum has to be used. However, this has no bearing on our later discussion and it is not worth complicating the matter by introducing the two weight factors that belong here.

The formula can become more vivid if one applies it to a number of well-known cases. It is known, for instance, that in counties where there are *more storks* there also are *more children*. This somewhat puzzling result is made more acceptable if a *distinction* between *rural* and *urban* counties is introduced as a test factor. It then turns out that within the two groups of counties the relationship between storks and children disappears: the two partials are zero. The original relationship emerges as the product of the fact that in rural counties there are more storks, and in these same counties the birth rate is higher.

Our introductory examples can also be easily reproduced in this formula. With religious programs the product of the [xt] [ty] relationships is positive, and the two partials very small; with discussion programs the product is negative and therefore, by necessity, the partials have to be larger than the original relationship. In the case of classical music the salient feature is that one partial is positive and the other negative. The first rows of figures in Tables 4-6 correspond to [xy]. The second rows correspond to the partials. [xt] can be obtained from Table 2. In Table 3 and in the footnote, we have the data to compute [ty] for each of the three program types.

Just to become better acquainted with the general formula, the reader is asked to apply it to a type of argument which is especially frequent in Durkheim's writing. At one point he says in essence: "Idiocy seems to be a deterrent of suicide. The idiots are much more common in the country than in the city, while suicides are much rarer in the country." A similar example can be found when Durkheim tries to prove that less literate people commit fewer suicides by the following argument: "We have seen that in all countries of the world women commit much fewer suicides than men. Women are also much less educated . . . they do not have strong intellectual needs. . . ." It will be noted that Durkheim never considers the partial relations. What effect does this have on his argument?

There are two cases in which the formula takes on a very characteristic form and which, therefore, deserve special attention. One case happens in a *controlled experiment* where we have two matched groups, one of which is exposed to a stimulus and the other is not. Let us call the exposure stimulus "x". The essence of matching can be precisely formulated in the frame of our discussion. For any conceivable test factor, the two matched groups should be alike, or, in other words, $[xt] = 0$; therefore, the third member in our basic formula will always be zero (matching is required for relevant test factors "t" only). Relevant factors are those which do have, or might have, a relationship with criterion "y". In the case of an irrelevant test factor, $[ty]$ would be zero, and again the final item in the formula would disappear.

In the case of the controlled experiment, therefore, the result of introducing a relevant test factor would be exemplified by

Form 2) $$[xy] = [xy;t]' \oplus [xy;t]'' \oplus [0] \cdot [ty]$$

The other case of special interest occurs when the two partials are zero and the original relationship is equal to the product of the relationship between the test factor and the two original variables. It is found, for instance, that men have more automobile accidents than women. If, however, the amount of mileage driven during the year is introduced as a test factor, it turns out that the partial relationship between sex and accidents disappears. In this case, then, the original relationship is shown to be equivalent to the product of two new ones which in turn might be made the object of further elaboration. The two relationships remaining here are usually called the marginals. They come about if we cross-tabulate the test variable against the two original variables; they do not require simultaneous tabulations of three variables, or in other words, they do not require partials.

Form 3) $$[xy] = [0] \oplus [0] \oplus [xt] \cdot [ty]$$

The difference between the last two cases is easily remembered. In Form 2, the partials remain and one of the basic relations $[xt]$ disappears. In Form 3, the marginals remain and the partials disappear. It is useful, therefore, to call the first case, *elaboration by partials* (P), and the case of Form 3, elaboration by marginals (M). (The term marginals becomes appropriate if one inspects Table 3 closer. $[xt]$ and $[yt]$ are formed by comparing age and listening habits of the two educational groups. This means comparing the marginal sums of the two partial fourfold Tables.)

For one who does not like to think in statistical terms, it might be easier to put it this way. In case P, the original relationship is maintained even after the test factor is introduced. In case M, the original relationship disappears and is substituted by new marginal relationships into which the test factor enters.

Here, then, is brought down to its logical skeleton a research operation familiar to every research laboratory. It consists of elaborating on a relationship between two variables by introducing a third one. We have already applied it to a number of concrete examples which, however, were all taken from empirical studies. Still, the way our examples run has a familiar tinge; going to texts that are held in high esteem by theorists, we find the same pattern. Dollard argues that upper-class Whites are fairer to Negroes than lower-class Whites because the former have less to fear from competition with the Negroes. Durkheim suggests that Catholics commit less suicide as compared with Protestants, because the Catholic community is more cohesive. These are important theoretical discussions, but if one looks at them quite closely, they too boil down to one scheme: two variables analyzed in the light of a third.

We already know everything that can be done with three variables. It is expressed in our main formula. Therefore, we ought to be able to derive from our formula anything which the theorists can do with two original variables and one additional variable. Or, in other words, we should be able to classify all theoretical thinking on three variables into a few major types, derived from the conditions of our main formula. This can actually be done, but, before proceeding, an additional consideration has to be introduced.

(To simplify the discussion, this analysis is restricted to three variables; if more than three variables are linked together, nothing changes basically, as can be shown fairly easily. We also restrict ourselves to dichotomies. If variables were introduced with three or more steps—for instance, young, middle-aged, and old people—the discussion would only become somewhat more complicated, but would not take a different form.)

THE ROLE OF TIME ORDER AMONG VARIABLES

A new aspect is introduced if we consider the time order between variables. The basic research operation from which we started required the classification of people according to certain attributes. The same classification is done mentally when we talk of people who do or do not live in competition with Negroes, or of the poor and rich neighborhoods, or of cohesive and uncohesive groups. (For the sake of simplicity, we shall restrict our examples to individual people.)

Very often these attributes are acquired at different times and therefore can be ranked accordingly. If, for instance, we relate length of engagement with subsequent marital happiness, the length of engagement comes earlier in the time order. If we relate parole breaking to some conditions of a criminal's adolescence, the latter again is prior in the time sequence.

Sometimes the time order is not as obvious, but it is clear enough for our purpose. Take such a result as that low-income people join fewer organizations. Even though a few people might have lost their money after they had joined, by and large we can assume that present economic status is acquired prior to present membership. The same would be true in many studies when we relate fairly permanent personality traits to achievements in school or on the job.

Some variables can be used in different ways, and therefore might change their place in a time sequence, according to the problem under investigation. The most typical example is age. People who are 60 years of age are characterized by certain physical handicaps, as compared to the 20 year olds. But, they are also characterized by the fact that they have been born and have grown up in the nineteenth century rather than after the first World War. Therefore, the timing of the variable depends upon the context. When we mentioned previously that older people are less educated, the thing that matters obviously was the period during which the people grew up. Therefore, age, as the indicator of time of birth, is prior to education. If, on the other hand we relate the age at which people die to the kind of climate they live in, age is subsequent to climate. A similar distinction can be made when we compare married people with single people. Being married can either mean the ability to have acquired a spouse, or it can mean living together under specific conditions as family members.

Finally, there are variables with undetermined time sequence. If we find, for instance, that the Democrats are more in favor of government interference in business than the Republicans, we cannot say offhand what the time sequence of party affiliation and opinion is. The same is true when we find that people use a certain product and listen to a certain radio program on which it was advertised. Very often, we have to use variables in our studies for which the time sequence is dubious. But this is due either to deficiencies in the manner in which we collect our information or to the fact that we use data that had been collected for other purposes. As a matter of principle, it is always possible to establish the time sequence of variables. Progress in research consists in getting this point straightened out. Although what one does with variables that are hazy regarding the time sequence would be an interesting topic of discussion it is not the topic of our present note. For the rest of the discussion, we shall assume that we deal with variables whose time sequence is established, and we shall choose our examples accordingly.

THE MAIN TYPES OF ELABORATION

We are now ready to present the decisive point. It is claimed that there are essentially four operations which can be performed with two original and one test variable. It makes no difference whether these operations are performed with actual data or whether they take the form of theoretical analyses. If a relation between two variables is analyzed in the light of a third, only these four operations or combinations thereof will occur irrespective of whether they are called interpretation, understanding, theory, or anything else.

The way the four cases originate will now be described. Let us assume that we start out with a relation between the two variables, x and y, with x being prior to y in the time sequence. Then test variable, t, is introduced. Two time relations are possible: either t lies in sequence between x and y, or it lies prior to x (including "simultaneity" of x and t here). Upon the introduction of t, two things can happen: either $[xt] = 0$, or it does not equal zero. If $[xt]$ is not zero, we shall assume for simplicity's sake that the partial relations between x and y are zero. This gives four main configurations

which are described in the following scheme by the symbols MA, PA, etc.
We shall turn to a description and exemplification of these four patterns.

	$[xt] = 0$ $[xy;t] \neq 0$	$[xt] \neq 0$ $[xy;t] = 0$
Position of "t"		
Antecedent	PA	MA
Intervening	PI	MI

In cases of the *type PA,* we usually call the test variable "t" a "condition".
General examples easily come to mind, although in practice they are fairly
rare and are a great joy to the research man when they are found. For
example, the propaganda effect of a film is greater among low than among
high educated people. The depression had worse effects on authoritarian
families than on other types.

Three general remarks can be made about this type of finding or reasoning: (a) It corresponds to the usual stimulus—disposition—response sequence, with "x" being the stimulus and the antecedent "t" being the disposition. (b) The whole type might best be called one of *specification.* One
of the two partials will, by necessity, be larger than the original relationship.
We, so to speak, specify the circumstances under which the original relationship holds true more strongly. (c) Usually we will go on from there and
ask why the relationship is stronger on one side of the test dichotomy. This
might then lead into one of the other types of analysis. Durkheim uses type
PA in discussing why married people commit suicide less than unmarried
people. He introduces as a test variable "a nervous tendency to suicide,
which the family, by its influence, neutralizes or keeps from developing."
This is type PA exactly. We do not experience it as much of an explanation
because the introduction of the hypothetical test variable, like the tendency
to suicide, sounds rather tautological. We want rather to know why the
family keeps this tendency from developing, which as we shall see later
leads to type MI.

The type PI is also easily exemplified. We study the relationship between
job success and whether children did or did not go to progressive schools.
We find that if the progressively educated children come into an authoritarian job situation, they do less well in their work than the others; on the
other hand, if they come into a democratic atmosphere, their job success
is greater.

The relation between type of education and job success is elaborated by
an intervening test factor, the work atmosphere. Following the example of
Paul Horst, we call such a test factor a "contingency". He points out that
in many prediction studies, the predicted value depends upon subsequent
circumstances which are not related to the predictor. Another example of
this kind is given by Merton who studied the relation between occupational
status and participation in the life of a housing community. White-collar
people participate more if they are dissatisfied whereas manual workers
participate more if they are satisfied with their jobs.

Just for the record, it might be mentioned that types PI and PA have a
simple relationship. If "t" is the condition (type PA) then "x" is a contingency. If "t" is a contingency (type PI) then "x" is a condition.

Actually, then, we have here only one major type of elaboration for which the word specification is probably quite appropriate. There are two sub-types of specification according to the time sequence of "x" and "t".

Type MA is used mainly when we talk of rectifying what is usually called a *spurious relationship*. It has been found that the more fire engines that come to a fire, the larger is the damage. Because fire engines are used to reduce damage, the relationship is startling and requires elaboration. As a test factor, the size of the fire is introduced. The partials then become zero and the original result appears as the product of two marginal relationships; the larger the fire, the more engines—and also the more damage.

When we start with a relationship which is psychologically puzzling, we usually stop at that point, but this same mode of elaboration is also used under different psychological circumstances. More people commit suicide during the summer than during the winter. (Incidentally, for a precise formulation, this relationship would have to be put somewhat differently: among the people sampled during the summer we find more suicides than among people sampled or counted during the winter.) Durkheim suggests, as a "t" factor for elaboration, increased social activities going on during the summer. (This is a nice example of how a concrete formulation clarifies the time sequence; the intensity of social life precedes the counting of people as well as the suicides.)

Our interest immediately shifts to the [ty] relationship, to wit: to the presumed fact that greater intensity of social life leads to more suicides. Actually, of course, whether this explanation which comes from Durkheim is correct would depend upon a disappearance of the partials. Durkheim would have to show that if intensity of social life is kept constant, the season does not make any difference in suicides.

Because he has no data on this point, he rather looks for other situations where he can presume that intensity of social life varies. He finds that there are more suicides during the day as compared with the number during the night, which he again explains with the help of the same test factor. This leads into the whole question of probability of inference which we do not follow up here.

At this point a terminological remark is in place. We use the term *"elaboration"* to describe the research operation expressed in our main formula. We also show that there are certain ways of reasoning that are identical with this formula; the only difference is that in reasoning we do not use precise figures—we make statements which essentially imply that certain partial or marginal relationships are larger or smaller than others, or they are approximately zero, or different from zero.

The term "elaboration" is useful because it is so colorless that it probably does not connote too many associations which would detract from the precise meaning it has in this paper. The terminology becomes more "touchy" when it comes to distinguishing the four types of elaborations. They too are precise as long as we realize that they represent certain research or reasoning operations. When we give them names, however, we are in danger of losing the focus of our discussion. It seems, for instance, reasonable to call Type MA an "explanation" because this word seems to be used often to describe the operation MA. But there is no doubt that many people have used the word "explanation" in different ways. It is, therefore, important to remember that "explanation" in this context is identical with the too-cumbersome term "elaboration of the Type MA." Whether the term should be used this way or not is a mere psychological question. Should future experience show that the term misdirects the reader, it could be dropped without any change in the argument.

This terminological difficulty becomes immediately apparent when we now turn to *Type MI,* for which many people will certainly have used the term "explanation". We, here, shall use the term *"interpretation"* for Type MI. The difference between "explanation" and "interpretation" in this context is related to the time sequence between "x" and "t". In an interpretation the "t" is an intervening variable situated between "x" and "y" in the time sequence.

Examples of Type MI have been given all through the paper. Living in a rural community is related to a lower suicide rate when compared with city dwelling. The greater intimacy of rural life is introduced as an intervening variable. If we had a good test of cohesion we would have to find that type of settlement is positively correlated to degree of cohesion, and degree of cohesion with suicide rate. But obviously some rural communities will have less cohesion than some urban communities. If cohesion is kept constant as a statistical device, then the partial relationship between the rural-urban variable and the suicide rate would have to disappear.

It might be useful to exemplify the difference between Type MA and Type MI by one more example. It was found during the war that married women working in factories had a higher rate of absence from work than single women. Here are a number of possible elaborations:

a. Test factor: more responsibilities at home. This is an intervening variable. If it is introduced and the two partial relationships—between marital status and absenteeism—disappear, we have an elaboration of Type MI.
b. Test factor: physical handicaps, as crudely measured by age; because it stands for amount of time, the physique of the respondents has already been exhausted. This is an antecedent variable. If it turns out when age is kept constant that the relation between marital status and absenteeism disappear, we would have it explained, probably call it spurious, and forget about it: Type MA.

The latter case suggests again an important point. After having explained the original relationship, our attention might shift to [ty]: the fact that older people show a higher absentee rate. This, in turn, might lead to new elaborations: is it really that older women have less physical resistance, be they married or single? Or, is it that older women have been born in a time where work is not as yet important for women and, therefore, they have a lower work morale. In other words, after one elaboration is completed, we will, as good scientists, immediately turn to a new one; but the basic analytical processes will always be the same.

An important statistical observation is in place here. In Types MA and MI, the two newly emerging relationships are always larger than the original one, as can easily be seen arithmetically. Therefore, we find that every elaboration has at least one correlation that is higher than the one with which we started. This has important psychological and logical implications but there will not be space to discuss them here.

One final point can be cleared up, at least to a certain degree, by this analysis. We can suggest a clearcut definition of the *causal relationship* between two attributes. If we have a relationship between "x" and "y"; and if for any *antecedent* test factor the partial relationships between x and y do not disappear, then the original relationship should be called a causal one. It makes no difference here whether the necessary operations are actually carried through or made plausible by general reasoning. This general reasoning, incidentally, will always consist of using one of the four basic operations discussed here, except in those cases where the reasoning is directed toward the disentangling of time sequences among badly chosen variables.

This definition has special bearing on the following kind of discussion. It is found that in densely populated areas the crime rate is higher than in sparsely populated areas. Some authors state that this could not be considered a true causal relationship but such a remark is often used in two very different ways. Some authors suggest an intervening variable: for instance, the increased irritation which is the result of crowded conditions. Even if their interpretation is correct, that does not detract from the causal character of the original relationship. On the other hand, the argument might go this way: crowded areas have cheaper rents and, therefore, attract less desirable elements. Here the character of the inhabitants is antecedent to the characteristics of the area. In this case the original relationship is indeed explained as a spurious one and should not be called causal.

2. OPINION FORMATION IN A CRISIS SITUATION

by S. M. Lipset

STUDYING THE OPINION making processes is the principal objective of public opinion research. In the main, however, such research has been forced to analyze the factors related to existing attitudes and sentiments rather than the formation of attitudes toward new problems or issues. The controversy at the University of California over the requirement that all faculty members sign an oath affirming that they were not members of the Communist Party created an opportunity to study the opinion forming process in a comparatively closed environment.[1] Both students and faculty were faced with the necessity of making up their minds about an issue that had not previously existed.

Between March 15 and April 21, 1950, a representative sample of the student body of the Berkeley campus of the University of California was interviewed concerning its opinion about the loyalty oath and the non-Communist hiring policy. Every fortieth student was selected systematically

Reprinted in part from the *Public Opinion Quarterly,* Vol. 17, 1953, pp. 20-46, by permission of the author and the publisher. (Copyright, 1953, by Princeton University.)

from the files of the Registrar. The study was planned after February 24, when the Regents issued their ultimatum to every non-signer of the oath to sign or get out. Interviewing began on March 15 and ended on April 21, the day that the Regents lifted the ultimatum and accepted the Alumni proposal of a contract form and committee hearing.[2]

The interview schedule was designed to obtain the students' opinions on the issue of the oath and the policy of exclusion of Communists from teaching. Information was also secured on various social background characteristics of the group, as well as on their attitudes on a variety of political subjects which were not specifically related to the issues of academic freedom and civil liberties. The attitudes of the students as a group paralleled the official position of the faculty and its supporters. That is, the students were opposed to faculty members being required to take an oath affirming that they were not members of the Communist party. They were, however, more divided on the issue of employing Communists in the university. Table 1 presents the results for the entire sample.

Table 1—Attitude of 480 Students to the Loyalty Oath and the Policy of Employing Communists*

Loyalty Oath		Communist Employment	
Approve oath requirement	26%	Oppose Communist employment	45%
Disapprove oath	64	Approve Communist employment	39
Don't know	10	Qualified approval	
No response	0	Approve if known as a Communist	4
		Approve if not a propagandist	4
		Approve if non-controversial subject	2
		Don't know	4
		No response	2

* For the purpose of analysis the students were divided into nine groups on the basis of their attitudes to both the oath and the policy. Only five of these groups contained enough cases to warrant inclusion. In succeeding tables these groups will be represented by letter abbreviations: PP-PO, pro-policy of barring Communists and pro-oath requirement; PP-AO, pro-policy and anti-oath requirement; AP-PO, anti-policy and pro-oath; AP-AO, anti-policy and anti-oath; and DK for the "don't knows" on either question.

Predispositions. Various studies have indicated that attitude formation is related to the basic predispositions of individuals. That is, attitudes on any given issue are rarely if ever independent of the general cluster of attitudes that people bring to any situation in which they participate. In the case of the loyalty oath controversy, one would expect that general political predisposition would have affected students' reactions to issues of academic freedom. In order to test this hypothesis, the respondents were asked about their past and present political preferences, and were presented with a six question attitude scale designed to rank them as conservatives or lib-

Table 2—Predisposition Groups

Attitude on Oath and Policy	Extreme Liberal (N:161)	Moderate Liberal (N:84)	Moderate Conservative (N:130)	Extreme Conservative (N:97)
PP-PO	5%	18%	25%	32%
PP-AO	25	23	18	26
AP-PO	2	6	10	8
AP-AO	58	34	29	24
Don't know	10	19	18	10
	100	100	100	100

erals.[3] The data shown in Table 2 appear to confirm the hypothesis that attitudes on the loyalty oath and non-Communist hiring policy were not independent of general political predispositions.

A similar pattern occurred when opinions on the two issues were compared with the respondents' party identifications. As compared with Republicans, Democrats were disproportionately against the loyalty oath and the policy of barring Communists. The supporters of minority political parties were, as one would expect, even more definitely in favor of the rights of Communists than were the Democrats. The differences between adherents of the two major parties were much less, however, when the question of liberalism or conservatism was held constant than when such partisans were compared independently. General liberalism or conservatism appears to have been more important than party affiliation as such. Nevertheless, Democrats as a group were more prone to oppose the loyalty oath than were Republicans.

Table 3 shows that seniors and graduate students, particularly the latter, were much more liberal on the academic freedom issues than the members of the three lower classes, but this difference also decreased when liberalism and conservatism were held constant. Most of the difference between the two groups of students was contributed by the variation in the proportion of liberals, the graduate students in particular being the most liberal group in their general attitudes. While there are few data which help to account for this fact, it is possible to suggest some hypotheses. During the course of the loyalty oath controversy, students were exposed to more propaganda from the liberal or faculty side than from the conservative or Regents' side. The data indicate that senior and graduate students had more information about the controversy than lower classmen. Upper classmen and graduate students, who had closer contact with their instructors than lower classmen, may have been exposed to more discussion about the issues. Public opinion research has suggested that propaganda is more effective with people whose basic predispositions are already in line with the propaganda themes, and, moreover, that its effectiveness is increased if it is conveyed at least in part through face to face contacts.[4] In this case, therefore, it may be suggested that seniors and graduate students received more of the preponderately "anti-oath, anti-policy" propaganda, received it most directly and effectively in the context of personal relations, and that this propaganda influenced most those individuals with liberal predispositions. The fact that the dis-

Table 3—College Class and Political Attitudes

Issue: Communists May Teach	FRESHMEN, SOPHOMORES AND JUNIORS			SENIORS AND GRADUATES		
	Conservative (N:65)	Moderate (N:111)	Liberal (N:49)	Conservative (N:49)	Moderate (N:103)	Liberal (N:95)
Yes	39%	44%	51%	33%	48%	73%
No	58	50	39	65	48	24
Don't know	3	6	10	2	4	3
	100	100	100	100	100	100
Loyalty Oath	(N:66)	(N:115)	(N:49)	(N:48)	(N:104)	(N:95)
Approve	39	33	16	36	31	2
Disapprove	54	53	76	56	54	93
Don't know	7	14	8	8	15	5
	100	100	100	100	100	100

tribution of attitudes among the moderates and conservatives differed only slightly from class to class becomes understandable in terms of this hypothesis, since one would expect that those with non-liberal predispositions would not be greatly affected by the liberal propaganda of the faculty.

The pervasive influence of basic predispositions can also be seen when

Table 4—Attitudes and Religion

Issue: Communists May Teach	CONSERVATIVES			LIBERALS			
	No Religion (N:8)	Catholic (N:17)	Protestant (N:83)	No Religion (N:55)	Catholic (N:11)	Jew (N:17)	Protestant (N:51)
Yes	37%	23%	36%	78%	27%	71%	54%
No	50	77	62	13	64	29	43
Don't know	13	0	2	9	9	0	4
Loyalty Oath							
Approve	25	53	36	5	18	6	8
Disapprove	63	41	57	89	64	94	88
Don't know	12	6	7	6	18	0	4
	100	100	100	100	100	100	100

the students are compared by religious background (Table 4). Considering religion alone, it would appear that, of the four religious preferences given, Jews were most liberal on the academic freedom issues, those with no religious preference next, followed by Protestants, with the Catholics most conservative. Breaking down religious preference by position on the political predisposition scale indicates, however, that, with the partial exception of the Catholics, the differences among the different religious denominations were in part contributed by the varying proportions of liberals or conservatives within them. The Catholics deviate with regard to permitting Communists to teach—even liberal Catholics were opposed to this; however, a majority of liberal Catholics are opposed to the loyalty oath.

One of the most interesting findings of this study concerns the 78 students who reported having no religious beliefs of their own, but gave their parents' religious affiliation. In each case, the students answering "none" were more liberal than those students who had a religious affiliation, but the direction of the differences among the three religious groups remained the same among those who reported no religion. That is, irreligious Catholics were more conservative than irreligious Protestants, who in turn were more conservative than irreligious Jews (Table 5). It is evident that the religious group into which one is born remains an effective determinant of attitudes even among those who have broken with the group.

In the *Authoritarian Personality*, R. Nevitt Sanford reports that subjects who were religious and reported the religion of their mothers were more prejudiced (ethnocentric) than those who reported a maternal religious affiliation but were irreligious themselves.[5] If the attitudes toward the academic freedom issues are correlated with ethnocentrism, then the findings of this study also indicate that breaking with a familial religious pattern is related to liberalism.

The Press. The newspapers of the San Francisco Bay area played an important role in the entire loyalty oath dispute. All of them agreed on the policy question—that is, that no Communists be employed by the University.

They divided sharply, however, on the question of the loyalty oath. The *San Francisco Chronicle* and the *San Francisco News* both vigorously supported the faculty's opposition to the non-Communist oath with many editorials and favorable news stories. The three Hearst papers in the area, the *San Francisco Examiner,* the *San Francisco Call-Bulletin,* and the *Oak-*

Table 5—Religious Affiliation and Attitudes Toward Academic Freedom Issues

Issue:	RESPONDENT'S RELIGIOUS AFFILIATION GIVEN			RESPONDENTS' RELIGIOUS AFFILIATION NONE—FATHERS' RELIGION		
Communists May Teach	Catholic (N:57)	Protestant (N:263)	Jew (N:24)	Catholic (N:10)	Protestant (N:58)	Jew (N:10)
Yes	33%	43%	75%	50%	64%	80%
No	63	53	25	50	29	10
Don't know	4	4	0	0	7	10
	100	100	100	100	100	100
Loyalty Oath						
Approve	37	31	4	20	19	0
Disapprove	53	60	92	60	71	90
Don't know	10	9	4	20	10	10
	100	100	100	100	100	100

land Post-Enquirer, supported the Regents in their efforts to impose a loyalty oath, and repeatedly denounced the faculty opposition as being Communist inspired. The *Oakland Tribune* took the same position as the Hearst press, but did not print as many editorials and was somewhat more objective in its news presentation. The *Berkeley Gazette* printed many objective news stories and avoided taking an editorial position. These were the papers which were being read by the student body while the controversy was on.

The students were asked which papers they had read in the last two days before being interviewed. The information obtained, shown in Table 6, gives some indication of the influence of the press on the attitudes of the student body.

There appears to have been a definite relation between the editorial opin-

Table 6—Newspaper Reading Habits*

Respondent's Attitude to Oath and Policy	Pro-Oath Hearst and Tribune (N:83)	Both Sides Chronicle, Hearst and Tribune (N:90)	Anti-Oath Chronicle and News (N:147)
PP-PO	34%	19%	12%
PP-AO	18	21	27
AP-PO	11	7	4
AP-AO	30	41	49
Don't know	7	12	8
	100	100	100

* The other combinations contain too few cases to be meaningful.

ions and news policy of the various newspapers, and the attitudes of their readers. One could not conclude from this fact alone, however, that the newspapers of the Bay area played an important factor in the development of opinion on the oath and hiring issues. It is possible that the readers of the different papers differentiated on other factors, such as class in school

or political sympathies. One would have expected that liberals would have
been more prone to read a liberal newspaper.

The study permits an approximation of a controlled experiment on the
influence of newspapers. The newspapers all agreed on the policy of barring Communists but differed on the oath issue. If the papers had any influence on students' attitudes, it should have been primarily on the issue of
the loyalty oath rather than the policy. The data indicate that readers of
the more conservative papers tended to be more conservative on the policy
issue of Communist employment than did the readers of the liberal papers.
This was at least in part a result of selective purchasing of newspapers, as
the readers of the *Chronicle* and the *News* were in general more liberal according to the attitude scale than the readers of the Hearst papers and the
Tribune. Holding respondents' positions on the non-Communist hiring policy
constant, readers of liberal papers were more opposed to the oath than were
readers of the conservative papers. The pro-policy people who read the
Chronicle and the *News* were almost two-to-one against the oath, while the
pro-policy students reading Hearst and the *Tribune* were almost two-to-one
for the oath. Over one-quarter of the students who were in favor of allow-
ing Communists to teach and who read the pro-oath papers were for the
oath, as compared to seven per cent of those who read the anti-oath papers
(Table 7). It is interesting that the majority of the students who answered
"no opinion" to the oath question also reported that they had not read any
newspapers during the two days before being interviewed.

Table 7—Newspaper Influence: Opinion on Hiring Policy Held Constant

	AGAINST COMMUNISTS TEACHING					FOR COMMUNISTS TEACHING				
Papers Read	N	Ap-prove Oath	Dis-approve Oath	Don't Know	Total	N	Ap-prove Oath	Dis-approve Oath	Don't Know	Total
Chronicle and News	(77)	34%	66%	0%	100%	(101)	7%	83%	10%	100%
Hearst and Tribune	(47)	64	36	0	100	(43)	26	70	4	100
Both sides	(48)	48	50	2	100	(57)	12	79	9	100
None	(36)	17	25	58	100	(25)	12	72	16	100

Readers of the anti-oath papers tended to be more liberal than readers
of the pro-oath papers. So far it is possible that the relationship indicated
in Table 6 is spurious—that, in other words, it is basic liberalism or
conservatism which is actually being compared, not the influence of the
papers. By holding political attitudes, as revealed by the predisposition scale,
constant, it should be possible to see whether the newspapers had an effect
over and above these other related attitudes; this is done in Table 8.

Though the number of cases is unfortunately small, the evidence shows
that, regardless of the newspaper they read, persons with similar basic
political attitudes did not differ greatly on the question of the right of Communists to teach. In other words, the newspaper read did not have an independent influence on this issue. This is not surprising, since the newspapers were all agreed on the question. On the oath question, however,
those reading the *Chronicle* or the *News* tended to be more pro-faculty than
those reading the Hearst press or the *Oakland Tribune,* even when basic
political attitudes were held constant. The newspapers which maintained a

Table 8—Newspapers Read and Attitudes on the Issues; Predisposition Constant

CONSERVATIVES

COMMUNISTS MAY TEACH

Papers Read	N	Yes	No	Don't Know	Total
Chronicle and News	(45)	33%	62%	5%	100%
Hearst and Tribune	(36)	28	69	3	100
Both sides	(23)	29	61	0	100

LOYALTY OATH

Papers Read	N	Ap-prove	Dis-approve	Don't Know	Total
Chronicle and News	(43)	28%	65%	7%	100%
Hearst and Tribune	(36)	47	47	6	100
Both sides	(25)	44	56	0	100

MODERATES

COMMUNISTS MAY TEACH

Papers Read	N	Yes	No	Don't Know	Total
Chronicle and News	(85)	51%	46%	3%	100%
Hearst and Tribune	(54)	42	41	7	100
Both sides	(53)	45	51	4	100

LOYALTY OATH

Papers Read	N	Ap-prove	Dis-approve	Don't Know	Total
Chronicle and News	(88)	21%	64%	15%	100%
Hearst and Tribune	(46)	52	44	4	100
Both sides	(53)	34	47	19	100

LIBERALS

COMMUNISTS MAY TEACH

Papers Read	N	Yes	No	Don't Know	Total
Chronicle and News	(63)	68%	27%	5%	100%
Hearst and Tribune	(22)	68	27	5	100
Both sides	(38)	66	29	5	100

LOYALTY OATH

Papers Read	N	Ap-prove	Dis-approve	Don't Know	Total
Chronicle and News	(63)	8%	87%	5%	100%
Hearst and Tribune	(20)	15	70	15	100
Both sides	(38)	3	92	5	100

barrage of slanted stories and editorials for the duration of the conflict appear to have had a real effect on student opinion. Liberals who read both sides were similar in their attitudes on the oath to the liberals who only read the anti-oath papers, while conservatives who read both sides were similar to conservatives who read the pro-oath papers. Apparently, when exposed to the cross-pressures of conflicting newspaper reporting and editorial policy, the students were more likely to accept the point of view which fitted in best with their basic political predispositions.

Since this relationship between newspaper policy and attitude appears to contradict the findings in some other public opinion studies, it should be worthwhile to see whether any other factors, other than general political attitude, may account for the differences in the attitudes towards the oath of the readers of the various papers.

The relationship between papers read and attitude toward hiring policy, holding class in college constant as in Table 9, is largely related to the fact that the more liberal students tended to read the *Chronicle,* while the more conservative ones tended to read the Hearst press or the *Oakland Tribune.* It is significant, however, that the relationship between newspaper read and attitude toward the oath was greater than the one between the paper and attitude toward the policy, suggesting again the influence of the newspapers on students' attitudes toward the oath. The same pattern holds true for political party as well. Democrats and Republicans reading the *Chronicle* or the *News* were far more likely to be opposed to the oath than were those who read the papers which supported the Regents.

The data of this study suggest that the newspapers had a great influence in this controversy. They do not prove this conclusively, however, as it is possible that a selective element other than the factors considered was pres-

Table 9—College Class and Newspapers Read

	FRESHMEN, SOPHOMORES AND JUNIORS					SENIORS AND GRADUATES				
			COMMUNISTS MAY TEACH							
	N	Yes	No	Don't Know	Total	N	Yes	No	Don't Know	Total
Chronicle and News	(64)	48%	47%	5%	100%	(113)	56%	42%	2%	100%
Hearst and Tribune	(61)	38	54	8	100	(40)	43	50	2	100
Both sides	(49)	43	49	8	100	(65)	54	43	3	100

			LOYALTY OATH							
	N	Ap-prove	Dis-approve	Don't Know	Total	N	Ap-prove	Dis-approve	Know Don't	Total
Chronicle and News	(81)	25%	63%	12%	100%	(113)	14%	78%	8%	100%
Hearst and Tribune	(62)	44	48	8	100	(40)	43	52	5	100
Both sides	(53)	38	58	4	100	(65)	19	66	15	100

ent and differentiated among the readers of the various papers. Liberal *Chronicle* readers, for example, may have been basically more "liberal" than liberal Hearst readers. A panel study in which the sample's members were interviewed as the controversy proceeded, would have been necessary to evaluate definitely the influence of the newspapers. It is also necessary to remember that all of the interviewees were college students and were exposed to repeated slanted news stories and editorials about a situation which was very close to them. One would expect that they read many of the detailed stories about the University controversy.

Socio-economic Status. Socio-economic status is one of the most important factors differentiating conservatives from liberals in the society as a whole. The means that a student uses to finance his way to school should be a clue to the socio-economic position of his family.[6] Presumably, the more well-to-do the family, the more likely that the student will be supported by his parents. If this assumption is true, then Table 10 confirms the relationship established between occupational position of parents and attitudes on academic freedom. Those students who relied completely on parental support were more conservative than those going through school by other means. Those working their way through school or completely dependent on the G.I. Bill contributed proportionately more to the anti-Regent group.

These data would seem to suggest that the higher the socio-economic position of the parents, the more likely the student was to be pro-Regent on the question of the oath or policy. This factor was also probably related to general conservatism-liberalism; that is, higher socio-economic status and general societal conservatism go together.

Table 10—How Financed Through School

Attitude on Issues	Work (N:64)	G. I. Bill (N:85)	G. I. Bill & Work (N:63)	Family & Work (N:97)	G. I. Bill & Family (N:48)	Family (N:93)
PP-PO	8%	18%	19%	18%	21%	26%
PP-AO	23	16	18	30	29	18
AP-PO	13	2	9	6	2	6
AP-AO	42	45	41	38	29	33
Don't know	14	19	13	8	19	17
	100	100	100	100	100	100

The status aspirations of the students may also have played a role in the development of their attitudes on the oath and other issues. Information was secured on the future job aspirations of the students and also on how much money they expected to earn ten years after leaving school. Table 11 appears to indicate that prospective teachers were more opposed to the Regents than students might have been expected to identify with members of their own future profession. Actually, however, this relationship appears to be spurious, at least in part. Almost all of the prospective teachers were majoring in the social sciences, the humanities, or the pure physical sciences. These three disciplines were the most liberal on the issues. If major subject is held constant, as in Table 12, there was little difference, especially on the oath issue, between the opinions of prospective teachers in these fields and those intending to go into other occupations.

Campus Activities. The students at the University of California are differentially involved in the campus life. Some of them simply attend classes and live with their parents or wives in various parts of the San Francisco Bay Area. Others spend their entire time at the University living in a fraternity house, a student cooperative, or a boarding house. These different out-of-class environments should affect student attitudes and interest in campus affairs. Students living at home should be affected more by general community opinion than those living on or near campus.

Table 11—Future Job Aspirations

Attitude to Oath and Policy	Teacher (N:124)	Engineer (N:41)	Independent Professional (N:78)	Salaried Professional (N:154)
PP-PO	14%	27%	18%	14%
PP-AO	22	17	21	26
AP-PO	4	5	9	7
AP-AO	47	24	40	39
Don't know	13	27	11	14
	100	100	100	100

Table 12—Occupations and Major Subject

Loyalty Oath	SOCIAL SCIENCES		HUMANITIES		PHYSICAL SCIENCES	
	Teachers (N:34)	Non-Teachers (N:79)	Teachers (N:37)	Non-Teachers (N:39)	Teachers (N:9)	Non-Teachers (N:27)
Approve	20%	20%	14%	13%	22%	26%
Disapprove	71	76	78	77	67	63
Don't know	9	4	8	10	11	11
	100	100	100	100	100	100

The data presented in Table 13 tend to confirm this hypothesis. The students who lived within the University community were more prone to support the faculty in the oath controversy than those living with their families at home. One might expect such a finding on the assumption that students living away from school would have been more likely to be exposed to pro-oath sentiments than those living on campus, while the students spending their entire school life within the school community would have been subject to influence by the faculty, and to the pro-faculty activities organized by various student groups.

Holding constant class in school, political attitudes, and political party affiliation did not invalidate the finding, as in each case students living within the University community were more likely to oppose the oath than either students in the same class or students who had the same political attitudes and party affiliations but lived away from the campus. Certain interesting differences appeared, however, when the two residence groups were compared holding parental socio-economic class constant. The children of "upper-class" fathers (professionals, proprietors, and business executives) who lived with their families were more prone to be against Communists teaching and in favor of the loyalty oath than persons from the same social class background who lived within the school community. There was, however, no difference between the children of wage workers living at home and those living around the school, as Table 14 shows. The original finding regarding

Table 13—Residence

Attitude to Oath and Policy	Lives with Family (N:195)	Lives with Schoolmates (N:275)
PP-PO	21%	16%
PP-AO	26	21
AP-PO	7	6
AP-AO	32	43
Don't know	14	14
	100	100

the residence groups, therefore, must be qualified in so far as it applies to the entire sample.

Looked at in another way, three of the groups in Table 14 had similar attitudes on both the oath issue and the non-Communist policy. Only one group, the children of persons with high socio-economic status who "live with family," was deviant. This finding may be related to a number of alternative hypotheses, none of which can be evaluated on the basis of the data. It may be possible that the community as a whole differed along socio-economic lines on the communist teacher or loyalty oath issues. The differences between the two groups of students living with their families may, therefore, have reflected exposure to different community reference groups. While there is no evidence concerning attitudes among the people of California, it is extremely dubious that a large proportion of persons on any socio-economic level was in favor of Communists being allowed to teach; the hypothesis that different social class attitudes as such were reflected in the student body does not satisfactorily explain the differences.

Table 14—Residence and Occupation of Parents

	UPPER CLASS		WAGE EARNERS	
Communists May Teach	Lives with Family (N:122)	Lives with Schoolmates (N:188)	Lives with Family (N:64)	Lives with Schoolmates (N:64)
Yes	37%	57%	55%	55%
No	59	41	36	40
Don't know	4	2	9	5
	100	100	100	100
Oath				
Approve	34%	22%	22%	23%
Disapprove	60	67	64	65
Don't know	6	11	14	12
	100	100	100	100

A second possible hypothesis is that the classification of "upper class" was too broad, and that the students living at home with their families actually belonged to a different layer of the "upper class" than those living on campus. This hypothesis, also, does not appear likely in terms of other related data. It is true, however, that those living at home differed from those in school according to home community. Those living at school came disproportionately from the smaller cities and towns of California, although many of them were from Los Angeles and from outside of the State. The variable of community of origin did not, however, differentiate students on the issue.

There is a third hypothesis, more plausible on the basis of impressionistic evidence, which assumes that an off-campus general community and a campus community constituted two alternative reference groups toward which students could orient themselves. There is evidence that off-campus community opinion was overwhelmingly against Communists teaching and generally unsympathetic to the faculty's position on the oath, while the campus opinion, shaped by the faculty's stand, was opposed to the loyalty oath. Moreover, a majority of students supported the right of Communists to teach.

Faced with this conflict between the two reference groups, "working-class" students, regardless of where they lived, and "upper-class" students living on the campus took the liberal position on both questions, thereby disproportionately orienting toward the campus community as the effective positive reference group on this question. The "upper-class" students living at home, however, disproportionately reacted toward off-campus opinion. This latter group was least exposed to the "climate of opinion" dominant on campus, and had least reason for taking their cues from the faculty, whose status in the non-academic community at large is not high compared with other more conservative authorities. For all of the workers' sons, including those who lived off campus, the university community was a locus and vehicle for their mobility aspirations and striving; as part of the total process of rising, they tended to assimilate the attitudes and orientations of the college community, and especially of its leaders.[7]

This hypothesis calls for direct evidence on the effective use of positive and negative reference groups by different groups of students, and especially points up the need for additional research on the comparative influence of multiple-reference groups operating at cross-purposes. The data here suggest that the social status of different reference groups, as compared with that of the subjects being analyzed, may be one of the principal variables determining which reference group will prevail in a cross-pressure situation.

Perception of the Situation. W. I. Thomas many years ago laid down the theorem: "If men define situations as real, they are real in their consequences." It has long been apparent that perception of an external phenomenon is largely determined by the frame of reference—the supplied context —within which it is perceived. Both perception and attitude formation are heavily affected by the nature of the meanings, the frame of reference, the predispositions that individuals bring to a situation. In the controversy over the loyalty oath and the issue of Communists teaching, one would expect that people not only differed in their opinions on the issues but also in their awareness of the presence of Communists. It is to be expected that persons who feared Communists most would "see" more Communists in their environment than would those who disparaged the Communist threat.

The data set forth in Table 15 tend to confirm this hypothesis. The students who supported the oath and the Regents' policy believed that there were many more Communists in the student body than did the students who were opposed to both. Over two-fifths of the pro-Regents students thought that there were over five hundred Communist students on the campus, as compared with less than a quarter of the anti-policy anti-oath group making a similar estimate. Here one can see the operation of a perceptual self-confirming hypothesis. Those fearful of Communism saw the justification for such fears in their social environment, while those who were not as fearful did not see the same picture of what should have been an objective fact—the number of Communists in the student body. The question, of course, was actually a projective question; no student, unless he were a member of the Communist Party, would have had accurate information on the number of Communists on the campus. The answers, therefore, give us some insights as to the sentiments and attitudes that different groups of students brought to the situation, including perhaps varying definitions of a "Communist." Those most fearful of the Communists may have operated under broader definitions.[8]

Table 15—How Many Students Do You Think Are Communists?

	Pro-Policy Pro-Oath (N:81)	Pro-Policy Anti-Oath (N:106)	Anti-Policy Anti-Oath (N:179)
Don't know	27%	18%	14%
Under 50	7	17	17
51-500	25	30	46
501 and over	41	26	23
	100	100	100

Perceptual framework can also be analyzed from the point of view of the controversy itself. One would expect that the opposing groups of students would differ in their conception of the faculty's and public's attitude on the oath as well as on their general information on the subject. The students were asked what per cent of the faculty they thought favored the oath. Almost all of the students recognized that the majority of the professors were opposed to the oath, but, as Table 16 shows, there were substantial differences in the proportions that different groups believed supported it.

Table 16—What Per Cent of the Faculty Favor the Oath?

	Pro-Policy Pro-Oath (N:86)	Pro-Policy Anti-Oath (N:108)	Anti-Policy Anti-Oath (N:183)
Don't know	17%	7%	9%
Under 1%	6	20	13
1-10%	18	30	36
10-25%	21	26	25
25-50%	23	14	10
Majority	18	3	7
	100	100	100

WHAT DO YOU THINK THE PUBLIC THINKS OF THE OATH?

	(N:85)	(N:108)	(N:183)
Don't know	7%	5%	11%
Support	51	30	44
Opposed	19	34	15
Not interested	16	23	27
Split	7	8	3
	100	100	100

The dominant view among the students was that the public supported the oath while the faculty opposed it. The pro-oath group, however, believed that a larger group of faculty members supported the oath than did the anti-oath students. The same pattern was true of estimates of the public's position; more pro-Regent than anti-Regent students believed that the public was in favor of the oath. The most interesting set of responses to these questions were the "don't knows" and those who said that the public was uninterested in the question. In this case, "don't know" and "no interest" were meaningful answers. Almost twice as many pro-oath students (17 per cent) as anti-oath students (9 per cent) said that they did not know what proportion of the faculty favored the oath. On the other hand, there were more "don't knows" among the anti-oath students (11 per cent) than among the pro-oath students (7 per cent) when it came to the question of the public's opinion about the oath. Over one-quarter of the anti-oath, anti-policy students also said that they thought the public was uninterested in the oath question.

With regard to the attitudes dominant in the two major communities of reference, disproportionate numbers in both the pro- and anti-oath groups apparently held a point of view which supported or at least did not conflict with their own position. This disproportionate ignorance and distortion of the facts is understandable in the light of the known connections between attitudes and perception. "Because perception is functionally selective, and because beliefs and attitudes play a role in determining the nature of this selectivity, new data physically available to an individual but contradictory to his beliefs and attitudes *may not even be perceived.*"[9] Moreover, "The lack of relevant facts and the frequent conflicting facts provided for us by different authorities frequently operate so as to force the creation or invention of facts that may bear no real relation to the external situation. Those pressures which work toward the formation of beliefs work in the absence of adequate data and may force the emergence of facts that support and are congruent with the beliefs."[10]

The majority of anti-oath students refused to recognize that the public was actually against them, while over one-third of the pro-oath students either regarded the faculty as on their side or said that they did not know the faculty thought. Given the fact that the faculty repeatedly, by almost unanimous votes, voiced its opposition to the oath, it is significant that fifty-six per cent of the pro-oath students either believed that over a quarter of the faculty supported the oath, or did not know the faculty's point of view. It seems clear that attitudes entered into and distorted the perception of some proportion of each of the major groups of students in directions that would tend to support attitudes already held.

Conclusions. This study indicates anew that opinion formation tends in large part to be a product of the activation of previous experiences and attitudes. Students at the University of California reacted to a crisis situation largely according to their group affiliations and other background characteristics. It would have been worth while to have had a panel study of opinion formation on the loyalty oath to see how this activation took place. The role of the University community, specific meaningful group affiliations, and the press, could have best been analyzed by repeated interviews with a panel as different events occurred.

The "deviant cases," those students who behave different from the majority of those with the same characteristic as themselves, suggest that deviation in behavior is a result of being exposed to cross-pressures. Liberal students who read pro-oath newspapers were more likely to support the oath requirement than those reading a paper consistent with their basic political attitudes. Students who were in favor of barring Communists from University employment but who read anti-oath papers were more prone to oppose the oath. Conservative students who resided within the University community were exposed to the majority opinion of the student body against the oath and were, therefore, more likely to be liberal on the academic freedom issues than their co-thinkers politically who were not as exposed to campus opinion. Catholic graduate students were probably exposed to pressure from the liberal graduate student body and were less favorable to restrictions on Communists than their undergraduate co-religionists.

Another effect of cross-pressures on students exposed to conflicting norms or expectations appears to have been a relatively high level of ignorance regarding the issues and their background. Ignorance here may have been serving the function of reducing the clarity, and thus the intensity, of the conflict; for example, this may have accounted for the greater lack of knowledge among the pro- than among the anti-Regents students. Cross-pressures not only directly affected the distribution of attitudes and the quantity and accuracy of information among different groups and categories of students, but also apparently influenced their active behavior in the controversy. In every category, those students who were against the Regents, but who had characteristics or were exposed to pressures which made for pro-Regents attitudes, were less likely to sign an anti-oath petition than those with homogeneous anti-Regents characteristics.

It is probably impossible to generalize from an analysis of the internal evidence available within one context the weight that any given item will have in a different cross-pressure situation. The two studies of student opinion on the Berkeley and Los Angeles campuses of the University of California suggest that a much larger proportion of the students at U.C.L.A. supported the position of the Regents in requiring a non-Communist loyalty oath.[11] It is extremely doubtful that the differences between the two campuses were a result of differing proportions of students in the categories that affected opinion on this issue. For example, there is no reason to believe that there were more conservatives or Catholics at Los Angeles. In fact, the past history of student political organization would suggest that, if anything, the U.C.L.A. campus is on the whole more liberal than Berkeley. The fact that the Berkeley faculty was more active than the Los Angeles one in opposing the oath, and the unanimous pro-Regents stand of the Los Angeles newspapers, as compared to division in the Bay Area, may have meant that the variables of University community influence and press influence had different weights in the two situations.

These differences point up a problem that arises in many opinion studies. We know, for example, that the proportion of workers or Catholics who are Democrats varies considerably from community to community, though in most cases these variables contribute to some degree to a Democratic predisposition. The analysis of why these same factors have different weights in different contexts must involve a study of the functional interrelationships among the variables which are handled in opinion research. Most such researches, including this one, necessarily handle these various factors atomistically. One cannot determine from survey data alone the ramifications for the rest of the system of changes in any one or several factors. This suggests the necessity for comparative institutional research which would attempt to locate those aspects of the social structure that result in the same nominal variable having quite different subjective meanings and objective weights in different contexts.

The evidence presented in this paper suggests that attitudes toward academic freedom are related to the same variables which influence attitude formation in other areas of life. Though supporters of civil liberties may hope that the belief in the rights of unpopular and even dangerous minorities is shared by persons regardless of personal political belief, the evidence does not warrant maintaining that hope. In general, those individuals who are characterized by the factors which make for conservatism, or who have conservative beliefs are opposed to the civil and academic rights of Communists. Those students who stand lower in socio-economic or ethnic group status, or who are liberals politically, tend to defend the rights of Communists.

It is possible, of course, to regard these patterns from another perspective. Historically, most violations of civil and academic rights in American society have been directed against liberals, leftists, trade unions, and members of minority groups. With the exception of the restrictions on Fascists during the last war, persons who are characterized by being well-to-do, having no interest in the labor movement, conservatives, white Protestants, Republicans, have not had to fear the possibility of social discrimination, loss of economic opportunities, or imprisonment as a result of their political opinions or group characteristics. American liberals, Jews, Negroes, Orientals, trade-union supporters, even though opposed to the Communist Party and the Soviet Union, may be more prone to consider the implications of any restrictions, even those directed against a totalitarian political party, as setting dangerous precedents which may afterward react against themselves. The individual members of these groups may not consciously analyze these long-term implications, but the historic experiences of their groups may have conditioned them to react in this way.

In addition to these general factors, the legal position of the Communist Party has become a political football in American politics. Conservatives and Republicans are attempting to use the widespread American antagonism towards the Communist Party against the politics of the Democrats, liberals, and Socialists. The non-Communist left-of-center groups, therefore, have painful and recent evidence for fearing that attacks on the Communist Party may be followed by attacks on themselves.

Catholics, though members of a minority group which has frequently been persecuted in this country, belong to a church which has made anti-Communism one of its principal activities. Discrimination and persecution of Roman Catholics in Communist-controlled countries has been severe, and Catholics, therefore, may be expected to react more strongly against Communists.

In interpreting the data of this study, it is necessary to recognize the danger of generalizing these findings beyond a student population. Students operating within the intellectual atmosphere of the university may react in more rational ways than the general population. Student members of underprivileged groups may, for example, be more inclined to make rational identifications between their own group and other groups under attack, an identification which underprivileged groups outside the campus may not make.

3. WHO WERE THE MOST CRITICAL OF THE ARMY'S PROMOTION OPPORTUNITIES?

by Samuel A. Stouffer and Leland C. DeVinney

[The first volume of *The American Soldier*, entitled *Adjustment During Army Life*, discussed, among many other topics, the degree of social mobility in the Army and the attitudes toward promotion policies and opportunities. Chances for promotion, for example, varied with education, longevity, age, and branch of service. The more highly educated men, those who had been in service longer, older men, and men in certain branches of service, such as the Air Force, had higher rates of promotion than others. In the selection which follows, the authors demonstrate that criticism of the chances for promotion in the Army was more a function of expectations than of objective opportunities.—ED. NOTE.]

DATA FROM RESEARCH SURVEYS to be presented will show, as would be expected, that those soldiers who had advanced slowly relative to other soldiers of equal longevity in the Army were the most critical of the Army's promotion opportunities. *But relative rate of advancement can be based on different standards by different classes of the Army population.* For example, a grade school man who became a corporal after a year of service would have had a more rapid rate of promotion compared with most of his friends at the same educational level than would a college man who rose to the same grade in a year. Hence we would expect, at a given rank and a given longevity, that the better educated would be more likely than others to complain of the slowness of promotion. The facts, as we shall see, tend to bear this out. The better educated, in spite of their superior chances of promotion, were the most critical.

A similar phenomenon appeared to operate between different branches of the service. This, along with the differentials by rank and education, is illustrated in Chart I. Here the responses of Military Police to the question, "Do you think a soldier with ability has a good chance for promotion in the Army?" are compared with responses of Air Corps men, in early 1944. Longevity is held roughly constant by taking only men who had been in the Army 1 to 2 years. It will be noted that more of the less educated, among both privates and noncoms in both branches, had favorable opinions than did the better educated. For example, among privates and Pfc's in the Military Police, 33 per cent of the less educated said that a soldier with ability had a very good chance for promotion, as compared with 21 per cent of the better educated privates and Pfc's. Finally, it will be seen, among both privates and noncoms in each educational group, that the Air Corps men tended to take a dimmer view of promotion opportunities for men of ability in the Army than did the Military Police.

Reprinted from *The American Soldier: Adjustment During Army Life*, Vol. I, pp. 250-258, by permission of the authors and the publisher. (Copyright, 1949, by the Princeton University Press.)

Without reference to the theory that such opinions by soldiers represent a relationship between their expectations and their achievements relative to others *in the same boat with them,* such a finding would be paradoxical, indeed. For chances of promotion in the Military Police were about the worst in any branch of the Army—among this sample of men in the Army 1 to 2 years, only 24 per cent of MP's were noncoms as compared with 47 per cent of the Air Corps men. The MP's felt, too, that as a *branch* the Military Police had been discriminated against in getting ratings, two thirds of them saying in answer to another question that MP's do not have as good a chance for promotion as men in other branches.

But consider a high school graduate or college man in the Military Police with Army longevity of 1 to 2 years. The chances of his being a noncom were 34 out of 100, based on the proportions of noncoms in this sample at this time. If he earned the rating, he was one of the top third among his fellows of equal educational status. If he failed to earn the rating, he was in the same boat with two thirds of his fellows with equal schooling. Contrast him with the Air Corps man of the same education and longevity. The chances of the latter's being a noncom were 56 in 100, based on the proportions in this sample at this time. If he had earned a rating, so had the majority of his fellows in the branch, and his achievement was relatively less conspicuous than in the MP's. If he had failed to earn a rating, while the majority had succeeded, he had more reason to feel a sense of personal frustration, which could be expressed as criticism of the promotion system, than if he were one of two thirds in the same boat, as among the MP's.

The process would work in the same way among the less educated. In both the Military Police Branch and the Air Corps, the promotion chances of the less educated were inferior to the chances of others. In the MP sample, only 17 per cent of the less educated were noncoms; in the Air Corps sample, the corresponding figure was 47 per cent. An MP who did not complete high school would feel unusually rewarded compared with others in his outfit in becoming a noncom; one who remained a private had so much company that he hardly could view discrimination against him as a reflection on his personal competence. In the Air Corps, those with ratings had almost as much company as those who remained privates—with less room for personal satisfaction over comparative achievement and more room for dissatisfaction over comparative failure to climb the status ladder.

While the psychological mechanisms seem to operate as described above in producing the pattern of opinions about promotion possibilities, we must not lose sight of the fact that on the average those with ratings had more favorable opinions about promotion than those without. Nor must we jump to the conclusion that men who were critical of promotion policy were necessarily dissatisfied with their Army jobs. True, cross tabulation, within a particular subgroup, of opinions about promotion and expressions of job satisfaction will almost invariably show that men who were most critical about promotions were also least satisfied with their jobs. But that is *within* a given subgroup. As between subgroups, the relationship may vanish or reverse itself. In the case of the comparison of the Military Police and the Air Corps it reverses itself. Although the Air Corps men were more critical of promotion, they also were more likely than the MP's to be satisfied with their Army job. For example, 36 per cent of the Air Corps men in this sample said they would *not* change to some other Army job if given a chance, whereas only 21 per cent of the MP's gave this response. Promotion opportunity was only one of many factors in job satisfaction. Other elements, such as the chance to learn something useful in civilian life, entered in, as did informal status factors such as the general prestige of the branch to which

Chart I—Opinions About Promotion Opportunity—Comparisons by Education and Rank Between Military Police and Air Corps (White Enlisted Men in the Army 1 to 2 Years, Continental United States)

QUESTION "Do you think a soldier with ability has a good chance for promotion in the Army?"

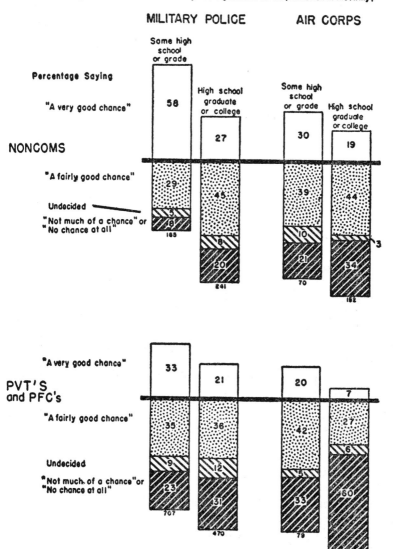

Military Police data from special survey of a representative cross section of MP's, S-107, March 1944. Air Corps data are a segment from a representative cross section of all white EM in United States, S-95, January 1944.

Chart II—Opinions About Promotion Opportunities by Force, According to Rank, Longevity, and Education (United States White Cross Section, July 1943, S-63 and S-64)

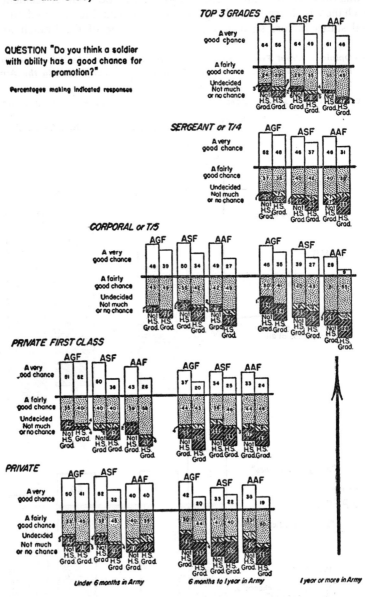

QUESTION "Do you think a soldier with ability has a good chance for promotion?"

Percentages making indicated responses

assigned. In general, Air Corps was a high prestige branch, Military Police a low prestige branch. One of the elements which contributed to making the difference in prestige was, no doubt, the difference in T/O[1] opportunities for social mobility.

The illustration presented in Chart I was based on a special cross-section survey of Military Police in March 1944 and the Air Corps segment of a cross-section survey of the Army at the nearest available date—namely,

January 1944. These data were especially selected to exhibit the structure of opinion on two sharply contrasting groups with respect to promotion opportunities in the Army. It is desirable to see whether the same general pattern holds up on a broader basis, where there is less contrast between groups.

The findings of a study based on a representative cross section of white enlisted men in continental United States in June 1943 are shown in Chart II. Here is charted, in a given vertical bar, the percentage distribution of response to the same question about promotion opportunity as was portrayed in the previous chart. Instead of MP's and Air Corps, we now compare Ground Force branches, Service Force branches, and Air Corps. The same educational groups are shown as in Chart I. Five ranks are shown, from private to top three grades, and three longevity periods—under 6 months, 6 months to 1 year, and 1 year or over.

The number of cases on which an individual bar is based is in many instances very small. No comparison is shown if the numbers in the sample for a particular rank, longevity, and education group fell below 30 for any one of the three Army Forces. Nevertheless, no particular inference should be drawn from a single pair of comparisons. It is rather on the *pattern as a whole*—on its regularities and irregularities—that we must focus attention.

In general, differences in opinion about promotion opportunities are rather small, tending in any individual case to be somewhat less striking than in the extreme illustration presented earlier, but a definite pattern is present, as can be seen by a general inspection of Chart II and confirmed by more detailed examination. Four findings emerge:

1. *For a given rank, the shorter the longevity the more favorable tends to be the opinion about promotion.* Compare, for example, less educated AGF privates in the Army less than 6 months with those in the Army 6 months to 1 year. The proportion of men who say that promotional opportunities are very good drops from 50 per cent to 42 per cent respectively. A total of 18 such comparisons can be made in Chart II and all 18 are in the same direction.

2. *For a given longevity, the higher the rank the more favorable tends to be the opinion about promotion.* For example, consider less educated AGF men in the Army a year or more. The number who say that opportunities are "very good" is 64 per cent among the top three grades, and it drops to 52 per cent among buck sergeants, and to 45 per cent among corporals. Thirty comparisons are possible between any two grades, in Chart II. Of these, 25 show the tendency indicated, 1 shows no difference, and 4 show the reverse tendency. (It must be remembered that many of the percentages are based on a small number of cases and are thus subject to a large sampling error. Moreover, the tie and reversals are all found in the Pfc-private comparisons.)

3. *For a given rank and longevity, the less the education the more favorable tends to be the opinion about promotion.* This, as are the two conclusions above reported, is in accordance with the expectation based on the analysis previously presented. Take AGF top three grades with over a year in the Army. Among the less educated, 64 per cent rated promotion opportunity "very good"; among the better educated, 56 per cent. There are 24

such comparisons possible in Chart II. Of these, 22 are in the direction indicated, 1 shows no difference, and 1 is a tie.[2]

4. *For a given rank, longevity, and educational level, the less the promotion opportunity afforded by a branch or combination of branches, the more favorable the opinion tends to be toward promotion opportunity.* This, again, is in accord with our previous discussion. On the average, promotion opportunity was very much better in the Air Corps than in either Service Force or Ground Force branches. It was somewhat better in Service Forces than in Ground Forces. Consider privates first class with less than high school education and less than 6 months in the Army. In Ground Forces, 51 per cent rated promotion opportunities "very good," in Service Forces 50 per cent, in Air Forces 43 per cent. Between Ground Forces and Air Forces, 16 such comparisons can be made in Chart II, and of these 14 are in the direction indicated and 2 are reversals. Of the 16 comparisons between Air Forces and Service Forces, 13 are in the direction indicated with 1 tie and 2 reversals. Of the 16 comparisons between Ground Forces and Service Forces, the Ground Force men are more favorable in 11, the Service Force men more favorable in 4, and in 1 comparison both are the same. These patterns of difference are statistically significant,[3] but the picture tends to become less decisive if looked at from some other viewpoints. For example, we know that promotion opportunities were best in Air Forces, intermediate in Service Forces, and least in Ground Forces. But in only 10 of the 16 comparisons do the proportions "very favorable" come out in exactly the reverse order. And the results, though still in the same direction, tend also to be statistically indecisive if comparisons between any two forces are made by combining the "very favorable" and "fairly favorable" categories. To be conservative, we should limit our conclusion by saying that a force with relatively less promotion chances tended to have a larger proportion of men speaking very favorably of promotion opportunities than another force with greater promotion chances.

As in our earlier discussion of the Military Police and the Air Corps, a caution must be sounded against assuming from these findings that a liberalization of promotion policy—which might reduce rather than raise the relative self-gratification of the successful men and increase rather than reduce the sense of defeat of the unsuccessful—would increase job satisfaction. What actually would happen we do not know, because this could be determined only from controlled experiments, which were never made. But it is relevant to point out that job satisfaction was highest in the Air Forces, intermediate in Service Forces, and lowest in Ground Forces—reversing exactly the direction seen in attitudes toward promotion. For example, using the question, "How satisfied are you with your Army job instead of some other Army job?" for the same men as shown in Chart II, AAF tends to have, in almost all subgroups, a larger proportion of men who say they are very satisfied with their job. Air Forces exceed Ground Forces in all 16 comparisons and exceed Service Forces in 14 out of 16 comparisons, with 1 tie and 1 reversal. Service Forces exceed Ground Forces in 13 out of 16 with 1 tie and 2 reversals.[4]

The strong role of status in job satisfaction is reflected in the fact that in 30 comparisons which may be made between job satisfaction of men at a given rank level with men at the next higher rank level (holding education, force, and longevity constant) 27 show the greater proportion of satisfied men among men with the higher rank.[5]

It has been possible to repeat the analysis shown in Chart II in other samples and at other periods in the war. No unusual or significant divergencies from the pattern there revealed of attitudes toward promotion have been observed. From one survey made in the Pacific, it was possible to compare the results from two questions, somewhat different in manifest content, which were asked on the same questionnaire. One was, "Do you think a soldier with ability has a good chance for promotion in the Army?"—the same question with the same check list of responses as was used in Chart II. The other was, "Do you think a soldier with ability has a good chance for promotion in your outfit?" As might perhaps be anticipated, for a given longevity differences by rank were sharper with the latter question than the former, as were differences by longevity for a given rank. But with respect to education and branch, the pattern of differences was the same with either question. Consistently, using either question and holding rank and longevity constant, the less educated tended to look more favorably on promotion opportunities than the better educated. Likewise, the men in Air Forces tended to look less favorably on promotion opportunities than men in Service Forces and, in turn, the latter tended to be less favorable than men in Ground Forces.

4. THE INTERPLAY OF DEMOGRAPHIC AND PSYCHOLOGICAL VARIABLES IN THE ANALYSIS OF VOTING SURVEYS

by Edward A. Suchman and Herbert Menzel

THE FIRST FINDINGS of a survey analysis are usually the discoveries of statistical associations between some easily identifiable demographic variable —like sex, age, occupation, place of residence, nativity, etc.—and some behavior, attitude, or experience which one would like to predict—in the instance to be reported, voting behavior in a presidential election. Such findings, while interesting descriptively, are only the bare beginnings of a quest for causal relationships. The following report from a study of the 1948 presidential election in Elmira, New York, illustrates that survey analysis can carry us a considerable distance toward the singling out of the social and psychological processes at work.[1]

It was found that members of ethnic and religious minority groups disproportionately favored one of the major political parties:

Table 1—Percentage Democratic of Two-Party Vote*

Italian-American	82	(94)
Negro	81	(84)
Jewish	67	(108)
Catholic†	65	(186)
but:		
White, native-born Protestant	19	(369)

* Percentages are computed on the basis of those who are recorded as Republican or Democratic only. Those who did not vote, did not answer the question, did not remember, or voted for minor parties are disregarded. The figures in parenthesis are the total frequencies corresponding to 100% in each case. E.g., 65% of the 186 Catholics in the sample voted Democratic.

† While the Italian-Americans are also Catholic, the Catholic group includes only a minority who are of Italian descent. The results presented are based upon two independent samples of Italian-Americans and Catholics.

The association between minority group membership and Democratic vote is unmistakable. When additional variables of a psychological nature are introduced into this correlation of a demographic background char-

This is a previously unpublished paper. The data on which this paper is based were collected and analyzed by the senior author. The interpretation which follows, prepared by the junior author, is largely the collective product of a seminar held at Columbia University under the joint sponsorship of the Planning Project for Advanced Training in Social Research and the Bureau of Applied Social Research. The seminar reviewed certain existing studies and tried to integrate some of their interpretations. James S. Coleman and William N. McPhee were especially active in the development of the ideas discussed here.

acteristic with political behavior, a striking fact appears. Not only did each minority group vote Democratic to a far greater extent than did the native-born White Protestants of Elmira; the Democratic vote was even stronger among those members of each of these minority groups who were most deeply involved in the group. In this respect, all of the minority groups showed surprising consistency with one another. For instance:

Table 2—Percentage Democratic of Two-Party Vote

Catholics who:

Chose religious group as among "most important"	66	(129)
Did not choose it*	58	(31)

* Psychological identification was here measured by whether or not the respondent included "religious group" in his answer to the question, "Which of these are the most important to you? Choose as many as you feel are very important to you: Your union, religious group, political party, social group, lodge, work group, race, nationality."

Thus Catholics voted Democratic more often than Protestants did, and the Democratic vote was especially high among those Catholics who regarded their religious group as among the most important to them.

The statistics on Jews are strikingly similar. Thirty-three per cent of the Jews in the sample voted Republican. What would happen when "importance of the religious group to the respondent" is introduced as a third variable?

Table 3—Percentage Democratic of Two-Party Vote

Jews who:

Chose the religious group as particularly important	72	(69)
Did not choose it	56	(39)

Just as was found to be the case among Catholics, the disposition to vote Democratic proved stronger among those members of this minority who regarded their religious group as important to them. If we now divide the Jewish sample according to their stand on religious customs, we obtain a very similar result:

Table 4—Percentage Democratic of Two-Party Vote

Jews who:

Attend religious services and favor Orthodox customs	76	(46)
Either attend religious services or favor Orthodox customs	61	(46)
Neither attend religious services nor favor Orthodox customs	42	(12)

Still a third measure of the in-group feeling of these voters is their response to the question, "In general, how friendly or unfriendly do you think Gentiles are toward the Jews?" When their reply is used to yield a breakdown of the religion-vote relationship, the outcome is consistent with the above findings:

Table 5—Percentage Democratic of Two-Party Vote

Jews who:

Think Gentiles are 'not friendly' or 'fairly friendly' to Jews	69	(86)
Think Gentiles are 'very friendly' to Jews	46	(13)

Again, those who are high on the measure of in-group feeling vote Democratic more often than the other members of the given minority group. And this phenomenon can not only be observed among Catholics and Jews, but among other minority groups as well. Nineteen per cent of the Negroes sampled, it will be recalled, voted for the Republican party. All the Negroes in the sample were asked a question parallel to the one just mentioned for Jews: "In general, how friendly or unfriendly do you think Whites are toward the Negroes?" Their party votes were distributed as follows:

Table 6—Percentage Democratic of Two-Party Vote

Negroes who:

Think Whites are 'not friendly' or 'fairly friendly' to Negroes	84	(71)
Think Whites are 'very friendly' to Negroes	61	(13)

Now to turn to still another minority group—the Italian-Americans. Only 18% of the sample of Italian-Americans voted Republican. The Democratic bent is especially visible among those who have an ongoing interest in affairs in Italy:

Table 7—Percentage Democratic of Two-Party Vote

Italian-Americans who:

Have 'quite a lot' of interest in what is going on in Italy today	90	(18)
Have 'not very much' or 'no' interest	79	(75)

Thus we see that the minority group trend toward the Democratic party is always strongest among those members who identify most strongly with the group. No matter which of the minority groups we study, and no matter which of the available measures of identification with the group we use, identification "intensifies" the group tendency.

Now what does this information add up to? Does it merely demonstrate the obvious—that whatever tendency is associated with a social category, will be stronger among those who belong to the category more? No—it seems rather to present a real finding, which poses an explanatory problem. For it is not at all clear what "belonging to a category more" means, nor whether it is adequately measured by the single dimension of psychological identification, as indicated by our questionnaire responses. Furthermore, the intensification of a group tendency by psychological identification with a group, far from being obvious, does not always occur. It did not occur, for instance, among the White Protestant "majority" of Elmira:

Table 8—Percentage Republican of Two-Party Vote

Protestants who:

Chose religious group as among the most important	80	(264)
Did not choose it	81	(140)

There is no significant difference between the two subgroups of Protestants in the way they voted. We do not know the reason. Perhaps the "intensification" observed among the minority groups is peculiar to group-conscious groups, or to groups among whom politics is regarded as a legitimate group affair, rather than as strictly a matter of everyone's private conscience; but these are only speculations.

Another line of speculation pursues the question, "what makes the intensification occur where it does occur?" What is it that makes those who show greater identification with the group fall in line with the group tendency more regularly? A number of hypothetical answers are possible.

1. One group of these answers says that the respondents who report strong identification with their group are affected by exactly the same factors that bring out the tendency among the rest, only more so. If, e.g., Negroes favor the Democratic party because they regard it as the champion of civil rights legislation, then those who identify more strongly with the Negro race will be more concerned with civil rights legislation and hence favor the Democratic party more strongly. If an explanation of the high Democratic vote among Catholics is to be found in the large proportion of Catholics among lower-than-average income groups, who tend to vote for the party of the New Deal, then perhaps a stauncher Catholicism is to be found among the very low income groups, who would have even more reason to vote Democratic. If Italian-Americans should turn out to favor the Democratic party frequently because of gratitude to a political machine that has favored them, then the more in-group-conscious Italian-Americans may show even more gratitude to the machine. In actuality, we do not know what factors are at work producing the high incidence of Democratic vote in each of the minority groups, nor is this the place to inquire what caused the gross correlation of minority group membership and Democratic vote. But as far as the intensification of this correlation by psychological identification with the group is concerned, one explanatory hypothesis that is suggested reads: identification is an indicator of greater exposure to whatever factors produce the original correlation.

2. Quite different are explanations which stipulate special processes peculiarly at work among those who identify strongly with their groups. Such explanations are quite diverse, but most of them fall into one or another of two classes:

One class of explanation says, essentially, that these people vote Democratic because they want to be like their fellows in their respective minority groups. Those who identify with the group most strongly have the greatest desire to be like their fellows in the largest number of ways. We may call this "the explanation by motivated conformity." We need not here go into the psychological details of what makes a person want to be like his fellow-members in a group to which he belongs; it is a very commonly observed phenomenon.

Another class of explanation says, in essence, that because so many of his fellow-Catholics are Democrats, each particular Catholic person is proportionately exposed to more pro-Democrat opinions, information, and informal social pressure than the individual Protestant is; similarly for Negroes, Jews, and Italian-Americans. And this is especially true for those who participate most in interaction within the group, and least in interaction with out-group members. We may call this "the explanation by differential exposure to communications."

3. Both of these explanations make the following two assumptions:

a. They assume that some other processes than those hypothesized have produced an initial attitude favoring the Democratic party among a significantly larger portion of Catholics than of Protestants, of Jews than of Christians, of Negroes than of Whites, etc. Motivated conformity and differential exposure explain only that *some* Catholics, Jews, and Negroes are pro-Democratic simply because so many other Catholics, Jews, and Negroes are. Why these others are Democratic must be explained by other factors—

ultimately by politically relevant factors associated with being a Catholic, Jew, or Negro.

b. Both hypotheses also assume that each of the minority groups examined constitutes a true group in a meaningful sense, either sociological or psychological. If a set of people is to affect the communications which reach its members, the members must interact socially more with the set than across its boundaries; in other words, the set must constitute a real social group. If, on the other hand, the members are to be motivated to act "like the group," then they must think of it as a group—i.e., it must have the psychological reality of a reference group.

It is possible to define categories of individuals which correlate with vote, but have social or psychological reality as groups only to a very limited degree. (Age categories may be of this nature.) There is then no reason to expect that our social or psychological processes should operate within such categories.

4. How can empirical evidence be brought to bear on the choice between these alternate explanations of "intensification"? Can survey analysis go further than establishing the fact of intensification—can it contribute something to the choice between its suggested explanations?

First, we want to decide whether the strongly identifying group members are affected merely by especially strong doses of the same factors that produce the overall group tendency; or whether they are subject to special processes. What sort of evidence could help us choose between these two conflicting hypotheses?

a. The second hypothesis—special processes—is favored if it can be shown that no matter what determinants of the overall tendency we stipulate, when measured directly they are far from adequate for accounting for the percentage of Democrats among the minority group members. There is ample evidence of this sort in the Elmira data. Whether we partial out occupation, income level, education, nativity, or political ideology, there always remains a strongly disproportionate number of Democrats among the minority group members in white-collar as well as working-class occupations, on high as well as low income levels, etc.

b. The hypothesis of special processes is strengthened whenever the correlation between the measures of identification and the measures of the politically relevant determinants is found to be low. The lower the correlation between group identification on the one hand, and occupation, income, education, and political ideology on the other, the less likely is it that identification raises the Democratic vote of Catholics merely because identification indicates something about their occupation, income, etc.

c. The hypothesis of special processes is weakened whenever intensification fails to appear when it is tested on each level of occupation, education, ideology, etc., separately. We saw, e.g., in Table 2, that Catholics who hold their religious group very important vote Democratic more often than those who hold it less important. Now suppose that when we divide these Catholics into three income levels, we find that on each income level separately it makes no difference to the vote whether or not an individual regards the religious group as important. That would certainly speak for saying that identification raised the Democratic vote of Catholics in Table 2 only because it happened to be correlated with income, and not because it has some powers of its own to cause individuals to adhere to the group norm.

d. On the other hand, the hypothesis of special processes does not require that identification with the group make exactly the same amount of difference to the Democratic vote of Catholics on each income level. In fact, this hypothesis of special processes is strengthened whenever it is found that identification with the group makes the biggest difference on the high income level—generally speaking, on that level where the politically relevant determinant (like income, ideology, occupation) and the pro-Democratic group norm are at cross purposes.

This is so because the hypothesis of special processes implies that politically relevant factors lead[2] to the pro-Democratic attitude of group members to whom they apply, making Democratic vote the group norm, and that special, politically irrelevant processes cause the remaining group members to adhere to this norm—provided that they identify strongly with the group. Low-income Catholics, e.g., vote Democratic for whatever reasons cause low-income people generally to favor the Democratic party; high-income Catholics are led to vote Democratic only insofar as they identify with the Catholic group.

5. Once we are satisfied that special processes are at work, how can we decide whether the special processes are those of motivated conformity, or those of differential exposure to pro-Democratic communications due to differential interaction with minority group members?

The answer, in principle, lies in the partialling out against each other of psychological identification with the group, and differential social interaction with it. Supposing that we measure the participation of Jews in Jewish organizations, and also their feeling of identification with Judaism; and that we find the number of Democrats among the strongly participating Jews to be higher than among the inactive ones, on each level of identification. We would then conclude that screening of communications by the social environment is at work. If, on the other hand, the number of Democrats among Jews goes up with the psychological identification with Judaism on each level of participation, we would conclude that motivated conformity is at work. (Both processes may, of course, operate simultaneously.)

In practice the correlation of participation and identification is probably so high that it is not possible, in a survey design, to vary one while the other remains constant. Refined quantitative measurements of both would be necessary to partial them out against each other statistically. This operation has not been performed for the Elmira data.

6. If the hypothesis of special processes can be accepted—if there are socio-psychological processes which will predispose an individual to vote Democratic simply because he belongs to a group in which most others vote Democratic—then we have here an explanation of potentially very wide application.

As indicated above, it appears from the Elmira data that such politically relevant factors as occupation, income level, education, nativity, and political ideology can account for most, but by no means all, of the disproportionate Democratic vote among the minority group members in Elmira. Motivated conformity and differential exposure to communications are suggested as explanations of the rest of the disproportionately Democratic vote of minority groups—that portion of it not explained by the politically relevant factors. Motivated conformity and differential exposure may also explain similar findings in other instances—whenever a given attitude is differentially prevalent in a group even among the members to whom explanations directly relevant to the issue at hand do not apply.[3]

7. A second and very similar problem may also be explained by these two processes. It is often found that an attitude will persist in a group when explanations by relevant factors can only be made historically; i.e., "good and sufficient reasons" for the group to adopt the attitude in question applied at one time, but do so no more. Such a situation exists, to some extent, with respect to the Democratic vote of at least some of the minority groups we have been considering. The pro-Democratic tendency of Catholic voters in America, for example, seems to have been perpetuated from an earlier time, when the politically relevant factors predisposing to Democratic vote were more prevalent among Catholics than they are today. We know that earlier in the century American Catholics consisted largely of new immigrants to the big cities, engaged in unskilled and poorly paid occupations. Since that time, upward social mobility has considerably attenuated the prevalence of these factors among Catholics, but much of the Democratic tendency has persisted beyond the factors that presumably caused it to begin with.[4]

One may thus hypothesize that social and psychological processes of the kinds described are generally responsible for the spread within groups of the predispositional effects of "relevant" factors beyond those individuals to whom they apply, and for the perpetuation within groups of these effects after the attenuation or extinction of the "relevant" factors. Multivariate analysis seems well suited to investigate whether or not these processes are at work in particular instances. Whenever they are, we will expect that the predisposition will be especially high among those members who identify strongly with the group, and among those who participate frequently in the group's activities. This "intensification" should be especially prevalent among those group members to whom factors intrinsically relevant to the predisposition do not apply.

8. An unexpected and interesting phenomenon becomes apparent in these data. So far, we have concentrated on the figures for minority group members, and have seen that identification and participation increase the percentage of Democrats among them. But we saw in Table 8 that identification and participation do not appreciably increase the percentage of Republicans among White, native-born Protesants. Why should this be the case?

If our interpretations above are correct, we are compelled to one or both of two conclusions: (1) that Protestants constitute less of a psychologically or socially real group than Catholics, Jews, Negroes, or Italian-Americans; (2) that among Protestants, political voting is somehow less regarded as a matter for conformity with one's religious group—perhaps as a strictly private, individual affair—than is the case among the several minority groups. (The fact that Protestants in this country are not regarded as a "minority group" may help explain both of these circumstances.) We are led to these conclusions by the following considerations:

If social and psychological processes were at work spreading Republican predispositions among Protestants beyond the work of politically relevant demographic and ideological factors, then they would reveal themselves in an increased percentage of Republicans among those Protestants who show the greatest identification with or participation in Protestant affairs. Since this is not the case, we conclude that these processes are not at work—or at least only so little that our measures of identification and participation cannot show up their effects.

But this means that the Republicanism of Protestants must be due much more exclusively to politically relevant factors than is true for the Democratic bent of, e.g., Catholics. Where the politically relevant factors pull the other way, we will expect Protestantism to have less hold over the politics of its followers than Catholicism. This means that we would expect to find proportionately more Democrats among Catholic businessmen than Republicans among Protestant workers; more Democrats among Catholic conservatives than Republicans among Protestant liberals; etc.

Conclusion. By merely introducing a series of third variables into our survey results—multivariate analysis at its simplest—it has been possible to shed considerable light on the effects of a social characteristic that is not very directly involved as such in political issues, but that makes a big difference in vote. Members of ethnic and religious minority groups vote differently from the White, native-born Protestants, and this difference is not simply a function of differing demographic or ideological positions. The processes through which this excess difference comes about, we have found reasons to believe, are peculiar to socially or psychologically real groups; and are probably especially strong among minority groups conscious of their status.

5. POLITICAL INTEREST AND VOTING BEHAVIOR

by Paul F. Lazarsfeld, Bernard Berelson, and Hazel Gaudet

[In 1940 an investigation of political attitudes and behavior was undertaken in Erie County, Ohio. Part of the analysis of these data concerned the question of political interest, in which it was shown that education, socio-economic status, age, and sex were related to interest. In the selection which follows, the authors discuss certain factors involved in non-voting.—ED. NOTE.]

Least Participation in the Campaign—the Non-Voter. The acid test for interest in the election is actual voting. In 1940 Erie County had the high voting record of 81%. This was almost perfectly reflected in our panel, where 82% of the 511 people finally interviewed reported that they had actually voted.

Reprinted from *The People's Choice,* pp. 45-49, by permission of the authors and the publisher. (Copyright, 1948, by the Columbia University Press.)

The greatest proportion of non-voters was indeed found on the lowest interest level. People with no interest in the election were 18 times as likely not to vote as people with great interest (Chart 1).

Non-voting is a serious problem in a democracy. It is therefore worthwhile to look at these non-voters somewhat more closely. The great majority of them were *deliberate* non-voters; in October, during the last interview before the election, 29% intended to vote and knew for whom they would vote, 7% intended to vote but did not yet know for whom, and 64% did not intend to vote. In other words, two out of three cases of non-voting were intentional and premeditated, according to the voters' own statements. But even in the other groups there were some non-voters who resembled the premeditated ones.

Chart 1—Non-Voting Is a Function of the Level of Interest.

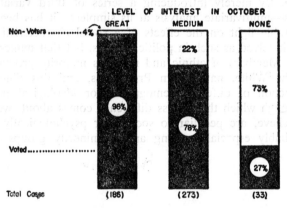

Of the people who did not carry through their preceding vote intention, only one-half had a legitimate reason: they were ill or had made a mistake about registration rules. The other half had never been interested in the elections and the reasons they gave were not at all convincing: "too busy sorting apples," "there were too many people waiting at the polls," and so on.

A few people could not decide how to vote right up to the last moment. Half of them liked or disliked the candidates equally, so they finally decided not to vote at all. The other half had such low interest records throughout the sequence of interviews and offered so little to explain their indecision that they, too, would be more aptly labelled deliberate non-voters. On the other hand, a few people in the group of deliberate non-voters were not without interest in the election; they saw no difference between the two candidates or they felt that voting is no remedy for current social ills.

As a net result, three-quarters of the non-voters stayed away from the polls deliberately because they were thoroughly unconcerned with the election. This sheds a new light on the whole problem of the non-voter. Only a small number of people were kept from the polls by a last-minute emergency. The possibility that the deliberate non-voters could have been made more interested during the campaign is slight; their decision not to vote was too persistent. A long range program of civic education would be needed to draw such people into the orbit of political life, and further studies are needed to unearth the specific nature of their lack of interest.

If we push the analysis of our own data a step further, we gain additional insight into the problem. Perhaps some primary personal characteristics are involved. But the difference in deliberate non-voting between people with more or less education can be completely accounted for by the notion of interest.

Once the interest level is kept constant, education does not make any

Chart 2—Once the Interest Level Is Held Constant, Education Does Not Affect the Proportion of Non-Voters

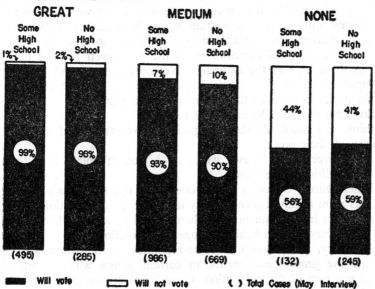

Chart 3—Sex Is the Only Personal Characteristic Which Affects Non-Voting, Even If Interest Is Held Constant. Men Are Better Citizens but Women Are More Reasoned: If They Are Not Interested, They Do Not Vote

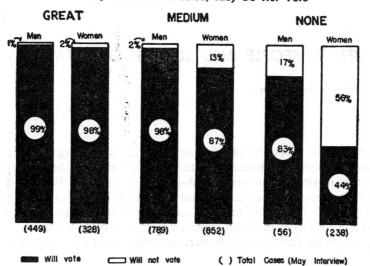

further difference (Chart 2). Deliberate non-voting increases greatly as interest decreases—but if a person is interested, he will vote irrespective of his formal educational level. On the other hand, if he is not interested, he is not likely to vote in any case.

A similar picture is obtained for people on different SES levels, for those with different residences, and for different age and religion groups. But the result is startlingly different for the sex of the respondents (Chart 3).

Sex differences, alone among the personal characteristics, affect non-voting *independently of interest*. The less a group is interested in the election, the greater will be the amount of deliberate non-voting among women as compared with men. If a woman is not interested, she just feels that there is no reason why she should vote. A man, however, is under more social pressure and will therefore go to the polls even if he is not "interested" in the events of the campaign. Not only is it true that women feel no compulsion to vote, but some of them actually consider their aloofness a virtue. Remarks such as these were not infrequent:

"I don't care to vote. Voting is for the men."

"I think men should do the voting and the women should stay home and take care of their work."

"I have never voted. I never will. . . . A woman's place is in the home. . . . Leave politics to the men."

In other words, although legal restrictions upon women's participation in politics were removed some twenty-five years ago, the attitude of women toward politics has not yet brought them to full equality with men. Changes in the mores have lagged behind changes in legislation.

In summary, then, efforts to extend political participation will have to overcome the general indifference to current affairs which seems characteristic for a part of the population. In addition, however, such efforts must refute the idea that public life is, by common consent, the man's realm.

6. FAITH IN PEOPLE AND SUCCESS-ORIENTATION

by Morris Rosenberg

THE FOLLOWING EXAMPLE of multivariate analysis is designed to illustrate the way in which a particular statistical relationship may hold with different degrees of strength among the sub-groups of a sample. Failure to recognize this fact may at times lead to faulty or vague inferences from the data, and may reduce our ability to make accurate predictions for certain groups. In addition, this type of multivariate analysis may often make us aware of the operation of variables which were not obvious in our original relation-

This is a previously unpublished paper.

ship. These points are illustrated in a study dealing with the relationship between faith in people and success-orientation.

Analysts of the American value system have emphasized the importance of "success," of social mobility, as a central social value. In the middle class, at least, the individual is encouraged to want to get ahead, to elevate himself in the status hierarchy. For example, Middletown believes "in being successful," say the Lynds.[1] ". . . a man owes it to himself, to his family, and to society to 'succeed' . . . one should be enterprising; one should try to get ahead of one's fellows, but not 'in an underhand way.' "[2] Merton observes that ". . . the [American] culture enjoins the acceptance of three cultural axioms: first, all should strive for the same lofty goals since these are open to all; second, present seeming failure is but a way-station to ultimate success; and third, genuine failure consists only in the lessening or withdrawal of ambition."[3] And in his discussion of the American value system, Williams has noted: "First, American culture is marked by a central stress upon personal achievement, especially secular occupational achievement. The 'success story' and the respect accorded to the self-made man are distinctly American, if anything is. Our society . . . has endorsed Horatio Alger and has glorified the rail splitter who becomes president."[4] This emphasis upon success has also been noted by Cuber and Harper,[5] Myrdal,[6] Fromm,[7] Horney,[8] Margaret Mead[9] and others.

A limited amount of evidence bearing upon this general proposition, in so far as it applies to young middle class people, is afforded in a study of Students' Values conducted in a large eastern university in 1952. A representative sample of students was asked: "How important to you, personally, is it to get ahead in life?"

Table 1—Important To Get Ahead

	Per Cent
Very important	45
Fairly important	43
Not very important	10
Very unimportant	2
N =	(1,552)

Although we cannot confidently draw any final conclusions regarding the value of success on the basis of a single question, these results do tend to suggest that the students accept the idea of getting ahead. As Table 1 indicates, 88 per cent of the sample considered it either very important or fairly important to get ahead, whereas only 10 per cent considered it not very important and only 2 per cent checked very unimportant. Although these results do not reflect a universally *burning* desire for success (only 45 per cent considered it very important), the value of success, in so far as it is reflected in the responses to the above question, does appear to be generally embraced by the membrs of our student sample.

If the value of success is actually general in the sub-culture under consideration, the question arises: Why do some people consider it more important to get ahead than others?

An attempt to provide a complete answer to this question cannot be undertaken here, but one factor was considered particularly important. This is the individual's basic attitude toward humanity, his faith in people. Horney has observed that an individual who has a basic hatred of people often develops a desire to dominate them, control them, master them, establish his superiority over them. In a world which is a jungle, inhabited by predatory beasts, the only safety lies in getting so much power and strength that one is invulnerable to the attacks of others.[10] Now such an attitude fits in neatly with the culturally-defined value of success, which is based largely on a competitive struggle for superiority. It was therefore hypothesized that part of the reason for the differential emphasis upon success could be accounted for in terms of the individual's degree of faith in people, i.e., those with low faith in people would consider it more important to get ahead in life than those with high faith in people.

In order to test this hypothesis, a "faith-in-people" scale, consisting of five items, was constructed. The items in the scale were the following:

1. Some people say that most people can be trusted. Others say you can't be too careful in your dealings with people. How do you feel about it?
2. Would you say that most people are more inclined to help others, or more inclined to look out for themselves?
3. If you don't watch yourself, people will take advantage of you.
4. No one is going to care much what happens to you, when you get right down to it.
5. Human nature is fundamentally cooperative.

The reproducibility of this scale, using the Guttman method, was .92. On the basis of these five items, six scale types emerged. Those respondents in ranks 1-2 were considered to have "high faith," those in ranks 3-4, "medium faith," and those in ranks 5-6, "low faith." The relationship between faith in people and desire to get ahead is shown in Table 2.

Table 2—Faith in People and Desire To Get Ahead

Important To Get Ahead In Life	High Faith	Medium Faith	Low Faith
Very important	38%	49%	57%
Not very important	62	51	43
N =	(673)	(618)	(251)

Students with low faith in people are clearly more likely to consider success in life "very important" to them than are those with high faith in people. Fifty-seven per cent of those with low faith made this choice, compared with 49 per cent of those with medium faith and 38 per cent of those with high faith.

This finding highlights the complexity of factors involved in striving after success. On the one hand, as our evidence suggests, it may in part involve a desire to master a humanity one despises. On the other hand, as Williams has noted, success in American culture tends to be used as a measure of achievement and as a standard of personal excellence. "Money comes to be valued not only for itself and for the goods it will buy, but as symbolic evidence of success and, thereby, of personal worth."[11] People who highly value success in American society may simply be seeking to demonstrate their worth in a manner highly acceptable to the society.

We would thus expect that the impact of faith in people upon one's desire to get ahead would tend to be strongest upon those who are not under strong cultural pressure to be successful. One simple fact which is over-looked surprisingly often in discussions of success is that the value is considered much more appropriate for men than for women. Women are much more likely to attain higher status through the success of their husbands than through their own achievements. This certainly tends to be the case among the members of our sample; only 28 per cent of the women, compared with 51 per cent of the men, considered it "very important" to get ahead in life. We would thus expect the influence of the individual's degree of faith in people on his success-orientation to be greater among the women than among the men since, in the former case, this relationship is less likely to be adulter-ated by a general social pressure to succeed. The results in Table 3 confirm this expectation.

Among the men, 59 per cent of those with low faith in people considered it "very important" for them to get ahead, compared with 52 per cent of those with medium faith and 48 per cent of those with high faith. The male's basic interpersonal attitude thus has *some* influence on his desire for suc-

Table 3—Faith in People and Desire To Get Ahead, by Sex

Important to Get Ahead	MEN			WOMEN		
			FAITH IN PEOPLE			
	High	Medium	Low	High	Medium	Low
Very important	48%	52%	59%	19%	34%	51%
Not very important	52	48	41	81	66	49
N =	(444)	(491)	(200)	(229)	(137)	(51)

cess, but it is not a very strong one; the difference between men with the lowest and highest degrees of faith in people is only 11 per cent. Even men with high faith in people often accept the cultural value of success quite completely. Among the women, however, fully 51 per cent of those with low faith in people were particularly anxious to be successful compared with only 19 per cent of those with high faith, a difference of 32 per cent, or nearly three times as great as that obtaining among the men. This example illustrates the general point that a relationship which obtains among two variables for a total sample may hold in different degrees among various sub-groups of that sample. Many men in American society, irrespective of their attitudes toward humanity, accept the idea that they should do their best to get ahead. Consequently, the relationship between these two vari-ables in this population subgroup, though significant, is considerably smaller than that among women, who are not exposed to the same amount of cul-tural pressure to get ahead.

7. THE EFFECT OF COLLEGE EXPERIENCE
ON SUBSEQUENT EARNING CAPACITY

by Ernest Havemann and Patricia S. West

[The following selection is drawn from a study of U. S. college graduates which was based on a nationwide survey. This study dealt with a wide variety of questions concerning the college graduate—his family life, his vocation, his political opinions, and so on. In the pages which follow, Havemann and West discuss the influence of attendance at certain institutions of higher learning on subsequent financial success.—ED. NOTE.]

IT WOULD BE PLEASANT to report that the boys from Podunk College, in just as great numbers as the boys from Princeton, go on in later life to become captains of industry and the professions. As a nation we like to think that all diplomas as well as all men are equal, that the little college at the edge of a small town is as sure an avenue to success as the university in the middle of New York or New Haven. We like to think so—but we are wrong.

When it comes to predicting a graduate's financial success, it develops that the wealth and prestige of his college are the best guide of all. The fact that he went to Princeton instead of Podunk means even more than the fact that he specialized instead of taking a general course, or that he was sent to school by his parents instead of having to work his own way. Our data show that the earnings of the graduates go up steadily as the wealth of their colleges, as measured by their endowment per student, rises from the lowest to the highest brackets. Even among the wealthiest colleges, it is the hallowed Ivy League that produces the richest graduates—and the prestigious "Big Three" of the Ivy League, Harvard, Yale and Princeton, that produce the richest of all. If we divide the men graduates into groups by the type of school attended, we get these sharp differences in median incomes:

THE BIG THREE $7,365
(Harvard, Yale, Princeton)

OTHER IVY LEAGUE   6,142
(Columbia. Cornell, Dartmouth, Pennsylvania)

SEVENTEEN TECHNICAL SCHOOLS   5,382
(California, Carnegie, Case, Detroit, Drexel, Georgia, Illinois, Massachusetts, and Stevens Institutes of Technology; Rensselaer, Rose, Virginia, and Worcester Polytechnic Institutes; Clarkson College of Technology, Cooper Union, Polytechnic Institute of Brooklyn, Tri-State College)

TWENTY FAMOUS EASTERN COLLEGES   5,287
(Amherst, Bates, Bowdoin, Brown, Clark, Colby, Franklin and Marshall, Hamilton, Haverford, Hobart, Lafayette, Lehigh, Middlebury, Rutgers, Swarthmore, Trinity, Tufts, Union, Wesleyan of Connecticut, Williams)

From *They Went to College*, pp. 178-185, by Ernest Havemann and Patricia Salter West, copyright, 1952, by Time, Inc. Reprinted by permission of Harcourt, Brace and Company, Inc.

THE BIG TEN	5,176
(Chicago, Illinois, Indiana, Iowa, Michigan, Minnesota, Northwestern, Ohio State, Purdue, Wisconsin)	
ALL OTHER MIDWEST COLLEGES	4,322
ALL OTHER EASTERN COLLEGES	4,235

Why should these wide differences—amounting to over $3,000 from the top to the bottom—exist? One reason for the low figures at the bottom is that the "all other" colleges turn out a disproportionate share of men who go into the low-paid fields of teaching and the clergy, and conversely a smaller share of graduates who enter the high-paid fields of business, law, medicine, and dentistry. But among the other groups of colleges there are no significant differences in the graduates' occupational fields. The Big Three of the Ivy League turn out only a few more doctors and lawyers than the Big Ten Schools, and not nearly so many businessmen as the technical schools with their engineering specialists. The fact is that job for job (as well as age for age) the differences still stand. If we consider only graduates who have entered business and wound up as proprietors and executives of one sort or another, we find that the following proportions were earning $5,000 a year or more at the time of the study:

Of the Ivy Leaguers, 84%.
Of the Big Ten graduates, 68%.
Of the "all other Midwest" graduates, 59%.

At the other extreme, if we consider only graduates who have gone into schoolteaching, we find that these proportions were earning less than $3,000:

Of the Ivy Leaguers, only 7%.
Of the Big Ten graduates, 18%.
Of the "all other Midwest" graduates, 24%.

The moral seems to be that if the Ivy Leaguers go into well-paying jobs they earn even more than any other graduates, while if they go into low-paying jobs they do not do so badly as the others.

Although we have noted that good grades may at least sometimes lead to good incomes, it develops that even the poorest students from the Ivy League share in the general prosperity—and do better than the best students from other schools. Of the Ivy Leaguers who just got by—the C and D students—42% had reached the $7,500 level. Of the A students from the Big Ten only 37% had hit that mark, and only 23% of the A students from the "all other Midwest" colleges. Even the great financial disadvantage of a general education, rather than a specific one, does not seem to hold back the Ivy Leaguers. Of the Ivy League humanities majors, 46% had reached the $7,500 bracket, and of the social scientists 50%. But even among the Big Ten's engineering graduates, with their highly specific training and all the advantages that go with it, only 23% had reached the $7,500 level.

What all this amounts to is that the differences in earning power between graduates of rich and famous schools and those from small and obscure schools are so great that they override everything else. Earning power rises steadily with each increase in wealth and prestige of the school. At the extremes, the Ivy League graduates do best of all financially even when they make poor grades and take a general rather than specific course, both of which are ordinarily handicaps—while the graduates of the smallest schools do not get up to the averages even when they make fine grades and take the type of specific courses which ordinarily produce the biggest incomes.

As we have already noted from time to time, earnings are by no means an exclusive measure of a college's success or its graduates' feelings of satisfaction. In fact this is one reason there are so many sorts of colleges, catering to young people seeking rewards ranging from a degree in animal husbandry to a husband. But on a simple cash basis, the figures we have been examining here are quite a testimonial to the rich and famous schools, and especially to the Ivy League. It is worth asking whether the figures are perhaps even more of a testimonial to the families of the boys who go there.

Knowing that the rich colleges tend to attract students from wealthy families, and that the wealthy boy tends to earn a bigger income in later life than the boy who works his way, can we write off all the college differences as really just a matter of family backgrounds? From a first glance at Table 1, one might be inclined to think so. Only one out of five Ivy League graduates had to earn the major part of his college expenses—against one out of two graduates of Midwest colleges. And one in every three Ivy Leaguers did not have to pay a cent toward his education, where only about one out of ten men from most Midwest colleges was so completely subsidized.

But the moral of the table is not so simple as that. In the Big Ten, mostly comprising state universities with low fees, 86 out of 100 graduates worked their way, wholly or in part. The proportion sent by their parents was just about as low as at other Midwest colleges. Yet as we have seen, Big Ten graduates do better financially than the graduates of our "other Midwest" and "other Eastern" schools. In their case it is definitely not a matter of a son's coasting to success on his father's financial momentum.

Moreover, we know that some poor boys do go to the rich schools; as the table shows, even in the Ivy League 19% of the graduates have earned more than half their expenses. The question now becomes: what about the relative earning power of graduates who went to different kinds of colleges, but whose economic backgrounds were just about the same? Table 2 shows the answer: the golden touch of the Ivy League falls on rich and poor alike. By the age of 40, chosen here because it implies a certain financial maturity, 50% of the students who worked their way through Harvard, Yale, Princeton, or some other Ivy League school have risen to the $7,500-or-over income level. This is as many, or more, as among the graduates who were supported by their families while getting degrees at our group of famous Eastern colleges, the Big Ten or the "other" schools.

In general, the different financial rewards of the rich schools versus the obscure ones are just as pronounced even when we separate the graduates by family background. At all types of colleges, the graduates from wealthy family backgrounds wind up making more money than those from poorer family bakgrounds. But among both the self-help students and the family-supported students, considered separately, the type of college plays a great part in later financial success.

It is not just the family; it must be the school—or the kind of students who go there. There are undoubtedly some factors working here that we cannot possibly measure, and many of them must revolve around the personalities, talents, hopes, and ambitions of the students. Although this is necessarily a matter of sheer speculation, we might get the best clue of all by thinking for a moment about some various young men who are leaving high school and faced with making a choice of colleges.

Certainly one type of student who can count on having all expenses paid by his family is the boy from a very rich and socially prominent family, whose parents and grandparents have been college graduates from time immemorial—and from the most famous schools at that. Such a boy might very well be expected, as a matter of course, to follow his father's footsteps at Yale or at Harvard. If he does not go to the Ivy League—but instead chooses some equally wealthy but smaller college, or a state university or a very small and obscure school—there must be a reason. Perhaps he is doubtful of his scholastic ability or his willingness to study, and wants the

Table 1—How Many Worked Their Way?

Per Cent of Graduates Who Earned:	Ivy League	20 Famous Eastern Colleges*	17 Technical Schools†	All Other Eastern Colleges	The Big Ten	All Other Midwest Colleges
More than half	19%	25%	26%	36%	43%	49%
Up to half	49	54	54	47	43	39
None (of all college expenses)	32	21	20	17	14	12

* Amherst, Bates, Bowdoin, Brown, Clark, Colby, Franklin and Marshall, Hamilton, Haverford, Hobart, Lafayette, Lehigh, Middlebury, Rutgers, Swarthmore, Trinity, Tufts, Union, Wesleyan, Williams.
† California, Carnegie, Case, Detroit, Drexel, Georgia, Illinois, Massachusetts, and Stevens Institutes of Technology; Rensselaer, Rose, Virginia, and Worcester Polytechnic Institutes; Clarkson College of Technology, Cooper Union, Polytechnic Institute of Brooklyn, Tri-State College.

Table 2—In Reaching Top Income Brackets, College Makes a Difference

	Ivy League	17 Technical Schools	20 Famous Eastern Colleges	Big Ten	All Other Midwest and Eastern Colleges
PER CENT OF GRADUATES, 40 AND OLDER NOW EARNING $7,500 OR MORE PER YEAR					
Those who as students earned more than half of all college expenses	50%	43%	40%	40%	23%
Those whose family paid all college expenses	76	64	50	49	32

safety of a school which is considered a little softer touch on the matter of grades. Perhaps he dislikes his family's social life, and all the social implications of the wealthier schools. Perhaps he is an intellectual rebel, and feels that he should go to a more "democratic" school and live a less profitable and more dedicated life than his father. Whichever of these possibilities or any others happens to be the reason, the chances are he is the type of young man who is less able or less interested in making money.

Within the lifetimes of our graduates another very common type of family-supported student has been the son of the self-made man. His father did not go to college; neither did his mother; but the family has made enough money to send the children to college and is eager to do so as a matter of prestige. They live in a small town or a small city; the father is a merchant, a traveling salesman, or a good insurance agent, or perhaps a factory superintendent or the owner of a small manufacturing firm. Although the family has a decent amount of money, it is not among the social elite even in its own community. Such a young man might well prefer a small and unpretentious college, or at the most his state university. If instead he elects to go to one of the famous wealthy campuses, or even to the Ivy League, he too must be something of an exception—motivated by unusual abilities or by extraordinarily high social or career ambitions.

In the case of boys who work their own way through school, it is always easiest to choose colleges where the fees and living expenses are low; and if there happens to be a college right in the home town, that is the easiest of all. For a young man in New Mexico with no means of support except what he can earn with his own hands outside the classroom hours, the thought of traveling all the way to Princeton, finding a job in a strange part of the country, and meeting the higher expenses of an Ivy League education is a pretty frightening thing. The boy who does it must be exceptionally confident, self-reliant, and ambitious to begin with. Moreover he must feel that the college course can give him something well worth straining for.

Very possibly the student bodies at the wealthiest and most famous schools are made up largely of young men who are in a sense the most determined to gain the highest positions in life—or the most likely to inherit them. The smaller and less noted schools possibly have a greater proportion of students who are less ambitious—or who would conceivably not want to have the presidency of a big corporation, and all the trappings that go with it, if it were handed to them on a platter. It may also be that four years of association with rich or ambitious young men on a wealthy campus intensify financial strivings more than four years of the more casual life on a smaller campus. Although we have found that extra-curricular activities as such bear no relation to financial success, perhaps personal associations and social contacts on the campus do. Some people believe, and they may be right, that the best way to make your son a financial success is to buy him a dinner jacket and then let him figure out how to pay his way into the places where he can wear it.

8. THE TWO PURPOSES OF DEVIANT CASE ANALYSIS

by Patricia L. Kendall and Katherine M. Wolf

THE ULTIMATE OBJECTIVE of many social research undertakings is to make it possible to *predict* the behavior of particular types of individuals under specified conditions. When, for example, we study the reading habits of middle-class adults, or the development of ethnic attitudes, we attempt to locate the factors which determine the behavior or the attitude in the cases which we examine so that we can predict, and perhaps modify, the reading habits or the ethnic attitudes of persons not included in our sample.

At the present time, however, there are few, if any, generalizations in social research which permit completely accurate predictions. Every time that we try to apply our predictive schemes, we discover that there are a number of cases which do not exhibit the behavior or the attitudes which we expected of them: the persons with low income who vote for Republican candidates, the college graduates who depend on the radio as their primary source of news information, and so on.

Until recently such *deviant cases,* as they are called, were considered little more than a source of embarrassment to the researcher. He tried to "explain them away" as best he could so that his findings would present a neat bundle with no loose ends.

During the last decade, however, Paul F. Lazarsfeld has pointed out[1] that the analysis of deviant cases can, by refining the theoretical structure of empirical studies, increase the predictive value of their findings. In other words, deviant case analysis can, and should, play a *positive role* in empirical research, rather than being merely the "tidying-up" process through which exceptions to the empirical rule are given some plausibility and thus disposed of.

First of all, through deviant case analysis the researcher is able to uncover relevant *additional factors* which had not previously been considered.[2] Predictive schemes can clearly be of greater or lesser complexity. At the one extreme are those which attempt to predict specified types of behavior on the basis of an allegedly exhaustive identification of *all* relevant factors. Such schemes, while the ideal of social research, are rarely attempted (and even more rarely achieved) because of the complexity of human behavior. At the other extreme are the schemes which attempt to predict behavior

---

Reprinted from "The Analysis of Deviant Cases in Communications Research," pp. 152-157, in *Communications Research, 1948-49,* edited by Paul F. Lazarsfeld and Frank Stanton, by permission of the authors, the editors and the publisher. (Copyright, 1949, by Harper and Bros.)

through knowledge of one or two factors which are postulated as "the" cause or causes. And it is these schemes, by far the most common in social research, which fail to account for the behavior of some of the individuals being studied.

The first function of deviant case analysis, then, is to move the latter type of predictive scheme in the direction of the former. Through careful analysis[3] of the cases which do not exhibit the expected behavior, the researcher recognizes the oversimplification of his theoretical structure and becomes aware of the need for incorporating further variables into his predictive scheme. For example, researchers of the Princeton Office of Radio Research[4] attempted to determine why one-third of the listeners to Orson Welles' dramatization of "War of the Worlds" considered it a news-broadcast rather than a play. It was first believed by the researchers that whether a given listener would regard the broadcast as a play or a news report could be predicted from knowledge of the time at which the given listener first tuned in; it was believed that those who tuned in at the beginning and heard the opening announcements would not be misled, while those who tuned in late and thus missed the opening comments might well think that they were listening to a news-broadcast. Examination of the case-studies largely confirmed this expectation, but a number of deviant cases nevertheless appeared: approximately 15 per cent of those who had listened from the beginning of the broadcast had nevertheless considered it to be news.

Close analysis of these cases revealed that one reason[5] for their deviation was that during the Munich crisis of 1938 (approximately one month before the Orson Welles broadcast) listeners had become accustomed to having regular radio programs interrupted by news bulletins irrelevant to the scheduled program. The researchers therefore realized that listeners' reactions to the broadcast could not be predicted completely accurately solely by determining whether they had heard the opening announcements. Accurate prediction also required information on listeners' expectations in regard to scheduled programs being interrupted for the dissemination of important news.

In Mirra Komarovsky's study, *The Unemployed Man and His Family,*[6] the analysis of deviant cases similarly extended the theoretical structure. Komarovsky originally predicted that men whose authority in their families was based on their abilities as "good providers" would more frequently lose that authority when they became unemployed than would men whose pre-unemployment authority rested on the love and admiration of their families. This prediction was borne out by a majority of the cases in her sample group. But in several families where the husband's authority had been based on his role as provider, the predicted loss of authority did not occur. Analysis of these deviant cases showed the necessity for including a further factor in the predictive scheme. Detailed study revealed that in most such families the wife was afraid of her husband and that this fear was so potent a factor that the husband was able to maintain his authority even when he could no longer act as provider.

The first function of deviant case analysis, then, is to correct the oversimplifications of predictive schemes by demonstrating the relevance of additional variables. The second function of this type of analysis is not to add anything to the scheme but rather to *refine the measurement of statistical variables used to locate the deviant cases.*

Virtually all social research assumes that it is valid procedure to use easily measured and easily manipulated indices in place of the complex and inaccessible concepts about which we should like ultimately to talk. The relative proportions of lawyers and ministers, for example, have been used as indices of the "secularization" of a community; Durkheim considered membership in specific religious groups, marital status, and rural-urban residence as indices of "social cohesion"; formal educational level is frequently used as an index of "mental sophistication" or "critical ability"; and so on. If social researchers questioned the legitimacy of substituting available indices for inaccessible concepts, they would soon be forced to close shop.

The crudity of the indices, however, sometimes prevents accurate prediction. When, for example, we predict that mentally sophisticated people will behave in some specified way, and attempt to confirm this expectation by examining the behavior of college graduates, we shall very probably discover a number of deviant cases. Analysis of these cases may reveal that formal education is not always the equivalent of mental sophistication, and that some of the college graduates whom we considered mentally sophisticated should more properly be classified as unsophisticated. Analysis of deviant cases will thus have indicated not the inadequacy of the basic predictive scheme, but rather the inaccuracy of classification procedures and the crudity of our indices.

Robert K. Merton, in his study of responses to the Kate Smith war-bond selling marathon,[7] predicted that listeners who were concerned about the safety of close relatives in the armed forces would be particularly vulnerable to Smith's accounts of the sacrifices which soldiers had made and were making in the war. Accordingly, he compared the responses of listeners who had close relatives in the armed forces and of those who did not. The findings largely confirmed his prediction but also revealed a number of deviant cases: listeners who had brothers, sons, and husbands in the armed forces, but who did not respond to the soldier-sacrifice theme. Re-examination of the interview records revealed that the crudity of the index used had led to the mis-classification of all of these listeners. The mere fact of having a close relative in the armed forces was found to be in and of itself no indication of concern about their safety. The kin mentioned by these listeners were not in any immediate danger: some were stationed in the United States, some were overseas but in inactive theaters, and one was home on leave at the time of the marathon.

This example is particularly interesting, for it demonstrates that the discovery and analysis of deviant cases, while pointing out the necessity for refining crude indices, can often thereby confirm the researcher's hypothesis more adequately than might be possible were there no deviations. If, for example, *all* of the listeners with relatives in the armed forces had been particularly responsive to the soldier-sacrifice theme, Merton could not have argued so convincingly that it was their concern, their anxieties and fears, about their relatives which motivated their response. Another analyst might have advanced the counter-argument that the response was not emotionally

motivated, but wholly rational—that these listeners recognized better than
others the need for equipment to be purchased through war-bond sales.
Deviant cases alone make it possible to choose between these two possible
interpretations.[8]

Deviant case analysis also served to refine the roughly constructed indices of the "invasion from Mars" study. As we remember, the analysts
predicted that listeners who tuned in to the Orson Wells broadcast at the
beginning would not mistake it for a news program. But, there were a number of early listeners who did make this mistake. Upon close analysis[9] the
researchers found that, while for some of these listeners their predictive
scheme was inadequate (familiarity with the practice of interrupting a
scheduled program with news bulletins needed also to be taken into account),
for other individuals it was the crudity of the indices which produced seemingly deviant behavior. The behavior of "tuning in at the beginning," was
intended as an index of "hearing the opening announcements" or "attending
to the broadcast from the beginning." But the researchers discovered that
this behavior was not an infallible index. There were some listeners who
said that, although they had tuned in the broadcast at the beginning, they
had missed the opening announcements because, in conformity with their
customary behavior, they disregarded the "opening commercials." By re-
classifying such listeners as latecomers, errors in prediction were decreased.

9. DEFINITIONS OF A SITUATION

by Robert K. Merton, with the assistance of

Marjorie Fiske and Alberta Curtis

[In 1943 Kate Smith went on the air in a marathon eighteen-hour broadcast for
the purpose of selling United States War Bonds. Robert K. Merton and his associates conducted a study among a sample of listeners designed to reveal the meaning and impact of Smith's appeals for the audience. Among various types of
listeners described in this study was one type called "the susceptible bond buyer,"
a group of people who were emotionally involved in the war, but had not intended
to buy bonds at the time of the broadcast; these people bought bonds under the
direct impact of Smith's broadcast. It was possible to isolate the various appeals
which affected the listeners. Some people with close relatives in the Armed Forces
tended to respond selectively to the sacrifice theme in the broadcast. In the selection which follows, the authors discuss this group and analyze those "deviant"
cases with relatives in the Services who failed to react in this manner.—ED. NOTE.]

WE HAVE NOTED that a central theme in the Smith broadcasts could be
summarized in these terms: Buy a bond and bring your boy back home. And

Reprinted from *Mass Persuasion*, pp. 125-129, by permission of the authors and the publisher.
(Copyright, 1946, by Harper and Bros.)

it was to this theme that these persons* chiefly responded. A series of interlocking data indicate that the context of this selective response was provided by their deep personal involvement in the war. To begin with, four of the listeners in this category were mothers of sons in the armed forces; the fifth had a brother in the service, and the sixth was himself a veteran of the first World War. In contrast, only 9 of the 22 others in the susceptible category had close relatives (son, brother, husband or father) in some branch of the service.

Table 1—Responses to Accounts of Soldier Sacrifice

Responded to Accounts of Soldier Sacrifice	CLOSE RELATIVES IN ARMED FORCES		
	Yes	No	Total
Yes	5	1	6
No	9	13	22
Total	14	14	28

Further data account for this selective response. These five persons were peculiarly beset by fears and anxiety concerning a son or brother who, in all five instances, was serving overseas. They were, therefore, peculiarly sensitive to Smith's vivid portrayals of the needs and sacrifices of men at the front. It was as though they visualized their own sons as the central figures in the dramatic episodes described by Smith. Phrases which were little more than cliches for others took on deep emotional significance for those who interpreted them in the light of their own longings and anxieties. Thus, almost echoing a Smith phrase, one informant in this category defined her bond purchase as a means of "bringing my brother home sooner."

Within this context of emotional stress, Smith's appeals were taken by mothers as presenting a means of coping with the apprehensions that crowded in upon them. They felt themselves at the mercy of incalculable circumstances. There was the ever-present imminence of fateful word from the War Department—We regret to inform you . . . Faced with these obsessive fears, it was psychologically difficult for them to arrive at the dispassionate judgment that nothing could be done to enhance the safety of their sons. All this generated a powerful need for "doing something" about an unendurable situation and, under the goad of this desperate anxiety, the bond purchase took on an almost magical character.[1] For, tormented by terrible forebodings, these mothers acted as though the *particular* bond they bought would directly safeguard their own sons in battle, as though *their* bonds would set in motion circumstances which would bring their boys safe through the war. *Something* was being done, and the sense of helplessness and lack of control over an unbearable, ego-charged danger gave way to a feeling of having introduced some measure of control.[2] Smith's vivid accounts of the horrors to which fighting men are exposed thus had a double-edged character: they virtually terrorized these mothers into an added bond purchase and by doing so, provided a behavior formula for temporary escape fom intolerable fears and anxieties.

Translating Smith's appeals into acutely personal terms, the anxious mother of a bombardier stationed in England felt that her bond was to serve as direct aid to her son.

"I remember she say, 'If you buy a bond, you buy a ticket for your son to come home.' [At this point, the interviewer was shown a photograph of her

---

* The susceptible bond buyers who responded to accounts of soldier sacrifice.

son.] She was just like speaking to me. Her voice . . . she helps mothers, our sons,
I cried all the time. [She asks the interviewer: You think maybe our boys come
home soon?] The way she speaks to mothers, it would break anyone's heart. I
think: I am going to buy a bond. *I'll buy a bond for my boy. I wouldn't NOT
have the money to help my son. I wouldn't be able to rest.*"

A Brooklyn housewife, whose only son was overseas, similarly supplied
a personal context for Smith's accounts of sacrifice, as the following excerpt
indicates:

"The way she was talking, I had all I could do to get to the phone quickly.
She was telling the story of a young fellow—I remember his name, Merrill—that
didn't have any legs or arms and was happy and wanted no sympathy and that
we should buy bonds in his name *and save some other boy from such a thing.
It touched very deeply. Not only what she said. But my son's in the service for
three years. . . .* It got me so. I ran from the phone right over to his picture and
started to cry. And I said: *'Sonny, if this will save one hair on your head,* I thank
God, and I thank God that I live in the United States.'"

In those instances where mothers had no knowledge of their sons' where-
abouts or of the risks to which they were exposed, anxieties were all the
more intensified. The absence of any secure basis for judgment gave free
rein to all manner of apprehensions which they sought to escape by actively
doing something for their boys:

"I tell you, I was pretty well upset. I sent my daughter to call her up. *I hadn't
heard from my boy for some time and I was worried.* [Informant gives way to
tears.] It's funny how some people don't give. It's only a loan. If I had more
money, I'd given it all. [Informant finds it increasingly difficult to speak.] I feel
foolish, but I can't help myself. I'm so upset about my son on the Flying Fortress.
*Every time she spoke, it meant more and more. I was so upset. It made me wish
I could have given her all—everything I had to give up for the boy.* I was trying
to get some money together to get curtains, but I put up with the old ones."

"I was listening to Kate's stories and started to think of my son. He trained in
the Seventh Regiment. It was just that she was asking for money and my boy
is in the war. *I don't even know where he is now. His A.P.O. number has been
changed.*"

But all this does not explain why only 5 of the 14 listeners with close
relatives in the armed forces responded in this fashion. What of the "deviate"
cases, those 9 who did *not* respond selectively to this phase of Smith's appeals? An analysis of the interviews provides the clue. The unresponsive
persons had little basis for acute fears or anxiety concerning the safety of
sons or brothers in the service. In five cases, their kin were stationed in
this country and, therefore, their situation did not evoke immediate anxiety.
And in another instance, where a son was overseas, he was far removed
from any active war theater. Nor could a chief gunner's mate, the husband
of another informant, be a source of anxiety, since at the time he was home
on leave and listening with his wife to the Smith bond drive. Thus, the
emotional context for selective listening was significantly different for the
two categories of informants, although both had close relatives in the Army
or Navy.

In review, then, the evidence suggests that susceptible listeners responded
selectively in terms of distinctive sets of determinants. By taking "close rela-

tives in the service" as a crude index of direct emotional involvement with the war, we found a tendency for those who were emotionally involved to respond particularly to the "sacrifice" theme of Smith's broadcasts. But this led to the problem of interpreting the absence of such selective response among some relatives of servicemen. A further refinement of our index in terms of those relationships which did or did not generate anxiety enabled us to account for such seeming "exceptions." It was against the background of acute anxiety concerning the safety of affectively significant persons in the armed services that some informants were particularly affected by the sacrificial theme.

10. THE PREDICTION OF PERSONAL ADJUSTMENT AND INDIVIDUAL CASES

by Paul Horst

ONE OF THE MOST INTERESTING and useful parts of a prediction study should be the investigation of cases which have been incorrectly predicted in a new sample. In this connection the case study method may be particularly useful. When the case method is used in attempting to determine the relevant factors associated with variation in a given activity, it is left to the discretion of the investigator to decide what individuals shall be included in the case study. In a study of incorrectly predicted cases, however, the cases are already selected, so that attention may be focused directly on the problem of determining why the formula was inadequate.[1] All factors making for inaccuracy of prediction should be carefully investigated with reference to each incorrectly placed person. The possibility of coaching, ambiguity of items, inadequate motivation, unusual physical conditions, or a number of other influences may be discovered. More important, however, the research worker is in a position to look for other prediction factors which had not previously been taken into account. In this connection, the case study of incorrectly placed individuals may have its most useful function, namely, that of discovering important factors which had formerly been neglected in the prediction system. A great deal of attention should be given to working out rather specific and controlled methods for investigating the misplaced cases, since this type of study can offer rich rewards in the way of suggesting revision of previous hypotheses and new hypotheses which can be further tested by statistical techniques.

In this connection, the statistical and case study methods may be used

Reprinted from *The Prediction of Personal Adjustment,* pp. 117-118, by permission of the author and the publisher. (Copyright, 1941, by The Social Science Research Council.)

profitably to supplement one another. The use of either method alone will probably yield less satisfactory results than when they are thus used in conjunction with one another. When the statistical analysis reaches a ceiling of prediction accuracy, it must await the aid of the case study. The investigator, by studying intensively those cases which he failed to predict correctly, may learn which factors previously used were irrelevant, which relevant factors were overlooked, and what particular relationships of factors should have been taken into account. By incorporating what has been learned into a new statistical analysis, mistakes previously made may be rectified, and new ideas may be tested for their contribution to prediction efficiency

11. THE INFLUENCE OF THE NORTHERN ENVIRONMENT ON THE INTELLIGENCE TEST SCORES OF NEGROES

by Otto Klineberg

THIS PART OF THE STUDY attempts to discover whether the admittedly superior northern environment has any effect in raising the intelligence-test scores of southern born Negro children. The method used was to compare the scores obtained by different groups of New York Negro children, all born in the South, but differing in the number of years which they had lived in New York City. If the environment has an effect, there should be a rise in intelligence at least roughly proportionate to length of residence in New York. If there is no environmental effect, and if the superiority of the New York City Negroes is entirely due to selective migration, length of residence ought to make little or no difference.

The present investigation includes nine distinct studies made under the direction of the writer by candidates for the degree of Master of Arts in the Department of Psychology in Columbia University. Together they represent the findings on 3,081 subjects, consisting of ten and twelve-year-old Negro boys and girls in the Harlem schools; three of the studies were made with the National Intelligence Test, scale A, form I; three with the Stanford-Binet; one with the Otis Self-administering Examination, Intermediate Form; one with the Minnesota Paper Form Boards; and one with an abbreviated Pintner-Paterson Performance Scale. The results of these studies will be presented separately, and also combined, wherever possible, so as to give a more general and at the same time more reliable picture of the environmental effect.

The three studies with the National Intelligence Test, scale A, form I, were made upon 1,697 twelve-year-old boys and girls in the Harlem schools in 1931 and 1932. In all three studies the subjects at the time of testing had passed their twelfth, and had not yet reached their thirteenth birthdays. The attempt was made in each case to secure every Negro boy or girl within this age range at the various schools at which the studies were made, and it is not likely that many were omitted. The scores were so combined as to make possible a comparison between a northern born control group and the southern born children who had been in New York one year, two years and so on up to eleven years. In every case note was

Reprinted in part from *Negro Intelligence and Selective Migration*, pp. 24-34, 40-42, by permission of the author and the publisher. (Copyright, 1935, by the Columbia University Press.)

taken of the average school grade of these various groups, so that degree of retardation or acceleration in school might also be used as a rough measure of present intellectual level. As might be expected, the intelligence-test scores and the school grades show a high degree of correspondence.

(1) The first of these studies was made by George Lapidus on 517 twelve-year-old boys between February and May, 1931; the subjects were all in attendance at three public schools and one junior high school in Harlem. The following table gives the average National Intelligence Test scores for each group.

It may be seen that in spite of minor fluctuations there is a very definite tendency for the scores to improve as length of residence increases. This result appears more clearly when the test scores of the subjects are combined into two-year groupings; the rise is now definite and regular.

Taking the northern born group as standard, there is a reliable difference in its favor over the one-two-year group and the three-four-year group, the difference divided by the sigma of the difference being equal to 5.33 and

Table 1—National-Intelligence-Test Score and Length of Residence (Lapidus)

Residence Years	1 Year	2 Years	3 Years	4 Years	5 Years	6 Years
No. of Cases	30	26	14	21	22	19
Average Score	64.43	63.96	54.50	75.09	76.72	67.21

Residence Years	7 Years	8 Years	9 Years	10 Years	11-12 Years	12 Years (Northern born)
No. of Cases	18	15	13	10	21	308
Average Score	86.61	79.93	74.00	79.10	93.85	86.93

These results are also presented in the following graph.

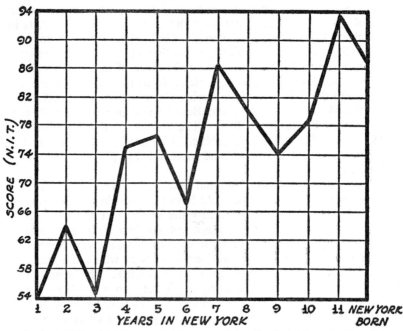

Graph 1. National-Intelligence-Test Scores and Length of Residence in New York.
Twelve-year-old Boys (Lapidus)

Table 2—Combined Groups (Lapidus)

Residence Years	1 and 2 Years	3 and 4 Years	5 and 6 Years	7 and 8 Years	9, 10 and 11 Years	12 Years (Northern born)
No. of Cases	56	35	41	33	44	308
Average Score	64.21	66.86	72.32	83.58	84.64	86.93
Standard Deviation	29.5	29.5	33.2	29.1	30.4	28.9
Reliability of Av.	3.94	4.98	5.18	5.06	4.58	1.64

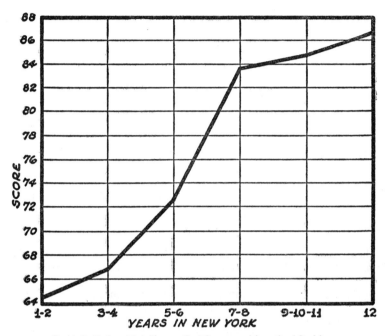

Graph 2. National-Intelligence-Test Scores and Length of Residence.
Combined Groups (Lapidus)

3.83, respectively.* The superiority over the five-six-year group is practically reliable (99 chances in 100); over those subjects who have been in New York seven years or more the superiority is small and unreliable.

Table 3 gives the average grade for these various groups and also the degree of retardation. (Note: a grade of 4B.60 means that the average child in this group is 60 per cent through 4B.)

It is clear in this case also that length of residence in New York has a very real effect upon scholastic level. Since 7A is the normal grade for twelve-year-old White pupils, it can be seen that the northern born group is only slightly more than three-fourths of a year retarded, and that the retardation is far more marked in the case of the recent arrivals from the South. This finding agrees with the experience of school authorities in the North, who have found it a very difficult problem to assimilate southern Negro children into their classes.

These results, which are in harmony with those reached in other investigations which form part of this study, correspond with the findings of

* When this ratio is greater than 3, the difference is conventionally regarded as a true or reliable one.

Table 3—Grade Retardation (Lapidus)

Residence Years	1 Year	2 Years	3 Years	4 Years	5 Years	6 Years
No. of Cases	30	26	14	21	22	19
Average Grade	4B.86	4B.96	4B.69	5A.96	5B.38	5B.00
Standard Grade	7A for average 12-year-old pupils					
Retardation Years	2.07	2.02	2.15	1.52	1.31	1.50

Residence Years	7 Years	8 Years	9 Years	10 Years	11 Years	12 Years (Northern born)
No. of Cases	18	15	13	10	21	308
Average Grade	5B.84	6A.06	6A.25	6A.89	6A.04	6A.44
Standard Grade	7A	. . . .	. . . .	. . . .	. . . .	. . . .
Retardation Years	1.08	0.97	0.88	0.55	0.98	0.78

Peterson and Lanier.[1] The latter report that the New York Negro boys whom they tested were retarded approximately half a school year, whereas in Nashville the retardation is more than twice as great. There is a correlation of $+0.49$ between school grade and years of residence in New York for all subjects not born in New York City (72 cases); when those who had lived in New York more than six years were eliminated, the correlation was increased to $+0.60$ (40 subjects). There is no correlation between grade and length of residence in the city for those children who have been in school only in New York.

The authors comment:

All of these facts seem to point rather clearly to the conclusion that there are certain advantages of instruction and motivation in the educational system of New York which are superior to what the Negro gets in the South and in the West Indies. . . . Another point about the retardation of the transient Negro in New York should be mentioned. It is well known that any child transferring from one school system to another tends to be placed in a grade lower than he would be in if he did not make the change. This may be due either to the poorer status of the first school or to differences in the curricula which make it necessary for the child either to go into the lower grade or to repeat a grade to avoid the omission of necessary training. As to the Negroes transferring from the South to New York, the teachers uniformly report that these children are very poorly trained. Any one who has given tests in Southern Negro schools knows that they do not have the facilities of the Whites, and so the comparative retardation of Southern Negroes in the New York schools is probably due largely to inadequate training, rather than to a more general tendency to place the newcomer back.[2]

(2) The second study with the National Intelligence Test was made between February and May, 1932, by Charlotte Yates on 619 twelve-year-old girls in the Harlem schools. The scores were combined in the same way as in the preceding study, and the results are presented in Tables 4-8, and Graphs 3-5.

The results are again quite clear and definite (especially in the case of the groups combined in two-year intervals (Table 5 and Graph 4). The difference between the northern born group and the southern group with one to two years' residence in New York is completely reliable; d/sigma d (that is, the difference divided by the standard error of the difference) equals 5.87. For the three-four-year group, d/sigma d equals 4.83. The difference in the case of all the other southern born groups is small and unreliable; in the case of the nine-ten-eleven-year group, the difference is in favor of the southern born, but is also small and unreliable.

Table 6 gives the average grade and the degree of retardation of these various groups. The normal grade for twelve-year-old girls is 7A.

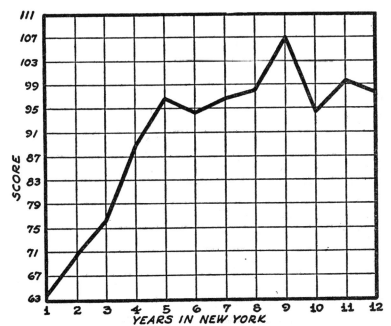

Graph 3. National-Intelligence-Test Scores and Length of Residence in New York. Twelve-year-old Girls (Yates)

Table 4—National-Intelligence-Test Score and Length of Residence (Yates)

Residence Years	1 Year	2 Years	3 Years	4 Years	5 Years	6 Years
No. of Cases	30	28	31	19	31	26
Average Score	63.66	70.43	76.25	88.78	96.58	94.38
Standard Deviation	25.3	34.96	18.78	26.23	24.79	21.24
Reliability of Average	4.61	6.60	3.55	6.02	4.40	4.16

Residence Years	7 Years	8 Years	9 Years	10 Years	11 Years	12 Years (Northern born)
No. of Cases	25	22	14	15	21	359
Average Score	96.56	98.09	106.85	94.67	99.23	97.86
Standard Deviation	20.46	25.88	18.10	29.76	27.95	29.7
Reliability of Average	4.26	5.51	4.83	7.69	6.1	1.5

It will be seen that there is again a very definite decrease in the amount of retardation, proportionate to length of residence in New York City. The retardation is appreciable only for those groups which have been in New York six years or less; for all other groups it is only a small fraction of a year. There is practically no school retardation in the case of Negro girls who have had all of their schooling in New York City.

In this study a comparison was also made between the scores of those girls coming from *urban* and *rural* communities in the South. Since the

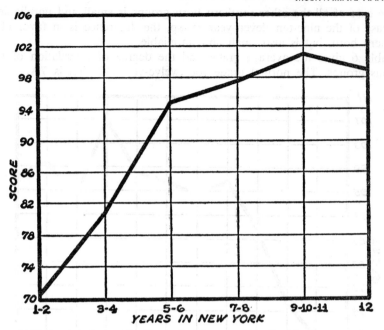

Graph 4. National-Intelligence-Test Scores and Length of Residence.
Combined Groups (Yates)

Table 5—Combined Groups (Yates)

Residence Years	1 and 2 Years	3 and 4 Years	5 and 6 Years	7 and 8 Years	9, 10 and 11 Years	12 Years
No. of Cases	58	50	57	45	50	359
Average Score	70.80	80.7	94.80	97.55	100	97.86
Standard Deviation	33.20	23	26.7	22.1	27.5	29.7
Reliability of Average	4.36	3.2	3.53	.32	3.87	1.5

Table 6—Grade Retardation (Yates)

Residence Years	1 Year	2 Years	3 Years	4 Years	5 Years	6 Years
No. of Cases	30	28	31	19	31	26
Average Grade	4B.92	5B.76	5B.79	6A.09	6A.38	5B.94
Retardation Years	2.04	1.12	1.11	0.95	0.56	1.03

Residence Years	7 Years	8 Years	9 Years	10 Years	11 Years	12 Years
Number of Cases	23	22	14	14	21	359
Average Grade	6B.88	7A	6B.75	6B.75	6B.99	6B.84
Retardation Years	0.06	0.00	0.13	0.13	0.01	0.08

Table 7—Migrants from City and Country (Yates)

	CITY BORN GROUP				
Residence Years	1 and 2 Years	3 and 4 Years	5 and 6 Years	7 and 8 Years	9, 10 and 11 Years
Number of Cases	47	37	33	37	36
Average Score	76	81.1	94.34	99.4	103.33
Standard Deviation	43.20	23.50	24.20	23.50	26.30
Reliability of Average	6.25	3.86	4.17	3.56	4.38
Average Grade	5B.89	5B.83	6A.45	6B.64	6B.88

Table 7—Migrants from City and Country (Yates)

Residence Years	COUNTRY BORN GROUP				
	1 and 2 Years	3 and 4 Years	5 and 6 Years	7 and 8 Years	9, 10 and 11 Years
Number of Cases	9	9	11	7	4
Average Score	49.6	67.4	84	104	101.5
Standard Deviation	15.30	11.5	27.4	28.7	18.13
Reliability of Average	5.1	3.83	8.3	3.72	17.55
Average Grade	4B.70	5B.75	6A.15	6B.54	6B.88

school facilities in the southern cities are usually far superior to those in the country districts, it was felt that there might possibly be some difference between these two groups of migrants. Unfortunately, it was not always possible to determine very accurately the earlier residence of each child. In many cases the families had moved about a great deal before finally settling in New York. It frequently happened, for example, that a family moved from the country to the city in the South before coming North, and in that event a girl might give the name of the city as her previous residence. A study of this kind would require a much more careful personal inquiry into the movements of each family than was possible in this case.

Table 7 and Graph 5 present these results. The number of cases is slightly smaller than those reported in the other tables, as many children knew only the state and not the exact locality of their birth. The classification into city and country groups was based upon the census of 1927; a population of 5,000 inhabitants was regarded as constituting a city.

In spite of the small number of subjects from the rural districts, the results are very striking. They suggest that while the rural children start out far behind those from the city, after a number of years of residence in New

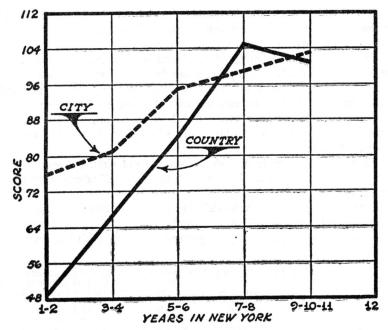

Graph 5. National-Intelligence-Test Scores and Length of Residence.
City and County Born (Yates)

York the difference disappears. In the case of the one-and-two-year groups, the difference in favor of the city born children is reliable; for the three-and-four-year groups it is almost reliable; for all the others it is small and unreliable.

Table 8 shows the degree of school retardation of city and country born children; there is again a marked difference between the city and country children who have been in New York only a short time, and no difference between the earlier arrivals.

Table 8—Grade Retardation (Yates)

	CITY BORN GROUP				
Residence Years	1 and 2 Years	3 and 4 Years	5 and 6 Years	7 and 8 Years	9, 10 and 11 Years
Number of Cases	47	37	33	37	36
Average Grade	5B.89	5B.83	6A.45	6B.64	6B.88
Retardation Years	1.05	1.09	0.53	0.18	0.06

	COUNTRY BORN GROUP				
Residence Years	1 and 2 Years	3 and 4 Years	5 and 6 Years	7 and 8 Years	9, 10 and 11 Years
Number of Cases	9	9	11	7	4
Average Grade	4B.70	5B.75	6A.15	6B.54	6B.88
Retardation Years	2.15	1.13	0.43	0.23	0.06

Table 9—The Three Studies Combined (Lapidus, Yates, and Marks)

Residence Years	1 and 2 Years	3 and 4 Years	5 and 6 Years	7 and 8 Years	9 Years and Over	Northern Born
No. of Cases	150	125	136	112	157	1017
Average Score	72	76	84	90	94	92

(3) As the three studies* with the National Intelligence Test were made under the same conditions, the results were combined to show more clearly the extent of the environmental effect.

The improvement with length of residence is clear and definite. The excellent showing of the one-two-year group in Marks' study raises the level of that group considerably, but not above that of any of the succeeding year combinations. It will be noticed that the range of average scores is from 74 for the one-two-year group to 92 for the control group; this suggests that the I.Q. remains constant only when there is relative constancy in the environment.

(4) One study was made of 536 twelve-year-old girls, between February and May, 1931, by Isabel D. Traver, with the Otis self-administering examination, Intermediate form.

These results are not nearly so definite as those obtained in the National Intelligence Test studies. There is practically no difference between the one-two, three-four and five-six-year groups; it is only with the seven-eight-

[* The third study using the National Intelligence Test, which is not included in this selection, was conducted by Eli Marks on 561 twelve-year-old boys. The relationship between National Intelligence Test scores and length of residence was less clear in this study than in the two previously cited, but the results were in the expected direction. The evidence was clear, however, in indicating that as years of residence in the North increased, the amount of school grade retardation decreased. These results were interpreted as testifying to the superior environment of the North. However, the question was raised whether the more recent migrants might be inferior to the earlier arrivals. By conducting two studies with similar subjects one year apart, it was shown that no evidence existed to indicate that the more recent arrivals were inferior.—ED. NOTE.]

year group that any correspondence between test score and length of residence in New York becomes evident. Whether this is a function of the test or of accidents of sampling, it is impossible to say. In any case there is still a very marked difference between the earlier arrivals (six years or less) and the later ones (seven years or more), and this is clearly in favor of the latter. While the environmental effect does not appear very early in this study, it is still there. The northern born group is reliably superior to the one-two, three-four, and five-six-year groups; it is definitely, but not quite reliably, superior to the seven-eight-year group, and only slightly and unreliably superior to those of more than eight years' residence in New York. The northern group as a whole is also reliably superior to the southern born group as a whole. There was no difference between the girls born in the West Indies (30 cases) and those born elsewhere in the South (170), and only a slight superiority of those born in New York City over those born elsewhere in the North. In general it may be said that these results are corroborative of those found in the National Intelligence Test studies.

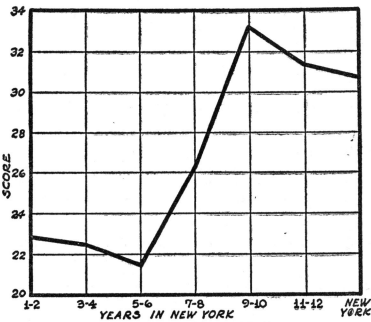

Graph 6. Otis Scores and Length of Residence.
Twelve-year-old Girls (Traver)

Table 10—Otis Scores and Length of Residence (Traver)

Residence Years	1 and 2 Years	3 and 4 Years	5 and 6 Years	7 and 8 Years	9 and 10 Years
No. of Cases	28	37	45	19	23
Average Score	22.8	22.5	21.5	26.2	33.1
Standard Deviation	12.6	9.6	10.6	13.7	13.7

Residence Years	11 Years and Over	New York Born	Total Southern Group
No. of Cases	18	243	170
Average Score	31.4	30.9	25.1
Standard Deviation	13.8	15.1	13.0

12. EFFECT OF INCOME CHANGES ON
THE RATE OF SAVING

by George Katona

THAT IN the short run changes in income influence consumption and saving has been dramatically emphasized by Keynes, who called the relationship between the two factors the fundamental psychological law and assigned to it a central place in his theoretical system.

The fundamental psychological law . . . is that men are disposed, as a rule and on the average, to increase their consumption as their income increases, but not by as much as the increase in their income. . . . A rising income will often be accompanied by increased saving, and a falling income by decreased saving, on a greater scale at first than subsequently.[1]

During the past twelve years most of the theoretical discussions of the problem concerned long-run effects of income changes which are not considered in this paper. The Keynesian thesis about the short-run relationship between changes in income and saving appears to have been accepted by most students.[2]

Empirical evidence for the validity of the short-run relationship may be sought, and was usually sought in the past, on the aggregative level, by comparing year-to-year changes in national income, aggregate consumption, and saving. The same relationship that prevails between aggregates may also be found, however, as expressly stated by Keynes, between changes in income and consumption of individual income receivers (or groups of income receivers). It is the latter problem that will be raised here: do recent studies of the financial behavior of families shed light on the relation between changes in income and changes in the amounts saved?

From the point of view of empirical studies of consumer behavior, the problem presents itself as follows: We consider three groups of families, A, B, and C; in Period 1 families A had a real income of $2000, B of $3000, and C of $4000; in the subsequent Period 2 all three have the same real income, namely, $3000. Then we ask: Will families A and families C change the amounts they save during Period 2? What will be the relation of such changes (more specifically of ΔS) to the changes in income (ΔY)? We may, however, also ask a second question, although that question has not been emphasized by Keynes: Will the three groups of families save the same amounts of money in Period 2? If not, how will their savings differ (more specifically, what will be the relation between S and ΔY)?

Reprinted by permission of the author and the publishers from *The Review of Economics and Statistics*, Vol. XXXI, 1949, pp. 95-103. Cambridge, Mass.: Harvard University Press, Copyright, 1949, by The President and Fellows of Harvard College.

The author has elaborated the contents of this article, and has added more recent data in support of the hypotheses printed in the article, in his book *Psychological Analysis of Economic Behavior*, McGraw-Hill Book Co., 1951.

Answers to both questions can be derived from the Keynesian thesis. The answer to the second question is: The amounts saved by the three groups will differ; A will save the most, C the least, and the amounts saved by B will occupy the middle position. This will be the case because those whose incomes increased will not increase their consumption proportionately and will therefore save the largest amounts; those whose income decreased will not decrease their consumption proportionately, and will therefore save the smallest amounts.

In the Surveys of Consumer Finances, conducted by the Survey Research Center of the University of Michigan for the Board of Governors of the Federal Reserve System,[3] from which the data presented in this article are taken, it was possible to obtain information relevant to the second but not to the first question.[4] Even with respect to the second question, the relationship was not tested in the general terms just stated. First of all, information is available for two years only, for 1946 and 1947. In using data obtained from the 1947 survey, the year 1945 was substituted for Period 1 and the year 1946 for Period 2, and in using data obtained in the 1948 survey, the year 1946 for Period 1 and the year 1947 for Period 2. Secondly, income within 1000-dollar brackets was substituted for the "$3000 income" in the previous statement. Finally, money income was used instead of real income; but two different rates of income increases were considered, one of which is undoubtedly larger than the increase in the price level from 1945 to 1946 or from 1946 to 1947.

The consumer units were divided into groups according to the changes in their income (see Table 1). Those whose money income in two consecutive years differed by less than 5 per cent were placed in one group which was considered as consisting of people with "no change in income." Those whose income declined in the second year by 5 per cent or more were considered as having suffered an income decrease. It was not possible to divide that group according to the size of the decrease because the subgroups would have consisted of such a small number of units that the results would have been unreliable. The number of units whose income increased from 1945 to 1946 and from 1946 to 1947 was, however, considerably larger than the number of those whose income declined. Therefore, it was possible to analyze two groups separately, one consisting of units with an income increase of at least 5 and at the most 24 per cent, and one consisting of units with an income increase of 25 per cent or more. Since the general price level undoubtedly did not increase by as much as 25 per cent in either of the two years, the latter group consists of units who had an increase in real income. From the point of view of changes in real income, therefore, the headings of Table 1 may be re-written as follows: (1) units with a large decline in real income (those with a decline in money income); (2) units with a small decline in real income (those with unchanged money income); (3) units with small changes in real income (those with a 5 to 25 per cent increase in money income); and (4) units with an increase in real income (those with an at least 25 per cent increase in money income).

Table 1 shows the percentage of consumer units who were dissavers (spent more than their income), who were zero savers (whose expenditures equaled their income), and who were small or large savers (saved less or more than 20 per cent of their income). Saving was measured by determining the "additions to savings" and the "withdrawals from savings" for a representative sample of consumer units. It is defined as the difference between income and expenditures. Purchase of a house is considered as saving, purchase of consumer durable goods as expenditures (see Note to Table 1).

In comparing the four groups with different income changes, considerable and consistent differences are found in the frequency of dissavers. First, with respect to the behavior of units whose money income declined, the results appear to be in accordance with what one would expect on the basis of the Keynesian principle. In both years and in each income group, more of those whose income declined dissaved than of those whose income remained stable. Although the two groups do not differ greatly with respect to the frequency of large savers, inspection of the table makes it clear that on the average people whose money income declined spent a larger proportion of their income than people whose money income did not change or increased to a small extent.

The smallest proportion of dissavers is found among people in the two middle groups. When the saving performance of those with an income increase of 25 per cent or more is considered, a relationship becomes apparent which is the reverse of that derived previously from theoretical considerations. People with an increase in real income, instead of saving most, dissaved frequently in 1946 as well as in 1947. Dissavers were much more frequent among consumer units with a large income increase than among units with stable income; and in some cases, as frequent as or more frequent than among units with an income decline. The differences between the proportions of dissavers among spending units with an income decrease and with an income increase of 25 per cent or more are not statistically significant.

When the proportion of dissavers in a given group is relatively large, the proportion of savers is usually small. But the proportion of large savers —those who save 20 per cent or more of their income—need not be small (because, in a given group, there may be relatively many dissavers, few small savers, and many large savers). Although in this respect the results are not clear in every one of the income groups, it appears that in 1946 and 1947 large income increases were associated both with frequent dissaving and frequent high rates of saving.

It is possible that income changes influence the saving behavior in different ways at different income levels. For instance, will the response to an income increase from $2000 to $3000 differ from the response to an income increase from $20,000 to $30,000? The survey data available at present do not permit us to answer that question.

A specific finding, obtained in one or two empirical investigations, cannot be used to confirm or to refute theoretical assumptions. But such a finding may well be utilized to reformulate the assumptions so as to make them more productive in future research. The statement on the effect of income changes on savings which formed the starting point of this paper has the disadvantage that it is an all-or-nothing proposition. Empirical research is better served by a hypothesis of the following type: under conditions A_1 behavior a_1 is most probable; under conditions A_2 behavior a_2

Table 1—Relation of Past Income Changes to Proportion of Income Saved (Percentage Distribution of Spending Units in Each Group)

Rate of Saving in 1946 or 1947	1947 SURVEY OF CONSUMER FINANCES. INCOME CHANGE FROM 1945 TO 1946				1948 SURVEY OF CONSUMER FINANCES. INCOME CHANGE FROM 1945 TO 1946			
	De-crease (—5% or more)	No Change (+5% to —5%)	In-crease (5% to 25%)	In-crease (25% or more)	De-crease (—5% or more)	No Change (+5% to —5%)	In-crease (5% to 25%)	In-crease (25% or more)
I. Units with Income between $1000-1999								
Negative	40	22	21	36	34	28	23	40
Zero	7	17	7	4	9	14	9	7
Positive, 1 to 19% of income	38	39	47	40	45	46	52	37
Positive, 20% or more of income	15	22	25	20	12	12	16	16
	100	100	100	100	100	100	100	100
II. Units with Income between $2000-2999								
Negative	41	26	23	45	38	26	27	32
Zero	2	2	3	4	4	7	4	1
Positive, 1 to 19% of income	38	49	52	27	41	52	51	39
Positive, 20% or more of income	19	23	22	24	17	15	18	28
	100	100	100	100	100	100	100	100
III. Units with Income between $3000-4999								
Negative	21	10	16	21	33	29	29	31
Zero	*	2	1	*	1	*	2	1
Positive, 1 to 19% of income	55	60	59	41	41	48	51	45
Positive, 20% or more of income	24	28	24	38	25	23	18	23
	100	100	100	100	100	100	100	100

* Less than 0.5 per cent.

NOTE: The data are taken from the 1947 and 1948 Surveys of Consumer Finances, each of which was based on a representative sample of consumers in Continental United States living in private households. The consumers were grouped in spending units, defined as all related persons living in the same dwelling who pool their incomes for their major expenditures. There are about 15 per cent more spending units than families because some families consist of two or more spending units.

The amounts saved, or dissaved, were determined by tabulating the answers to 73 questions. For the list of positive and negative items included, see Federal Reserve Bulletin, August 1948, pp. 928 ff. The most important difference between the definition of saving as used in the Surveys and that of "personal saving" as used by the Commerce Department (computed as the difference between aggregate personal income and consumer expenditures) is that the latter does and the former does not include depreciation on farms and non-farm homes. According to both concepts, purchases of consumer durable goods are included among expenditures and not savings.

Spending units whose "withdrawals from saving" (reduction in liquid assets, amounts borrowed, etc.) exceeded their "additions to saving" were classified as dissavers; those whose "additions to saving" exceeded their "withdrawals from saving" as positive savers. It follows that dissavers are those units whose expenditures exceeded their income; and positive savers are those units whose income exceeded their expenditures. The term "income" refers to total annual money income before taxes.

The behavior of the middle income group, those with incomes between $1000 and $5000, who represented over 70 per cent of all units in both years, is shown. The sample surveys did not yield a sufficient number of cases in the lower and upper income brackets to permit reliable calculations of the saving performance of high- and low-income units with different income changes. Study of high-income units would be particularly interesting because of the possibility that their saving behavior is less influenced by income changes than that of other units.

etc. In this way it is not assumed in advance that the behavior will be identical under all circumstances; for instance, irrespective of the extent of income changes, of the new income level, of the age of the families, or at different phases of the business cycle. The nature of circumstances that produce different or even abnormal forms of behavior can then be studied.

A reformulation of the original hypothesis so as to make it more fruitful for empirical studies also appears necessary because of psychological considerations. It may suffice to say here briefly that in the light of psychological findings it is not to be expected that the effects of "reward" and "punishment" will be just the reverse of each other. Discarding an established habit may, for instance, be relatively easy if conditions become more favorable, while there may be a stronger tendency to maintain habits if conditions become less favorable. The Keynesian formulation, according to which increases and decreases in income are treated similarly (though with different signs), cannot be presumed to be correct a priori.

On the basis of psychological considerations and of certain empirical evidence taken from detailed interviews, two contradictory hypotheses may be formulated.

(1) The inertia hypothesis. We tend to do what we have done before under similar circumstances. If conditions change, our habits may change too, though slowly. Therefore, for a while consumers will tend to maintain their previous habits and standards of expenditures when their incomes change. The older the established habit of expenditure and the smaller the income change, the stronger will be that tendency.[5]

(2) Consumers in general have many unsatisfied needs. They need and desire automobiles, household appliances, furniture, medical care, entertainment, etc. beyond the quantities with which they provide themselves. When their incomes increase, they become aware of the possibility of satisfying some of their needs and desires. Thus, in the short run, an increase in income may lead to large, unusual expenditures. The larger the income increase the more probable is it that this will be the case even at the expense of saving.[6]

The first hypothesis applies both to increases and decreases in income, the second, however, only to increases. Both hypotheses are incomplete because they do not specify the conditions under which the postulated behavior is likely to occur. In just that sense they may be called fruitful because they point the way for empirical research intended to clarify those conditions.

Since, according to Table 1, large income gains and negative rates of saving frequently occurred together, it seems that in 1946 and 1947 some families behaved in a way corresponding to the second hypothesis. Many of these families were young (heads less than 35 years of age) and were war veterans.[7] Before raising the question as to whether the behavior found in 1946 and 1947 was caused by deferred wartime demand or even by special needs of veterans that arose immediately or shortly after their discharge, a more general problem will be taken up: under what conditions did the various kinds of saving behavior occur?

In formulating the original hypothesis, and also in Table 1, an assumption was made which requires further study in the light of psychological considerations. All increases and decreases in income were considered jointly as if they had only one possible meaning. From the point of view of objective changes in the situation, an income increase from $2000 to $3000, for instance, experienced by family A is, of course, the same as an increase from $2000 to $3000 experienced by family B. It is, however, not the objective impact (the stimulus) that determines the behavior (the response), but how the objective impact is understood by the person who responds. The "meaning" of the stimulus is determined by the greater whole of which the stimulus forms a part. This greater whole includes past experiences and expectations or, to put it differently, the frame of reference and the attitudes of the person.[8]

As a first approximation to the analysis of the frame of reference within which income changes were perceived in 1946, two aspects of the "greater whole" will be singled out for study: the question of the subjectively temporary or permanent nature of income changes and the role of income changes at the phase of the business cycle which most (or many) people assumed to prevail at the given time.

The rationale of the first investigation may be presented as follows: An income increase from $2000 in 1945 to $3000 in 1946, as represented by the solid line in Chart 1, may have different meanings according to the

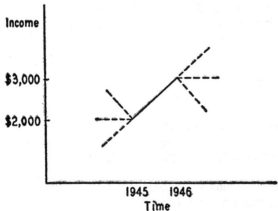

Chart 1. Schematic Presentation of Different "Meanings" of the "Same" Income Change (Income Increase from $2,000 in 1945 to $3,000 in 1946)

income developments before 1945 and the expected developments after 1946. Assume, for instance, that a person had a still lower income before 1945 and expected to have a still higher one after 1946; in that case he may have seen his income increase in 1946 as a part of a steady advance toward higher levels. If, however, the income of a person had dropped to the 1945 level and, after an advance from 1945 to 1946, was expected to drop again, that advance may have appeared to him as a temporary interruption in a downward income trend. Many further "meanings" of the same income increase may be derived from the schematic chart presented and, similarly, varied conditions may prevail with respect to income declines.

Changes in income before 1945 are not considered in this paper, because in the 1947 Survey of Consumer Finances it was not deemed possible to investigate income changes that had occurred before 1945. On the basis of preliminary studies it was thought that inquiries referring to the distant past would be subject to great memory errors.[9]

The effect of income expectations on the rate of saving was, however, studied. The results of these studies are shown in Table 2, in which the joint effects of past and expected income changes are considered. The term "past income change" refers again to the change from one calendar year to the next year in which the saving performance was measured. Expected income changes refer to changes expected to occur from the calendar year in which saving was measured to the next year.

Although the information presented in Table 2 must be called tentative because it is derived from a joint consideration of all consumer units in the middle income ranges and is nevertheless based on relatively few cases, the following conclusions appear to be warranted:

(1) Income expectations have an effect on the saving performance. If those with past income declines are divided into three groups according to their income expectations, differences are found in the saving data; similarly, if those with past income stability or past income increases are divided into three groups, the savings of the three groups are not the same; and these findings were made for both 1946 and 1947. As to the direction of the differences, it can be stated that there were more dissavers among those who expected income increases than among those who expected income decreases (in both years), and more high savers among those who expected income decreases than among those who expected income increases (in 1947).

(2) The largest proportion of dissavers is found (in both years) among those with a past income decrease and an expected income increase. In other words, an income decline that is believed to be temporary was frequently associated with spending more than one's income.

(3) The smallest number of dissavers is found (in both years) among those whose income did not change and was not expected to change. Income stability was not associated frequently with spending more than one's income.

The low rate of saving of people with temporary income declines and, more generally, the apparent effect of optimistic income expectations on reducing the rate of saving, must be understood within the framework of the economic situation as it appeared to most people in 1946 and 1947. It was found in the surveys that income increases were much more frequent than income decreases in both years. Therefore, many of those whose income declined may have felt that their personal financial situation developed contrary to the general trend. Furthermore, most people thought (a) that 1946 as well as 1947 were good, prosperous years and also (b) that good times would continue. Expectation of income increases was, then, usually thought to be in accordance with the general trend of the economy. Whether under different conditions, for instance at a different phase of the business cycle, income increases or optimistic income expectations would have had different effects on people's spending and saving decisions cannot be determined at present.

In analyzing the saving performance, the units who dissaved and who saved were considered separately. The greatest difference in effects of the various forms of income changes occurred in the frequency of dissaving. The relationship between that frequency and large income gains calls for further analysis (while the relation between dissaving and income declines will not be considered further). Therefore, the forms of dissaving will be studied and the question raised whether there is an aspect of dissaving which is specifically related to increase in income.

Table 2—Relation of Past and Expected Income Changes to Proportion of Income Saved (Percentage Distribution of Spending Units with $1000 to $3999 Income in Each Group)

I. 1948 SURVEY OF CONSUMER FINANCES

Rate of Saving in 1947	1947 INCOME SMALLER THAN 1946 INCOME 1948 income expected to be smaller*	same	larger	1947 INCOME SAME AS 1946 INCOME 1948 income expected to be smaller*	same	larger	1947 INCOME LARGER THAN 1946 INCOME 1948 income expected to be smaller*	same	larger
Negative	33	32	44	32	23	36	30	28	32
Zero	7	3	6	7	17	7	3	2	6
Positive, 1 to 19% of income	39	44	37	40	50	46	43	53	45
Positive, 20% or more of income	21	21	13	21	10	11	24	17	17
	100	100	100	100	100	100	100	100	100

II. 1947 SURVEY OF CONSUMER FINANCES

Rate of Saving in 1946	1946 INCOME SMALLER THAN 1945 INCOME 1947 income expected to be smaller*	same	larger	1946 INCOME SAME AS 1945 INCOME 1947 income expected to be smaller	same	larger*	1946 INCOME LARGER THAN 1945 INCOME 1947 income expected to be smaller*	same	larger
Negative	32	26	44	**	18	32	28	26	31
Zero	4	2	2		9	6	4	4	2
Positive, 1 to 19% of income	44	51	35		47	37	42	45	43
Positive, 20% or more of income	20	21	19		26	25	26	25	24
	100	100	100		100	100	100	100	100

NOTE: The data are taken from the 1947 and 1948 Surveys of Consumer Finances. In a small sample survey, subgroups may become too small to permit measurement of group performance. When the spending units interviewed in the Surveys were divided according to (a) past income changes and (b) expected income changes, groups of such small sizes resulted that their further division by (c) income level and (d) rate of income change became impossible. Therefore in Table 2, in contrast to Table 1, those with large and small income increases are not separated and all units in the middle income brackets are considered together.

The subgroups presented in the 17 columns of Table 2 consist of interviews with 80 to 450 spending units. Six groups consisting of only 80 to 150 cases are marked with an asterisk to indicate that those data are less reliable than the data in the other columns. Two asterisks indicate a group which consisted of so few cases that saving data could not be computed for it.

Because of the small number of cases involved, many of the differences between two groups are not statistically significant at the 95 per cent probability level. The conclusions derived from the table represent probable tendencies and not proven facts. They are reinforced, however, by the similarity of differences found in two consecutive surveys.

"Same" refers to less than 5 per cent change in income, "larger" to increases beyond, and "smaller" to decreases under 5 per cent.

Income expectations were determined at the end of the year. The heads of the consumer units were asked whether they expected their income in 1948 (or 1947) to be larger, the same, or smaller than their 1947 (1946) income.

Dissaving may occur because of illness, accidents, or other emergencies which necessitate large, unusual expenditures. It may occur, further, because of unemployment or retirement. Both aspects may be ruled out in the present connection because they would hardly represent factors leading to or arising from gains in income. But dissaving may also occur because of large expenditures for consumer durable goods. The purchase of automobiles, furniture, refrigerators, and other household implements was frequently financed through borrowing or drawing on previously accumulated liquid assets. The proportion of families who purchased durable goods in 1946 and 1947, and especially the proportion of those who spent large amounts on durable goods, was much higher among the dissavers than among the positive savers. It is then conceivable that the purchase of durable goods was related to income gains.

In four consecutive nationwide surveys, which were independent of each other, the finding was obtained that more consumer units whose income had increased purchased durable goods than units with stable or declining income (Table 3, part I). Further, more units who expected income increases purchased such goods than units who did not expect income gains (Table 3, part II). These differences were found consistently in the various income groups, among people in the lower and middle brackets as well as among people in the higher brackets who bought durable goods most frequently.

Consumer optimism was also measured by separating people who expected prosperous times to continue from those who anticipated a business recession. Again, there were more purchasers of durable goods among the former than among the latter. Finally, planned purchases of durable goods were related to consumers' general economic outlook and their income expectations. It was found, in 1947 as well as in 1948, that those who expected income increases or good times to come planned to spend larger amounts on durable goods than those who were uncertain or pessimistic about the future course of their income or of the general economy.[10]

These findings shed some light on the decision formation by consumers.

Table 3—Relation of Income Changes to Purchases of Consumer Durable Goods
(Percentage Distribution of Spending Units in Each Group)

I. PAST INCOME CHANGES
(Income in period in which durable goods were purchased
compared to income in preceding year)

	DIRECTION OF PAST INCOME CHANGES		
	Decrease	*No Change*	*Increase*
Bought automobiles in first half of 1948*	7	9	13
Did not buy	93	91	87
Bought other durable goods in first half of 1948*	20	20	29
Did not buy	80	80	71
Bought automobiles and other durable goods in 1947†	40	35	48
Did not buy	60	65	52
Bought automobiles and other durable goods in first half of 1947‡	27	28	38
Did not buy	73	72	62
Bought automobiles in 1946 §	9	7	14
Did not buy	91	93	86
Bought other durable goods in 1946 §	27	23	32
Did not buy	73	77	68

II. EXPECTED INCOME CHANGES
(Income expected in next year compared to income in
year in which durable goods were purchased)

	DIRECTION OF EXPECTED INCOME CHANGES		
	Decrease	*No Change*	*Increase*
Bought automobiles and other durable goods in 1947†	40	40	51
Did not buy	60	60	49

* Data from a survey conducted in July 1948.
† Data from the 1948 Survey of Consumer Finances.
‡ Data from a small survey conducted in July 1947.
§ Data from the 1947 Survey of Consumer Finances.
NOTE: In further tabulations, the amounts of expenditures for durable goods were also taken into account. It was then found that more consumers whose income increased or who expected income increases spent large amounts on durable goods than consumers whose income declined or who expected income declines. When durable goods expenditures of less than $200 were considered, no differences were found between the various groups.

Need and desire for durable goods, which probably prevail at present in the United States among all groups of people irrespective of their financial situation and their attitudes, cannot be transformed into effective demand except if certain "enabling conditions" are present. But even if family income is sufficient, or the family has liquid assets, or is able to borrow (and the desired goods are available), the purchase will be made only under certain conditions and not under others. Income increase, past as well as expected increase, appears to be one of those conditions or one of the incentives for freer use of discretionary purchasing power. To be sure, it is not the only condition. Millions of consumers who suffered income declines and were pessimistic about their future did buy durable goods in 1946 and 1947 as shown in Table 3. Some of them, possibly, had to buy a car to reach their place of work, and others might have been influenced by persuasion or considerations of prestige. The analysis of consumer motivation is still in its very beginning. But income gains and optimism, even though they are only some of the factors helping to transform need into effective demand,[11] deserve special attention. Should the findings made during the last few years be confirmed in the future, especially under different economic conditions, such as a period in which depression is generally anticipated or low business activity prevails, they would serve to clarify the role of consumers in influencing business cycle fluctuations.

With respect to the developments in 1946 and 1947, the findings on the relationship between the frequency of durable goods purchased and income gains help to explain the frequency of dissaving among people who either experienced or expected an income increase. Furthermore, they tend to cast doubt on the assumption that the relatively high frequency of dissaving in 1946 and 1947 was caused exclusively by a unique factor, the wartime deferred demand. The latter assumption would be correct only if it were true that people who experienced (or expected) income increases after the end of the war had greater deferred demand than other people. Finally, the relatively large proportion of young people among the dissavers can now be explained: demand for durable goods is much more frequent among younger than among older people.

The findings discussed in this article will be summarized in the form of three hypotheses formulated in a tentative way. They are presented here not because they are known to be valid but because they can guide further research. They are formulated in terms of the short-run relation of income changes to saving, although psychologically it is consumer expenditures— for durable goods as well as for many other goods and services that have not been considered in this paper—which are probably influenced by the income changes.

Hypothesis 1. A decline in income will tend to lead to a reduction in the amounts saved or to a change from saving to dissaving. This will be the case particularly if those whose income declined are optimistic (consider the decline in their income temporary).

Hypothesis 2. An increase in income, and especially a large increase, may result in a reduction of the amounts saved or even in a change from saving to dissaving. In place of a smooth adjustment to the new income level, such behavior may occur especially if people believe that their financial situation improved permanently or if they anticipate further income increases.

Hypothesis 3. Expected income declines will tend to increase the amounts saved, irrespective of past income changes.

These hypotheses have the advantage of linking the analysis of the consumption function with business cycle theory. This means, however, that they must be tested at different phases of the cycle, so that the conditions under which they are valid may be determined.

13. "FRIENDS AND NEIGHBORS"—THE APPEAL OF LOCALISM IN VOTING BEHAVIOR

by V. O. Key

[In his book *Southern Politics,* Key has analyzed the structure of political parties in southern states, and has examined the factors influencing voting behavior. In the selection which follows, the author demonstrates the manner in which he employs ecological voting data to examine the influence of localism on electoral behavior in Alabama.—ED. NOTE.]

A POWERFUL LOCALISM provides an important ingredient of Alabama factionalism. Candidates for state office tend to poll overwhelming majorities in their home counties and to draw heavy support in adjacent counties. Such voting behavior may be rationalized as a calculated promotion of local interest, yet it also points to the absence of stable, well-organized, statewide factions of like-minded citizens formed to advocate measures of common concern. In its extreme form localism justifies a diagnosis of low voter-interest in public issues and a susceptibility to control by the irrelevant appeal to support the home-town boy. In some instances, of course, localism may reflect concern about some general state issue bearing on the area.

If the factions within the Democratic party of Alabama amounted to political parties, a candidate's strength in the vote from county to county would not be influenced appreciably by his place of residence. A well-knit group of voters and leaders scattered over the entire state would deliver about the same proportion of the vote to its candidate wherever he happened to live. A concern for issues (or at least for group success) would override local attachments. In well-developed two-party situations localism is minimized, if not erased, by a larger concern for party victory. The classic case is that of Duchess County, New York, the home of Franklin D. Roosevelt, a Democrat of some note. The county, traditionally Republican, stub-

Reprinted from *Southern Politics in State and Nation,* pp. 37-41, by permission of the author and of Alfred A. Knopf, Inc. (Copyright, 1949, by Alfred A. Knopf, Inc.)

bornly held to its partisan attachments and repeatedly failed to return a majority for even its most distinguished son. Radically different voting

Table 1—Friends and Neighbors: Home-County Strength of Candidates for Democratic Nomination in Alabama's Eighth Congressional District, September 24, 1946

Candidate	His Home County	Per Cent of Home County Vote for Local Boy	Per Cent of District Vote for Him	Per Cent of County Vote to Outsider with Highest Vote
Johnson	Limestone	65.1	15.0	22.0
Jones	Jackson	97.5	22.7	0.9
Meadows	Morgan	47.4	8.5	24.7
Pounders	Lauderdale	40.2	4.5	28.7
Smith, Jeff	Madison	70.1	17.8	14.4
Smith, Jim	Colbert	62.1	19.5	2.9
Twitty	Colbert	30.1	12.0	2.9

behavior characterizes battles within the Alabama Democratic primaries. A candidate for governor normally carries his own county by a huge majority, and the harshest criticism that can be made of a politician is that he cannot win in his own beat or precinct. If his friends and neighbors who know him do not support him, why should those without this advantage trust a candidate?

A special primary held in Alabama's eighth congressional district in September, 1946, provides an extreme illustration of the friends-and-neighbors effect. Each of six of the district's seven counties was represented by at least one candidate for the nomination. Each home-town candidate led the polling in his own bailiwick in the first primary. In one county the local candidate was credited with 97.5 per cent of the vote. The other counties manifested less of an urge toward unanimity but in every instance outsiders fared poorly against the local candidate. The details are set out in Table 1. In this district it is plain that no dual system of district-wide factions existed. The controlling factors in voting were local pride and patriotism, reinforced perhaps by county machines and by the candidates' personal followings.

The same type of localism appears in state contests. In a sense the battle of state politics is not a battle between large party factions. It is rather a struggle of individuals—perhaps with the support of their county organizations—to build a state-wide following on the foundation of local support. This localism appears most clearly in the so-called "first primary," which is a contest to determine the two strongest contenders who "run off" the race for the nomination in the second primary. In these first races, usually involving a multiplicity of candidates, the fluidity of factions shows itself most sharply. In the second primary, limited to two candidates, voters are compelled to divide into two camps and the underlying localism becomes blurred.

The pattern of localism emerges vividly in the pair of maps in Figure 1, which identify the counties of peak strength of "Big Jim" Folsom and Judge Elbert Boozer in the first gubernatorial primary of 1946. "Big Jim's" strength clustered around two counties: Coffee and Cullman. Born in southeastern Alabama in Coffee County, he spent his young manhood there and married the daughter of the probate judge, a functionary of great political importance in Alabama. In later life he lived in Cullman County, in northern Alabama, and in traveling the surrounding counties as an insurance salesman built up a wide acquaintance. In the 1946 primary, he polled 72 per cent of the popular vote of Cullman County, a remarkable tribute by his fellow citizens. In the surrounding counties his strength tapered down, and in the state as a whole he drew only 28.5 per cent of the vote.[1]

The second map in Figure 1 delineates geographically the popular strength of Judge Elbert Boozer, a self-made man of wealth who, having become probate judge of Calhoun County, aspired to the governorship. In the state he polled only 15.9 per cent of the total vote, running fourth in a field of five candidates. In his own county and a couple of adjacent counties, he managed to attract more than 50 per cent of the vote, and his highest popular strength appeared mainly in counties clustered about his home bailiwick.

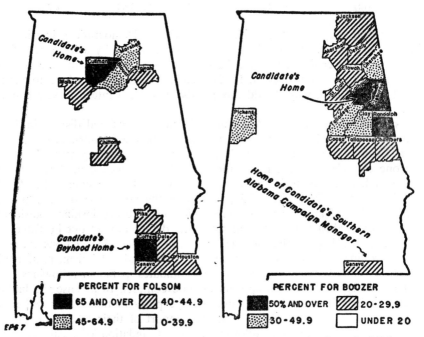

Figure 1. Friends and Neighbors: Areas of Concentration of Popular Strength of Folsom and Boozer in First Alabama Gubernatorial Primary, 1946

An endless number of illustrations of the friends-and-neighbors effect could be presented. Another pair of examples is mapped in Figure 2. In keeping with an Alabama custom, Chauncey Sparks in 1938 ran for governor presumably with the hope that he might make enough of a showing to try again in 1942 and win. The good people of Barbour County gave their fellow-citizen Sparks 84.7 per cent of the vote, a truly heroic performance when viewed against the 23.7 per cent of the vote he received in the state as a whole. R. J. Goode, another candidate at the 1938 primary, attracted 71.6 per cent of the vote of his home county and only 22.4 per cent of the state vote.

Not every candidate for state-wide office profits from a heavy friends-and-neighbors vote, but nearly always such a following constitutes a nucleus around which an aspirant for a state-wide office attempts to build a faction. The voters of the larger cities apparently do not have the same sense of loyalty toward a local candidate as do those who dwell in small towns and in the rural areas. The frequency of the friends-and-neighbors pattern points to the personal factor in the transient factions of southern state politics. At times it also points to control of a local machine or perhaps to incapacity of election officials to restrain from slanting their arithmetic for the benefit of the home-town boy. More important than all these factors, the friends-and-neighbors pattern reflects the absence of well-organized competing factions with stable and state-wide followings among the voters. Almost any local leader with any prospects at all who aspires for state office can cut into the strength of established state leaders or factions within his own immediate bailiwick. He gains support, not primarily for what he stands for

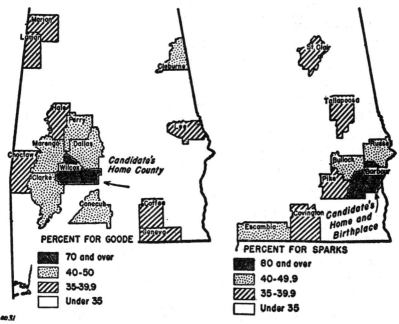

Figure 2. Friends and Neighbors: Areas of Concentration of Popular Strength of Sparks and Goode in Alabama Gubernatorial Primary of May 3, 1938

or because of his capacities, but because of where he lives. A more or less totally irrelevant appeal—back the home-town boy—can exert no little influence over an electorate not habituated to the types of voting behavior characteristic of a two-party situation.

Auxiliary Readings

A. THE GENERAL IDEA OF MULTIVARIATE ANALYSIS

C. I. Lewis and C. H. Langford, *Symbolic Logic* (New York: Dover Publications, Inc.), Chapters I-IV.

> Gives an elementary introduction to the calculus of classes, as developed by modern logic. Includes an historical introduction to Boolean algebra which helps in understanding its revelance for the problems of this section.

G. Yule and M. G. Kendall, *Introduction to the Theory of Statistics* (14th ed.; New York: Hofner Co., 1950), Chapters I-V.

> Is still the classical presentation of attribute statistics. The matters treated there were not developed further because for a long time statisticians were mainly interested in quantitative variables. Modern social research has again directed attention to the early chapters of this text.

W. J. Goode and P. K. Hatt, "Some Problems in Qualitative and Case Analysis," *Methods in Social Research* (New York: McGraw-Hill Book Co., Inc., 1952), Chapter XIX.

> Gives leads to the use of IBM procedures so that the student can go on from there to a more systematic study. Should be accompanied by laboratory work on IBM machines. The chapter also gives several examples of the principles discussed in Selection (1) of this section.

Hans Zeisel, "Tools of Causal Analysis," *Say It With Figures* (New York: Harper & Bros., 1947), Chapters 8-9.

> Gives numerous concrete examples organized in terms of the general scheme developed in Selection (1).

B. SPECIAL ASPECTS OF MULTIVARIATE ANALYSIS

S. Asch, "Values and Limitations of Sociological Data," in *Social Psychology* (New York: Prentice Hall Co., 1952), pp. 531 ff.

> A critical discussion of multivariate analysis; the lack of psychological insights is deplored. Raises the important problem of the relation between "psychological mechanisms" and the "survey approach" in social research.

H. A. Weeks, "Male and Female Broken Home Rates by Types of Delinquency," *American Sociological Review*, Vol. 5, 1940, pp. 601-609.

> Previous studies have shown that young female delinquents are much more likely to come from broken homes than young male delinquents. This was usually explained in terms of the greater importance of the home for girls. The present paper shows that if type of delinquency is introduced as a third factor, the matter becomes considerably clarified. Males commit more property violations, while females are more frequently turned over to the courts because of immorality, ungovernability, etc. The latter violations occur more often in broken homes for both male and female. In other words, the relation between types of homes and sex of delinquents is accounted for by the type of violations which, on the one hand, are more likely to generate in broken homes, and, on the other hand, are more likely to be committed by girls.

G. Belknap and A. Campbell, "Political Party Identification and Foreign Policy," *Public Opinion Quarterly*, Vol. XV, 1951-52, pp. 601-623.

> Raises the question of how one may analyze, in a cross-sectional survey, the extent to which people's attitude to foreign affairs contributes to, or derives from, their party affiliations.

H. H. Hyman and P. B. Sheatsley, "Some Reasons Why Information Campaigns Fail," *Public Opinion Quarterly*, Vol. XI, 1947, pp. 412-423.

> Like Selection (2) of this section, it shows various ways in which the effect of exposure to propaganda can be isolated through multivariate analysis.

C. DEVIANT CASE ANALYSIS

H. Gosnell, *Getting Out the Vote* (Chicago: University of Chicago Press, 1927), Chapter 10.

An experimental study showing that letters to prospective voters increase registration. Chapter 10 discusses districts in which the letters were not successful.

E. W. Burgess and L. S. Cottrell, *Predicting Success or Failure in Marriage* (New York: Prentice-Hall, 1939), pp. 300-310.

Although a relatively high correlation was found between the adjustment score and the prediction score, it was considered necessary to analyze those cases in which disparity in scores appeared. Case studies revealed that the observed differences could be accounted for by personality and unique biographical factors which the predictive items had reflected inadequately.

C. Friedrich, "The Agricultural Basis of Emotional Nationalism," *Public Opinion Quarterly*, Vol. I, No. 2, 1937, pp. 51-61.

In 1929, a referendum was held in Germany on the Young Plan. The nationalistic opposition was highly correlated with the proportion of farmers in all districts under investigation. Exceptions, however, were found which are partly explained in terms of historical circumstances, and partly in terms of specific influences like the role of the Catholic church.

D. THE TESTING AND VERIFICATION OF HYPOTHESES

E. Durkheim, "Suicide and Cosmic Factors," *Suicide* (Glencoe, Ill.: The Free Press, 1951), Book I, Chapter III.

A variety of geographical factors, such as climate and change in temperature, are considered as possible causes of suicide. The authors who make these imputations are criticized. The available data are marshalled in an effort to show that "social causes" are the real determinants of suicide.

O. D. Duncan, "Is the Intelligence of the General Population Declining?" *American Sociological Review*, Vol. 17, 1952, pp. 401-407.

Examines the thesis of a competent geneticist that the average intelligence quotient of the English and American people is declining in each generation due to the inverse relationship between size of family and IQ scores. The author calls into question the research instruments employed and certain assumptions underlying the argument, concluding with the presentation of empirical data which tends to disconfirm the hypothesis.

E. Pessen, "Did Labor Support Jackson?: The Boston Story," *Political Science Quarterly*, Vol. 64, 1949, pp. 262-174; and R. T. Bower, "Note on 'Did Labor Support Jackson?: The Boston Story'," *Political Science Quarterly*, Vol. 65, 1950, pp. 441-444.

Data were collected in Boston classifying wards as to their economic level and the number of votes they gave to the Jacksonian candidates at various elections around 1830. In no wards did the Jacksonians have the majority, but their relative strength correlated highly with economic level. The controversy between the two authors centers around these two findings and their proper interpretation.

H. M. Case, "Two Kinds of Crystallized Occupational Choice Behavior," *American Sociological Review*, Vol. 19, 1954, p. 85.

In previous studies of occupational choices stress was laid upon the distinction between "true" and "pseudo" plans. Here, criteria are developed to distinguish the two types. Adolescents in the two groups actually differ in the direction which previous speculations had anticipated.

S. C. Dodd, "Can the Social Scientist Serve Two Masters?" *Research Studies of the State College of Washington*, Vol. XXI, No. 3, 1953.

Shows that studies undertaken to solve practical problems may at the same time test basic scientific hypotheses. Examples drawn from concrete investigations are presented.

SECTION *III*

The Analysis of Change
Through Time

Introduction

In the world of the social scientist, change is important from three points of view. As an active human being he thinks of a desirable future society and would like to know how to bring it about. As a reflecting intellectual, he would like to know how society has come to be what it is now. As a scientist, he is interested in the study of change as a means of discovering causal interrelations and lawful regularities. The study of social change can be sketched on a broad canvas; transitions from one historical phase to the next, general principles of stability, changes in the relations between economic and cultural factors can be made the objects of inquiry. But one can also approach the problem of change on a microscopic level. How do people make up their minds on a particular subject, how are saving and employment related, how has a specific piece of legislation been passed—these, too, can be made the objects of empirical investigation.

The present section restricts itself to the narrower approach. This does not imply that inquiries dealing with general dynamic principles or covering broad spans of time do not have their own methodology; it just has not been clarified to the point where it can be systematically transmitted. This Reader is restricted to areas where some degree of methodological codification has already been achieved. In terms of this criterion, three groups of studies seem eligible for inclusion: trend, panel, and prediction studies. They will be briefly described as our selections of characteristic examples are explained.

A. *Trend studies*. In these studies the investigator follows a small number of variables through time and interprets their relationships. Our first two selections are typical examples, differing mainly in the kind of characteristics under investigation. Dorothy Thomas, in Selection (1), deals with an economic and a demographic variable— harvest and migration. Her study is remarkable because of the very clear-cut result to which her careful analysis leads. Hamilton, in Selection (2), relates an economic to a cultural factor. He studies how the content of sermons changes during periods of prosperity and depression. His study is an example of what many social scientists would consider a wave of the future, for he shows the connection between an economic and a "symbolic" variable.

The next two selections are of a somewhat different nature. Here one variable is of a qualitative character. In Selection (3), Cantwell deals with the public discussion of Roosevelt's proposal to change the composition of the Supreme Court. He interrelates various phases of the activities of Congress with available repeated public opinion polls. In Selection (4), Stouffer relates newspaper circulation to changes in living habits and, particularly, to the appearance of radio on the American scene. Stouffer's study is remarkable in that he starts not with the data but with a set of systematically developed hypotheses which he wants to test. And his test is quite sophisticated inasmuch as it requires the comparison of urban and rural areas relative to trends in newspaper circulation.

No discussion of trend analysis can omit a reference to Stuart Rice's handbook on *Methods in Social Research.* This monumental work appeared just when the depression occupied everyone's mind and therefore did not have the impact it deserved. The technique developed by Rice consisted of selecting outstanding investigations and having them discussed by other authorities in the field. In his Section VIII on "attempts to determine relations among measured experimentally uncontrolled factors," trend data are dealt with. All the essays included there form a valuable background for the present section.

B. *Panel studies.* During the last fifteen years the so-called panel technique has developed, consisting of the analysis of repeated interviews with the same respondents in order to investigate the factors which make for change in attitudes. Many of these studies have, so far, been conducted during political campaigns. Selection (5) explains the main purpose of panel studies under such circumstances. It is characteristic of repeated observations to greatly increase the number of interrelations which can be investigated. The terms "process analysis" and "dynamic social research" have been properly applied to this procedure. Some of its technical aspects are further exemplified in Selection (6). There Glock gives typical examples of panel tables taken from a variety of studies on race attitudes, buying habits, career patterns of soldiers, etc. He discusses the description of change (turnover), the conditions under which it takes place, the way influences can be traced and, finally, the interaction of two or more variables.

Quite a number of these examples are particularly apt in pointing up the differences between panel studies and the analysis of concurrent trends. In the latter case, we are restricted to a comparison of the way in which each variable develops over time. In a panel study we weave back and forth between the variables and their values at different periods. Selection (7) is taken from Rosenberg's analysis of questionnaires administered to the same students two years apart. Students were twice asked what occupation they intended to enter and, at the same time, the details of their occupational goals were ascertained in a variety of ways. The mutual interaction between changes in the students' values and changes in their occupational plans is the focus of this selection.

C. *Prediction studies.* Trend analysis and panel analysis are the two main devices which enable us to derive generalizations from data collected through time. But there is another use of such data which is of great practical importance and has interesting methodological implications. In recent years, a large number of prediction studies have been made in various fields. It is useful to distinguish two types: those which predict future action from people's intentions and those which predict from correlated characteristics. Prediction from intentions is exemplified by John Clausen's study of the post-war plans of American soldiers in Selection (8). It was possible to ascertain, on the basis of a follow-up study, which soldiers had actually chosen the occupations they had planned on during the war. As a result, alternative ways of predicting can now be evaluated in retrospect. In Selection (9), Burgess and Cottrell summarize their work on the prediction of marital success. The paper clearly traces their methodological considerations and thus needs no further comment here. It is a typical example of prediction from correlates.

It is well known that a prediction instrument works better for a whole group (prediction of rates) than for a single individual. Mistakes made in individual cases tend to cancel out, thus making prediction useful mainly when large numbers are involved, so that the effort pays off in the statistical aggregate. But even there a serious problem remains: On what side should we err if a choice can be made? Is one parole breaker as great a social cost as fifty good men kept too long in prison, or 100 such men? Or is it better to let many undeserving go free so that no one suffers unjustly? These kinds of questions have led to extensions of the formalism underlying the prediction problem which Goodman explains in Selection (10).

The content of this section can be utilized by the teacher in a variety of ways. In regard to trend studies he will want to stress the parallels with business cycle analysis and to raise the question of what special variables the sociologist would be interested in. A special scrutiny of chapters on social change in current textbooks would also be rewarding. For example, the question could be raised: How could the general ideas usually expressed in such books be translated into more precise research terms?

Panels can be developed easily in the classroom. Students might, e.g., keep records on the kind of personal contacts they had during a certain number of days and the satisfaction they feel with their own work (using a simple graphic rating device); or they might, in a similar way, keep score on how well they slept and their mood. Once such data are collected for a number of successive periods, they lend themselves to exercises in analysis which would extend the type of examples given in Selections (5) to (7). The difference between panel studies and multivariate analysis, as discussed in Section II, Group A, of this Reader also needs to be elaborated; in a panel study the time sequence of variables is established by successive interviews, while in surveys it has to be surmised.

In the same way the logic of prediction studies can be related to the study of deviant cases (Group C of Section II). The teacher will also want to stress that prediction studies usually make no causal imputations, while panel studies more often try to do so. There are, however, many transitions between the two. Since problems of index formation are so basic in social research, they will reappear in all sections of this volume. For example, Clausen's study (8) contains a nice example of the reduction of an attribute space in classifying the certainty of post-war plans and a comparison of the index so obtained with a direct self-rating. Finally, the relation between all selections in this section and controlled experiments deserves class discussion, even though the latter have not been included in this Reader.

1. THE IMPACT OF THE HARVEST
ON POPULATION CHANGE

by Dorothy S. Thomas

[In *Social and Economic Aspects of Swedish Population Movements, 1750-1933*, the author examines Swedish population trends and population structure. Various factors implicated in the determination of births, deaths, and migration are analyzed. In the present selection Dr. Thomas discusses the impact of the harvest on marriage, death, and fertility rates, and indicates the relationship of Swedish emigration to the Swedish harvest and to American business conditions. —ED. NOTE.]

THE IMPACT OF THE HARVEST

IN THE DAYS before industrialization, when scientific agricultural technique was unknown and grain production predominated, the welfare of the Swedish people was intimately bound up with the state of the harvest. Years of super-abundance provided no security against inevitable and all-too-frequent years of famine, for excessive crops could neither be stored adequately nor transported readily to other localities. Over-consumption and waste followed every extraordinarily good harvest; under-consumption and want, every seriously deficient harvest.

Sundbärg claimed that neither the revolts and struggles for political power nor the trade cycles in the 18th century meant much in comparison with good or bad harvests.

Irrespective of which party had gained control, or whether the King himself was on the throne, if the harvest was good, marriage and birth rates were high and death rates comparatively low, that is, the bulk of the population flourished. On the contrary, when the harvest failed, marriage and birth rates declined and death devastated the land, bearing witness to need and privation and at times even to starvation. Whether the factories fared well or badly or whether the bank-rate rose or fell—all these things *at this time,* were scarcely more than ripples on the surface.[1]

Sundbärg's hypothesis can, to some extent, be tested by statistical analysis, for an index of the adequacy of the harvests is available by years from 1748, and since 1865 has been based on official crop reports. This index is

Reprinted from *Social and Economic Aspects of Swedish Population Movements, 1750-1933,* pp. 81-92. (Copyright, 1941, by the Macmillan Company and used with their permission and with permission of the author.)

Chart 1

CYCLES OF HARVEST INDEX AND MARRIAGE RATES
1753 - 1783

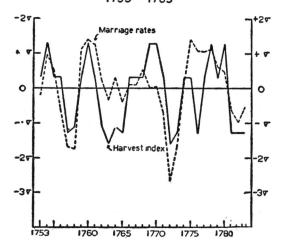

in the form of a rating scale with values from 0 representing a severe famine, through 6 representing an average or adequate harvest, to 9 representing superabundance. Although the ratings cannot be taken as quantitatively

Chart 2

CYCLES OF HARVEST INDEX AND DEATH RATES
1753 - 1783

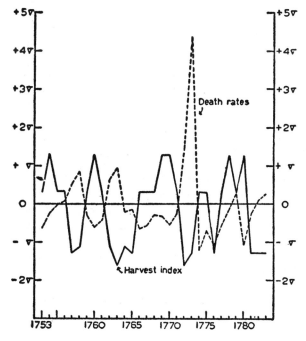

exact, they do give a fair picture of relative distress and prosperity, in terms both of the extent and of the quality of the harvest. The correlation between annual fluctuations in this index and those in birth and death rates, marriage and fertility rates (after secular trends have been eliminated), is consistently very close for the thirty year period after the middle of the 18th century. Not only marriage rates but crude birth rates and married and unmarried fertility rates rose following adequate harvests and declined in years following harvest failures; whereas death rates showed an equally strong tendency to rise after a failure and decline in periods of abundance. During the early years, the strength of the correlation (represented by coefficients ranging from .42 to .61) between the harvest index and all these vital indexes is a striking demonstration of the impact of the harvest, as Charts 1 and 2 indicate for marriage and death rates. The lessening of the impact with time is also quite apparent. The last significant correlations of harvest indexes with marriage, birth, and fertility rates appeared in the period 1815-1838 and a diminishing or inconsistent correlation is apparent in subsequent periods.[2] The death rate tended to be negatively correlated with the state of the harvest for every period and subperiod, but after the 1780's the coefficient attained probable statistical significance in only one subperiod, 1863-92.

In consideration of the many variables influencing these vital rates, the strength of the early correlations and the consistency of their pattern are surprising. Of all the correlations, that of the marriage rate with the harvest index is most readily interpreted, for marriage is a relatively volitional matter, which the prudent will tend to postpone from bad times to years when the prospects of providing for a family are brighter. Death is, however, for the bulk of the population, far less a matter of volition and the negative correlation should probably be interpreted in terms of malnutrition and its secondary effects. These secondary effects may well have been of greater importance than actual starvation for, in times of famine, the outbreak of epidemics was frequent. We have attempted to eliminate the major epidemics from the correlations, but it was impossible to eliminate the long periods of persistent cholera and dysentery, which were common through the 1880's, or the sharply rising trend in deaths from tuberculosis. Nor could we allow for the increase in mortality which undoubtedly followed periods of extensive misuse of potato brandy, which were characteristic of the early 19th century.[3]

The correlation between the crude birth rate and the harvest index has a plausible explanation, for the crude birth rate is a variable dependent to an appreciable extent upon fluctuations in the marriage rate. The fact that fertility rates, which are less dependent on the marriage rate, are so highly correlated with the state of the harvest is, however, less readily explained. It is quite probable that at least three factors operated to produce this correlation: (1) variations in the marriage rate, which would tend towards a relative deficiency of the younger and presumably most fertile women in the whole fertile age group in times of harvest failure and a relative excess in years of abundance; (2) variations in physical stamina associated with severe malnutrition, which might affect the ability to carry pregnancies to successful completion, and (3) variations in contraceptive usage. If the first of these factors were of primary importance, a negative relationship between unmarried fertility and the harvest index might be expected since the unmarried groups would have excesses of the fertile ages in periods of harvest failure. The correlation between the harvest index and unmarried fertility is, however, significantly positive for approximately the same periods as is the correlation between the harvest index and married fertility. The striking covariation in the two fertility series is shown in Chart 3. This suggests that the second or the third factor (one involuntary and the other voluntary) was of considerable importance. It is indeed highly probable that both of these factors played some role. Birth control is no new invention; and the violence of the fluctuations in the death rate in early years suggests that the physical stamina of the people might have been strongly affected by malnutrition and disease during famine years. The relative weights at any one time, or changes over periods of time in these and other factors cannot, of course, be determined on the basis of these statistics.

It is quite probable that correlation coefficients under-represent the impact of the harvest in the earlier years, partly because of difficulties in calculating the secular trend accurately, partly because minor fluctuations in

Chart 3

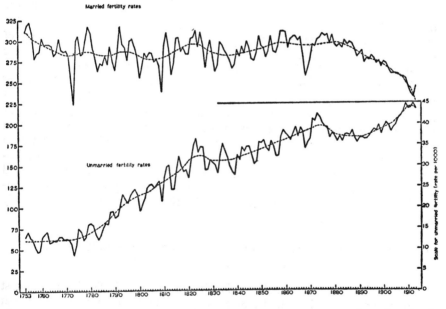

FERTILITY RATES AND TRENDS, 1753-1913

the harvest index may reflect changing methods of rating rather than real differences in the adequacy of the harvest. If we disregard small differences in the ratings and simply consider any rating of 5.4 or less as indicative of failure, and any rating of 5.5 or more as indicative of adequacy, we can relate every year of failure to the immediately preceding normal year and throw light more directly upon the impact of failures.

There were 39 years of harvest failure between 1753 and 1850. A reduction in the marriage rate deviations followed 37 of these failures; and a reduction in married fertility, unmarried fertility, and crude birth rate deviations, and an increase in death rate deviations followed 30 of these failures, irrespective of wars or epidemics. After 1850 and up to 1913, there were only 12 years which conformed to the stated definition of harvest failure. Of these, 8 were followed by reductions in the marriage rate, but only 4 by reductions in married fertility, 7 by reductions in unmarried fertility, 4 by reductions in the crude birth rate, and 8 by increases in the death rate deviations. Thus, although there is some slight evidence of persistence in the effects of harvests, the impact of failure upon vital indexes, and particularly upon birth and fertility rates, had spent most of its force well before the turn of the 20th century.

The reduction in the *number* of harvest failures has been noted. The reduction in the variability of the harvest cannot be so clearly demonstrated, because of gradual changes in the methods of rating. Nevertheless, the decrease in the standard deviations of the harvest index from around 60% in the latter half of the 18th century (1753-1807), to 34% in the first half of the 19th century (1808-62), to 12% in the period from 1863 to 1913 undoubtedly reflects more than a mere change in rating methods. All of the vital rates also showed marked reductions in variability: marriage rates from 8% to 7% to 5% for the same periods as those noted for the harvest index; married fertility rates from 5% to 4½% to 3%; unmarried fertility rates from 10% to 7% to 3%; crude birth rates from 5½% to slightly over 4½% to 2½%; and death rates from 15% to 11% to 5%. That many factors have operated to produce the reduction in the variability of marriage, birth, fertility, and death rates is obvious; but that *one* of these factors is the lessening impact of the harvest seems highly probable.

With the development of scientific agriculture, the success or failure of a harvest was less dependent upon weather alone; with diversification of production, consumption demand became more elastic and substitutes or other foods more possible; and, with the extension of inland transportation and of foreign trade, and the development of storage facilities, a local crop failure could be more readily compensated from more favored regions. Towards the close of the 19th century, failures became less frequent, and those that occurred were less severe. Waste was no longer a necessary concomitant of abundance, nor did severe deprivation and distress inevitably follow failure of the crops.

EMIGRATION AND POPULATION PRESSURE IN AGRICULTURE:
THE "PUSH" AND THE "PULL"

The great outflow of peoples which began in the 1850's drained almost a million and a third from the Swedish population, and represented a net loss of well over a million in the sixty years up to 1910. This notable emigration is far too complicated a phenomenon to be explained simply in terms of population pressure in agriculture. However, the rapid population increase, the damming up of young people in the country, the slow expansion of opportunities for making a living from the land, and the late development of industrialization and urbanization had unquestionably produced a latent push towards migration upon the surplus population and this was enhanced by the severe hardships suffered during recurrent harvest failures. This push had, of course, existed for decades and, at times, in a very acute form before relief through emigration became possible. Not until reports of the expanding opportunities in the New World[4] had achieved a certain credibility, and access to this goal had been facilitated by improvements in transoceanic transportation, did the movement attain magnitude. Once under way, however, it proceeded with great rapidity, not the least important factors in its progress being reports of success, and financial contribution towards the costs of the journey, from earlier emigrants; solicitation by American agents; and growing dissatisfaction with certain non-economic conditions of Swedish life, among them compulsory military service, limitations on political participation, and lack of religious freedom.[5]

As Chart 4 indicates, the movement did not progress evenly to a maximum nor having spent its strength, decline gradually to a minimum, but proceeded rather in a series of great waves. The first great wave began in 1867, reached its crest in 1869, and declined to a trough in 1874-77. There followed another upward movement in 1878, reaching a crest in 1882 and a trough in 1884-85. The last of the great waves began its upward swing immediately, reached a crest in 1887-88, and declined irregularly to a minimum in 1894. Emigration had spent its major force by the 'nineties, except for a temporary recrudescence in 1902-3.

Chart 4

NET EMIGRATION PER 100,000 POPULATION 1851-1914 AND TREND 1861-1908

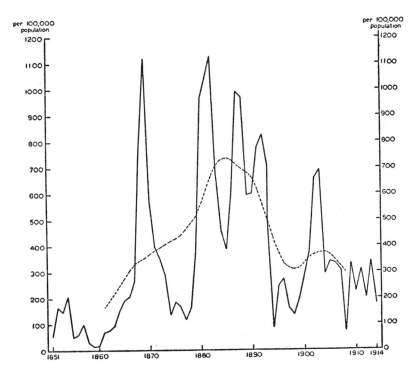

Well before the turn of the 20th century, the latent push in agriculture had found an outlet in expanding industry within the country. Up to the 'nineties, however, this latent push was strengthened by the pull of opportunity in America. The push from agriculture was at this time more or less constant, whereas the pull to America varied greatly from one phase of its pronounced business cycles to another. The impact of the harvest had been continuously diminishing during the 19th century, as was indicated in the preceding section, and a temporarily enhanced push resulting from a harvest failure played a very minor role, compared with a temporarily enhanced pull resulting from business prosperity in America. In fact, the correlation between net emigration and the harvest index was practically 0 from 1870 to 1908, whereas the correlation between net emigration and American business cycles was +.67. That the temporary push played an appreciable role in the late 'sixties, however, is suggested in Chart 5, and a probably significant negative correlation (—.35) between the harvest index and net emigration is found for the period 1867-82. Due possibly to the importance of the harvest in the lives of the people during these earlier years, the correlation of emigration with business cycles is somewhat less (+.63) from 1870 to 1882 than for the years from 1883 to 1908 (+.71).

There were only seven years of pronounced temporary "push" from agri

Chart 5

CYCLES OF NET EMIGRATION, 1867–1908, HARVEST INDEX, 1867–1882, AND AMERICAN BUSINESS CONDITIONS, 1870–1908

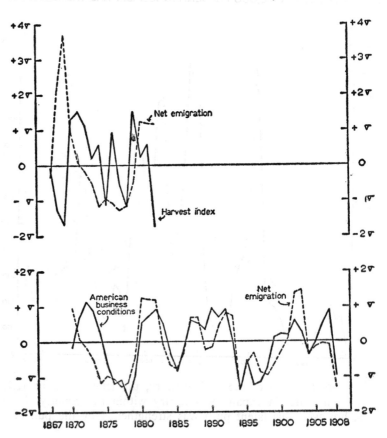

culture for the whole period 1867-1908. Of these, two coincided with a pull from America, but the other five coincided with uncertain business conditions or depression in America, i.e., the push was not strengthened by a consistent pull. On the other hand, no less than 15 years of prosperity in America coincided with adequate or abundant harvests in Sweden, i.e., the pull was operating without a concomitant temporary push from agriculture. It seems reasonable to conclude, from the present analysis, that the main push from agriculture was latent and lasted well through the 'eighties; that the temporary, recurring pushes due to harvest failures played a very slight role after the 'seventies, and that the rise and decline of American prosperity was a major factor in the wave-like movement of emigration from the early 'seventies through 1908.

2. SOCIAL OPTIMISM AND PESSIMISM IN AMERICAN PROTESTANTISM

by Thomas Hamilton

A MOVEMENT away from the "social gospel" with the introduction of a note of social pessimism seems observable in the preaching of American Protestant ministers during the period from 1929 to 1940. Since the pulpit is of some importance in the formulation of public opinion such a trend is worthy of note by students of that subject. If the change in the nature of the utterances of ministers were found to be paralleled by similar alterations in the disseminations emanating from other formulators of public opinion the phenomenon at hand would be of even more significance as part of a larger pattern.

Much of the American religious thinking of the early '20's was concerned with the problem of "the Kingdom of God on Earth" and man's improvement of his worldly lot. This tendency to equate religion with contemporary social movements or with anything temporal or human has been rejected by a group now prone to speak of the former position as "defunct liberalism," and to charge it with failure to recognize great qualitative differences between the temporal and the eternal. W. M. Horton in commenting upon Karl Barth in this connection says: "Such pessimism as this was no doubt irreligious according to liberal Christian notions, but as Barth despairingly searched the Scriptures it struck him that a certain pessimism about human affairs was characteristic of their teachings; and when he

Reprinted in part from *The Public Opinion Quarterly*, Vol. VI, pp. 280-283, by permission of the author and the publisher. (Copyright, 1942, by Princeton University.)

turned to the Biblical commentaries of Luther and Calvin he was pleased to discover that these men of faith viewed the secular scene pretty much as he did. Perhaps, after all, it was not wrong to be 'embarrassed' when one attempted to make God intelligible in terms of contemporary social movements; perhaps a God who could be discovered on the human plane would not be God; perhaps 'embarrassment,' inability to talk without involvement in verbal contradictions and rational paradoxes, was something one was *bound* to experience in the presence of the true and living God who is 'wholly other' (totaliter Aliter) than all our ideas of him. Perhaps theology itself is but the 'description of this embarrassment.' "[1]

The Material. Since October, 1929 there has been published a monthly magazine called *The Christian Century Pulpit.* Each issue has contained six or seven sermons delivered by Protestant ministers of the various denominations. It is probable that some of these sermons were revised and polished before being submitted for publication and thus may vary from their original form. Since this study is not concerned with audience reaction the fact that the oral, not the written, word is the natural medium for communicating sermons is not relevant.

It should also be pointed out that editorial predilections might shape the content of these magazines. However, inquiry among informed sources indicated that the sermons printed were not selected on the bases of *what* was said. The sermons appearing come generally from two sources: (1) ministers who are widely known; (2) young ministers with whom the editors are personally acquainted.

While no contention is made that the sermons which furnish the basis for this study are strictly representative of all the sermons delivered from Protestant pulpits in the United States, a word should be said of the influence which this magazine may have on preachers whose sermons are not printed. The publishers have reported that "nearly all" of the circulation of this magazine is among ministers. Conversation with several ministers indicated that the publication is rather closely read and that its influence upon future sermons is probably considerable. On the bases of these factors it was decided that this magazine might fruitfully be used for purposes of analysis as long as the limitations are remembered when conclusions are stated.

The Method. From each issue of *The Christian Century Pulpit* one sermon was selected for analysis. The method of selection was simply to rotate the order in which sermons appeared in the publication. A sentence classification for social optimism and social pessimism was constructed and is given below. If in a given period the sentences of social pessimism outnumber those of social optimism the period shall be characterized as socially pessimistic, contrariwise—socially optimistic.

SOCIAL OPTIMISM

I. Sentences about science and education.
   A. The desirability of applying the "scientific spirit" to religion.
   B. Imputing a high value to science.
   C. Holding that religion should abandon that which is disconfirmed by science.
   D. Indicating that Christianity must keep up with the times.

    E. Stating that social problems can be solved by application of intelligence.

    F. Imputing a high value to education.

II. Sentences about religion and worldliness.

    A. Asserting that the church must not be "other-worldly."

    B. Giving to orthodoxy, dogma, and ritual a negative value.

III. Sentences about the solution of social problems.

    A. Holding that we make progress.

    B. Urging an optimistic view of the future in spite of obstacles.

    C. Approving particular solutions.

    D. Emphasizing social rather than individual responsibility for the problems of society.

    E. Asserting that the task of the church is the building of the kingdom of God on earth.

SOCIAL PESSIMISM

I. Sentences about faith.

    A. Indicating that "true" faith should be imposed by force if necessary.

    B. Asserting the necessity for complete obedience to authority.

    C. Affirming that after authority has made its decision discussion should cease.

    D. Affirming the need for an all-powerful authority.

II. Sentences about man.

    A. Holding that discipline is needed because men are weak.

    B. Affirming man's need for mysticism and ritual.

    C. Discrediting leaders who display affection toward followers.

    D. Averring that men are becoming more evil.

    E. Indicating the necessity for absolute standards.

    F. Holding that the sinfulness of man is the root of our social problems.

III. Sentences about science and education.

    A. Discrediting scientific point of view.

    B. Indicating the futility of measurement.

    C. Minimizing the value of analyzing religion.

    D. Indicating the futility of education.

    E. Holding that there is a need for more religious training in education.

IV. Sentences about the environment.

    A. Indicating that trouble is universal.

    B. Holding that a troubled environment is in itself a good thing.

The Results. In Figure I the two classifications are plotted as "matching" curves, the better to show their relationship. From these presentations certain conclusions can be stated, subject however to the limitations previously mentioned.

1. The material analyzed showed an increase in the number of sentences of social pessimism in relation to those of social optimism from 1929 to 1940.

2. Two years showed exception to the "long" curve mentioned above. These were 1933 and 1937.

3. In order to locate more exactly the locus of the shift of 1938, 1939, 1940, the mean for each classification was computed for the first nine

years and for the last three. The locus can be said to be in those classifications of sentences where the two means vary most in the direction
of the "long" curve described above. Calculated on this basis, the
greatest decrease in sentences of social optimism was in classifications
III E(—13 1/9), III C(—11 8/9), I D(—8 7/9) and I A(—8 2/9);
the greatest increase in sentences of social pessimism was in classifications II C(+6 4/9), II E(+3), and I C (+2 2/3).[2]

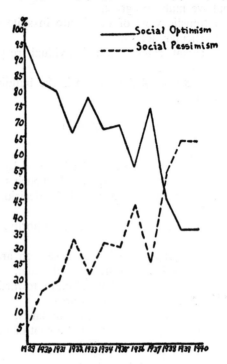

Figure 1

4. The above conclusions suggest certain lines which further investigation might follow profitably.
   a. This paper might be checked by analysis of papers read at minis-
      ters' conferences, professional journals, books on theology most
      widely read by ministers, etc.
   b. A few studies of an earlier period on the lay attitude toward the
      role of the church exist. Tests might now be made to see if this
      attitude has changed in the same direction as have pulpit utter-
      ances. It is recognized that scantiness of data would make a com-
      parative study difficult.
   c. It would be useful to collect a series of sermons for an earlier
      period comparable to those printed by *The Christian Century Pul-
      pit*. A comparison of present results with an analysis of the early
      '20's would be particularly interesting. Certain generalizations might
      be tentatively put forward if sermons of the early years of the first
      World War showed a tendency to contain a greater number of

sentences of social pessimism in relation to those of social optimism.

d. A more intensive study of sermons for the years 1933 and 1937 might reveal certain hypotheses about the relationship between political and economic conditions and sermons. Investigation as to why these years were marked by an upswing of social optimism would be valuable.

3. PUBLIC OPINION AND THE LEGISLATIVE PROCESS

by Frank V. Cantwell

THE ROLE PLAYED by public opinion in a democracy, particularly as it affects the legislative process, has long been a subject for speculation by political scientists. The advent of controlled quota sampling permits of the study of this important relationship in measurable terms. The object of the present discussion is to trace the interaction of public opinion and the executive and legislative branches of government as they have dealt with a single public question—reorganization of the Supreme Court, as presented to Congress for consideration by President Roosevelt on February 5, 1937. Enlargement of the Supreme Court from nine to fifteen members was the most controversial feature of the general reorganization of the federal judiciary proposed by the President, aimed at speeding up the process of clearing cases through the federal court system, and making the system more "representative" of the wishes of the people.

The debate on enlargement of the Supreme Court provides a useful and interesting case study for several reasons. The case as a public issue has a definite beginning and end, ranging from the proposal of the judiciary reform bill by the President on February 5 to the death of Senator Joseph T. Robinson on July 14, 1937. As it was debated by public and legislators, the issue was a relatively clear-cut one, uncomplicated by side issues or utterly foreign events that might have influenced the course of either legislators or the public. Finally, and of decided importance, the American Institute of Public Opinion made weekly measurements of opinion toward the proposal during the entire period that reorganization of the Court was a public question. This permits the correlation of reliable opinion samplings with events in the debate and the observation of their relationship.

From this observation it is hoped to throw light on several specific ques-

Reprinted from *The American Political Science Review*, Vol. LV, 1946, pp. 924-935, by permission of the author and the publisher. (Copyright, 1946, by The American Political Science Association.)

tions: (1) What is the general nature of the relationship between the public and its legislators? (2) What are the forces at work which determine the direction that public opinion will take in a debate of this type? (3) Is there a noticeable tendency on the part of legislators to follow the guidance of public opinion, and if so, to what extent do legislators take their lead from the public? (4) To what extent do legislators attempt to swing opinion to their way of thinking? (5) Are there any phases of the relationship between the public and legislators that might be improved so as to make it more effective in approaching the process of deciding public policy?

THE DEBATE ON THE COURT BILL

From accounts of the Court debate as carried in the *New York Times,* the following short outline of leading developments in the debate has been prepared:

Chronological Listing of Events in the Court Debate

February 5—President Roosevelt sends message to Congress recommending reorganization of the federal judiciary, including increasing the membership of the Supreme Court from nine to fifteen members. President reported "calm and confident," reflecting his conviction that he has a huge popular mandate for what he is doing. Message creates shock throughout country.

March 1—The Supreme Court upholds Congressional resolution abrogating payments in gold. Decision is of aid to New Deal.

March 4—President Roosevelt, in Democratic Victory Dinner speech, calls for party loyalty on the Supreme Court issue.

March 8—The President, in a fireside chat, assures Americans that, in proposing reorganization of the Court, he is seeking to protect them from the Court's usurpations.

March 9—Homer Cummings, Attorney-General, opens Administration arguments before Senate Judiciary Committee, saying the bill will restore the governmental machinery to its proper balance.

March 22—Senator Burton K. Wheeler opens opposition arguments before Senate Judiciary Committee and reads a statement from Chief Justice Charles E. Hughes saying enlargement of the Court is "unnecessary." Statement is said to have the approval of Justices Brandeis and Van Devanter.

March 29—The Supreme Court reverses Adkins v. Children's Hospital decision and holds constitutional minimum wage law of the state of Washington. Adkins case specifically overruled by 5-4 decision. Decision opens way for federal minimum wage legislation.

April 12—In handing down decisions in four specific cases, the Supreme Court upholds the National Labor Relations Act (Wagner Act). Decision in chief case is 5-4.

April 28—Senators Hatch, McCarran, and O'Mahoney, members of the Senate Judiciary Committee previously uncommitted on Supreme Court Bill, announce opposition on basis of testimony offered before the Committee.

May 10—Washington reports say that Justices Brandeis and Van Devanter will retire from Court in June.

May 18—Justice Willis Van Devanter, 78, retires.

May 24—The Supreme Court upholds the Social Security Act in ruling on three cases, two by 5-4 decisions.

June 14—The Senate Judiciary Committee reports unfavorably to the Senate on the Court bill, terming the proposal "a needless, futile, and utterly dangerous abandonment of constitutional principle." Vote is 10-8 against proposal.

July 14—Senator Joseph T. Robinson, majority leader of the Senate, dies suddenly. Supreme Court Bill will be abandoned.

Charts 1 and 2 have been prepared from two questions asked weekly by the Gallup Poll during the debate. The first question, recorded in Chart I, was asked during the period from February 15 to April 5, and reads: "Are you in favor of President Roosevelt's proposal regarding the Supreme Court?" The second question, recorded in Chart 2, covers the period from April 12 to June 7, and reads: "Should Congress pass the President's Supreme Court plan?" In both questions, the Supreme Court plan was stated to be "President Roosevelt's." Possibly the use of the President's name might have introduced a bias, although throughout the debate, in the newspapers, on the radio, and in the halls of Congress, the plan was also identified with the President. In view of this very common identification, the possibility of such a bias is minimized. In any event, any tendency toward bias would not affect the validity of the figures as used in this study, since a bias would be constant.

Phase One of the Debate. The initial period in the debate extends from the introduction of the President's proposal on February 5 until the week immediately preceding the two speeches made by the President. As may be seen from Chart 1, in this early period public attitudes toward the proposal divided equally, 45 per cent of the people expressing approval of the proposal, and 45 per cent expressing disapproval, with 10 per cent in the "no opinion" category. These figures are from the Gallup Poll taken during the week of February 15. At approximately the same time, the *New York Times* reported that an informal poll of senators made by *Times* reporters showed that 32 senators were on record as favoring the proposal, 28 as against the proposal, while 35 remained uncommitted. Thus, while 90 per cent of the public had put themselves on record as favoring or disapproving the proposal, only 63 per cent of the senators had taken a definite stand. One week later, on February 17, the *Times* news columns carried this statement from a Washington staff member: "Conservative Democrats . . . especially those in the Senate, gagged at the proposals. . . . Many of them maintained a prudent silence, waiting to see how the cat of public opinion would jump."

In this first stage of the debate, newspapers and radio commentators began to take definite stands on the proposals, and senators and other public figures began to make statements setting forth their positions. Senator Norris declared against the bill; former Governor Alf Landon, who had carried the Republican standard in the presidential election a few months earlier, came out against the proposal; Senator Champ Clark declared against the scheme; and Senators Glass and Wheeler denounced it. The only figure of magnitude to raise his voice in favor of the proposal was Senator La Follette. In the face of this cumulation of official opinion against the proposal, public opinion began to turn against the plan, and by March 1 the Gallup Poll reported that the anti-proposal vote had grown to 48 per cent, while the pro-proposal vote had slumped to 41 per cent—a difference of 7 percentage points. The President and his advisers became aware that public sentiment was turning away from the proposal.

As early as February 15, the *Times* reported that Attorney-General Cummings and Senator Sherman Minton were planning to make appeals for public support of the plan. The *Times* news columns said: "The frank object of all these appeals is to induce the backers of the President to send telegrams and letters to their senators and representatives to offset the thousands received at the Capitol in the last few days in opposition to his sweeping plan for remaking the Supreme Court with more liberal-minded men." On February 19, the *Times* said: "On the showing of informal polls that the Administration's judiciary reform bill may hang on the decision of less than a dozen senators, President Roosevelt and the forces identified with him, particularly organized labor, intensified their efforts to insure its passage as a prerequisite to further New Deal legislation. . . . The opposition strategists in the Senate . . . were . . . making preparations for one of the stiffest legislative battles of recent years. They were making no particular effort to dig into the dwindling reservoir of unpledged senators, leaving that to the weight of the letters and telegrams still coming in from all parts of the country." Phase One of the debate may be summarized by saying that the President introduced the proposal with the hope that public opinion, which had given him a handsome victory in November, would provide the pressure necessary to push the proposal through Congress. This public pressure was not forthcoming, and the public had become increasingly hostile. Opposition senators were biding their time as they watched public opinion swing behind them. So far as the Administration was concerned, a counterattack was necessary to win back public favor to the proposal.

Phase Two. The second phase of the debate may be entitled the Administration drive for public support. The outstanding development during this phase was the entry of the President directly into the discussion. With opinion turning away from the proposal, it became obvious that use of the most powerful weapon in the New Deal arsenal was indicated—a personal appeal from the President. Consequently, the President made two speeches to the nation within five days, an address at the Democratic Victory Dinner on March 4 and a fireside chat on March 8. The *New York Times* reported the fireside chat in these words: "He had no intention of packing the Court with 'spineless puppets.' He simply proposed to return the Court to its 'rightful and historic place' and save the Constitution from 'hardening of the arteries.' " On the morning following the fireside chat, Attorney-General Cummings opened the Administration case before the Senate Judiciary Committee, saying that the proposal would restore the governmental machinery to its proper balance. The Gallup Poll for the week of March 1 immediately registered the impact of the President's speeches. As may be seen from Chart 1, the anti-proposal vote fell to 47 per cent and in two weeks dropped precipitately to 41 per cent, the lowest point reached by the No vote at any stage of the debate. On the other hand, the pro-proposal vote began a climb that was to last until March 29, rising from 41 to 45 per cent during the month. Success had apparently crowned the effort of the Administration to win the favor of public opinion, for the Yes vote now held a slim margin over the No vote. However, as will be seen, this margin was to prove far from decisive.

Phase Three. On March 22, the opposition forces swung back into action as Senator Burton Wheeler, chief of the anti-court reorganization forces, opened the opposition arguments before the Senate Judiciary Committee. As the first opposition witness, Senator Wheeler read a statement from Chief Justice Charles E. Hughes saying enlargement of the Court was "unnecessary"; and the statement was said to have the approval of Justices Brandeis and Van Devanter. Chart 1 shows that during that week the No vote turned again and began a steady climb upward which was to mount almost steadily until the proposal was finally killed. Evidently, opposition arguments before the Judiciary Committee were sufficiently convincing to solidify the No vote, and Chart 2 shows the constant strength of the oppositionists among the public from this date onward.

Phase Four. The turning point in the debate was reached on March 29. On that day, the Supreme Court handed down a decision reversing an earlier decision in the Adkins v. Children's Hospital case. The effect was to hold constitutional the minimum wage law of the state of Washington, thus paving the way for federal minimum wage legislation, one of the chief objectives of the New Deal. The effect on public opinion of the switch by the Supreme Court was nothing short of profound. An examination of both Charts 1 and 2 reveals that the Yes vote, or those in favor of reorganization, began a sharp slump from which it never fully recovered. In terms of percentages, the Yes vote dropped from a high of 45 per cent in the week before the reversed decision in the Adkins case to a low of 31 per cent on May 17. It is safe to say that the Administration lost its case before the public on the day when the Supreme Court did its famous about-face. It is to be noted, however, that the Yes vote which became estranged from the proposal did not shift into the No group, but fell into indecision and became allied with the No Opinion group. Charts 1 and 2 show that the growth of the No Opinion group almost matches, point for point, the decline in the Yes group. This phenomenon will be enlarged upon below.

From the beginning of Phase Two onward, the Senate Judiciary Committee had been holding extensive hearings at which educators, farm and labor leaders, women's group leaders, and the representatives of almost every special interest group in the nation appeared and presented their case. To what extent the members of the Judiciary Committee were "holding off" from presenting the bill for a formal test on the Senate floor is difficult to tell with exactness. During this period, opinion was in a state of flux, and the Judiciary Committee served a valuable function by permitting opinion to crystallize. Some evidence of political maneuvering to take advantage of a favorable climate of opinion is revealed in a charge made by Senators Wheeler and Van Nuys on April 3, five days after the Supreme Court handed down the decision in the Adkins case. The *New York Times* reported the two Senators as charging Attorney-General Cummings with a "gag" attempt, based on reports that Mr. Cummings had hinted that he would like to see the Judiciary Committee bring the hearings to a close. The *Times* reported the Senators as saying: "There is no doubt the Attorney-General would like to close public hearings on this issue. . . . Hundreds of American citizens, holding responsible positions at the bar, in universities, and in the molding of public opinion have asked to be heard . . . it is the duty of the Senate Judiciary Committee to continue these hearings until every cross-section of public opinion has been given an opportunity to present its views." Senator Wheeler was astute enough to realize that the tide of opinion was running against the proposal, and that time was playing into the hands of the opposition, just as Mr. Cummings knew that time was playing against the Administration. The two opposition Senators realized the impact of the Supreme Court decision of March 29 on the public and were willing to continue the hearings of the Judiciary Committee until such time as the increased opposition they expected from the public should have an opportunity to register itself through witnesses at the hearings and through senatorial channels of sounding opinion. The Judiciary Committee did continue its hearings, and reports continued to furnish the bulk of newspaper and radio accounts of the reorganization debate. The incident is illustrative of the dependence that both sides placed upon the pressure of public opinion to furnish the force needed to carry the day. Opponents and proponents alike realized that without the backing of public opinion they were lost, and were anxiously trying to win opinion to their side, while waiting for opinion to crystallize sufficiently so that a clear-cut case of public support would be forthcoming.

On April 12, with the No vote holding a six per cent margin over the Yes vote, the Supreme Court handed down a decision upholding the National Labor Relations Act in rulings on four specific cases. In the chief case, the decision was five to four in favor of the act. Strangely enough, the effect of this decision on public opinion was the reverse of that in the Adkins case, as Chart 2 shows. The No vote went down slightly while the Yes vote mounted slightly. This reversal of opinion can be traced to the fact that the Administration immediately made capital of the two successive favorable decisions of the Court, following a series of reverses for the New Deal—maintaining that the two decisions proved the point that the Court was actually composed of human beings who were subject to error and could see the error of their ways. The Administration raised its famous cry that Court decisions rested on whether a Justice came down heads or tails, which indicated the need for a larger Court membership. This argument, although it had an immediate effect, was not powerful enough to change the trend of opinion, and the following week (April 19) the No vote rose three percentage points, while the Yes vote sank two points.

Phase Five. The next development of note in the debate occurred on May 10, when reports from Washington circled the country to the effect that Justices Brandeis and Van Devanter intended to retire from the Court in June. Chart 2 shows that the effect of this report was to increase public indecision, which had been mounting steadily from the introduction of the proposal, and after the report had gained credence the No Opinion group stood at a high of 25 per cent on May 17. It is worth pausing to note the state of opinion at this time.

Table 1—Shift in Vote on Court Reorganization, February 15-May 17*

	February 15	May 17	Difference
Yes, favor reorganization	45%	31%	—14%
No, oppose reorganization	45%	44%	— 1%
No opinion	10%	25%	+15%

* February 15 represents roughly the introduction of the proposal. May 17 is representative of the period following circulation of reports that Justices Brandeis and Van Devanter would retire in June.

Table 1 shows that the opposition group had held its own, despite sharp dips. The Yes group, proponents of reorganization, had lost a total of 14 percentage points; the No Opinion group had risen from 10 per cent to 25 per cent; and the table shows that those who lost faith in their position did not feel powerfully enough affected to jump into the opposite camp, but that their reaction was to fall into a state of indecision. The gain for the No Opinion group represents the total defection from both the Yes and No groups. In other words, the public was still not clear upon a course of action, although the number of Yes people who were growing increasingly doubtful of their position was very much larger than the respective No group. The importance of this observation lies in the assumption that members of the Senate were idling along, waiting for a popular reaction. This was not to be forthcoming, since the people were becoming increasingly indecisive. But for the next event unfolding on May 18, it is difficult to say how long this deadlock between the people and their legislators, each waiting for the other to act, might have lasted.

Phase Six. The deadlock was broken on the date mentioned with announcement of the retirement from the Supreme Court of Justice Willis Van Devanter at the age of seventy-eight. Chart 2 shows that this announcement immediately cleared the atmosphere, and both opponents and proponents of the court reorganization proposal were enabled to make up their minds definitely. Opinion had at last crystallized. The retirement of Justice Van Devanter meant that the President would be able to appoint to the Court a Justice more in sympathy with New Deal objectives. In turn, this appointment, together with the recent "liberalization" of the Court in the Adkins and Wagner Act decisions, meant that for all practical purposes the Court had been reorganized. De facto reorganization apparently was satisfactory to the public, and the No vote rose quickly until on June 7 opponents of court reorganization had 50 per cent of the public behind them, while only

Table 2—Shift in Vote on Court Reorganization, February 15-June 7

	February 15	June 7	Difference
Yes, favor reorganization	45%	35%	—10%
No, oppose reorganization	45%	50%	+ 5%
No opinion	10%	15%	+ 5%

35 per cent favored reorganization. The No Opinion vote sank rapidly from 25 per cent on May 17 to 15 per cent on June 7.

Table 2 shows that after the retirement of Justice Van Devanter, opinion crystallized more rapidly in the direction of opposition to the proposal than in favor of it. A total defection of 10 per cent of those originally favoring reorganization can be noted, five per cent of these people switching their vote into opposition, while five per cent were unable to come to a decision and moved into the No Opinion group.

This evident satisfaction of the people with the changed court situation came as a great relief to legislators, who were now able to deal with the delicate problem of de jure court reorganization. On June 14, with the battle of public opinion decided, and with opinion firmly behind it, the Senate Judiciary Committee reported unfavorably (ten to eight) to the Senate on the Judiciary Reorganization Bill, terming the measure "a needless, futile, and utterly dangerous abandonment of constitutional principle." Reorganization of the Court was no longer a public issue; and whatever lingering inclination there might have been on the part of the Administration to press for court reform in the face of public opposition was dissipated by the death on July 14 of Senator Joseph T. Robinson, majority leader of the Senate, who had thrown all of his strength into the fray on behalf of the proposal.

CONCLUSIONS

Having examined in some detail the interplay between public opinion and events in the court debate, it is now possible to form conclusions as to the general nature of the relationship between the public and its legislators as they deal jointly with a public question. In many respects, the debate on the Court is typical of the problems which present themselves for solution in our democracy. For this reason, the conclusions which follow have been cast in such a form that they may be applied to understanding the nature of any similar debate on a public question. At the same time, it must be borne in mind that so many diverse factors operate while a question runs its public course that these conclusions have applicability only in so far as the phenomena at work in a given situation are taken into consideration. Further study of the type of relationship under consideration will permit the understanding with considerable exactness of how public opinion and the legislative process affect each other. This, in turn, will enable the public and legislators to operate together at full efficiency; for it is undeniable that national questions must be solved by the joint action of the people and their elected legislative representatives.

1. *Legislators display an inclination to "wait on" public opinion to shape itself before dealing formally with questions.* This does not mean that senators were content merely to follow the lead of public opinion, for many made an effort to mold opinion to their way of thinking through radio addresses and personal appearances. It does mean that the great majority of senators were keenly aware of the existence of public opinion and hesitant to take action so long as its final direction was not absolutely certain. Although many senators committed themselves publicly during the course of the debate, at no time did either side show determination to force a showdown on the floor of the Senate, such hesitation seeming to stem from the uncertain condition of public opinion, which never registered above 50 per cent either for or against the proposal.

The function of the Senate Judiciary Committee as a sounding board is interesting. As long as any doubt remained about public sentiment toward the bill, the committee remained in session, and only when it was perfectly plain that public support for the proposal would not be forthcoming did it make its unfavorable report. During the extended period of public hearings, an amazing array of witnesses appeared before the committee and every possible type of argument for and against the proposal was brought forth. Doubtless this varied array of witnesses gave to the senators valuable clues as to public feeling on the proposal, and it was on the basis of testimony offered before the committee that Senators Hatch, McCarran, and O'Mahoney announced their opposition to the bill. The most useful function of the committee seems to have been to hold in abeyance the necessity of making a formal decision while senators waited in the hope that public opinion would develop in a decisive direction and render unnecessary a decision on the Senate floor.

2. *Events played a more important role than Congress or the President in shaping the direction of public opinion.* The six leading determinants of opinion in the debate were: (1) the President's Victory Dinner speech and fireside chat on the fourth and eighth of March; (2) the opening of the

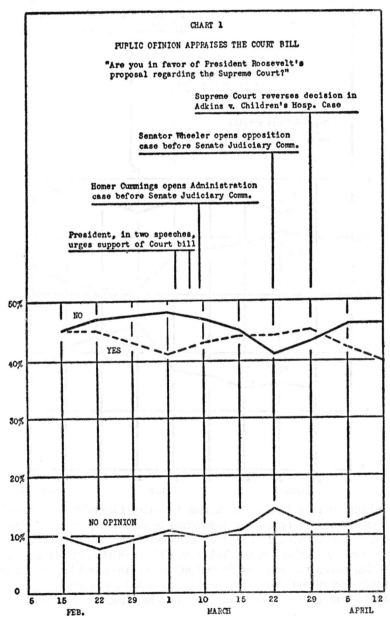

CHART 1

PUPLIC OPINION APPRAISES THE COURT BILL

"Are you in favor of President Roosevelt's proposal regarding the Supreme Court?"

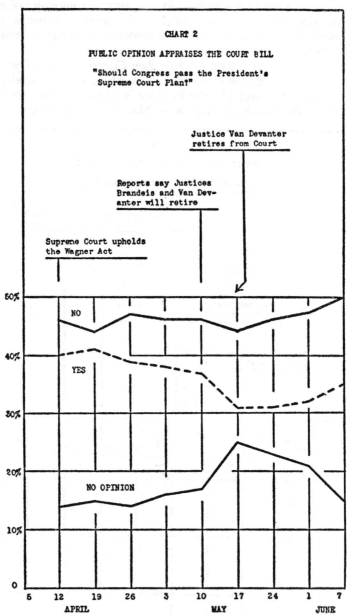

CHART 2

PUBLIC OPINION APPRAISES THE COURT BILL

"Should Congress pass the President's
Supreme Court Plan?"

Justice Van Devanter
retires from Court

Reports say Justices
Brandeis and Van Dev-
anter will retire

Supreme Court upholds
the Wagner Act

Administration case before the Senate Judiciary Committee on March 9;
(3) the opening of opposition arguments against the proposal before the
committee on March 22; (4) the decision of the Supreme Court over-
ruling an earlier decision in the Adkins v. Children's Hospital case on March
29, which paved the way for federal minimum wage legislation and broke
the succession of anti-New Deal decisions handed down by the Court; (5)
Washington reports, beginning on May 10, that Justices Brandeis and Van

Devanter were planning to retire; and (6) the retirement on May 18 of Justice Van Devanter.

Of these six steps in the downfall of the Court proposal, three were attempts by government officials (the President and senators) to mobilize opinion in a particular direction. The other three were events in the sense of being unanticipated happenings beyond the province of either proponents or opponents of the proposal. While the President's speeches and the arguments given before the Senate Judiciary Committee affected public opinion measurably, they were incapable of affecting it decisively. The major event in opinion-determination was the decision of the Court in the Adkins case. From the time of this decision, the public Yes vote dropped off steadily, while the No vote rose. The second most important step in opinion-determination was the retirement of Justice Van Devanter, with the effect of crystallizing opinion which had been drifting into indecision as the debate wore on. As Cantril has said, "opinion is generally determined more by events than by words—unless those words are themselves interpreted as an "event."[1]

3. *Public opinion cannot propose a course of action, and a healthy public opinion requires leadership.* Throughout the course of the debate, as shown by the accompanying charts, public opinion was responsive to political moves and events. At no time was there observable any great spontaneous movement of opinion in a direction which would have indicated to legislators the necessity for taking a particular course of action that would have broken the deadlock. It is characteristic of public opinion that it cannot generate a proposal or series of proposals serving to satisfy its needs. Public opinion can indicate very powerfully the general area of its needs, but it remains for an individual or group of individuals to come forward with specific proposals toward which opinion can display approval or disapproval. We have seen how, during the course of the debate, the public support that fell away from both the Yes and No sides of the discussion tended to gather in the No Opinion category, where it remained in a state of indecision awaiting some new determining factor that would move it once more into the realm of decision. Those legislators who waited in the hope that public opinion would show them the way were waiting in vain. Public opinion in a democracy responds to leadership, and needs the stimulus of leadership in order to crystallize one way or the other on specific proposals. Legislators are perfectly correct in sounding opinion so that they may determine whether or not they are moving in a direction calculated to meet popular needs. It is completely fallacious for legislators to wait on public opinion to tell them what to do, because public opinion waits on leadership to supply the grist of fact and suggestion so that it can fulfill its function, which is the acceptance or rejection of proposals. In a sentence, when faced with a specific problem, public opinion will respond to proposals, but cannot generate them; generation of proposals is the function of the legislators.

4. THE EFFECTS OF RADIO UPON NEWSPAPER CIRCULATION

by Samuel A. Stouffer

THE LONG-TERM TREND IN NEWSPAPER CIRCULATION

THE MOST TEMPTING WAY to study the effect of radio on newspaper circulation would be to analyze the existing circulation figures, but three major difficulties make an interpretation very hazardous:

1. If newspaper reading increases or decreases, radio will be only one of several causes. The growing importance of foreign affairs, the breakdown of rural isolation, and other factors will have to be kept steadily in mind.

2. Radio can affect newspaper reading in various ways. News broadcasts might make the news content of the paper more or less interesting. But listening to any kind of program could occupy the time formerly available for newspaper reading, and all sorts of stimulations coming over the radio (for instance, dance orchestras broadcasting from night clubs) might change the entire pattern of the public's leisure-time activities. Again, radio touches the destinies of newspapers by competing for a place in businessmen's advertising budgets.

3. Newspaper reading is not synonymous with news reading. The remarkable development in the picture form of news reporting might have an influence upon newspaper circulation which would spuriously be attributed to radio if it were overlooked.

Apart from these general factors there is a special reason why inferences about radio's long-time effects are dangerous when derived from general newspaper-circulation data. Circulation figures relate to the total number of papers sold, not the total number of families taking newspapers. Many families may take two or three papers. If many of these families, because of the radio, reduced the number of papers taken, the papers' circulations might drop, even if the radio encouraged a large number of non-newspaper-reading families to take newspapers for the first time. The newspaper figures might in this case show a loss; at the same time there would be an increase of news reading among the public.

It is likely that the radio first invaded families able to take a daily newspaper. By the time of the 1930 census, radio ownership varied from 12 per cent of the families in the East South Central states to 55 per cent in New England. By 1938, according to the estimates by the Joint Committee on Radio Research, radio ownership had risen to 60 per cent in the East South Central states, to 92 per cent in the Middle Atlantic and New England states, and to 95 per cent on the Pacific coast. By this time practically all

This selection was prepared by Samuel A. Stouffer for Paul F. Lazarsfeld's *Radio and The Printed Page*, and is reprinted from pp. 266-272 of that work by permission of the author and the publisher. (Copyright, 1940, by Duell, Sloan and Pearce, Inc.)

the regular newspaper subscribers undoubtedly had radios. The growth in radio ownership since 1930 probably represents an accretion, year by year, of successive groups who even before they possessed radios were less ardent newspaper readers than the groups preceding them in radio ownership. The effect of the radio on newspaper circulation among these people would be particularly important to study, but there would be no way of interpreting the trends to indicate whether there was an increase or decrease in newspaper reading after these people obtained radios. As indicated before, any increase of reading in this group might cancel a decrease in the circulation of extra papers among the earlier radio owners and stauncher newspaper readers; or the reverse might be true.

If, however, a rather special hypothesis can be set up, general newspaper-circulation figures cautiously handled may be of some interest. Here are three such hypotheses and the actual findings concerning them:

1. *Expectation:* If, as studies previously published seem to show, the radio's advantages to rural listeners were greater relatively than its advantages to urban listeners, then one would expect the circulation for newspapers to increase more or to decline less (say, between 1929 and 1937) in the immediate trade area of the city than in the outlying territory.

Findings[1] (limited to cities of 15,000 and over, all of whose papers were Audit Bureau of Circulations [ABC] papers in both 1929 and 1930): Table 1 divides 181 cities into two groups, one of increasing and the other of decreasing aggregate newspaper circulation. About half of the cities with an increasing circulation showed greater increases in the rural areas than in local and suburban areas. Those factors that make for an increase (for

Table 1—Changes of Newspaper Circulations in Central and Outlying Areas of 181 Cities[2]

| | NUMBER OF CITIES FOR WHICH CIRCULATION CHANGED MORE IN: | |
	Local and suburban area	Outlying Area
Cities with *increasing* aggregate circulation	60	60
Cities with *declining* aggregate circulation	10	51

example, improved service) seem, then, unrelated to special circulation areas. The decrease of circulation, however, is much more likely to take place in outlying areas. Five-sixths of the cities which lost newspaper circulation lost more heavily in outlying areas, where the time advantage of radio is likely to be more effective. A special tabulation (not reproduced here) showed that the same relationship holds true also if the circulation figures are analyzed separately for the Eastern, Western, and Southern parts of the country.

2. *Expectations:* Since radio news tends to favor national news at the expense of local affairs, the local newspaper might hold up more successfully because it still performs a function which radio has not taken over.

Findings (all daily circulation, ABC and other, pooled for each city): Table 2 shows that for three regions alike, conforming to expectation, newspaper circulations in the smaller cities held up better. Only about half of the big cities' newspapers increased their circulations between 1929 and 1937, while more than two-thirds of the small-town papers showed such an increase.

Table 2—Per Cent of Cities of Different Size Showing an Increase in Daily Newspaper Circulation in Different Areas[3] (1929 to 1937)

	REGION		
Size of city	East	West	South
100,000 and over	50	45	65
25,000 to 100,000	59	56	78
15,000 to 25,000	68	68	84

3. *Expectation:* The afternoon papers probably get the major news breaks —especially on foreign and national political news, and in the Central and Western time zones—but may not have so much time as the morning paper for the preparation of detailed interpretive materials. Since the newspaper's news-break value, in comparison with its feature value, is reduced by radio, the morning paper should be benefited at least in the local areas.

Findings: (a) The percentage of morning circulation in the total morning and evening circulation has increased on an almost straight-line trend ever since the World War. The pattern is about the same since 1930 and before. (b) In a sample of cities for which data were available by special analysis at the Audit Bureau of Circulations between 1929 and 1937, the morning papers in 25 out of 45 cities (56 per cent) held up better than the evening papers in local and suburban circulation. This is perhaps the fairest comparison of morning and evening papers, since the evening papers necessarily have a different and shorter radius of distribution from the center of a city. These findings seem to conform with the expectation that morning papers may suffer relatively less damage from the radio than evening papers. However, the results are not decisively corroborative, and further studies are called for.

General circulation figures, then, give certain leads if they are studied under special conditions. The analysis attempts to create a kind of semi-experimental situation by dividing areas according to the differential role radio is likely to play. The trends selected in the preceding samples can be summarized as follows:

The newspaper fared better in urban as compared with rural areas; this phenomenon could be due to the time advantage that radio has outside the centers of distribution of print. The newspaper fared better in small than in large cities; this might be because the radio does not compete in the presentation of routine personal news items of local interest. The morning newspaper did somewhat better than the evening paper, and this might be due to the fact that the morning paper is frequently "analytical" and therefore less subject to radio's competition than the afternoon paper, which is more dependent upon its straight news content at least in regard to current daily events.

to vote for the
frequently than
"Don't knows"
a considerable 1
predictions.

Such "extern
ment. Turnover
We can pick o
social situation
respondents wei
among those w
individuals with
pectations expre
were usually th
the process one
final decision:
picked as the w
variables which

The table [c
specific influenc
let us focus our
did not intend t
fitted their actic
November. But
inaction to an i
dates. The influe
The field staff i
the Republican
cratic. And, ind
go to the polls,
Republican part

Thus, by stud
we can analyze
havior. This, in
what people rea
changes in mind
a specific readin
interviews cond
statistical analys
(These techniqu
lication.)[1]

In the preser
important influe
machine this is
challenge. The
of behavior are
tion of types of
examination of :
seem to produc
called dynamic

B. } **PANEL ANALYSIS**

5. THE PROCESS OF OPINION
AND ATTITUDE FORMATION

by Paul F. Lazarsfeld, Bernard Berelson and Hazel Gaudet

Dynamic Social Research. Public opinion research is frequently misunderstood at the present time. From poll findings published in magazines and newspapers, laymen, and even colleagues in other social science fields, have gained the impression that such research is content to describe how people feel about a given issue at a particular time. Actually, the scope of this new discipline is much broader. Social scientists want to know the process by which the various sectors of public opinion influence legislative action and other decision-making in government. Furthermore, we are eager to discover in what ways attitudes themselves are formed. *The People's Choice* focused its attention on this latter problem, the formation, change and development of public opinion.

A group of social scientists remained in Erie County, Ohio, from May until November, 1940, in order to observe the progress and effect of the presidential campaign in that community. A large number of people were interviewed, but the study centered around a panel of 600 respondents who were questioned every month for a period of seven months.

The panel subjects fell into two main groups: those who did not change their political opinion during the period of the study and those who changed in any of a variety of ways. Some shifted their party allegiance, others could not make a decision until the end of the campaign, and still others claimed a definite vote intention but did not go to the polls. These various types of changers and shifters were the central interest of the study, for they were the people in whom the processes of attitude formation and change could be observed. They were compared with the "constant" people. Their personal characteristics, their contacts with other people, and their exposure to radio and newspapers were carefully examined. The reasons they gave for their changes were related to their objective social-economic positions. The positions they had at one time were contrasted with what they stated at both previous and subsequent interviews. In other words, we did not describe opinion; we studied it *in the making.*

Now let us consider one phase of this dynamic analysis in order to discover its essential elements. The panel was interviewed for the sixth time

durin
electi
the e

Table

This
for a
ducte
ally t
per c
for th
for it
attitu
table
tende
Th
week
opini
beha
gand
If
may
sions
Does
At w
it ag
case,
Whe
Ai
differ
chan
indiv

Qu
here
in O
reach
They
socia
For
robo

But the picture is not completed by knowledge only of who changes and in response to what influences. We also want to know the directions of the changes: Do they result in a random redistribution of opinion, or is there some discernible pattern? Turnover analysis in the present study provided preliminary, but revealing, answers to this question. For particular subgroups within the community, attitude change led to greater uniformity and *homogeneity:* individual changes brought members of specific subgroups into closer agreement with each other. For the community as a whole, however, attitude change produced greater diversity and *polarization:* individual changes brought the members of one subgroup into sharper disagreement with members of other subgroups. We shall consider this process in greater detail in a later section of the foreword. The point to emphasize here is that, through the kind of dynamic research employed in the present study, problems such as the development of group cleavages or increasing awareness of class interests become amenable to social research.

Social Research as a Continuing Endeavor. We are frequently warned that the results of a specific study are valid only for the time and place where it was conducted. Does this mean that the findings of one study can never be duplicated in another? Should we expect different results, even under similar conditions? Questions of this kind suggest that terms such as "repetition" and "corroboration of evidence" need to be considered more carefully. In fact, when similar studies are available, comparative analyses can serve three positive functions:

1. The comparison may indicate that the findings of both studies are the same. This we shall call "the function of *corroboration.*"

2. The comparison may indicate that, although the statistical results of the two studies differ, consideration of the specific conditions under which the results were obtained will lead to the same general conclusions. This we shall call "the function of *specification.*"

3. A negative result in the first study may be clarified by new findings in the second one. This we shall call "the function of *clarification.*"

It happens that the present study can be compared with a similar one. A second but briefer panel study was conducted during the 1944 presidential campaign, four years after the one dealt with in this volume. The Bureau of Applied Social Research, in cooperation with the National Opinion Research Center, then at the University of Denver, conducted two interviews with a nation-wide cross-section of about 2,000 people: one interview before the election, the other after. What will a comparison of these two studies yield? We shall select several examples to illustrate and clarify the functions of comparative analyses.

A first example deals with the corroboration of findings. In the Erie County study, there were 54 party changers, persons who shifted their allegiance from one party to the other. Here again the question about the direction of attitude change arose. Did these party shifts bring the changers in closer harmony with other members of the subgroups to which they belonged, or did the changes occur in some other direction?

In order to answer this we made use of the fact already referred to, namely, that the poor, the urban residents, and the Catholics are more likely to vote the Democratic ticket, while the well-to-do, the Protestants, and the rural dwellers are more frequently found in the Republican camp. On the basis of these three social characteristics, indications of membership in different social groups, it was possible to construct an "index of political predisposition." The index, in turn, permitted us to classify the social backgrounds of all individuals as conducive to either a Democratic or a Republican vote. It was thus possible to distinguish between two types of individuals: those whose vote intentions were in harmony with their social backgrounds, and the deviate cases whose intentions were at variance with those of the subgroups to which they belonged.

When the 54 party changers were studied, it was found that, before their shifts in party allegiance, 36 individuals had expressed intentions at variance with their social environments, while, after their shifts, only 20 were deviate cases. We thus came to the conclusion that party changes are in the direction of greater consistency and homogeneity within subgroups.

Because the 1944 study covered only the final few weeks of the campaign, when party changes are rare, it found an even smaller number of shifters. Moreover, an index of political predisposition is less valid when applied to a nation-wide sample than when applied to the residents of one county. And yet, despite these limitations, the results of the second study are an almost *a fortiori* corroboration of those in the first. In 1944 it was possible to study 36 changers. Before their shifts, 22 expressed intentions which deviated from the prevailing opinion climate of their social environments; after the shifts, only 14 deviated.

A comparison of similar studies can thus increase our confidence in findings which might be considered doubtful if only one of the studies had been carried out. Without such corroboration, a finding based on 54 cases in one study and on 36 in a second would be so unreliable that we would question its validity. With the corroboration made possible by successive studies, we are more inclined to accept the result.

Comparative analyses can also confirm general conclusions by indicating that statistically different results are the outcome of different specific conditions. In order to illustrate this function of "specification" we shall return once more to a group of changers already considered: those who said in their pre-election interviews that they would not vote, but who finally went to the polls. In the Erie County study all such individuals voted Republican, while in the 1944 study a majority of these changers voted Democratic. At first glance this might appear to be a contradiction of findings. But is it? In 1940 the Erie County Republican machine was by far the stronger; in 1944 the Political Action Committee was active throughout the nation. Furthermore, P.A.C. concentrated on getting low-income people to the polls on the assumption that, if they voted at all, they would vote Democratic. The figures of the 1944 study prove that assumption correct. Of 20 people (largely from low-income groups) who did not intend to vote but who finally did, 3 cast a Republican and 17 a Democratic ballot.

Thus comparative analyses of studies carried out under different historical or social conditions can lead to much the same sort of confirmation as does actual duplication of results. A comparison of the final decisions of last-minute voters in an election where the Republican machine is strong, with the similar decisions made by similar voters in an election where pro-

Democratic forces are active leads to one general conclusion: the machine which makes a strong last-minute effort to get stragglers to the polls can be of great assistance to its party.

Finally, a comparison of similar studies can lead to the clarification of results. In the 1940 study there was some indication that the party changers were the more indifferent voters. This finding was an unexpected one, for political experts have frequently asserted that, during a campaign, the more intelligent and concerned voter will shift his allegiance from one candidate to another as he learns more about their platforms and as he is better able to appraise their qualifications to deal with the foreign and domestic situations which arise. Because the relationship between party changers and indifference was unanticipated, the plan of the 1940 study did not make adequate provisions for examining it.

This was corrected in the 1944 study. Then all respondents who expressed a vote intention in their preelection interviews were asked two questions: Were they much concerned whether or not their candidate won? and, Did they believe there were any important differences between the two candidates? Analysis of the answers to these questions revealed, in fact, that the party changers (those who voted for one candidate after having said they intended to vote for the other) were considerably *less* concerned with the election than were the "constant" voters (those who actually voted as they had previously intended to): 38 per cent of the changers, as contrasted with 21 per cent of the constant voters, said it made little difference which candidate won the election; 65 per cent of the changers, as contrasted with 46 per cent of the constant voters, could see no real differences between the candidates. It is important to recognize that these expressions of indifference are not post-factum rationalizations of party changes; they were obtained *before* the change took place.

We can thus clarify a result in the earlier study. The people who change their political opinion are not greatly concerned about the campaign or its outcome. Their indifference makes it difficult for them to reach a lasting decision, for they are easily swayed by fortuitous influences. A conversation with a friend today sways them toward one candidate; a persuasive radio talk yesterday had convinced them to vote for the other party. It is not impossible, in fact, that some of the indifferent voters have not reached a real vote decision even as they enter the polling booths.

We were able to compare only two studies and these only at several points. Yet the comparative analysis was productive. It did increase our confidence in results of the individual studies, and it did confirm some of the broader interpretations. Clearly, then, social scientists have missed a valuable opportunity for adding to the fund of basic knowledge by failing to repeat the same type of study under constant and varying conditions. Panel studies lend themselves particularly well to such repetition: their logic is clear, and comparable aspects of different situations can easily be isolated and contrasted.

Our discussion thus far has indicated research methods and plans through which sociologically relevant and scientifically precise data can be obtained. But social research does not stop with the collection of such information. What is needed further is a systematic integration of the data in a theoretical context. Only then can we expect that the data will, on the one hand, be applicable in concrete social situations, and will, on the other hand, point out the directions in which future research work should move.

Empirical Data and Social Processes. The Erie County study resulted in a number of generalizations which should be relevant to any research concerned with short-range changes in attitude or behavior. These do not yet form a coherent system. They are generalizations which form a bridge between the facts as they are observed and a more systematic theory which still awaits development. They are statements about social processes, and are, thus, high-order generalizations when contrasted with statements of empirical fact, low-order generalizations when contrasted with the theoretical formulations toward which social research aims.

All of our conclusions about the social processes through which attitude changes occur are closely interrelated, but for our present purposes it will be sufficient to discuss them separately.

1. A first point concerns the stability of attitudes. The subjects in our study tended to vote as they always had, in fact, as their families always had. Fully 77 per cent of the panel members said that their parents and grandparents had voted consistently for one or the other of the major political parties, and they maintained these family traditions in the 1940 election. This stability was made possible by a sort of protective screen built around central attitudes. Despite the flood of propaganda and counterpropaganda available to the prospective voter, he is reached by very little of it. And, when we examine what exactly does reach him, we find that he elects to expose himself to the propaganda with which he already agrees, and to seal himself off from the propaganda with which he might disagree.

2. Such stability cannot be explained by reference to the "stubbornness" or "inertia" of human nature. Whatever other social or psychological functions may be served by the preservation of basic attitudes, it provides a source of great satisfaction to individuals in their group contacts. By maintaining their attitudes intact, they are able to avoid or to minimize conflicts and disagreements with the persons in their social environments who share these attitudes. Thus attitude stability is instrumental in preserving feelings of individual security.

3. These individual tendencies are supplemented by group processes. While the individual preserves his security by sealing himself off from propaganda which threatens his attitudes, he finds those attitudes reinforced in his contacts with other members of his group. Because of their common group membership, they will share similar attitudes and will exhibit similar selective tendencies. But this does not mean that all of the members of a group will expose themselves to exactly the same bits of propaganda or that they will be influenced by precisely the same aspects of common experiences. Each individual will have his private fund of information and his private catalogue of experiences, even though these are selected and judged according to common standards.

In their mutual interactions, each individual makes public some of the private information and a few of the private experiences which support common attitudes. Thus all individuals become subject to a broader range of selected influences. The interactions serve to increase the isolation of any one individual; they provide him with additional arguments to support his position. The end result of such interactions among group members, then, is a reinforcement, a mutual strengthening, of common attitudes.

4. And yet, change does come about in some cases. It is important, therefore, to determine the conditions under which attitudes lose their stability, and the processes through which the change takes place.

One process depends on the activation of previous experiences and ideas. Every individual carries around with him germs of observations and half-forgotten experiences which are in a sense "recessive," usually because they do not fit into the prevailing traditions or interests of the group to which he belongs. Under certain circumstances, however, during a crisis or during a period of intensive propaganda, these can be brought to the fore. They can then lead to a restructuring of attitudes, and, perhaps in some cases, to a change in group affiliations.

5. Such predispositions to change are more typical for individuals in whom cross-pressures operate. In our complex society, individuals do not belong to one group only. They have a variety of major social affiliations: their social class, their ethnic group, their religious group, the informal associations in which they participate. These various affiliations will make conflicting claims on some individuals: an upper-class Catholic, for example, may find that his religious affiliation pulls him in one direction, while his class position pulls him in the opposite direction. And when concrete situations, such as an election campaign, require him to make a definite decision, he must also decide which of his group loyalties should take priority.

The problem of determining how these cross-pressures are resolved is one of the main tasks for social research. The following questions are relevant in this connection: In which of his various group affiliations does the individual experience such conflicting claims? Are there any general rules for predicting which claims will prove the stronger, when several are in conflict? The reader will find that many of the specific findings in the present study are pertinent to this problem, although no safe generalizations about so complex a topic can be made on the basis of a single investigation. The method developed in the Erie County study, however, should provide the means for answering the question. What kind of behavior does an individual under such cross-pressures exhibit? We found in the present study that, compared with the rest of the Erie County population, individuals who experienced cross-pressures took considerably longer to arrive at a definite vote decision. But such delay is not the only possible reaction. Other alternatives range all the way from individual neurotic reactions, such as an inability to make any decisions at all, to intellectual solutions which might lead to new social movements. Many of the baffling questions about the relationship between individual attitudes and social environment may be answered when these problems of cross-pressures and reactions to them are thoroughly and properly studied.

6. But when talking about an individual and his environment we oversimplify the problem, for the environment consists of other individuals. How are their attitudes developed? Or, to put it somewhat differently, through what mechanisms and processes does a group develop common attitudes?

Again the problem leads us in several directions. We are led, first of all, to study opinion leaders. In every social group there are some individuals who are particularly active and articulate. They are more sensitive than others to the interests of their group, and more anxious to express themselves on important issues. It is relatively easy to locate these individuals, and thus to study how they differ from the majority of their group.

In the present study we found that one of the functions of opinion leaders is to mediate between the mass media and other people in their groups. It is commonly assumed that individuals obtain their information directly from newspapers, radio, and other media. Our findings, however, did not bear this out. The majority of people acquired much of their information and many of their ideas through personal contacts with the opinion leaders in their groups. These latter individuals, in turn, exposed themselves relatively more than others to the mass media. The two-step flow of information is of obvious practical importance for any study of propaganda.

The concept of opinion leadership is, incidentally, not a new one. In the many studies of "power," "influence," and "leadership," we are reminded that every community can point to important men and women who set the fashions and are imitated by others. But our investigation suggests that this familiar concept must be modified. For we found that opinion leadership does not operate only vertically, from top to bottom, but also horizontally: there are opinion leaders in every walk of life.

7. Opinion leadership, however, is only one of the mechanisms through which the attitudes of a group are formed. Another is what has been called the "emergence" or "crystallization" of opinion. Social situations, of which a political campaign would be one example, constantly demand actions or opinions. And the members of a group meet these demands, even when there is no particularly articulate individual on whom they can rely for advice. For, above and beyond opinion leadership are the mutual interactions of group members which reinforce the vague feelings of each individual. As these interactions take place, a new distribution of articulate opinions and attitudes is crystallized.

In essence, then, the process of emergence is another phase of the process of reinforcement discussed above in point (3). When prior attitudes exist, mutual interactions will reinforce them; when no prior attitudes but only vague feelings exist, mutual interactions will crystallize these feelings into definite opinions.

Such emergences of attitude or action have usually been studied only in panic situations, or in attempts to understand "mob behavior." The same processes are at work in many other situations, however, and they do not always lead to turbulence or violence. They occur whenever a stream of propaganda inundates a community, when an important event takes place, or if a group decision is to be made. And, because of their generality, it is important to study under what conditions and in what way these emergences develop.

It is interesting to note that, formulated in this way, questions about the formation of opinion are similar to problems with which economists have struggled for many years. For example, they frequently view the stabilization of price levels as a function of the interactions between supply and the demands of a number of individuals. This is logically similar to considering the distribution of opinion in a group a result of the interactions of many individuals. In neither case can the final result be explained by the previous actions or opinions of individuals considered separately. In both cases the final result is a function of interactions which have as their by-product something which had not existed before.

8. There is still another factor in opinion change. Opinions seem to be organized in a hierarchy of stability. In the course of a campaign, the more flexible ones adapt themselves to the more stable levels. Each political party holds a set of tenets which it tries to impress upon voters. At the beginning of a campaign quite a number of people give "Republican" answers to some questions and "Democratic" answers to others. But as the campaign goes on, there is a tendency for the opinion structure of more and more people to become more and more homogeneous. When the changes are studied, the topics can be ranked according to their degree of flexibility. Vote intention is most stable; attitudes on more specific topics tend to become consistent with party position. Among these topics, in turn, there are some which seem to be dragged along by others. In the 1940 campaign, for instance, opinions on the personalities of the candidates were relatively more stable, and opinions on specific issues, such as the role of the Government in economic affairs, were likely to be adjusted to the evaluation of the men.

These are only some of the processes through which opinions are formed and modified. But they should help to answer a question raised previously, namely, whether shifts in attitudes move in any definite direction. For, whether the process of change involves the resolution of cross-pressures, the influence of opinion leaders or external events, or mutual interactions, the result of change is increased consistency, both within groups and within individuals. As these processes mold and modify opinions, the group members find themselves in closer agreement with each other; there is thus the simultaneous movement toward increased homogeneity within groups and increased polarization between groups which we described earlier. And correlatively, as the individual conforms more closely to his social environment, as he resolves his cross-pressures and finds vague feelings crystallized into definite opinions, many of the inconsistencies in his private set of attitudes will disappear.

Finally, while these generalizations refine the results of the present study, it is important to recognize their preliminary and tentative character. Investigations of other specific situations may lead to new generalizations or may indicate the need to modify those outlined here. One must keep in mind the relation of a specific study and the type of generalization which we consider. They summarize the information thus far collected, but they are not only summaries. They operate also as guides in new researches, for, with them in mind, we know from the start what to look for. Such generalizations, however, are always too general. The concepts which they imply must be translated into specific indices adapted to the concrete situation. It is through new researches and a constant interplay between data and generalizations that systematic progress is achieved.

Avenues of Further Research. There are four major questions which require further investigation and clarification.

First of all we should like to repeat the present study under different political conditions. Are vote decisions arrived at through different processes when the election centers around important issues? In recent presidential campaigns, such as those studied in 1940 and 1944, there have been few issues on which the major parties were split. As a result, party tradition and machine politics have been potent factors in vote decisions. But there is growing evidence that the Republican and Democratic parties are now moving toward sharper conflict on such basic issues as labor legislation. Future presidential campaigns, then, should provide an opportunity to study how attitudes toward specific issues are crystallized, and how these attitudes are related to vote traditions and group influences.

Much the same sort of information can be obtained by conducting similar studies in local elections. We know that in most of these attention is focused on local issues and that in many of them temporary combinations of interested groups cut across party lines. Under such conditions, party activities are reduced. Before the individual can reach a vote decision, he must make up his mind about specific issues and policies. He may therefore be open to persuasion from various sources, and the processes through which he develops a vote decision may be different from those which operated in recent presidential campaigns.

Secondly, we should like to learn more about the personalities and social backgrounds of individuals who change their attitudes. This would require detailed case studies of both "shifters" and "constants." In the Erie County study, special interviews were conducted with the changers, but limitations of funds did not permit us to go as far as we would have liked or as is necessary.

A third problem concerns the relation of the influences uncovered through panel analysis to the total flow of influences and decision within the community. Panel results can often be understood only when the general background of the community is considered. One of the limitations of the present study, for example, resulted from our failure to study the total community in greater detail. Toward the end of the interviewing we learned from our respondents how important the local Republican machine was in influencing the formation of opinion. By that time, however, it was no longer feasible to study the political situation adequately.

A similar shortcoming was our failure to study the opinion leaders more thoroughly. When the panel subjects mentioned that they had received information or advice from other persons, that fact was recorded and the total incidence of personal influences was determined. But there was no attempt to interview the opinion leaders themselves.

This was remedied in a later research, the results of which will soon appear. Here again the study centered around a panel of respondents, this time in an Illinois community.[2] But here, the opinion leaders received special attention: anyone mentioned by a panel member as being influential was asked a series of special questions designed to determine his sources of information and opinion. In this way we were able to obtain a clearer picture of the flow of influence in that community. We did not view it only through the eyes of individual panel members, but were able to trace it along a series of vertical and horizontal chains.

The fourth challenge is of a methodological nature. Neither the values nor the limitations of panel methods have been fully explored as yet. How long can a panel be retained? On what topics can repeated interviews be used safely, and on what other subjects will repetition bias the information collected in later interviews? Would we gain further insights if we analyzed panel results according to the sophisticated mathematical techniques developed by the time-series analysts? How is current laboratory experimentation on attitude formation related to field studies in which repeated interviews are used?

Even during the preliminary phases of the Erie County study it became clear that the technique of repeated interviews was in no way restricted to studies of political propaganda. It is a general method, applicable to any study of attitudes which develop over a period of time. For example, if we want to correct ethnic attitudes, or modify consumer wants, or improve international understanding, we must do more than describe attitudes. We must also study how such attitudes are developed and how they can be influenced. These are all problems for the kind of dynamic social research exemplified in the present study.

6. SOME APPLICATIONS OF THE PANEL METHOD

TO THE STUDY OF CHANGE

by Charles Y. Glock

IN RECENT YEARS, social scientists at our universities and research people associated with both public and private organizations have given increasing attention to the use of the panel method of repeated interviewing in carrying on their research. Briefly, the panel method involves recruiting a sample of individuals representing the universe to be studied and interviewing these people at two or more different points in time on the problems under consideration. The method has been most frequently employed to study trends in consumer brand preferences, listening and reading habits, and in some cases, to collect data on opinions and attitudes. Considerably less attention has been given to the applications of the technique to the study of short-term changes in attitude and behavior patterns for which panel studies are particularly suited.

The following remarks are designed to call attention to some of the recent developments in the application of the panel process to investigating and understanding the phenomena of change.[1] Among the questions relevant to

Reprinted from the American Society for Testing Materials, Symposium on Measurement of Consumer Wants, *Special Technical Publication No. 117*, 1951, pp. 46-54, by permission of the author and the publisher. (Copyright, 1951, American Society for Testing Materials.)

studies of social change, whether undertaken by the social scientist, the business man or the civil servant, are three which are perhaps of primary importance:

1. What was the effect of a stimulus in producing change?
2. What are the conditions which produce differential changes in attitudes or behavior among various groups in a population?
3. What is the mutual interaction between attitudes or behavior patterns which occur simultaneously?

The panel method, because of the special modes of analysis it permits, can provide answers to these questions; answers not readily obtainable from cross-sectional polls. The first attribute of panel analysis important in this respect is that it enables the analyst to identify individual changers objectively. If it develops that a respondent reports an attitude or habit, which differs from that reported in a previous interview, then he is a "changer" and can be studied as such. Cross-sectional polls must rely on the respondent's memory to identify him as a "changer."

Second, the panel process permits the analysis of turnover. Polls may report that there are 3 per cent more persons with a Republican vote intention on November 1 than there were on October 1. But this can be the net result of 15 per cent changes from Democrat to Republican and 12 per cent changes from Republican to Democrat. In another case, the same difference might be the result of, let us say, 45 per cent changes in two directions. The size and nature of the turnover, which is discernible through panel analysis, is of great importance to the study of change.

Finally, there is another analytical advantage of the panel method which should be mentioned. There are certain indices which can only be formed by repeated interviews. Whether someone is brand-loyal or brand-shifting, for example, is a question which involves data extending over a long period of time, and it therefore seems to require repeated interviews. One could think of many other examples of such concepts involving time for which panel analysis is particularly suited.

The Effect of a Stimulus in Producing Change. These are the general advantages of panel analysis. We turn now to the specific modes of analysis involved in providing answers to the three broad questions posed earlier. If the effect of some specific event, or stimulus, is to be studied, we have the first type of situation in which the panel method may be used. To answer a question on the effect of a particular stimulus in producing change, we need information regarding an attitude or behavior pattern before and after the stimulus has been applied. Panel studies concerned with this type of question therefore proceed in the following steps:

1. test of criterion in the first interview.
2. test of criterion in the second interview.
3. determination of exposure to stimulus in second interview.

In an attempt to determine what effect, if any, exposure to the film "Gentlemen's Agreement" had on reducing the level of anti-Semitism,[2] a sample of 503 white Christians living in and around Baltimore was interviewed in November, 1947, prior to the local exhibition of the film. Among the questions asked was a series designed to permit classification of those exhibiting a high, medium, or low level of anti-Semitism.[3]

In the second interview, carried out in May 1948, a measurement of respondents' level of anti-Semitism was again made. In addition, they were asked whether or not they had seen "Gentlemen's Agreement" which had been shown in Baltimore theaters during the period between the two interviews. The level of anti-Semitism exhibited at the time of the first and second interviews for those who had and those who had not seen the film are presented in Table I.

Table I—Percentage Changes in Level of Anti-Semitism Among Those Exposed and Those Not Exposed to the Film, "Gentlemen's Agreement."

Level of Anti-Semitism in Following May	LEVEL OF ANTI-SEMITISM IN NOVEMBER					
	HIGH		MEDIUM		LOW	
	Saw "GA"	Did Not	Saw "GA"	Did Not	Saw "GA"	Did Not
High	63	70	16	45	5	14
Medium	19	15	46	20	9	16
Low	18	15	38	35	86	70
Total Cases	32	132	26	76	57	173

It turns out that the level of anti-Semitism is more likely to be reduced among those who had seen the film than among those who had not. In order to insure that this finding was not the result of selective exposure, educational level was controlled and the results were shown to be the same on all educational levels.

Table I is suggestive in another respect. The fact that we find as much exposure as we do among those whose attitudes deteriorated might be considered evidence that there are a multitude of conflicting influences impinging on the individual.[4] One factor inducive to change in a favorable direction is counterbalanced by another, perhaps stronger, pressure for change in a less favorable direction. How such conflicting pressures might be identified and studied in panel analysis will be discussed later.

In actual day-to-day affairs, we are perhaps more often interested in the effect of a combination of stimuli rather than of a single stimulus. The business man, for example, is often as interested in the effect of a complete marketing campaign as he is in a single advertisement. The public health official responsible, let us say, for educating the public about the character of venereal disease wants to know how effective his entire educational program has been in increasing public knowledge as well as finding out the effectiveness of a single pamphlet or radio program. The same type of panel process used for the measurement of single stimuli is applicable here.

Several organizations[5] interested in arousing public interest in international affairs and the United Nations jointly undertook an educational program in Cincinnati, Ohio, in the winter of 1947-48 to achieve this purpose. Prior to the inauguration of the educational program, in September, 1947, a sample of 588 residents of the city was interviewed on their knowledge about and interest in such problems.[6] An index of level of interest was derived from this interview which permitted respondents to be classified as exhibiting great, medium, or little interest in these subjects.[7]

In March, 1948, following the program, the same respondents were interviewed again and the question on level of interest repeated. In addition, a number of questions were asked to measure the degree of exposure to the educational program; on the basis of these questions the respondents were classified as exposed or not exposed.[8] Table II reports the results in terms of the proportion of respondents in the exposed and unexposed groups whose level of interest had increased, remained the same, or decreased in the period between the first and second interviews.

Table II—Changes in the Level of Interest in International Affairs and the United Nations Among Those Exposed and Unexposed to an Educational Program

Level of Interest	Exposed	Unexposed
Increased between first and second interviews, per cent	30	24
Remained the same, per cent	49	54
Decreased between the first and second interviews, per cent	21	22
Total cases	256	133

We see that, regardless of exposure, the level of interest of most respondents remained the same between the two interviews. However, among those who did change, the exposed respondents were somewhat more likely to increase their level of interest, suggesting that the educational program did have some positive effect. As in the previous example, however, we note that even among the exposed individuals there were some whose level of interest had decreased between the two interviews. This suggests that these individuals may have been exposed to conflicting stimuli during the period of the educational program which exerted an even stronger influence on their behavior.

There exist many such situations in which conflicting stimuli are likely to complicate the analysis of an individual or group of stimuli in producing change. How, for example, does the consumer resolve the host of conflicting claims concerning the qualities of competing products? When exposed to the ideas of conflicting political parties, how does the individual make up his mind about his own voting behavior? The panel process enables us to obtain some insight into problems of this order.

In a study of political behavior conducted in Elmira, N. Y., in 1948,[9] 204 respondents were found to have shifted in their vote inclination between interviews conducted in August and October; 102 shifted toward the Republicans and 102 towards the Democrats. In seeking to explain these shifts, it was felt that those persons who had been exposed to primarily Republican influences would tend to shift Republican, while those exposed to primarily Democratic influences would tend to shift Democratic. However, what about those who were exposed relatively equally to arguments from both sides? Among a number of factors examined to answer this question was the political orientation of the respondent's three closest friends. Table III shows the direction of the shift of vote inclination among those whose friends

Table III—Shifts in Vote Inclination According to Political Orientation of Three Closest Friends

AUGUST TO OCTOBER SHIFTERS	POLITICAL ORIENTATION OF THREE CLOSEST FRIENDS		
	Republican	Mixed	Democratic
Shifted toward Republicans, per cent	56	49	39
Shifted toward Democrats, per cent	44	51	61
Total cases	107	46	51

were all Republican; all Democratic; and those whose friends were mixed in their political orientation.[10]

Those whose friends are of the same inclination tend to shift their vote inclination in that direction. However, those exposed to conflicting pressures from their friends are as likely to shift one way as the other. The index used here is, of course, a crude one and we have used it merely to illustrate the character of the analytical procedures involved. A more refined analysis would have to take into account, as well, the nature of the respondent's interaction with his three friends as well as other factors likely to influence his vote inclination.

Conditions Producing Differential Changes. Some evidence has now been offered illustrating the way in which panel analysis can help us to answer questions concerning the effectiveness of single, multiple, or conflicting stimuli in producing change.[11] We have seen, however, that people do not all behave in the same way when exposed to the same stimulus. Some people who saw "Gentlemen's Agreement" reacted differently to it than others; some individuals whose friends were Republicans shifted their vote inclination accordingly while others did not. It often becomes important, therefore, to understand the conditions under which differential changes in attitude or behavior occur.

To answer this, our second question, we need first to have some means of identifying change and, second, to know the conditions existing prior to the occurrence of the change. In terms of panel analysis, we need to determine the conditions at the time of the first interview and, to identify change, we must administer an equivalent test of the criterion in both the first and second interviews.

In studies conducted during the war of the behavior of the American soldier, Stouffer and his associates gave some attention to the factors affecting social mobility in the Army.[12] They found that even when such factors as age, seniority, and education, factors related to both ability and promotion, were held constant some soldiers were more likely to obtain promotions than others. Studies of soldier attitudes toward the Army showed that higher ranking men had better attitudes than others. This did not necessarily permit the inference to be made that higher ranking men had better attitudes than others prior to promotion. However, the hypothesis was offered that this was in fact the case.

To test this hypothesis, 336 privates were interviewed in November 1943 on their attitudes toward the Army. On the basis of these interviews, the soldiers were rated as to the degree of their conformity to the attitudes considered favorable from the Army's point of view.[13]

In March 1944, the records of 318 of the 336 soldiers interviewed previously were examined to determine which had received promotions. Table IV shows the proportion of soldiers on each level of the conformity scale who had received promotions during the intervening period. We see that other conditions being equal, soldiers whose attitudes were most conformist were most likely to be promoted subsequently.

In the example, panel analysis was used to help explain the factors influencing a change in status. The previously mentioned Elmira study provides us with an example along the same lines where panel analysis was used to

Table IV—Proportions of Soldiers Receiving Promotions on Each Level of a Conformity Scale

Distribution of Conformity Scores Among Privates in November 1943	Number of Cases	Percentage of These Promoted by March 1944
Relatively high score	68	31
Medium score	138	28
Relatively low score	112	17

help explain a change in attitude. It was found that some respondents indicating a Republican or Democratic vote intention in August, 1948 failed to carry out their intentions in their actual voting behavior in November. In seeking to explain this shift, attention was given to the conditions under which the August vote intention was stated. On the assumption that respondents' position in the class structure may have conflicted with their vote intention (that is, persons in the working class with a Republican vote intention, and persons in the middle class with a Democratic vote intention) respondents were asked to indicate which party they thought would do the best job for people in their class. Table V reports the actual voting behavior of those who were for Dewey and those for Truman in August in terms of whether their intention was in conformity or conflicted with their class interest.

Among those people who planned to vote for Dewey in August, those whose class interest was in conflict with their vote intention were much more likely to abandon Dewey than those where such conflict did not arise. The conflict between the vote intention and class interest apparently led to a considerable shift in actual vote. We see here the applications of panel analysis to studying the conditions producing varying changes in attitudes among different groups in a population. This example is significant in another context as well. We saw previously how panel analysis can be applied to study the effect of conflicting stimuli on behavior. Here, we have seen that it is also applicable to study conditions of cross pressures operating on behavior patterns.

Table V—August Preference and November Behavior by Party Which Would Serve Class Interest*

	AUGUST-DEWEY SUPPORTERS		AUGUST-TRUMAN SUPPORTERS	
	Republicans Do Best For Class	Democrats Do Best For Class	Republicans Do Best For Class	Democrats Do Best For Class
Voted Dewey, per cent	81	48	(30)	3
Voted Truman, per cent	6	21	(50)	76
Did not vote, per cent	13	31	(20)	21
Total cases	286	73	10	161

* This table reported in another context in Helen Dinerman, "1948 Votes in the Making—A Preview," Public Opinion Quarterly, Winter, 1948-49, pp. 585-598.

Panel analysis along these lines applies to a considerable number of other situations as well. Theodore Newcomb, for example, in his study of Bennington college students found that those students initially in disagreement with the atmosphere of a community were more likely to change than others, so that they conform better to the prevailing socio-political orientation.[14] In a study now under way at the Bureau of Applied Social Research on operational problems in panel studies, it has been noted that those women who discontinue participating in consumer panels are more likely to be unsystematic in their buying behavior than those who continue to participate.

Mutual Interaction between Attitudes or Behavior Patterns Occurring Simultaneously. The social scientist frequently deals with results where the causal link between two correlated variables is not only ambiguous but the two variables may have an effect on each other. Suppose we cross-tabulate two items from a cross-sectional survey; we find, for instance, that there is a positive correlation between reading an ad in a magazine and owning the product which it advertises. The naive interpretation would be to interpret the correlation entirely as an effect of the advertising. However, it frequently happens that the observed correlation is at least partially spurious, due to the fact that those groups which, because of their characteristics are most likely to buy the product, are also frequently most likely to be exposed to the advertising campaign. Even after the spurious part of the correlation is removed by controlling the sample, the remaining nonspurious part cannot *a priori* be interpreted as being due only to the effect of seeing on buying. There will generally also be an effect of buying on seeing; people may look at an advertisement because they already buy the product and are therefore interested in it. In a panel study this time sequence can be set straight. If we have two interviews, we can always single out those people who owned the product before they read the ad and those who read the ad before they owned the product.

Such analysis applies to a considerable number of problems in which two or more factors are interrelated. To apply panel analysis to the study of the mutual interaction of attitudes or behavior patterns which change concurrently, it is necessary to have information on the interacting variables at both interviews.

In an attempt to study the mutual interaction between changes in reaction and changes in mood, an experimental study was undertaken with 500 college students from various institutions throughout the country.[15] In two interviews taken one month apart, the investigators sought, on the one hand, to obtain a measure of the respondent's mood at the time of each interview[16] and on the other hand, to obtain his reaction to three annoying situations: being made to wait for a lunch date, seeing someone push ahead in a line waiting to get into a movie theater, and being jostled by a stranger in a subway.[17] Respondents were categorized into four groups representing different classes of mood over the two interviews:

+ +   Those who were in a good mood during both interviews.
+ —   Those who were in a good mood during the first and in a bad mood during the second interview.
— +   Those who were in a bad mood during the first and in a good mood during the second interview.
— —   Those who were in a bad mood during both interviews.

The proportion of respondents in each of these four groups who responded in an unaggressive way to each of the criterion questions at both the first and second interviews was then determined. The results are presented in Table VI.

There is a marked tendency for changes in reactions to follow mood changes. Those in a consistently good mood show a constant lack of aggression and those in a consistently bad mood are more aggressive and constant in their response. The two groups of mood changers reveal degrees of unaggressiveness which correspond to their moods at the time of each interview.

Table VI—Interaction Between Mood and Attitude Patterns at Two Different Times

| | PER CENT IN EACH MOOD CLASS GIVING UNAGGRESSIVE REACTIONS | | | | | | | |
| | (+ +) | | (+ —) | | (— +) | | (— —) | |
	Int. I	Int. II	Int. I	Int. II	Int. I	Int. II	Int. I	Int. II
Waiting for date	71	68	58	37	46	69	40	34
Waiting for movie	68	67	70	53	50	63	58	57
Travelling in subway	82	75	71	54	64	78	63	66
Average	73.7	70.0	66.3	48.0	53.3	70.0	53.7	52.3

In this case, changes in mood have been related to changes in answers to questions of essentially a "subjective" character. Further research is indicated to see to what extent changes in answers to "objective" questions might also be correlated with changes in mood.

There are many other situations in which panel analysis of this kind might be applied. To what extent, for example, are brand shifts of, let us say, coffee purchases related to shifts in the purchase of other products? How are changes in vote intention regarding major candidates related to shifts concerning minor candidates? What is the relationship between a change in the newspaper which a person reads and a change in his political orientation?

In using the panel to study such changes as these and others that we have outlined in this paper, it is not necessary that we limit ourselves, as we have done, to situations in which only two variables and two panel interviews are involved. Such analyses can be extended to apply to other situations in which more than two variables or more than two interviews are involved as well. We might, for example, divide people into those who use a given product and those who do not according to information obtained in a first interview. Then in the second interview we can subdivide each group according to whether or not they saw a particular film in which the product was advertised. The four groups so obtained can then be interviewed a third time, and we can study whether they maintained or changed their buying behavior, according to whether they had or had not seen the film.

We might divide Republicans and Democrats, and further subdivide them according to the party which they expect will win. In a second interview we could see whether people who expected their own party to win are less likely to change than those who are less optimistic about their rival party. This would furnish a good test of the "bandwagon effect." But it still leaves open the question as to whether a man who expects the opposing party to win is not weaker in his own convictions. This objection might be met by adding one or two preceding interviews to get a measure of stability of opinion.

It is obviously impossible in this brief paper to follow all of the ramifications of the analysis of repeated interviews. We would stress, however, that the primary advantage of the panel method lies in its applicability to the study of change, and not in its providing easy access to respondents.

Technical Difficulties. Certain operational problems connected with the use of the panel method are troublesome, and we might comment upon them briefly since they perhaps explain why the panel method has not been more widely adopted.

Panel studies have the same initial problem as single interview studies in recruiting people to participate. Some people who, according to the sample design, should be contacted never are, or, when contacted, refuse to grant the interview. People who are willing to participate have been found to differ in many respects from those who do not participate. Efforts have been made to compensate for this original participation bias by substituting people with equivalent characteristics for those who do not participate. However, this procedure does not eliminate the danger of a psychological bias: the higher-educated participant is probably quite different from the higher-educated nonparticipant in most of these cases.

The problem of bias is further aggravated in panel studies since, once the membership of the panel has been recruited, there is still the danger that not every participant will cooperate in every interview and as a result there will be a varying participating group from one interview wave to the next. This mortality within the panel raises the question of whether or not the group which continues to cooperate is still representative of the original panel.

A third problem is whether or not continued participation in a panel has a conditioning effect on replies to questions. One danger is that repeated interviews may make the respondent more than ordinarily aware of the problems involved in the subject matter of the interviews. This may result in his becoming more susceptible to influences leading to change or contrariwise, make him more inclined to resist such influences in order to provide consistent replies.

Work is going ahead on the study of these operational problems in panel research. With continued efforts we can expect to learn how to minimize and perhaps eventually to eliminate them. Despite these present limitations, however, it is evident that, with proper safeguards, the panel method is a most valuable tool in the study of change.

7. FACTORS INFLUENCING CHANGE
OF OCCUPATIONAL CHOICE

by Morris Rosenberg

IT IS GENERALLY RECOGNIZED that an individual's decision to enter a particular occupation is dependent upon a number of rather complex factors, including, among others, one's interests, capacities, and values, and certain

---

This is a previously unpublished paper.

"reality factors."[1] Somewhat less attention, however, has been devoted to an examination of those factors bringing about *change* of occupational choice. This report undertakes to investigate certain factors contributing to such change among a sample of college students.

Two studies of students' values were conducted with representative samples of the undergraduate population of a large eastern university in 1950 and 1952. Since a number of people filled out both questionnaires, it was possible to investigate the changes in attitudes and values which had occurred among them during the two-year span. Among questions dealing with a variety of topics were several designed to investigate occupational values and occupational choices; some of these questions, phrased identically, were included in both studies. It was thus possible to examine certain factors influencing change of occupational choice.

THE INFLUENCE OF VALUES AND IDEOLOGY

Values. Although there is wide variation in the values which people entering the same occupations hope to fulfill, we nevertheless find a decided tendency for members of certain occupations to hold certain value orientations.[2] For example, students who want to become teachers or social workers tend to choose "people-oriented" values ("give me an opportunity to work with people rather than things" and "give me an opportunity to be helpful to others"); students planning to enter one of the fields of business emphasize more than others the extrinsic rewards of work ("provide me with a chance to earn a good deal of money" and "give me social status and prestige"); artists, natural scientists and dramatists are relatively concerned with "self-expression" ("permit me to be creative and original" and "provide an opportunity to use my special abilities and aptitudes"). What influence do these values exercise on change of occupational choice?

Let us take those respondents who, in 1950, said they would like to become teachers. As noted above, these students tended more than others to select "people-oriented" values. Our expectation would be that those teachers* ranking one of the "people-oriented" values high in importance in 1950 would be less likely to abandon the field of teaching in 1952 than would those teachers who had not ranked one of the "people-oriented" values high. The data bear out this expectation.

Table 1—Occupational Values and Change of Occupational Choice Among Teachers*

| | OCCUPATIONAL VALUES OF TEACHERS, 1950 | |
	"People-oriented"	"Non-people-oriented"
Remained teachers, 1952	57	19
Left teaching, 1952	43	81
N = 100%	(82)	(26)

* Percentage difference statistically significant at .01 level.

The first point to note is that people desiring to enter teaching in 1950 characteristically ranked one of the "people-oriented" values high; of the 108 teachers at that time, 82 chose one or both of these occupational values

---

* References to "teachers" and "businessmen" are to those students who indicated that they would *like* to become teachers and businessmen, except where otherwise indicated.

and 26 did not. Of particular importance, however, is the fact that of those teachers who did select "people-oriented" values in 1950, 43 per cent had left teaching two years later; but among the teachers who did not hold these values, 81 per cent had changed their occupational choices. Put in other terms, people in the former group were exactly three times as likely to *maintain* their occupational choices as were those in the latter group. As far as teachers are concerned, it is evident that if people are not concerned with satisfying those occupational values predominantly held in the occupation they have chosen, they are more likely to desire a different occupation two years later.

Now let us examine whether people who did *not* choose teaching in 1950, but selected "people-oriented" values, were more likely to *become* teachers in 1952 than were non-teachers who did *not* select "people-oriented" values.

Table 2—"People-oriented" Values and Choice of Teaching, Among Those Who Were Non-Teachers in 1950*

| | OCCUPATIONAL VALUES, 1950 | |
	"People-oriented"	"Non-people-oriented"
Became teachers in 1952	7.5	4.2
Remained non-teachers in 1952	92.5	95.8
N = 100%	(451)	(385)

* Percentage difference statistically significant at .05 level.

Because of the small number of non-teachers who switched to teaching between 1950 and 1952 absolute differences are naturally small; therefore, we have computed the percentages to one place beyond the decimal point. It turns out that non-teachers holding "people-oriented" values are significantly more likely to switch to teaching than non-teachers who fail to hold these values.

Thus, the fact that teachers holding "people-oriented" values are more likely to *remain* teachers than those who hold other values exclusively, and that non-teachers holding "people-oriented" values were more likely to *become* teachers than other non-teachers, points clearly to the influence of occupational values on change of occupational choice. These data strongly suggest the existence of a trend toward greater "psychological consistency" between occupational values and occupational choice.

Do values also lead to change of occupational choice in other fields? Let us examine the occupational area of business. We noted above that one outstanding fact about the business group, which broadly distinguishes it from the professional group, is its concern with the instrumental values of money and status. One interesting finding is that these values are not only associated with the original occupational choice, but are clearly an important factor in the ultimate decision to remain in the occupation or to leave it.

Table 3—Occupational Values and Change of Occupational Choice Among Businessmen*

| | OCCUPATIONAL VALUES OF BUSINESSMEN, 1950 | |
	Money-status values	Non-money-status-values
Remained businessmen, 1952	57	32
Left business, 1952	43	68
N = 100%	(42)	(37)

* Percentage difference statistically significant at .05 level.

It is evident that among businessmen, too, holding the occupational values characteristic of the group influences change of occupational choice. Although there are many businessmen who do not hold the money-status values, businessmen as a group are more likely to make this choice than are members of any other occupational group. It is thus interesting to note that among the businessmen who selected these values in 1950, 57 per cent continued to choose business as their desired occupation two years later, compared with 32 per cent of the businessmen who did not emphasize the values of money or status. It is plain that it is not a particular set of occupational values, but rather the values dominant within the group, which influences change of occupational choice.

This point is further accentuated when we combine teachers who chose "people-oriented" values with businessmen who selected the occupational values of money and status and compare them with teachers and businessmen who failed to make the choices characteristic of their group.

It may be observed that 57 per cent of those agreeing with the dominant value complex in their own groups remained in their chosen occupations

Table 4—Dominant Value Complex Among Teachers and Businessmen and Change of Occupational Choice*

	TEACHERS AND BUSINESSMEN, 1950	
	Agreed with dominant value complex, 1950	Disagreed with dominant value complex, 1950
Remained in occup., 1952	57	27
Changed occup., 1952	43	73
N = 100%	(124)	(63)

* Percentage difference statistically significant at .01 level.

two years later compared with 27 per cent of those who disagreed with the dominant value complex of the occupational group. Since the combination of occupations increases the size of our N's, the percentage differences here are easily significant at the .01 level. In other words, occupational values do influence change of occupational choice, but this influence is exercised in terms of the *norms* of the group, *not in terms of specific values.*

Ideology and change of occupational choice. The literature on occupational choice has devoted relatively slight attention to the factor of socioeconomic ideology. In many occupational areas ideology is clearly irrelevant to the technical skills required for performance. It may be that occupational activity for the engineer or the physicist may not differ materially in a capitalist or socialist society, but the same cannot be said for the businessman. The style and ends of occupational action of the businessman depend entirely on the maintenance of capitalism, based on the principle of private investment for profit. The businessman aspirant who, for whatever reason, happens to hold a liberal socio-economic point of view is under cross-pressures. On the one hand, there are pressures rooted in the nature of the occupational activity pulling him in the conservative direction; on the other hand, he has adopted certain liberal convictions. Just as cross-pressures predispose people to change their vote decision, so do such cross-pressures operate to produce a change of occupational choice. Concretely expressed, businessmen who have a conservative ideology are significantly more likely to remain faithful to their occupational choices over a two-year span than are those who hold a relatively more liberal political view.

For example, students who planned to enter the field of business in 1950 were asked to agree or disagree with the following statement: "Democracy depends fundamentally on the existence of free business enterprise." Fifty-three per cent of those who agreed with the statement remained faithful to their choice of business in 1952, while only 29 per cent of those who disagreed or were undecided held to their choice of the field of business. Similar results were yielded when these students were presented with the following statement: "The 'welfare state' tends to destroy individual initiative." Fifty per cent of those who agreed with the statement were businessmen constants, compared with 28 per cent of the disagree-undecided group. Questions dealing with labor also showed that the more liberal respondents were more likely to shift away from the field of business. Confronted with the statement, "The laws governing labor unions today are not strict enough," 63 per cent of those who agreed were unchanging businessmen, compared with 35 per cent of those who disagreed or were undecided. Finally, students were asked to agree or disagree with the following statement: "Labor unions in this country are doing a fine job." Fifty-five per cent of those who disagreed with the statement were constant businessmen, compared with 35 per cent of those who agreed or were undecided. The N's in each case are not large, but the results are highly consistent.

It is possible to combine the answers to these four questions into a score of conservatism. Twenty-two people, or 28 per cent of the businessmen, gave the conservative answer to all four questions, whereas only one man, or 1.4 per cent, was liberal on all four questions. Thus it would not be just to speak of conservative and liberal businessmen, but rather to speak of more conservative and less conservative groups. When we compare those who gave consistently conservative answers with those who gave occasionally conservative answers, we can observe the impact of socio-economic ideology on change of occupational choice very clearly.

Table 5—Conservative Ideology and Change of Occupational Choice Among Businessmen*

	CONSERVATIVE IDEOLOGY	
	Very conservative	Not very conservative
Remained businessmen, 1952	73	36
Left business, 1952	27	64
N = 100%	(22)	(56)

* Percentage difference statistically significant at .01 level.

The less conservative businessmen are clearly more likely to change their occupational choices than are the more conservative businessmen. Although ideology may be irrelevant in many occupations, it is clearly an important factor with regard to the field of business.

Dedication to Career. We have noted that the values an individual hopes to satisfy in his work will importantly influence his change of occupational choice. It is also possible to examine the influence of values in terms of the wider context of one's anticipated major source of life satisfaction. There is one question in our study which may serve as a measure of the importance of work within the individual's total value-system.

Students were asked: "What three things or activities in your life do you expect to give you the most satisfaction?" The alternatives presented were: your career or occupation; family relationships; leisure-time recreational activities; religious beliefs or activities; participation as a citizen in the affairs of your community; participation in activities directed toward national or international betterment. Respondents were then instructed to rank these alternatives in order of importance. Most of the respondents, both male and female, checked "family relationships" as most important; a much smaller number checked "your career or occupation"; and very few checked any of the other four alternatives.

If a young person, looking into the future, expects to obtain his major life satisfactions from his work, then it is reasonable to describe him as "dedicated" to his work. One occupational group which we might expect to be dedicated to their careers would be those people planning to become doctors. The training required for the study of medicine is so onerous and time-and-money consuming that one would expect only a person firm and unwavering in his occupational direction to resist the temptation to take an easier course. Are the more 'dedicated' doctors indeed more likely to maintain their occupational choices?

Table 6—Main Source of Life Satisfaction and Change in Choice of Medicine*

| | MAIN LIFE SATISFACTION | |
	Career or occupation	Family relationships
Still chose medicine, 1952	80	33
Left medicine, 1952	20	67
N = 100%	(20)	(27)

* Percentage differences statistically significant at .01 level.

Such dedication proves to be an important factor in adhering to the field of medicine. Among those students who were medical aspirants in 1950, 20 chose "career," 27 chose "family," and 5 chose "others." Of those choosing "career," 80 per cent still wanted to be doctors two years later; of those choosing "family," only 33 per cent wanted to be doctors two years later, a difference of 47 per cent. Adhering to, or shifting away from, the field of medicine is thus clearly related to how important career is within one's total life framework. Those who tend to view their work simply as a way to make a living in order to enjoy a satisfactory family life would be more disposed to seek easier ways to fulfill this aim.

A somewhat more direct way of determining the student's dedication to his career is to note whether he enters his field reluctantly or willingly. The person who would like to enter one occupation, but who, for various reasons, actually expects to enter another, is doubtlessly less dedicated to his work than the student who expects to enter the field he desires. In our sample, the largest proportion of reluctant recruits turned out to be in the field of business. Many of these people preferred to become doctors, lawyers, journalists, etc.; however, since most of their fathers were businessmen, they were induced, either through various direct or indirect pressures or simply through the smoothing of their occupational paths, to select this field. They did so, however, with a longing backward glance toward other occupations. What is the outcome of this conflict?

The results indicate that the reluctant businessmen were clearly more likely to change their occupational expectations than were the willing businessmen. Two years later, only one out of five expected to enter the field of business, compared with over three out of five of the willing businessmen. If we make the reasonable assumption that a conflict between aspirations and expectations leads to reduced dedication, then it is plain that the less dedicated people are more likely to change the fields they expect to enter. These results emphasize, incidentally, the sense of "free choice" felt by the young American college male in his occupational choice.

Table 7—Attitude toward Business as an Occupation and Change of Occupational Choice*

| | ATTITUDE TOWARD BUSINESS, 1950 | |
	Reluctant businessman	Willing businessman
Remained in business, 1952	20	61
Left business, 1952	80	39
N = 100%	(46)	(44)

* Percentage difference statistically significant at .01 level.

We have seen that values and ideology may have an important influence upon the individual's decision to change his occupational choice. There is also evidence to suggest that personality factors and capacities may also be implicated in this decision.

For example, the student sample was asked: "How important is it for you to have your plans for the future rather clearly known to you in advance?" It may be that people who consider it very important may tend to have a life-view oriented far into the future (the "far-sighteds"), whereas the opposite type, tending to view matters within a day-to-day context (the "myopics"), would show little perdurance in their decisions and plans. And we find, in fact, that the teachers, engineers, and doctors who find it very or fairly important to have their plans known in advance are less likely to change their occupational choices in the two-year span than those who consider it not very important or not at all important. The percentage difference for the combined occupations is statistically significant at the .01 level. These findings suggest that change of occupational choice is in part attributable to an individual's general way of planning his life.

Another factor which one might expect to influence stability or change of occupational choice would be the relationship between the individual's *capacities* and the requirements of the occupation. For example, it is common knowledge among those who hope to become doctors that a high academic level is a minimal requirement for acceptance to medical school. Consequently, we would expect a man with an undistinguished academic record to soon abandon his hope of becoming a doctor. Such turns out to be the case. Among medical aspirants with relatively good grades in 1950, 75 per cent still hoped to become doctors in 1952; but among those with relatively poor grades in 1950, only 27 per cent made this choice two years later.

It is thus evident that the relationship between one's capacities and the requirements of the occupation will influence the stability of choice. People who are going into business, for example, do not need high college grades for occupational success. Thus we find that among those planning to enter business in 1950, those with poorer grades were *less* likely to change their occupational choices than those with superior grades. The latter tended to move in the direction of the professions. Thus certain capacities which may bring about change in one field may produce stability of choice in another.

THE TREND TOWARD INCREASING PSYCHOLOGICAL CONSISTENCY

We noted above that people who hold the values most commonly selected in their occupations are less likely to change their occupational choices than are those who failed to hold these values. This raises the question of whether one can expect an increasing "psychological consistency" between values and choices in the course of time. For example, we would expect that people holding values inconsistent with their choices would tend to do one of two things: they would either change their occupational values in a direction consistent with their occupational choices, or they would change their choices in a direction consistent with their values. If this were the general pattern, then we would expect that a relationship between values and choice in 1950 would increase by 1952. Is this expectation borne out by the data?

Previous analysis had revealed that members of certain occupations tended to de-emphasize "people-oriented" occupational values. Certain of these occupations involved work with "impersonal matter" (farming, engineering, architecture, and natural science); others involved the use of creative self-expression (art and journalism-drama); and the remainder dealt with business activities (business [unspecified], real estate-finance, and sales-promotion). Students choosing other occupations tended to place greater stress on "people-oriented" values (i.e., those desiring to enter social work, social science, teaching, medicine, personnel, housewife, secretarial, food-hotel, advertising, government work, and law). We will call the first group the "non-people-oriented" occupations (or NPO Occ.) and the second group the "people-oriented" occupations (or PO Occ.). "People-oriented" values will be called PO Val. and "non-people-oriented" values, NPO Val.

We know in advance that PO Occ. is positively related to PO Val. in 1950. The question is whether this relationship among the same group of people increases by 1952. If so, this would indicate a tendency toward increased psychological consistency between occupational choice and occupational values.

Table 8—Relationship between Occupational Values and Occupational Choice in 1950 and 1952

Choice	PO Val.	1950 VALUES NPO Val.	Total	Choice	PO Val.	1952 VALUES NPO Val.	Total
PO Occ.	226	89	315	PO Occ.	226	66	292
NPO Occ.	166	231	397	NPO Occ.	154	266	420
Total	392	320	712	Total	380	332	712

It will be noted that in 1950 there were 89 people with NPO Val's who chose PO Occ's, and 166 people with PO Val's who chose NPO Occ's. In terms of the general relationship between occupational values and occupational choice, these 255 people were the psychologically inconsistent group, and constituted 36 per cent of the panel members.* By 1952, however, there were 66 NPO Val's with PO Occ's and 154 people with PO Val's choosing NPO Occ's. In other words, there were now 220 inconsistent people, or 31 per cent of the sample. The percentage differences between "inconsistents" on the two waves are statistically significant at the .05 level. Another way

---

* We have omitted those answering "don't know" on either wave.

of expressing this trend is to note that in 1950 the coefficient of association between occupational choice and occupational values was Q = +.559, whereas by 1952 the coefficient of association had increased to Q= +.711.

There is thus a significant trend toward increased psychological consistency, although it is admittedly not a large one.

The trend noted above, however, does not reveal the complete picture of turnover. In order to observe all the combinations of occupational choice and occupational values in 1950 and 1952, it is necessary to present the data within the framework of a 16-fold table.

Table 9—"People-Oriented" Occupational Values and Occupational Choices in 1950 and 1952

Occup. Values and Choices, 1950	PO Occ. PO Val.	PO Occ. NPO Val.	NPO Occ. PO Val.	NPO Occ. NPO Val.	Total
	OCCUP. VALUES AND CHOICES, 1952				
PO Occ.-PO Val.	163	15	30	18	226
PO Occ.-NPO Val.	21	29	8	31	89
NPO Occ.-PO Val.	36	8	73	49	166
NPO Occ.-NPO Val.	6	14	43	168	231
Total	226	66	154	266	712

Let us examine the people who were inconsistent in 1950. There were 255 such people, 89 PO Occ.-NPO Val's, and 166 NPO Occ.-PO Val's. These people might behave in one of three possible ways. The first possibility is that they might have changed either their occupational choices or their occupational values so that they now hold a psychologically consistent position. It turns out that, of those 255 originally inconsistent people, 137, or 54 per cent, had now become consistent. The second possibility would be that these people would maintain their original inconsistency, changing neither occupational choice nor occupational values. It turns out that 102 people, or 40 per cent of these respondents, did so. Finally, it is possible that these inconsistent people might change both values and choices, thereby achieving an inconsistent position which was the diametric opposite of their original position. This turns out to be the rarest phenomenon of all, with only 16 cases, or 6 per cent, manifesting this behavior. There is thus an evident tendency for people with psychologically inconsistent positions to become more consistent with the lapse of time.

This change is in striking contrast to those who were originally consistent; these people tended to maintain their same consistent position. Of the 457 consistent people in 1950, 331, or 72 per cent, maintained the same consistency in 1952; 102, or 22 per cent became inconsistent; and 24, or 5 per cent, changed to the opposite pole of consistency.

It is thus evident that people who are originally consistent tend to *remain* consistent. However, it may be noted that there are relatively few "complete reversals," *i.e.,* inconsistents who change both choice and values to become inconsistent in the opposite way, or consistents who change both choice and values to become consistent in the opposite way. If changes occur, these are usually changes of either choice *or* values, but rarely both.

Having noted that occupational choice and occupational values increased in consistency between 1950 and 1952, the question we now wish to raise is: Is this increased consistency achieved by people changing their values to accord with their occupational choices, or is it achieved by people changing their choices to accord with their values? This can be determined by observing the subsequent behavior of those who were originally inconsistent.

Table 10—Inconsistent People in 1950 Who Became Consistent in 1952

	1952	
1950	PO Occ. PO Val.	NPO Occ. NPO Val.
PO Occ.-NPO Val.	21	31
NPO Occ.-PO Val.	36	49

It will be seen that those people in the upper left-hand cell and in the lower right-hand cell maintained their occupational choices, but altered their values in a direction consistent with these choices; this occurred among 70 people. Conversely, those people in the lower left-hand and upper right-hand cells maintained their values but altered their occupational choices in a direction consistent with the values; this occurred in 67 cases.

It is thus plain that the trend toward increased consistency is a consequence of both a change of values to suit the occupational choices and a change of choices to suit the occupational values. Both choices and values appear to exercise approximately equal influence in bringing about the increase in consistency.

In sum, we have seen that the hypothesized trend toward psychological consistency between occupational values and occupational choice does occur. In the course of the two-year span between waves, the inconsistents tended to become more consistent, and the consistents tended to remain consistent. Both occupational values and occupational choice appeared to be about equally influential in producing the increased consistency.

8. THE PREDICTION OF SOLDIERS' RETURN
TO PRE-WAR EMPLOYMENT

by John A. Clausen

[The following selection, drawn from *Measurement and Prediction:* Studies in Social Psychology in World War II, is an example of the prediction of people's behavior on the basis of their stated intentions. Among several prediction studies undertaken by members of the Research Branch of the Information and Education Division of the War Department were those dealing with the studies of the postwar plans of soldiers. Efforts were made to predict soldiers' plans to return to school, to return to previous employers, to engage in farming, to become business owners and to enter governmental employment. In order to compare the predictions with the postseparation performance, mail questionnaires were sent to a sample of separatees from four widely scattered separation centers asking about their occupational activities, interests, and efforts. In the following selection, John A. Clausen discusses the procedure employed to predict soldiers' plans to return to their previous employers.—ED. NOTE.]

APPROXIMATELY FOUR FIFTHS of the Army's male personnel had worked for an employer just before entering the service. The Selective Service Act of 1940 assured reemployment rights to all personnel entering the Armed Forces after May 1, 1940, who were occupying nontemporary jobs in the civilian economy as of the time of induction or enlistment. Some men, however, had left their regular jobs either to take jobs in war industry or to take vacations before entering the service. Once the war was under way, many men entering war industry were replacing others who had enlisted or been inducted.

There was no accurate knowledge of the number of men in service who had reemployment rights to their preservice jobs. Estimates generally ran between 20 per cent and 30 per cent and were based largely on guesswork, as the following quotation suggests:

"When allowance is made for those veterans, now probably 40 per cent of the total, who entered military and naval service without previously having had gainful employment, for the large number who will have no reemployment rights because they occupied temporary positions or were unemployed at the time of induction, for those whose jobs will be wiped out by business

Reprinted in part from Samuel A. Stouffer, Louis Guttman, Edward A. Suchman, Paul F. Lazarsfeld, Shirley A. Star, and John A. Clausen, *Measurement and Prediction*, Studies in Social Psychology in World War II, Vol. IV, pp. 623-638, by permission of the author and the publisher. (Copyright, 1950, by the Princeton University Press.)

failures or technological changes, for those so disabled that they will not be able to resume their old occupations, and for those jolted out of a customary way of life, whom new maturity, skills, or ambitions will tempt to greener pastures, the number of veterans with effective rights to reinstatement is estimated at about 20 per cent of the total."[1]

The estimate that 40 per cent of all military personnel had not previously been gainfully employed was at least double the actual figure, but there was no way of knowing how many veterans had occupied temporary jobs or how many desired to find new jobs. Moreover, many employers indicated that they would attempt to reemploy not merely those veterans who had legal rights to a job, but all veterans who had been in their employ at the time of induction or enlistment. It seemed relevant, therefore, to inquire into the number of men in service who planned to return to work for their previous employers.

Ascertaining Plans to Return to Previous Employer. The problem of multidimensionality of plans was nowhere more difficult to deal with than in the area of plans to return to work for one's previous employer. Some men wanted to return to the exact niche they had previously occupied; others wanted to return to the same employer but in a different (and usually a better-paying) job; still others were interested in working in the same occupation but with a different employer, yet were considering the possibility of going back to work for their former employer if other opportunities were not readily available. For a large proportion of the Army's personnel who had previously been gainfully employed, it appeared that the possibility of returning to work, at least temporarily, for one's previous employer was not to be completely dismissed even though other pastures might seem greener. A survey conducted in December 1943 to elicit attitudes toward postwar vocational guidance included three questions relating to interest in doing the same or a different kind of work with the same or a different employer after the war. More specifically, the questions asked were:

1. Whether the respondent *would like to go back* to his old job with his old employer, a different job with his old employer, the same kind of work with a different employer, or a different kind of work with a different employer.
2. What kind of work the respondent *would like to do* after the war.
3. What kind of work the respondent *actually expected to do* after the war.

It was found that of men who had previously been employed, a slight majority (54 per cent) said they would like to do the same kind of work, and of this group, about three fourths said they would like to work for their previous employer. Among the 46 per cent of all previous employees who said they would like to do a different kind of work, however, nearly half were doubtful as to whether they would actually do a different kind of work, and a fourth thought they would probably return to work for their previous employer. Clearly this was not a unidimensional problem.

Considerable difficulty was encountered in attempting to phrase questions simply enough to be intelligible to the soldier with only fifth or sixth grade education yet precisely enough to specify the dimensions desired for classification. For example, the expression "go back to your old job after the war," was interpreted by a majority of soldiers as referring to a job with their last employer prior to induction, but some men took this expression to mean the same general occupation, regardless of employer, and some took it to mean precisely the same occupation with the same employer. The man who hoped to go back to a somewhat different job with his previous employer was frequently at a loss to know how he should classify himself. To get around this problem, it was decided to ask separate questions about type of work or occupation, and about prospective employer.

Another major difficulty was encountered in inconsistencies among responses to questions which were designed primarily for men who had been employed just before their induction. Such questions usually carried an answer category, "I was *not* working just before I entered the Army," but some men who had not previously been employed failed to check this category and instead checked that they planned to do a different kind of work than they had previously done. Other men, not employed just before induction but employed at some earlier date, further confused the picture with respect to probable reemployment of those drafted or volunteering for the service from their jobs subsequent to the spring of 1940. To meet this problem it seemed desirable first of all to ascertain employment status prior to induction and then in this area to study the plans only of those men who had occupied full-time jobs prior to their induction.

In the world-wide survey conducted in the summer of 1944, men were classified first as to whether or not they had been employed just prior to induction or enlistment, then by their judgment of whether they could get work with their previous employer and, finally, whether they expected actually to return.[2] They were also asked to describe the kind of work they expected to do, and this was coded as "similar to" or "different from" the kind they had previously done. These data were used as a basis for estimating the minimum number of soldiers counting on going back to their old jobs and the maximum number considering returning to work for their previous employers. The method of classification is described in the following quotation from the survey report:

"Those enlisted men who say both that they plan to do the same kind of work and that they *expect* to return to their old jobs may be considered a minimum estimate of the proportion definitely counting on going back to their old jobs. These comprise a fourth of the white enlisted men who worked as employees before they entered the Army. Those men (fourteen per cent of former employees) who are planning to return to the same kind of work and who say they *may* return to their former employers also seem more likely to try to get their old jobs back than to make a change. The estimate of the maximum number of men who are considering returning to their former employers includes all other men (twenty-one per cent) who say that they *may* go back to work for the employer they worked for just before they entered the Army. Some of these men are undecided about their postwar plans, and many of them are seriously considering alternative plans—a different type of work for an employer, full-time school, self-employment, etc.—but they do not feel sure enough about the alternatives to rule out going back."[3]

It appeared likely then, on the basis of their plans, that about 40 per cent of the soldiers who had previously been employed might return to work for their former employers. There was some doubt, however, as to the desirability of using the dimension "type of work" as a criterion for estimating probable extent of return to previous employer. A man might desire a change in occupational category yet primarily be intent on securing a job with his old employer. Subsequently, therefore, the use of this dimension was discontinued and a different criterion for distinguishing between probable returnees and others was established.

Plans of Separatees in December 1945. The questionnaire administered to separatees used the same basic questions for a classification of plans to return to preinduction employer with but one modification of any importance: in answer to the question, "Do you think you actually will go back to work for the same employer . . . ?" the previously used response category, "I may, but I'm not sure" was replaced by two new categories: "Yes, I probably will" and "I may, but I probably will *not.*" It was hoped that under conditions favorable to prediction from stated plans, this change would permit discrimination between one group of which more than half the members would actually return and another group of which somewhat less than half would return. On the assumption that errors of individual prediction would to a considerable extent counterbalance each other, the new categories gave a cutting point for a total percentage prediction as well as for individual prediction. The classification scheme, along with the two questions on which it was based, is given below.

Question 24: Do you think you could get work with the employer you worked for before you came into the Army, if you wanted to?

Question 25: Do you think you *actually will* go back to work for the same employer you worked for before you came into the Army?

Classification	Answer to question 24	Answer to question 25
Definite plans to return	Yes, I'm almost sure I could	Yes, I'm almost sure I will
Tentative plans to return	Yes, I'm almost sure I could	Yes, I probably will
	or	
	Yes, I think so, but I'm not sure	{ Yes, I'm almost sure { Yes, I probably will
Considering returning but not planning to	Yes, I'm almost sure I could Yes, I think so, but I'm not sure	I may, but I probably will *not*
Not considering returning	All other combinations	

Among December separatees slightly over four fifths had been gainfully employed at full-time jobs and about 3 per cent had been employed part-time before entering the service. The preinduction employment experience of the December separatees approximated that of the total Army as revealed by earlier world-wide surveys. This was in accordance with expectation, since they were being released about midway in the demobilization process and in most characteristics were fairly close to Army averages as of peak strength.

Table 1 presents a comparison of the plans of white enlisted men surveyed in the world-wide cross examination of summer 1944, and those of December separatees at the time of discharge. December separatees were planning to return in higher proportion than were enlisted men who had

Table 1—Comparison of Plans of White Enlisted Men to Return to Previous Employer among Men in Service in Summer 1944 and Men Separated from Service in December 1945 (Per Cent)

	Men in service Summer 1944	Separatees December 1945
Total	100	100
Had worked full time for an employer	80	82
Definite plans to return	(23)	(29)
Tentative plans to return	(26*)	(17)
Considering returning		(13)
Not considering returning	(31)	(23)
Had not worked full time for an employer	20	18

* Wording of answer category was such as to include all those considering returning but not definitely planning to do so.

been surveyed in the summer of 1944. The first question to be answered, in evaluating the use of soldiers' plans as predictors, was whether the differences reflected the effect of different characteristics within the sample groups, or whether there had been real shifts in the plans of soldiers with similar characteristics.

An analysis of characteristics associated with plans to return to one's preinduction employer revealed that such plans were held in highest proportion among older men, those with relatively short service in the Army, and those longest employed in the job held just before induction. The last-mentioned variable, however, was found to account for all of the correlation between age and plans to return and most of the correlation between length of Army service and plans to return.

Table 2—Plans to Return to Previous Employer, by Duration of Previous Employment December 1945 Separatees (Per Cent)

	LENGTH OF PREVIOUS EMPLOYMENT			
	Less than 1 year	1-2 Years	2-5 Years	Five Years or more
Total	100	100	100	100
Definite plans	18	35	47	64
Tentative plans	22	24	17	16
Considering returning	17	19	13	13
Not considering returning	43	22	23	7

Performance of Separatees. In order to establish the relationship between plans expressed at separation and performance defined in terms of an attempt to carry out those plans, the follow-up questionnaire asked not only about current employment status but also about efforts to return to preinduction employer. The question asked and the distribution of responses of December separatees are reported in Table 3.

The extent of return of December separatees to work for their preinduction employers was very closely in accordance with predictions made on the basis of their plans. Among December separatees 46 per cent had expressed plans indicating that they were leaning toward return, and within three to four months after discharge 42.3 per cent had returned, another 4.3 per cent still planned to return, and 3.6 per cent had tried to return but had been unable to do so. Thus, 50.2 per cent may be classified as having returned or tried to return.

Actually, the accuracy of the prediction of return to preinduction employer

Table 3—Responses of December Separatees to Question Relating to Return to Preinduction Employer as of Two to Four Months after Discharge

Question 6: Since you got your discharge, did you go back to work for the employer (company, person, etc.) you worked for before you entered the Army?	December separatees (per cent)
Total	100.0
I wasn't working for an employer before I went into the Army	12.1
Yes, I got a job with my old employer and I am working there now	38.2
Yes, I got a job with my old employer but I am not working there any more	4.1
I tried to get a job with my old employer, but couldn't	3.6
No, I asked about a job but decided not to work there	6.0
No, I haven't started working there yet, but I plan to go back with my old employer	4.3
No, I didn't try to go back and I don't plan to	29.1
No answer	2.6

was probably somewhat higher than indicated by the above figures. It appears that about 2 per cent of the group of separatees was comprised of men who reported that they had returned or had tried to do so, yet who had at the time of discharge indicated that they were not employed immediately prior to their induction. In classifying plans to return, it will be recalled that men not employed full-time *immediately* prior to induction were not included, since they presumably had no real claim to jobs.[4]

It will also be noted that answers to the category "I wasn't working for an employer before I went into the service" give a considerably lower estimate of the number not gainfully employed than was given by questions in the questionnaire administered at the separation centers. (See Table 1.) Some men employed only part-time before induction answered the follow-up question in terms of their relation to their part-time employer. Some men not employed at all prior to induction checked "I didn't try to go back" instead of checking that they had not been employed; others simply did not answer the question. All of which again indicates the problem of maintaining exact specification of dimensions in asking such questions.

The Adequacy of Plans as a Basis for Prediction. In addition to the questions already described as the basis of classification of soldiers' plans to return to previous employers, the "summing up" question toward the close of the questionnaire* was also used as a basis for estimating the probable rate of return. The first answer category was "I will probably work for the employer I was working for just before I came into the Army." This question was followed by another which asked about the degree of certainty of the

---

* [The questions referred to are the following:

"68. In this questionnaire we have asked you a lot of questions about your plans for after your discharge. Now that you have thought them over a little more, try to take everything into consideration and check the one thing you will most probably do *first of all*—after you have gotten your discharge and taken a vacation.

1....I will probably work for the employer I was working for just before I came into the Army.
2....I will probably work for salary, wages, or commission for some other employer.
3....I will probably go to full-time school or college.
4....I will probably farm for myself or with my family.
5....I will probably go into business for myself.
6....I am undecided what I will do.

69. How sure do you feel that this is what you will try to do *first of all*? (Check one)
1....I am very sure.
2....I am pretty sure, but might do something else.
3....Chances are about 50-50 that this is what I will try to do.
4....I'm really not at all sure what I will do."

Quoted from page 705 of *Measurement and Prediction, op. cit.*]

soldier's plans. To be classified as having definite plans to return to work for one's previous employer, by this scheme, a man had to check the appropriate category in the question involving alternatives (Q 68) and check

Table 4—Comparison of Alternative Methods of Classification of Separatees' Plans to Return to Previous Employer

Interest in returning to previous employer	Separatees December 1945 (per cent)	
First Method (direct questions)		
Definite plans to return	29	
Tentative plans to return	17	} 46
Considering returning	13	
Other (including men who had not been employed)	41	
	100	
Second Method (final alternatives)		
Definite plans to return	27	
Tentative plans to return	20	} 47
Other plans	53	
	100	

"I am very sure" (that this is what I will do first of all after discharge) in answer to the question relating to degree of certainty. All other men who checked that they thought they would probably return to work for their preservice employer (but who were not "very sure") were classified as having tentative plans to return. A comparison of the proportions of men classified as having plans to return to their previous employers, based upon the alternative methods of classification, is given in Table 4.

It will be noted that predictions based upon the alternative methods were closely similar—assuming that most men with definite or tentative plans would carry out those plans and that roughly compensating numbers who had not planned to return would actually do so.

As would be expected, there was a high degree of consistency in classifications based on the two methods. Thus, of 1,713 December separatees who had worked for an employer just before entering the Army, the same prediction—whether return or nonreturn—was given by the two methods in 1,489 or 87 per cent of the cases. See Table 5.)

Table 5—Extent of Consistency of Prediction Using Alternative Methods of Plans Classification, and Extent of Return to Previous Employer for Each (December Separatees)

Prediction based on original method of classification	Prediction based on second method of classification	Number of separatees	Per cent who actually returned*
Return	Return	841	83
Return	Nonreturn	118	49
Nonreturn	Return	106	60
Nonreturn	Nonreturn	648	26

* Or planned to return or had tried to return as of three to four months after discharge.

The two groups of men whose expression of plans was inconsistent, by the criterion of alternative classification, tended to counterbalance each other and to return to their previous employers in reasonably similar proportions.

Of the errors in prediction of return, only about a third came from the two rather small groups which appeared inconsistent in the expression of their plans. The other two thirds came from the larger groups who had consistently reported plans to return or consistently reported plans not to return. It would appear, therefore, that while manifest uncertainty of plans expressed at the time of discharge was a significant source of error in prediction, the modification of plans after discharge was probably of greater importance as a source of predictive error.

Population Characteristics and Prediction of Return. As has already been mentioned, the most important characteristic associated with plans to return to preinduction employer was the length of time a man had been with that employer. In addition to its relationship to *plans* expressed at the time of discharge, duration of previous employment was also found to affect the extent of *actual return* by men who expressed similar plans. That is, among men with definite plans (or tentative plans, or no plans) to return to their previous employer, those longest employed went back in higher proportion than those employed for a shorter period (Table 6).

Table 6—Rate of Return to Previous Employer per Hundred Separatees Reporting Specified Plans to Return and Specified Duration of Previous Employment

| Duration of previous employment | RATE OF RETURN BY PLANS EXPRESSED AT SEPARATION | | | |
	Definitely return	Probably return	Possibly return	Plan not to return
Less than one year	76	63	41	21
One year up to two years	83	72	56	23
Two years up to five years	86	}77*	}53	}29
Five years and over	93			
Average rate for plans group	(85)	(70)	(49)	(24)

* Combinations made where single classes contained fewer than fifty cases.

For December separatees, tabulations to show extent of return, by length of Army service, by age and by education, holding constant plans and length of previous employment, revealed no significant relationships. That is, among groups of comparable plans and comparable duration of employment, older men were no more likely to return than were younger men, men in the Army less than three years were neither more nor less likely to return than were those in the Army for longer periods, high school graduates and college men were no more likely to return than were soldiers whose education had not extended beyond grade school. There was a slight tendency for those high school graduates who had *not* planned to return to their previous employers to stand by their plans (i.e., not to return) to a somewhat greater degree than was the case among men with only grade school education, but this was the only group for which rate of return seemed to be related to education.

Type of Employer and Rate of Return. The questionnaire administered at the separation centers had asked for a report of the type of employer for whom the men had worked in their last civilian jobs—whether a private employer with fewer than fifty employees, a private employer with fifty or more employees, or a branch of Federal, state, or local government. An analysis of the extent of return to previous employers, by type of employer, of December separatees revealed that 40 per cent of the men who reported they had worked for small private employers, 61 per cent of those who reported they had worked for larger private employers, and 52 per cent of those who said they had been governmentally employed[5] actually returned to their former employer. In part, these differences reflect a difference in the plans of the three groups. Even with duration of previous employment held constant, plans to return to their preinduction employer were more frequently expressed by men who had worked for larger companies than by those who had worked for companies or individuals employing less than fifty persons. Part of the greater degree of return by the employees of larger companies, however, seems to be independent of plans expressed at separation. Consistently higher rates of return were noted for the employees of larger companies when plans and duration of previous employment were held constant.[6]

Of men who had worked for more than three years for companies employing fifty or more workers, nearly four fifths planned to return and a slightly higher proportion actually returned. Only three fifths of the men who had worked for smaller companies for a comparable time planned to return, and the same proportion actually returned. It is interesting to note that a number of industrial giants have reported the return of more than 90 per cent of their former personnel who entered the service.[7] The number of governmental employees involved was too small to permit the use of controls adequate to support any generalizations in this respect.

9. THE PREDICTION OF ADJUSTMENT IN MARRIAGE

by Ernest W. Burgess and Leonard S. Cottrell, Jr. *

THE PROBLEM

WE DO NOT FEEL IT necessary to justify an effort to increase skill in guessing right about the future. Particularly is this true of fields of experience wherein correct guesses are relevant to immediate acts of personal adjustment. Hence without apology we submit a brief outline of an exploratory effort at predicting adjustment in marriage.

Briefly stated, the problem in this study was to discover what prediction as to adjustments in marriage could be made from a knowledge of certain items in the background of prospective husbands and wives. The back-

Reprinted in part from *The American Sociological Review*, Vol. I, 1936, pp. 737-751, by permission of the authors and the publisher. (Copyright, 1936, by The American Sociological Society.)

* The authors wish gratefully to acknowledge the financial assistance given this study by the Social Science Research Committee of the University of Chicago. They wish also to thank the students and colleagues and the many anonymous husbands and wives whose cooperation was vital in this study. Special thanks are due Mr. Richard O. Lang of the University of Chicago.

ground items selected were those which would not require the subtle powers of the psychologist or psychiatrist to detect, but were chosen purposely on the basis of the ease with which the information could be elicited from persons willing to cooperate in the study.

Such a choice of items should in no sense be taken to imply that we discount the importance of more elusive psychological and physiological factors in marital adjustment. Indeed, in the work of collecting schedule data we accumulated information on personality factors in marital adjustment that appeared more basic than any of the items on our schedules.

We wish to reiterate, however, that we were after background material which would be easily obtainable and which could be used for predicting the probabilities of successful adjustment in marriage. A precise description of the relationships obtaining between our various items and marital adjustment was not the central interest in this study.

[The sample consisted of] a roughly homogeneous, middle class, native-white, urban American group.

The data on this group were collected on eight-page printed schedules that were filled out anonymously. Many students, colleagues, friends and a few social organizations participated in getting nearly 7000 schedules into the hands of possible subjects. About 1300 couples responded. Of these, 526 conformed to the requirement that they be residents of Illinois and that their marriage date be not less than one year and not more than six years in the past at the time of filling out the schedules. Most of the schedules were collected during 1931-33.

We may now turn to a description of the way the materials were handled.

A CRITERION OF ADJUSTMENT IN MARRIAGE

Any attempt at predicting adjustment in marriage calls for some definition of what is meant by adjustment, and some method of indicating varying degrees of adjustment.

A highly generalized definition of a well adjusted marriage might be the following: A well adjusted marriage is a marriage in which the attitudes and actions of each of the partners produces an environment which is highly favorable to the proper functioning of the personality structures of each partner, particularly in the sphere of primary relationships.

Four corollaries follow from this definition: 1. The degree to which the indicated conditions are met would be the degree of adjustment realized. 2. Since personality structures differ from individual to individual it follows that a particular combination highly favorable to a given personality would be entirely unsuited for another. 3. Since personalities are not unitary but are composites of role patterns, a marriage which is favorable to the functioning of one part of the personality may not be favorable for another part of the structure. 4. Since personalities are not static but are in process of development, a combination favorable to the functioning of the personality at one time may not be so for a later period in the development; and hence recurring periods of poor adjustment are necessary conditions of "growth" until a relatively mature and stable level of personality organization is achieved.

Setting aside all questions of the relative adequacy of this definition and its corollary propositions, it is quite evident that it would be extremely difficult, if not impossible, to give it a direct quantitative expression. However, in this as in other instances where a numerical index is desirable, it is possible to give symptoms of adjustment a quantitative expression even though we may not be able to measure directly the variables operating in adjustment. This means, of course, that we do not measure adjustment directly but must be content with an inferential criterion. Moreover, we are measuring present adjustment only.

In constructing a numerical index of adjustment it was necessary to make certain assumptions. We assumed that those subjects whose marriages approximated our definition would make statements which would indicate: 1. That the individual regards his marriage as happy. 2. That there is essential agreement on critical issues in the relationship. 3. That there is a substantial amount of common interests and activities. 4. That there are frequent demonstrations of affection. 5. That there is a minimum of regret concerning the marital choice and a minimum of complaint about the marriage or the partner.

If our assumptions are correct, then we should expect replies to questions centering around the above points to have some value for indicating the degree of adjustment realized in a given marriage. Moreover, if the replies to such questions were appropriately weighted or scored, a composite of these individual weights should give at least a rough numerical index of the degree of adjustment in marriage.

Proceeding on such an assumption we assigned numerical values to the various types of replies on a list of twenty selected questions. At first we were disposed to assign values arbitrarily but finally decided on a more empirical method. We correlated replies to each of the selected questions with the way the subjects rated the degree of happiness of their marriages. The replies were then weighted according to their correlation with happiness ratings. How these weights were assigned and the score computed is described below.

Since the ratings of happiness in marriage were used as a guide in the assignment of weights to the various replies, we should first devote our attention to these ratings. We asked each subject to rate his marriage on a scale with five steps designated as "very happy," "happy," "average," "unhappy," "very unhappy."

Now happiness is a nebulous and elusive affair, especially when one attempts to define it. Offhand one would expect a great deal of variability in the way a subject would rate the happiness of his marriage from time to time. It might be expected also that husbands and wives would rate the marriage differently. Moreover, one would expect that an outsider's rating of a marriage would differ from that of the marriage partners.

Thus far these expectations have not been borne out by our experience. The following data show that there is a rather consistent agreement in: 1. Independent ratings given by the two partners in a given marriage. 2. The ratings given by outsiders more or less familiar with the marriage and one of the marriage partners. 3. The rating of a given marriage by two outsiders. 4. The rating given by the same person at different times.

Table I shows a comparison of the way husbands and wives independently rated their marriages.

Of the 252 pairs of ratings 180, or 71.4 per cent, agree; 62, or 24.6 per cent, disagree by only one step, and only 10, or 4.0 per cent, disagree by two or more scale steps. The tetrachoric correlation between the two sets of ratings is +.89.

Table II shows the comparison of ratings of a marriage, one rating being by one of the marriage partners and one being by an outsider who is well acquainted with the couple. The ratings were of course given independently, and the persons who were being rated were not aware of the fact.

In this comparison we find that 132, or 48.5 per cent, are identical ratings; 116, or 42.7 per cent, vary by only one scale step; and 24, or 8.8 per cent, disagree by two or more scale steps. The tetrachoric correlation coefficient for the table is +.91.

Table I—Comparison of the Way Husbands and Wives Rated the Happiness of Their Marriage

RATINGS	HUSBAND'S RATING						
	Very unhappy	Unhappy	Average	Happy	Very happy	Total	Percentage Distribution
WIFE'S RATING:							
Very happy	1		3	24	112	140	55.6
Happy			12	38	12	62	24.6
Average		3	14	7	6	30	11.9
Unhappy	1	11	2			14	5.5
Very unhappy	5	1				6	2.4
Total	7	15	31	69	130	252	100.0
Percentage Distribution	2.8	5.9	12.3	27.4	51.6	100.0	

On a small number of cases (34) we made careful reports of case interviews. These interviews, properly disguised were read by two competent judges. The judges gave what they regarded as a correct rating of the happiness of the marriages. In all the comparisons made: between rating of judge number one and the rating by the subject; between judge number two and the subject; and between the ratings of the two judges, there was very close agreement. None of the coefficients of correlation fell below +.95.

A small number of subjects (38) were available for a second rating after a lapse of time varying from eight months to two years.[1] A comparison of the first and second ratings of this group showed that only four of the ratings differed by as much as two scale steps. The correlation coefficient was +.86.

This study of happiness ratings suggests that the rating scale has sufficient reliability and validity to allow its use as a guide in selecting questions which

Table II—Comparison of the Rating of Marriages by a Marriage Partner and an Outsider

RATINGS	MARRIAGE PARTNER'S RATING						
	Very unhappy	Unhappy	Average	Happy	Very happy	Total	Percentage Distribution
OUTSIDER'S RATING:							
Very happy			4	16	57	77	28.3
Happy		2	4	31	35	72	26.5
Average	1	4	6	16	8	35	12.9
Unhappy	10	27	20	3		60	22.0
Very unhappy	11	11	5	1		28	10.3
Total	22	44	39	67	100	272	100.0
Percentage Distribution	8.1	16.2	14.3	24.6	36.8	100	

discriminate between good and poor adjustment and in assigning proper weights to the various answers to such questions.

By correlating the replies to each of our questions with the happiness ratings, we were able to select twenty questions. These questions elicited replies that were indicative of the degree of adjustment.

The twenty questions include such things as the following: (a) Extent to which couple engages in common activities. (b) Extent of agreement on a number of points such as, handling finances, recreation, friends, dealing with in-laws, manners, intimate relations, etc. (c) Extent to which affection is demonstrated. (d) Extent to which partners confide in one another. (e) The number of complaints listed regarding the marriage or the partner.

Replies to each question were given numerical values which varied with the proportion of "very happy" subjects giving the reply. Thus, if in our sample, 40 per cent of those who rated their marriage as very happy gave answer "a" to question "x" and only 5 per cent gave answer "b," the numerical value assigned to answer "a" would be roughly 8 times as great as that assigned to answer "b." This procedure can best be illustrated by showing a table in which replies to certain of the questions are correlated with the ratings of happiness.

In Table III the replies to the question on extent of agreement in ways of dealing with in-laws are correlated with the rating of happiness.

Table III—Comparison of Ratings of Happiness in Marriage with Extent of Agreement on Ways of Dealing with In-Laws. Percentage Distribution

	RATING OF HAPPINESS					
EXTENT OF AGREEMENT	Very unhappy	Unhappy	Average	Happy	Very happy	Number of Cases
Always Agree	3.8	2.7	11.5	19.2	62.7	182
Almost Always Agree	4.5	6.3	17.1	29.7	42.3	111
Occasionally Disagree	7.7	20.0	23.1	20.0	29.2	65
Frequently Disagree	18.6	25.6	23.2	16.3	16.3	43
Almost Always Disagree	20.0	50.0	20.0	5.0	5.0	20
Always Disagree	38.2	38.2	11.8	8.8	2.9	34
All Cases	9.1	12.9	16.0	20.5	41.5	455

As one might expect, replies indicating essential agreement on the in-law question are much more frequent among those who rate their marriage as very happy or happy than are replies indicating serious disagreement.

In the "very happy" column the percentage of those who checked "always agree" is about twenty times as great as the percentage who checked "always disagree." Hence we may assign a value of twenty to the answer "always agree" and zero to the answer "always disagree." We followed this procedure in principle. When the distribution on all of the "agreement" questions were averaged and the two scale steps "almost always disagree" and "always disagree" were combined to get enough cases to make the proportion stable, we found it desirable to give a maximum value of ten to the answer "always agree" and zero to the answer "always disagree" for all questions of that type.[2] The intermediate answers were given values graded down evenly from ten to zero.

This procedure was followed for each of the twenty selected questions, and resulted in a numerical value for each possible reply to each of the questions. This done, it was possible to take a schedule properly filled out and compute a marriage adjustment score by summing up the numerical values on replies to the twenty questions.

Table IV—Frequency Distribution of Marriage Adjustment Scores by Happiness Rating Categories

ADJUSTMENT SCORE	Very unhappy	Unhappy	Average	Happy	Very happy	No rating	Total	Percentage Distribution
180-199				7	65		72	13.7
160-179			5	31	118	1	155	29.4
140-159			12	34	32	1	79	15.0
120-139	2	9	27	24	6	2	70	13.3
100-119	3	13	23	8			47	8.9
80- 99	13	19	5	3		1	41	7.8
60- 79	15	17	3		3		38	7.2
40- 59	7	8	1				16	3.2
20- 39	2	5	1				8	1.5
Total	42	71	76	108	224	5	526	
Percentage Distribution	8.0	13.5	14.4	20.5	42.6	1.0		100.0

Mean score = 140.8; σ = 38.8

Table IV shows the frequency distribution of adjustment scores for the whole group and for each happiness rating group.

As would be expected the adjustment scores show a fairly close correlation with the ratings of happiness, since the ratings were used as guides in assigning the score values to the individual questions. The tetrachoric coefficient of correlation between scores and ratings is +.92.[3]

Table V shows that the score does discriminate between groups who are divorced or separated on the one hand and those whose marriages have not

Table V—Distribution of Marriage Adjustment Scores by Groupings into those Who Are Divorced, Separated, Have Contemplated Divorce or Separation and Have Not Contemplated Divorce or Separation

ADJUSTMENT SCORE	Divorced	Separated and not Divorced	Have contemplated Divorce or Separation	Have not contemplated Divorce or Separation	No Reply	Total
180-199				64	8	72
160-179	3		4	141	7	155
140-159	1	6	8	54	10	79
120-139	9	6	19	29	7	70
100-119	10	13	13	11		47
80- 99	15	12	9	4	1	41
60- 79	12	18	4	3	1	38
40 59	6	8	2			16
20- 39	5	2	1			8
Total	61	65	60	306	34	526

been broken on the other. Furthermore, among those not divorced or separated the score discriminates between those who state they have considered breaking their marriage and those who claim not to have contemplated this step.

This table would suggest that our score has considerable validity.

Some evidence of the reliability of the score is seen in the fact that scores computed from schedules filled out independently by husbands and wives have a fairly high correlation ($r = +.88 \pm .03$).

Having constructed a score to measure indirectly the present marital adjustment, we then attempted to use certain background information to predict the adjustment score.

CONSTRUCTION OF A PREDICTION SCORE

The schedules used in this study called for information on certain items in the premarital backgrounds of husband and of wife. This information covered such things as age; place in the family; health; education; occupation; employment history; earnings; amount saved at time of marriage; religious affiliation and activity; participation in other organized social groups; friendships with men and women; length of courtship and engagement; attachments to and conflicts with parents; happiness of parents' marriages; and certain items on the occupation, religion, education and social-economic status of the parents of each.

Our problem with respect to these data was to devise a method of combining the information on each of the schedules into single numerical expressions, whose variations would correlate as closely as possible with the variations in the marriage adjustment scores.

The procedure followed in constructing such a prediction score was similar in most respects to our procedure in constructing the adjustment score. Since we were trying to predict the adjustment score we used that score as a guide in assigning numerical values to replies on questions regarding premarital information.

Each item of information on the premarital backgrounds of husband and wife was correlated with the adjustment score. Those items which showed a significant relationship were selected for use in constructing the prediction score. Twenty-one items in the husband's background material and twenty items in the wife's background were selected for this purpose. Each type of reply was then given a numerical value in accordance with its frequency in the "very high" adjustment score group.

Table VI illustrates the procedure. In this table is presented the relationship between level of educational achievement at the time of marriage and marriage adjustment score.

The data in this table indicate that in our sample the higher the educational level at the time of marriage the greater the chances are that the marriage adjustment score will be high. It also seems that contrary to certain recent pronouncements on the college girl as a poor marriage risk, the wife's educational achievement makes more difference in the chances for a high adjustment score in marriage than does the husband's.[4]

The numerical values assigned to the different educational levels were determined (with certain variations that we do not have space here to discuss) by the procedure already described in the discussion of the adjustment score. In the case of husbands, we gave twenty points to replies stating that the husband was in a graduate level of educational achievement at the time of marriage; fifteen if he was in, or had completed, college; zero if he was in, or had completed, high school; and five points if his education did not exceed the grades.

In the case of the wife's schedule we gave forty points for the graduate

Table VI—Percentage Distribution of Marriage Adjustment Scores at Different Educational Levels

	MARRIAGE ADJUSTMENT SCORE*				Number of Cases
	Very Low	Low	High	Very High	
HUSBAND'S EDUCATION					
Graduate Work	3.8	8.6	36.2	51.4	105
College	9.8	15.1	26.8	48.3	205
High School	15.1	24.3	27.0	33.6	152
Grades only	21.6	19.6	21.6	37.2	51
No reply					13
WIFE'S EDUCATION					
Graduate Work	0.0	4.8	38.7	56.5	62
College	9.2	18.9	22.9	48.9	227
High School	14.4	16.3	32.2	37.1	202
Grade only	33.3	25.9	25.9	14.8	27
No reply					8
All Cases	11.8	16.7	28.4	43.2	526

* For convenience in presentation, the adjustment scores were grouped as follows: Very low, 20-79; low, 80-119; high, 120-159; very high, 160-169.

level at time of marriage, thirty for collegiate level, twenty for high school level, and zero for the grade school level.

This procedure was followed for each of the forty-one items used in constructing the premarital background or prediction score. It is an admittedly crude procedure and doubtless has a number of serious fallacies. It is encumbered with such apparent inconsistencies as giving more value to a grade school level of education of the husband than to a high school level. The differences in score values cited were not great, but they violate one's feeling for consistency. However, we preferred to be consistent in our empirical procedure rather than violate that procedure for the sake of consistent weightings in some of our items.

It will be noted that the maximum score values vary from item to item and are not the same for the same item for husbands' and wives' answers. In each case the maximum score is approximately equal to the difference between the highest percentage and the lowest percentage in the column headed "very high" adjustment scores.

By following this method we were able to assign values which varied roughly in accordance with the discriminal value of the item.

Table VII—Relation Between the Prediction Scores and Marriage Adjustment Scores. Percentage Distribution

	MARRIAGE ADJUSTMENT SCORE*				Number of Cases
PREDICTION SCORE	Very Low	Low	High	Very High	
700-779	0.0	10.0	10.0	80.0	10
620-699	1.5	12.1	25.8	60.6	66
540-619	5.8	21.9	29.2	43.1	137
460-539	27.6	29.4	25.9	17.1	170
380-459	39.8	31.1	15.1	14.0	93
300-379	57.2	25.7	11.4	5.7	35
220-299	75.0	25.0	0.0	0.0	8
Total					519*

Mean prediction score = 516.0; σ = 98.8.
* Seven cases thrown out because subjects failed to answer a sufficient number of background questions for computation of their scores.

With a numerical value determined for all types of answers to questions on the 41 selected items, we were in a position to take any given schedule on which a couple had answered the required questions, assign the numerical value to the replies, sum them and thus compute a background or prediction score. The background scores were computed for each of the 526 couples and these scores were correlated with the marriage adjustment scores. The Pearsonian coefficient of correlation was +.51.

Table VII gives a better idea of the relation between the two scores.

It was of course to be expected that, since the adjustment score was used as a guide in assigning numerical values to the replies upon which the premarital score is based, the two scores would correlate fairly closely. However, our confidence in the prediction value of the score is increased somewhat by noting the relation between the background score and the status of the marriage. Table VIII shows the percentage distribution of prediction scores for 73 divorced couples; 61 separated couples; 64 couples who state they have considered divorce or separation; and 342 couples who claim not to have contemplated breaking their marriage.

With our scoring procedure established, the important question was whether or not the scores would behave the same way when applied to a new sample. Schedules were collected from a new sample of 155 couples in the same general social-economic level from which we drew our first group. Their replies were scored in the manner described above. Notwithstanding the fact that the ranges in the adjustment and prediction scores were narrower than those of the original sample, the correlation coefficient was +.48.

Table VIII—Percentage Distribution of Prediction Scores for Those Who Are Divorced, Separated, Have Contemplated Divorce or Separation and Have Not Contemplated Divorce or Separation

| | | | MARITAL STATUS | | |
PREDICTION SCORE	Divorced	Separated	Have contemplated Divorce or Separation	Have not contemplated Divorce or Separation	Number of Cases
700-789	0.0	0.0	9.1	90.9	11
620-699	2.9	0.0	5.9	91.2	68
540-619	2.9	4.3	6.5	86.3	139
460-539	13.9	15.0	13.9	57.2	173
380-459	25.0	17.0	16.0	42.0	100
300-379	34.2	21.9	21.9	21.9	41
220-299	50.0	37.5	12.5	0.0	8
Number Cases	73	61	64	342	540*

* Fourteen cases were added to the original sample of 526.

While our procedure will doubtless either amuse or irritate the sensitive statistician, there is no denying that the study does point to possibilities of a more thorough and adequate application of prediction techniques to the problem of marriage adjustment.

10. GENERALIZING THE PROBLEM OF PREDICTION

by Leo A. Goodman*

SOME VERY INTERESTING research has been reported on prediction instruments.[1] We would like to suggest some slight generalizations of the concepts which appear in the statistics literature, but which might not be known to the general reader. We would also like to make a practical suggestion to facilitate the actual use of these generalizations.

Albert J. Reiss, Jr., has pointed out that "the central problem of the theory of prediction is to make the best prediction for each case." The question we would like to raise is whether or not it is desirable to concern ourselves with this central problem of prediction, or whether we should be concerned with a somewhat more general problem.

Consider the following very much simplified illustration of prediction in criminology. We are interested in presenting information to the parole board to aid them in deciding whether or not they wish to parole a person P who has appeared before them. We have had the opportunity of classifying P into one of two categories I or II on the basis of a group of factors F which are obtained from tests, records, and reports. We have also found that studying 100 parolees using the factors F led to the following experience table:

Table 1

	Non-Violators	Violators
I	40	50
II	10	0
Total	50	50

Using F for prediction, we would first note whether the person was classified as I or II. If I, we would then predict that he would violate; if II, we would predict that he would not violate. For the original 100 parolees, predicting in this way would lead to $40 + 0 = 40$ errors of prediction.

Now suppose we were able also to classify P into one of two categories A or B on the basis of another group of factors G which are obtained from tests, records, and reports. (We might also like to consider this new classification G as simply another basis for making predictions—possibly, a different way of scoring the original factors of F.) For the original one hundred parolees the use of factor G led to the following experience table:

Table 2

	Non-Violators	Violators
A	0	10
B	50	40
Total	50	50

Reprinted from *The American Sociological Review*, Vol. XVII, 1952, pp. 609-612, by permission of the author and the publisher. (Copyright, 1952, by The American Sociological Society.)

* This work was prepared in connection with research supported by the Office of Naval Research.

Using G for prediction, we would then note whether the person was classified as A or B. If A, we would predict that he would violate; if B, we would predict that he would not violate. For the original one hundred parolees, predicting in this way would lead to $0 + 40 = 40$ errors of prediction.

From the point of view of prediction, G is as good and as useful as F. The accuracy of F equals the accuracy of G, and the efficiency of F equals the efficiency of G. However, it seems clear that F, when looked at from a slightly more general point of view, is better than G. In both cases, there were 40 errors of prediction. For F, the 40 errors consisted of stating that the parolees would violate when, in fact, they did not violate. For G, the 40 errors consisted of stating that the parolees would not violate when, in fact, they did violate. We think most people would agree that it is more important to be able to predict violations than to predict non-violations. Hence we would prefer F to G.

Now suppose we give some consideration to the factors which led us to believe that it is more important to be able to predict violations than to predict non-violations. Let us, for example, consider the case in which the violation is a murder. In such a case the community protests and the family of the murdered person protests. On the other hand, if we had not placed the violator on parole, we would have had to consider the financial cost of continued incarceration. In the case of a second kind of error, that is, keeping a non-violator in prison, the non-violator protests, his family protests, and his imprisonment is a financial cost. On the other hand, if we had paroled the non-violator, we would have had to consider the financial cost of parole. That is, we attempt to make more explicit our conceptions of the possible consequences, which are usually thought of implicitly, of the available decisions. These considerations might make more explicit the bases for the policy decisions of a parole board. Consider for the moment the case in which we agree that the social cost (not necessarily in monetary units) may be described by the following table of social costs:

Table 3

	Non-Violation	Violation
Not paroled	2	1
Paroled	0	100

We are all interested in minimizing the social cost. Since there were 50 violations and 50 non-violations, the social cost of paroling the 100 original parolees is $0 \times 50 + 100 \times 50 = 5000$. The social cost of not having paroled these 100 persons would be $2 \times 50 + 1 \times 50 = 150$. Hence it is clear that if we must choose simply between having them all paroled or all not paroled, we would choose not to parole them, selecting the smaller social cost of 150.

Consider now the social costs of using factors F. We would not parole those classified as I, incurring a social cost of $2 \times 40 + 1 \times 50 = 130$, but we would parole those classified as II, incurring a social cost of $0 \times 10 + 100 \times 0 = 0$. Hence the total cost of using the information based on a person's classification with respect to factors F is 130. The savings in social cost is $150 - 130 = 20$ or $20/150 = .13 = 13$ per cent.

Let us next consider the social costs of using factors G. We would not parole those classified as A, incurring a social cost of $2 \times 0 + 1 \times 10 =$

10; and we would parole those classified as B, incurring a social cost of
$0 \times 50 + 100 \times 40 = 4000$. Thus the total social cost of using the information based on a person's classification with respect to factors G is 4010.
The saving in social cost is $150 - 4010 = -3860$ or $-3860/150 = -.26$
$= -26$ per cent.

The conclusion of the analysis using Table 3 is that the use of F results
in a savings of 13 per cent and the use of G results in a loss of 26 per cent.
Hence it seems we would do better to use an over-all decision for the group
of parolees than to use factors G, but would do still better if we used factors F.

The careful reader will note that in the preceding analysis the factors F
and G were used in conjunction with a specific rule for making decisions.
For example, since Category B consisted of 50 non-violators and only 40
violators, we decided to parole those classified as B. The social cost of this
decision we saw was 4000. We could have used factors F and G in conjunction with other rules for making decisions, for example, the rule for
deciding in such a way as to minimize social cost. For the case of Category
B we might note that if we had decided not to parole those in this class,
the social cost of this decision would have been $2 \times 50 + 1 \times 40 = 140$.
Therefore we would decide not to parole those in Category B.

Let us now reconsider using factors F to aid us, attempting to minimize
the social cost. If we decide not to parole all those classified as I, the social
cost is $2 \times 40 + 1 \times 50 = 130$. If we do parole those classified as I,
the social cost is $0 \times 40 + 100 \times 50 = 5000$. Thus it seems clear that
we must decide not to parole those in Classification I, choosing the smaller
social cost of 130. If we decide not to parole those in Classification II, the
social cost is $2 \times 10 + 1 \times 0 = 20$; and if we do parole this group, the
social cost is $0 \times 10 + 100 \times 0 = 0$. Hence we would decide to parole
those in Classification II, choosing the smaller social cost of 0. The total
social cost of using the information based on a person's classification with
respect to factors F is $130 + 0 = 130$. The saving in social cost is $150 -
130 = 20$ or $20/150 = .13 = 13$ per cent.

Let us now reconsider using factors G to aid us. If we decide not to
parole all classified as A, the social cost is $2 \times 0 + 1 \times 10 = 10$. If we
do parole those classified as A, the social cost is $0 \times 0 + 100 \times 10 =
1000$. Therefore we would decide not to parole those in Classification A,
incurring a smaller social cost of 10. If we decide not to parole those in
Classification B, the social cost is $2 \times 50 + 1 \times 40 = 140$; and if we do
parole this group, the social cost is $0 \times 50 + 100 \times 40 = 4000$. Hence
we would decide not to parole those in Classification B incurring the smaller
social cost of 140. The total social cost of using the information based on
a person's classification with respect to factors G is $10 + 140 = 150$. The
saving in social cost is $150 - 150 = 0$ or $0/150 = 0 = 0$ per cent.

The conclusion of this analysis is that the use of F results in a savings of
13 per cent, and the use of G results in a savings of 0 per cent. Hence we
still see that factors F should be used.

Someone might not agree completely with the numbers in Table 3. Let
us take another table of social costs:

Table 4

	Non-Violation	Violation
Not paroled	90	1
Paroled	0	100

If we are interested in the social cost as described in Table 4, then we see that the social cost of paroling the 100 original parolees is $0 \times 50 + 100 \times 50 = 5000$, and the social cost of not having paroled these people is $90 \times 50 + 1 \times 50 = 4550$. Therefore if we must choose simply between having them all paroled or all not paroled, we would choose not to parole this group of men, incurring the social cost of 4550.

Now reconsider using factors F to aid us. If we decide not to parole all those classified as I, the social cost is $90 \times 40 + 1 \times 50 = 3650$. If we do parole those classified as I, the social cost is 5000. Hence we would decide not to parole those in Classification I, choosing the social cost of 3650. If we decide not to parole those in Classification II, the social cost is $90 \times 10 + 1 \times 0 = 900$; while if we do parole this group, the social cost is equal to 0. Thus we would decide to parole those in Classification II, choosing the social cost of 0. The total social cost of using the information based on a person's classification with respect to factors F is 3650. The saving in social cost is $4550 - 3650 = 900$ or $900/4550 = .20 = 20$ per cent.

Let us reconsider using factors G to aid us. If we decide not to parole all classified as A, the social cost is $90 \times 0 + 1 \times 10 = 10$. If we do parole those classified as A, the social cost is 1000. Hence we would decide not to parole those in Classification A, incurring the social cost of 10. If we decide not to parole those in Classification B, the social cost is $90 \times 50 + 1 \times 40 = 4540$; and if we parole this group, the social cost is 4000. Hence we would decide to parole those in Classification B, incurring the smaller social cost of 4000. The total social cost of using the information based on a person's classification with respect to factors G is $10 + 4000 = 4010$. The saving in social cost is $4550 - 4010 = 540$ or $540/4550 = .12$ or 12 per cent.

The conclusion of the analysis using Table 4 is that the use of F results in a saving of 20 per cent and the use of G results in a saving of 12 per cent. Using either Table 3 or Table 4, we would conclude that F is better than G.

One might raise a question as to whether Table 3 or Table 4 or some other table is the appropriate one to be used in the analysis. The following suggestion is an attempt to answer this question.

The parole board in making these decisions does implicitly, if not explicitly, give some consideration to the various consequences of its decisions. One might hold a meeting of the board to discuss in some detail the kinds of social costs involved. Probably the board members would all agree that the greatest social cost occurs when there is a violation, and the least social cost occurs when a parolee is a non-violator. Let us assign the numbers 100 and 0, respectively, to these occurrences. We might ask each member of the board what number he would assign to the social cost of not paroling a non-violator and then average the values suggested by all the board members. Suppose this average is 87.6. We might then ask each member what number he would assign to the social cost of not paroling someone who would have been a violator had he been paroled. Suppose the average of the values suggested by all the board members was 1.3. The new table of social costs would be the following, which could be used in the analysis of parolees and in the comparison of factors such as F and G.

Table 5

	Non-Violation	Violation
Not paroled	87.6	1.3
Paroled	0.0	100.0

It may be worth noting that if the following table of social costs were used we would be dealing with the usual problem of prediction.

Table 6

	Non-Violation	Violation
Not paroled	100	0
Paroled	0	100

The writers who deal with the usual problem of prediction implicitly accept this table of social costs. The reader may or may not agree with it.

The careful reader will see that the particular case we have considered can be easily generalized. The problem of social costs suggests immediately the importance of classifying violations with respect to their severity—at least into major and minor violations. Hence we would then be dealing with a 2×3 social cost table and also a 2×3 experience table. If we also have, say, 10 scores for factors F rather than two (I and II), we would have a 2×3 social cost table and a 10×3 experience table. The procedures and measures suggested here for the 2×2 tables can be easily generalized to the $m \times n$ tables.

We admit that we have taken rather an oversimplified and extreme example. This has been done in an effort to make the comments clearer. We believe the points made herein will also be of importance in less extreme cases.

We would like to refer the reader to some of the statistics literature on the subject discussed herein. Traditionally, the central problem of statistics has been to draw inferences, that is, to make reasonably secure statements on the basis of incomplete information. A newer theory of the foundations of statistics centers about the problem of statistical action rather than inference, that is, deciding on a reasonable course of action on the basis of incomplete information. The problem of parole is clearly a problem calling for statistical action. The exploration of this theory of statistics was begun by Abraham Wald and is treated in his book.[2] Some general exposition of the theory and an original example are given an elementary treatment in a recent journal article by R. Clay Sprowles.[3] An informal exposition of the field to which this theory pertains has been presented by L. J. Savage.[4]

Auxiliary Readings

A. TREND STUDIES

W. F. Ogburn, *Social Change* (New York: B. W. Huebsch, Inc., 1922), pp. 210-236.

Analyzes the lag between the material conditions of culture and the adaptive culture in a study of workmen's compensation as a means of dealing with industrial accidents. Examines data to show that workmen's compensation laws lagged about half a century behind the time the conditions of industry required them.

A. L. Kroeber, "On the Principle of Order in Civilization as Exemplified by Changes in Fashion," *American Anthropologist,* 1919, New Series, 21, pp. 235-263.

For a period of 150 years, measurements are taken on women's dresses available from fashion plates. Indices such as lengths and widths of skirts and heights and widths of waists are used. Characteristic periodic shifts are shown to exist. They are analyzed in terms of cyclic variations and related to broader social patterns.

H. Goldhamer and A. W. Marshall, *Psychosis and Civilization: Two Studies in the Frequencies of Mental Disease* (Glencoe, Ill.: The Free Press, 1953).

The question is raised as to whether, during the last century, the rate of mental diseases has really increased. The study is particularly enlightening in regard to the use of historical statistical data. Such factors as availability of hospitals and families' attitudes toward mental diseases greatly affect the interpretation of reported rates.

S. A. Stouffer and P. F. Lazarsfeld, *Research Memorandum on the Family in the Depression* (New York: Social Science Research Council, 1937) Bulletin 29, pp. 24-66.

An effort is made to answer, by the use of available data, the question of how employment chances for married and single women compared with each other and with those of men. The need for preliminary speculations and the difficulty of final conclusions are stressed.

B. PANEL ANALYSIS

P. L. Kendall, *Conflict and Mood—Factors Affecting the Stability of Responses* (Glencoe, Ill.: The Free Press, 1954).

Questionnaires on a large variety of topics were answered by the same people within an interval of two months. The replies varied greatly according to the nature of the question and certain characteristics of the respondents. Answers to questions which created a conflict in the respondent were markedly unstable; this was found to be true for several different ways of measuring conflict. Changes in general mood were found to relate to changes in specific attitudes of criticism.

E. A. Suchman, "Factors Determining Which Men Got Promoted," in S. A. Stouffer, et al., *The American Soldier: Adjustment During Army Life,* Vol. I (Princeton: Princeton University Press, 1949), Chapter 6, Section III.

A panel of about 500 soldiers was interviewed twice within a period of six months in regard to their attitudes toward various aspects of army life. Soldiers who are more conformist are shown to be more likely to be subsequently promoted, and, inversely, promotion has the effect of making soldiers at all levels of criticism more favorable toward army life.

T. M. Newcomb, *Personality and Social Change* (New York: Dryden Press, 1943).

The first major study based on repeated interviews, it is very rich in psychological interpretation of the findings. The first part gives statistical results, while the later parts are based on case studies. A reformulation of the results and ideas in the light of systematic panel analysis would be fruitful.

Hans Zeisel, *Say It with Figures* (New York: Harper & Bros., 1947), Chapter X.

Offers a good introduction to the treatment of repeated interviews.

J. Tinbergen, "Economic Business Cycle Research," *Readings in Business Cycle Analysis*, The American Economic Association (Philadelphia: The Blakiston Co., 1944), Part I, pp. 61-86.

Shows how the economist approaches process analysis. The parallels with panel analysis deserve careful study and discussion.

C. PREDICTION STUDIES

L. E. Ohlin and O. D. Duncan, "The Efficiency of Prediction in Criminology," *American Journal of Sociology*, Vol. 54, 1948-49, pp. 441-451.

Establishes an index of predictive efficiency and compares a large number of studies in the field of criminology in terms of this index. Of particular importance is the discussion of the differences which appear between predictions applied to the samples from which the original experience tables were derived and those applied to new samples.

E. W. Burgess and P. Wallin, "Predicting Success in Marriage," *Engagement and Marriage* (New York: Lippincott Co., 1953), Chapter 16.

Provides a comparative survey of all major marriage prediction studies. An interesting distinction between predicting and forecasting is made. All through this text tables are reported which are pertinent to this section, because engaged couples are reinterviewed several years after their marriage.

L. S. Cottrell, Jr., "The Aftermath of Hostilities," in S. A. Stouffer, et al., *The American Soldier: Combat and Its Aftermath*, Vol. II (Princeton: Princeton University Press, 1949), Chapter XII.

During the war the Research Branch of the Army made a number of predictions as to how the soldiers would behave at the time of demobilization. These predictions were checked by actual research. Reasons for success and failure of predictions are discussed. This chapter represents the most advanced use of prediction studies for sociological analysis.

A. Kaplan, A. L. Skogstad, and M. A. Girschick, "The Prediction of Social and Technological Events," *Public Opinion Quarterly*, Vol. 14, 1950, pp. 93-110.

Discusses a number of factors which may be considered if one is to speak of the success of a prediction. Develops a variety of success criteria and applies them to actual data.

F. Mosteller, et al., "Report of the Committee on Analysis of Pre-Election Polls and Forecasts," Appendix A-2, *The Pre-Election Polls of 1948* (Social Science Research Council, Bulletin 60, 1949).

A group of social scientists reanalyzed the 1948 polls to find out why they mispredicted the election. The appendix selected gives the general findings. The other papers of the various contributors are equivalent to a very systematic discussion of problems involved in prediction from intention.

Formal Aspects
of Research
on Human Groups

Introduction

In THE FIRST three sections we have covered the basic operations underpinning much of social research. We need variables; we have to analyze their relations; and we want to follow their change through time. For the social scientist, however, there exists a very important distinction as to the objects to which these procedures apply. These objects may be individuals; they may be small groups; they may be larger and more formal institutional structures; or, finally, they may be large collectives such as nations or cultures. For the sake of simplifying our variables, we have taken it more or less for granted in the first three sections that our units are mainly individuals (although some of our selections went beyond this restriction). In this section, on the other hand, we focus our attention on groups, seeking to provide material to answer two questions: To what extent do the basic methodological ideas apply, irrespective of whether our unit of analysis is an individual or a group? What new and special problems arise in the latter case?

When we deal with characteristics of individuals, some distinctions are habitual: between an attitude, a personality trait, a biological characteristic such as height, an economic characteristic such as income, etc. When it comes to group characteristics, however, their logical structure is more obscure. If an author discusses the transition from feudal to industrial society, he implicitly claims that if he were presented with a large number of societies he could order them according to their degree of

"feudalism." How would he proceed? We can infer from his writings that sometimes he would use the average of each individual's attitude, if he had the necessary information; sometimes he would make inferences from cultural products like churches and writings; sometimes he would use interpersonal relations as indicators for "feudalism." And just as in the use of a personality test, pertaining to an individual, he might be called upon to combine seemingly contradictory indicators into an index. It is true that most of the time our author has not enough data and therefore does not become aware of what could be done with his concept of "feudalism"; and what he does is just right for his purpose. The methodologist, in the long run, will not be permitted to avoid the larger task; he should show what is common to the formal nature of group characteristics on all levels. As a beginning, we have restricted ourselves to selections which refer to small groups only. The writings on the institutional and cultural level are usually not too clear and, in any case, the formal analysis of the simpler material is a necessary first step to the broader task.

A. *The nature of group characteristics.* Several authors have tried to develop general systems of group properties—none with special success. Our first two selections are especially pertinent to smaller groups. They both stress the difference between *aggregative properties,* which are derived from information about each individual and, on the other hand, *global properties,* which deal with a product of the group without reference to any individual member's contribution. But beyond this the emphasis is somewhat different. Kendall and Lazarsfeld, in Selection (1), distinguish aggregative properties according to whether the basic characteristic of the individual is a variable or a qualitative attribute. They do this because the group property, then, is in the one case a distribution and in the other case a rate; and intellectual trends in social theory can often be classified as to which of these two group properties they emphasize. Cattell, in Selection (2), also starts with aggregative properties but then becomes more concerned with another distinction: many group characteristics, e.g., "cohesion," may be built up from the relation between pairs of members; or, like "stratification," may be founded on relations between subsets. Such relational group properties obviously lie behind many of the terms used by social theorists. A fairly satisfactory systematization might develop by combination of the approaches proposed in these two selections, especially if additional attention were given to global characteristics of collectives, such as literary products and prevailing rules of conduct.

B. *Propositions about groups.* Groups are characterized for the purpose of developing propositions about them. The language of multivariate analysis applies to groups as well as to individuals. This should sound obvious, were it not for the fact that, especially in our older tradition, collectives were mainly studied in isolation: one community or one tribe. The student therefore needs training in the idea that statistical correlations can be established, the elements of which are themselves collectives; as a matter of fact, they are among the fastest developing products of modern social research.

Goodacre, in Selection (3), orders a number of army platoons along two variables; one variable is cohesion and the other is performance in maneuvers. He finds a positive correlation between these two characteristics of the groups. Irrespective of the merit of the variables, the point to see is that although this relationship deals with the characteristics of *groups* as such, it does not differ in principle from one in which *individuals* are the unit of analysis where a positive correlation might be shown between, let us say, education and reading ability. The same consideration holds true for Selection (4), where Murdock cross-classifies tribes according to a political and a residential characteristic. In Selection (5), Bavelas relates the seating arrangements of small groups to their efficiency in solving collective tasks. It is interesting to note, incidentally, that we were not able to find studies where three group properties were analyzed simultaneously.

C. *The notion of property space, as applied to group characteristics.* Obviously, the general rules of index formation, to which Section I of our Reader was devoted, apply to group characteristics as well as to individual properties. We have singled out one special phase of this process for renewed emphasis in the present section. Teaching experience has shown that the student has difficulties when he has to apply the idea of multi-dimensional classification to groups. In Selection (6), Hemphill and Westie give a careful report of the way they developed and tested fourteen dimensions along which small groups can be described. They show that the notion of "profile" can be properly and profitably applied to such material. Once groups are located in a property space, then all the operations like reduction and substruction, as they have been especially described in Selection (5) of Section I, can be applied. This becomes especially clear through Selection (7). There, Miner reviews the efforts to classify communities by the degree to which they have departed from the type of folk society. A careful reading of his discussion shows that the anthropologists are trying here to reduce a multi-dimensional property space into a one-dimensional sequence—the Gesellschaft-Gemeinschaft continuum.

D. *Analysis of interpersonal relations.* All the preceding selections applied to procedures in the analysis of collectives which are also applicable to individuals. But in the analysis of groups there appears one new element: the social relation. By this term we mean either the relationship between two members of the group or between one member and his associates in general. This interest has led to a variety of research efforts which are here exemplified by two different selections. Bales and his students have paid attention mainly to the *content* of interactions. They have developed a series of categories and used them to classify behavior in a wide variety of controlled situations. Selection (8) by Bales therefore exemplifies an important trend in modern social research. Many feel that developing an appropriate kind of classification, staying with it for a long time, and applying it to the analysis of a broad range of situations is necessary for the development of substantive knowledge of group behavior. Bales is, undoubtedly, the foremost exponent of this position. Selection (9) serves a more *formal* puprose. The interpersonal relations in a group can become very complex. Earlier writers used mainly graphic devices. Recently, algebraic procedures have been developed to classify and count cliques, to distinguish chains of interaction, and so on. Festinger and his colleagues provide an elementary presentation of these techniques. This selection is representative of a new trend in sociometry.

The final selection, No. 10, serves to show how a variety of indices can enter into the same investigation. The authors of the Westgate study dealt with a number of small courts and barracks-type apartment houses in a housing project. Each court or building was characterized according to the homogeneity or heterogeneity of opinions among its residents. Here, then, we have the property of a collective, the housing unit. The residents, in turn, were divided into deviates and conformists; for each resident a number of sociometric choice indices were also developed. These then provide individual properties of various kinds. The study shows how the properties of the residents are related to the distribution of attitudes within the courts and buildings.

The topics covered in this section are still not fully organized, and therefore much has to be left to the utilization by the teacher. We have already emphasized that the systematizations in Group A need further clarification which has to be attained by seminar discussions. The propositions in Group B themselves introduce a variety of group properties. The student should be asked to analyze them in detail and to put them into a more systematic context. The main purpose of this section is to sensitize the students to the notion of group properties and their interrelations. This effort can be helped by drawing on material from other social sciences. The anthropologist deals with the notion of patterns of culture; the historians are concerned with climates of opinion. It will be a useful exercise to study such more discursive writings and to see how some of their contents can be translated into a language of group properties and their indices.

The teacher will also want to utilize the many parallels between this section and Section I. The discussion on integration of cities and its measurement given in Selections (I-1) and (I-8) has special bearing here. For the reason that ecological research is well described in many textbooks, it has not been included among our selections. One aspect of it, however, has special bearing on the problem of systematization. The ecologist characterizes an individual according to the properties of the area in which he lives as well as by his own personal properties. The formal problems thus resulting have been discussed in a few papers which were especially singled out in our auxiliary reading list. The teacher will note that while the word ecology is not used there, the matter enters quite clearly into the data of Selection (10) in the present section. This might also be the place to reiterate that we have excluded from our Reader more difficult mathematical formalizations which are especially notable in the field of small group research.

1. THE RELATION BETWEEN INDIVIDUAL AND GROUP CHARACTERISTICS IN "THE AMERICAN SOLDIER"

by Patricia L. Kendall and Paul F. Lazarsfeld

IN SURVEY WORK, we generally use several items to indicate the particular concept with which we are dealing. We feel more confident that a respondent really is optimistic about the future if he indicates this in answer to a number of questions, rather than in answer to only one. But this requires the construction of an index. The multiple items must be grouped into classes which are both meaningful and easily manageable.

Usually the Research Branch analysts* combined their items into the familiar kind of scales, grouping together those respondents who had given specified responses to the same number of questions, without respect to the particular questions thus answered. Through this technique, they developed a number of attitude and behavior scales which are used extensively throughout the two volumes. For example, they worked out a scale of conformity to the Army (I, 265, Chart XI), a scale indicating degree of vindictiveness toward the enemy (II, 163, Table 15), another concerned with job adjustment (II, 502, Table 21), still another dealing with confidence and pride in one's outfit (II, 336, Chart IV), and a score of fear symptoms. (II, 179, Table 20)

The theory and technique of such combinations of items into scales has been greatly advanced by the Research Branch. In the fourth volume of their series, called *Measurement and Prediction*, Stouffer and his staff report on the basic principles underlying their scale construction. It does not seem necessary, therefore, to discuss the matter any further in the present context; the main purpose of this paper is to codify those operations which are implied, but not explicitly formulated, in *The American Soldier*. There is one aspect permeating many of the examples which deserves special atten-

Reprinted from "Problems of Survey Analysis," pp. 186-196, in *Continuities in Social Research: Studies in the Scope and Method of "The American Soldier,"* edited by Robert K. Merton and Paul F. Lazarsfeld, by permission of the authors, the editors, and the publisher. (Copyright, 1950, by The Free Press.)
* Research Branch, Information and Education Division, U. S. Army. The analysis of Research Branch data which is discussed in the present selection is that reported in *The American Soldier: Adjustment During Army Life,* Vol. I, and *The American Soldier: Combat and Its Aftermath,* Vol. II. In this discussion, references to the first and second volumes of *The American Soldier* are referred to as I and II respectively. Page numbers are indicated by Arabic numerals. For a narrative summary of the major findings of these volumes, see P. F. Lazarsfeld " 'The American Soldier': An Expository Review," *Public Opinion Quarterly,* Vol. 13, 1949, pp. 377-404. A previous reading of this paper might help the student to see the numerous examples cited here in their substantive context.

tion. The matter is best introduced by the notion of "level of complexity" according to which indices can be viewed.

The Correspondence between Personal and Unit Data. Let us start out with the fact of promotion. First of all, we can ascertain whether a soldier who entered the Army as a private has been promoted. This is typical of the items which might be included in a scale of Army success; other indicators with which it might be combined are the citations and decorations which he received, the way in which his superiors evaluate him, and so on. Secondly, confining our attention to promotion only, we can count how often each soldier was promoted. In that case, the number of promotions, summed over a period of time, would be used as an index of success. We can go still further, and determine how many men in a whole unit have been promoted during a specified time period. This would be an index of the opportunities which a given unit provides. The incidence of a single promotion, the index of success pertaining to a man and the index of opportunity pertaining to a unit differ in their complexity: the second index comes about by summing the first over time; the third comes about by summing the second over the population.

It can be seen quite easily that the notion of complexity is a relative one. We cannot speak of the complexity of a single index, but only of the relative complexity of two indices. If a second index is formed by some procedure of combination in which the first index is an element, then the second index is said to have a higher level of complexity. A detailed discussion of the numerous consequences which derive from this notion of complexity would go beyond the limits of this paper. We shall restrict ourselves to a discussion of the relation between an individual index and a group index of just one higher degree of complexity. We thus exclude cases where combinations are formed over other units than groups, and we also exclude the discussion of more than two complexity levels. Even then, the necessary considerations are rather intricate.

In order to have a uniform and neutral terminology, we shall use the following expressions. A *personal datum* is a fact predicated about a single individual. If several personal data about the same person are combined in some way, we shall talk of a *personal index*. Any kind of aggregate of persons will be called a *unit*. A group of people, for instance, who interact with each other, form a unit; but an aggregate of people who serve in a regiment together or who live in the same census tract will also be called a unit, irrespective of whether or not they are in contact with each other. A *unit datum* is any fact predicated about a unit. If a number of unit data are combined to characterize a single unit we shall talk of a *unit index*. Units as well as persons can form the elements of a statistical analysis. (The statistics in many studies of urban ecology, for instance, have units as elements.)

Our main interest here is directed toward the *logical relationship between personal data and unit data*. In order to be as concrete as possible we start with data taken from Table 18 in II, 450.

Here four Army divisions, each a unit, are compared in a variety of ways. The first row shows the proportion of malaria cases in the four divisions and the second row the proportion of soldiers exhibiting a pre-established number of neurotic symptoms. A glance at the two rows shows the greater the

Table A—Anxiety Symptoms and Certain Related Factors among Combat Infantrymen
in Four Divisions in the South and Central Pacific Areas (March-April 1944)

	Division A S. Pacific	Division B S. Pacific	Division C Cen. Pacific	Division D Cen. Pacific
Percentages who have had malaria	66	41	2	2
Percentages receiving critical scores on the Anxiety Symptoms Index	79	63	56	44
Median number of days in combat	55	31	19	3
Number of cases	1,420	1,388	1,298	643

incidence of malaria the greater also the incidence of neurotic cases. Let us look at the character of the data in the first row. On an individual level, the only possible distinction is between those who have had malaria and those who have not. But a unit of soldiers (in this case, a division) can be characterized by the proportion of soldiers with malaria. The personal datum, *incidence* of malaria, is an attribute.[1] To it corresponds as a unit datum the malaria *rate* which is a continuous variable. This correspondence will be called that of *Type I*.

Now let us turn to the unit datum in the third row. Each individual soldier was obviously characterized first by a continuous measure—the length of time he had been in combat. The unit is characterized by an average formed over the personal data, in this case the median. If the personal datum is a variable and the corresponding unit datum an average of the same variable we shall talk of correspondences of *Type II*.[2]

On a somewhat impressionistic level, the two types mentioned so far have something in common. The personal datum and the corresponding unit datum have what one might call psychological similarity. We use practically the same terms in talking of the malaria-beset soldier and the malaria-infected division or in talking of the veteran soldier and the veteran division. We shall see presently that the similarity does not need to be as great as the linguistic usage suggests.

If the personal datum is a variable, then there can be still another correspondence. It is entirely possible that two divisions have the same "median number of days in combat" and still differ in an important respect. One division might be quite homogeneous in that most of its soldiers had the same amount of combat experience. The other division might have received many replacements, so that some of its soldiers have much more than the median amount of combat experience, while others have hardly any. It is quite obvious that this homogeneity of combat experience can only apply to a division; by the logic of the way it is measured, homogeneity can only be a unit datum and never a personal datum. We shall talk of correspondence, *Type III,* when the unit datum is a standard deviation, a measure of skewness or any other parameter of a distribution derived from a personal datum variable.

In the three types discussed so far, the personal data could be attributed to individuals without any reference to the unit. Number of days in combat, number of psychoneurotic symptoms, incidence of malaria are typical examples of this kind. There are, however, certain personal data which imply either a reference to other members of the unit or to the unit as a whole. While not used in *The American Soldier,* the best examples to draw on here are so-called sociometric measures. Whether a person chooses as a friend a man in his own unit or one in another unit; whether a man is chosen as a friend by many people in his unit or by few—these would be typical examples of what one might call relational personal data. They are predicated about individuals but refer to the unit in their definition. The corresponding unit data can be of three kinds, repeating, as it were, the previous three correspondences. The structure of a unit, for instance, could be characterized by the even distribution of sociometric choices over all members of the unit or by the concentration on a few "leaders." The cohesion of the group might be characterized by the ratio of choices made within and outside the unit. We shall lump together as *Type IV* all those cases where the personal datum is of a relational nature, and the corresponding unit datum is any kind of aggregate of an individual relational datum. In a more systematic discussion this would not be justified, but in the present context Type IV is mentioned only for the sake of completeness. It will not be taken up again because no examples are provided in *The American Soldier*.

There is, finally, one kind of unit datum which is distinguished by the fact that no individual datum can correspond to it. Table A conveys the general impression that the divisions are arranged according to the amount of battle strain they have undergone. Suppose we were to construct a general unit index of strain to characterize a division. We would combine the different pieces of information into a scale, just as in common test practice various items of information pertaining to a single individual are combined into a scale. But if we form a strain index for a division, a new kind of material can be introduced. One item which we might use, for instance, is a measure of the extent to which the mess equipment of the division is worn out. Homogeneity of combat experience can only be predicated about a unit, but the datum is formed on the basis of information collected from each member of the group. The state of mess equipment, however, is something which, even as a datum, pertains only to the unit and never to the individual. In such cases we shall talk of *Type V*.

We thus have five main correspondences between personal and unit data. A clear distinction of these different types of relationships between per-

Nature of the Personal Datum	*Nature of the Corresponding Unit Datum*
I. An attribute pertaining to one person only.	I. A rate.
II. A variable pertaining to one person only.	II. An average.
III. As in Type II.	III. A parameter of the distribution of the variable, *e.g.*, standard deviation or measure of skewness.
IV. In characterizing an individual, a reference is needed either to other members of the unit or the unit as a whole.	IV. Any of the statistical aggregates used in the previous types.
V. No information introduced about a single individual.	V. The unit item characterizes the group only, but belongs in a meaningful context with data of the previous type.[3]

sonal and unit data is important to many sociological discussions, and indispensable for a clear understanding of much of the work reported in *The American Soldier*. This understanding can be increased by considering how unit data are used in the two volumes.

The Interchangeability of Personal and Unit Data. The most common use of unit data is as a substitute for personal data which, for one reason or another, are not available. In this case the analysts will always deal either with Type I or II. The classic example of this kind in social research is the use of voting data prior to the development of polls. Because an individual's vote is secret, the only way to find out whether Al Smith received more support from poor than from rich people in Chicago was to relate the proportion of Democratic voters to average rent paid in all of the voting precincts. The kind of statistical analysis carried out in such a case leads to the types of problems which are characteristic of all survey work; spurious factors, for example, are especially likely to enter into correlations between unit data. The only difference is that the statistical element in an "ecological" analysis is the precinct and not the voter.

The Research Branch had so much information about individual soldiers that they were not forced at any point to rely on correlations between unit data without any reference to the constituent individuals. Suppose this were not the case, however. Suppose that in setting up the table quoted above, the analysts discovered that they lacked information as to how long each man had been in combat. It is still conceivable that there would be general agreement as to how the four divisions, as units, ranged themselves according to combat exposure. Then the third row would most likely be used as evidence that increased exposure to combat makes for an increase in neurotic symptoms. Consciously or unconsciously, everyone would accept the correlation between the two sets of unit data as a substitute for a correlation between two corresponding sets of personal data.

Very frequently, the Research Branch turned to a closely related application: they used both types of data to reinforce specific findings. The most elaborate parallel example can be found in II, Chap. I. This is a chapter dealing with the predictability of combat performance from paper and pencil tests. Section 1 is based on unit data. The average morale score obtained from units in training is related to the rate of battle fatigue cases during the Normandy invasion. It turns out that the average test score permits us to predict fairly well the non-battle casualty rate. In the second section of this chapter, the same relationship is established for two sets of personal data. Here the attitude score of the individual soldier is related to the combat rating he later obtained from his fellow soldiers and his superior officers. In I, Chap. VII, another instructive double check can be studied. Chart II shows that soldiers who chose their own assignments liked their jobs much better than those who did not. Chart I shows that in branches where a large proportion chose their jobs there was also a large proportion of soldiers who liked to be in that branch. On an individual level (Chart II), we only have four-fold tables. On a group level (Chart I), we have a correlation diagram between two variables which permits a more refined analysis.[4]

An important question is *whether a correlation between unit data and one between the corresponding personal data must always give the same result.* Stouffer and his associates are very much aware of the problem and at various points stress that this does not need to be the case. We shall make an effort here to collate the pertinent examples in *The American Soldier,* and to derive from them some general methodological considerations. The following three examples provide the best basis for induction.

(1) In I, 290, Chart II, it is shown that soldiers who chose their own assignments liked their jobs better than those who did not. Chart I shows that units where a large proportion chose their jobs also have a large proportion of soldiers who liked to be in that branch. Here an association of two attributes (personal data) corroborates the result derived from the correlation between two proportions (unit data).[5]

(2) Chart IX in I, 252, shows on a personal level that soldiers who were promoted were, as one would expect, considerably more optimistic about general promotion chances in the Army than those who were not promoted. But, in addition, a unit comparison between Military Police and the Air Corps is also presented. We learn that the promotion chances in the Military Police were much poorer than in the Air Corps. And yet the satisfaction with promotion in the Military Police was considerably higher among all subgroups. That is to say, using personal data, promotion is positively related to satisfaction; using unit data, satisfaction is negatively related to promotion chances.[6]

(3) In I, 357, Table 17, 12 Air Force fighter groups, each of them treated as a statistical unit, are compared. We know what proportion in each group complain about their food, and we also know the proportion satisfied with their Army work. There is no interrelationship between these two sets of unit data; the variation in food supply seems to have little effect on general satisfaction and dissatisfaction. No corresponding personal data are given, but from many similar results in *The American Soldier* and from other studies we can take it for granted that on an individual level there would be an association. Soldiers who complain about food are also more likely to complain about other matters, like the job they have.

Let us first fasten on the difference between the third and the first examples. Variations in the rate of food complaints from one unit to another are likely to reflect actual differences in the objective situation; variations in complaints from one soldier to another are more likely to reflect personality characteristics of the individual soldiers. We are not surprised to find that job satisfaction has one kind of relationship with a personality trait and a different relationship with an external situation. The personal data and the unit data in the third example stand for different factors, despite their formal correspondence. In the first example, the personal information that the soldier has chosen his job and the unit rates of soldiers who report this are likely to reflect objective differences equally well. We are not surprised therefore that, in this case, the two sets of data have the same relation to job satisfaction.

The most interesting example is the second one. Here the personal datum of having been promoted as well as the promotion schedule of the various units are both objective facts. But the one reflects individual experiences and the other what one might call *experiences of the whole unit.* The authors analyze in considerable detail (I, pp. 250-258) how the experience of the unit might affect the expectations and evaluations of the individual: the promoted man in an advantageous unit enjoys his own promotion less and the non-promoted man resents his setback more. This would explain the positive association between promotion and approval of the promotion system based on personal data, and the negative correlation between promotion chances and approval based on unit rates.[7]

Before a complete codification of this whole problem could be attempted, a much larger array of examples is needed. But the few instances permit us at least to preview the kind of generalizations which might develop. At this point we can state one general expectation: *If individual data are more likely to reflect an attitude and unit data an objective reality, then they will not necessarily have the same relationship to a third set of data.* If the personal data and the unit data are likely to reflect the same objective reality and the same experience, it will be safe to use them interchangeably. This, however, will not be the case if the unit data not only reflect each person's experience but also the experience of other people in the unit, which might have quite different meaning for the people directly and those more indirectly involved.

A Further Problem. The last qualification, so well illustrated by our second example, is really a transition to a quite different relationship between personal data and unit data. So far we have questioned whether the two types of data can be used interchangeably and whether the results necessarily must corroborate each other. In all of our examples we compared corresponding statistics where, on the one side, the elements were individuals characterized by individual data and, on the other side, units characterized by unit data. There is, however, one further connection which, from a sociological point of view, is probably the most interesting one.

There is no reason why unit data cannot be used to characterize individuals in the unit. A man who does not have malaria in a unit where the incidence of malaria is very low probably feels differently about his state of health than does the man who has no malaria but serves in a unit with high incidence and therefore is surrounded by malaria cases. A man who could not choose his job in a unit where the rate of free choice is very high would feel differently than the one working with people who also were denied a choice. In the same way, a man not promoted in a unit with a tight promotion scheme would feel differently than a soldier with the same experience serving in a unit where every other man was promoted.

In terms of actual analysis the matter can be restated in the following terms: just as we can classify people by demographic variables or by their attitudes, we can also classify them by the kind of environment in which they live. The appropriate variables for such a classification are likely to be unit data. A survey analysis would then cover both personal and unit data simultaneously.[8]

2. TYPES OF GROUP CHARACTERISTICS

by Raymond B. Cattell

[The author has spent many years developing a system of basic personality traits through factorial analysis of a large number of tests. He is now working on a similar program to derive basic group characteristics. In an introduction to a progress report on his statistical work, which is reprinted below, he discusses the systematization of group properties.—ED. NOTE.]

ANY ATTEMPTS AT SCIENTIFIC PREDICTION of group behavior must employ some scheme of measurement of group characteristics and performances, *i.e.*, of traits of the group as a whole. An infinite number of possible variables exists. Consequently, for the sake of economy as well as to insure interaction among various researches, it is necessary to settle upon a limited number of important parameters. To get effectiveness as well as economy, it is necessary not only to agree on a limited set of standard parameters but also to discover those which correspond to functional unities in group response behavior and structure.

By these scientific canons some of the early group research has got off to a false start by arbitrarily assuming such popular dimensions as degree of sociability, of democratic organization, of democracy, strength of morale, general group ability, degree of aggressiveness, *etc.* It may *seem* enough if such variables are sufficiently operationally defined to be reproducible in other experiments, but (1) they are generally lacking in such precision: the criteria of democracy, for example, have been different in different experiments on this supposed parameter; (2) even when precisely reproducible it is questionable whether a certain dimension or factor loads the same individual variables in the same way in different groups—just as we measure intelligence by different tests in nursery school children and adults, so morale may weight certain observations differently, for example, in large and small groups; and (3) a variable may avoid both of the above objections and still be of no particular relevance or predictive value on group behavior. To say the variable is relevant to a theory is not particularly impressive, since at this stage of perception, theories are far more likely to be wrong than right. The field of variables needs to have some of its structure revealed before we can profitably make tentative hypotheses or theories.

At the time this research was begun, no proof had been offered that the operational measurements used to measure any of these descriptive categories constituted a unitary pattern other than in the experimenter's imagination. The basic research now to be described sets out to measure groups on a wide variety of performances and characteristics, to intercorrelate these group variables, and to determine by factor analyses what *functionally unitary "traits" exist for groups* of the given size and organization.

Reprinted in part from "Determining Syntality Dimensions as a Basis for Morale and Leadership Measurement," pp. 16-22 in *Groups, Leadership, and Men*, H. Guetzkow, ed., by permission of the author, the editor, and the publisher. (Copyright, 1951, by the Carnegie Press.)

The pursuit of any comprehensive research upon this problem of determining what may be called group *syntality* dimensions (syntality meaning for a group what personality does for an individual) is best planned in two stages, as has been done in the corresponding inquiries on factors in individual *personality*. The first and more flexible stage is a survey of the verbal categories and symbols that have come into popular use in describing groups of all sizes and sorts. The second calls for greater precision by passing to objective measurement of the variables finally chosen as most important and representative of the pragmatic verbal field and by introducing factor analysis to order these variables. Thus the first "rating" stage reconnoiters the whole situation and gives a perspective within which the exact behavioral measurement can proceed.

As a matter of research strategy, we may note parenthetically that the *behavioral* measurement research will at first hold constant some of the multifarious directions of variation found in the *verbal* survey, *e.g.*, size, membership motivation, degree of overlap with other groups. In this vaster task of determining objective measurement parameters, studies must proceed in planned rotation or sequence, holding some sets of variables constant in each, as, for example, age has been held constant in most of the initial factorizations of ability in the individual personality. Thus each experiment must confine itself to a population of groups of fixed size and type.

At the time the present objective measurement research began (1948), some verbal surveys were already started elsewhere, notably at Ohio State, which fortunately issued in a very comprehensive and well organized set of dimensions.[1] However, our variables were already set up partly on the basis of a pioneer study in our own Social Psychology Research Institute,[2] and it remains for our further experiments to take advantage of some of the realms of variation uncovered by these verbal studies. Incidentally we shall distinguish in the rest of this article between variables and dimensions. Dimensions are special variables which have been selected by factor analytic or other methods to represent more variables than themselves, to be substantially independent of one another and to correspond to the chief significant directions of variation which characterize the entities measured.

At present the hundred or more variables recorded in the objective study subtend all three "panels" of group characteristics, namely, (1) performances of the group acting as a whole, (2) particulars of internal structure and interaction, and (3) characteristics of the population (mean and sigma on various personality factors and attitude-interest measures). The first we shall call "syntality" variables; the second, "structure" variables; and the third, "population" variables. Later we shall attempt to get crisper definition of factors by factorizing these three realms in isolation, but in this initial exploration it seems desirable to intercorrelate all in a single pool to determine the over-all functional relations.

These three panels require little further definition. Population variables are simply means of the personality factor or other measures of the component members. By contrast, syntality variables deal with emergents from the population variables. Thus a group of low general intelligence with a highly intelligent leader may have a lower population measure but a higher syntality measure, on intelligence. Structure variables are harder to distinguish from syntality variables because they also characterize the group as a whole, but syntality can be measured without any observations on the *internal* interaction of the group.

Examples of the three classes of variables from the present study are as follows:

1. *Syntality variables:* Accuracy of conclusion in committee-like debate on given data; reduction of strength of pull when tug-of-war rope is electrified (a "morale" variable); time to construct a large wooden structure to given specifications; extent of cheating in competition with other groups; extent of deviation from prior group decision as a result of emotional appeals.

2. *Structure variables:* Degree of formalization of leadership; assessment of leadership along a directive-non-directive continuum; orderliness of behavior; amount of expressed criticism of the group; amount and kind of interaction, as determined by an interaction-process analysis; permissiveness of atmosphere; degree of change of individual opinions after expression of group opinion; degree of emergence of "lieutenants" between formal "captain" and rest of group; frequency of change of formal leader at periodic voting; and a variety of sociometric scores.

3. *Population variables:* Here we attempted to determine the more important dimensions of personality by the fewest possible measurements. Consequently, we assessed such ability, dynamic and temperament factors as general intelligence, emotional stability (vs. neuroticism), surgency, schizothymia, as well as interests and attitudes on some important issues, *e.g.,* radicalism-conservatism, and some background data. The present research was aided by recent advances in the degree of definition of these factors through a research for the United States Public Health Service simultaneously being carried out by this Research Unit. Most dependence has been placed on the 16 Personality Factor Questionnaire. For each group the mean and the dispersion (sigma) for some twenty personality aspects of the population were thus obtained directly and some twenty more were obtained from individual behavior observed in the group.

About one hundred and fifty variables, comprising some sixty syntality variables, fifty structural variables, and forty population variables, were thus measured for eighty groups of ten men each. An attempt was made to get a wide range of subjects and finally the eight hundred persons were taken about equally from Air Force officer candidates (courtesy of Air Force Human Resource and Development Branch), university students, and men enlisting in the Navy.

It seems important, in spite of difficulties, to insure that in experiments on groups, the groups formed are real in some sense other than that of being arbitrarily brought together for the experiment. This does not mean that they must have traditions or long duration, but they must have real dynamics. Our definition of a group is *a set of people who satisfy their needs consciously and unconsciously through the existence and instrumentality of this set of people.* That is to say, the group must operate as the best means by which each individual can satisfy certain individual desires. In this experiment, each individual hoped to gain ten dollars which he could do only by joining up in one of these groups. In addition to three to four hours of individual testing, each individual shared nine to twelve hours of group activity and testing which was divided into three sessions on three different days spread over a week or more. The present study is thus confined to *traditionless groups* which for the first session were *without,* and in the last two sessions *with formally elected and defined leadership.*

The almost innumerable further problems to which a positive solution is opened up by a sound factorization of group dimensions may be illustrated by issues going popularly under the rubric of leadership problems. Our thesis is, first, that the effectiveness of a leader is only to be measured in terms of *the performance of groups under him.* As part of the preliminary exploration, Dr. Saunders in this Unit is making an analysis of variance in group performances to see what fractions are associated respectively with leader variance and with population variance. When this is done we propose to correlate syntality measurements, *e.g.,* on the morale factors, the general ability factor, *etc.,* with the measured personality factors in leaders, the structural (sociometric) characters of the group, and the mean value of these characteristics for the population.

The kinds of questions which the comprehensiveness of the data in this study will enable us to answer in quantitative terms may be illustrated by the following outstanding ones:

1. To what extent do the syntal characters of the group depend upon population characters? We already have evidence that the mean individual level in general neuroticism is strongly correlated with the level of group morale obtained.

2. How are the syntal characters related to leader behavior dimensions, *e.g.,* domination, imitation, integration, as worked out by the Ohio researchers?[4]

3. What is the correlation between syntal dimensions and measures of interpersonal communications as worked out, for example, by Festinger, Schachter, Back and their co-workers?[5]

4. What are the correlations between syntality measures and various sociometric measures of internal interaction (other than strictly communication variables as in [the work of Carter, Haythorn, and Howell].[6]) This may link up with the study of administrative conference process by Marquis since two of the situations in which our groups were tested were designed to involve administrative kinds of activity.

5. What are the personality characteristics which distinguish leaders from non-leaders statistically broken down with respect to various types of group syntality, particularly with regard to successful and unsuccessful groups as measured on various dimensions? This aspect of the analysis can be brought into close relation with the work of Carter[7] on leadership personality in relation to other variables.

6. How is the degree of shift of individual toward group opinion related to (a) division of opinion in the group as in the work of Asch,[8] (b) the personality characteristics of the individual, and (c) the syntality dimensions of the group?

7. What is the relative rate of learning on various performances and internal integrative activities (comparing our third with our first session) of groups of different syntality, leadership structure, and mean population characteristics? This integrates with the morale and productivity studies of French and Katz.

It will be seen that in general the analysis seeks to interrelate, without prejudice as to the direction of causation, three measured aspects of the group: syntality, internal structure (deduced from function), and population characters.

Our argument is that really effective hypotheses can best be formed when factorization has structured the variables in these areas into a dozen or so putative functional unities, any one of which is likely to extend across all three areas. These factors will themselves be interrelated and can profitably form the basic concepts for more precise and interpretative hypotheses dealing with the manner of their interrelation. Prior to this revelation of the main factor structure, it would seem as unprofitable to attempt ambitious hypotheses as to speculate about cellular structure before the use of the microscope.

3. THE USE OF A SOCIOMETRIC TEST AS A PREDICTOR OF COMBAT UNIT EFFECTIVENESS

by Daniel M. Goodacre, III

THE INSTITUTE FOR RESEARCH IN HUMAN RELATIONS, under contract with the Personnel Research Section of the Adjutant General's Office, was assigned to "develop measures of effectiveness for small combat units." A Moreno technique, the Sociometric Test, was one of the predictors developed. A field problem for scout squads of reconnaissance platoons was developed as a criterion of the effectiveness of that squad's field performance. The scout squad is made up of six armed men with full field equipment and two jeeps; one jeep contains a radio and the other has a light machine gun mounted upon it. Under "normal" combat conditions the squad leader and two of his men ride in one jeep while the assistant squad leader rides in the other jeep with the remaining two men. The field problem consisted of twelve tactical situations, such as an air attack, the outposting of a road junction, a withdrawal, etc., which were constructed to represent battlefield conditions, as nearly as possible. These twelve situations had been agreed upon by a group of military experts to be representative of the normal combat functioning of this type of unit. The field problem required about six hours to complete and was run over a circular course covering a wide variety of terrain features. All of the twelve squads used in the problem were from the same regiment, had had about the same amount of training, and were tested at the same military reservation. The rating of combat behavior was done by personnel from the Institute and the military on a standardized rating form while closely following the squads in the field. The squads to be tested were first given the various predictors, including the Sociometric Test, and were then taken to the problem area and conducted through the field problem.

The purpose of constructing the Sociometric Test was to develop a paper and pencil measure of group cohesion; the assumption being that group cohesion and group performance are related. It was further hypothesized that Army social interactions may be categorized into three areas of interaction. These areas are:

First, a *Non-Military Area* that is thought to consist of social interactions that take place outside of the military structure while on a leave or pass

Reprinted from pages 148-152, *Sociometry*, Vol. XIV, 1951, Editor, J. L. Moreno, Beacon House, Inc., by permission of the author and the publisher.

status off the reservation. This area is represented in the Sociometric Test by the following questions:

If you were going on pass what man (or men) would you *want* to go on pass with and what man (or men) would you *not want* to go with?

If you were going to a party or dance tomorrow what man (or men) would you *want* to have there and what man (or men) would you *not want* to have there?

If you had a leave to go home what man (or men) would you *want* to invite to your home and what man (or men) would you *not want* to invite to your home?

Second, a *Garrison Area* consisting of on the reservation social interactions that occur within the military structure but which are of a non-tactical nature. This is represented by the following questions:

If you were going to chow what man (or men) would you *want* to sit with and what man (or men) would you *not want* to sit with?

If your outfit was having a good movie tonight what man (or men) would you *want* to go with and what man (or men) would you *not want* to go with?

If you were told to pick the men whom you wanted to live in a tent or barracks with what man (or men) would you *choose* and what man (or men) would you *not choose?*

Third, a *Tactical or Field Area* of social interactions occurring "in the field" which are structured by a tactical military situation. This area is represented by the following questions in the test:

During an attack what man (or men) would you *choose* to share a foxhole with and what man (or men) would you *not choose* to share a foxhole with?

If you were to lead an advance through an enemy town what man (or men) would you *choose* to cover you and what man (or men) would you *not choose* to cover you?

If you were wounded what man (or men) would you choose to help you back to an aid station and what man (or men) would you *not choose* to help you back to an aid station?

The nine questions above were selected from a collection of suggested items gathered by interviewing combat veterans of World War II. The criteria for the selection of the items were that they:

1. Tap situations that occur with a high degree of frequency in all Army combat units.

2. Overlap as little as possible.

3. Be worded so that it would be both possible and logical for the respondent to make a positive, negative or no response choice.

Three different scores can be arrived at by assigning a unit weight to each of the positive and negative responses and summing different combinations of these responses. The three different scores and the methods of obtaining them are:

1. A score indicating the expressed attitude of one member of the group towards the rest of the group may be obtained by summing all of that individual's responses.

2. A score indicating the expressed attitude of the group towards any member of the group may be found by adding all of the responses made by others about that particular individual. This score may be thought of as an index of leadership or leadership potential.

3. A score indicating the extent of group cohesion may be derived by adding all of the responses the group made. This score is the one which is to be considered here.

The present format was developed in an attempt to minimize three factors which often have been found to be quite bothersome in the construction of sociometric tests. These three factors or difficulties are the halo effect produced in subsequent items by the patterning of previous responses, the tendency for a respondent to change a choice already made after discovering that the question has another aspect to it (either positive or negative), and the paucity of responses when written responses are required of a non-verbally oriented population such as we are dealing with here. These three difficulties have been somewhat minimized in this format by:

1. Putting each item on a separate page to reduce the "halo effect" of previous responses.

2. Presenting the entire question, both the positive and negative side of it, first as a unit, and then asking for the positive or negative choice *after* both aspects have been considered, to reduce the tendency of some respondents to change responses after they have once been made.

3. Having the respondent write each man's name only once to reduce the possibility of limiting the number of responses as a result of the respondent's resistance to a writing situation.

A rank order coefficient of correlation was run between the total score (the index of group cohesion) received on the Sociometric Test by each squad and the total received on the field problem by each squad. This correlation produced a rho of .77 which is significant for a N of 12 (squads) above the 1% level of confidence. Other rho coefficients found were:

Criterion and Garrison area	.62
Criterion and Social area	.78
Criterion and Tactical area	.79

As would be expected from the above statistics these three areas of social interactions are highly intercorrelated, with the Tactical and Social Areas correlating highest (rho of .84) and the Garrison Area correlating somewhat lower with the other two areas (rho's of .68 and .76). The lower correlations of the Garrison Area with the other two areas may be partially understood when the rho's between each question and the criterion of field performance are examined. It was found that two of the garrison questions (going to chow and going to a movie) had rho's of only .46 and .44 while the other seven of the questions all correlated with the criterion with rank order coefficients of correlation ranging from .63 to .75. It is felt that the two "weak sisters" in the Garrison Area are weak because they involve social interactions of a less intimate degree of association than the other items. This is manifested in the observation (at the military reservation where the testing was conducted) that inter-personal choices in these two situations (going to chow and going to the movies) are made relatively casually and indiscriminately as compared to, say, those made when going on a pass.

It is regrettable that reliability coefficients cannot be reported for the Sociometric Test but a rapid turnover of personnel in the units used in the study occurred shortly after the testing as a consequence of the outbreak of hostilities in Korea. This prevented re-testing of the original sample.

Index of Group Cohesion and Total Field Problem Score for Each Squad

Squad	Index of Group Cohesion	Total Field Problem Score
A	210	85
B	193	82
C	256	77
D	160	74
E	178	68
F	185	66
G	185	65
H	171	64
I	186	63
J	119	58.3
K	38	57.8
L	108	57

The correlation of .77 indicates that the group cohesion score received on the Sociometric Test is related in a positive manner to performance on the Scout Squad Field Problem. It is felt that this Sociometric Test could be applied with equal facility to any other Army combat unit and with changes of terminology in a few questions it could be applied to almost any small organized unit in the armed forces or industry as a predictor of group performance. Further research, however, would have to determine the effectiveness of that prediction of other groups.

4. STATISTICAL RELATIONS AMONG COMMUNITY CHARACTERISTICS

by George P. Murdock

[In 1941 George P. Murdock undertook an analysis of certain aspects of social structure, placing strong emphasis on the statistical treatment of data referring to various cultures. Particularly significant was the fact that he started with total human societies as his units of analysis. The Cross-Cultural Survey at the Institute of Human Relations, Yale University, had built up a file of geographical, social and cultural information on about 150 societies. Dr. Murdock utilized the data on 85 of these societies and, in addition, secured data on 165 other societies. In the selection which follows, the author examines the nature of the community in various societies, using the total community as the unit of analysis.—ED. NOTE.]

ANTHROPOLOGISTS from Morgan to Lowie have shown far more interest in the forms of the family, the sib, and the clan than in the organization of social groups upon a strictly local basis. Sociologists, on the other hand,

Reprinted in part from *Social Structure*, pp. 79-83, 85-90. (Copyright, 1949, by The Macmillan Company and used with their permission and with the permission of the author.)

have for some time manifested a strong interest in community organization, and a parallel concern has recently been developing in anthropology,
with especially noteworthy contributions from Steward[1] and Linton.[2]

The sociological term *community* is here chosen in preference to less
definite or less descriptive alternatives, such as "local group" and "band,"
as the generic designation for groups organized on a predominantly local
basis. It has been defined as "the maximal group of persons who normally
reside together in face-to-face association."[3] The community and the nuclear
family are the only social groups that are genuinely universal. They occur
in every known human society, and both are also found in germinal form
on a sub-human level.

Nowhere on earth do people live regularly in isolated families. Every-
where territorial propinquity, supported by divers other bonds, unites at
least a few neighboring families into a larger social group all of whose
members maintain face-to-face relationships with one another. Weyer,[4] in
demonstrating this fact for the Eskimo, has pointed out that community
organization provides individuals with increased opportunities for gratification through social intercourse, with more abundant sustenance through
cooperative food-getting techniques, and with insurance against temporary
incapacity or adversity through mutual aid and sharing. To these advantages
may be added protection through numbers and the economies possible
with specialization and a division of labor. The chances of survival thus
seem to be materially enhanced through community organization, and
this, together with the directly perceived gains, doubtless accounts for its
universality.

Communities differ in type with their mode of life. Where subsistence
depends largely upon gathering, hunting, or herding, which usually require
migration from place to place at different seasons of the year, the local
group consists typically of a number of families who habitually camp
together. This type of community is called a *band*. Agriculture, on the other
hand, favors more permanent residence in a single settlement, though exhaustion of the land may compel the community to move to a new site every
few years. Fixed residence is also consistent with a fishing economy and
even with a hunting economy under exceptional conditions where game
is plentiful and non-migratory. With more or less settled residence, the
community may assume the form either of a *village,* occupying a concentrated cluster of dwellings near the center of the exploited territory, or of
a *neighborhood,* with its families scattered in semi-isolated homesteads, or
of some compromise between the two, like the rural American town with
its dispersed farm homesteads and its local center with church, school, post
office and general store. It is also possible for people to live in settled
villages at one season of the year and in migratory bands at another. Of
the 241 societies in our sample for which information is available, 39 are
organized in bands, 13 in neighborhoods lacking prominent nuclei, and
189 in villages or towns.

In size, the community at its lower limit, approached for example by
the Reindeer Chukchee, consists of two or three families. The upper limit
is seemingly set by "the practical impossibility of establishing close contacts
with developing habitual attitudes toward any great number of people."[5]
For this reason, presumably, large urban aggregations of population tend

to become segmented, when geographical mobility is not excessive, into local districts or wards which possess the outstanding characteristics of communities. A study by Goodenough[6] reveals a maximum range of from 13 to 1,000 in average community population, with 50 as the mean for tribes with migratory bands,[7] 250 for those with neighborhood organization, and 300 for those with settled villages. The normal size of the community was shown by the same study to depend largely upon the prevalent type of food quest. Under a primarily hunting, gathering, or fishing economy, for example, the community averages somewhat fewer than 50 persons, whereas under an agricultural economy with animal husbandry it attains a mean population of about 450.

The community appears always to be associated with a definite territory, whose natural resources its members exploit in accordance with the technological attainments of the culture. Under a hunting or gathering economy, the lands of the community are ordinarily owned and exploited collectively,[8] although in some instances, as Speck[9] has shown for many of the Algonquian tribes of northeastern North America, they are divided into individual family tracts. The situation tends to be similar in herding societies. Under agriculture, the tillable land is sometimes collectively owned and periodically redistributed among families. Much more frequently, however, it becomes allocated as feudal or private property, although the non-agricultural portions of the community's territory may continue to be collectively owned and utilized. The territorial basis of the community survives even under a mercantile or industrial economy, despite the decline in the relative importance of land as a source of livelihood.

In consequence of its common territory and of the interdependence of its constituent families, the community becomes the principal focus of associative life. Every member is ordinarily acquainted more or less intimately with every other member, and has learned through association to adapt his behavior to that of each of his fellows, so that the group is bound together by a complex network of interpersonal relationships. Many of these become culturally patterned, yielding standardized relationships like those of kinship and those based on age and sex status, which facilitate social intercourse, and many are aggregated into clusters around common interests, forming groups such as clans and associations which help to bind the families of the community to one another.

Since it is mainly through face-to-face relations that a person's behavior is influenced by his fellows—motivated, cued, rewarded, and punished—the community is the primary seat of social control. Here it is that deviation is penalized and conformity rewarded. It is noteworthy that ostracism from the community is widely regarded as the direst of punishments and that its threat serves as the ultimate inducement to cultural conformity. Through the operation of social sanctions, ideas and behavior tend to become relatively stereotyped within a community, and a local culture develops. Indeed, the community seems to be the most typical social group to support a total culture. This, incidentally, provides the theoretical justification for "community studies," a field in which anthropologists, sociologists, and social psychologists alike have shown a marked interest in recent decades.

Under conditions of relative isolation, each community has a culture of its own. The degree to which this is shared by neighboring local groups depends largely upon the means and extent of intercommunication. Ease of communication and geographical mobility may produce considerable cultural similarity over wide areas, as, for example, in the United States today, and may even generate important social cleavages which cut across local groupings, as in the case of social classes. For most of the peoples of the earth, however, the community has been both the primary unit of social participation and the distinctive culture-bearing group.

United by reciprocal relationships and bound by a common culture, the members of a community form an "in-group,"[10] characterized by internal peace, law, order, and cooperative effort. Since they assist one another in the activities which gratify basic drives, and provide one another with certain derivative satisfactions obtainable only in social life, there develops among them a collective sentiment of group solidarity and loyalty, which has been variously termed syngenism, we-feeling, *esprit de corps,* and consciousness of kind.

The extension of personal relationships beyond the community may be facilitated by various cultural devices, e.g., local exogamy, blood brotherhood, safe-conduct, and market peace. It may be regularized by the development of social groups which cut across community lines, e.g., sibs, religious sects, and social classes. Finally, it may be consolidated by political unification, by the organization of a number of local groups under a single district, tribal, or state government. While many societies have followed this last course, an approximately equal number have developed no genuine political integration transcending the community. Evidence on pre-European governmental organization is available for 212 of our sample societies. In 108, each community is politically independent; in 104, definite governmental institutions unite several or many communities into larger organized groups of varying magnitude.

Among the factors favoring wider political organization, settled life appears to be peculiarly important. Table 1 shows that the bands of migratory tribes are usually politically independent, whereas the villages and settlements of sedentary populations are more commonly organized into larger aggregates.

Table 1

Community Organization	Bands	Neighborhoods	Villages	Totals
Politically independent	28	8	68	104
Politically dependent	5	4	93	102
Totals	33	12	161	206

The problem of achieving concerted action and maintaining law and order becomes far more complex in a larger political society than in a single community. Informal modes of consensus, reciprocity, and social control do not operate where face-to-face association is lacking, and must be supplemented by formal mechanisms and procedures. The interpersonal relationships which bind the members of the larger society together are, of necessity, relatively abstract or conventional rather than concrete or face-to-face. To be sure, they are ordinarily patterned after the intimate relationships developed within the community, but these become formalized and stereotyped as they are extended. The habits of personal interaction which largely govern the relationship of a villager and his local headman, for example, are conventionalized in terms of formal etiquette and of explicitly defined rights and duties when they are extended to apply to the impersonal relationship of a subject to his tribal chief or king. Similarly, rules of judicial procedure tend to supplant informal discussion, systems of taxation and tribute to replace gift-giving, and specialized officials to take over the several functions of the unspecialized local headman.

Even with complex governmental organization, the community normally survives as a political unit, albeit a subordinate one, and a relative simplicity and face-to-face quality still characterize, as a rule, its regulative forms.[11] For this reason, comparative studies of community organization are not vitiated by differences in political complexity. One may, however, seriously question the validity of those comparative studies of government which deal with the largest political aggregates in diverse societies, whether they be communities, organized tribes, or complex states. The Arunta band and the Inca empire, for example, are not comparable units, although it might well be profitable to compare the former with the local Peruvian *ayllu,* or the governmental institutions of the Incas with the Dahomean monarchy.

No special analysis of political structures was made for the present study, and none will be attempted here. The community, however, is one of the social groupings which operates significantly in the channeling of kinship nomenclature and sexual behavior, and for this reason it has been necessary to analyze it in its relations to the larger political society as well as to its constituent kin groups.

One type of social structure which often transcends the community is the organization into social classes. Information on class stratification was assembled in the hope that the material might prove significant in the interpretation of sexual and kinship behavior. Although this hope has not on the whole been realized, the data are summarized in Table 2 as possibly of general interest.

Table 2

Social Class Stratification	Slavery Present	Slavery Absent	No Data on Slavery	Totals
Complex structure of social classes	16	14	2	32
Hereditary aristocracy and commoners	15	18	6	39
Social classes based directly on wealth	10	5	0	15
Wealth distinctions without formal classes	7	16	3	26
Social classes absent	0	72	2	74
No data on class stratification	14	8	42	64
Totals	62	133	55	250

Slavery is distinguished in the table from other types of class structure, and the societies possessing and lacking slaves as a definite status group are enumerated in separate columns according to the class typing of the rest of the population. When war captives receive little differential treatment and are speedily adopted into the tribe, a society is considered as lacking a true slave class. A class structure is ranked as complex if it includes three or more definitely stratified groups other than slaves, or if it is complicated by the presence of hereditary and endogamous castes. A distinction is made between types of class structure based predominantly upon wealth and those in which privileged status is reported as primarily hereditary. For a number of societies, differences in wealth are reported to exist but to be associated with no important differences in behavior, thus resembling individual distinctions in skill, valor, and piety rather than status gradations in the stricter sense. These have been distinguished in the tabulation from other classless societies on the one hand and from wealth-stratified societies on the other.

As might be expected, social stratification is especially characteristic of sedentary populations. Slavery, for example, is reported present in 55 societies with settled villages or neighborhoods and absent in 94, whereas it occurs in only 3 of the tribes organized in migratory bands and is specified to be absent in 33. Genuine social classes appear in none of the societies of our sample that are organized in bands, but occur in a majority of those with settled communities, as Table 3 reveals.

Table 3

Class Stratification	Bands	Settled Communities	Totals
Complex structure of social classes	0	31	31
Hereditary aristocracy and commoners	0	38	38
Social classes based directly on wealth	0	14	14
Wealth distinctions without formal classes	7	19	26
Social classes absent	27	44	71
Totals	34	146	180

Social classes operate not only to unite members of different local groups but also to segment the community itself and to complicate its social structure. Thus a village may be divided into nobles and commoners or into a number of castes. Participation tends to be greater within such groups than between them, and significant cultural differences may emerge. It has been shown by Warner, for example, that a typical New England city is segmented horizontally into six social classes, each with its distinctive cultural characteristics, that intimate social participation is confined primarily to members of the same "clique" within a social class and secondarily to persons belonging to cliques in the same stratum, and that intercourse between classes takes place largely through more formal associations which override class boundaries.

Probably the most significant differences in the internal organization of the community result from the varying ways in which its structure is integrated with that of the varying types of kin groups. In many instances the community itself may be a kin group. Local groups of this type may be collectively designated as *kin-communities*. Among the 222 societies in our sample for which sufficient information is available on community organization, there are 81 with kin-communities. They include 15 with endogamous bilateral demes, 13 with exogamous patri-demes, 2 with matri-demes, 45 with patrilocal clan-communities, 2 with matrilocal clan-communities, and 4 with avunculocal clan-communities. In some other societies the community is normally divided into a number of clan-barrios. Local groups of this type may be called *segmented communities*. In our sample, 36 societies are characterized by segmented communities—27 with patrilocal clan-barrios, and 9 with matrilocal clan-barrios. Local groups which are neither segmented into clans, nor themselves organized as clans or demes, may be called *unsegmented communities*. In our sample, 105 societies possess unsegmented communities. In 48 of them neither clans nor extended families are present, and in 17 others clans are absent and extended families unreported. If clans are absent but extended families are present, the community can be regarded as only partially rather than completely unsegmented. This is the case in 40 of our societies—7 with bilocal extended families, 19 with patri-families, 10 with matri-families, and 4 with avuncu-families.

Communities of any of the above types may be further classified, on the basis of the presence or absence of social classes, as *stratified communities* or *unstratified communities*. In our own society, for example, communities are normally stratified but unsegmented.

The classification proposed by Steward[13] for band organization may be compared with that presented above. Steward's "patrilineal band," which is said to be characterized by "land ownership, political autonomy, patrilocal residence, band or local exogamy, and patrilineal land inheritance,"[14] includes both our patri-deme and our patrilocal clan-community. His "matrilineal band" embraces our matri-deme and our matrilocal clan-community. His "composite band," which is stated to differ from the "patrilineal band" in not having "band exogamy, patrilocal residence, or land inheritance by patrilineal relatives,"[15] would include both the endogamous deme and the unsegmented community in our classification, and probably the segmented community as well.

A recurrent feature of community organization, noted by Linton,[16] is an internal division into factions, usually two in number. We need instance here only the famous Tartharol and Teivaliol divisions of the Todas, the rivalrous districts of Faea and Ravenga on the tiny isle of Tikopia, the "hostile" and "friendly" factions among the Hopi, and the moiety cleavages of the Apinaye and many other tribes. Miner[17] has described a striking dual alignment in a rural French-Canadian parish, based ostensibly on affiliation with different political parties.

So widespread are such factional divisions, so frequently is their number precisely two, so commonly do they oppose one another in games and other activities, and so often are their reciprocal relations marked by rivalry, boasting, and covert forms of aggression that the phenomenon seems scarcely accidental. Ethnocentrism suggests a possible common function. A dual organization of a community, or of a larger social group, may provide a sort of safety valve whereby aggression generated by in-group disciplines may be drained off internally in socially regulated and harmless ways instead of being translated into out-group hostility and warfare. If this highly tentative hypothesis is valid, opposing factions should be more characteristic of peaceful than of warlike communities. Perhaps herein lies the fundamental social justification of a two-party political system in a modern democratic state.

5. COMMUNICATION PATTERNS IN TASK-ORIENTED GROUPS

by Alex Bavelas

WHEN THE NATURE of a task is such that it must be performed by a group rather than by a single individual, the problem of working relationships arises. One of the more important of these relationships is that of communication. Quite aside from a consideration of the effects of communication on what is generally called "morale," it is easily demonstrated that for entire classes of tasks any hope of success depends upon an effective flow of information. But on what principles may a pattern of communication be determined which will in fact be a fit one for effective human effort? Administrative thinking on this point commonly rests upon the assumption that optimum patterns of communications for a task-group may be derived from the specifications of the task to be performed. Students of organization, however, have pointed out repeatedly that working groups—even if one considers only communications relevant to the work being done—invariably tend to depart from formal statements of the patterns to be employed. One may take the view that this departure is due to the tendency of groups to adjust toward that class of communication patterns which will permit the easiest and most satisfying flow of ideas, information, and decisions. In groups which are free of outside control, it is clear that the interaction patterns which emerge and stabilize are products of the social process within the group. A group which exists as a part of a larger organization, however, seldom has the freedom to make such an adjustment. In most organizations the maintenance of the stated—and presumably optimum—patterns of communication is regarded as a first principle of effective performance. It is easy to understand this tendency of administration to inhibit changes in formal communication patterns. One need only remember how intimate the relation is between communication, control, and authority.

In these organizational situations, the imposed patterns of communication may determine certain aspects of the group process. This raises the question of how a fixed communication pattern may affect the work and life of a group. Do certain patterns have structural properties which may limit group performance? May it be that among several communication patterns —*all logically adequate for the successful completion of a specified task*— one will result in significantly better performance than another? What effects might pattern, as such, have upon the emergence of leadership, the development of organization, and the degree of resistance to group disruption?

These questions have prompted a series of exploratory studies which have

Reprinted from *The Policy Sciences,* edited by Daniel Lerner and Harold D. Lasswell, pp. 193-202, by permission of the author, the editors, and the publishers, Stanford University Press. (Copyright, 1951, by the Board of Trustees of Leland Stanford Junior University. One of the Hoover Institute Studies made possible by a Carnegie Corporation grant.)

grown into a program of research. The findings are incomplete at present, but are of interest in their possible implications. In this chapter, the attempt will be made to describe the areas of present experimental activity and the general direction which the work is taking.

Some Geometric Properties of Communication Patterns. If we consider who may communicate with whom in a task-group, without regard for the nature or medium of the communication, we can ask a number of simple but important questions. Let us vary the ways in which five individuals are linked[1] to one another (it being understood that every individual in the group will be linked to at least one other individual in the same group). What different kinds of communication patterns may we produce, and how may we describe quantitatively the differences between them? Obviously, this would more properly be an exercise for a topologist. For the social scientist it is more to the point to ask, "What differences among these patterns appear (quite intuitively) to be of a kind that would affect human beings in some way?" If we look at the patterns shown in Figure 1, we find

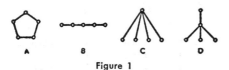

A B C D

Figure 1

that intuitive notions come easily—perhaps, too easily. Students commonly remark, upon seeing patterns *C* and *D* for the first time, that pattern *C* is "autocratic," while pattern *D* is a typical "business set-up." Actually, of course, in so far as linkage goes they are identical, the only difference being the arrangement of the dots on this paper. Among patterns *A, B,* and *C,* however, we may point to some real differences. For instance, in pattern *A* each individual can communicate with two others in the group directly— that is, without relaying a message through some other person. In patterns *C* and *D* there is only one individual in the group who can communicate directly with all the others.

To make another comparison, any individual in pattern *A* can communicate with any one of the others with no more than a single "relay." In pattern *B,* two individuals must relay messages through three others in order to communicate with each other.

In a sense, the comparisons just made involve the notion of "distance" between individuals in a pattern. If we adopt some method of counting the "distances" between individuals, we can make some statements regarding differences between and within patterns. In Figure 2 a method of counting is illustrated as applied to pattern *B* in Figure 1. The summation of all internal distances for pattern *B* is 40 ($\Sigma d_{x,\,y} = 40$). In a similar way, we find that the same summation for pattern *A* is 30 and for pattern *C,* 32. (Fig. 3 shows the tabulations of distances in pattern *C.*)

Turning to the question of differences among positions in the same pattern, we see clearly that position *q* in the pattern shown in Figure 2 is different from position *p* in the same pattern. One aspect of this difference is shown by the tabulation in Figure 2: $d_{p,\,x} = 10$, $d_{q,\,x} = 7$. Position *q* in Figure 2 has a total distance of 7, just as position *q* in Figure 3. In this case the distance from *q* to all others does not differentiate between the two positions. Yet we cannot but feel from an inspection of the patterns that there

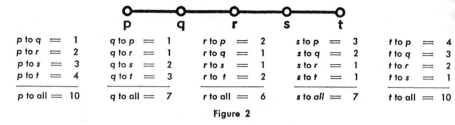

p to q =	1	q to p =	1	r to p =	2	s to p =	3	t to p =	4
p to r =	2	q to r =	1	r to q =	1	s to q =	2	t to q =	3
p to s =	3	q to s =	2	r to s =	1	s to r =	1	t to r =	2
p to t =	4	q to t =	3	r to t =	2	s to t =	1	t to s =	1
p to all =	10	q to all =	7	r to all =	6	s to all =	7	t to all =	10

Figure 2

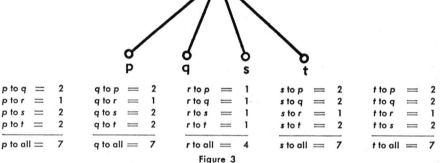

p to q =	2	q to p =	2	r to p =	1	s to p =	2	t to p =	2
p to r =	1	q to r =	1	r to q =	1	s to q =	2	t to q =	2
p to s =	2	q to s =	2	r to s =	1	s to r =	1	t to r =	1
p to t =	2	q to t =	2	r to t =	1	s to t =	2	t to s =	2
p to all =	7	q to all =	7	r to all =	4	s to all =	7	t to all =	7

Figure 3

is a difference between the two q positions. We could, of course, point to the fact that in one case q has two "neighbors" and in the other case has only one. But let us consider further the question of distance as such. Since the two patterns in question have different $\Sigma d_{x,\,y}$ values, it may help if we express the distance "q to all others" in a relative manner. One way of doing this is to calculate for each position the value of the expression:

$$\frac{\Sigma d_{x,\,y}}{\Sigma d_{q,\,x}}.$$

For position q in Figure 2, this quantity would be equal to 5.7; for position q in Figure 3, the quantity would be equal to 4.6. In Figure 4 are shown such similar values for each of the positions in patterns A, B, and C of Figure 1.

If we were to summarize the preceding discussion, we could say that comparisons between two patterns might be made on the basis of "dispersion" (sum of internal distances) defined as $\Sigma d_{x,\,y}$; and that comparisons between positions within the same pattern might be made on the basis of "relative centrality" defined as

$$\frac{\Sigma d_{x,\,y}}{d_{x,\,y}}$$

(the sum of all internal distances of the pattern divided by the total sum of distances for any one position in the pattern).

Operational Possibilities of Patterns. Let us turn now to the question of how these patterns of communication might be used by a group. Any sensible discussion of "operation" must, of course, be in terms of some specified task. A simple but interesting one would be the following: each of five subjects is dealt five playing cards from a normal poker deck and has the task of selecting from his hand the one card which, together with the four cards similarly selected by the other four subjects, will make the highest-ranking

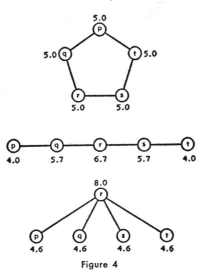

Figure 4

poker hand possible under these conditions.[2] The cards may not be passed around, but the subjects may communicate over the indicated channels, in the particular pattern being tested, by writing messages.

It is clear that pattern B in Figure 1 may be operated in a number of ways, or "operational patterns." Two of the possible operational patterns for communicating necessary information are shown in Figure 5. Obviously, it is possible for pattern B to be so operated that the subject in any one of the five positions will be the one to have all the necessary information first (and presumably decide which card each subject should select). There are no linkage strictures which would force a given method of operation into use. We might ask, however, whether there are differences in efficiency between different operational patterns. Two measures of efficiency come naturally to mind: the number of messages required for task completion, and the time required for task completion.

With respect to the number of messages required, it is possible to make a general statement. In terms of the task given above, one may say that each of the subjects has in his possession one-fifth of the information necessary for a solution. Also, all of the information must at some time be present at one position in the pattern. It can be shown that four messages are necessary and sufficient to accomplish this. Since each subject must know the correct card for him to select, an additional four messages will be required. One may say, therefore, that for any patterns with *symmetrical linkage* the number of messages required will be equal to 2 $(n-1)$, where n stands for the total number of positions, and that this requirement is completely independent of the linkage pattern as such.

With respect to the time it would take to reach a solution in different pat-

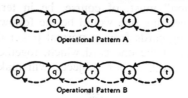

Operational Pattern A

Operational Pattern B

⟶ = Information regarding cards held
⟶ = Information regarding the card selection to be made

Figure 5

terns, we have a somewhat different situation. We must, of course, for any general discussion of speed of solution assume some standard unit of time to be associated with a message.[3] Let t equal the time it takes for information to go from one person to another when they are linked, i.e., when they occupy neighboring positions in the pattern.

(Before going on to a consideration of the patterns under discussion, a relationship between t and the number of individuals in a group should be pointed out. If any linkage pattern is allowed, then it may be stated that the minimum time for solution will have the following relation to the number of individuals in the pattern:

$$t^{min} = x + 1 \text{ when } 2^x < n \leq 2^{x+1}.$$

This relationship leads to some rather interesting conclusions. Let us consider two groups with unrestricted linkage—one group of nine members and one group of sixteen members. With a task such as that of selecting the best poker hand, the minimum time necessary for completion would be the same for both groups, although in the first case we would have nine individuals each possessing one-ninth of the information, and in the second case we would have sixteen individuals each with one-sixteenth of the information.)

With t defined in this way it is easy to see that operational pattern A in Figure 5 will require 8 time units, while operational pattern B in the same figure will require 5 time units. Obviously, when more than one message is sent in the same time unit, time is saved. However, if individual p sends a message simultaneously with individual r (as in Fig. 6), his message to q cannot possibly contain the information contained in the message from r.

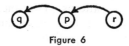

Figure 6

We can expect, therefore, that in certain patterns time will be saved at the expense of messages; and doing the task in minimum messages will involve the use of more time units. This is nicely illustrated by pattern A in Figure 1. In this pattern the problem may be done in as few as 3 time units, but to do this requires 14 messages; if the problem is done in 8 messages (the fewest possible), the number of time units required increases to 5.

Some Experiments with Selected Patterns. An analysis such as this must sooner or later lead to the question: "Granted that a kind of difference has been demonstrated between one pattern and another, is it a difference which will make a difference?" Such a question can be answered only by experiment. Without attempting a detailed account, a brief mention of two experimental studies would be helpful here.

Sidney Smith conducted an experiment[4] at Massachusetts Institute of Technology with eight groups of college students using patterns A and B shown in Figure 1. He gave his groups a task which in its essentials was similar to the poker-hand problem described earlier. Instead of playing cards, each subject was given a card upon which had been printed five symbols taken from among these six: ○ ★ * □ + ◈. While each symbol appeared on four of the five cards, only one symbol appeared on all five cards. Each group's task was to find the common symbol in the shortest time possible. In each subject's cubicle was a box of six switches, each switch labeled with one of the six symbols. The task was considered finished when each member of the group indicated that he knew the common symbol by throwing the appropriate switch. The switches operated a board of lights visible to a laboratory assistant who recorded individual and group times and errors (an error being the throwing of an incorrect switch). The subjects communicated by writing messages which could be passed through slots in the cubicle walls. The slots were so arranged that any desired linkage pattern could be imposed by the experimenter. No restriction whatever was placed upon the content of the messages. A subject who had the "answer" was at liberty to send it along. The cards upon which the messages were written were coded so that a reconstruction of the communicatory activity could be made.

Each experimental group worked on fifteen successive problems. The same six symbols were used throughout, but the common symbol varied from trial to trial. Four groups worked in pattern A, and four other groups worked in pattern B. No group worked in more than one pattern.

Of the detailed analysis which Smith made of the experimental data, only two findings will be presented here: errors, and the emergence of recognized leaders (see Table I and Fig. 7).

Table I

Error Category	Pattern A	Pattern B
Average total errors	14.0	7.0
Average group errors	5.0	1.5

Total errors = number of incorrect switches thrown.
Group errors = number of problems which on completion contained at least one error.
(All figures are averages from the performance of four groups in each pattern. Each group did 15 problems.)

With respect to the emergence of recognized leadership, Smith had each of his subjects answer a questionnaire immediately after the end of the fifteenth trial. One of the questions read: "Did your group have a leader? If so, who?" The answers are shown in Figure 7.

While no good theory could be formulated for the differences in numbers of errors, the findings suggested that the individual occupying the most central position in a pattern was most likely to be recognized as the leader. Also, from observation of the subjects while they worked, it appeared that morale was better in pattern A than in pattern B, and that the morale of the individuals in the most peripheral (least central) positions of pattern B was the poorest.

In order to explore these possibilities further, Harold Leavitt did a more detailed study[5] of the same two patterns plus two others. The four patterns he used are shown in Figure 8. Leavitt used the same problems and the same experimental setting used by Smith. His findings on errors and lead-

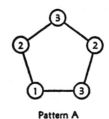

Pattern A

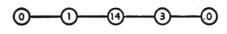

Pattern B

Figure 7. The number at each position shows the total number of group members (in the four groups in that pattern) who recognized the individual in that position as the leader.

ership recognition are presented in the same form as Smith's data (Table II and Fig. 9).

Leavitt's findings considerably strengthen the hypothesis that a recognized leader (under the conditions of the experiment) will most probably emerge at the position of highest centrality. His findings also lend some support to the hypothesis that errors may be related to pattern properties.

In addition to errors and leadership, Leavitt was interested in the question of morale differences between and within patterns. His subjects were asked two questions to which they responded by ratings from 0 (very unfavorable) to 10 (very favorable). The data are given below in averages of all ratings for subjects in the same pattern (Table III).

In order to check the hypothesis that morale differences exist within patterns and are related to relative centrality, the following analysis of the responses to the same two questions was made (Table IV). The ratings of men who occupied the most peripheral positions in patterns *B, E,* and *F* were averaged together; the ratings made by men in the most central positions of the same three patterns were also averaged together. All ratings made by subjects in pattern *A* were omitted from these calculations for the obvious reason that no one is most central or most peripheral in that pattern.

On the basis of a detailed study of all the data yielded by his experiments, Leavitt makes the following comments:

Pattern F^6 operated as expected in all five cases. The peripheral men sent their information to the center where the answer was arrived at and sent out. This organization usually evolved by the fourth or fifth trial and was maintained unchanged throughout the remaining trials.

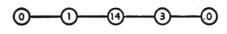

A   B   E   F

Figure 8

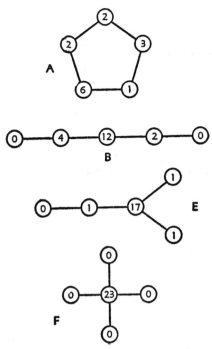

Figure 9. Emergence of recognized leaders

Table II

Error Category	PATTERNS			
	A	B	E	F
Average total errors	17	10	3	10*
Average group errors	3	2	1	1

* Leavitt attributes almost all of this error figure to one of the five pattern F groups which became confused over the meaning of one member's method of reporting his information.

Pattern E operated so that the most central man got all the information and sent out the answer. Organization evolved more slowly than in pattern F, but, once achieved, was just as stable.

Pattern B was not as stable as patterns E and F. Although most of the times the answer was sent out by the individual in the most central position, this function was occasionally performed by one of the men on either side of him. Organization was slower to evolve than in patterns E and F.

Pattern A showed no consistent pattern of organization. Subjects, for the most part, merely sent messages until they received or could work out the answer themselves.

A Proposed Experiment Using the Same Patterns but a Different Task. In the Leavitt experiment, the normal behavior of a subject in working toward a solution was to send to the others a list of the five symbols appearing on his card. Occasionally, however, something quite different would occur. The subject would send, instead, the one symbol (out of the total six symbols)[7] which was *not* on his card. The advantages of this method in saving time and avoiding possible error are obvious. In a sense this procedure is a "detour" solution of the problem confronting the subject. The whole task

Table III

Questions	AVERAGE RATING BY PATTERN			
	A	B	E	F
How much did you like your job?	6.6	6.2	5.8	4.7
How satisfied are you with the job done?	8.0	5.8	6.0	5.4

Table IV

Questions	AVERAGE RATING BY POSITION IN PATTERN	
	For 35 Individuals in the Most Peripheral Positions*	For 15 Individuals in the Most Central Positions†
How much did you like your job?	3.2	8.8
How satisfied are you with the job done?	4.6	7.8

* As represented here (black dots):

† As represented here (black dots):

situation was such as to suggest strongly the straightforward action of sending along the symbols one had, rather than the symbol one had not. Although the frequency of occurrence of this insight was fairly even in the groups, its adoption by the groups as a method of work was not. It was used by two of the five groups in pattern *A*, by one of the five groups in pattern B, and by none of the groups in patterns *E* and *F*. While these differences could not be demonstrated to be significant, they excited considerable speculation. In individual psychology it has been shown repeatedly that an individual's frame of reference may be such as to effectively inhibit the solving of a problem requiring a detour. With the groups in question the insight invariably occurred to some member or members. Why, then, did it not spread throughout the group in every case? Might it be that in certain communication patterns the probability of effective utilization of the insights that occur is greater than in others? It was felt that if a more suitable task could be devised, some relationship between the occurrence and utilization of insights and communication pattern might be uncovered.

A task has been constructed which seems to be a step in the right direction. Preliminary trials with it are encouraging. The task consists essentially of forming squares from various geometric shapes. In Figure 10 are shown the fifteen pieces which make up the puzzle and how they go together to form five squares.

Out of these shapes, squares may be made in many ways. Some of the possible combinations are: *c c a a, e a a a a, e a a g, f f a a a a, f f c a, f f g a a, i c a,* etc. However, if, using all fifteen pieces, five squares must be constructed, there is only one arrangement that can succeed—that shown in Figure 10. In the experimental situation the pieces are distributed among the five subjects. They are told that the task will be successfully completed when each subject has a square before him and no unused pieces. Messages and pieces may be passed along open channels.

The initial distribution of the pieces may be made so that the probability of "bad" squares being formed is increased ("bad" squares being any which, perfect in themselves, make a total of five squares impossible). A possible distribution is given in Figure 11.

Figure 10

As can be seen, the pieces with which an individual starts may suggest a particular composition. Or, the pieces an individual starts with may suggest nothing at all and therefore be speedily traded. Let us look at the situation at position *A* in Figure 11. The pieces *i, h, e* do not readily suggest a combination of themselves. We may assume that the subject will pass one of the three to position *B*. At position *B*, however, the situation is quite different. The combinations *a, c, e* or *a, a, a, h* or *a, c, i* all form squares which if completed will lead to group failure, so that any piece received from position *A* merely suggests possible "wrong" squares. In preliminary trials the "bad" squares appear with great regularity. The point of the experiment is what happens, once these deceptive "successes" occur. For an individual who has completed a square, it is understandably difficult to tear it apart. The ease with which he can take a course of action "away from the goal" should depend to some extent upon his perception of the total situation. In this regard, the pattern of communication should have well-defined effects.

A formal experiment using this task has not yet been done. Preliminary runs (making use of various communication patterns and concerned pri-

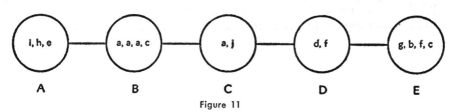

Figure 11

marily with experimental method) have revealed, however, that the binding forces against restructuring are very great, and that, with any considerable amount of communication restriction, a solution is improbable.

Concluding Remarks. The studies so briefly discussed in this chapter, if they do nothing more, suggest that an experimental approach to certain aspects of social communication is possible and that, in all probability, it would be practically rewarding. Although the problem of effective communication is an old one, recent trends are bringing to it a new sense of urgency. More and more it is becoming clear that any fundamental advance in social self-understanding must rest upon more adequate intercommunication. In areas where effective and highly integrated social effort is required, the problem is particularly critical. This is nowhere better illustrated than in scientific work. In many fields, it has become impossible to think in other terms than research teams. These groups, aside from the ordinary problems of communication which attend organization, face a whole new set of problems arising from the current emphasis upon "security." In practice, security is invariably translated into "communication restriction." In a sense, the experiments discussed above explore precisely this question: what happens to the performance and morale of working groups when communication is restricted in one way rather than in another?

The experimental evidence is provocative. Generalization at such an early stage of work is dangerous, but one is tempted to make a tentative step. It would seem that under the conditions imposed in the experiments, differences between certain patterns very probably exist. The differences most clearly revealed by the experiments are with respect to (a) the location, in the pattern, of recognized leadership; (b) the probability of errors in performance; and (c) the general satisfaction of group members.

Further, we note that in patterns with a high, localized centrality, organization evolves more quickly and is more stable, and errors in performance are less. At the same time, however, morale drops. It is conceivable that poor morale would, in the long run, affect stability and accuracy negatively. The experimental runs of fifteen trials conducted by Smith, if extended to a larger number of trials, might well begin to show this effect.

More speculative, at present, is the question of the occurrence and utilization of insight. The preliminary trials with the "five squares" puzzle, while few, are dramatic. Every group succeeded in forming two, or three, or four squares. But the ability to restructure the problem, to give up the partial successes, varied widely from pattern to pattern. If the indications of the few experimental runs that have been made to date are any guide, both occurrence and utilization of insight will be found to drop rapidly as centrality is more and more highly localized. In one group, the individual to whom the necessary insight occurred was "ordered" by the emergent leader to "forget it." Losses of productive potential, in this way, are probably very common in most working groups, and must be enormous in the society at large.

6. THE MEASUREMENT OF GROUP DIMENSIONS

by John K. Hemphill and Charles M. Westie

THIS PAPER DISCUSSES the construction of a series of scales developed for the purpose of objective description of group characteristics. These scales have been developed for use in the study of relationships between the behavior of leaders and characteristics of groups in which they function.[1]

We may accept provisionally a definition of a social group offered by Smith.[2] He defined a social group as "a unit consisting of a plural number of separate organisms (agents) who have collective perception of their unity and who have the ability and tendency to act and/or are acting in a unitary manner toward their environment." If one is to differentiate between what can be called a group and what can not, certain terms in the definition above need operational specification. For example, we must determine when separate organisms have a "collective perception of their unity" or when they have "a tendency to act or are acting in a unitary manner." This problem of the precise delineation of the concept "group" might be met by devising objective measures of a number of basic characteristics of groups, such as those reflected by the terms in Smith's definition. Certain arbitrary values of these objective measurements might be then established which would permit one to specify with reasonable precision what is or is not a group so defined. On the other hand, if one had such measures he might find it more meaningful to speak of degrees of "group-ness," rather than in terms of the all-or-none dichotomy imposed by group or non-group.

A. Selection of Characteristics to Describe Groups. The potential number of concepts or terms which can be used to describe characteristics of a given group is immense. In attempting to devise a system of group descriptions, it is necessary to choose from all available descriptive concepts a limited number which meet certain criteria relating to their probable usefulness for a given purpose. The following four criteria serve as guides in the selection of the group characteristics to be described in this paper: (*a*) each characteristic should be meaningful within a sociological or psychological framework; (*b*) each characteristic should be conceived as a continuum varying from the lowest degree to the highest degree; (*c*) each characteristic should refer to a relatively molar[3] rather than a molecular property of a group; (*d*) each characteristic should be relatively orthogonal or independent of all other characteristics in the descriptive system.

Reprinted from the *Journal of Psychology*, Vol. 29, 1950, pp. 325-341, by permission of the authors and the publisher. (Copyright, 1950, by The Journal Press.)

Fourteen characteristics of groups were found which appeared to meet the above criteria. These characteristics were selected and defined after gathering and carefully examining descriptive words and phrases from the works of a number of writers who have described the nature of groups. Descriptions of characteristics which seemed to overlap one another or otherwise failed to meet any one of the above criteria were discarded. Definitions of the characteristics finally selected are given below. These characteristics will hereafter be referred to as group dimensions.

1. *Autonomy* is the degree to which a group functions independently of other groups and occupies an independent position in society. It is reflected by the degree to which a group determines its own activities, by its absence of allegiance, deference and/or dependence relative to other groups.

2. *Control* is the degree to which a group regulates the behavior of individuals while they are functioning as group members. It is reflected by the modifications which group membership imposes on complete freedom of individual behavior and by the amount or intensity of group-derived government.

3. *Flexibility* is the degree to which a group's activities are marked by informal procedures rather than by adherence to established procedures. It is reflected by the extent to which duties of members are free from specification through custom, tradition, written rules, regulations, codes of procedure, or even unwritten but clearly prescribed ways of behaving.

4. *Hedonic Tone* is the degree to which group membership is accompanied by a general feeling of pleasantness or agreeableness. It is reflected by the frequency of laughter, conviviality, pleasant anticipation of group meetings, and by the absence of griping and complaining.

5. *Homogeneity* is the degree to which members of a group are similar with respect to socially relevant characteristics. It is reflected by relative uniformity of members with respect to age, sex, race, socio-economic status, interests, attitudes, and habits.

6. *Intimacy* is the degree to which members of a group are mutually acquainted with one another and are familiar with the most personal details of one another's lives. It is reflected by the nature of topics discussed by members, by modes of greeting, forms of address, and by interactions which presuppose a knowledge of the probable reaction of others under widely differing circumstances, as well as by the extent and type of knowledge each member has about other members of the group.

7. *Participation* is the degree to which members of a group apply time and effort to group activities. It is reflected by the number and kinds of duties members perform, by voluntary assumption of non-assigned duties and by the amount of time spent in group activities.

8. *Permeability* is the degree to which a group permits ready access to membership. It is reflected by absence of entrance requirements of any kind, and by the degree to which membership is solicited.

9. *Polarization* is the degree to which a group is oriented and works toward a single goal which is clear and specific to all members.

10. *Potency* is the degree to which a group has primary significance for its members. It is reflected by the kind of needs which a group is satisfying or has the potentiality of satisfying, by the extent of readjustment which would be required of members should the group fail, and by the degree to which a group has meaning to the members with reference to their central values.

11. *Size* is the number of members regarded as being in the group.

12. *Stability* is the degree to which a group persists over a period of time with essentially the same characteristics. It is reflected by the rate of membership turnover, by frequency of reorganizations and by constancy of group size.

13. *Stratification* is the degree to which a group orders its members into status hierarchies. It is reflected by differential distribution of power, privileges, obligations, and duties and by asymmetrical patterns of differential behavior among members.

14. *Viscidity*[4] is the degree to which members of the group function as a unit. It is reflected by absence of dissension and personal conflict among members, by absence of activities serving to advance only the interests of individual group members, by the ability of the group to resist disrupting forces, and by the belief on the part of the members that the group does function as a unit.

B. The Preliminary Scales. Items were written to be used as indicators of varying degrees of the above dimensions. Suggestions for these items were obtained by examination of responses given by more than 500 individuals to a free-response type questionnaire.[5] Each respondent described a group of which he was a member by answering more than 50 open-end questions about the nature of his group and his relation to it. The scales for the measurement of group dimensions were developed from approximately 1100 items directly suggested by responses to these questionnaires.

The method used in constructing the scales was influenced by the criteria which guided the selection of group dimensions. In addition to the obvious requirement that an item discriminate between high and low degrees of a given dimension, each item which was retained had to meet two other requirements; (*a*) that the item appear relevant to the nature of the dimension to which it was assigned and (*b*) that the item be independent of all other dimensions in the descriptive system. Items which pertained equally well to two or more of the group dimensions were considered undesirable because of the likelihood of introducing correlation between dimensions. The first screening of 1100 items was designed to remove from further consideration those items which could not meet the requirement of pertaining to one and only one of the group dimensions.

Item Homogeneity. Five judges[6] were used to screen items for relevance to a single dimension. Each of the judges considered each of the 1100 items for relevance to each of the 14 dimensions. They were instructed to read the definition of a dimension and then to sort the 1100 items into three categories. Items which definitely applied to the dimension were placed in one category. Items about which the judge was undecided were placed in a second. Items which definitely did not apply to the dimension were placed in a third category. Each judge worked independently. He considered all items for relevance to each dimension, one dimension at a time. The order in which the judges considered the dimensions was varied.

An index of homogeneity of placement[7] was computed for each item on which at least three of the five judges agreed that the item pertained to the same dimension. This index was adopted to give a single numerical evaluation of each item with respect to its homogeneity. Agreement among judges that the item applied to a dimension and agreement that it did not apply to other dimensions in the description system were given approximately equal weight in the value of this index.[8] An arbitrary value of the index[9] was selected as a cutting point for the elimination of items from further consideration.

Three-hundred and fifty-five items were edited and placed in a preliminary composite instrument entitled *A Study of a Group.* Items were placed in this preliminary form in a random manner irrespective of the dimension to which they belonged. The number of items for a dimension ranged from nine for the Hedonic Tone dimension to 47 for Permeability.

In the preliminary instrument items were presented in the form of simple declarative statements followed by five-point scales as illustrated in Table 1.

Table 1—Rating Scale Following Each Item

5	4	3	2	1
Definitely True	Mostly True	Undecided Don't Know Doesn't Apply	Mostly False	Definitely False

The respondent was instructed to check a point on the scale which would best describe his group. If he marked point 3, he was further requested to check one of the three alternative meanings of the middle response.

The Sample. Two-hundred descriptions were obtained involving 35 groups by using this preliminary form. No attempt was made to select a single representative of any particular population of groups. Effort in sampling was directed toward obtaining a variety of groups in which two or more members described the same group. The names of the groups, their approximate size, and the number of members describing them are given in Table 2.

These descriptions were obtained to be used in a quantitative evaluation of the group dimension scales. They provided data for (*a*) an estimation of the reliability for dimension total scores, (*b*) an internal consistency type of item analysis, (*c*) an examination of the intercorrelation among the dimension scores, and (*d*) an examination of the agreement between respondents who described the same group.

Supplementary Analysis of the Items. It was thought desirable to supplement the quantitative material mentioned above by a more qualitative appraisal of each of the items. This was done by obtaining elaborated comments from five persons for each item, directed toward determining why the respondent had selected a given response rather than another. The elaborations were collected from individuals who had just previously completed description of a group. Ambiguities and misunderstandings were frequently pointed out and suggestions for improvement of items were given.

A third processing of the 355 items involved editing for readability. A trained readability technician[10] examined each item and made suggestions for rewording so as to make them as easy to comprehend as possible. This was done to widen the range of application to respondents from groups in which the average educational level was not above the seventh or eighth grade.

The final selecting and editing of items was done after consideration of the quantitative information about the items, the qualitative remarks from five respondents telling why they responded to an item as they did, and the readability analysis suggestions.

C. Reliability of the Dimension Scales. The first step in the quantitative analysis of the dimension scales was the construction of *a priori* scoring keys for the items assigned to each of the group dimensions. Weights were assigned to each of the five points on the scale so that the highest degree of the dimension indicated by the item received a value of 5, the lowest degree received a value of 1, and the intermediate points were given values of 2, 3, or 4.

The first 100 descriptions were scored according to these *a priori* scoring keys. Split-half reliability estimates were made for each of the dimension scores on a basis of these first descriptions. The estimates of reliability for each of the dimension scores are presented in Table 3.

All reliability estimates were considered adequate for the establishment of "high" and "low" categories for internal consistency analysis.

D. Internal Consistency Item Analysis. The internal consistency item analysis was delayed until the entire sample of 200 descriptions had been obtained and scored according to the *a priori* keys. A "high" and a "low" group of 100 descriptions each was then established for each dimension on the basis of total scores. The "high" categories included those descriptions on which the score for a given dimension was above the median value, while the "low" categories included those descriptions on which the dimension score was below the median.

The ideal procedure of correlating the response to each of the 355 items with high-low categories for each of the dimensions was not undertaken for practical reasons.

Fifty-four items were examined for each total dimension score categorization. These included (*a*) all items which had been keyed as belonging

Table 2—Groups Described by Members Using "A Study of a Group"

Kind of Group	Number of Members	Number of Descriptions
1. An interdisciplinary graduate seminar	12	10
2. Professional staff of a social service organization	11	9
3. A neighborhood	72	8
4. A graduate seminar	9	7
5. Total office group of a research organization	11	6
6. Professional staff of the same research organization	8	3
7. The staff of a psychology department	30	8
8. The staff of a sociology department	19	14
9. A high school class	12	11
10. A second high school class	23	20
11. A woman's church club	43	2
12. An informal group which meets at a tavern	50	2
13. A division of a research organization	6	3
14. A young people's church club	25	2
15. A couple's club associated with a church	30	3
16. A night-school typewriting class	17	2
17. A boy scout fraternity	65	7
18. A graduate club in a college department	30	4
19. A military department	31	14
20. The staff of an economics department	54	3
21. A Kiwanis Club	51	2
22. An entire large university	27,000	7
23. A social sorority	23	2
24. Committee "A" within a college of a university	11	6
25. Committee "B" within the same college of a large university	11	9
26. Committee "C" within a college of a large university	6	5
27. A student government class	10	2
28. A Sunday School class	40	6
29. A college in India, the staff of	28	1
30. A school teaching staff	65	6
31. A high school teaching staff	140	1
32. A high school teaching staff	100	3
33. A scholastic fraternity	45	8
34. A social club	51	2
35. A dramatics fraternity	21	2

Table 3—Estimates of Reliability of Dimension Scores (N = 100 Descriptions)

Dimension	Number of Items	Estimate of Reliability*
1. Autonomy	25	.83
2. Control	19	.75
3. Flexibility	30	.78
4. Hedonic Tone	9	.59
5. Homogeneity	27	.71
6. Intimacy	28	.82
7. Participation	30	.76
8. Permeability	47	.74
9. Polarization	19	.73
10. Potency	28	.76
11. Size	1	—
12. Stability	11	.64
13. Stratification	24	.80
14. Viscidity	33	.87

* Corrected for full length of the scale.

to the dimension, plus (*b*) five items assigned at random from dimensions other than the dimension which determined the high-low categorization, plus (*c*) a varying number of items on which one or two of the five judges had indicated that the item might pertain to the dimension but the other judges had not concurred.

The degree of relationship between an item and the high-low categories was determined by computing four-fold correlation coefficients[11] between the item score, dichotomized at the point of maximum differentiation, and the total (high-low) score of the dimension. Table 4 presents the range and median value of these coefficients: (*a*) for items keyed as pertaining to the dimension, (*b*) for randomly assigned items not in the dimension, and (*c*) for items not keyed but possibly pertaining to the dimension.

Table 4—Fourfold Point Correlation Coefficients for Three Types of Items Included in the Item Analysis

Type of Item	Range	Median
Items keyed for the dimension	.03 — .78	.36
Items possibly related to the dimension	.00 — .50	.15
Items randomly selected from other dimensions	.01 — .36	.12

It will be noted that the median value of the keyed items is far above that of the randomly selected items and of those where only one or two judges had considered the item to be relevant. The randomly selected items rarely exceeded very low values. These findings may be viewed as substantiating the judgments of the five individuals who had originally considered the items for application to each group dimension. It also justifies the compromise with the ideal of examining all items for relation to each dimension.

E. Intercorrelation of the Dimension Scores. The intercorrelations among the dimension total scores were examined by computing tetrachoric correlation coefficients[12] between the high-low categories of each pair of dimensions. These coefficients are comparable to the product-moment correlation coefficients, because the dimension scores are known to be continuous; and inspection of the distribution of these scores revealed close approximation to normal distribution. Table 5 presents intercorrelations between dimension scores.

Table 5—Intercorrelations Among Fourteen Group Dimension Scores* (N = 200)

	1	2	3	4	5	6	7	8	9	10	11	12	13
1. Autonomy													
2. Control	−.06												
3. Flexibility	.29	−.29											
4. Hedonic Tone	.16	−.37	−.16										
5. Homogeneity	.12	.10	−.02	.40									
6. Intimacy	.12	.19	−.21	.38	.31								
7. Participation	−.25	−.12	−.25	.38	.12	.21							
8. Permeability	.46	−.29	.07	.19	−.02	.10	−.53						
9. Polarization	.03	−.02	−.31	.40	.28	.19	.49	−.10					
10. Potency	−.34	.03	−.46	.25	.07	.28	.69	−.51	.34				
11. Size	.03	.19	−.46	.07	−.16	.10	−.10	.19	−.16	−.02			
12. Stability	.00	−.19	.25	.19	.25	−.02	.00	−.06	.28	−.16	−.54		
13. Stratification	−.40	.21	−.10	−.49	−.31	−.12	.29	−.51	−.16	.34	.10	−.12	
14. Viscidity	.19	−.46	−.02	.81	.38	.03	.38	.16	.38	.19	−.16	.21	−.46

* The probability of securing a correlation value of .29 or larger by chance is .01.

While the majority of the intercorrelations among dimension scores are small enough to meet the criterion of independent dimensions, others were considered high enough to demand further attention. In the final selection of items for each of the scales another attempt was made to reduce overlapping in cases of dimensions which showed the highest intercorrelation. The content of the items going into the final scales was examined for clues as to reasons for overlaps. The content of the five recorded elaborations pertaining to each item was also examined in an effort to detect reasons for intercorrelations among these dimensions. Doubtful items were reworded or eliminated from the final scales. However, it is anticipated that there may still remain a substantial degree of overlap among such dimensions as Viscidity and Hedonic Tone, or Participation and Potency.

F. Agreement Among Respondents Who Described the Same Groups. In obtaining descriptions of groups an effort was made to obtain a description from more than one member of each group. This was done in order that the agreement among members as to the nature of their group could be examined. Within the first 100 descriptions, eight groups were obtained where a minimum of five members had described a single group. These groups were Nos. 1, 2, 3, 4, 5, 7, 8, and 9 as listed in Table 2. The total number of respondents involved in the description of these eight groups was 65. The dimension scores were examined to determine the degree to which members who described the same groups agreed. The variation among each of the group dimension scores was analyzed in two parts, (*a*) variation associated with differences between groups and (*b*) variation associated with description of the same group. Table 6 presents the *F* ratios expressing a comparison of these two variances, together with the extent of agreement between respondents as expressed by an unbiased correlation ratio.[13]

The descriptions given by respondents who described the same group agreed to an extent which exceeded chance expectations on each of the group dimensions. This result may be interpreted as indicating that the characteristics expressed by the group dimension scores are perceived in common by members of the same group. Responses to the items composing these scales are determined by other than individual attitudes of members belonging to the same social aggregate. The objectivity of measurement of group characteristics must rest on demonstrations of agreement between observations of the same social phenomena.

Table 6—F Ratios and Unbiased Correlation Ratios Expressing the Degree of Agreements among Respondents Describing the Same Group

Group Dimension	F Ratio*	Correlation Ratio
1. Autonomy	5.15	.56
2. Control	10.62	.72
3. Flexibility	7.52	.65
4. Hedonic Tone	6.03	.60
5. Homogeneity	8.37	.67
6. Intimacy	7.77	.65
7. Participation	4.49	.53
8. Permeability	11.84	.74
9. Polarization	3.60	.47
10. Potency	6.67	.62
11. Size	—	—
12. Stability	9.33	.69
13. Stratification	8.54	.67
14. Viscidity	11.16	.73

* The probability of obtaining an F ratio of 3.00 or larger is less than .01.

G. Evidence Bearing on Scale Validity. A *posteriori* evidence ot the validity of these dimension scores as descriptive of group characteristics can be obtained by comparison of the descriptions made by the members of different groups. As one example, we may examine the scores describing a military department (group No. 19, Table 2) and scores for Committee "B" within a college of a large university (group No. 25). The military department was composed of officers engaged in training students at a large university. This group might be characterized in a general manner as one which is well organized, somewhat overworked, and having the objective of training college students for reserve officer commissions. Committee "B" was one of a number of similar committees in a democratically administered college within the same university. Democracy in this particular college might well be described as a central prevailing ideology. The particular committee had as its purpose the consideration of many diverse issues concerned with student problems.

In making the comparison between these two groups, raw dimension scores were transformed into standard scores based on the entire 200 descriptions as a normative sample. Figure 1 presents in the form of a dimension profile the mean standard scores from the members' descriptions of their respective groups.

Inspection of Figure 1 will show many of the differences which would be expected between these two groups, portrayed in a striking manner. The military department is more highly stratified, has less autonomy, has higher control over member behavior, has less flexibility; (i.e., is more formal), and shows a higher degree of participation than the college committee.

In this first example two groups which were expected to be quite different have been compared. As a second example, we may compare the dimension scores of two groups expected to be very similar. The dimension scores of the committee we used in our first example are compared with those of a second committee "A," within the same college of the same university (group No. 24, Table 2). This committee exists within the same

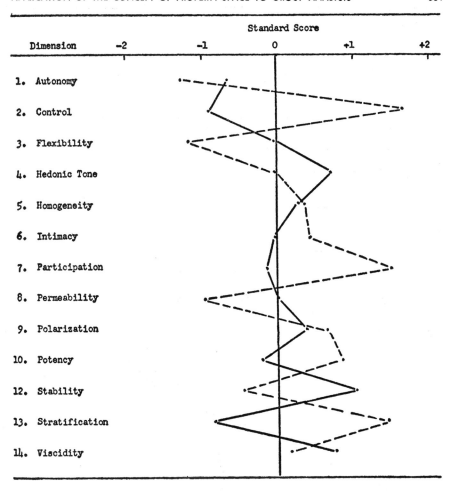

Figure 1. Dimension Scores (Standard Score Form) Describing the Characteristics
of Two Quite Different Groups

atmosphere of democratic ideology, but differs from Committee "B" in being
one echelon higher in the administrative hierarchy, and in having among its
membership several individuals having higher academic rank. Committee
"A" functions as a supervisory committee of other committees within the
college, receives reports from other committees, and generally functions to
safeguard basic policy. Figure 2 presents the mean standard scores for
these two groups in the form of profiles.

The profiles of these two committees have very similar forms. The greatest differences appear in the scores for intimacy and stratification. Committee "A" is slightly more stratified and slightly less intimate. Other
slight differences involve lower stability and permeability and higher con-

trol in the case of Committee *"A."* These small differences seem to be consistent with known facts about the committees. Greater differences in academic rank may account for greater awareness of stratification and less intimacy among members. Permeability of a committee in an administratively higher echelon is likely to be less than of those in lower echelons. The lower stability score may have as its basis the fact that members can be on Committee *"A"* only two years in succession while no such rules exist for the first committee. Higher control in Committee *"A"* may also be related indirectly to greater differences in academic rank.

Dimensions scores appear to be consistent with general knowledge about the nature of these groups.

H. Final Scales. It is not possible to reproduce here all of the scales in their final forms. Instead, sample items from each scale will be given. The

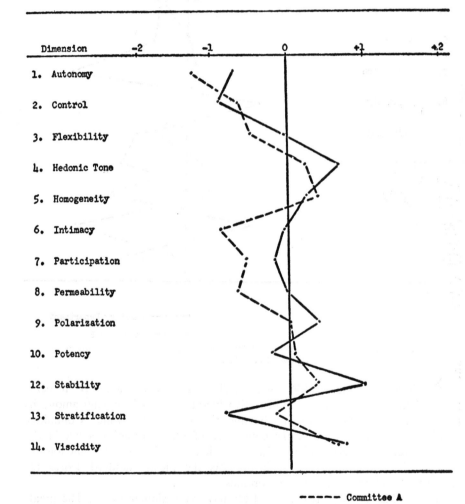

```
----- Committee A
───── Committee B
```

Figure 2. Dimension Scores (Standard Score Form) Describing the Characteristics
of Two Similar Groups

items have been arranged in five different series of scale forms suitable for use with *IBM* Answer Sheets. The same five point "Definitely True—Definitely False" format has been retained, with the exception that the middle category has been simplified to "Undecided."

1. SAMPLE ITEMS

Autonomy
1. The group works independently of other groups.
2. The group is under outside pressure.
3. The things the group does are approved by a group higher up.

Control
1. Activities of the group are supervised.
2. No explanation need be given by a member wishing to be absent from the group.
3. Members fear to express their real opinions.

Flexibility
1. The group is very informal.
2. There is a recognized right way and wrong way of going about group activities.
3. The group meets any place that happens to be handy.

Hedonic Tone
1. A feeling of failure prevails in the group.
2. There are frequent intervals of laughter during group meetings.
3. Members continually grumble about the work they do for the group.

Homogeneity
1. Members of the group are all about the same age.
2. The group includes members of different races.
3. Members of the group vary widely in amount of experience.

Intimacy
1. Members of the group do small favors for one another.
2. All members know each other very well.
3. Members address each other by their first names.

Participation
1. Each member of the group is on one or more active committees.
2. The group has a reputation for not getting much done.
3. Every member of the group does not have a job to do.

Permeability
1. The group engages in membership drives.
2. No applicants for membership in the group are turned down.
3. People interested in joining the group are asked to submit references which are checked.

Polarization
1. The group divides its efforts among several purposes.
2. The objectives of the group have not been clearly recognized.
3. Each member of the group has a clear idea of the group's goals.

Potency
1. A mistake by one member of the group might result in hardship for all.
2. Each member would lose his self-respect if the group should fail.
3. The activities of the group take up over half of the time each member is awake.

Size

1. Number of members in the group —.

Stability

1. There is a large turnover of members in the group.
2. Members are constantly leaving the group.
3. The group is rapidly increasing in size.

Stratification

1. Opinions of members are considered as equal.
2. The group is controlled by the action of a few members.
3. The older members of the group are granted special privileges.

Viscidity

1. Members of the group work together as a team.
2. One part of the group is working against other parts.
3. There is constant bickering among members of the group.

I. Summary and Conclusions. The development of a series of group dimension scales has been described. A large number of specific items descriptive of group characteristics has been assembled into scales measuring 14 dimensions of groups. The scales have adequate reliability, yield scores showing a high degree of agreement between respondents describing the same group, and with a few exceptions have low intercorrelations among themselves. The first step of the construction of the scale illustrates a method of utilizing judgments of experts in the assignment of items to dimensions making up a descriptive system. The preliminary scales thus constructed were subjected to conventional internal consistency item analysis. These refined scales may provide tools for the objective study of variation found among social groups. It is only in their final utility as tools of research that their validity can be established.

7. THE FOLK-URBAN CONTINUUM*

by Horace Miner

An evaluation of the utility of the *folk* ideal type and its contrast with the urban societal type seems appropriate at this time. Developments in the past two years ambiguously indicate both a decline and a resurgence in the use of the continuum. On one hand, there is Oscar Lewis' critical restudy of Tepoztlán,[1] the community in which Robert Redfield made the

Reprinted from the *American Sociological Review*, Vol. 17, 1952, pp. 529-537, by permission of the author and the publisher. (Copyright, 1952, by the American Sociological Society.)
  * The suggestions of Dr. Werner Landecker led to a more lucid presentation of several sections of this article.

initial tentative formulation of the folk concept.[2] Relevant also is Redfield's own restudy of Chan Kom, in which volume he seems to have abandoned the folk as a conceptual tool.[3] But on the other hand, Redfield and Asael Hansen have become advisory assistants to a new ambitious program of research in Yucatan cast in the folk-urban frame of reference.[4] Armand Winfield of Washington University is also planning to test hypotheses stemming from the continuum in a study of two Missouri communities.[5]

The conceptual scheme is now over twenty years old. Some aspects of it seem still to be misunderstood and some of the limitations which have become apparent have not yet been adequately stated. It is our purpose to examine the basic propositions of the folk-urban continuum in the light of experience and criticism, in an effort to determine its inherent advantages and limitations for research and theory building.

Briefly stated, Redfield's scheme defines an ideal type, the *folk society,* which is the polar opposite of urban society. The ideal type is a mental construct and "No known society precisely corresponds to it. . . ."[6] It is "created only because through it we may hope to understand reality. Its function is to suggest aspects of real societies which deserve study, and especially to suggest hypotheses as to what, under certain defined conditions, may be generally true about society."[7]

The folk type of society is characterized as follows:

Such a society is small, isolated, nonliterate, and homogeneous, with a strong sense of group solidarity. The ways of living are conventionalized into that coherent system which we call "a culture." Behavior is traditional, spontaneous, uncritical, and personal; there is no legislation or habit of experiment and reflection for intellectual ends. Kinship, its relationships and institutions, are the type categories of experience and the familial group is the unit of action. The sacred prevails over the secular; the economy is one of status rather than of the market.[8]

Redfield concerns himself largely with the folk pole of the continuum. It is the characteristics of the folk society which receive his descriptive attention. These are derived by discovering the common traits of those societies which are least like our own.[9] The definitive qualities of the urban type are then left as the logically opposite ones to those which characterize the folk. Urban society is never actually discussed here as an ideal type and is not explicitly named. Redfield usually refers to it as "modern urbanized society" or some variant of the phrase. Implicit in the use of this pole as an ideal type, however, is the idea that it stands for urbanized society in general and that modern Western society represents the specific case most closely approximating the polar category. The term "urban society" would appear to represent the content of the ideal type more adequately.

The folk-urban continuum developed, of course, from earlier conceptual schemes. Maine, Tönnies, and Durkheim contributed important dichotomies of societal characteristics. Redfield's formulation took elements of these characteristics and others which he saw to be related and put them together as the definitive traits of the polar types. A factor influencing the research work of Redfield was that of concern with empirical method. To this interest must be attributed the fact that he executed, in Yucatan, one of the rare field projects in which a series of communities was selected and studied to test a specific hypothesis. Consistent with the express purpose of the formulation of the ideal type, its characteristics suggested the hypothesis. Concerning the Yucatañ study, Redfield writes:

The problem is seen as one of the relation among variables. No one of these is the sole cause of the others, but it is assumed, subject to proof, that, as certain of these vary, so do others. *For the purposes of this investigation** the isolation and homogeneity of the community are taken together as an independent variable. Organization or disorganization of culture, secularization, and individualization are regarded as dependent variables. The choice of isolation and homogeneity as independent variables implies the hypothesis that loss of isolation and increasing heterogeneity are causes of disorganization, secularization, and individualization. Even if this should be established, it would not follow that these are the only causes of these effects or that these are the only co-variant or causal relationships to be discovered in the same data.[10]

Consideration of the data from Yucatan leads Redfield to the conclusion that ". . . increase of contracts, bringing about heterogeneity and disorganization of culture, constitutes one sufficient cause of secularization and individualization."[11] No formal generalization is attempted with regard to the nature of the processes through which the variables affect one another, although the analysis of the data is full of demonstration of their specific interdependence in Yucatan. Comparison of the Yucatan material with that from Guatemala leads Redfield to the final conclusion that ". . . there is no single necessary cause for secularization and individualization."[12]

The pertinent research in Guatemala is that of Sol Tax. It is essentially exploratory in nature—an attempt to discern if, in another cultural milieu than Yucatan, the variables of the ideal type are related in the same way. Tax says Guatemalan societies are "small . . . homogeneous in beliefs and practices . . . with relationships impersonal . . . and with familial organization weak, with life secularized, and with individuals acting more from economic or other personal advantage than from any deep conviction or thought of social good."[13] As trade and commerce were important in Guatemala even in pre-Spanish times, Redfield regards Tax's observations as suggesting that the development of important commerce and a money economy may be another sufficient cause of secularization and individualization.[14] Tax points out that there seem to be two aspects of culture which cut across the dichotomy of the continuum. He finds the Guatemalan Indian "world view" or "mental apprehension of reality" to be folk in character but their kind of social relations to be those of the civilized (urban) type.[15]

Turning to other relevant research, Redfield's introduction to the writer's study of a comparatively isolated, French-Canadian community points out that this culture is intermediate on the continuum.[16] (He originally used the term "folk" to indicate this sort of society rather than the polar type, as Oscar Lewis has pointed out.) The Quebec study was not oriented toward any proposition explicitly related to the folk-urban continuum, but the writer agrees with Redfield's further observations that as the folk-like community lost its isolation, through contact with the city, it became more heterogeneous, a market economy developed, and indications of disorganization appeared.

In a subsequent study of Timbuctoo, French West Africa, the writer did

---

* Italics mine.

try to determine whether or not this densely populated, heterogeneous, non-isolated community showed social disorganization and was characterized by secular behavior and impersonal relationships, even in the absence of influences from Western civilization. As the report of this work is not yet available,[17] the following comments must, for the moment, be taken at their face value as evidence of the author's experience with and involvement in the folk-urban conceptual scheme.

The previous lack of interest, among anthropologists, in the urban pole of the continuum has already been alluded to. This polar type is logically also an ideal type, yet its characteristics have frankly been derived from a consideration of our own society. Further, in the series of Yucatan communities, decreasing isolation was in fact due to increased contact with Western urban civilization. This was explicitly recognized by Redfield.[18] But inherent in the continuum, as a hypothesis-provoking construct, is the idea that increased contact with any dissimilar society, not just with Western urban society, results in change in other variables of the ideal type. The Timbuctoo study was an attempt to avoid the limitations of the Yucatan research and of relevant rural-urban studies which have also been made in situations of rural contact with cities of Western civilization.

Briefly, the theoretical implications of the Timbuctoo data are that lack of isolation, marked population density and heterogeneity seem to be accompanied by disorganization, secularization and impersonalization, even in the absence of Western influences. The market economy appears as the system which makes possible the basic ecological conditions, holds the diverse cultural elements together, and mediates most relationships among them. Having said this, certain qualifications are immediately required. Evidence of disorganization and of secular and impersonal behavior, is most evident in relationships between members of different ethnic elements of the community. Familial relationships within each group seem to be strong, sacred and personal. Other intra-ethnic relationships are only somewhat less folk-like in character. Any attempt to characterize the whole society, and to compare it with others, highlights the fact that the folk-urban continuum deals with problems of the relative degree of presence or absence of polar characteristics, which vary not only between cultures but within them, and that no adequate methodological techniques exist for operationalizing and quantifying the characteristics themselves. To this point we shall want to return.

Certainly the most adverse comment on the utility of the folk-urban continuum is Oscar Lewis' critique which concludes his restudy of Tepoztlán. Both because this is a restudy of a community analyzed earlier by Redfield and because of the limited amount of research conducted with the continuum explicitly in mind, Lewis' comments deserve careful consideration.

Lewis points out that the folk concept is an ideal type and hence a matter of definition. It is upon its heuristic value that the type and its related continuum must be judged. He makes the following six criticisms of the conceptual framework, with regard to its utility for the study of culture change and for cultural analysis:[19]

(1) The folk-urban conceptualization of social change focuses attention primarily on the city as a source of change, to the exclusion or neglect of other factors of an internal or external nature. . . .

We would agree that Redfield's writing and research does neglect other sources of change than urban contact. We can not agree that the folk-urban continuum excludes other conceptualization. Most social scientists believe that the evolution of cities and civilizations has resulted from increased cultural interaction and interdependence. The operation of this process is evident in Tax's Guatemalan data and in the Timbuctoo material. However, it would be erroneous to say that even loss of isolation need always be considered the independent variable in change. Any other variable might do, so far as the continuum is concerned. The very consideration of what other characteristics might be so employed leads immediately to the fruitful observation that some of the type traits seem to presuppose others. For example, great heterogeneity in the division of labor requires a large population, while a large population may exist with a relatively unelaborate division of labor.

(2) . . . culture change may not be a matter of folk-urban progression, but rather an increasing or decreasing heterogeneity of culture elements. For example . . . the incorporation of Spanish rural elements, such as the plow . . . did not make Tepoztlán more urban, but rather gave it a more varied rural culture. . . .

The fact that Lewis says "may not be a matter of folk-urban progression" can be taken to mean that homogeneity and the other variables of the ideal type are interrelated only in certain circumstances. His phraseology also suggests an identification of the concepts "folk" and "rural."

While it is possible that homogeneity may vary independently from the other variables, the following excerpts from Lewis' monograph demonstrate that this was not the case with regard to the increase of heterogeneity resulting from the addition of plow cultivation to hoe agriculture in Tepoztlán.

The differences between hoe culture (*tlacolol*) and plow culture are not limited merely to the use of different tools; each system has far-reaching social and economic implications.[20]
Tlacolol is practiced on communally owned land and necessitates a great deal of time and labor but very little capital. Plow culture is practiced on privately owned land and requires relatively little time and labor but considerable capital. In the former, there is dependence almost exclusively upon family labor; in the latter, there is a great dependence upon hired labor.[21]
Tlacolol is essentially geared to production for subsistence, while plow culture is better geared to production for the market. It is significant that most families who work *tlacolol* are landless and that *tlacolol* has traditionally been viewed as the last resort of the poor.[22]
[An informant says of Tepoztlán during the Diaz regime,] ". . . The presidents of the municipio, in agreement with the *caciques,* forbade the sowing of *tlacolol* and so the poor had no way of helping themselves. This prohibition was due to the fact that if the poor planted *tlacolol,* the rich or *caciques* would not have the peones during the rainy season to seed their lands. . . ."[23]
. . . in the years immediately following the Revolution, that is between 1920 and 1927, relatively few individuals became *tlacololeros.* The population of the village was still small (the Revolution having reduced the population to about half its previous figure) and there was a relative abundance of rentable land. . . .
In 1927 the municipio lost control of the *tlacolol* lands, which passed to the jurisdiction of the forestry department. . . . With the rapid increase of population in the thirties, the shortage of land became acute and the need for the *tlacolol* land urgent. Many individuals began to open *tlacolol* plots and were fined.

In 1938 a group of Tepoztecans . . . stated that they would open *tlacolol* even if it meant violence and arrest. Following this demonstration the *tlacololeros* were allowed to work without government interference, and the number of *tlacololeros* increased.[24] . . . one of the crucial problems in Tepoztlán . . . (now is) the rapid increase of population with no accompanying increase in resources or improvement in production techniques. On the contrary, the increase in the number of *tlacololeros* represents a return to a more primitive type of production in an effort to escape the devastating effects of a money economy during a period of inflation. . . . Although it is helping to resolve the immediate problem, it by no means offers a satisfactory solution. In fact, it increases the problems to be faced.[25]

The writer knows of no better demonstration than that above of the manner in which two tools and their associated techniques form the core of social subdivision within a society. While it would certainly be unjustifiable to attribute the land-use system and its attendant problems in Tepoztlán solely to the co-occurrence of plow culture and *tlacolol,* it is equally unjustifiable to say that they are unrelated. Lewis' material indicates specifically that the introduction of plow agriculture and its co-existence with hoe agriculture is directly related to phenomena of population density, family cooperation, market economy, group solidarity, and conflicts indicative of social disorganization. What is more, this heterogeneity of technique seems to be related to shifts in the other variables away from the folk and, hence, toward the urban type. Tepoztlán is rural, in that it is an agricultural community, but it has a rural culture which shows definite urban influences and characteristics.

(3) Some of the criteria used in the definition of the folk society are treated by Redfield as linked or interdependent variables, but might better be treated as independent variables. . . .

The argument supporting this statement cites Tax's work and Lewis' own material showing that commercialism is accompanied by little evidence of family disorganization in Tepoztlán. This point is obviously a more generalized statement of that immediately preceding it. The only comment required is to note that the continuum, as defined, does not require that the type traits change at the same rate or that they are all interdependent in the same way in all circumstances. This is implicit in Redfield's statement, ". . . the societies of the world do not range themselves in the same order with regard to the degree to which they realize all of the characteristics of the ideal folk society."[26] It is explicit in his comparison of the Yucatan and Guatemala evidence.[27]

(4) The typology involved in the folk-urban classification of societies tends to obscure . . . the wide range in the ways of life and in the value systems among so-called primitive peoples. . . . the criteria used . . . are concerned with the purely formal aspects of society. . . . Focusing only on the formal aspects of urban society reduces all urban societies to a common denominator and treats them as if they all had the same culture. . . . It should be clear that the concept "urban" is too much of a catchall to be useful for cultural analysis. Moreover, it is suggested here that the question posed by Redfield, namely, what happens to an isolated, homogeneous society when it comes into contact with an urbanized society, cannot possibly be answered in a scientific way because the question is too general and the terms used do not give us the necessary data.

What we need to know is what kind of urban society, under what conditions of contact, and a host of other specific historical data.

We should amend two of these statements slightly to bring them in line with the facts before discussing them. Obviously the reduction of "all urban societies to a common denominator" treats them as though they had *something in common,* but not "as if they all had the same culture." Secondly, we see again a confusion between the conceptualization of the continuum and Redfield's research concern with a particular kind of loss of isolation, namely urban contact.

Granted that it is desirable to study the total configuration of a society and the specific historical factors which gave rise to that pattern, limiting our interests to such inquiry produces a methodological and descriptive science, such as linguistics. If we want to develop a social science with general principles applicable to all societies, despite their cultural differences, we are forced to abstract categories of phenomena which are applicable to all cultures.

Differences in ethos are important in understanding culture, as Lewis says in his discussion, citing the individualism and competitiveness of the Plains Indians. But because the urbanite and the Indian hunter share these features, does this mean we should cease to consider individualism and competition as specifically related to other aspects of urban life? It may also argue that we need to know how and in what circumstances individualism is systematically related to other systems than the urban.

As for the polar types being "catchalls," too generally defined for scientific investigation, Lewis seems to be restating Redfield's remarks:

> The problems suggested in that earlier paper defining the types are too comprehensive in scope and too vague in definition to be suitable guides for research. Nine or ten characters, each simply denoted by a phrase or two, are thrown together and called a "type." It is not clear how we are to determine how any particular society partakes more or less of any of these characters. It is not made clear how we are to determine which of these characters is naturally associated with any other. It is necessary to ask many more special questions, and to relate them to particular fact, to define more precise lines of inquiry.[28]

The continuum is an oversimplification, but at least it is a simplification of a mass of data on cultural variation and change. As a rudimentary conceptual device, the continuum requires elaboration—elaboration which will produce a different conceptual scheme. Science does advance by asking the general questions. The crude answers to the general questions are the basis of increasingly more specific inquiry. The real query is, do we have a better initial answer than the folk-urban continuum to the general question of how to account for the similarities and differences observable among societies?[29]

(5) The folk-urban classification has serious limitations in guiding field research because of the highly selective implications of the categories themselves and the rather narrow focus of problem. The emphasis upon essentially formal aspects of culture leads to neglect of psychological data and, as a rule, does not give insight into the character of the people. . . .

The new element of critique here is that the continuum is not specifically concerned with psychological variables. This is perfectly true. The continuum does, however, invite the use of any body of theory which can explain the nature of the interrelationships among the variables.

(6) Finally, underlying the folk-urban dichotomy as used by Redfield, is a system of value judgments which contains the old Rousseauan notion of primitive people as noble savages, and the corollary that with civilization has come the fall of man. . . . It is assumed that all folk societies are integrated while urban societies are the great disorganizing force. . . .

To the extent that this is a criticism of Redfield rather than the continuum, we are not here concerned with the argument. This is, in part, the case, for there are no explicit value judgments placed on the polar types in their definition. The organization-disorganization variable, however, does lead to questions of value orientation. The concepts of "function" and what Merton calls "dysfunction," along with the idea of "degree of integration," are all closely allied in this problem. Social scientists do sometimes treat organization, function, and integration as though they were better than disorganization, dysfunction, and lack of integration. Much of our theory about culture change relies upon the belief that people experience conflict as punishing and that they restructure their behavior so as to eliminate the conflict. The fact that culture change often introduces new conflicts gives us pause to consider, but we still use this motivation of conflict-reduction as an essential element in explaining culture change. The basis for such motivation in the non-cultural reactions of organisms is quite clear. The value connotation of "organization" and "integration" seems to be a quality of data, not of the investigator, and as such is not bias.

Quite a different consideration concerning disorganization as a feature of urban society is that this characteristic may not be dependent upon the other variables of the polar type but may be a function of the rate of social change. Such an explanation is consistent with change theory and might explain why ancient urban civilizations seem to have been less disorganized.

The foregoing discussion has introduced many of the sorts of inadequacies which some social scientists have seen in the folk-urban concept. Rather than to continue here piecemeal treatment, further questions will be introduced into any attempted systematic formulation of all of the arguments, with a view to making some judgment as to what the status of the continuum might profitably be in our theoretical thinking.

Criticisms of the folk-urban concept might be classed under three general headings: (1) the problem of lack of fit between the empirical evidence on particular societies and the nature of these societies which one might expect from the ideal type construct, (2) the problem of definition of the characteristics of the ideal types, (3) the limited theoretical insight provided by the continuum.

(1) *The problem of fit.* Redfield deals with the ideal type as a mental construct which will be productive of testable hypotheses concerning society. This construct itself is commonly referred to as a hypothesis. It is the testing of this hypothesis which we here refer to as "the problem of fit." The fundamental hypothesis inherent in the formulation of the ideal type and the related continuum is that "There is some natural or interdependent relation among some or all of these characters (of the ideal type) in that change with regard to certain of them tends to bring about or carry with it change with

respect to others of them."[30] Implied also is a general tendency for the characters to change in the same direction.

A. L. Kroeber raises two questions which essentially involve problems of fit.[31] One, which he does not develop, concerns the nature of the characteristics of the neglected urban polar type. He asks if we can project the urban characteristics "forward into the future to a vanishing point." In other words, how can we conceive of a completely non-isolated, secular, heterogeneous, individualistic society? Kroeber's question is also applicable to the folk pole, although somewhat less so. While we might conceive of a completely isolated, sacred, personal, and kin-oriented society, what is a completely small or homogeneous society? These questions do not destroy the rationale of the continuum. They point up the fact that the empirically possible polarities must be located short of the logical extremes. Answers to the problem of what the minimal and maximal societal requisites are in this regard involve important knowledge about the basic nature of society.

Kroeber's other concern is the fact that if culture change is considered as movement along the continuum, it is an irregular progression, sometimes reversing its trend and moving at varying rates. These facts about culture change would only vitiate the continuum if it contended that change is always at the same rate or in the same direction. This it does not do. The fact that the direction of most change along the continuum corresponds with the ethnocentric idea of "progress" also suggests to Kroeber the possibility of bias. The conflict between this point and Lewis' view that Redfield has a value bias in favor of the folk pole makes it apparent that this sort of value judgment is not really inherent in the continuum.

The diffuseness of the hypothesis implied by the continuum is such that many specific cases of lack of fit do not in themselves invalidate the concept. If, considering all known societies, there is shown to be no general tendency for the elements of the type to co-occur, then obviously the ideal type is not valid. So far as the writer knows, no one has claimed that the general tendency does not exist.

There is another problem of fit which became apparent in the studies of Guatemala and Timbuctoo and in the restudy of Tepoztlán. This concerns the fact that the continuum requires that the investigator characterize a whole society as to the degree to which it partakes of each trait of the ideal type. The continuum states that some cultures are more folk-like than others; it admits that some characteristics of a single society may be more folk-like than other characteristics of the same society. What the continuum does not take into account is the fact that a single characteristic varies in its degree of folkness in different aspects of life in a single society. To ignore this fact in a summary characterization of the whole society blurs differences which are relevant and probably important. This observation seems to imply a need for the addition of some new dimension to the continuum.

(2) *Definition of characteristics.* Attempts to find the degree of fit between actual societies and the ideal type presupposes a precise definition of the characteristics of the type. The definition must be operationalized so that all observers of societies can categorize the cultural characteristics in the same way. Inasmuch as the traits of the ideal type are variables, there must be some way not only to identify them but also to quantify them, or at least to rank the variations of each trait in some consistent fashion.

Widely different societies conceivably might be ranked by judicious rule-of-thumb methods. There is definite evidence, however, that even this procedure is unsatisfactory. The difference between Redfield and Lewis in their conclusions concerning Tepoztlán is in large part attributable to the use of different standards by the two workers. It is even questionable if Redfield and Tax share a common standard, although they worked in close cooperation. Redfield seems to have had some reservations as to Tax's characterization of Guatemalan culture as secular and individualistic with weak familial institutions.[32]

Tax points out that the Indian *municipios* are highly specialized among themselves and in continuous intercommunication.[33] He characterizes each *municipio*, however, as being internally homogeneous.[34] This homogeneity is then used as characterizing Guatemalan societies. The designation of the community pattern as the societal pattern would appear to be legitimate only in instances in which the communities are isolated or in which they are undifferentiated and intercommunity structure is undeveloped. The writer would be inclined to regard Guatemalan society as heterogeneous.

The study of Timbuctoo may also be open to different interpretation from that which the writer has made. The attention given to cases of conflict may be seen by others as observer bias. Actually instances of conflict were specifically sought, as they were regarded as indicative of disorganization. There is nothing novel about this approach but it suggests that some scale of conflict indexes should be applied to the whole range of the organization-disorganization variable, instead of using it solely at one pole. Past practice has often been to categorize organization by a "see how well it all fits together" description. This led, for example, to the anomaly of Lewis discovering that there were over a hundred cases of crime in Tepoztlán during the time that Redfield was observing the integrated nature of folk culture there. In his later work Redfield came to recognize four different categories of organization.[35] Disorganization, in the sense of lack of internal consistency, stands as the polar opposite to only one of these. All four need some uniformly applicable and scalable treatment.

Others of the characteristics of the ideal type lend themselves to more explicit handling than has been accorded them. Population size and density are easily metricized. Indices of amount of isolation could be developed on the basis of amount of movement of persons and goods in and out of the community, as well as the amount of mail and mechanical communication. The degree of functional importance of these contacts to the society is less readily dealt with, but this factor is probably more significant than the gross quantity of contact.

The presence of three distinct culture groups in Timbuctoo, and their organization in a ramifying division of labor and class structure, was used as indicative of marked heterogeneity. An itemization of distinctive roles based on kinship, economy, politics, religion, etc., might fruitfully be derived from such data for single numerical comparison with similar material from other societies. Taking population size into account, one would have an index of heterogeneity of roles. It is not suggested that this is the only important kind of heterogeneity, but its relevance to degree of individualization and impersonalization is clear.

It should be said in passing that the Yucatan study suffers less from scaling difficulties than the other studies. In the first place, Redfield was familiar with most of the communities studied and his personal definition of the variables could be applied in each case. More important, the communities all presented varieties of traits with a common historical basis. It is relatively easy to judge the significance of traits which have been added to or dropped out of a particular ceremony. It is much more difficult to compare cross-culturally the significance of differences between utterly unrelated *rites de passage.*

The weight of evidence seems to be that, irrespective of the merits of the folk-urban continuum for theory building, the characteristics of the ideal type must be operationalized before relevant theory can be reliably tested cross-culturally.

(3) *The limited theoretical insight.* G. P. Murdock has criticized the folk-urban concept because it does not make use of historical, functional or psychological theory and method.[36] Melville Herskovits antedates Lewis in dissatisfaction with the type categories because they emphasize form rather than process.[37] These criticisms point up accurately the basic nature of the continuum. It does deal with the form rather than with the content of culture traits. As a predictive device it is a weak hypothesis. This doubtless accounts for the fact that Redfield does not refer to it as a hypothesis at all.

It will place the continuum in its proper perspective if we ask what utility remains for it, if it provides little exact fit or predictive value and if no theory concerning function or process is involved. To answer simply, we can only rephrase Redfield's original exposition. The ideal type is a conceptual recognition of a general tendency for certain formal characteristics of cultures to vary together. The continuum stands as an insistence that social science has something to explain here. Any body of theoretical knowledge in the social sciences can be related to the continuum if it can contribute to our understanding of the processes through which the characteristic traits are interrelated.

We note the Spencerian principle that as population density increases, so does differentiation, i.e., heterogeneity. This principle must be refined by the addition of Durkheim's idea of "social density," or frequency of contact and interchange within a population. This essential intervening variable lends itself not only to ecological treatment[38] but also to socio-psychological considerations of communication. In other words, there are bodies of theory which, when applied to the heterogeneity of population, and size and density characteristics, can go a long way toward explaining the processes through which they tend to vary together.

Probably the most valuable feature of the continuum is the fact that it provides a framework within which various theoretical fields may be integrated to provide greater understanding of the nature and course of culture change. It is clear that such theoretical progress will involve the clarification, refinement, and addition of important variables in such change. Whether or not these developments take place with the continuum specifically in mind, they will, of necessity, have to take into account the cultural facts upon which the continuum rests. It is hardly prophetic to predict that the linear continuum will evolve into a more complex and more insightful construct. The ideal types are useful as a basis for such development.

8. SOME UNIFORMITIES OF BEHAVIOR IN SMALL SOCIAL SYSTEMS

by Robert F. Bales

Introduction. There is a growing emphasis in several of the social sciences on the microscopic study of social interaction in small face-to-face groups. Children at play, classroom and discussion groups, committees, planning groups, work groups, therapy groups, and many others are being studied by direct observation. This work requires standardized methods of observing, analyzing, and comparing the behavior which goes on in widely different sorts of groups under different sorts of conditions.

For several years at the Laboratory of Social Relations at Harvard a number of researchers have been engaged in the development of a method for the recording and analysis of social interaction.[1] Up to the present time we have observed a variety of different kinds of groups, including some from other cultures, but our main experience has been with what could be called decision-making or problem-solving conferences of persons, ranging from two to ten, of our own culture. We are interested in the kinds of differences which appear under different experimental conditions. But our major interest has been in the understanding of certain approximate uniformities of interaction which seem to appear in spite of rather wide differences in experimental conditions. The uniformities reported below are all related to the fact that any particular piece of social behavior is always a part of a larger organized system of actions and reactions of more than one person. This inclusion in a system of interdependent activities affects the present character of each act and its probability of repeated occurrence.

A Standard Diagnostic Task. One of our basic assumptions is that there are certain conditions which are present to an important degree not only in special kinds of groups doing special kinds of problems, but which are more or less inherent in the nature of the process of interaction or communication itself, whenever or wherever it takes place. In aggregates of cases where the special conditions associated with individual cases are varied enough to approximate randomness, one would expect the effects of those interaction system tendencies that are due to inherent conditions to become apparent. We have used averages of large numbers of cases to help us form hypotheses

Reprinted from *Readings in Social Psychology*, revised edition, Guy B. Swanson, Theodore M. Newcomb, and Eugene L. Hartley, eds., pp. 146-159, by permission of the authors, the editors, the Society for the Psychological Study of Social Issues, and the publisher. (Copyright, 1952, by Henry Holt and Company, Inc.)

as to what such tendencies of interaction systems might be, and have then tried to set up conditions in the laboratory, in the form of a certain type of task, of personnel, etc., which will produce actual results like our averages.

Gradually we have evolved a laboratory task for groups which does tend to produce typical results in this sense. In this task the subjects are asked to consider themselves as members of a staff who have been requested by their superior to meet and consider the facts of a case, a human-relations tangle of some sort in his organization. The staff committee is asked to advise him as to why the people involved in the case are behaving as they do and what he should do about it. Each subject is given a summary of the case material. After each has read his summary, the typed copies of the case are collected by the experimenter. The manner of presentation is such that the subjects are made uncertain as to whether or not they possess exactly the same facts but are assured that each does possess an accurate, though perhaps incomplete, factual summary.

It should be noted that this particular concrete task has certain abstract characteristics which are important in eliciting a range of diversified behavior. It emphasizes certain *communication problems* (or conditions) which are present to some degree in all social interaction. The communication problems of *orientation, evaluation,* and *control* are each to a major degree unsolved at the beginning of the meeting and can typically be solved to some partly satisfactory degree for the members of the group during the period they are under observation. More specifically:

(*a*) With regard to *orientation,* members of the group have some degree of ignorance and uncertainty about the relevant facts, but, individually, possess facts relevant to decision. Their problem of arriving at a common cognitive orientation or definition of the situation must be solved, if at all, through interaction.

(*b*) With regard to problems of *evaluation,* the members of the group will ordinarily possess somewhat different values or interests, and the task is such that it typically involves several different values and interests as criteria by which the facts of the situation and the proposed course of action are to be judged. Again, the problem of arriving at common value-judgments necessary to cooperative action can only be solved through interaction.

(*c*) With regard to problems of *control*—that is, attempts of the members directly to influence each other's actions and to arrive at a way of controlling or influencing their common environment—the acceptance of the task sets up, in most instances, a moderately strong pressure for group decision, with the expectation that the excellence of the decision can and will be evaluated by each of them as well as by the experimenter, and, in this way, affect their status. The members typically face a number of possible alternative decisions or solutions, with uncertain degrees of potential frustration or satisfaction associated with various choices.

It is likely that these problems of orientation, evaluation, and control, with emphasis varying according to particular circumstances, are characteristic of a wide range of social interaction. They have much the same form and emphasis in a great many group conferences, work groups, committees, and the like that we find in our experimental groups. When group problems or tasks lack or greatly minimize any of these three abstract characteristics, we speak of them as being "truncated." When they are all present, and appreciably so, we speak of the problem as "full-fledged." All the uniformities to be described are apparently most characteristic of interaction in newly formed (initially leaderless) small groups, engaged in a "full-fledged" task. This raises such *problems of organization* as those of determining the number of leaders there shall be, the parts or roles each member shall play in the process, and the status or prestige order.

Whether or not the members are explicitly aware of these problems of communication and organization, the necessity of some way of coping with them is inherent in the experimental conditions which have been set up, and this necessity will affect the character and course of the members' interactions. The members and their overt activities can be said to constitute a *social system*. This conception implies that the group cannot steadily move toward making decisions unless *all* the problems rising from both of these sources are solved. It also implies that the members' attempts to solve some of the problems will tend to make unsuitable the solutions they have already obtained on certain others.

But group members do not have *problems of communication* unless they have reasons to communicate. Faced with a "full-fledged" task, members of newly formed small groups are confronted with two major conditions requiring them to talk to each other. The first condition is that they want to perform the task. The second condition follows from the first: to perform the task, the experimenter requires them to reach a joint decision; and to do this they must find some way of forming and maintaining a social-emotional organization.

As people try to handle these interdependent problems or conditions of communication and group organization (which tend to change and evolve with each new act as it emerges), the overt focus of their activity tends to "circulate" among members and to "oscillate" from one problem to another, converging (in successful groups) toward some sort of "satisfactory" final body of mutually consistent solutions. Thus the interaction tends to go through both minor and major "phases" in which attempts to adjust to one kind of problem create certain other disturbances, attempts to readjust to these disturbances, in turn, create further disturbances, attempts to readjust in turn to these second-order disturbances, and so on. The idea of an interdependent system of members and their overt activities tending to reach or maintain some sort of appropriate and mutually consistent solutions to their problems is the basic concept that appears to lead to an understanding of a whole series of persistent uniformities in social interaction which hold over a fairly wide range of minor differences in social setting.

We shall discuss the way three types of uniformities of interaction arise in this process: first, uniformities pertaining to the "Profile"—the way in which qualitatively different sorts of acts tend to reach a sort of balance with each other; second, those found in the "Matrix"—the way in which the different members of the group tend to reach a sort of balance with regard to the relative amounts and qualities of activities they initiate and receive; third, uniformities seen in the "Phase Movement"—the way in which the members' activities are typically distributed through time in such a way as to produce a balance of work on problems of orientation, evaluation, and control. In each of these three ways of looking at the interaction process we should anticipate some kind of "give and take" which tends toward the solution of all major communication and organization problems facing the group in such a way as to maintain, or constantly regain, the members' ability to work together. Let us first, however, describe the method for observing interaction to obtain the data we need. A concrete example may help.

Description of the Method. A special room is available in which groups can meet and be observed from an observation room through a set of large one-way mirrors. Let us imagine we are observing a group of five persons who are meeting to come to a decision about a point of policy in a project they are doing together. What does the observer do, according to the present method?

The heart of the method is a way of categorizing behavior at the time it occurs, act by act. The data are analyzed later to obtain summary measures descriptive of the group process, from which inferences can then be made

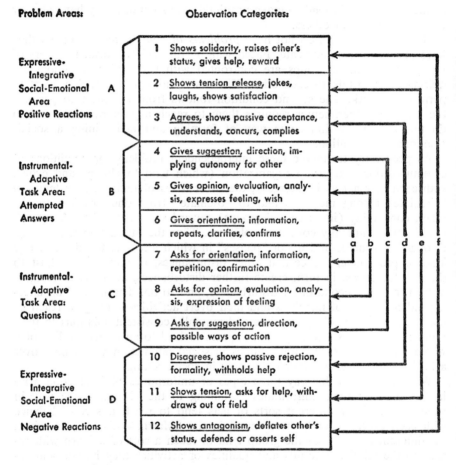

Figure 1. Set of categories used for direct observations of the interaction process.

A subclassification of system problems to which each pair of categories is most relevant:

a Problems of orientation   d Problems of decision
b Problems of evaluation   e Problems of tension-management
c Problems of control   f Problems of integration

as to the nature of underlying factors influencing the process. The set of categories as it actually appears on the observation form is shown in Figure 1. The outer brackets and labels do not appear on the observation form, but, rather, show how each category is related to the problems of communication and organization which all such groups are theoretically supposed to encounter. The set of categories is held to form a logically exhaustive classification system. Every act that occurs is classified into one of the twelve categories. All of the categories are positively defined—that is, none of them is treated as a residual or wastebasket category for "leftovers." With competent observers and hard training, correlations between observers ranging from .75 to .95 can be obtained.

Let us turn now to a concrete example. We will suppose that this particular meeting is very orderly and will describe it in terms of a series of three phases. Each of the major problems of operation that groups typically face has been made into an implicit "agenda item."

Phase 1. Emphasis on Problems of Orientation: (deciding what the situation is like). The chairman brings the meeting up to date with a few remarks. He says, "At the end of our last meeting we decided that we would have to consider our budget before laying out plans in greater detail."

The interaction observer looks over the set of twelve categories and decides that this remark is most relevant to the problem of orientation and, specifically, that it takes the form of an "attempted answer" to this problem, and so he classifies it in Category 6. The observer has already decided that he will designate the chairman by the number 1, and each person around the table in turn by the numbers 2, 3, 4, and 5. The group as a whole will be designated by the symbol 0. This remark was made by the chairman and was apparently addressed to the group as a whole, so the observer writes down the symbols 1-0 in one of the spaces following Category 6 on the observation form. In this one operation, the observer has thus isolated a unit of speech or process which he considers a proper unit for classification, has classified it according to its quality, identified the member who performed the act, and the person or persons to whom it was directed.

As the chairman finishes his remark, Member 2 asks the chairman, "Has anybody gone over our expenditures to date?" The observer decides that this is a "question" indicating that a problem of orientation exists, and so should be classified in Category 7. He so records it by placing the symbols 2-1 in the space following Category 7.

The chairman replies, "I have here a report prepared by Miss Smith on the expenditures to date." The observer marks down the symbols 1-2 following Category 6, indicating an "attempted answer" to the previous question. As the chairman goes over the report the observer continues to score, getting a good many scores in Categories 6 and 7, but also occasional scores in other categories.

Phase 2. Emphasis on Problems of Evaluation: (deciding what attitudes should be taken toward the situation). As the chairman finishes reviewing the items on the report he may ask, "Have we been within bounds on our expenditures so far?" The observer puts down a score under Category 8.

Member 3 says, "It seems to me we have gone in pretty heavily for secretarial help." The observer puts down a score in Category 5.

Member 4 comes in with the remark, "Well I don't know. It seems to me . . ." The observer puts down the symbols 4-3 in Category 10 to indicate the disagreement, and continues with scores in Category 5 as Member 4 makes his argument. The discussion continues to revolve around the analysis of expenditures, with a good many scores falling in Category 5, but also in others, particularly Categories 10 and 3, and interspersed with a number in Categories 6 and 7 as opinions are explained and supported by reference to facts.

Phase 3. Emphasis on Problems of Control: (deciding what to do about it). Finally the chairman says, "Well . . . what do you think we should do about that piece of equipment?" The observer scores 1-0 in Category 9. Member 2 says, "I think we should get it." The observer scores 2-0 in Category 4. As Member 2 begins to support his suggestion, Member 3 breaks in with a counterargument, and the discussion begins to grow heated, with more disagreement. Presently the observer notices that Member 5, who has said little up to this point, sighs heavily and begins to examine his fingernails. The observer puts down a score under Category 11.

In the meantime, Member 3, the chronic objector, comes through with a remark directed at Member 2, "Well, I never did agree about hiring that deadhead secretary. All she's got is looks, but I guess that's enough for Joe." The others laugh at this. The observer scores the first and second remarks under Category 12 as showing antagonism, and scores the laugh which follows as tension release in Category 2.

At this point Member 5 comes in quietly to sum up the argument, and by the time he finishes several heads are nodding. The observer scores both the nods and the audible agreements in Category 3. Member 3, the chronic objector, who is also the chronic joker, comes in with a joke at this point, and the joking and laughing continue for a minute or two, each member extending the joke a little. The observer continues to score in Category 2 as long as the laughing continues. As the members pick up their things one of them says, "Well, I think we got through that in good shape. Old Bill certainly puts in the right word at the right time, doesn't he?" The observer marks down two scores for the speaker under Category 1, shows solidarity, and after a few more similar remarks the meeting breaks up.

The idea that groups go through certain stages or phases in the process of solving problems, or that problem-solving would somehow be more effective if some prescribed order were followed, has been current in the literature for some time. However, the distinction between predicting an empirical order of phases as they will actually take place under some specific set of conditions, and prescribing an ideal order in terms of value judgments has not always been clearly drawn. It has typically not been recognized that different types of conditions or problems may result empirically in different sorts of phase movement. We have found that there are, indeed, *certain* conditions which must be quite carefully specified, under which a group problem-solving process essentially like that sketched above does tend to appear. These conditions can be set up experimentally in the laboratory, and have already been described above as the standard diagnostic task around which our other generalizations all revolve.

Unfortunately, space does not permit the presentation of the evidence in detail. In general, the patterns described and illustrated can be understood to refer to approximate or average uniformities in aggregates of large numbers of cases under randomly varying external conditions, and in addition, they can be understood to hold more uniformly and in particular under the full-fledged conditions of the standard diagnostic task described above.

Profiles. One of the important characteristics of interaction is the distribution of total number of acts among the twelve categories listed in Figure 1. A distribution of this kind, expressed in percentage rates based on the total number of acts, is called a profile. An illustrative and typical comparison of group profiles of two five-man groups working on the standard diagnostic task is shown in Figure 2.

Different kinds of groups operating under different kinds of conditions produce different types of profiles. In the present illustration the "successful" group attained a higher rate of suggestions and more often followed these with positive reactions, rather than with negative reactions and questions, than did the "unsuccessful" group.

Figure 2—Profiles of "Satisfied" and "Dissatisfied" Groups on Case Discussion Task

Category	Satisfied*	Dissatisfied†	Av. of the two	Av. rates by sections
	MEETING PROFILES IN PERCENTAGE RATES			
1. Shows solidarity	.7	.8	.7	
2. Shows tension release	7.9	6.8	7.3	25.0
3. Agrees	24.9	9.6	17.0	
4. Gives suggestion	8.2	3.6	5.9	
5. Gives opinion	26.7	30.5	28.7	56.7
6. Gives orientation	22.4	21.9	22.1	
7. Asks for orientation	1.7	5.7	3.8	
8. Asks for opinion	1.7	2.2	2.0	6.9
9. Asks for suggestion	.5	1.6	1.1	
10. Disagrees	4.0	12.4	8.3	
11. Shows tension	1.0	2.6	1.8	11.4
12. Shows antagonism	.3	2.2	1.3	
Raw score total	719	767	1486	100.0

* The highest of sixteen groups, identified as HR2-2. The members rated their own satisfaction with their solution after the meeting at an average of 10.4 on a scale running from 0 to a highest possible rating of 12.
† The lowest of sixteen groups, identified as HR3-3. Comparable satisfaction rating in this group was 2.6.

The profiles produced by groups, however, are not completely and radically different from each other. The profile produced by the average of these two illustrative groups is more or less typical of averages of larger aggregates. "Attempted Answers"—that is, giving orientation, opinion, and suggestion—are nearly always more numerous than their cognate "Questions"—that is, asking for orientation, opinion, or suggestion. Similarly, "Positive Reactions"—that is, agreement, showing tension release, and solidarity—are usually more numerous than the "Negative Reactions" of showing disagreement, tension, and antagonism. Intuitively, one would feel that the process would surely be self-defeating and self-limiting if there were more questions than answers and more negative reactions than positive.

On the average, for the groups we have examined, the relative proportions of different kinds of interaction are about as they are in Figure 2. Although the illustration makes no breakdown to show changes over time, note how the final balance among the proportions suggests that it might be the end result of a series of small sequences which consists of (1) an initial disturbance of a system (precipitated by the introjection of a new idea, or opinion, or suggestion into the group) followed by (2) a dwindling series of feedbacks and corrections as the disturbance is terminated, quenched, or assimilated by other parts or members of the system. "Attempted Answers," or, as one might call them for the moment, "Initial Acts," account for a little over half (or 57 per cent) of the total activity, with "Positive and Negative Reactions" and "Questions" accounting for roughly the other half. One might say that quantitatively (as well as qualitatively, by definition) interaction is a process consisting of action followed by reaction. Sometimes a single positive reaction restores the "balance." At other times a longer sequence is necessary. Consider the rates in the following way. Looking at the reaction side alone, and assuming it to be 50 per cent of the total, about half (or 25 per cent) is "Positive" and presumably terminates the disturbance introduced by the initial action. This leaves a portion of about 25 per cent which fails to terminate the disturbance. Of this nonterminating portion, about half (or 12 per cent) consists of "Negative Reactions," which typically precipitate further "Attempted Answers," thus beginning a repetition of the cycle. Of the remaining hypothetical 13 per cent or so, about half (or 7 per cent) are "Questions," which also, typically, precipitate "Attempted Answers." If about 7 per cent of "Attempted Answers" are in direct response to "Questions," these might well be called "Reactions," thus leaving the balance of "Initial acts" to "Reactions" about 50-50, as assumed above.

When tabulations are made of the frequency with which specific acts tend to lead to other types of specific acts the mechanisms by which the gross distribution of the profile arises become apparent. "Attempted Answers" tend to lead to "Positive Reactions" which in turn tend to return to more "Attempted Answers." When "Negative Reactions" appear, they tend to lead back to more "Attempted Answers." When "Questions" appear they tend to lead to "Attempted Answers." "Questions" seldom lead directly to either "Positive" or "Negative Reactions." These tendencies appear to be more or less inherent in interaction that is purposeful and goal-directed, if indeed it is "getting anywhere" and producing "satisfaction" even in a minimal way for the participants. The interesting differences between groups tend to be relatively minor variations on this general pattern, as in Figure 2.

Who-to-Whom Matrix. Another important direction of analysis deals with the way in which participation is distributed between members. The total number of different possible combinations of who is speaking and to whom for a given time period is called a matrix. Figure 3 shows a matrix containing all the interaction initiated by and directed toward the members of eighteen different six-man groups.

The pattern of distribution for particular groups is different in detail under different conditions. For example, groups with no designated leader generally tend to have more equal participation than groups with designated leaders of higher status. However, in spite of these differences, the distribution of total amounts each member tends to address to the group as a whole, as well as the amounts men in each rank tend to talk to men in each other rank position seem to be subject to system-influences, which tend to produce similarities from group to group, and some regular gradations by group size.

These generalizations may be illustrated in part by reference to Figure 3. Although this is an aggregate matrix for eighteen different groups, each of which has been rank-ordered before adding, it is sufficiently like those of particular groups to serve as an illustration. If the personnel for a particular

group are arrayed in rank order according to the total amount they speak
we then find that they are spoken to in amounts proportionate to their rank

Figure 3—Aggregate Matrix for 18 Sessions of Six-man Groups, All Types of Activity

Rank of Person Originating Act	TO INDIVIDUALS OF EACH RANK						Total to Individuals	To Group as a Whole 0	Total Initiated
	1	2	3	4	5	6			
1		1,238	961	545	445	317	3,506	5,661	9,167
2	1,748		443	310	175	102	2,778	1,211	3,989
3	1,371	415		305	125	69	2,285	742	3,027
4	952	310	282		83	49	1,676	676	2,352
5	662	224	144	83		28	1,141	443	1,584
6	470	126	114	65	44		819	373	1,192
Total received	5,203	2,313	1,944	1,308	872	565	12,205	9,106	21,311

order. In general, each man receives back about half as much as he initiates in
total. It will be remembered from the data in the profile that something like
half of all interaction is "reactive" in a qualitative sense. Each man spends
a certain portion of his time reacting to the initial acts of others. This amount
of time differs, however, according to the rank of the member.

Matrices have been constructed for particular categories of activity. The
most frequent initiator of acts tends to give out more information and opinion to specific individuals than he receives, while, on the contrary, initiators
with low frequencies give out more agreement, disagreement, and requests
for information than they receive. The profiles of participants tend to change
systematically as we proceed downward in rank. High-ranking men tend to
have more "Initial Actions" (Section B) in their profiles, while low-ranking
men have more "Reactions," both positive and negative. These qualitative
differences are important for the social organization of the members. *Quantitative* differentiation in participation is accompanied by, or is symptomatic
of, *qualitative differentiation of roles* of members.

If this is true one might expect quantity of participation to be related to
the status hierarchy of the members. We typically find that the order produced by ranking individuals according to their total amounts of participation is the same as the order produced by their own ratings of each other
as to "Productivity"—who has the best ideas and who does the most to guide
the discussion effectively, as well as the order of "popularity" produced by
their own ratings of whom they most like and dislike. Similar findings are
reported by Norfleet[2] and Bass[3] with correlations of about .95 in each case.
Strodtbeck[4] finds, in addition, a fairly dependable connection between amount
of activity initiated and probability of winning in contested decisions (which
is a kind of measure of power or influence). The empirical correlation between status as the participants feel it and amounts of participation given
out and received under the conditions described seems to be pretty well established. The explanation of this regularity apparently lies in understanding the values ascribed by the members to the qualitative differences in roles
which are usually connected with quantity—not in the sheer quantity alone.

Size of group is obviously an important condition affecting the distribution of activities. From present indications it appears that the top man in
groups larger than five or so tends to speak considerably more to the group
as a whole than to specific individuals in the group, as in Figure 3. All other
members tend to speak more to specific individuals (and particularly to the

top man) than to the group as a whole. Each man tends to speak to each other man in an amount which is a probability function of both his own rank on outwardly directed remarks, and the rank of the other on the receiving of communication.[5] As groups increase in size, a larger and larger relative proportion of the activity tends to be addressed to the top man, and a smaller and smaller relative proportion to other members. In turn, as size increases, the top man tends to address more and more of his remarks to the group as a whole, and to exceed by larger amounts his proportionate share. The communication pattern tends to "centralize," in other words, around a leader through whom most of the communication flows.

The tendency toward centralization is illustrated in Figure 4, which shows the relation of men in each rank position as to total acts initiated, by groups of increasing size. The matrix for each individual session was put in rank order and then all matrices for groups of a given size were added together. The points plotted thus represent aggregate or average rates of activity for men in each rank position. (The groups included in this graph were all observed before the present standard task was evolved, and include a wide

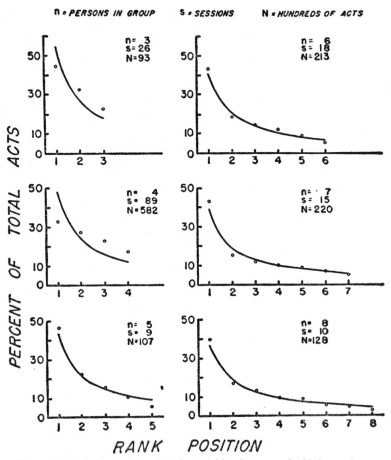

Figure 4. Rank ordered series of total acts initiated, compared with harmonious distribution, for groups of sizes three to eight.

variety of types. Data gathered on the standard task are expected to show similar tendencies but probably smoother curves and smoother gradations by size.) The points are plotted against a mathematically derived curve, the so-called "harmonic distribution," or "rank-size" curve for purposes of visual comparison. (This curve is of some general interest to social scientists, since it is often found to be a fair approximation of the distribution of factors such as income in large social systems.) In the present case the fit, although visually helpful, is not actually acceptable in a statistical sense. One of the reasons the fit is not good is precisely because of the tendency for communication to centralize and for a "leader" to appear. The points indicate that groups of size three and four tend to have a relatively "flatter" or more even distribution of amounts of participation between members, while the groups of larger size tend to show the rank 1 man with a higher amount of participation than the harmonic curve predicts. The prominence of rank 1 men in the larger groups is striking.

If the situation is one in which *inter*action is expected by the participators, however, there would seem to be a ceiling on amount of participation for the top man somewhere around 50 per cent, apparently connected with the general tendency for interaction under such expectations to come to a system-closure, such that each "action" of one member as it were, tends to be countered with a "reaction" from some other. Even if the top man is initiating most of the action, he still has to expect that he will receive a "feedback of reactions," of both a positive and negative sort, that will tend to equal the amount of action he initiates. It may very well be that the expectation of "equality" which is so often present in groups of our culture, is based on an expectation of an over-all balance of action and reaction rather than to an equality of amounts of output of all members, which in practice is practically never found.

Phase Movement. Changes in quality of activity as groups move through time in attempting to solve problems may be called phase patterns. The pattern of phases differs in detail under different conditions. However, these changes in quality seem to be subject to system-influences which produce similarities from group to group. An increase of task-oriented activities in the early parts of a meeting—that is, "Questions" and "Attempted Answers,"—seems to constitute a disturbance of a system "equilibrium" which is later redressed by an increase in social-emotional activities—that is, both "Positive" and "Negative Reactions."

Part of our observations prior to the development of the standard diagnostic task were kept by time sequence. Each available meeting was divided into three equal parts, and the amount of each type of activity in each part of each meeting was determined. The meetings were divided into two kinds: those which were dealing with full-fledged problems (essentially problems of analysis and planning with the goal of group decision as described for the standard diagnostic task), and those dealing with more truncated or specialized types of problems. Those groups dealing with full-fledged problems tended to show a typical phase movement through the meeting: the process tended to move qualitatively from a *relative* emphasis on attempts to solve problems of *orientation* ("what is it") to attempts to solve problems of *evaluation* ("how do we feel about it") and subsequently to attempts to solve problems of *control* ("what shall we do about it"). Concurrent with these transitions, the relative frequencies of both *negative reactions* (disagreement, tension, and antagonism), and *positive reactions* (agreement, tension release, and showing solidarity), tends to increase. The reasons why both negative and positive reactions have to increase are given below. It should be remembered that they are both "reactive." Figure 5 presents the summary data for all twenty-two group sessions examined in the phase study.

The underlying theory as to why the phase movement just described is characteristic of full-fledged conditions is again the same "system-equilibrium" rationale depending on the "interdependence of problems" in systems of social interaction. Consider first those problems immediately concerned with

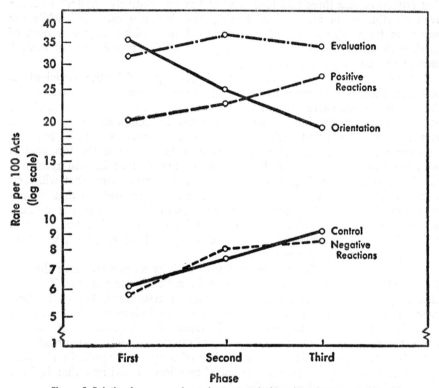

Figure 5. Relative frequency of acts by type and phase based upon 22 sessions.

the task. An individual may be cognitively oriented to a situation and speak of it to others in cognitive terms without committing himself (or the other when the other agrees), either to evaluation of it or an attempt to control it. But in speaking to the other in evaluative terms he attempts to commit both himself and the other to some assumed previous orientation, and further, if he suggests a way to control the situation by joint cooperative action, he assumes a successful solution has been obtained for problems of both orientation and evaluation. When the problems of arriving at a common orientation and evaluation of the situation have not been substantially solved by the group members, attempts at control will meet with resistance on the part of the others and frustration on the part of the person attempting to exercise the control. Probably generally, unless there are contrary cultural, personality, or group organizational factors, the interacting persons tend to avoid or retreat from this frustration-producing type of interaction by "backtracking" toward orientation and evaluative analysis until the prior problems are solved.

In addition to their task problems, the members of any cooperating group have problems of their social and emotional relationships to solve and keep solved. Efforts to solve problems of orientation, evaluation, and control as involved in the task tend to lead to differentiation of the roles of the participants, both as to the functions they perform and their gross amounts of participation. Some major features of this differentiation have already been described in the presentation of findings about the matrix. Both qualitative and quantitative types of differentiation tend to carry status implications which may threaten or disturb the existing order or balance of status relations among members. Disagreement and an attempt to change existing ideas and values may be necessary in the effort to solve the task problem but may lead, nevertheless, to personalized anxieties or antagonisms and impair the basic solidarity of the group.

This impairment, or the threat of it, we may assume, tends to grow more marked as the group passes from emphasis on the less demanding and more easily resolved problems of cognitive orientation on to problems of evaluation, and still more acute as it passes on to its heaviest emphasis on problems of control. Thus, a series of disturbances in the social-emotional relationship of the members tends to be set in motion by pressures arising initially from attempts to meet the demands of the external task or outer situation. These social-emotional problems tend to be expressed in a kind of status struggle as they grow more acute—hence the increasing rate of negative reactions.

However, at the extreme end of the final period, assuming that the members' attempts at control over the outer situation and over each other are successful and a final decision is reached, the rates in Categories 1, 2, and 3 also rise to their peak. In other words, the successfully recovering group tends to confirm its agreement and to release in diffuse ways the tensions built up in its prior task efforts, repairing the damage done to its state of consensus and social integration.

We note joking and laughter so frequently at the end of meetings that they might almost be taken as a signal that the group has completed what it considers to be a task effort, and is ready for disbandment or a new problem. This last-minute activity completes a cycle of operations involving a successful solution both of the task problems and social-emotional problems confronting the group. The apparent incongruity of predicting a peak for both negative and positive reactions in the third phase is thus explained. Negative reactions tend to give way to positive reactions in the final part of the third phase. The arbitrary division of the meeting into three equal periods of time is too crude to show the final dropping off of negative reactions in the third phase as solution is reached.

Conclusion. It may be that average tendencies like those presented can be taken as representative of typical social-system effects under full-fledged conditions. In experimental designs, then, where a full-fledged problem is used as the basic testing situation, deviations from empirical norms might be used as evidences of the effects of known or experimentally introduced conditions. For example, the experimental introduction of persistent difficulties of communication or orientation by placing together in the same group persons of widely different value standards might upset the profile, matrix, and phase sequence expected on the basis of the internal tendencies of the interaction system alone. Conversely, in using the method for clinical analysis or training of particular groups, groups might be set up under full-fledged conditions, and the deviations from the empirical norms used as diagnostic indicators of otherwise unknown characteristics of the group or the members.

The uniformities of the profile, matrix, and phase movement are all interdependent. They are manifest evidence that interaction is not a random collection of acts, but constitutes the observable process of a social system.

9. MATRIX ANALYSIS OF GROUP STRUCTURES

by Leon Festinger, Stanley Schachter, and Kurt Back

[In July, 1946 a study was undertaken in a new housing project established for married veteran students who were attending Massachusetts Institute of Technology. Part of this housing project, named Westgate, consisted of 100 single-family houses grouped in nine distinct court units. The court units, named Tolman, Howe, Main, etc., consisted of from seven to thirteen houses each. In the selection which follows, the authors indicate how they applied a matrix approach to analyze the patterns of group structure within these courts.—ED. NOTE.]

IN THE STUDY of groups by means of sociometric data much attention has been given to the exact pattern of connections among individuals. The need to describe and analyze the patterning of these connections has been apparent. It is not only important to know how many friendships exist in a group and what proportion of them are mutual friendships, but it is also important to know who a particular person's friends are, what his relations are with the friends of his friends, and what tendencies to subgroup or clique formation exist. We need to know how many paths of influence exist among members of a group, who can influence whom, over how much of a group a person's influence extends, and what is the nature of the indirect influence chains that may exist. If an item of information enters a group it is not only important to know how many people will eventually hear about it but also to know exactly who will hear it and from whom and how far removed from the original source it will be by the time a specific person hears about it.

    Without an adequate representational technique of handling such data

Reprinted from *Social Pressures in Informal Groups,* pp. 132-147, by permission of the authors and the publisher. (Copyright, 1950, by Harper and Bros.)

the analysis of the exact patterns of interconnections among members of a group is virtually impossible unless the group is very small. As the size of the group increases, the complexity of the pattern generally makes it difficult to comprehend by mere inspection. The result has been the relative neglect of this kind of analysis. Investigators have, by and large, contented themselves with analyzing sociometric patterns in such terms as the number of choices people receive, the kind of people who get most choices, the proportion of the choices inside the group, and other such summary measures which serve to relate the sociometric choices to other variables.

The major portion of this selection will be devoted to the development of a method of treating sociometric choices which makes it possible to analyze more complex interrelationships. By the use of some of the standard and relatively simple manipulations of matrix algebra we are able to analyze such things as subgroup formations, cliques, and indirect chains of influence from one person to another. The application of this analysis technique to the sociometric data from the Westgate courts yields some important insights into their structure.

PREVIOUS METHODS OF ANALYSIS

Initial attempts at the analysis and description of the exact patterning of interconnections in a group took the form of drawing complicated diagrams where the connections were represented by lines, with arrows on them, between individuals. Such diagrams might, for example, be drawn for the patterns of interconnections within Tolman Court and within Howe Court, as shown in Figures 1a and b. Some things become readily apparent from an inspection of and comparison between these "sociograms." Both courts seem very similar. In each court there are seven or eight people who give several choices among each other and four other people who are relatively or completely separated from the larger subgroup of seven or eight. Also, in each court there are one or two complete isolates who neither give nor receive any choices within the court. It is extremely difficult to determine more than this from inspection of these diagrams.

It is understandable that such a diagram would become unwieldly if the number of members increased or if the number of choices made by each member increased to any appreciable degree. There are no operating rules for such diagrams. One merely arranges them by trial and error so as to make the diagram look as simple as possible and then one further examines it with the hope that he will be alert enough to see what is to be seen. The differences between these two courts, which we shall later clearly show to exist, are difficult to perceive in these diagrams. Indeed, we were not aware of them until the sociometric patterns were subjected to a more systematic and rigorous form of analysis.

It was the recognition of these difficulties that led Northway[1] and Cook[2] to attempt to formulate a system which would order the sociometric diagram so as to make it more easily understandable. These attempts, however, still left the analysis of sociometric patterns in a vague and relatively unsystematic state. A large step forward was taken by Forsyth and Katz[3] in suggesting the use of a matrix and some of the manipulations of matrix algebra for the analysis of sociometric patterns. Their idea was to represent the sociometric pattern in a matrix form and then to rearrange this matrix, according to certain principles, in order to have it reveal what subgroupings were present. Figure 2a shows the representation of the sociometric pattern of Tolman Court in matrix form and Figure 2b shows the result of the consequent rearrangement manipulations of this matrix. The matrix presentation is simply performed by listing the individuals in the group along the rows and along the columns in the same order. The choices that any individual makes are then indicated by the number 1, in one of

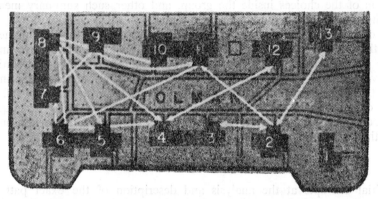

Figure 1a. Pattern of Sociometric Connections in Tolman Court

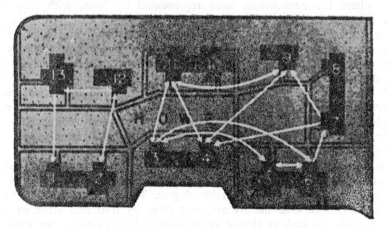

Figure 1b. Pattern of Sociometric Connections in Howe Court

the squares, so that the row corresponds to the person making the choice and the column corresponds to the person receiving the choice. The squares along the main diagonal of the matrix are, of course, left blank, since individuals did not choose themselves. Looking across any row reveals who was chosen by that person and looking down any column reveals from whom that person received choices.

The presentation in this form offers little advantage over the more complicated sociometric diagram for direct inspection. Some manipulations of the matrix, however, tend to simplify it. The suggestion of Forsyth and Katz is to rearrange the order of the members of the group so that the numbers in the matrix cluster are as close as possible along the diagonal. More technically, they suggest rearranging the order of the rows and columns so as to minimize the square of the perpendicular deviations of the numbers from the diagonal of the matrix. This rearrangement will show, clustered together, those people who choose each other frequently and, relatively separated, those who do not choose each other. Thus, in Figure 2b we can see which individuals in the group cluster together and which are far apart. This enables us to separate subgroups, and would seem to be a plausible means of analyzing changes in the pattern of connections in a group from one time to another. It does not, however, seem to be too helpful a method for comparing two different groups, and the labor involved in obtaining the ordering of the matrix which will cluster the choices most closely along the diagonal is quite tedious.

MEASURES OF THE PATTERN OF INTERCONNECTIONS

Before considering the methods of matrix manipulation which can satisfactorily handle these problems, let us examine briefly the kinds of measures and the patterns of interconnections which seem valuable to us and which these matrix manipulations will yield.

1. *Two-step indirect connections among people:* If we deal with the concept of a social structure or a group, rather than with relationships between pairs of people, the one-step connections between people (direct choices which they make) are clearly inadequate for a full description. The social group in which a person moves extends beyond his immediate friends. It also extends to the friends of these friends. These indirect connections are thus two-step ones. The character and behavior of the immediate group

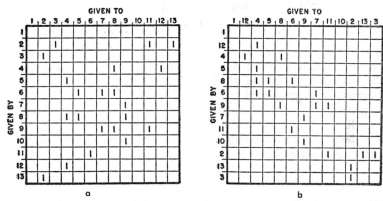

Figure 2a. Matrix Presentation of Sociometric Pattern in Tolman Court
Figure 2b. Canonical Matrix Presentation of Sociometric Pattern in Tolman Court

will depend in part upon these indirect connections. The way influence or information spreads through a structure will also be determined by such indirect connections. The exact determination of all such indirect two-step connections among people can be simply determined by matrix multiplication.

2. *Three-step or more indirect connections:* The same meanings and importances which apply to two-step connections logically apply to more indirect chains of connection among people. By matrix multiplication, it is possible to determine in simple, non-trial-and-error fashion all the chains by which influence or communication might spread through a group.

3. *Tendencies toward subgroup formation:* A major dimension on which

groups may differ from one another is the extent to which the total group is structured into subgroups. Finding such subgroups necessitates looking at the interrelations among a number of people. As will be seen later, by means of the same matrix multiplications which show us the existence of chains of indirect connections, we may also determine clearly and unequivocally the existence of various degrees of subgrouping.

THE METHOD OF MATRIX MULTIPLICATION

When the sociometric pattern is presented in a matrix form, an analysis of some aspects of the structure of the group can be performed by the relatively simple means of squaring and cubing this matrix.[4] Let us follow through these operations to see how they are performed and what type of information they will yield. In Figure 3a are shown, side by side, the original matrices for Tolman and Howe Courts. Figure 3b shows the squares of these two matrices and Figure 3c shows the matrices cubed. The squared matrix is readily obtained in the following way: to obtain the number which goes into the cell designated by column c and row r of the squared matrix, we multiply each cell in column c of the original matrix by the corresponding cell of row r and then add these products up. The cells in any row which "correspond" with the cells of any column are easy to determine. For example, the corresponding cells of the third row and the fourth column are such that if person 3 chooses someone who in turn chooses person 4, this will cause a 1 to appear in the squared matrix cell designated by row 3, column 4. The general equation for this multiplication might be written as follows:

$$A^2_{rc} = A_{1c}A_{r1} + A_{2c}A_{r2} + A_{3c}A_{r3} + \ldots + A_{nc}A_{rn}$$

In this equation A^2_{rc} refers to the number in the cell of the squared matrix in the r row of the c column; $A_{1c}A_{r1}$ refers to the product of the number in the cell in the first row of the c column and the number in the r row of the first column of the unsquared matrix, and so on.

This procedure is carried out through a short cut. The products of the corresponding cells of a row and a column will yield numbers other than zero only if a 1 appears in both cells which are being considered. Thus, a two-step connection where individual 2 chooses individual 11, and 11 chooses individual 6 (as in the case in the matrix of Tolman Court) will contribute a number in the row 2, column 6 cell of the squared matrix. Thus, to obtain the numbers which, for example, go in row 8 of the squared Tolman matrix, we observe that row 8 in the original matrix has 1's in columns 4, 5, and 9. We then look down each column of the original matrix successively looking only for numbers in the corresponding rows 4, 5, and 9. Column 1 has nothing in either 4, 5, or 9 row, nor do columns 2 and 3. Column 4 has a 1 in row 5 and so we write a 1 in the fourth column of the eighth row of the squared matrix. If a column of the original matrix contained 1's in two or all three of these rows a 2 or 3, respectively, would be written in the appropriate position of the squared matrix.

Each figure in this matrix represents the number of two-step connections that exist between the specified two members of the group. Thus the one in the eleventh column of the third row of the squared Tolman Court matrix in Figure 3b indicates that there is one two-step connection from number

3 to number 11. Looking at the original matrix we can easily locate this connection. Number 3 chooses number 2 and individual number 2 chooses number 11. It is clear, of course, that this relationship need not be symmetrical, just as the one-step connections need not be symmetrical. Here for example, there is not any two-step connection from number 11 to number 3.

The numbers that appear in the diagonal of this squared matrix have a special meaning. They indicate the number of two-step connections that exist from a person back to himself, or, in other words, they indicate the number of mutual sociometric choices in which this person was involved. Thus, the number 2 in the fourth row of the fourth column of the squared Howe Court matrix indicates that individual number 4 had two mutual choices. Looking back at the original unsquared matrix we readily see that these mutual choices were with individuals numbers 9 and 11. It is immediately clear in comparing the two courts that while about the same number of people in each court were involved in mutual choices, the number of

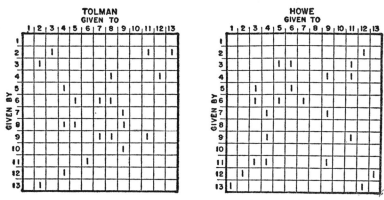

Figure 3a. Matrices of Sociometric Patterns for Tolman and Howe Courts

such mutual choices were considerably greater in Howe Court than in Tolman Court.

The meaning of these two-step connections between different people is quite important. For example, if the original sociometric choice indicates influence from Mr. A to Mr. B, the squared matrix would indicate the extent of indirect influence which Mr. A has and exactly which other people he influences indirectly. If the original sociometric data indicated channels of communication for information, the squared matrix would tell us, for example, that an item of information starting with number 8 in Tolman Court would be heard by numbers 4, 7, 11, and 12 in two steps, and if started with number 12 in Howe Court would be heard in two steps only by number 1. In Tolman Court, individual number 8 could communicate to number 4, 5, and 9 and from these people the information would spread to the others. In Howe Court, individual number 12 could communicate to numbers 2 and 13 but the information would not travel far. Number 2 could communicate to no one except back to number 12. Number 13 could communicate back to number 12 and also to number 1. Individual number 1 would thus be the only one to have heard it in two steps. It is interesting to note that this would be the end of the circulation of this item of informa-

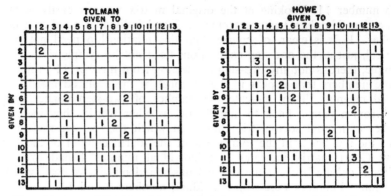

Figure 3b. Squared Matrices of Sociometric Patterns for Tolman and Howe Courts

tion in Howe Court since individual number 1 has no connections with anyone other than 13, his original informant.

While most people in these two courts had more indirect two-step connections than direct one-step connections, there were some who did not. Thus, number 2 in Tolman Court had three one-step connections with other people but only one two-step connection with anyone else. Thus, while communications or influences (assuming the connections imply communication or influence) would tend to spread farther and farther if started with most people; if started with someone like number 2 in Tolman Court, it would probably taper off quickly and not spread far at all.

The cube of the matrix is Figure 3c, which gives information on three-step connections, is obtained by multiplying the original matrix by the squared matrix in the same way that the original matrix was multiplied by itself. The formula for obtaining the values of the cells of the cubed matrix would be written similarly as:

$$A^3{}_{rc} = A_{1c}A^2{}_{r2} + A_{2c}A^2{}_{r2} + A_{3c}A^2{}_{r3} + \ldots + A_{nc}A^2{}_{rn}$$

The actual calculation is again performed rather simply. To obtain the numbers which appear in the seventh row of the cubed matrix of Howe Court, for example, we note that in the original matrix there are 1's in the

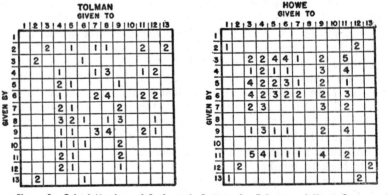

Figure 3c. Cubed Matrices of Sociometric Patterns for Tolman and Howe Courts

fourth and ninth columns of the seventh row. We then look at each column of the squared matrix to see if there are any numbers in the fourth and ninth rows. Column 1 has zero; column 2 has zero; column 3 has a 1 in the fourth and a 1 in the ninth row and consequently a 2 appears in the cubed matrix; column 4 has a 2 in row four and a 1 in row nine and consequently a 3 appears in the appropriate cell of the cubed matrix, and so on.

The meaning of the figures in this cubed matrix is similar to their meaning in the squared matrix. They indicate the number of three-step connections that exist between any two people. The numbers in the diagonal of the matrix now indicate the number of three-step connections from a person back to himself. The implications of these numbers in the diagonal of the cubed matrix will be elaborated on shortly.

It is apparent that these matrices may also be raised to higher powers to obtain the four-step or five-step or even more indirect connections among the members of a group. If we are concerned with a question such as how many people will hear a given item of information in three or fewer steps if it is started with any particular person, the answer may be obtained by adding together the original, the squared, and the cubed matrices. We can obtain information such as who influences the greatest number of people in less than a specified number of steps, which people are influenced by the greatest number of people and which individuals are only subject to the influence of a few, which people in the group are most indirectly connected to each other and how indirect this connection is, or what proportion of the possible connections among the various people actually exists. Being able to handle conveniently and efficiently these aspects of group structure and patterning of connections should make it feasible to study their effects on such processes as communication, influence, social pressures, and many others.

THE DETERMINATION OF CLIQUES

The manipulation of matrices by means of raising them to the third power can, with complete accuracy, determine the existence of cliques of various sizes and with various degrees of "cliquishness." Let us begin by defining an extreme instance of clique formation within a group and then see how we may determine whether or not such cliques exist in any given structure. We shall define this extreme type of clique as three or more individuals all of whom choose each other mutually. In other words, direct one-step symmetrical connections exist between every possible pair of members of such a clique. Clearly, in order to determine the existence of such a clique we would concern ourselves with the symmetrical submatrix consisting only of mutual choices and not with the complete matrix of connections. If we raise such a symmetrical submatrix to the third power we will obtain all the three-step connections that exist between any two people which involve only mutual choices. What would then be the meaning of a three-step connection from a member back to himself which involves only symmetrical choices—that is, what will be the meaning of the numbers which appear in the main diagonal of this cubed symmetrical submatrix? Numbers will appear in the main diagonal of this cubed matrix if and only if there exists a clique, as defined above, within the group. If such a clique does exist then numbers will appear in those positions on the diagonal which correspond to those persons who are members of the clique. If only one clique exists in the group or if more than one clique exists but they contain different members, then the number which appears in the diagonal for a particular individual will bear a given relationship to the number of people in the clique. If the clique is composed of n members, the number appearing in the diagonal for each of the members will be equal to $(n-1)$ $(n-2)$. We may thus immediately determine from this cubed matrix whether or not cliques exist, who belongs to these cliques if they exist, and how many members each clique has.

Let us examine the cubed symmetrical submatrices for Tolman and Howe courts which are presented in Figure 4. In Tolman Court it is immediately clear there were no cliques at all, since there are no numbers occurring in the main diagonal. In other words, in Tolman Court there was no subgroup as tightly knit as the requirements of our definition imply. In Howe Court, on the contrary, we observe that six people have numbers in the main diagonal and that all of these numbers are 2's. Since the number 2 occurring in the main diagonal of this matrix indicates the existence of a clique of three people we may immediately conclude that in Howe Court there were two nonoverlapping cliques of three people each. We may separate the two cliques very quickly with reference to the original matrix. There we may

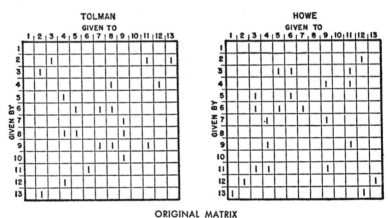

ORIGINAL MATRIX

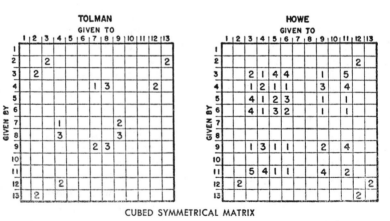

CUBED SYMMETRICAL MATRIX

Figure 4. Original and Cubed Symmetrical Sub-matrices for Tolman and Howe Courts

observe that number 4 chose number 9 and number 11. We consequently know that 4, 9, and 11 comprise one clique and that 3, 5, and 6 comprise the other. Since indirect three-step connections exist in the matrix between the two cliques, we may also conclude that there was at least one mutual choice made between them. Since the greatest number of indirect connections exist between number 3 and number 11, it is highly likely that this is the direct connection. Looking at the original matrix we indeed find a mutual choice between number 3 and number 11. It is clear that these two courts differed markedly with respect to cliques although we found them to be similar in many other respects.

It is also possible to distinguish subgroups which are not extreme cliques. These subgroups may be defined on the basis of mutual choices or on the basis of the complete matrix. We shall give some examples of such more moderate subgroup formations. If we look at the cubed symmetrical submatrix of Tolman Court we see that numbers 3, 2, and 13 are linked together. Here direct choices between numbers 3 and 13 are completely lacking. If we look at the cube of the complete matrix of Tolman Court we find that three, and only three people have 1's in the main diagonal. These three, numbers 4, 5, and 8, are consequently tied together in a circle. Anyone can get back to himself in three steps via the other two. One can, however, only go around this circle in one direction. The best criteria for distinguishing subgroups of less than the extreme degree must still be determined but it is clear that once defined, they may be relatively easily found by means of matrix multiplication.

10. THE OPERATION OF GROUP STANDARDS*

by Leon Festinger, Stanley Schachter, and Kurt Back

THE TERM *group standard*, or *group norm*, has been used freely either to describe or to explain the rather well substantiated finding that members of the same face-to-face group exhibit relative uniformity with respect to specified opinions and modes of behavior. The use of the term, whether in a descriptive or an explanatory manner, has generally carried with it the meaning that this observed uniformity derives in some manner from influences which the group is able to exert over its members. The fact that members of some social set all have relatively similar tastes in, for example, selecting recreational activities, has generally been explained on the basis of inter-

Reprinted from *Group Dynamics: Research and Theory*, edited by D. Cartwright and A. Zander, Chapter 16. Copyright, 1953, by Row, Peterson, and Company. Reproduced by permission of the copyright owners, the authors and the editors.

* This selection is a condensation of Chapters 5 and 6 of the book by the same authors entitled *Social Pressures in Informal Groups* (New York: Harper and Bros., 1950.)

individual or group influences rather than on the basis of similar circumstances producing similar but independent reactions in a number of people.

There is no question any longer that individuals and groups do exert influences on others which can and do result in uniform opinions and behavior patterns. There have been many studies which have demonstrated the existence and importance of this phenomenon. The classic experiment by Sherif[1] clearly demonstrated that, at least in a situation which was almost completely unstructured, the individual was virtually entirely dependent upon the group for forming a stable mode of response. The strength of the group influence was plainly sufficient to override most individual factors.

It has also been shown, by a series of independent studies,[2] that people's aspirations and goal-setting behavior are strongly influenced by information they possess about how others behave and their relationship to these others. All of these influences produce changes in the individual's behavior which result in his being more similar to other members of the group to which he feels he belongs.

Once we depart from the well-controlled laboratory situation it is no longer easy to claim unequivocally that observed uniformity is due to group influence. Newcomb,[3] for example, in his study of a college community which had a reputation for being liberal found that students consistently became more liberal with increasing length of attendance at the college. It is possible plausibly to maintain that these changing attitudes resulted from group pressures and influences once the student became a member of the community. It would also, however, be possible to maintain that these changes occurred in different people independently as a result of the similar experiences, curricular and otherwise, to which they were all subjected in the rather unique college. The demonstration that a group standard existed would indeed be difficult. Such demonstration would have to rest upon a series of empirical facts concerning the means by which the group enforces the standard, the relation between the pattern of conformity and the group structure, and the relationship to the group of members who deviate from the standard.

The study to be reported here undertook to investigate the nature and operation of group standards in two housing projects. These two projects, Westgate and Westgate West, were occupied by families of students of the Massachusetts Institute of Technology. The homes in Westgate were houses arranged in U-shaped courts. Those in Westgate West were apartments in rows of two-story barracklike structures. The same tenants' organization served both projects. The court in Westgate, and the building in Westgate West, had become the unit of social life in these projects by the time of the study. Friendship groups formed mainly within the court and within the building. The backgrounds and interests of the residents were relatively homogeneous throughout both projects and the assignment of houses or apartments to particular people had not been made on any kind of selective basis. It was also clear that there had been no differential treatment of courts or of buildings. The study of group standards might consequently be pursued fruitfully by carefully examining the reasons for differences in behavior among these social units where such differences emerged.

It was found that differences between courts did exist to a rather marked extent on matters concerning the Westgate tenants' organization. This organization was, at least potentially, of equal relevance and importance to all residents of Westgate and Westgate West, and all residents were urged to support it. Representation in the Westgate Council was on the basis of courts and buildings, and consequently called for action from each court and each building. Yet, in spite of this equality of relevance, some courts and buildings supported the organization, others were overtly hostile, while still others were indifferent. We shall proceed to examine the determinants of these differences among courts and among buildings to see whether group standards were or were not operating and, if they were, how they made themselves effective.

ATTITUDES TOWARD THE WESTGATE COUNCIL

By May of 1947, when interview data concerning the attitudes of residents toward the Westgate organization were collected, the Council had almost completed the first semester of active existence. Since the turnover in residents occurred mainly at the break between semesters, practically all residents who were living there at the time of the interview had been living in the project when the Council started its active program.

All of the 100 Westgate families and 166 of the 170 Westgate West families were asked, as part of a larger interview, "We understand there is a tenants' organization here. What do you think of it? Are you active in it?" The interviewers were instructed to follow these questions with non-directive probes until they were satisfied that they had obtained an adequate picture of the attitude toward the organization and the degree and kind of participation in its activities. These data were then categorized in the following way:

ATTITUDES TOWARD THE ORGANIZATION

Favorable. People who considered the organization primarily a good thing. Usually they endorsed both the idea of organization as such and some aims of the Council. Statements ranged from warm approval, "I am definitely in favor of it. It's a worth-while project. It's functioning well," to a vaguely approving, "It's all right."

Neutral. People who mentioned specific good and bad points about the organization so that no definitely favorable or unfavorable attitude could be assigned. In effect, this category included borderline people who had some basic attitude, but saw many points contrary to it. Examples are: "I guess it's all right if they accomplish something—I don't think they have as yet." "It's a good idea, but there are not too many problems for the community to deal with."

Apathetic. People who said they had not been interested enough to find out anything about the organization. In a sense this is a mildly unfavorable attitude —the organization did not concern them. On the other hand, they did not express any directly unfavorable opinion: "Don't know anything about it. Haven't been to any of the meetings or anything. Not knowing, I wouldn't want to say anything."

Unfavorable. People who expressed a definitely unfavorable opinion about the organization, saying that it was a waste of time, that the people in it were objectionable, that they never would achieve anything. "A large majority of the members are reactionary. They give no attention to wider aspects." "It's unnecessary and highschoolish."

ACTIVITIES IN THE ORGANIZATION

Active leader. People who took a definite part in the activities of the Council as a whole, as representatives, committee members, or doing volunteer work.

"We've been to meetings as delegates two or three times. I volunteered as bartender for the block party." "I am one of the court representatives. I'm a member of the welcoming committee greeting new residents."

Active follower. People who, though not active in the sense of the previous category, had attended more than one court meeting. They cooperated with the Council as it was set up on the court level. They went to the meetings in which the representatives were elected. They listened to the representatives' reports of the Council's actions and gave their suggestions and complaints to be taken up in the next meeting. They were, therefore, a necessary working part of the organization, although they took no part in the workings of the Council as such. "We have been to the building meetings; that's as far as it goes." "We go to the meetings. Everybody goes to them."

Inactive. People who did not make any effort to keep in contact with the organization. This included both the people who belonged (that is, they considered themselves represented by the Council) and those who did not feel even a formal connection with the Council. From the point of view of actual behavior, these two groups are indistinguishable. "To be truthful, I'm not active. Splendid idea, but I'm too busy." The principal answer from this group was a curt "No." These people did not even attend court meetings.

The questions about attitudes and activity measure two different aspects of a person's relation to the organization. His attitude may stem from a variety of interests and beliefs. He may view the Council as a way of having certain needs satisfied, as a way to meet his fellow tenants, as unrelated to his needs, or as a childish pastime. It is clear that some of these ways of looking at the Council will lead more readily to activity than others. But a resident's actual activity will also depend on other factors—whether he has time, whether a neighbor draws him into some work, whether he sees something that he personally can do. It is therefore possible that attitude and activity may occur together in all combinations, although some are more likely than others. They are distinct, though correlated, variables.

PATTERNS OF ATTITUDE AND ACTIVITY

There were differences from one court to another in attitude toward and activity in the tenants' organization. This implies that within any one court there was relative homogeneity with respect to both of these factors. In the extreme case, where all members of a court coincided exactly on both of these dimensions, the demonstration of homogeneity would be a simple matter. This extreme case does not occur, of course, and some method must be devised for describing the pattern within any court both with respect to the content of the pattern and the degree of homogeneity. That is, is it a favorable and active court or is it an unfavorable and inactive court? Do 80% of the court members show this behavior and attitude combination, or do only 60% of the court members show it?

It seemed feasible, from the nature of the data, to distinguish four possible types of court patterns: namely, favorable-active, favorable-inactive, unfavorable-active, and unfavorable-inactive. Once it was determined in which of these categories a court was located, the number of people in the court who conformed to or deviated from the court pattern could then be easily computed. When this was done it would be possible to proceed to a careful examination of whether or not the observed degree of homogeneity within courts was worthy of note, and whether or not it could be attributed to the existence of group standards.

If only these four types of patterns are to be distinguished we must, for this purpose, do some additional combining of the original categories into which the data were classified. This presents no problem for the activity dimension. Clearly the active leader and active follower categories should both be called active; but the combination of the attitude categories presents somewhat more of a problem. The extreme categories, favorable and un-favorable, clearly fall into their proper place. The categories of apathetic and neutral are not quite so clear. It was reasoned that the apathetic people were at least mildly unfavorable to the organization, since they either did not care to know about it or else had simply remained sufficiently out of things not to have heard about what was going on. On the basis of this reasoning, the apathetic people were classed as unfavorable.

The few residents who were classified as neutral were really borderline cases. To some extent they were favorable and to some extent unfavorable. Whatever the court pattern happens to be, in this sense they both conform to and deviate from it on the attitude dimension. In accordance with this view, the neutral people were not considered in determining the court pattern. In any event there were too few people thus categorized to have affected this determination much. Once the court pattern was determined, these neutrals were regarded as conformers if they fell into the proper activity category and were, of course, considered deviates if they did not.

Table 16.1—Attitude-Activity Distributions (Percentage)

	Active Leaders	Active Followers	Inactive	Unclassified	Total
			a. Westgate (N = 100)		
Favorable	22	14	18		54
Neutral	2	6	4		12
Apathetic		1	15		16
Unfavorable	2	2	13		17
Unclassified			1		1
Total	26	23	51		100
			b. Westgate West (N = 166)		
Favorable	16	38	24	1	79
Neutral		2	1		3
Apathetic	1	2	8		11
Unfavorable	1		3		4
Unclassified		2	1		3
Total	18	44	37	1	100

NOTE: Significance of difference between Westgate and Westgate West:
Attitude $x^2 = 37.86$; $p = .01$
Activity $x^2 = 12.42$; $p = .01$

We shall describe the method used for determining the court pattern by using Tolman Court as an example. Looking first at the activity dimension, we found that 12 residents were active and only one was not. On the attitude dimension, nine residents were favorable and two were unfavorable. The classification of this court, then, is "favorable-active." In this case, following our procedure for neutrals, we shall consider anybody who was neutral and active as conforming to the group standard. Of the two neutrals in the court, one followed the group standard and the other did not. The conformers include everybody who was favorable or neutral and active. There were 10 conformers and three deviates from the pattern.

A different type of pattern is shown in Main Court. Here six of the seven residents were inactive, while five were either apathetic or unfavorable. The pattern is therefore "unfavorable-inactive." As the only neutral resident was active, he cannot be considered as conforming to the pattern; he and the favorable inactive resident were deviates. The five inactive residents, who were either apathetic or unfavorable, conformed to the pattern.

This procedure was carried out for each of the nine Westgate courts and for each of the 17 Westgate West buildings. In Westgate, five of the courts showed a favorable-active pattern, one court showed a favorable-inactive pattern, and three courts showed an unfavorable-inactive pattern. Wide differences did exist among the courts. Also, within each court there was relative homogeneity. Five of the nine courts had a small proportion of deviates. In all but one of the courts the majority conformed to the court pattern.

In Westgate West the degree of homogeneity within the building was perhaps even more striking. Only four of the 17 buildings had as many as 40% deviates from the building pattern, and nine of the buildings had only one or two such deviates. In contrast to Westgate, however, there were no marked differences among the patterns in different buildings. Thirteen of the buildings had favorable-active patterns and four of them had favorable-inactive patterns. There were no buildings with an unfavorable pattern. While in Westgate there was evidence for homogeneity within the court, and heterogeneity among the courts, in Westgate West there seems to have been the same amount of homogeneity among buildings as was found within the building.

If we combine all courts into an over-all Westgate pattern, and all buildings into an over-all Westgate West pattern, this difference between the projects emerges even more clearly. These over-all patterns for the two projects are shown in Table 16.1. In Westgate, no homogeneous over-all pattern exists. Favorable attitudes were displayed by 54% of the residents, unfavorable or apathetic attitudes by 33%, while 49% were active and 51% inactive. If we use the same criteria for determining the over-all pattern here as was used for the individual courts, we would conclude that Westgate had a favorable-inactive pattern from which 78% of the residents deviated. Clearly, the greatest concentrations were in the favorable-active and the unfavorable-inactive quadrants. Even if we depart from our rigorous method of determining patterns and regard the pattern in Westgate as favorable-active, we still find that a majority (56%) of the residents were deviates.

The situation in Westgate West is clearly different. Here 79% of the residents were favorable and only 15% were unfavorable or apathetic, while 62% of the residents were active and 37% were inactive. The over-all pattern is favorable-active. Most of the deviation that did occur from this pattern was on the activity dimension, with little deviation on the attitude dimension.

What may we conclude from this analysis of the patterns within Westgate and within Westgate West? Do we as yet have any evidence for asserting the existence or nonexistence of group standards? With regard to Westgate we can clearly say that there was no group standard for the project as a whole. There were obviously opposing subgroups within Westgate with regard to both attitude and activity. Can one, however, maintain that there were group standards within each court? At this point this conclusion would seem plausible, although it is by no means unequivocally demonstrated. We must, however, find some explanation why different courts, each composed of the same kinds of people in similar circumstances, reacted so differently from each other toward the organization and why, in spite of different reactions from different courts, there was relatively homogeneous behavior within each court. We at least are led to suspect that group standards or group norms were operating.

In Westgate West, however, we cannot come to the same conclusions. Here it is possible that a group standard existed for the project as a whole; it is possible that group standards existed within each building; and it is possible that no group standards or norms existed at all, but that the obtained high degree of uniformity was due to similar independent reactions of the residents to the same state of affairs. As we have pointed out before, the hypothesis that the uniformity in Westgate West resulted from similar independent reactions of the residents seems probable on the basis of several considerations: Unlike the residents of Westgate, who had been living there up to 15 months and had had four months' actual experience with the organization, the residents of Westgate West were all relative newcomers. The oldest residents of Westgate West had only been living there about five months, and their contact with the Westgate organization had been limited. It was only about one month prior to the collection of these data that Westgate West actually joined the organization. We might expect, then, that in Westgate West, where the social groupings had not had time to form into cohesive units, and where the contact with the tenants' organization was only recent, group norms would not have developed to any considerable degree. The tenants, however, all in the same situation and pretty much the same kinds of people, tended individually to react favorably to the organization.

THE EVIDENCE FOR GROUP STANDARDS

On the basis of an examination of the actual distribution of conformity to and deviation from patterns of majority behavior, we have arrived at hypotheses concerning the reasons behind the observed degree of uniformity. It has seemed reasonable to suppose that group standards existed in the Westgate courts but that none existed in Westgate West. If this is true, there should be other differences between these two projects which would support these hypotheses. One derivation may immediately be made. If the behavior in Westgate was determined largely by group influences while the behavior in Westgate West was determined largely by individual reactions, then individual differences on relevant factors should show more relationship to attitude and activity in Westgate West than in Westgate.

The personal reasons which residents of the two projects gave for their attitudes, and for whether or not they participated in the activities of the organization, were numerous and varied. Some people had special interests which were aided by the organization; some did not believe in organized activities in general; some said they had no time; some felt that their efforts would be fruitless for the short time that remained for them to stay in the project. All these factors, and others of the same kind, were influences acting on the individual, independently of the group to which he belonged. It would have been desirable, but almost impossible, to obtain reliable indications as to whether or not each of these factors was operating on a particular individual.

Reliable data are at hand, however, concerning the length of time they expected to remain in the project. This, of course, coincided with the length of time they expected to remain in school and was fairly frequently mentioned as a reason for not participating in the activities of the tenants' organization. These data reveal that there was hardly any difference in attitude between long-term and short-term residents in either Westgate or Westgate West.

The breakdown by activity tells a different story. In Westgate, again, little difference was found. The shortest time group—those moving out in June—could not be affected by any medium or long-range program of the Council. In spite of this, 9 out of 16 cooperated with the Council. The group expecting the longest residence—those who intended to stay at least for a year and were frequently indefinite about how much longer—cooperated even a little less with the Council; only 14 out of 29 fell into these categories. The differences are not statistically significant.

In the activity ratings of the Westgate West residents, however, we find that length of expected residence made a difference. Among the short-term residents, 50% were actively cooperating with the Council, while 72% of the long-term residents were. The median expected residence for the active leaders was 17 months; for the inactive residents 12 months. These differences are significant at the 5% level.

We thus find our derivation borne out. The data support our hypotheses concerning the difference between Westgate and Westgate West. In Westgate West, where individuals were reacting more or less independently in terms of their own needs and preferences, we find a significant and appreciable degree of relationship between how much longer they expected to stay in the project and whether or not they became active in the affairs of the tenants' organization. In Westgate, group influences were important. A major determinant of an individual's activity was whether or not others in his group were active. There was, consequently, no relationship at all between how long one expected to stay there, or how much benefit one would derive from the organizational activities, and whether or not one became active. We may reaffirm our hypotheses with somewhat more confidence now and look for the next testable derivation which we can make.

To be able to create and maintain group standards, a group must have power over its members. This power, the ability to induce forces on its members, has been called cohesiveness. If the group uses this power to make the members think and act in the same way, that is, if there are group standards, the homogeneity of the attitude and activity patterns should be related to the cohesiveness of the group. Correspondingly, if no relation exists between cohesiveness and homogeneity of the pattern, the group does not use its power to induce the members to conform, and we may take it as indicative of the absence of group standards.

The power of a group may be measured by the attractiveness of the group for the members. If a person wants to stay in a group, he will be susceptible to influences coming from the group, and he will be willing to conform to the rules which the group sets up.

The courts and buildings in Westgate and Westgate West were mainly social groups. The attractiveness of the group may, therefore, be measured by the friendships formed within the group. If residents had most of their friends within the court, the group was more attractive to them than if they had few friends within the court. The former situation will imply a more cohesive court, which should be able to induce stronger forces on its members. This should result in greater homogeneity within the more cohesive court than within the less cohesive one.

The necessary measures for determining the relationship between the cohesiveness of the court and the effectiveness of the group standard are easily obtained. Sociometric data from a question regarding who the residents saw most of socially may be used here. Thus, if the members of one court give a total of 30 choices, 18 of which are given to others in their own court, the percentage of "in-court" choices is 60. This court is then considered more cohesive than some other court which gives a total of 32 choices, only 16 of which are to others in the same court. The homogeneity of the court, or how effective the group standard is, may be measured simply by the percentage of members of the court who deviate from the court pattern. The more effective the group standard and the more homogeneous the court, the

Table 16.2—Cohesiveness of Court and Strength of Group Standard (Westgate)

Court and N of Residents		% Deviates	Choices in Court ——————— Total Choice	Choices in Court — ½ Pairs ——————— Total Choice
Tolman	13	23	.62	.529
Howe	13	23	.63	.500
Rotch	8	25	.55	.523
Richards	7	29	.47	.433
Main	7	29	.67	.527
Freeman	13	38	.48	.419
Williams	13	46	.53	.447
Miller	13	46	.56	.485
Carson	13	54	.48	.403
R.O. correlation with % deviates			−.53	−.74
t*			1.65	2.92
p			.15	.02

* Testing significance of file and rank order correlation as suggested by Kendall, M. G., *The Advanced Theory of Statistics*. London: Charles Griffin and Co., Limited, Vol. I, p. 401, 1943.

lower will be the percentage of members who deviate. The second and third columns of Tables 16.2 and 16.3 show the percentage of deviates and the proportion of "in-court" choices for each court in Westgate and for each building in Westgate West.

From our hypotheses concerning the existence of group standards in the Westgate courts and the absence of group standards in the Westgate West buildings, we would expect to find an appreciable negative correlation in Westgate and no correlation in Westgate West between the percentage of deviates and the proportion of "in-court" choices. In Table 16.2 it may be seen that the correlation is —.53 in Westgate. Here, the more cohesive the court (that is, the greater the proportion of "in-court" choices) the smaller the proportion of people who deviated from the court standard. As we expected, this correlation is virtually zero in Westgate West (Table 16.3). Here the proportion of people who deviated from the building pattern had little or nothing to do with the cohesiveness of the building group.

Table 16.3—Cohesiveness of Building and Strength of Group Standard (Westgate West)

Building	% Deviates	Choices in Building Total Choices	Choices in Building —½ Pairs Total Choices
211-20	10	.58	.50
221-30	10	.66	.59
201-10	11	.60	.54
231-40	20	.80	.64
241-50	20	.70	.61
251-60	20	.74	.63
281-90	20	.80	.68
311-20	20	.66	.53
261-70	25	.57	.46
271-80	30	.47	.38
341-50	30	.62	.50
351-60	30	.85	.76
321-30	33	.62	.52
361-70	40	.67	.56
291-300	50	.59	.50
301-10	50	.72	.64
331-40	70	.42	.35
R.O. correlation with % deviates		—.20	—.27
t		.79	1.09
p		not significant	

The measure of cohesiveness which we have used may, however, be considerably improved. The major uncertainty in the measure, as it stands, lies in our inability to distinguish between the cohesiveness of the whole group and the cohesiveness of subgroups. For example, a group of eight people all making choices within the group might or might not have high cohesiveness as a total group. As an extreme illustration, there conceivably might be two subgroups of four people each, every member within each subgroup choosing every other member, but without any choices at all between the subgroups. In this case each of the subgroups may have great cohesiveness, but the cohesiveness of the group as a whole would be low. Similarly, if in a group of eight or ten people there is a subgroup of three, the total group would be less cohesive than if no subgroup existed. It appears that if a strongly knit subgroup includes a large majority of the group, the cohesiveness of the whole group may still be high.

This effect of tendencies toward subgroup formation may be taken into account in our measure by correcting for the number of mutual choices which occurred. If there were no tendencies at all toward subgroup formation within a group, then the number of mutual choices which we would expect to occur would be quite low. In a group of ten people with each person giving, say, two choices within the group, we would only expect to obtain two mutual choices in the complete absence of tendencies toward subgroup or pair formation. As the tendencies toward subgroup formation increase, we shall expect to find more and more mutual choices. Thus, the existence of mutual choices to some extent decreases the cohesiveness of the group as a whole.

We may check further on whether or not this relationship was a property of the group as a whole. A corrected measure of cohesiveness, obtained by subtracting half of the number of mutual pairs of choices, is certainly meaningful only as a measure of the group as a whole. The fact that mutual choices occurred certainly does not detract from the personal attractiveness of the individuals involved in these mutual choices. We should then expect the correlation with the measure of prestige of the subgroup to increase when the corrected measure of cohesiveness is used. This correlation in Westgate is .75, representing an appreciable increase in relationship. In Westgate West, where the buildings did not constitute really functional social units, the correlation remains unchanged—still very close to zero.

THE SOCIAL STATUS OF THE DEVIATE

What are the conditions which produce deviates? When pressures and influences are being exerted on people to adopt a certain way of thinking or a certain pattern of behavior, some people conform quite readily while others are able entirely to resist these influences. The mere knowledge that these "individual differences" exist does not explain the reasons for them or the factors which are responsible for producing deviates. To learn this, we must examine the means by which group influences may be resisted.

The pressure which a group exerts on its members may be overt and sometimes even formalized. Laws, rules, mores, etiquette, and so on exemplify some of these overt pressures. The pressures which induce men to open doors for women, to dress in certain special ways on certain special occasions, or to enter their fathers' businesses are all overt and recognized. It is likely, of course, that before a group norm or standard can become thus openly formalized it must be in existence for a long time, or else must be of such a nature that deviation from the standard is harmful to the group. Such open pressures are generally also accompanied by open punishment for deviation in the form of censure, overt disapproval, or even rejection from the group.

On the other hand, the pressures which a group exerts on its members may be subtle and difficult to locate. The weight of others' opinions, the gradual change in one's ideas of what is the "normal" thing to do simply because everyone else does it, the mutual influences of people who share their ideas and their attitudes, also serve effectively as pressures toward conformity with the behavior pattern of the group. Under these circumstances the consequences of nonconformity are also more subtle. These consequences may merely be a tendency to prefer those people who are not "different."

There is no indication that in Westgate there was any overt or formalized pressure on court members to conform to the court standard. Many of the residents realized that the people in their court were different from the people in some other court, but the influences which created and maintained these differences among courts were indirect and nonovert. Members of the courts were being influenced in their opinions and behavior merely by virtue of their association with others in their courts, without any formalized "group intent" to influence.

The strength of the influence which the group can exert in this manner depends partly upon the attractiveness of the group for the member and partly on the degree to which the member is in communication with others in the group. No matter how attractive the group is to a particular person, it will be impossible for the group to exert any influence on him if he is never in communication with the group. We may now examine some of the conditions under which individuals will be able to resist these influences.

1. The group may not be sufficiently attractive to the member. Under these circumstances, the relatively weak influence which the group exerts cannot overcome personal considerations which may happen to be contrary to the group standard. An example will illustrate this phenomenon:

(*Mr. and Mrs. C, in Williams Court.*) We don't have any opinion at all about the organization. We're bad ones for you to interview. We have no need for an organization because we're pretty happy at home. We're socially self-sufficient. Others in the court feel it is wonderful and we discovered many that felt that way. We have friends in this and other courts but our main interests are in the home.

2. There may not be sufficient communication between the member and others in the group. Under these conditions the pressures from the group are simply not brought to bear on the member although, if they had been exerted, they might have been very effective. In such instances the deviate may not even be aware of the fact that he is different from most of the others in his group. An example of this type of deviate follows:

(*Mr. and Mrs. S, in Freeman Court.*) The organization is a good idea, but the trouble with people like us is that we don't have time. That's why we haven't had anything to do with it. I think it's the consensus of opinion that people here don't have the time. [Actually the majority of the people in the court were active.] There are wonderful people living here, but it seems peculiar to Westgate that people are hard to get to know. A lot of people come here expecting to make friends without any trouble, and then find it isn't so easy. It would be a good thing if the organization helped people to get acquainted.

3. The influence of some other group to which the people belong may be stronger than the influence which the court group is able to exert on them. Under these conditions the person who appears as a deviate is a deviate only because we have chosen, somewhat arbitrarily, to call him a member of the court group. He does deviate from his own court, but he conforms to some other group to which he actually feels he belongs. Such a group may, of course, be outside of Westgate altogether. There are instances, however, of people belonging to groups other than their own court, but still within the limits of Westgate:

(*Mr. and Mrs. M, in Carson Court.*) We think the organization is fine and Mrs. M is the chairman of the social committee which is holding its first big event tomorrow night. I don't see much of the others in this court. My real friends are in the next court over there, in Tolman Court. There are only two people living in this court that do anything for the organization, myself and one other person. It's generally understood that the others have different interests. The people in Tolman Court are more active. Carson Court people aren't as sociable as people in Tolman Court.

THE DEVIATE IN WESTGATE

These three types of conditions do, then, appear to produce deviates; at least we were able to locate deviates who seemed to exhibit such patterns of relationship between themselves and the group. If these are the major factors which make for nonconformity, we should also be able to demonstrate their relevance for all of the deviates rather than for a few selected examples. The two variables, attractiveness of the group for the member and amount of communication between the member and the group, should be reflected in the sociometric choices which people gave and received. We should expect that deviates would give fewer choices to others in their court and would receive fewer choices from them. Whether this happened because they were not in full communication with the group or because the group was not attractive to them, the result in the sociometric choices should be essentially the same—the deviates should be sociometric isolates in their court.

Table 16.4 shows the average number of "in-court" choices given and

Table 16.4—Average Number of "In-Court" Choices of Deviates and Conformers in Westgate

	N	Choices Given	Choices Received
Deviates	36	1.25	1.11
Conformers	64	1.53	1.61

received by the 36 deviates and the 64 conformers in Westgate. It is readily apparent that the deviates were more isolated sociometrically than were the conformers. They both gave and received fewer choices than did the conformers.[4] Moreover, the conformers tended to receive more choices than they gave, while the deviates tended to receive fewer choices than they gave. Deviates tended to choose conformers more than conformers chose deviates. This might be called relative rejection by the conformers.

Deviate status, then, was accompanied by a smaller degree of association with others in the court. It is still possible, however, that these deviates were not true isolates, but merely members of groups other than the court group. In our case studies we saw two examples of this sort. An examination of all sociometric choices exchanged with people outside the court, however, reveals that this was not true of the deviates as a whole. Table 16.5 shows the average number of "out-court" choices given and received by the deviates and conformers. It is clear that the deviates, in the main, were not members of groups other than those of their own court. They gave only as many choices to people outside their own court as did the conformers, but received considerably fewer choices from outside than the conformers.[5] We

Table 16.5—Average Number of "Out-Court" Choices of Deviates and Conformers in Westgate

	N	Choices Given	Choices Received
Deviates	36	1.14	.89
Conformers	64	1.16	1.55

must conclude that these deviates, who had fewer associations within their own court, also had fewer associations with others in Westgate—at least, insofar as this is reflected by the number of choices they received.

Choices given by deviates to people outside their own court tended to be given to the conformers in other courts. These conformers tended not to reciprocate the choices. The deviate, who was perceived as being different from the others in his court, was not as often chosen by outsiders. This is consistent with our knowledge that the court is perceived as the basis for social grouping in Westgate. People who were on the fringes of their own group were also on the fringe of social life between courts. While conformers in Westgate received an average of 3.16 choices from others, the deviates received an average of only 2.00 such choices. The deviates were relative isolates. It is clear that this isolation was not wholly voluntary on the part of the deviates, since they gave only slightly fewer choices than the conformers.

It is possible to examine the situation of the deviate more closely if we restrict ourselves to the six full-size courts in Westgate. Ten of the houses in these six courts faced onto the street rather than into the courtyard area, so that the people living in these houses had fewer contacts with others in the court. Of the other 68 people living in these courts only 34% were deviates, while 7 of the 10 corner-house residents were deviates. It appears that the isolated geographical position in which these 10 found themselves, and the resultant lack of contact between them and the rest of the court, made it difficult for the court to exert influence on them. The lack of contact suggests that mainly chance factors would determine whether they would show the pattern of attitude and behavior that had become the standard in the court.

Table 16.6 shows the "in-court" choices for these six full-size courts with the corner-house deviates separated from the others. The lack of contact between the court and the deviates in these corner houses is readily apparent. They both gave and received only about one-third as many choices as did the others in the court.[6] It is not surprising that they had remained uninfluenced by the group standard in their particular court.

Table 16.6—Average Number of "In-Court" Choices of Deviates and Conformers for the Six Large Courts in Westgate

	N	Choices Given	Choices Received
Deviates in corner houses	7	.57	.43
Deviates in inner houses	23	1.52	1.39
Conformers	48	1.52	1.60

The other deviates in the court did not suffer from such lack of contact. They gave as many choices to the others in the court as did the conformers. As was true for all the deviates in Westgate, however, they tended to receive fewer than they gave, while the conformers tended to receive more choices than they gave.[7]

Table 16.7, again, shows that these inner-house deviates were not members of groups other than the court group. They gave only as many choices to people outside their own court as did the conformers and, again, received many fewer.

The deviates stood out as relative isolates, not only within their own court, but in Westgate as a whole. The corner-house deviates received, from all sources, an average of only 1.57 choices, the other deviates received an average of 2.26 choices, while the conformers received an average of 3.18 choices. The conformers were more closely involved with the social life in Westgate than were the deviates. Whether relative isolation brings about deviate status (as seems to be the case for those living in corner houses), or whether deviate status tends to bring about isolation through "rejection by others" (as might be the case with the deviates living in inner houses), the two things seem to go hand in hand.

THE DEVIATE IN WESTGATE WEST

We concluded above that there was no relation in Westgate West between the uniformity of behavior within a building and the cohesiveness of the

Table 16.7—Average Number of "Out-Court" Choices of Deviates and Conformers for the Six Large Westgate Courts

	N	Choices Given	Choices Received
Deviates in corner houses	7	1.29	1.14
Deviates in inner houses	23	1.13	.87
Conformers	48	1.17	1.58

building, and that group standards were not operating in Westgate West. The opinions of the people about the tenants' organization and their degree of activity in it would, consequently, not be determined by pressures or influences from the group. The behavior of the individual would be more a matter of individual reaction and influence from other individuals than of group pressures.

We may well examine the sociometric status of those people who were different from the majority in their building, although we should not expect the isolation which we found among the deviates in Westgate. These people were deviates only in the sense that they reacted differently from most of the residents, and not in the sense of having successfully resisted group pressures to conform.

Few people in Westgate West expressed unfavorable attitudes toward the organization. Consequently, few people differed from the pattern of their building on the attitude dimension. The great majority of the deviates differed only on the activity dimension from the others in their building. Thirteen of the seventeen buildings had "favorable-active" patterns, and most of the deviates were people who felt favorably inclined, but had merely not attended the meetings of their building. It is plausible to expect, then, that we would find these deviates not to be isolates in the community despite their absence from building meetings. The data corroborate these expectations. Altogether, deviates and conformers both gave an average of about two and one-half choices, and both received an average of about two and one-half choices. We may thus conclude that in the absence of strong group formation, and in the absence of group standards, being different from the people in the group did not result in isolation.

SUMMARY

In order to conclude that observed uniformity in behavior of a number of individuals is the result of the operation of group standards or the existence of "social norms," we must be able to show the existence of psychological groups which are enforcing such standards. A collection of individuals with a relatively high number of sociometric linkages among them may constitute such a psychological group, or may merely constitute a series of friendship relationships with no real unification of the group as a whole. It is highly likely, of course, that such a series of friendship relationships among a number of people will in time make for the development of a cohesive group. In Westgate West, where there had not been time for this process really to develop, evidence indicating the absence of group standards was found.

When a cohesive group does exist, and when its realm of concern extends over the area of behavior in which we have discovered uniformity among the members of the group, then the degree of uniformity must be related to the degree of cohesiveness of the group, if a group standard is operative. The more cohesive the group, the more effectively it can influence its members. Thus we have found that in the more cohesive groups in Westgate there were fewer deviates from the group pattern of behavior. The cohesiveness of the court group as a whole was the important determinant of the number of deviates. Subgroup formation within the larger group, no matter how cohesive these subgroups may have been, tended to disrupt the cohesiveness of the larger unit.

Although, on the basis of the data available to us, we have not been able to separate clearly the different means by which people can resist group influences and thus become deviates, there is abundant evidence that the attractiveness of the group and the amount of communication between the member and the group are major determinants. It also would seem likely that these two factors would generally not occur separately, but would operate together in most situations. The sociometric status of the deviate is clearly different from that of the conformer—isolation seems to be both a cause and an effect of being a deviate.

Auxiliary Readings

A. SYSTEMATIZATION OF GROUP PROPERTIES

S. C. Dodd, "A System of Operationally Defined Concepts for Sociology," *American Sociological Review*, Vol. IV, 1939, pp. 619-634.

This is one of the many publications by the author in which he proposes a system of classification by which complex group properties can be reduced to a few simple elements.

G. A. Lundberg, "Some Problems of Group Classification and Measurement," *American Sociological Review*, Vol. V, 1940, pp. 351-360.

Three types of basic interpersonal relations between two people are discussed: mutual attraction, repulsion, and indifference. From these relations, group structures are built up and formulae for their possible frequencies are derived.

W. S. Robinson, "Ecological Correlations and the Behavior of Individuals," *American Sociological Review,* Vol. 15, 1950, pp. 351-357, and H. Menzel, "Comment on Robinson's 'Ecological Correlations and the Behavior of Individuals,'" *American Sociological Review,* Vol. 15, 1950, p. 674.

> Robinson discusses the conditions under which an ecological variable like "a district with a high rate of illiteracy" and an individual property like being "illiterate" cannot be interchanged without affecting empirical findings. Menzel points out that it is not only a question of interchangeability. Ecological variables sometimes stand for structural characteristics which have to be considered in their own right.

E. Durkheim, "Anomic Suicide," *Suicide* (Glencoe, Ill.: The Free Press, 1951), Book II, Chapter V, Section IV.

> A distinction is made between countries where there are many divorces and people who are divorced. Easier divorce laws affect the divorce probabilities of men and women differently.

B. INTERRELATIONSHIP OF GROUP PROPERTIES

A. P. Hare, "A Study of Interaction and Consensus in Different Sized Groups," *American Sociological Review,* Vol. 17, No. 3, 1952, pp. 261-267.

> Tests various hypotheses concerning the relationship of group properties. Shows, for example, that "as the size of a discussion group is increased from five to twelve members, the amount of consensus resulting from group discussion will decrease."

R. H. Van Zelst, "Validation of a Sociometric Regrouping Procedure," *Journal of Social and Abnormal Psychology,* Vol. 47, 1952, pp. 299-301.

> An impressive demonstration of the practical application of the sociometric procedure in the production of a housing project. Relates group cohesion to such group properties as labor turnover rate, labor cost, and materials cost.

J. L. Moreno, *Who Shall Survive?* (Washington: Nervous and Mental Disease Publishing Co., 1934), pp. 96-103.

> The standard exposition of the sociometric method. In the selection cited, the author characterizes *groups* as introverted, extroverted, balanced, outward aggressive, inward aggressive on the basis of sociometric choices or rejections, and relates these characteristics to group morale, *esprit de corps,* proportion of runaways, group malbehavior, etc.

C. Goodrich, B. W. Allin, and M. Hayes, *Migration and Planes of Living, 1920-1934* (Philadelphia: University of Pennsylvania Press, 1935), pp. 13-25.

> An attempt to establish a rough index of economic well-being which would permit comparisons of counties over the entire nation and in all types of communities. Considered a number of indicators and discarded all but three: number of federal income tax returns; number of residence telephones; and number of families who reported radio sets in 1930. A formula for weighting these factors, based on the national averages, is given, and a total score, roughly indicative of economic welfare, is computed.

C. THE APPLICATION OF THE CONCEPT OF PROPERTY SPACE TO GROUP ANALYSIS

W. J. Goode, *Religion Among the Primitives* (Glencoe, Ill.: The Free Press, 1951), pp. 227-239.

> A number of primitive tribes, as total cultural units, are ranked with reference to religious personnel, societal matrix, sacred entities, ritual, and belief, and the basis for such ranking is indicated. By combination and reduction of these dimensions a typology is developed.

C. P. Loomis and J. A. Beegle, "A Typological Analysis of Social Systems," *Sociometry,* Vol. 11, 1948, pp. 147-191.

> The distinction between familistic Gemeinschaft and contractual Gesellschaft is broken down into a number of dimensions. An Amish farm family, New Mexico Ditch Association, and a division of the U. S. Department of Agriculture are compared according to these dimensions. This paper parallels the ideas exemplified in Selection (5) in Section I. It deserves careful study because it implicitly applies the notion of property space to collectives.

W. E. Henry and H. Guetzkow, "Group Projection Sketches for the Study of Small Groups," *Journal of Social Psychology*, 1951, 33, pp. 77-102.

A projective test, similar in principle to the TAT, is developed for the purpose of analyzing and describing groups. A large number of categories descriptive of group properties are established, e.g., communication clarity, content-procedure ratio, goal concentration, tension level, participation spread, role-differentiation, in-group feeling, creativity of group product, etc.

D. THE FORMAL ANALYSIS OF INTERPERSONAL RELATIONS

E. D. Chapple (with collaboration of C. M. Arensberg), "Measuring Human Relations: An Introduction to the Study of the Interaction of Individuals," *Genetic Psychology Monographs*, Vol. 22, 1940, pp. 9-147.

A systematic approach to the objective description of human interactions. Includes a discussion of the interpersonal relations obtaining in the family, the factory, and political institutions.

G. A. Lundberg and M. Steele, "Social Attraction-Patterns in a Village," *Sociometry*, Vol. I, Jan-Apr. 1938, pp. 375-419.

The analysis of the sociometric structure of a small Vermont village, based on a house-to-house canvass. Describes the system of interpersonal relations in the community, and demonstrates that the "stars" tend to have higher socio-economic status, as measured by the Chapin living-room scale, than the satellites.

R. M. Stogdill, "The Organization of Working Relationships: Twenty Sociometric Indices," *Sociometry*, Vol. XIV, No. 4, Dec. 1951, pp. 336-373.

A sociometric study of the personnel of a naval bureaucratic unit, using the criterion of time spent in getting work done, is presented. Notes how hierarchical level within the formal organization, degree of responsibility, power to delegate authority, etc., determine the degree and nature of interaction. Includes a discussion of the interrelationships among various sociometric scores.

R. R. Sears, "Experimental Studies of Projection: I. Attribution of Traits," *Journal of Social Psychology*, Vol. 7, 1936, pp. 151-163, and E. Frenkel-Brunswik, "Mechanisms of Self-Deception," *Journal of Social Psychology*, SPSSI Bulletin, 1939, *10*, pp. 409-420.

Sears asks the students in a class to rate each other in regard to certain personality traits. As a result he knows how each student sees himself, how the others see him, and how he judges the average of his fellow students. The question is raised: To what extent and under what conditions does a person project his own traits onto others? Simultaneously with this study done at Yale, Frenkel-Brunswik investigated the same problem with students at Vienna, but utilized to a greater extent participant observations and detailed interviews with her subjects. A comparison between the strictly quantitative approach of Sears and the more qualitative approach of Frenkel-Brunswik provides a fruitful exercise in methods.

M. W. Riley and S. H. Flowerman, "Group Relations As a Variable in Communications Research," *American Sociological Review*, Vol. 16, 1951, pp. 174-180.

The reading and listening habits of children are related to the sociometric position they have among their age peers.

The Empirical Analysis of Action

Introduction

So FAR we have dealt with a type of research which puts any interpretation at the end of an analytical chain. The objects under investigation were characterized by a series of variables; these in turn were interrelated—sometimes through time—by statistical procedures; finally, conclusions were drawn from the findings: they were taken either as a special case of a more general law or they were used as guides for more intricate relations to be further investigated. But this left out a whole other world of research procedures where "connections" are investigated more directly. The clinical psychologist deals with one person at a time and traces, let us say, his emotional difficulties back to his childhood experiences. The historian links the events of the French Revolution back to the social factors which characterized the old regime. The anthropologist links a tribe's ideas about magic to the ways it makes its living in a specific environmental setting. There the crux of the intellectual task lies not in *finding* regularities, but in *applying* available knowledge to the understanding of a specific case—be it a person or a collective.

Everyone knows the large and often controversial literature written around the methodological problems which such kinds of work involve. The present section does not intend to cover this discussion. Rather it concentrates on a very specific type of research, restricted enough so that its procedures can be fairly clearly understood, and yet of such a nature that it clearly involves the problem of causal analysis in a single case.

The studies selected here all have to do with actions many people perform repeatedly and under somewhat comparable circumstances. They buy food and they choose what movie to attend; from time to time they vote and they change their residence; and some of them occasionally get into automobile accidents or commit crimes. As a result, there has developed a body of studies which can be combined under the title, "the empirical analysis of action," if the term action is used in a somewhat broad sense. The purpose of such a study may be formulated in a variety of ways. Social reformers want to keep people from committing crimes; advertisers want to know how people can be made to buy their products; occupational counsellors study how people choose their jobs, because they want to turn one man's experience into another man's guidance. Whatever the purpose, all these studies have one central topic in common: What are the factors which account for the choices which people make among a specified number of alternatives?

We have used a similar phrase in the Introduction to Section II. But the studies included in the present section are different in one crucial respect which has to be understood at the outset. Take, as an example, Lipset's study of the University of California Loyalty Oath controversy (Selection (2) in Section II). In this study, it was concluded, on the basis of statistical analy-

387

sis, that certain newspapers influenced their readers toward the oath. In the course of the investigation, the only thing we knew of each individual was what newspapers he read, what attitudes he had, and so on. The causal inference regarding the relationship between exposure and effect was made at the end of the study and was based on the pertinent classification of individuals in a multivariate system. In the studies here under review, *the causal inference is made on each single individual separately* and at a much earlier stage of the investigation. Here, too, we often end up with statistical results telling, for instance, that the influence of friends is more frequent than the influence of newspapers. But whether a newspaper did or did not influence a specific reader has to be assessed in each case separately.

The purpose of this section is to acquaint the student with such studies so that he can see the paradigm behind them. It is not claimed, of course, that this paradigm is directly applicable to the broad scale studies of the historian or the subtle case reports of the clinical psychologist. But they exhibit elements which the more complex approaches also contain and which will be indispensable once methodology for the latter approaches is developed. In this sense our selections are on the borderline of the area which our Reader tries to represent: the methodology has not been completely formalized, but some advances have already been made. This will become apparent as soon as we single out the five typical steps through which empirical analysis of action usually proceeds.

STEP 1.

Certain *typological distinctions* must be made so that only cases which are fairly comparable are treated within the frame of one's study. For example, if we ask about causes of crime, it is obvious that the commission of a first crime certainly has a different constellation of determinants than the performance of a professional criminal who commits one of a long series of repeated criminal acts. The Democrat who votes for a Republican candidate for the first time is likely to give us information on his reasons which are quite different from those of the Republican voter who has voted for his party all his life.

STEP 2.

Once we have agreed on the specific sub-type of action, we also have to decide on the set of factors we intend to take into account. It is well known that the general question "why" leads to an infinite regress. In any concrete study, however, we are usually interested in assessing the causal role of but a small number of factors. Was it chiefly a desire for freedom or for economic gain which brought the Pilgrims to America? Was it a teacher or a parent who influenced a youngster more in his occupational choice? The set of elements to be considered may be called an *accounting scheme*. The purpose of such an accounting scheme is not only to limit the scope of the study, but also to order the elements under consideration into a number of categories. In migration studies, for instance, we distinguish the pushes which drove a man away from his former place of residence and the pulls which attracted him to the new place. Within each of these categories we will then want to decide which of a series of pushes and which of a series of pulls was more effective. It is, incidentally, a still undecided question whether it is also feasible to make causal assessments *between* categories — whether, for instance, the push or the pull was more decisive.

STEP 3.

Once we have established our categories we have to decide on *the best interviewing methods* to get the necessary information from each respondent. There are two factors to be considered here. On the one hand, we have to make sure that the respondents considered all the elements which we have in our scheme. A voter who has shifted from one candidate to the other might only mention the attractive features of the new choice if we do not specifically ask him about the weaknesses of the candidate he stopped favoring. On the other hand, we require what might be called "surplus information." We do not want to rely exclusively on the actor's own assessment of what determined his choice. We have to introduce specifying and check questions, so that in the end the investigator can make his own assessment of each single case.

STEP 4.

Once all of our material is collected, we have to make the crucial *causal assessment*. In principle, it is not difficult to state the issue involved. A person has been subject to a situation x and performed an act y. Would he have done y without the occurrence of x? Actually, the matter is quite complicated. What do we mean by "without the occurrence of x?" Were there other substitutes for x, say z, easily available; e.g., if a man had not read a story in the newspaper would he have heard it over the radio anyhow? Is there something in the disposition of the respondent which would make him search out actively a substitute z for x? And, in any case, is the likelihood of y following z about the same as the likelihood of it following x? To this we have to add the reminder that such assessment has to be made for every element or category of the accounting scheme. If, in a case of migration, the "push" is famine, the "pull" is a specific job, and the "link" the letter from a relative, then a separate assessment has to be made on each of these factors. The whole procedure is still far from clear. But one point will be clearly seen from the selections in this section. By proper use of the preceding three steps—preclassification, specification of the accounting scheme, and well-directed collection of data (e.g., through interviews), the task of causal assessment is greatly elucidated and facilitated.

STEP 5.

Once the causal factors have been assessed in each single case, all cases in the sample are combined into a *statistical result*. Two matters have to be understood in this step. First, the result can never be *one* table of "reasons." There will be as many tables as the accounting scheme contains categories, and cross-tabulations between the categories are very much in order. Consumers, for instance, who are influenced by advertising might be affected by different arguments than people who are influenced by friends. Secondly, the student should realize that the kind of statistical results obtained in such empirical action studies are of a peculiar nature. Suppose we find that 10% of the voters who changed their minds within a specific week of the campaign were influenced by the speech of one of the candidates. This can mean that either a large number heard the speech and a few were affected; or it can mean that the speech reached a small audience but was very effective among those who heard or read about it. It is this final step where sometimes an indirect verification of the assessment procedure is possible. We never can tell whether we were right in a single case. But we sometimes might have objective evidence that in a given situation one factor affected more people than another. The question then can be raised —and sometimes answered—whether the proportion of cases in which the two factors were assessed as causally important, agrees with this external information.

The sketching of these five steps was necessary because no systematic presentation of the empirical analysis of action is yet available. In order for the matter to acquire vivid meaning, however, the teacher will have to trace the various elements in the selections of this section.

A. *The study of buying as a paradigm for empirical analysis of action.* The first three selections are intended to provide a rather general picture of this area. It is, incidentally, no coincidence that they are all taken from the field of consumer research. There the problems have been worked through in considerable detail. This is so partly because much work has been done in consumer research, and partly because the relatively simple act of buying lends itself well to the development of a basic paradigm. The first selection should show this very clearly. It emphasizes how various techniques can be derived by following an activity in progress over time and in examining the interplay of various causal categories. The second selection, by Smith and Suchman, exemplifies the necessity of distinguishing various types of action (Step 1) and shows one way in which the causal assessment is carried out (Step 4). The third selection, dealing with advertising effectiveness, considers the question of appropriate interviewing techniques (Step 3), and the way in which statistical results might be verified (Step 5). All three selections, however, touch on the other elements of the whole operation.

A word should be inserted here on the resistance which social scientists sometimes feel when they are asked to be concerned with findings from consumer research. It is undoubtedly true that other topics are more important than what brands of merchandise people buy. But this is also the case for such questions as whether one of two lifted weights is heavier, or whether a rat moves left or right in a maze. Often, simple insignificant situations lend themselves best to initial exploration. The task is, of course, not to stop forever at places where it is easy to dwell. But to avoid them as a matter of principle might well impede the progress toward more worthwhile sites.

B. *The development and use of accounting schemes.* The next three selections highlight the idea of accounting schemes. The material for Selection (4) are the reports of people who became excited when they heard Orson Welles' broadcast, "The Invasion from Mars." In preparation of a large-scale study, Herzog had to decide on what elements of the whole sequence to focus: the frightening feature of the script, the predisposition of the listener to believe, the social situation which prevent-

ed checking up on the reality of the event, etc. In Selection (5), Gaudet reports how an accounting scheme is developed step by step. It derives, on the one hand, from the purpose of the study: what makes voters shift from one candidate to another; on the other hand, repeated pre-tests with respondents show at what points their answers do not provide the data for which the investigator is searching. Selection (6) presents an unusual application of the whole idea. The problem there is to find a useful scheme for reporting automobile accidents and to allocate causes for them. It is interesting to see how engineers end up with the solution which the social research methodologist would anticipate: various aspects of the case have to be distinguished; within each of these broad categories, specific alternatives have to be considered; the accident does not have "*a* cause"; the different elements of the situation—condition of the road and of the car, behavior of the driver, etc.—have to be assessed in their causal impact.

C. *The assessment and statistical analysis of causes.* The assessment procedure is the focus of attention in the next two selections. Komarovsky, in Selection (7), traces the effect of unemployment on the status of the man in his family. (Her term "discerning" is equivalent to the term "assessment" adopted in this Reader.) Hers is probably the most self-aware account available in the literature as to how an investigator decides on a causal imputation.

Selection (8) provides a systematic example of the statistical end result of an assessment procedure. Rossi selects a number of complaints people have about their previous place of abode. They all have moved. What is the causal role of these complaints in the respondents' decisions to change their residences? Because Rossi deals with several complaints, he has to have a standardized procedure to assess their impact relative to each other. It is interesting to compare this procedure with the one used in Selection (2). There Smith and Suchman use a rating scale in order to summarize all the diversified information they have about the impact of a radio program on a purchase. Rossi uses the combination of three specific questions for the same purpose. Selection (8) helps also to remind us of the difference between the general question "why"—which can hardly be given any meaning—and the very concrete, although still troublesome query of whether a specific factor played a causal role in a specific course of events.

D. *Other ways of tracing influences.* The specific procedures to which this section is devoted cover only a small sector of possible ways of tracing the role of various elements in an activity in progress. Lest the student be misled, at least two other approaches should be represented. One is much broader than the formal "analysis of action" and Selection (9) is a good example. Here, Dollard discusses the way a clinical psychologist takes into account the role which the broader community plays in the life history of individuals. Inversely, Selection (10) exemplifies a narrower topic than the one to which the preceding selections were devoted. During the war, it was desirable to trace the effect which indoctrination films had upon the attitudes of soldiers. Merton and Kendall report the techniques which were used in an effort to determine the reaction of audiences at the time they were exposed to motion pictures devised to convey the war goals of this country and its allies.

In using the selections of this section the teacher might want to make some further cross references to other sections. In I (E), the classification of "reasons" as obtained in questionnaires was discussed; in some of the examples, clear use was made of the accounting scheme idea. In II-A, the main theme was how to explain statistical relationships; the student should be able to distinguish clearly between that task and the task of explaining an individual performance. In II-C, we dealt with the analysis of deviant cases; there is an obvious similarity between the procedures exemplified there and the main topic of this section. The panel technique presented in III-B has for its purpose the explanation of change. The student should consider how the study of individual cases of change could be built into and used in panel studies. Within the present section most of the selections inevitably utilize several of the five steps we have just sketched. It is a useful exercise to identify in any of the concrete studies at which point any of these steps come into play. Finally, it should be remembered that simple actions are performed by us all the time. It is easy and useful to derive therefrom a class exercise. Each student might be asked, for instance, to write down in some detail all that he remembers about how he made up his mind when he went to the movies the last time. This material then can be used to go through all the steps of a complete action analysis, including the final statistical collation.

1. THE ANALYSIS OF CONSUMER ACTIONS

by Arthur Kornhauser and Paul F. Lazarsfeld

THE NEED FOR A SYSTEMATIC APPROACH

THE TECHNIQUES of research may be divided into two broad classes: we shall call them "master techniques" and "servant techniques." The master techniques are those used in planning and organizing research, in controlling it, in interpreting the findings. The servant techniques are employed in the actual operations of digging up facts and assembling them.

As one looks over the market research field the question arises whether the master techniques and the servant techniques have received their respective dues. It is our strong suspicion that attention has focussed disproportionately upon the servant techniques—upon the details of gathering and tabulating bits of information. Certainly these details are crucially important. The formulation of master techniques may prove even more important. The latter go far toward determining the nature of the servant techniques to be employed; they supply the standards for judging how well the subordinate tools are functioning; they provide the rational framework within which the research materials are given orientation and meaning.

There is little doubt what the servant techniques of market research include: procedures for constructing questionnaires, conducting interviews, choosing statistical samples, tabulating inquiries, extrapolating from trend curves, formulating buying power indexes, and so on. These matters have been extensively and ably discussed in a number of places. Certain special problems of these servant techniques we shall consider later. For the moment, however, we shall direct our attention to the master techniques.

First of all, what are they? The master techniques of the engineer are his mathematical and physical principles, his procedures for testing and experimentation, his professional engineering knowledge as a whole. The master techniques of the physician lie in the fields of physiology, bacteriology, and pathology. And what of the market researcher? What for him corresponds to the scientific equipment of the engineer or the doctor? Our answer—and we shall try to support it in the following pages—is knowledge of psychology —especially the psychological analysis of action.

We recognize fully the present limitations of psychological knowledge.

Reprinted from "The Techniques of Market Research from the Standpoint of a Psychologist," The Institute of Management Series, *Institute of Management 16* (1935), pp. 3-15, 19-21, by permission of the authors and the publisher. (Copyright, 1935, by the American Management Association, Inc.)

We are not able to offer it as an adequate answer to the market research man's prayers. All that we are suggesting is: first, that market research needs general, orienting, intellectual techniques, even more at the present time than it requires everyday digging tools; and second, that these larger techniques are supplied in considerable part, though not at all exclusively, by psychology. *We suggest simply that a systematic view of how people's market behavior is motivated, how buying decisions are arrived at, constitutes a valuable aid in finding one's way around midst the thousand and one questions of specific procedures and interpretations in market research.*

This need for a psychological view grows out of the very nature of market research. For that research is aimed predominantly at *knowledge by means of which to forecast and control consumer behavior.* It is a matter of ascertaining sales opportunities in order that these opportunities may be utilized and developed on the basis of the facts. Sales opportunities exist—or fail to exist—in people's minds. Hence the task is essentially psychological. It is a matter of gaining detailed understanding of specific human reactions.

There is, to be sure, another type of market research. It makes use of census data, descriptions of what people buy, and purely statistical predictions based on past buying. These methods assume that people will continue to buy as they have bought, or that they will continue to change in the directions in which they have been moving. The techniques of these statistical predictions lie mainly outside the scope of this paper, though, even in these studies, the collection of data and their classification frequently present problems that are psychologically challenging.

Most market research goes beyond purely statistical predictions. It seeks underlying explanations or interpretations. For guidance in these studies psychological master techniques appear indispensable. Systematic explanatory concepts should serve, here, to help market inquiries avoid fragmentary and distorted market pictures. They should encourage continuing research which goes beyond the first partial and trivial answers, too often accepted as though they were grand final conclusions.

Clearly the point of view here suggested is in sharp contrast to that which insists on the exclusive use of objective data; only the facts of buying behavior! But what does one do with the facts? How does one know what facts are worth gathering? How tell what further types of evidence to seek? How fit the picture together? How interpret? How put meaning into the material? Questions like these point unmistakably to the need that is here emphasized.

We turn, then, to consider what the psychologist can offer toward the filling of that need.

AN ACTION SCHEMA

What we offer is an analysis of action—an analysis of how the individual's market behavior is determined.

Any bit of action is determined on the one hand by the total make-up of the person at the moment, and on the other hand by the total situation in which he finds himself. This relationship is represented in Figure I. The action is a joint product of factors in the individual and factors in the situation. Explanations must always include both the objective and the subjective, and these are always in inseparable interrelationship. Hunger and available food are equally indispensable causes of eating. Likewise the advertisement which attracts one's attention and the subjective interest, attitude, or habit, which produces the attentive response.

THE INDIVIDUAL

MOTIVES

MECHANISMS

THE ACTION

THE SITUATION
THE PRODUCT
SALES
        INFLUENCES
OTHER
    INFLUENCES

Figure I

What a person *is* at any moment governs what he *does in the given circumstances*. What he "is," on the side of action possibility, comprises "motives" and "mechanisms." Hunger or a desire for a new red necktie are motives; the ability to walk, used in entering a restaurant, say, or the mental equipment used in reading an advertisement or in recalling one's lack of funds, are mechanisms. These mechanisms, it should be noticed, are not independent of the motives, but are directed by them. Motives and mechanisms are different aspects of the same total individual make-up which determines action at any moment.

By "motives" we mean to refer to the set of inner guiding processes which determine the movement of behavior toward ends or goals. The processes may be conscious or unconscious. They consist of some condition of tension or disequilibrium within the person, with the ensuing conduct serving to relieve the tension or to re-establish equilibrium. In mental terms this means that we have cravings, desires, wishes which, once they are aroused, insistently demand gratification.

The use of motives in explaining conduct is aided by having a working classification of these motives. Classifications have been offered by many psychologists, and while they differ among themselves, a considerable amount of agreement remains. Any reasonably carefully drawn list of motive categories is useful practically. It calls attention to the varied impulses that lead to a given type of action and thus indicates a range of possible explanations to be investigated. By thoughtfully running through the classification, one finds his mind directed to reasons for action which, although they had not occurred to him spontaneously, now appear well worth testing by the collection of further evidence.

We recall the surprise of a market research executive in the motor car field, for example, when he came upon the motive category, "desire to be alone." *He* had not felt this urge, and hence the thought that persons might want automobiles partly as a means of getting away from people, had never occurred to him. Similarly we have repeatedly observed how university students, even those quite mature, are aided in finding new explanations for people's buying as they do, and new appeals to be used, when they employ a systematic motive classification.

Our actual buying behavior is largely an expression of *specific attitudes,* that is action-tendencies toward particular objects, reflecting the varied directions of motivation as these have been molded in the courses of experience. One's negative attitude toward a certain store, for example, may be an expression of injured pride occasioned by a domineering salesman. The attitude, in turn, leads one to avoid the store, to criticize it, perhaps to praise the leading competitor, and to concentrate one's buying there. Business affairs are conducted in a world of these attitudes. They are the form in which motives immediately enter into people's conduct and speech. They directly determine market behavior. The attitudes that lead to buying hence lie at the very heart of market research problems.

But "mechanisms," too, play an important role. An analysis of action must include more than motives alone. The motives operate in a way that is determined by other structures and processes as well. All these other processes may be lumped together under the name "mechanisms." Thus one division of mechanisms comprises the sensory capacities which determine what we can and cannot see or hear or taste. The halitosis "psychosis," for example, is no more dependent upon the desire for cleanliness or fears for our social acceptability than upon the fact of olfactory adaptation which prevents our being aware of our own breath because of continued exposure to it. Motor or muscular capacities of all sorts, and intellectual powers and limitations, are further important mechanisms which settle the course of conduct. Suffice it, by way of illustration, to mention the strenuous efforts to adapt motor cars and household conveniences to the natural physical abilities of people; and the deep interest of the advertising profession in questions of literacy, memory, and intelligence levels of consumers. Under mechanisms, too, belongs all our knowledge—knowledge of products, brands, prices; knowledge of how to judge merchandise; knowledge of the number of dollars in our pocket and the number of creditors on our heels; knowledge of the consequences of our purchase; and so on indefinitely.

We may note, in passing, how clear the motive-mechanism classification makes the distinction, so often overlooked, between *familiarity* with a brand name (a matter of knowledge—a mechanism) and *attitude toward the brand* (a motive). Thus a recent inquiry into this relation revealed such discrepancies as the following: Toothpaste A, while most familiar to 16 per cent of the women tested (the brand they first thought of) received only 8 per cent of top rankings when these women expressed their attitudes toward the several brands. Toothpaste B, in contrast, was first thought of by only 5 per cent but was most favorably rated by 11 per cent. Similarly one brand of toilet soap had percentages of 12 and 26 for familiarity and preference respectively, while another had corresponding percentages of 23 and 15. It is, of course, necessary to go back of such figures to find their meaning and their significance for future sales of the products. But even these gross findings do illustrate clearly the importance of measuring *both* knowledge and attitudes—both mechanisms and motives.

So much for a first sketch of the factors in the *individual,* which explain action. A word, now, about the *situation.* People's buying is governed by the influences playing upon them from outside no less than it is by their inner dispositions. These external factors may be thought of as centering in the product itself, and spreading from that center to a vast range of other influences more and more remote. Next to the attributes of the product, the influences most significant for purchase are the selling methods, advertising, store, and generally, conditions surrounding the sale. Beyond these influences lies the whole world—though obviously certain parts of the world are more closely related to people's buying behavior than other parts, and hence are more valuable to investigate. To mention only one illustration, investigation of the part played by advice of friends is often of utmost importance.

In general, then, one proceeds in his analysis of any bit of action by analyzing those motives and mechanisms that appear significant, and also by studying the outside conditions which appear most clearly related to those inner dispositions. Explanations are found by working back and forth between individual dispositions and external influences. The behavior of the moment is always governed by both.

THE IMPORTANCE OF THE TIME-LINE

The preceding analysis of action deals only with the *immediate* explanatory factors, with the *present* determinants of buying behavior. But the actual purchase is the end-point of a long-continued process. Back of this final response lies the *history* of the desires and attitudes which now dominate conduct. The task becomes that of accounting for the familiarity with the product and for the specific desires that eventually lead to the purchase. In market research, these earlier preparatory stages are no less significant than the last. Useful analysis must cover the temporal course of the act, not merely a single cross-section.

Figure II offers a schematic representation of this developmental or biographic analysis of action. It calls attention to two essential facts: The first is that present action can be understood only by reference to what went before; the complete buying act must be seen in a sequence of stages along an extended time-line. The second point is that each stage in the growth of the readiness to buy is itself a bit of response determined jointly by the person as he *then* is and by the then existing influences. The relationship pictured in Figure I, in other words, repeats itself over and over again in the sequence constituting the complete action. At each successive stage along the time-line, however, we are dealing with a changed person, different by reason of what has occurred at preceding stages and also, of course, we have new influences that have come into operation to affect the on-going action.

In Figure II, we begin with the individual I_1, as he is, say, at the time he first has his attention called to X-toothpaste or Y-automobile. He is already an extremely complex combination of motives and mechanisms—a man with deep-seated desires and prejudices, stores of information and misinformation, specific, felt needs for having an up-to-date car, for saving money, and so on. In a particular situation S_1, now, this man encounters some influence, perhaps an advertising appeal, which stops him and elicits the response A_1.

His response is not an immediate purchase; it is a favorable feeling toward Y make of car or a belief that X dentrifice will protect his teeth. This A_1 response is always a joint effect of I_1 and S_1, and it leaves the individual a changed person. He is now no longer I_1 but he has become I_2, a person familiar with and favorably inclined toward X or Y.

This changed person I_2 some time later (it may be minutes or weeks) hears a friend comment enthusiastically about the product (S_2). This then is the second significant step: the I_2 and S_2 combination results in a further state of belief and acceptance. It is to be noted that the S_2 situation (friend's remarks) might have fallen on deaf ears if A_1 had not previously occurred. The sequence and interrelationship of occurrences along the time-line are crucially important.

The further altered person I_3 now encounters other influences. They may be akin to those already illustrated or it may be merely that the individual yields to a leisurely thought-encouraging situation S_3, where he deliberates about the new car or the dentifrice and definitely decides to buy (the decision is A_3). The final purchase occurs, then, when the person (now I_4) with an attitude of readiness to purchase (A_p) finds himself in a situation S_4 containing the precipitating influence to induce the purchase (I_{np}).

This longitudinal analysis of action may begin at stages near to, or remote

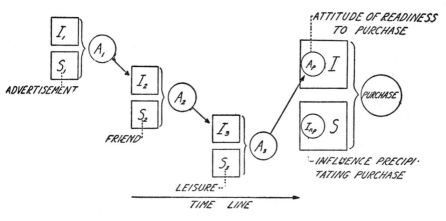

Figure II

from, the final purchase. Practically, it is wise to take as a starting point for inquiry the stage where the want and the means to its gratification are first clearly conscious. Sometimes, as in the above example, this means beginning with a particular advertising or sales influence; at other times, with the influence of friends or family, or an outsider's chance remark; in still other cases, the initial condition arises in the course of one's own observations and activities. Whatever the starting point, however, a complex background already exists in the make-up of the person—itself a summary of vast ranges of preceding experiences. It is necessary, consequently, to begin at the point chosen, with whatever understanding of the then-existent individual one may possess or discover, and to proceed by tracing the most significant steps leading from that point to the final buying act.

In dealing with the market behavior of people in general, or with large sections of the population, our understanding of the individuals whose buying acts are to be traced comes from our organized knowledge about human nature—knowledge of the motives and mechanisms earlier discussed. Beginning with this psychological background, the problem is to analyze the steps by which people move to the attitudes and buying responses in which the interest of a particular investigation centers. At each stage, the analysis corresponds to that described in the preceding section and represented in Figure I.

THE ROLE OF INTERPRETATION

The procedure to be followed under the proposed pattern of inquiry is guided by two additional principles. The first of these may be called the *principle of differential explanation.* It calls attention to the fact that a market research study is not interested in *complete* explanations, in accounting for *all* aspects of buying behavior. It is always a matter of explaining particular features of what people do, as contrasted with certain alternative possibilities. Otherwise the inquiry would be literally endless. The principle, then, stated most bluntly is: *Specify precisely what is to be explained for present practical purposes.* This will mean specifying why, in the course of action, this alternative occurs rather than that. With respect to even very simple buying behavior, a large number of *different* explanation-seeking questions can be asked. Much muddled work arises from failure to keep the several questions separate.

Thus in the simple matter of soap-buying, the inquiry may aim at learning any one or all the following things about *this* purchase (and there are still numerous other causal questions still unmentioned):

Beginning far back on the time-line, such questions as
    (a) Why the consumer buys soap at all
    (b) Why she likes soap of a particular color, odor, hardness, etc.
    (c) Why she believes all soaps are equally good
Somewhat nearer the purchase, and more concretely
    (d) Why she buys soap of the X-type and price
    (e) Why she buys X-soap specifically
    (f) Why she buys one cake instead of several
    (g) Why she buys at this particular time
    (h) Why she buys at this particular place
    (i) Why she buys as she does now (this month or this year) as contrasted with other months or years
    (j) Why *she* buys (i.e., why this kind of person rather than others, different as to sex, age, location, economic class, etc.)

If the investigation seeks explanations for several of these facts, it is none the less essential that they be definitely thought out separately, so that each portion of the inquiry will be clear about what it is trying to explain. If we are investigating the buying of Ford automobiles, one part of the study deals with reasons for purchasing low-priced cars; a quite different set of questions and tabulations is needed to ascertain why people buy Fords instead of Chevrolets; still other lines of inquiry must be pursued if we wish to learn why Fords are bought in preference to used cars, or why *any* car is bought, or why the Fords are bought at the times and places they are. Research results which seek to explain buying actions without clear specification of what part or aspect of the action is to be explained are foredoomed to confusion. If the "why" questions are to be clear, one must see the varied alternatives to the behavior studied; the specific alternative actions must be held in mind in planning the study. This is the first of the two guiding principles.

The other principle has to do with *the use of tentative interpretations.* It stresses the role of hypotheses, suggested explanations, psychological theories and bits of psychological insight in guiding market investigations. Explanations are never mere tabulations of observations; we never get useful explanations merely by "collecting the facts." Interpretations are indispensable in addition—interpretations in terms of the motives and the mental mechanisms which determine conduct in given situations. The practical spadework of market inquiry and analysis must be preceded and guided by hypotheses, by understanding of *probable* explanations of the specific features of conduct in question. The second principle, then, may be epitomized to read: *Use tentative interpretations in planning the inquiry and let the collection and analysis of data aim at checking upon and modifying these preliminary views.*

The interpretations are attempts at psychological understanding; they seek to find the *meaning* of the facts collected. Two broad classes of interpretations may be distinguished. The first is concerned with the dynamics of action, with explaining the causal sequences in buying behavior. This sort of interpretation falls into the pattern already sketched, but it requires detailed and specific applications within that general framework. The second type of interpretation attempts to account for similarities and differences in behavior among groups, and to understand the factors related to these similarities and differences. The nature of both classes of interpretation and their interconnection may be seen from a few illustrations.

The various categories in a classification of motives provide valuable, though too general, interpretations of the first class. These are supplemented by the more revealing interpretations having to do with specific attitudes and with the unconscious and indirect operation of hidden motivations. The motivation hypotheses range from the most ordinary to the most subtle and unusual. Research into the purchase of a particular brand of soap may be guided in part by simple notions that the soap is bought because of people's preference for its odor, shape, or price. One may inquire, too, how far purchases are affected by women's belief that the soap either injures or improves their health, beauty, or social acceptability. Less obviously, it may be that the soap is regarded as especially "masculine" or "feminine"; or it may carry vague memories of hospitals and sick-rooms; or its name may arouse half-conscious national loyalties or antipathies.

In addition to interpretations which turn upon features of motivation, there are others which have to do primarily with "mechanisms"—though the two are always intertwined. For example, one may wisely guess, on the basis of psychological knowledge, that an advertising campaign is pitched at too high an intellectual level, that a peculiarly shaped bottle is too inconvenient to handle or a carton too difficult to open. A psychologist using the type of procedure here suggested would almost certainly have seen the *problem* of opening cigarette packages wrapped in cellophane—*before* the package was on the market.

All such suggestions of course are *hypotheses;* they are guesses to be checked upon. Evidence is collected to show the truth or falsity of each.

But unless one has these—and many additional—possible interpretations in mind, there is little likelihood that he will discover significant evidence at all. The more plausible and comprehensive the preliminary interpretations, the greater the probability of arriving at a sound, practically useful, understanding of the buying in question.

The other type of interpretation centers in statistical tabulations and comparisons. The aim is still to understand the actions of people in the market, but often it is necessary to divide the people into groups according to age, sex, buying power, intelligence, personality peculiarities, or what not, in order to reach a sound interpretation of the buying behavior under investigation. Frequently, too, the buying is associated with other observable facts; it occurs among people in certain localities, at certain seasons, after exposure to certain types of advertising, after previous use of the same product, and so on. Hence the market investigator requires guiding interpretations with respect to kinds of people and the measurable characteristics related to their conduct quite as much as he needs interpretations of the first type.

A first illustration pertains to age in relation to milk-drinking among adults. Tentative interpretations suggested that habit differences between different age groups and between groups differing in education might well cause differences in milk consumption. A simple analysis showed that remarkable differences do exist in milk consumption between groups with different levels of schooling. Among college educated people, more than 70 per cent drink milk; among people who have attended only grade school, less than 50 per cent; high school graduates lie in between. In another part of the study it was shown that milk consumption decreases markedly with age. However, and this is the significant use of interpretation in the case, there is in America today a clear correlation between age and education among adults. Amount of schooling has rapidly increased during recent decades. Hence, when the persons interviewed are divided into age groups, the younger ones will have the better schooling; conversely, if the sample is grouped according to schooling, the better educated are younger on the average. Hence an adequate interpretation demanded a further analysis of age and schooling to see which was primary. It turned out that the apparent influence of education was completely accounted for by the age difference. A special check made sure that it was really the age and not the educational difference which mattered. In a selected sub-sample with constant average age for all three educational groups, the educational differences in milk consumption disappeared.

Another illustration of statistical interpretation may be taken from the same study. It was found that persons who had been forced by their parents to drink milk against their will are more frequent among non-drinkers than among milk drinkers. The off-hand interpretation might be that coercion in childhood leads to distaste for milk as adults. But the alternative hypothesis is equally plausible, that since all parents believe in milk drinking, those whose children dislike it have to force them to drink it. Additional information is needed in this instance before one or another interpretation can be accepted. One might seek evidence, for example, concerning children who disliked milk but who were not coerced into drinking it or who were influenced by more subtle methods; likewise cases of children who liked milk but who were coerced to drink more.

At all events, whatever the limitations in a particular instance like this last, the necessity is constantly present to find meaning in the results as far as feasible, and to see where further data are needed. Giving "merely the facts" usually means giving an assortment of observations, more or less relevant as the case may be, together with trivial, vague, or incorrect interpretations instead of sound ones, which have been critically considered and based on careful psychological analysis.

The essential outlines of a "master technique" have now been sketched. The collection of market research data and the analysis of results are to be carried on within the broad framework provided by a psychological analysis of action. Within that framework it is further necessary that the inquiry be directed to specific limited aspects of the action—the choice to be dictated by the practical purposes that are paramount. The particular points of action to be investigated are most clearly defined by seeing *with what alternatives* they may be contrasted. The search is for causes why people act *this* way and in response to *this* type of influence rather than in *different* ways and in response to *different* influences. The research into these differential explanatory factors within the whole pattern of action is, finally, directed by tentative interpretations; it aims to collect evidence which will suggest more definite and specific psychological hypotheses about the phases of activity in question and which will then support or deny the validity of these interpretations.

The actual collection of information presents no end of additional problems of technique, even when the investigation is directed by the above guide-posts. The problems are ones of detail—albeit most important detail. Questionnaire and interview procedures, methods of direct observation, experimentation, attitude rating devices—all are utilized in the spade-work of research. The "master techniques" tell *where* to dig and what to dig *for;* they do not prescribe the exact tools or digging methods.

Here let it be stressed, however, that in whatever specific ways the evidence is secured, the investigator always has the problem of seeing the picture *whole.* Only thus can he know what parts or aspects of the market behavior deserve attention and what parts may be omitted. In planning the research, it is his job to canvass the entire range of external influences and of dispositions in people that may plausibly appear to play a significant part in the activity studied. Singly and separately, the various motives, mechanisms, and external influences to be weighed are obvious enough. But it is the open-minded, comprehensive, attention to *all* of them that is easily neglected. A psychological approach stresses the appreciation of the complete picture, where each separate influence can be assigned its proper place. The psychological analysis guards against over-simple, misleading emphasis on this or that factor, and against the neglect of other factors which may prove more important.

We can imagine that by this time the reader is saying to himself: Nonsense! The plan is far too elaborate. We can't ask the consumer to give us his life history in order to find out why he buys soap. We can't ask him a hundred questions. The answer is: You don't need to. We assume you will not. Then *why,* you ask impatiently, all this talk about what should be covered? And the answer is: The explorer must know far more of the country than the spot where he pitches his tent. You may survey tentatively scores and scores of points that might be inquired into—and you may end with an interview schedule of five questions. But those five questions will be vastly different from the ordinary ones. You will have explored and decided the *best* spot to pitch camp; not guessed. You will have determined what is worth asking and to what questions it is reasonable to expect usable answers. By analyzing the *whole* act, one sees what part is significant for his present purpose. He has a map by means of which to locate his present position. Only thus can he judge the meaning of his observations—and decide upon practical next steps.

SOME SPECIFIC APPLICATIONS

The next problem to which we wish to apply our theoretical approach has to do with the statistical analysis of interview and questionnaire responses. This field has been much neglected in theoretical discussions, in spite of its great practical importance. With any interview questions other than the simplest and most formal, a great variety of answers will be received. We take, for example, 200 questionnaires which contain the question, "What are the essential features of good oil?" and we find that 167 different comments are recorded. These comments have a certain direct value for the copy writer; he is to a certain degree justified in assuming that the language in which the consumers speak will be the language in which they can most easily be spoken to. But when it comes to drawing general conclusions from these varied answers, the necessity arises for grouping them. This involves the process of coding.

We shall not take time to deal with the astonishing mistakes in coding which occur in many studies. To cite only one illustration: The class *"bought for a member of the family"* is made to include, in one study, both the food asked for by the father and the food the mother judged might be good for the baby. The market significance of the cases is altogether different, though both are covered by the word "for." Many such examples could be given. But even leaving aside actual mistakes, we all have seen tables containing long lists of words with following frequency figures, with which no one really knows what to do. The psychologist has this advice to give: Group the data in such a way that they reflect the structure of the concrete act of purchase to which they pertain, and thus prepare them for the final job of interpretation.

Let us take as a first example the oil questionnaire mentioned above. In going through the comments we find such words as, "clear color," "not too thin," and others like "should be durable," "won't carbonize." These words can at once be referred, in our chart of the buying act, to the two groups of factors—motives and mechanisms. Apparently the second group of words like "should be durable" pertain to what we want the oil to do for us; the first group pertains to how we recognize its qualities. The *effects* of the oil correspond to our purposes or motives; the *features* of the oil correspond to our ways of judging its suitability. It is found that 75 per cent of the answers refer to effects, 25 per cent to features. Now we take the answers of the same 200 people given to the same question but pertaining to gasoline. Here 90 per cent speak about effects and 10 per cent about features. Thus we at once detect an interesting difference in the way people buy oil and gasoline though further data are needed for a detailed interpretation.

Before attempting a more general formulation we give another example. Women are asked why they bought their last dress in the store they did. Some say, "because the merchandise is good there," or "because I had agreeable experiences with the salesgirls"; others refer to an "advertisement," to "convenient location," or to "a special sale." Again we are reminded of a distinction in our basic scheme—the division of the situation into influences arising from the product (in this case the store) and other influences. We now group the reasons, according to that distinction, into "characteristics of the store" and "additional influences." The fact that, among 700 women, 41 per cent give responses of the first class and 59 per cent give responses of the second class is not yet important. But now we select two groups of 200 women each who patronize two different stores and find the following differences:

	Characteristics of the Store	Additional Influences
Store B	39	61
Store C	60	40

Here our grouping reveals a very significant difference in the standing of these two stores. Store "C" stands apparently much more on its direct merits than does Store "B."

A final example leads us to the most fundamental distinction we have made in our scheme. Women are asked what made them decide to send their laundry out of the house instead of washing it at home as they had done in the past. Typical answers are, "the baby was ill," "unexpected guests came," "wanted to have more time for myself." We realize that the last answer is of the character of a motive, the first two of the character of influences, in the sense of our chart. Altogether we find in this study 81 per cent of influences and 19 per cent of motives mentioned as answers to the question regarding the decision to send the laundry out. Therewith the ground is laid for a tentative interpretation to the effect that this special group of women is still reconciled to the idea of doing laundry at home, and that it requires unusual situations to cause them to change the habit.

Now a more general formulation can be made of the consequences of our analysis of action for the statistical handling of responses. *It seems to be advisable to group answers parallel to the general structure of the act.* The main distinctions given in our charts can be followed in such a grouping: individual dispositions versus influences (the laundry case), motives versus mechanisms (the oil case), the product versus other influences (the stores). By such a grouping we prepare the way for interpretations since the results are thus formulated in terms of the action which the study aims to understand as a basis for later control of that action.

We shall call this entire proceeding "complementary grouping." Complementary grouping means, then, to combine a great number of comments into a few groups corresponding to the main elements of the "act of purchase" in our chart. Our material might pertain to a general decision, as for instance, the laundry example did. It might pertain to the selection of a special outfit, as in the department store example. These two examples would be located on very different parts of our "time line"—the general decision much earlier than the special selection of an outfit. But, even for two such different phases of a purchase we use the same scheme of joint determination by individual and situation, and the main elements we have singled out therein.

In addition to the *complementary grouping* there is another which we shall call the *supplementary grouping*. This grouping pertains to subdivisions within some one heading in our analysis of the purchase. The sales influences, for instance, might be grouped into "newspaper advertisement," "magazine advertisement," etc. The specific motives which the gasoline has to satisfy might be grouped into "desire for quick pick-up," "desire for long mileage, (i.e., economy)," etc. Many criticisms against the statistical treatment of consumers' comments are connected with confusions of complementary and supplementary groupings. The supplementary groupings are only sensible as partial breakdowns of the main complementary groups.

The results which appear in supplementary groups can apparently be used immediately; we can derive from them, with the usual caution necessary in all use of statistical results, the relative importance of different media, the relative importance of different appeals, and so on. The complementary groupings cannot be used so directly, because we always have to take into account that they result from different interpretations our respondents gave to our questions. The complementary groups are valuable, however, in such directions as indicating how explicitly (a) features of the product, and (b) sales influences, have been recognized by consumers, and how influential each of these has been; how far the buying is impulsive or emotionally motivated rather than being careful, deliberate, and informed; how far the buying occurs as a natural expression of desires and how far it is due to special causes in the external situation. Both forms of grouping are useful; it is only their confusion that is disastrous.

2. DO PEOPLE KNOW WHY THEY BUY?

by Elias Smith and Edward A. Suchman

THE STANDARD WAY of showing the influence of radio upon people's buying habits consists in presenting a four-fold table which divides the sample into listeners and non-listeners on the one hand, and buyers and non-buyers on the other hand.[1] For instance, in a telephone survey made in March 1938 in Syracuse, New York, people were called up during the time Boake Carter (who was then advertising Philco radios) was on the air, and asked for the program to which they were listening at the moment of the call, and also the make of radio they owned.[2] The following four-fold table

Reprinted from the *Journal of Applied Psychology*, Vol. XXIV, pp. 673-684, by permission of the authors and the publisher. (Copyright, 1940, by the American Psychological Association, Inc.)

Table 1—Relation between Owning a Certain Brand of Radio Set and Listening to a Program which Advertises It

LISTENED TO BOAKE CARTER	OWNED A PHILCO RADIO Yes	OWNED A PHILCO RADIO No	Total
Yes	104	130	234
No	208	322	530
Total	312	452	764

resulted. The tetrachoric correlation of this table is .1. This shows a slightly positive relationship, indicating that people who listen to Boake Carter are more likely to own a Philco radio.

There are a number of practical and theoretical objections to be raised to such a table. Practically, the collection of the information necessary to compile such a table is quite expensive, especially if the survey is not restricted to telephone homes. Theoretically, one is free to challenge the causal interpretation of such a table: it might be either that people listen to Boake Carter because they own a Philco (and not the other way around), or that there is a spurious factor involved, for example, that wealthier people are more likely to own a Philco and also to listen to Boake Carter.[3]

Obviously, it would be a great improvement upon this type of a survey to ask those people who both own a Philco and listen to Boake Carter directly whether the commentator influenced them in their purchase of a radio set, provided that the information so obtained is valid. The problem stated in this generality is of momentous importance because it implies the whole question of the validity to be attached to people's explanations of their actions. It will take years of coordinated research to give a final answer, and even then it would have to be conditional upon many qualifications such as, for example, the nature of the product being investigated, the time of the interview, etc. The experiment to be reported here purports to formulate the problem of this direct interview more clearly and to show that its investigation is not so hopeless as may often be thought.

The purpose of the investigation, then, is to find out, from a number of people who own Philco radios and listen to Boake Carter, the proportion who can be considered to have bought their radio because they listen to the program. We shall attempt to show how, through the use of these personal interviews, it is possible to approach the same result concerning the effectiveness of the Boake Carter advertising arrived at from the extensive telephone survey given in Table I.[4]

The task divides itself into three steps: 1) getting all possible relevant information on each individual purchase; 2) formulating clearly what is meant by the phrase, "A person buys because . . ."; 3) looking for a criterion of validity for the final result.

HOW CAN WE OBTAIN THE NEEDED INFORMATION?

In order to get a maximum of useful information, a specific kind of questionnaire must be developed. This sort of questionnaire has been described elsewhere in its more detailed aspects.[5] Here only a brief topical summary of the elaborate form developed in this study is given. The main idea is that there are different types of purchasers and the task of the interview consists in first ascertaining to which type the specific respondent belongs and then asking him those questions most closely adapted to his type. The main distinction to be made is whether the respondent knew beforehand that he wanted a Philco or whether he decided on the brand only at the time of actually purchasing the radio set.

In the first case the main problem is whether the program has influenced his choice of brand from the start. Sometimes in beginning the interview with the question, "Why did you buy this brand?" certain respondents immediately refer to the advertising. It is more likely, however, that they will refer to certain advantages of this brand, in which case the interviewer must follow up with the question, "Where did you learn about those things?" At this point some will refer to the radio plug, but others will mention friends or other influences; then, to make certain that no possibility is overlooked, this question must be added: "Do you remember having read or heard anything else about the Philco radio?" (If Yes) "What was it about? Where did you see or hear it?" At this point we shall have learned about everything a respondent of this particular type is able to tell us.

In dealing with people whose choice of brand was not determined before the purchase but developed as they shopped around, the adequate process of interviewing is somewhat different. These respondents are likely to tell the interviewer about salespeople who influenced them, or about how impressed they were by the Philco they saw in a store. To make certain that no possible influence of Boake Carter's advertising has been overlooked, the task of the questionnaire now is to ascertain very concretely every phase of this shopping process and to ask at each point whether any preliminary knowledge of Philco's quality was remembered at the time the decision was made. (For example, "When the salesgirl showed you the Philco, was it the first time you had heard about it, or had you known about the brand before? If so, from what source did you learn about it?" etc.)

There are always specific situations to which the attention of the interviewer has to be drawn by the questionnaire. For instance, it is important to ascertain whether the respondent has established in his mind a range of eligible makes which he takes for granted, *e.g.,* that he would choose only a nationally known brand. If so, it is important to find out whether previous advertising has contributed to putting Philco into this eligibility range, even though the respondent may not have mentioned it specifically when reporting the purchase.

The main idea of such a questionnaire, then, is to visualize the primary psychological types of purchasers, to anticipate for each the role which the advertising under investigation *can play,* and then to ask for each type those questions which are most likely to bring out the role it actually did play. After having first spoken about the purchase and traced its possible determinants, we then turn around and review the whole situation once more by starting from the advertising itself. A series of questions is asked starting from the more general and becoming more and more specific so that no preceding answer can pre-judge the next.

"Can you recall ever seeing or hearing an advertisement for Philco before making the final purchase?" If yes, more detailed information is asked: if no, we proceed:—

"Have you ever heard any Philco advertising over the radio?" If yes, details are asked: if no, we proceed:—

"Did you ever listen to Boake Carter? Do you know what product he advertises?"

As a third approach, we try throughout the interview to learn what weight the respondent himself gives to the different factors mentioned. At several points the question is inserted: "What influence would you say this (factor just mentioned) has had upon your purchase?" At the end of the interview a question is added which tries to summarize the impression which the respondent has given of the total cause of his purchase as far as the role of the radio program is concerned.

As a result of each such interview—which, incidentally, is not unpleasant for the respondent and does not take very long—we have a great amount of structuralized information on the purchase; and although the respondent might have forgotten or "repressed" a great deal, at least all the screens which are so frequently due to misunderstandings have been eliminated and all the respondent himself can possibly know about the cause for his purchase has been brought to light.

WHAT IS TO BECOME OF THE INFORMATION THUS COLLECTED?

We are interested in knowing how many Philco owners have been influenced by Boake Carter to buy their radio set. We call "influenced" any person who otherwise would not have bought a Philco. If it were technically possible, an experiment should be set up dividing people at random into two groups: the one group should be made to listen to the program and the other to refrain from listening. How many more Philco sets would be found in the former group after a certain period of time? This experiment, of course, is technically impossible. To what extent, then, can the information collected by our interview procedure be substituted for the experiment?

In order to answer the above question it is necessary to be able to analyze each of the questionnaires in great detail for any influence Boake Carter may have had. The problem to be solved in relation to the interview technique, then, is "How do we know when Boake Carter was the determining factor in the purchase?" While it is always very difficult to decide "yes" or "no" as to this influence for a single case, it is quite another matter to be able to decide for two cases whether the one case is more or less influenced than the other. In other words, it is not an impossible task to establish a continuum upon which all the cases are ranked from decreasing to increasing Boake Carter influence. This continuum in turn may arbitrarily be broken into any number of groups, depending upon how sharply we wish to distinguish one group from another.

As people tell us about their experiences in buying their radios, this continuum seems to fall most naturally into four groups, graded according to the degree of influence of the program.

Grade 1: People who remember only after being prompted that they heard about Philco on the Boake Carter program. Their report clearly shows some other factor to be the outstanding influence, and we can find no relation between the program and their choice of brand. In most cases, the Philco was not decided upon until the actual purchase was made.

Grade 2: Boake Carter is mentioned by the respondent as a source of information in the early parts of the interview; he feels that the program may have influenced him somewhat, but is sure that he would have bought a Philco even if he had not listened to the program. The presence of other factors contributing to the purchase is brought out clearly in the interview.

Grade 3: Here the program is mentioned immediately as a source of information and definitely as an influence; but there are other factors which seem equally important, and no decision as to the main influence is possible. The respondent himself feels that even without Boake Carter, he might have purchased a Philco radio. While the importance of Boake Carter is felt, it is not decisive.

Grade 4: The importance of Boake Carter is acknowledged almost as soon as the interview opens—usually spontaneously. The program is mentioned as the main reason for buying a Philco; no other factor is mentioned as decisive and the respondent states that he would not have bought a Philco if it had not been for Boake Carter.

In relation to our problem of deciding when we can attribute the purchase to Boake Carter, we see that the real difficulty comes in determining where to draw the line between Grade 3 and Grade 4. The main distinguishing characteristic between the two grades lies in their answers to the question, "Would you have bought a Philco were it not for Boake Carter?" In order to be classified as Grade 4, a respondent would have to answer "No" to this question. Let us examine comparative accounts of two respondents, one of whom falls into Grade 3 and the other into Grade 4.

GRADE 3	GRADE 4
History of Purchase	
Respondent was dissatisfied with old radio and wished to get a more up-to-date model. Knew about Philco through Boake Carter program but inquired among friends as to how satisfied they were with their radios. At the time of the purchase itself, they were convinced that Philco was the best buy, and went to the store intending to buy one. Their knowledge of Philco is rather limited and comes from Boake Carter and their friends. They listen to Boake Carter regularly and had been doing so for one year before making the purchase.	Respondent could not remember exactly why purchase was made at that time, stating that he just needed a new radio. When they went to make the purchase they had definite intentions of buying a Philco. They had heard about Philco from friends, through newspaper advertisements, and through Boake Carter. They definitely knew that it was the kind of radio they wanted, knew it to have a good tone and to be a well-constructed machine. Their knowledge of Philco was quite definite, mainly because of Boake Carter. They listened to him five times a week and had been listening to him for three years before purchasing the Philco.
Analysis of All Factors	
Recommendation by friends and knowledge of Philco through Boake Carter were the two influences present in this case. Boake Carter aroused the interest in Philco and led to further investigation. The recommendation by friends confirmed Boake Carter's advertising and led to the purchase.	Three possible influences can be detected: the friends' recommendation, newspaper advertisements, and Boake Carter. The goodwill towards Philco is apparent throughout the interview and is due probably to all three of the above factors. However it is also apparent from the respondent's own statement that this good-will was due mainly to Boake Carter. The following statement shows this clearly: "My attention was first called to Philco through Boake Carter's program and I got to thinking that Philco must be a pretty good buy. Boake Carter has a good program and is an expert commentator. I don't think he would advertise a product that wasn't excellent or work for a company that wasn't completely reliable."
Determination of Main Influence	
The fact that the respondent sought confirmation of Boake Carter's statement shows that although this influence was present and important, it was not the determining one. Were it not for favorable reports from various friends, the respondent would probably not have bought a Philco. While both factors are of great importance, the determining factor seems to be "recommendation."	This statement by the respondent indicates clearly the main influence. In conclusion, the respondent states that were it not for Boake Carter he probably would not have bought a Philco.

From the above comparison it can be seen how we can place one respondent higher on the scale of Boake Carter influence than the other. While the decision that one is definitely a Boake Carter influence and the other is not must be arbitrary, we feel that if we were to limit the Boake Carter influence to Grade 4 only, we would be getting at those people who really "would not have bought a Philco without Boake Carter advertising it."

In regard to all four grades, a careful analysis of all the cases resulted in the following distribution:

Table 2—Degree of Influence of Boake Carter's Program On 155 Purchases of Philco Radio Sets

Degree	Proportion of Cases
1 (lowest)	48%
2	20
3	13
4 (highest)	19
Total per cent	100
Total number of cases	155

It is the cases of influence-degree No. 4 which seem to correspond to what we would call colloquially, purchases caused by Boake Carter's advertising. We are therefore inclined to state that of these 155 cases, 19 per cent were induced by radio advertising to buy a Philco set. This means that, to the best of our general psychological knowledge, we feel that this proportion of respondents would not have bought a Philco if it had not been for Boake Carter's program.

Practically, the figure is of great importance as soon as we add two other items of information available from the records of most advertisers. If the approximate size of the audience to a program and the number of Philco owners in the total population is known, it is possible to calculate whether the particular advertisement is paying its way in view of the knowledge that 19 per cent of this audience would not buy the product were it not for the program. Restricting ourselves here to the psychological aspect of the problem, we do not enter into the somewhat intricate statistical considerations which are suggested by this last remark.

HOW CAN THE RESULT BE TESTED FOR VALIDITY?

There is one relatively simple way of doing this. It consists in using several judges for the classification of the interviews. Two additional judges were made thoroughly familiar with the criteria we used to ascertain the highest degree of influence, and then were asked to classify the cases in their own way. One ended up with 21 per cent of the purchases induced by the program and the other with 18 per cent. These figures do not deviate too much from the 19 per cent found by the first judge.

But it can be objected that this is only an agreement on bias because all three judges proceeded on the same basis of a common sense analysis. It would be highly desirable to find more objective tests which could be applied to determine validity in such cases.

The best type of check would be a tie-in with one of the major advertising tests being made from time to time by business agencies. Two test cities are usually selected, in only one of which an advertising campaign is put on. Then the sales are observed and if they rise in the city covered by the campaign the advertising is considered promising. It would be highly desirable to interview those people in the campaign city who bought the product and ask them why they bought it. The number of people who, on the basis of interviews such as the one discussed in this paper are finally considered to have been influenced by the program, should be equal to the difference in customers between the campaign city and the control city.

As a substitute for such a procedure we used a situation which offered itself through a lucky coincidence. In the Spring of 1938 the change from standard to daylight time forced a change of time in the Boake Carter program which we were studying. The commentator came on an hour and a quarter earlier than he had been broadcasting previously. When another telephone survey was made two weeks after the change in time, the correlation between Philco ownership and Boake Carter listening was higher. In a four-fold tabulation of 773 cases parallel to the one given at the beginning of this paper, the tetrachoric correlation between Philco ownership and Boake Carter listening was .3 whereas it was .1 just two weeks previous to the change of time.[6] There were, then, two samples of people who showed to varying degrees an objective association between two characteristics. If our interviews and the classification based upon them were valid, then in the second sample more people should report that they were induced by Boake Carter to buy a Philco.[7]

And indeed it turned out that according to our interviews 15 per cent of the first group were classified as "buying because of Boake Carter" and 23 per cent of the second group.[8]

We have here, then (for the first time as far as we know), an objective test of the validity of direct interviews intended to ascertain the influence of a specific series of advertisements upon the buying habits of people. The objective test and the results of the interviews corroborate one another.

SUMMARY

Two samples were available, each of which could be arranged in a four-fold tabulation indicating the correlation between listening to a commentator program and owning the make of radio set which this program advertised. The tetrachoric correlation in the one sample was .1 and in the second sample, .3. In each sample the people who listen to the program and own the advertised brand were interviewed as to how they came to buy their radio sets. The answers were classified into four degrees of sales influence which could be attributed to the commentator. Degree 1 indicated no influence at all, whereas degree 4 was given to those cases where three judges agreed that this special make of radio would not have been bought were it not for the influence of the program. The purchasers of influence degree 4 could therefore be considered those who, we would say colloquially, bought their sets because of the commentator's influence.

The main purpose of the study was to see whether the statistical result of such judgments would be corroborated by the objective correlation between ownership and listening. Therefore, after the classification of our cases into influence grades was made, the cases were divided into those coming from the first sample and those from the second sample. In the sample having the correlation .1, we found 15 per cent who had "bought because of the radio program," whereas in the sample with the .3 correlation, we found 23 per cent of these cases. This result was taken as one piece of evidence that by appropriate direct interviews we can measure the selling influence of a radio program, if by this influence we understand the difference in sales between a group which is and a group which is not exposed to this program.

3. EVALUATING THE EFFECTIVENESS OF ADVERTISING BY DIRECT INTERVIEWS

by Paul F. Lazarsfeld

THERE HAS BEEN much discussion among psychologists about whether there is any point in asking people why they buy, or why they do certain other things with which a market research study might be concerned. The problem in all its generality cannot be treated in a short article. One aspect of it has had special prominence in market studies which attempt to test the effect of advertising. Is there any chance, by means of direct interviews, of evaluating the role played by advertising in a specific group of purchases? This paper is restricted to this aspect of the problem and to a clarification of the following questions involved:

1. What does it mean to speak of advertising as having played a role in a certain purchase?
2. What kind of interviewing technique is likely to bring out pertinent information?
3. What meaning does a statistical analysis of such reasons have?
4. How can results in this field be verified?

What does a "reason for buying" mean?—The meaning of the word, "reason," is notoriously vague; it proves helpful just as with most other concepts having a causal connotation, to link it up with the idea of a controlled experiment. Let us assume that we are dealing with a group of people who have been divided into two groups by a completely random procedure, so that no single characteristic will give any individual more of a chance of belonging to one, rather than to the other group. Next, one of these two groups is exposed to certain advertising, but the other is not. Then, after some time has passed, if the exposed group buys more of the advertised product than the unexposed group, we can say that the advertisement has caused increased sales. This, of

Reprinted from the *Journal of Consulting Psychology*, Vol. V, 1941, pp. 170-178, by permission of the author and the publisher. (Copyright, 1941, by the American Psychological Association, Inc.)

course, is a definition, and other students may prefer to use other starting points for this kind of discussion. As long as we do not deviate from this definition through the discussion, however, it will not be difficult to relate other approaches. It should be kept in mind that we are dealing with two groups which have been made comparable by random selection and subsequent exposure; this is quite different from comparing two groups who have or have not been exposed to advertising by their own choice.

The simplest scheme for presenting the relationship between exposure and effect is the fourfold table. Table I gives a schematic example of this

Table I—Relationship between Exposure and Effect in Advertising

	Bought	Did Not Buy Product	Total
Mail was sent	500	500	1000
Mail was not sent	250	750	1000
Total	750	1250	2000

kind of designed experiment, assuming that 2,000 people have been divided at random into two groups of 1,000 each; and that one of these groups has been sent a mailed advertisement, while the other has not. If after some time it is found that 500 members of the exposed group now own the product advertised by this mailed circular and only 250 members of the unexposed group have bought it, the mailed advertisement can be considered the cause of the difference in the purchases of the product between the two groups.[1]

Such an effect can be measured with all the various coefficients which have been developed to gauge the correlation of a fourfold table.[2] All these measurements go back to one simple idea. If the exposure being studied had not had any effect, then the exposed and the unexposed people would have made the same number of purchases. Of the group unexposed to the advertising, 25 per cent bought the product. Twenty-five per cent of the exposed group could then also have been expected to buy the product without the instigation of the advertisement. But actually 50 per cent of the exposed group did so. The 25 per cent difference, therefore, can be attributed to the advertising. To speak of persons, not per cents, it can then be said that 250 of the exposed group who bought the product would have bought it anyway. The other 250 bought it "because" of the advertising campaign. From now on these 250 cases will be referred to as "*b*-cases." The 25 per cent buying difference between the exposed and the unexposed group will be used as a measure of the effect, F, of this special campaign.

Still referring to this imaginary example, we originate the psychological problem if we ask the following question: *By means of direct interviews, is it possible to single out these 250 b-cases?* So far we know only that among those people who were exposed and bought the product, there are these 250 *b*-cases. But, from the statistical analysis, we cannot say whether it was Mrs. Smith or Mr. Jones who belongs in this group. Would they be able to tell us? As far as we can see, this is the only way to formulate the problem of whether people know why they buy: If a controlled experiment, of the kind described above, were made, would we be able to single out, by means of appropriate interviews, these 250 *b*-cases which we find by statistical cross-analysis?

The question can be put in still another form, by giving the number of *b*-cases a slightly different interpretation. The correlation between exposure to the mailed advertisement and buying is by no means perfect. As a matter of fact, in practical work, even if it is at all significantly above zero, we should consider the campaign quite successful. The correlation is not high because it does not make much difference to the buying habits of most of the people whether or not they receive the advertisement. On the other hand, for a few people, it makes all the difference in the world. They would not have bought this merchandise if the advertisement had not reached them. Theoretically speaking, then, the people we are studying were of two kinds. Some find themselves in such situations, or in such moods, or have such personal characteristics, that there is a correlation of $+1$ between their buying and their exposure to our advertising campaign. For the rest of them the correlation is zero, indicating that they would or would not have bought, regardless of their exposure. It could be shown algebraically, but it is obvious even by meditating about the matter, that the number of *b*-cases is simply the number of people in our exposed groups who have those characteristics pertinent to a correlation of $+1$ between exposure and action.

However one looks at it, then, the question of whether a certain advertisement was a reason for a person's buying a commodity is equivalent to a question such as this: When the person was exposed to this influence, was the situation such that without this exposure he would not have bought the article, whereas since he was exposed his buying necessarily followed according to all the "rules of psychology" we were able to apply to this case?

Interviewing techniques to detect the role of advertising. Certain interviewing techniques can be derived as necessary from the preceding analysis. According to it, the art of asking why consists in getting enough information about the situation in which the respondent was exposed to advertising so that a reasonable estimate can be made of whether or not he would have bought the advertised product even if he had not been exposed. We put ourselves, so to speak, back to the time of the exposure, and try to forecast in each single case what would have happened. This point of view allows a scrutiny of the actual information to determine whether it is complete enough to permit such a prediction.

A friend comes to visit me late at night, and when asked why he has come, he answers, because he "feels lonely." Putting ourselves in his situation at home when he felt lonely, we see immediately that from that point we could not have predicted his visit to me if we did not have any further information of this sort: Does he have other friends as well? If so, why is the visit to me more suited to a feeling of loneliness than a visit to someone else? What is it in his personality or in the quality of his feeling of loneliness which makes him want to see a friend rather than go to a movie or get drunk? It should be observed that we do not want to know how these things developed biographically. We need merely additional information at the time of his loneliness to "understand," or to have predicted for this phase of the development, that in the end he would come to visit me.

More examples of this kind can now be treated with fewer of the details.

A respondent says he didn't vote because it rained on election day. That might or might not be an acceptable statement, according to the following additional information which would be needed. Is his health frail so that he is always afraid of going out in the rain, and therefore the rain actually would have led us to predict his not voting? Or is he just not interested in politics and any other excuse would have been as good? Or was the rain so bad that, according to prevailing standards, no one without a special means of transportation would be expected to go out on the street?

A housewife uses a brand of soap she has not used before. In an interview she reports that she could not get her usual brand, and so bought the one which she found at her dealer's. Whether availability at the dealer is to be noted as a reason depends mainly upon the question of whether the new soap was really the only one which the dealer carried at the time of her purchase. If this is not the case, then, had we observed her at the store, we would need some more information for prediction: It might have been the only soap the name of which was known to her from advertisements; or the only soap available within a certain price-range; or the soap displayed nearest to where she stood in the store. Questions directed toward such information would be indispensable in making the interview complete.

A man says he votes for the Democratic Party because Roosevelt is for the poor fellow. But so are the Townsendites and the Communists. We therefore need additional information of this kind: Does the man know of other parties? Does he think that a vote for small parties is a wasted vote? Has he examined the other parties and found shortcomings in them which negate their attitude toward the poor fellow? Again, only with such additional information can we decide the weight which Roosevelt's social policies have had for this man's vote. It might well be that in the course of such a scrutiny, the whole picture would change, and other reasons would emerge into the foreground.

Even an answer which is usually quite meaningless and comes only from bad interviewers can make sense with this sort of examination. Suppose we study why people choose certain items on a menu, and someone tells us that he chose shrimp salad because he likes it. This answer might be meaningful if it is qualified, upon further questioning, somewhat like this: He liked shrimp better than anything else on the menu that day; or he liked it best in the price-range he was prepared for; or there are other things on the menu he likes as well, but he had eaten these foods recently.

In order to work such techniques into a formal questionnaire to be used for a specific problem, it is usually necessary first to make trial interviews and to scrutinize the way the consumer, himself, looks at the situation. Taking as an example a questionnaire on gasoline purchases, it was found for instance that when people were asked how they started to use their present brand, they usually gave one of five reasons. Either they spoke (1) about their personal reasons, such as the relationship to station attendants, (2) about convenient location, (3) they just tried around and then got used to a brand, (4) they mentioned recommendation of friends, or (5) finally advertising. The research problem then consists in devising such a questionnaire that no matter what starting point the respondent takes of his own initiative, provisions are made to check back to see whether additional factors played a role which the respondent overlooked under the impact of the first factor which came to his mind. The pertinent part of such a questionnaire, then, would consist first of a general question, "Why?" and a check list of the reasons which can be expected on the basis of the pretest. Then the list of *specifying questions* would be added. From the schedule used in the gasoline study we present the specifying questions as an example (without regard to any particular spacing).

IF—(1): *Personal Reasons* (*Friend or relative in station, etc.*)
    a) What sort of connection do you have with the attendant?
    b) Do you care what gasoline you buy provided it is a known brand?
    c) (If yes to *b*) What is your preferred brand?
    d) (If *c* is answered) How did you happen to get interested in this brand?

IF—(2): *Convenience*
    a) Are other brands as conveniently located?
    b) (If yes to *a*) Why then did you select this brand?
    c) (If no to *a*) Why is there just this one?
    d) Are there many stations with your brand, thus making it convenient?
    e) What other advantages besides convenience has this station (or brand)?

IF—(3): *Trial*
    a) (If chance) How did you happen to try it?
    b) (If deliberate) What other brands did you try?
    c) (If deliberate) About how long did you experiment?
    d) (If deliberate) What made you finally decide in favor of this brand?

IF—(4): *Recommendation of friends or acquaintances*
    a) Who was the adviser (i.e., personal friend, relative, business acquaintance)?
    b) Did he tell you about the product or did you just follow his example?
    c) (If the former—*b*) What argument made you follow his advice?

IF—(5): *Advertising*
    a) Was it just one advertisement or a series of advertisements?
    b) Just what advertisement was it that impressed you most?
    c) Can you remember when you saw or heard it?
    d) (If radio—do not ask) Where was it?
    e) What were the sales points that impressed you most?
    f) Can you give more details as to how the advertisement impressed you and made you buy this brand?

After these interviews are turned in, it is then usually possible, with a great degree of safety, to divide those cases where it seems that advertising was a cause of a purchase from those where it does not seem to have been a cause. In one study, for example, five judges were used to make this decision on the same material. Among them an average tetrachoric correlation of .85 was obtained.[3]

Statistical analysis of reasons.—Suppose, then, that we find that 20 per cent of a number of people who bought the product acknowledged the effect of advertising. What does this figure mean?

In order to give the answer, we must go back to the original fourfold table, reproduced here in a somewhat more general form.

Table II—Effect of Advertising on Buying

	Bought Product	Did Not Buy Product	Total
Exposed	q	t	e
Not exposed to advertisement	s	v	$n-e$
Total	a	$n-a$	n

One way to express the effectiveness, F, of exposure to advertising upon buying, would be the formula:

$$F = \frac{q}{e} - \frac{s}{n-e}$$ (Differences in proportion of buyers between exposed and unexposed people.)

The *number* of b-cases would be expressed by the formula:

$$b = eF$$

where e equals the number of exposed people.

The number of *b-cases*, then—that is to say, *the number of people who say they bought because they were exposed—equals the effectiveness, F, of the advertising, times the extent of exposure.* This is an important result. It shows that if we have interviews which are able to reconstruct the past so well that the information we have is equivalent to a controlled experiment, then the statistical result we get is the product of two factors: the extent and the effectiveness of an advertising campaign. The same number of b-cases might be found if very many persons are exposed to the advertisement even though its effectiveness is rather small, or if relatively few people are exposed to a campaign which is extremely effective, in the sense of getting exposed people to come to the store. The number of b-cases, then, measures what one might call the *impact* of an advertisement, which is the product of its extent and its effectiveness.

To round out this analysis, it is necessary to visualize some concrete research situations in which we are likely to use direct interviews. It can be that we have access only to people who would buy the product—as would be the case, for example, with a mail-order house, or when the respondents are already in the store, or when we are dealing with subscribers to a magazine. Using the symbols of Table II, this would be a situation where we have only the "a-people" who bought, but where we do not know how many people did not buy, and therefore cannot know the size, n, of the complete sample. In this case, interviews would tell us only the relative impact of two advertising media. For instance, if we have ascertained that b_1 people bought a product under the influence of the radio, and b_2 people bought it under the influence of the newspaper, then the ratio of b_1 to b_2 would be our main result.

The question must be raised whether such a result, even if it measured up to the highest standards, is of practical importance. There are a number of reasons why the answer should be "yes." It is true that the most interesting piece of information would be the effectiveness, F, itself. We should like to know what increases in sales a campaign brings about among those people who are exposed to the advertisement. Very often, however, it is enough for practical purposes to know only the impact. If an advertiser puts a certain amount of money into radio and another amount into newspaper advertising, he would like to know which medium got him more additional sales, and he wouldn't care whether a difference is due to the two media reaching the same number of people, but the one is more effective with those it reaches; or whether it is because the two media are equally effective but the one has a larger audience, or both of these. Also, in certain cases, additional material might permit an estimate of the exposure, e, for the two media. We might, for instance, know the approximate size of the audience to a certain program and the approximate readership of a magazine. If, then, an appropriate sample is interviewed and we find out how many buyers of the product have been influenced by the program and how many by the magazine, we can take into account the amount of exposure for the total population from which the sample has been taken and then compute directly the effectiveness, *F*, of the two media. *F* would tell us what increase of sales the medium would lead to in a controlled experiment.

If the research situation is such that we know how many people in our complete sample bought the product, and also know how many have been exposed to the different advertisements, we can immediately construct Table II, and then it would seem that no direct interviews would be needed. This, however, is not always correct. Even where a complete fourfold table can be drawn up, the direct interviews may add decisively to our knowledge. Results have been reached, for example, showing that people who are exposed to advertisements also use more of the advertised products.[4] In these studies we do not know to what extent exposure leads to use, or use to exposure. One way to disentangle the two factors is, again, the direct interview. The same is true in regard to spurious factors. People might listen to a program *and* buy the product because they are well-to-do. Direct interviews would lead to a number of *b*-cases smaller than could be expected from a fourfold table. A spurious correlation would thus be corrected and wrong interpretation avoided.

How to test the validity of reasons. We turn to the last of our four points. So far we have assumed that our interviews yield results equivalent to a controlled experiment, and our concern has been to clarify the relationship between the statistical results obtained by the two methods. Can we expect, however, that direct interviews will ever reflect the process of a concrete purchase so clearly that a decision can be made as to whether a certain piece of advertising was or was not an influence? Much has been said about people not knowing why they act, and many a market research man feels that it is an impossible task to find this out. Here again, the schematic analysis of the problem presented here will help to clarify the matter.

First, it must be remembered that we are not dealing with the rather meaningless general question of why people buy, but with the task of tracing the effect of specific advertising upon concrete purchases with the help of retrospective interviews. In such cases, where do the difficulties lie?

In the first place, it may be that people forget that they have been exposed to advertising. The interviewing technique sketched above tries to follow possible exposure into situations where the respondent might have overlooked mentioning it. Whatever the respondents mention—role of price, or influence of salesperson, or special qualities of the product—we check back to see whether advertising entered by forming their idea of the quality, or giving advice of the salesperson additional support. This should reduce mistakes in remembering exposure considerably, probably leaving only those cases where such exposure would not have had any actual influence, and thus the omission would not change the results in any case.

In those cases where exposure has been established, errors can be made in appraising the effect. We shall certainly be frequently wrong in making the statement that, in a given situation, buying was or was not to be expected, because the psychological rules which we more or less explicitly apply are not very safe. But there still might be a chance of our erring sometimes on the positive and sometimes on the negative side, and that in the end the misjudgments would probably cancel out and the statistical results would be valid.

As a matter of fact, the only conceivable test of the validity of reasons is a statistical one. For obvious reasons, it is not possible to verify whether a certain purchase would have been made even without a specific advertising influence having been introduced. We can test only whether the number of b-cases which we ascertain by direct interviews is corroborated by the number of b-cases derived from a controlled experiment. This innocent little sentence implies a vast research program. In order to settle whether reasons for buying obtained in an interview are valid data, it would be necessary to set up controlled experiments and parallel them by direct interviews. Opportunities are not lacking. Quite frequently advertising campaigns are tested by comparing two trade areas, one of which is covered by the campaign, and the other of which is not.[5] In each of these situations, direct interviews could be added and their results compared with the objective test.

Such opportunities have not been used so far and one of the tasks of applied psychologists is to stress the desirability of this procedure whenever they are connected with a pertinent test situation. At present, therefore, only crude substitutes for such tests can be reported and used for exemplification.

In a market study, the problem was to find out why people do not buy at a certain department store. One reason to be tested was the location of the store. People were divided into two groups, according to whether they lived in the rather immediate neighborhood of the store, or in a more distant area which was defined by several criteria such as number of miles and transportation facilities. As a result of cross-analysis, a fourfold table of the following kind was obtained.

Table III—Regularity of Buying in Relation to Distance of Store

	Buy Regularly	Do Not Buy Regularly	Total
Live near the store	277	116	393
Live at some distance from store	135	302	437
Total	412	418	830

From a computation identical to the one given in Section 1 above, we can conclude that there should be 158 b-cases,[6] that is to say people who, upon being interviewed, would reply that they do not buy at this store because it is located inconveniently for them. The 418 people who did not buy at the store or did not buy there regularly were interviewed, and 40 per cent, or 167, said that their reason for not buying was the inconvenient location of the store. This is indeed a corroboration of the expectation derived from the fourfold table, which can be considered relatively satisfactory in view of the crudeness of the data.[7]

Another reason investigated in this study was: poor opinion of the store. In regard to this poor opinion a somewhat different kind of test was made.

Somewhere during the interview each respondent who only bought occasionally at the store was asked to judge it according to the following seven aspects: style of merchandise, interior arrangement, salesclerks, price of merchandise, quality of merchandise, services, customers.

The answers to these questions can be used as a crude attitude-test by classifying people according to the number of items on which they express criticisms. The most favorable attitude would be that of the respondent who had no criticism to make on any aspect. The least favorable attitude would be exhibited by respondents who had criticisms on all these items. In classifying people according to this test, we perform an operation comparable to the one we performed when we classified people according to location. The score permits people to be grouped according to their critical attitude toward the store, and this grouping can be used for the purpose of studying the validity of people's reasons. We would expect that the more critical groups would more frequently mention bad opinion of the store as their reason for not buying there. The figures bear out this expectation as shown in Table IV.

Table IV—Relation between Expressed Criticisms and Reasons for Not Buying

Criticism Score (Number of Items Criticized)	Total Number of Cases	Proportion of Respondents Giving Bad Opinion of Store As Reason for Not Buying
None	55	25%
One	45	48
Two	29	64
Three or more	47	78

We see that the number of criticisms increases in proportion to the number of people who give poor opinion of the store as their reason for shopping there only occasionally.[8]

It has to be kept clearly in mind that neither of these two examples contains any circuitous reasoning, as one might assume at first glance. The information on residence and attitude toward the store is collected independently of the quest for reasons. Logically, it might be that residence and attitude, on the one hand, and reasons on the other hand, have no relationship. That they actually do is an inferential test for the validity of the reasons. Furthermore, it is important to realize that such factors as where a person lives and the attitude he has, have the logical character of an "exposure"; they take on the character of "reasons" if in an individual case they are linked up with not buying at the store on the ground of the respondent's retrospection and the psychologist's evaluation of it.

It seems from this and a few other available examples,[9] that using personal interviews to test the effect of advertising is not impossible. On few points could a psychologist be of more service to the men of action than by refining this type of interview and studying the extent and the limits of its applicability. The entire complex of problems, however, of which we have been able to present only a small segment, is difficult and will require a wide diversity of interconnected studies, beyond the working capacity of a single psychologist. Its obvious practical importance might warrant the coordinated efforts of applied psychologists as a whole.

4. WHY DID PEOPLE BELIEVE

IN THE "INVASION FROM MARS"?

by Herta Herzog

[On the morning after the famous Orson Welles broadcast, Frank Stanton, then Research Director of the Columbia Broadcasting System, commissioned a small number of detailed interviews. The purpose was to discover the main factors which accounted for people becoming excited under the impact of the broadcast. The present selection is a memorandum written to Dr. Stanton by Dr. Herzog, who was in charge of these interviews. Her observations are clearly organized around an accounting scheme in the sense of this section. Subsequently, a major study was carried out and published by Cantril, Herzog, and Gaudet, *The Invasion From Mars* (Princeton: Princeton University Press, 1940).—ED. NOTE.]

THIS IS A REPORT of thirty very detailed interviews which have been made in Orange, New Jersey. The respondents were, on the average, middle-class people and we learned before the actual interview from friends and neighbors, that they had been greatly affected by the broadcast.

The purpose of the interviews was to bring out those psychological aspects which would seem useful for an analysis of the whole event. Our thirty cases, of course, do not permit a reliable statistical evaluation. The results, however, are given in such a form that the reader can visualize how tables would look if the study were conducted on a broad basis.

An analysis of the total situation leads one to expect that the following psychological factors have to be considered:

a. What in the past experience or personality of our respondents made them inclined to become perturbed?

b. What in the program was especially conducive to taking it for a real news broadcast?

c. Which listener situations were especially likely to facilitate a misunderstanding of the program?

d. How did people influence one another when they were listening in groups or got in contact with each other?

e. What possibilities of checking upon the nature of the broadcast did the listener have and what use did he make of these possibilities?

The sections of this report correspond to the points just enumerated and can be considered as tentative answers to these questions.

A. THE TIME IS OUT OF JOINT

The idea that everyone today is prepared to believe unusual and grue-some events is the theme which, in many variations, runs through the inter-views. The interviews contain remarks like:

"The people's nerves are pitched up."
"These times are not normal."

Without being asked expressly, each respondent mentions at least one factor in his preceding experience which might have made him ready to take the program for a news broadcast. The following list of factors is arranged ac-cording to the frequency in which they have been mentioned:

The permanent talk about war
The strange developments of science
The recent floods
Religious beliefs
Individual experiences of a number of respondents

Very often one interviewee would give a number of concurrent factors which, in his opinion, made him susceptible to taking the broadcast seriously. The following pages include a number of quotations for each major group and an effort is made to put them in the correct psychological context.

The War Scare in Europe. The great majority of respondents mentioned, in one way or another, the recent political events. There are three different ways in which this factor seems to play a role. Some people point to the general atmosphere of uncertainty which has been created by the Czecho-slovakia crisis and similar events.

"I have never been in any accident or catastrophe. But the war news has every-body so tense we more or less believe everything we hear. I could not believe the Martians were coming down but I thought it was some physical disaster and evi-dently the end of the world had come."

Other people seemed to feel more specifically that the political situation would make an invasion by an enemy quite believable.

"I was all excited and I knew that Hitler did not appreciate President Roose-velt's telegram a couple of weeks ago. While the United States thought everything was settled, they came down unexpected."
"The Germans or the Japs are the nations about which you hear things of that kind (poison gas attacks), and they do not need any reason for declaration of war. America is a fruitful country. If they want it, they will take it."

A third group feels that the special technique of relaying news over the radio prepared them to believe any bad news which would come to them in such a form.

"It was made up like a news flash exactly the way as it was made during the war crisis. I thought it was some sort of a disaster. One never knows what is going to happen these days."

Experiences with Science. That the political situation during the last years created a feeling of uneasiness, a readiness to be afraid, will not be a sur-prise. It is interesting to see, however, that the development of science of which we are so proud, in general, is also likely to create this potential anxiety.

Incidental reading about Mars is mentioned by quite a number of people in this connection. People have heard that Mars might be inhabited, that it is next to the Earth, Mt. Wilson Observatory was a familiar name to one respondent, "Life" had brought out pictures of how the world could come to an end, etc. Evidently the man on the street is sometimes more bewildered than elated by scientific progress. Mrs. C., it seems to us, formulates the psychological problems very aptly:

"I have no education. I do not know what can happen and what cannot. That's up to the scientist. I care for the children and my family. And if *he* says it happened! Also they mentioned those 'mirrors' of those armored men. Well, I learned about the Middle Ages. And I have seen an X-ray machine when my boy had a broken leg."

Buck Rogers and his feature stories in the newspapers are mentioned by several people. Is it the outcome of a spy scare that made Mrs. B. think for a moment that Buck Rogers had given the Mars people the idea to come to fight us?

"It's foolish I know, but somehow I thought: Buck Rogers had always put those things into the funnies. Maybe the Mars people have seen it. Maybe they are so smart and actually do it. Anything can happen and there is so much tenseness around anyhow."

It is quite likely that such a magic attitude toward science will prove, upon further study, a major determinant of the preparedness to believe in a real event. Some incidental information collected on people who did not get frightened shows that some training in the cultural evaluation of social or natural events was most likely to prevent people from believing in the disaster. It would at least be very valuable in case of further studies to check upon this point because of its implications for education toward rational behavior in emergencies.

Recent Natural Catastrophes. Some people feel that hearing of hurricanes and tidal waves contributes to giving a general feeling of lack of security.

"I hated to make myself think that the end of the world had come but there were such unusual things happening in the world, like floods, that I thought it was possible."

Religious Beliefs. Certain trends in religious thinking are another factor contributing to a general expectation of disaster. Evidently the religious aspect can either come in, in a rather rational way as exhibited by the first quotation or in an irrational and emotional way as exemplified by the second quotation given for this group:

"My husband and sons weren't as excited as I was but they had their doubts. They are both pretty calm people. While it was going on, they tried to figure it out. At the beginning of the broadcast, my older son said, 'It sounds like a Buck Rogers story,' but as time went on he became more convinced that it was real. He tried to explain to me while the excitement was on that that's the way the world balances itself—either by floods or wars and that this was some other form of God-sent elimination of people."

"I thought our Lord was punishing us for something we did to displease Him. I tried not to get panicky. You have to face things."

Individual Experiences. In addition to general influences like war and scientific awe and the natural catastrophes, and religious thinking, we find that a number of people had more special grievances into which the present event seemed to fit. Two active Republicans intimated that Roosevelt had so badly mismanaged foreign affairs that one could not be surprised if some foreign country had come and cracked down upon the United States.

A Jewish woman reports:

"The first thing that came to my mind while my sister-in-law was talking was that there was an uprising against the Jews."

One respondent had heard recently of a meteor actually falling down in New Jersey and another heard a broadcast describing the explosion of an oil tank in Linden. So special events seem to have increased their preparedness for Sunday night. Occasionally, people would mention an incident immediately preceding the broadcast which increased their credulity later on: One man was just reading a mystery story when he tuned in during the program and one group of people had just been discussing natural catastrophes.

Altogether, one is surprised to see the great amount of *potential anxiety* which seems to be embedded in the minds of many of our respondents. Whether this feeling of insecurity is characteristic of all of us or whether it is especially great for those people who became disturbed by the broadcast cannot be decided without further research.

B. WHAT MADE IT SO REALISTIC?

The preparation of people to believe in a disaster is only one aspect of our problem. Another question is: What were the features of the broadcast which made it so believable? Each of our respondents gave his own impression of the program. The replies were classified in rather large units, not taking every single word but the main ideas expressed by the informants. Although people spoke a lot on this point, we were able to reduce each statement to two or three major features. For a classification of a greater number of cases the following list of features will probably prove helpful. They are ranked according to the frequency in which they were mentioned in our cases.

a. The authenticity of places and persons mentioned.
b. The technical realism of the performance.
c. Some special sentences mentioned.
d. Some more general aspects of the performance.

a. *Regarding Names.* Many people were especially impressed by the appearance of government officials or scientists. Some mentioned particularly that no federal official would get mixed up in something if it were not an authentic situation. Other people mentioned that they were especially impressed by the fact that names were so familiar, that they had been to all of those places, and that they were so nearby. Here is an especially interesting comment for this group.

"One thing was the local names. Watchung Mountains is a name known only to the people who live there. But by the way, I wonder if Welles did not want to give his wife's friends a thrill; he married a girl from my neighborhood."

b. *Regarding Technical Features.* These comments seem to be equally divided between those who say that interruptions in the night club and the shifting of the news flashes from spot to spot made the illusion so perfect; and those who mentioned acoustic items of the program. A majority of comments in the latter group mention the gasping voice of the announcer, his muffled scream when he was about to break down. Evidently the announcer is a cardinal feature in such a situation.

c. *Regarding Phrases.* For a psychological interpretation it should be worthwhile to study especially the phrases and actual quotations which people can remember as decisive features which made them believe in the broadcast. It is interesting, for instance, that the one statement of an "official" is mentioned several times. "It is incredible but true." It is psychologically quite understandable that people are more likely to believe a strange tale when the narrator himself stresses the incredibility. Many of the other sentences especially mentioned by our informants were those where the "government people" stressed that they would take the leadership in the emergency and give all necessary advice. If it could be proved in a larger study that just such remarks were important, it would point to an interesting psychological interpretation: in an emergency we are especially inclined to believe in people who promise that they will take from us and unto themselves the responsibility of coping with the situation.

d. *General Comments.* Of the cases belonging here the greater part said that they did not think there was any reason to doubt the broadcast: they felt that such a story was quite likely anyway. Some people mentioned the special confidence they have in radio as an institution. It should be worthwhile to quote a few comments made in this connection:

"We have so much faith in broadcasting. In a crisis it has to reach all people. That's what radio is here for."

"The announcer would not say it if it were not true. They always quit if something is a play."

"I put credence on news bulletins. I feel that the radio is the official organ to let people know of tragedies—this sort of broke my faith in radio."

"I always feel that the commentators bring the best possible news. Even after this I will still believe what I hear on the radio."

C. THE SITUATIONAL CONTEXT

How could they have believed it, was the question which a number of people asked after it was all over. And, indeed, neither the potential anxiety nor the realistic features of the program would fully account for the effect. We have to include in our analysis the special moment at which the people started to listen; here is a list of the main situations in the order of frequency in which they occurred in our sample.

Dialed in by coincidence after the program had begun
Family members or friends rushed in and made them listen
Were urged over the telephone to listen
Happened to enter a room where the program was on
Listened from the beginning

As was to be expected, only a very few cases listened from the beginning among our respondents who were selected because they were known to have been upset. The majority were dragged into the situation by other people either directly or by telephone. Very revealing are those cases who heard from the beginning that it was a Mercury Theater Play because they evidently furnish examples of a loose kind of radio listening. They report that they did not listen very carefully and when the flashes came, they were so upset that they forgot what they had heard just a few minutes before. Relatively near to this psychological situation is the case of some people who had been listening to other programs when they were called to listen to WABC. Here again, the sudden impression of the flashes made them overlook the fact that everything was being carried on in an orderly fashion over the other station. (It might be, however, that the stressing of "scoops" in radio publicity made it plausible that one station reports the end of the world during the dance program of another station.)

D. THE ROLE OF OTHER PEOPLE

Our material does not permit us to do more than utter a few hunches as to how people mutually influenced each other. It seems that in most of the cases the husband behaved critically or at least much more calmly than the wife.

"My husband was so calm even when he thought that the end of the world was coming that he made me mad. He did not even put his arm around me."

"I got furious at my husband because he did not want to drive home quicker. . . . Then he stayed in the car to listen and I was pacing the floor inside."

On the other hand, when a man got panicky he seems to have especially impressed others in his environment. In one case a usually calm and intellectually conceited brother had telephoned and said very excitedly that he was leaving his home with his family. That a person who was considered apparently an intellectual authority told about the event evidently made for immediate acceptance. Another group of cases are those people who are usually sheltered and not used to making decisions of their own. When they happened to be caught by the broadcast without their usual guides the situation was especially difficult.

"I rushed downstairs to phone my husband to come home and decide what it was and what should be done. . . . Children were crying, 'Mother, where will we go?' But I got them dressed and said, 'Wait until daddy comes, he will know.'"

Were people more likely to be scared when they tuned in for themselves or when other people made them aware of the event? Our evidence is contradictory. In some cases the excitement of others seemed to have increased the critical faculties of certain people; in other cases people felt they would never have believed it if they had been alone. On the other hand just because they were alone, some others were just in the mood to fall for exciting news.

E. EVERYTHING FITS INTO THE PICTURE

Altogether, it is one of the surest but, of course, most obvious results that most of those people who were upset had started to listen to the program after it had begun. The much more important psychological problem is to what extent people were able to check up on the authenticity of the broadcast. Here lies probably one of the most important aspects of the event from a social point of view: To what extent will an emergency deprive people of the intelligent use of a rational means of behavior?

Objectively, they could tune in to other stations, look into the newspaper, or check for information over the telephone. Most of the people did something of this kind but for a very interesting reason, only about half of them succeeded. The following list gives the main patterns in the order of frequency in which they occurred with our respondents:

Abortive check-ups were made which seem to prove that the program was a real broadcast.

Station identification or information from other people came so quickly that no major panic could develop in spite of the respondent believing the news.

People acted immediately under the impact of fear without further control.

The ten cases of people who checked up and found their suspicions corroborated show how great the danger is that a state of panic distorts our rational thinking. The issue is important enough to enumerate what happened in those cases:

One man mistook the sight of the neon lights in Newark streets as fire shining.

One woman looked out of the window and saw a "greenish eerie light" which later on proved to be the lights on the car of the maid who had just come home.

In two cases people were told over the telephone about the event and by coincidence tuned in to WABC for a check up. As a result, they had no more doubts.

In one case, the police were called so early that they had no information yet and were worried themselves.

In three cases a strange coincidence seemed to corroborate the fear of the one who tried to check up.

A boy telephoned to his mother at a party where she was supposed to be. When no one answered, he was sure that the fumes had overtaken all the people in that apartment. Later on, it turned out that the party had gone to an empty apartment in the same building where they could dance better.

In one home, there were two radios and the parents checked up on the radio of the boy; they knew that the boy always listened to Charlie McCarthy at this time Sunday night and when they heard the Mercury Theater program over the radio, they were sure that all stations carried the disaster.

One man looked at the newspaper and evidently got the wrong program because he found music announced for the time for which he was looking.

How definitely people interpreted all evidence in the light of their own apprehension is strikingly shown by the following two quotations:

Mrs. B. tells: "We looked out of the window and Wyoming Avenue was black with cars. People were rushing away."
Mrs. O. tells: "No car came down my street. 'Traffic is jammed,' I thought."

There was no way out. Many cars or no cars, all seemed equally to indicate the worst.

The great role those abortive controls played has not been mentioned as far as we know in the newspaper discussions of the event. It seems to be a factor which could come out only from such a detailed kind of interview.

How about the five people who did not check up at all? One family was in a car and drove home horrified; they arrived there when the play was over. Two people ran out of the house immediately and stayed out until they finally learned that there was nothing to it. In two cases, the people just stayed paralyzed until the end of the program relieved them of the terror. In one of the cases, the respondent did not think he could tune in to other stations because the announcer had said that his station was the only one not yet destroyed.

F. THE THRILL OF DISASTER

The analysis of the factors leading to the "Mars scare" would not be complete if we did not point out some definite elements of enjoyment which radiate through a number of the reports we have collected. It is not alien to modern psychological theory to assume that interspersed in their experience of fear, people had experiences of relief and elation.

In some cases, the language of the respondents is astonishing. One woman tells how she and her husband were "glued to the radio." One young man did not turn to another station for a checkup because he did not want to miss anything. One man says that "although we were not scared, we could not stop listening."

In three cases, the people refused for quite some time after the broadcast to believe it was not true. It is almost as if they did not want to abandon something valuable and which they had to protect against the other people in their environment who wanted to rob them of it.

"They all dismissed it but I did not really believe that it was a play until I saw the newspapers the next morning. I went to bed still thinking that something was going to happen."

The following rather hazardous assumptions could be made and an example furnished here and there.

a) Some people felt important for participating in such a momentous event irrespective of the danger involved.

Mrs. C. says so explicitly:	"I urged my husband to listen and said it was a historical moment possibly and he would be sorry afterwards to have missed it."
Mrs. J., without knowing it, describes how she behaved as a messenger of great importance:	"I stood on the corner waiting for a bus and I thought that every car that came along was a bus and I ran out to get it. People saw how excited I was and tried to quiet me, but I kept saying over and over again to everybody I met, 'Don't you know that New Jersey is destroyed by Germans—it's on the radio.'"

b) Our daily lives are full of frustration and some people might have experienced the disaster as a release from all the prohibitions surrounding us.

Mrs. J. tells how she came home, knees shaking and hardly able to walk the stairs:

"I looked in the icebox and saw some chicken left from Sunday dinner and that I was saving for Monday night dinner. I said to my nephew, 'We may as well eat this chicken—we won't be here in the morning.'"

c) In some cases where people felt personally worried, it might have been a relief to see one's own plight, so to say, taken over by the community. We do not have a case where that is expressed textually but the case of the Jewish woman mentioned previously comes very near to it:

"I realized right away that it was something that was affecting everybody, not only the Jews, and I felt relieved. As long as everybody was going to go, it was better."

d) Finally, one cannot but feel that in a few cases an element of the sadistic enjoyment of a catastrophe is involved. One woman described how people were drowning "like rats" in the Hudson River and another said they were "dying like flies." Another woman was described by the interviewer in the following terms: "She is the kind that enjoys sensations (impressed by massacres in Spain). The expression on her face as she tells of her anxiety reveals her enjoyment." This report was given without any idea that in the final analysis we would look for this kind of evidence.

The following description of what was reported over the radio should be joy for any psychoanalyst:

"They (the monsters) were like snakes—the little ones were crawling out of the pit and multiplying."

The most striking indication of such psychological implications is given by Mrs. S. Her behavior, as well as her wording, might intimate the voluptuous element we are thinking of:

"Then, also, my husband tried to calm me and said, 'If this were really so, it would be on all stations,' and he turned to one of the other stations and there was music. I retorted, 'Nero fiddled while Rome burned.'"

5. A MODEL FOR ASSESSING CHANGES
IN VOTING INTENTION

by Hazel Gaudet

[The following paper was prepared as a memorandum to guide interviewers in assessing changes in voting intention. The purpose of the study was to investigate the role of radio as a means of political propaganda—a problem which was fairly new in 1939, when these instructions were written. They show how the general ideas of action-analysis are applied to a concrete study and can be adapted to use by an average field interviewer.—ED. NOTE.]

WHENEVER THE INTERVIEWER DISCOVERS that a respondent has changed his opinion on a political question since the last interview, he is supposed to determine the influences which led to that change. Ordinary interviewing requires a considerable amount of tact and skill, but ascertaining the full reasons for a change in opinion is more difficult. It requires special knowledge and perception of what constitutes a complete answer. It requires a special definition of the possible components of a change. Interviewers should be made especially alert and aware on this point so that they will

This is a previously unpublished paper.

never accept the first answer given by a respondent if it is incomplete without following it up with further questioning.

REASONS FOR DIFFICULTY

One of the chief reasons why it is so difficult to get at this type of a response is that the respondent takes for granted that we know part of the reason for his change of opinion, and he answers us only superficially. Not knowing that we are interested in knowing details that seem obvious or trivial to him, it is the task of the skilled and sensitive interviewer to draw him out, question by question, until the actual reasons have been reached. This is especially difficult because there is no one set of questions which will cover the countless types of situations in which the interviewer may find himself after asking the first question. It is necessary for him to weigh the implications of the first response that he receives, determine how closely it approximates the complete reason for the respondent changing his mind, and after he has located the gaps in the information he has received, to select appropriate questions which will draw out the further information which is necessary to make up a full answer to the question.

Another reason why the task is so complex is the fact that it seems psychologically more suitable to ascertain reasons for change as indirectly as possible. It might not make for the best *rapport* to challenge the respondent at the outset with the fact that the change is known to the interviewer. The first question should work around the subject, should ask opinions of the old choice or the new. Only where this type of indirect discussion does not elicit the desired information on changes should direct questions be ventured.

The more specific the original question the greater chance there is that the respondent will give a complete account of himself of his own accord. For instance, a good starting point is always to refer the first question to the respondent's new choice—to ask, "Why do you think Roosevelt is best?" in order to lend concreteness to the individual's thinking. Similarly, the answers to "What is the reason for this change?" can never be expected to be as complete or as specific as the answer to such a question as, *"What is the reason for this change since the last interview?"* Wherever possible, the interviewer should *limit the question to a particular area so the respondent will know more precisely what is expected of him.*

ELEMENTS OF COMPLETE ANSWERS

In the autumn of 1939 a trial set of 1,000 interviews were made to study methods of securing reasons for change of opinion. Analysis of the try-out questions led to laying down certain elements which must be present in every complete answer accounting for a reason for a change.

By presenting a few examples of complete and incomplete answers to these types of questions on change of opinion it is hoped that the elements constituting a complete answer will be made clear. These cases could be analyzed indefinitely in great detail. This paper purports to present only the minimum outline of the requirements for a complete answer. *Ideally, responses should be supplemented by as much additional information as the interviewer can possibly elicit from each respondent.*

(1) *Old Choice or New.* Responses were given either in terms of the old

choice or the new. Even when the chief reason for a change lies in dissatisfaction with the old choice, however, this is not sufficient reason to account for the direction of the new choice. In other words, *there must always be a reason for the new choice being made somewhere in the answer.* The only place where this principle does not apply is in instances where the respondent changed from the choice of a definite man or party to uncertainty of opinion or answered "don't know." In such a case some argument against his old choice is a sufficient answer. For instance, a person may change from Garner to Roosevelt chiefly because he just learned Garner's age and considers him too old to be president, but this still does not account for the respondent fixating on *Roosevelt* rather than some *other* Democrat. On the other hand, if he had changed from Garner to "don't know," it would be satisfactory for the interviewer to accept an answer which dealt with the old choice exclusively.

(2) *Occurrence or Source. The interviewer should always make certain that he has learned the occurrence, event or piece of new information which has brought about the change of opinion. He should also determine, if possible, the source or channel which brought this information* to the attention of the respondent. The two are not mutually exclusive, will frequently occur together in the same answer, but are not always both necessary to the complete response. As a matter of fact, it is frequently impossible to secure both but, wherever possible, the interviewer should do so. For instance, if the outbreak of war caused a respondent to change his opinion on the suitability of presidential candidates, it is difficult or impossible to isolate one particular source of information for such a great world-shaking event. News of it was present in every source of information open to the respondent, so it would be probably impossible for him to name the place where he learned it. On the other hand, if someone has just learned that Mr. X is a crook, there should be no difficulty in determining the particular source of such specific information.

Some respondents will answer with the channel of information and others with the event which changed their opinion. If they answer in terms of the former (source), interviewers should always go on to ask them what they learned which led them to this opinion. If they answer in terms of the latter (the event or occurrence), it is possible to ask where they learned it, but it is not possible to expect them to be able to indicate the channel on all occasions. *Complete answers should always include the new information which led to the change of opinion and, in addition, should add the source of the information wherever possible.*

There is one exceptional type of case in which it is possible that the interviewer will not be able to get the actual information which changed the respondent's opinion: that is an instance in which the mere prestige of the channel or source of information was sufficient to make the change. It might happen that a husband's opinion on the subject was influential in changing the wife's choice of candidates without the wife being able to name any particular argument which was used to sway her. In this case it would not be presenting a wrong picture to credit the husband as being the chief influence rather than any particular piece of information which he passed along. An interviewer should not accept a mere channel of information as being sufficient reason to account for the change without having made the attempt to delve further into the content of what was actually said or advised.

(3) *New Information or Attitude.* Finally, information should be gathered on the type of change which went on in the respondent. A man may change his mind about political issues in two chief ways: (a) *new information* may cause him to think differently of the qualifications of the different candidates or parties and (b) his whole system of thinking may have changed so completely that a new candidate may fit into his ideas. His ideas about the man may not have changed but his new attitude may make the man suitable. These two types of changes may occur either together or separately. Naturally more people change because of a new valuation of the candidate or political party than because their own systems of thinking have altered. An example of a revaluation of a choice is a respondent who changed from Dewey to Hoover at the outbreak of the war because the latter was more experienced and better fitted for the presidency during times of strained international affairs. The respondent's ideas of what constitutes a good president did not necessarily change, and his evaluation of Dewey and Hoover as men did not vary, but the new world situation made a different type of man more suitable at the present time. An example of the second type, the change of attitude, may occur when an individual who has always been opposed to centralized government decides he is in favor of concentrating power in Washington. He was formerly very opposed to the New Deal, but with his changed ideas in government he then becomes in favor of Roosevelt for another term. *Every answer should include a clue to whether the respondent has learned new facts about his choice, or whether his own ideas have changed so as to make the new choice suit him better.*

Summary. To summarize, the following three groups of elements which must occur in a minimum account of a change of political opinion have been outlined.

(1) The answer must usually be stated in terms of the new choice. If the respondent has changed from a candidate or party to a state of uncertainty, however, a reason for change may be stated in terms of the old choice.

(2) The answer must include the incident, occurrence or piece of new information which caused the change in opinion and, wherever possible, should indicate the source of this information. It is frequently possible to give the influence without being able to name the source definitely. The only cases in which the source of information might be given without a definite piece of information which changed the opinion would be in cases in which the prestige of the source of information was sufficient to change the respondent's mind no matter what the specific facts of the matter were.

(3) The type of change should be specified; that is, the interviewer should find out whether this change occurred because of a new estimate of the candidate or party in question, or whether some fundamental principle of the respondent's has undergone change.

A complete answer should always include a minimum of one element from each of these three groups, and usually should include more than that. It should tell who they are talking about, what information influenced them and if possible where they learned that piece of information, and finally how this influence changed their thinking. An interviewer should never be content with an answer unless it answers all of these questions: who, what, where and how. The answer to these four questions should constitute a complete "why," within the limitations set for the present study.

A GRAPHIC DEVICE FOR CHECKING RESPONSES

The various elements which constitute a complete answer to a reason for change of opinion which have just been outlined may be graphically presented, as shown in Chart 1.

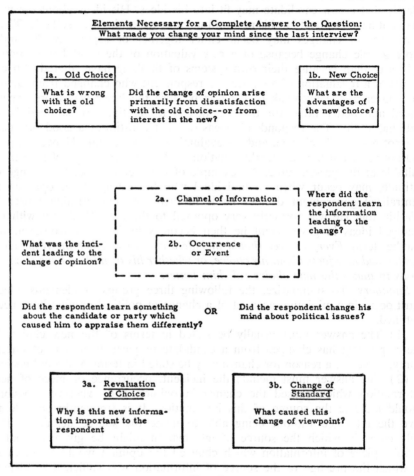

Elements Necessary for a Complete Answer to the Question:
What made you change your mind since the last interview?

1a. Old Choice		1b. New Choice
What is wrong with the old choice?	Did the change of opinion arise primarily from dissatisfaction with the old choice--or from interest in the new?	What are the advantages of the new choice?

2a. Channel of Information

Where did the respondent learn the information leading to the change?

2b. Occurrence or Event

What was the incident leading to the change of opinion?

Did the respondent learn something about the candidate or party which caused him to appraise them differently?   OR   Did the respondent change his mind about political issues?

3a. Revaluation of Choice	3b. Change of Standard
Why is this new information important to the respondent	What caused this change of viewpoint?

Chart 1

By plotting some of the actual answers to questions on reasons for change secured in the preliminary interviews, it is possible to illustrate graphically what constitutes a complete answer and to show the shortcomings of various incomplete answers, as well as to illustrate ways in which the interviewers should have attempted to enrich the responses by seeking further specifying questions.

The minimum essentials for an answer on change of political opinion appear in Chart 2.

The first diagram is a graphic representation of the type of answer which is phrased in terms of the new choice, which tells the occurrence or new information which influenced the decision, and the change is a revaluation of the candidate rather than a fundamental change in the standards of judgment of the respondent. This type of response constituted the largest group of fairly complete responses which were secured in the preliminary try-out interviews. An example of this sort of response is one man who changed from Garner to Roosevelt and accounted for it by saying:

Since the war he has handled things so well, has done a wonderful job to keep us out of it so far.

The respondent is talking about Roosevelt (1b—new choice) whom he has revalued over Garner (3a) because of his handling of our foreign affairs

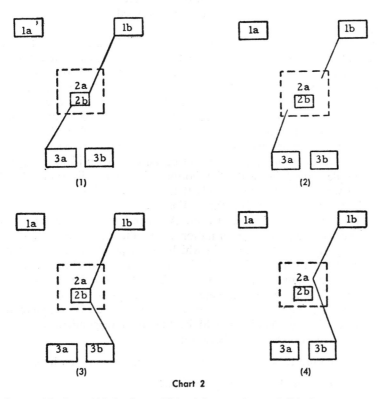

Chart 2

Any combination which involves additional features is permissible but no answer with fewer elements than these can be considered as giving a complete account of the reasons for the change.

since the outbreak of the war (2b). The only missing piece of information that might be especially pertinent here would be to ascertain if possible the chief sources of information about Roosevelt's policies. Since, however, the respondent has probably met his subject matter at every turn, it is probably impossible to get him to answer this question. It would be possible, of course, to ask if Garner had done anything to lose favor with him, but the chances are that it is a case of "not loving Garner less but loving Roosevelt more" so he would not be able to give an answer to such a query.

A response which would be presented graphically similar to the next diagram (2) would be the following:

(McNutt to Hull) Read his World's Fair speech; does not want this country in war.

The response is in terms of the new choice (1b), the new information—the fact that Hull does not want to get this country into war—is the specific occurrence which brought about the change of the opinion (2b), he learned about it through reading his World's Fair speech (2a) and through these influences revalued his opinion of Hull (3a). One might ask this respondent where he read the speech and he might be able to answer specifically or generally, but outside of that, this can be considered quite a complete answer to the question which does not need to be followed up by further specifying questions to any great extent.

The two lower diagrams on the chart (3 and 4) are similar to the two just illustrated except that they pertain to instances in which the respondent has completely changed his standard of judgment. This occurs so rarely that there were no actual examples of these types of response in the preliminary interviews. Theoretically, the first one (3) would occur in an instance of a respondent changing from Browder to Thomas at the time of the Russo-German non-aggression pact because he himself suddenly became an isolationist. In other words, his change of candidates occurred not because of any revaluation of the men but because his own ideas changed. The same example would illustrate the bottom right-hand diagram (4) if the respondent were able to say definitely that he secured this information which caused the change through *The Daily Worker.*

"Don't Knows" Are Special Cases. As mentioned before, all complete answers must contain some information about the new choice of candidate or political party except in cases in which the respondent has changed from a specific choice to uncertainty (don't know). The old choice may always be mentioned as supplementary to the information on the new choice, but it is never sufficient for a complete answer except in the one instance of change to uncertainty. An example of a response which is complete without a mention of the new choice would be that of a respondent who changed from Hoover to "don't know" because:

Hoover is too pro-British so the war has changed my mind on him.

It would be persented graphically in Chart 3.

The answer is in terms of the old choice, Hoover, (1a), it was occasioned by the outbreak of the war (2b), and resulted in a revaluation of the old candidate (3b) and a resultant state of uncertainty; it would be impossible to secure any information from him on his "new choice."

CLASSIFICATION OF ACTUAL RESPONSES

In a trial set of interviews, wherever a change of opinion was found, the blunt question was asked, "Why did you change your mind?" or "What was the reason for this change?" The type of answers which resulted from this simple direct questioning form the best illustration of the inadequacy of this method. Not only is one question usually insufficient to elicit a complete

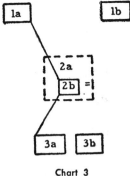

Chart 3

answer, but this particular direct question is not the one which produces the best results.

The responses to this trial study were divided according to the number of factors in the foregoing scheme. The results appear in Table 1.

Out of 632 responses, 105 individuals or 16.6 per cent were not able to answer at all. There is every reason to believe, however, that if the interviewers had asked them more specific questions, they might have cut down this number considerably. It was difficult to classify 39 cases (6.2 per cent). Of the remaining cases which were classified, 69.8 per cent (441) gave incomplete answers and only 7.4 per cent approached completeness according to the criteria which we have just set up. Some examples of the incomplete answers which were received most frequently will serve to clarify the table. For instance, the most frequent type of response concerned only the occurrence which had brought about the change of opinion. The most usual occurrence mentioned was the war. In one case, a man changed from McNutt to Roosevelt because of "war conditions." He failed to give the relation of war conditions to his new choice, or what he thought of war conditions; the answer is obviously incomplete.

Almost as frequently respondents would mention an occurrence in connection with their new choice, but even so, they frequently neglected to mention what it was about the new candidate which decided them. For instance, one man changed from Dewey to Taft because Taft "seems to be coming forward." The respondent did not mention any characteristics of Taft which caused him to change his mind. We still do not know what the respondent thinks of Taft, nor how his reasoning is related to his own attitudes.

Another category which accounted for many of the responses was the third, in which respondents gave only some characteristic of their new choice as the reason. For instance, the man who changed from "don't know" to Garner because he was "more conservative than the present regime" gives no intimation of what happened *since the last interview* to cause the change.

A similar answer—but one which is even more meaningless—is the man who accounted for his change from Dewey to Taft by saying, "I think he's best so far." He did not say why he thought he was best, or why he decided against Dewey, or what influenced the change since the last interview.

A reference to Table 1 shows that 43 people answered only in reference to the new candidate and the channel of their information (fourth in the list of incomplete responses). Typical of these responses is one respondent who changed from Dewey to Vandenberg because he has "read more about him." He refers to his new choice and to the channel but he neither tells *what* the source of information was or *what* the new information about Vandenberg was which caused him to change his mind. Furthermore, he gave no inkling as to whether the information caused him to think better of Vandenberg or whether he made a fundamental change in his own attitudes which made Vandenberg more suitable to him.

One more example of incomplete response will serve to show the prac-

Table 1—Classification of Actual Responses (1939 pre-test)

Classification		Number
INCOMPLETE RESPONSES		
1. Occurrence		75
War	60	
General conditions	9	
Other	6	
2. New candidate and occurrence		74
Roosevelt and war	33	
Vandenberg and neutrality	3	
Other	38	
3. New candidate		66
Roosevelt	11	
Garner	10	
Dewey	8	
Other	37	
4. New candidate and channel		43
Print	17	
Private discussion	4	
Other	22	
5. Change of standard		22
6. Channel of information		22
7. Old candidate and occurrence		20
8. Old candidate and revaluation of choice		20
9. New candidate and revaluation of choice		15
10. Old and new candidates and revaluation of choice		13
11. Old candidate		11
12. Other miscellaneous combinations		60
Total Incomplete Responses		441
COMPLETE RESPONSES		
1. New candidate, occurrence, and change of standard		15
2. Old candidate, occurrence, and revaluation of choice*		7
3. Old and new candidates, occurrence, and revaluation of choice		6
4. New candidate, occurrence, and revaluation of choice		4
5. Old candidate, occurrence, and change of standard*		4
6. Old and new candidates, occurrence and change of standard		3
7. New candidate, channel of information, and revaluation of choice		2
8. Other miscellaneous combinations		6
Total Complete Responses		47
UNCLASSIFIABLE		39
NO ANSWER		105
GRAND TOTAL		632

* Changed to "don't know."

tical difficulties in the way of the interviewer. As an example of the fifth group of individuals in the table of incomplete responses, 22 in number, is one man who changed from Roosevelt to McNutt because he "decided against the third term." In order to make a complete response of such an answer, an interviewer should find out what influences led to the decision against the third term, whether it was an incident, new information, a particular channel of information, and whether he turned chiefly against Roosevelt or in favor of McNutt.

Examples of More Complete Responses. Reference to the table of complete responses shows that the most frequent adequate responses concerned (1) the new candidate or choice, (2) an occurrence and (3) a change of attitude or standard. An example of this most frequent group may be the man who changed from Hull to Roosevelt and accounted for it as follows: "The way the war is going I am beginning to think we should get into it. I am beginning to agree with Roosevelt's intervention policy and I was always an isolationist before. I want Roosevelt for president for this reason." His responses may be presented graphically as in Chart 4.

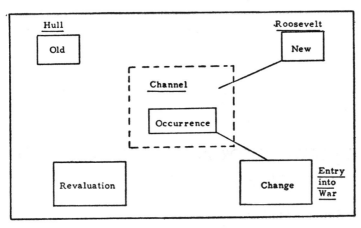

Chart 4

This is a complete response because it tells the event which caused the change of attitude and how Roosevelt fits into this man's ideas—in other words, what he likes about Roosevelt. The answer represents elements from three levels on the diagram and may be considered to be quite complete.

The next most frequent type of response which meets the minimum of our requirements were those concerned with (1) old candidate, (2) an occurrence and (3) revaluation of choice. As mentioned before, this type of response can be adequate only in instances in which the respondent has changed from a definite name to uncertainty or "don't know." Whenever a change has been made to a definite person, it is imperative that the reason for changing to the *new* choice be included in the reason, no matter what additional information is obtained about the old choice. An example of this second type of adequate response may be the man who changed from Roosevelt to "don't know" and said, "It looks as if Roosevelt was getting us into war. I don't believe we should help the Allies, so I have changed my mind about Roosevelt since the war began. I don't know who I want now—just somebody who will keep us out of war." His response may be presented graphically as in Chart 5.

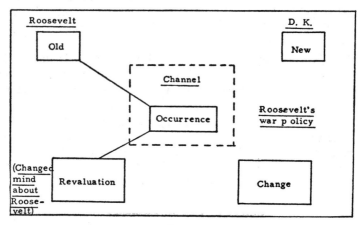

Chart 5

6. A FRAMEWORK FOR ASSESSMENT OF CAUSES OF AUTOMOBILE ACCIDENTS

by J. Stannard Baker

TRAFFIC ACCIDENTS: WHAT THEY ARE

IF YOU ARE SERIOUSLY INTERESTED in traffic accidents and their prevention, you ought to understand more than the ordinary person about what traffic accidents are and how they happen.

You will know that a traffic accident is not just a collision between a couple of cars, but rather a whole series of events, one leading into the other. A collision is only one of these events. More important still, you will clearly realize that when you have found a law violation or some other single condition which contributed to the accident, you cannot yet say that you know its cause! Finding causes is not so simple as that. Almost all

Reprinted from *The Traffic Institute's Basic Training Manual on Accident Investigation: Traffic Accidents,* publication No. 799, 1952, pp. 1-13, by permission of the author and the publisher. (Copyright, 1952, by The Traffic Institute, Northwestern University.)

accidents have many causes; direct causes, mediate causes that lead to the direct ones, and deep in the past, accidents have roots in many early or remote causes.

Especially if you ever have to investigate one, you need a clear idea of what makes an accident, how one cause leads to another, just how the road, the vehicle, and the driver can contribute to the mishap, and what the results may be. In fact, the main purpose of investigation is to find out exactly these things.

In the present discussion, we do not intend to tell you how to investigate accidents. Nor will we name over the many circumstances common in the traffic accidents today. These are all the subject of special publications. We will try only to look at accidents a bit more closely than most people ever bother to do. We will take them apart, as it were, in a professional way and examine them as experts. By so doing our thinking about accidents will be less fuzzy. We can then talk about them, not in vague general terms, but with precision. All who deal with traffic accidents professionally must strive for common, clear ideas about them. Otherwise the facts dug up by investigators are not truly summarized by statisticians; the engineers do not quickly see what improvements they must make in cars and roads; and driver license authorities do not have a firm basis for dealing with problem drivers.

Accidents involving vehicles may occur in places other than on a trafficway. Persons involved in these accidents may also be prosecuted and convicted of certain violations of the Uniform Vehicle Code. These violations include manslaughter, negligent homicide, driving while intoxicated, leaving the scene of an accident, and reckless driving.

Investigators may investigate accidents which involve vehicles and which occur on private property as well as those which occur on a trafficway. All accidents have much in common with traffic accidents. But many accidents are traffic accidents and here we are discussing only the latter.

CONDITIONS NECESSARY TO MAKE A TRAFFIC ACCIDENT

First, let us review what it takes to make a traffic accident. To do this, we will have to define some of the terms which are often used carelessly. There are four conditions which must be met before we can say that a happening or series of events is a traffic accident.

1. There must be *surprise*. Like any other kind of accident, a traffic accident is unintentional and unexpected. It has in it, therefore, an important element of surprise. If a smash-up on the highway were done on purpose, it would be no accident. If an intentional wreck resulted in death it would be homicide or suicide.

2. It must happen on a *trafficway*. A trafficway is "the entire width between property lines (or other boundary lines) of every way or place of which any part is open to the use of the public for purposes of vehicular traffic as a matter of right or custom. A trafficway and a public way are synonomous." A traffic accident may, therefore, occur not only on any of the public property included in streets and highways, but also on some private roadways such as those at railroad stations. You can have a collision of two automobiles without having a traffic accident. This happens

when they are entirely on private property as, for example, within the gates
of a manufacturing plant, on a construction project, or even a farm or
home driveway.

3. It must *involve traffic*. Traffic is "pedestrians, ridden or herded animals, vehicles, streetcars, and other conveyances either singly or together
while using any highway for purposes of travel." This means that the vehicles and people must be traveling on the highway. There must be some
motion of some highway unit in a traffic accident. An automobile can be
smashed up on a trafficway without being in a traffic accident. This can
happen, for example, if a storm blows a tree on a standing car or if a parked
car catches on fire. You can also have a traffic accident without a motor
vehicle being involved. For example, if a boy coasting down a sidewalk on
a bicycle hits a dog and gets hurt in the spill, it is a traffic accident, but
not a motor vehicle accident, of course.

4. It must do some *injury or damage*. A car can skid into a terrific spin
on a trafficway, but so long as nobody is hurt or nothing is hit, there is no
accident. A car can even go over a bank and have to be pulled back on
the road by a tow truck and still it is no traffic accident unless the car is
damaged or somebody is hurt before the car comes to rest. Probably the
most common surprise to a road user on a trafficway is simply running out
of gasoline. This is an accident, but not a traffic accident. A blowout or
other breakdown of the vehicle in traffic is also an accident, but unless
there is other damage or injury, it is no traffic accident. However, running
out of gasoline, blowouts, and breakdowns can be mediate causes of traffic
accidents in which someone is hurt or damage is done. Perhaps we might
say that a traffic accident must result in damage, injury, or *death*. Death in
traffic accidents rarely occurs without injury. Therefore, let it be understood that when injury is mentioned, it also includes death. A traffic accident may involve very little damage. The amount of damage makes no
difference except in requirements for reporting. In some places you do not
have to *report* accidents with less than a certain amount of damage. In
many commercial vehicle fleets, on the other hand, every contact with another
vehicle, whether it results in visible damage or not, is reportable as an
accident.

So, however much traffic accidents differ as to cause, circumstances, and
results, they all have four things in common: they involve *traffic* on a *trafficway, surprise,* and *damage* or *injury*.

TRAFFIC ACCIDENTS BACKWARDS AND FORWARDS

We See Most Traffic Accidents Backwards. Unless you are involved in
it, you usually learn first the *result* of the traffic accident. You read in the
papers ". . . died early Wednesday from injuries received in an automobile
accident." You see a wrecked car in the junkyard. Even if you hurry out
to investigate an accident at the scene, the first thing you see is the damage
and injury.

You can usually find out what collision or other key event led to the
result, and you can get some idea of the direct cause of this key event. What
led, in turn, to the direct causes is harder to learn and still earlier acts or
conditions, even when they are very important to the accident, are generally

lost in the past. Thus, what we see most clearly is the result or end of the accident. We have to imagine, in most cases, the early causes, remote in the past, which are the real beginning of the mishap. We see most traffic accidents backwards.

Knowing so much more of the end of accidents than of the beginning is unfortunate because to stop accidents we must get at their causes. We can do little about the results. Getting the facts from which we can know the direct causes and at least guessing sensibly at the earlier causes is the main aim of accident investigation.

You will probably never know the true beginnings of a single real traffic accident, but if we study many of them closely we can get good enough ideas of the underlying causes of traffic accidents in general to be very helpful in preventing them.

Looking at an Accident from Beginning to End. To understand how a series of events makes up a traffic accident, we can study an imaginary accident from beginning to end. By this means, you can see how some of these events are the causes of others and how certain ones are used to fix the precise place, type, and time of the accident. A simple accident will do as an example. The facts of such an accident are listed and labeled in Exhibit One. You should follow the chart [appearing below]. You should examine the information on this chart closely before reading farther.

CAUSES OF ACCIDENTS

If you knew all of the facts about an accident—even those acts and conditions which a long time before helped set the stage for it—you would realize clearly at once how many different things contributed to it. In other words, you could find many causes of an accident, perhaps hundreds of them. Study these causes a little and you will see that some are closer to the accident than others although not necessarily more important. Some of the contributing acts or conditions lead *directly* to the mishap. These are easy to discover. Others are early causes remote from the accident. Such causes are very difficult to learn about in any particular accident. In between are middle or mediate causes. They lead from the remote to the direct cause. They are, if you please, the result of remote causes, and the causes of the direct cause.

All causes of accidents have one thing in common. You must be able to say of each cause that, "if it had not existed, the accident would not have happened."

Early or remote causes are contributing conditions which made possible the chain of events which we speak of as a traffic accident. They also include the acts which created these conditions or neglect which failed to do away with them. Many different accidents can arise from the same early causes, but it is often difficult to connect any particular accident to those early causes.

The conditions which we think of as remote causes of accidents often result from acts of the public and public officials which result in conditions of street and highway transportation which are favorable for accidents, and failure to create other conditions to prevent them.

These conditions are reflected in turn, of course, in the acts of teachers of drivers, engineers who design and build cars and highways, police who supervise traffic, courts which fail to create a sufficient deterrent to violations, and driver license authorities who do not correct or remove unsafe drivers.

Early causes also include conditions not quite so remote. These conditions are noted in the acts, and especially the neglect, of drivers—in planning trips, failure to maintain vehicles, drinking before driving, failing to prepare for emergencies, and many other things which, *after* an accident, can be seen so clearly as contributing factors, and become sources of deep thought, often secret regret, and remorse.

Mediate or Middle Causes are:

1. Conditions which exist at the time and the place of the accident,
2. The acts or neglect which lead quickly up to the surprise, and
3. The acts after surprise which make the situation worse, or the failure to take action to mitigate or reduce the seriousness of the accident.

The Story of An Accident

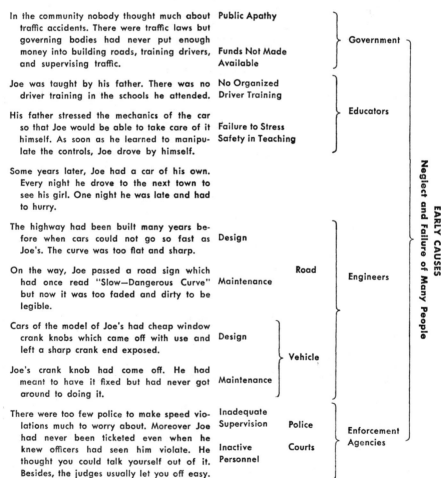

In the community nobody thought much about traffic accidents. There were traffic laws but governing bodies had never put enough money into building roads, training drivers, and supervising traffic.
Public Apathy
Funds Not Made Available
} Government

Joe was taught by his father. There was no driver training in the schools he attended.
No Organized Driver Training

His father stressed the mechanics of the car so that Joe would be able to take care of it himself. As soon as he learned to manipulate the controls, Joe drove by himself.
Failure to Stress Safety in Teaching
} Educators

Some years later, Joe had a car of his own. Every night he drove to the next town to see his girl. One night he was late and had to hurry.

The highway had been built many years before when cars could not go so fast as Joe's. The curve was too flat and sharp.
Design

On the way, Joe passed a road sign which had once read "Slow—Dangerous Curve" but now it was too faded and dirty to be legible.
Maintenance
Road
Engineers

Cars of the model of Joe's had cheap window crank knobs which came off with use and left a sharp crank end exposed.
Design

Joe's crank knob had come off. He had meant to have it fixed but had never got around to doing it.
Maintenance
} Vehicle

There were too few police to make speed violations much to worry about. Moreover Joe had never been ticketed even when he knew officers had seen him violate. He thought you could talk yourself out of it. Besides, the judges usually let you off easy.
Inadequate Supervision
Inactive Personnel
Police
Courts
Enforcement Agencies

Neglect and Failure of Many People } EARLY CAUSES

Mediate causes usually determine the contribution of the vehicle, the road, and the driver or the pedestrian to the accident.

Example: Driving under the influence of intoxicating liquor; but the drinking which resulted in being under the influence is an early cause.

Example: Rain which makes the pavement slippery.

Example: The fact that a sign cannot be seen is a mediate cause; but failure to remove bushes which hide it is an early cause.

Example: A tire blowout is a mediate cause; but the neglect of the driver to keep his tires inflated so as to avoid blowouts is an early cause. The failure to keep a car under control after a blowout is another mediate cause.

Example: Violations of the rules of the road are mediate causes, but violations of laws relating to vehicle condition, driver licensing, and similar matters are early causes.

The direct cause of an accident is the unconventional behavior of a vehicle, pedestrian, or passenger which leads directly to the key event. There

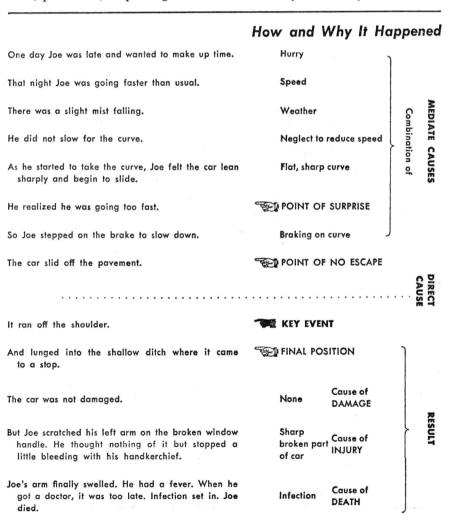

How and Why It Happened

One day Joe was late and wanted to make up time.	Hurry	
That night Joe was going faster than usual.	Speed	
There was a slight mist falling.	Weather	
He did not slow for the curve.	Neglect to reduce speed	
As he started to take the curve, Joe felt the car lean sharply and begin to slide.	Flat, sharp curve	
He realized he was going too fast.	☞ POINT OF SURPRISE	
So Joe stepped on the brake to slow down.	Braking on curve	
The car slid off the pavement.	☞ POINT OF NO ESCAPE	
It ran off the shoulder.	☞ KEY EVENT	
And lunged into the shallow ditch where it came to a stop.	☞ FINAL POSITION	
The car was not damaged.	None	Cause of DAMAGE
But Joe scratched his left arm on the broken window handle. He thought nothing of it but stopped a little bleeding with his handkerchief.	Sharp broken part of car	Cause of INJURY
Joe's arm finally swelled. He had a fever. When he got a doctor, it was too late. Infection set in. Joe died.	Infection	Cause of DEATH

MEDIATE CAUSES — Combination of

DIRECT CAUSE

RESULT

is, for practical purposes in one-car accidents, only one direct cause. We find this in what the car did. Why the car did it is a mediate cause. If we were watching a car from outside we could see this unconventional behavior. Of course, not all such behavior which we would see would result in accidents, because the driver or some other driver or pedestrian may be successful in avoiding the accident after the surprise.

Example: Skidding on a curve is a direct cause. The slippery paving or high speed is a mediate cause.

Example: Failure to stop for a red light; but the inattention of the driver or his wilful disregard of the signal are mediate causes.

Example: Failure to slow down in approaching a blind corner; the high speed which required the slowing is a mediate cause.

THE Cause. You must be careful how you speak of *the* cause of an accident. People often mention any cause of an accident as *the* cause; worse still, they often carelessly think that when they know one circumstance which contributed to it they know the cause. This is only true when you speak of the *direct* cause. You cannot say, for example, that drunken driving was the cause of the accident. It was a mediate cause. There was at least a direct cause resulting from it and early causes, such as driving after drinking, and drinking with the knowledge that there was driving to be done after it.

The only way you can speak or think of *the* cause as covering anything but the direct cause is to think of the cause as that *combination* of circumstances which resulted in the accident. It takes the *combination* to make the accident. One cause alone is not enough. For example, there can be drunken driving that results in no accident. The accident follows only when drunken driving combines with other things such as speed. In fact, there can be accidents in which the driver is intoxicated in which driving under the influence is not a cause, because the intoxicated condition contributed nothing to the accident. That is, the accident would have happened even if that condition had not existed.

LANDMARKS IN THE CHAIN OF EVENTS

If the cause of an accident, properly speaking, is a *combination* of causes —direct, mediate, and early—then the accident itself, strictly speaking, is a series of events. Among these events some are picked out as reference points or landmarks. We say that other events are before or after them, or that they occurred a certain distance away from the key event on the road. We must agree on the names for these events if we are going to talk technically and precisely about accidents. We must be technical if we are to be successful in investigating individual accidents and in understanding traffic accidents as a whole.

We will mention here the reference points in the series of events in the order in which they usually occur. This is not the order of importance.

Point of surprise is the moment when a driver or pedestrian realizes that something is going wrong. It is not the moment when danger develops, because danger may develop before the driver is aware of it. Not all accidents have a point of surprise. For example, if a driver falls asleep and runs into a heavy fixed object on the roadway, he may be killed without ever knowing that he was in an accident.

The point of surprise is used mainly in trying to evaluate the contribution of drivers to the accident. Did the driver do anything or fail to do anything before this point which contributed to his surprise? Inattention is probably the most common contribution the driver makes to his own surprise. But there are also others, including speed. The point of surprise is particularly useful in trying to find out what the driver did or should have done but did not do after surprise to avoid the accident or to make it less serious. Many accidents are prevented by prompt and proper action after surprise, but most good drivers strive to avoid the surprise in the first place.

Point of no escape is that place in time after or beyond which the accident cannot be prevented. Nothing the driver can do will save him from this point on, although he still may be able to mitigate the accident, for example, by slowing down as much as possible before a collision. Sometimes the point of no escape and the point of surprise are the same. Sometimes the point of no escape comes before the point of surprise, for example, in the driver-asleep accident. Often the point of no escape comes after the point of surprise and this indicates faulty judgment on the part of the driver in his attempt to prevent the impending accident.

Key event is a most important landmark in the series which makes up an accident. It is usually not hard to locate. It is the only event which is bound to be the same for all vehicles involved in a multiple car accident.

The key event is the event by which we classify the accident as to type and exact time and place.

1. In all collisions on the roadway or shoulder, the key event is the first contact between the colliding bodies.

2. If a vehicle leaves the roadway and shoulder before striking anything or overturning or having any other difficulty leading to injury or damage, leaving the shoulder is the key event.

3. If the accident involves neither collision nor leaving the roadway, the key event is usually the same as the direct cause.

Example: A moving car catches fire and burns. The key event is the start of the fire.

Example: A boy falls from a moving truck. The key event is the loss of contact with the truck. This is also the direct cause of the accident.

Key events involving motor vehicles are officially listed as these:

1. Collision with pedestrian.
2. Collision with another motor vehicle.
3. Collision with a railroad train.
4. Collision with streetcar.
5. Collision with bicycle.
6. Collision with animal-drawn vehicle.
7. Collision with animal.
8. Collision with fixed objects.
9. Collision with other object.
10. Non-collision, overturning on the roadway.
11. Non-collision, running off the roadway.
12. Other non-collision.

In traffic accidents not involving motor vehicles, there are additional similar key events.

Sometimes the key event is spoken of as the "first event." This refers only to which of the twelve events listed above occurs first in an accident.

Maximum engagement is the time and place in which vehicles, pedestrians, or other objects in a collision are pushed together as far as they will be. The position of the vehicles and other objects at this point is quite important in reconstructing many accidents. Maximum engagement always follows the key event.

Final position is the place and time when objects involved in the accident come to rest. This is the position *before* anything is moved to help the injured or salvage the vehicles. It is very important in investigating accidents, but fortunately it is usually easy to determine before vehicles have been moved. Often the final position of passengers or freight carried by a vehicle is quite different from that of the vehicle itself. The final position of vehicles and other objects, as well as their location, is helpful in figuring out what happened.

The exact time and place. To identify an accident it is well enough to say in general where and when it happened. For example, we say that the accident happened at 4:30 P.M., May 15, 1955, at Fifth and Main Streets, Springfield, Illinois. This prevents confusion of this accident with any other accident. However, to reconstruct the chain of events which is an accident, we may have to know how many feet from certain points in the intersection of Fifth and Main the accident took place, and how many seconds there were between the point of surprise and the key point. For exact purposes, the key point is nearly always taken as the reference. It is zero time and distance for the accident. Seconds and feet are measured and computed before this point to the beginning of skidmarks, for example, and after it or beyond it to final positions.

Sometimes the exact position of the key point is important in determining whether the accident is to be counted on private property, or on one side or the other of a county or municipal boundary. This fact may determine in what jurisdiction law cases arising from the accident may have to be tried, which people investigate it, whether it is to be counted as a traffic accident, and against the records of which community it will be charged.

RESULTS

The results of an accident are always death, injury, or damage; otherwise there is no accident. The amount and kind of damage are important in settling liability claims. Billions of dollars change hands every year in the United States on the basis of the analysis of the kind and amount of damage and injury in automobile accidents.

Very important in investigating accidents is the examination of damage to vehicles. This is often the key clue to what happened and who was to blame. It very often confirms or contradicts the testimony of witnesses. The causes of damage and injury when discovered and accurately reported are of greatest assistance in the improvement of the design of vehicles, and in the construction of roadways to make them safer and easier to drive on.

A part of any full understanding of an accident must, therefore, involve a study of causes and results.

MULTIPLE ACCIDENTS

So far, our discussion has been based on simple single accidents involving only one highway user unit. What about the accidents involving two cars or a car and a pedestrian—that is, involving two or more highway user units? These are multiple accidents. A two-car accident is actually two accidents and should be treated as such. Except, of course, they are reported on the same accident report form. Each driver and each car is in an accident. For each driver, the other vehicle is part of the problem—something to be seen, evaluated, and avoided if possible. Only by looking at accidents in this way is it possible to evaluate the contribution to accidents of both drivers and both vehicles, and the part of the road that each traveled upon successfully. The two accidents always have in common the key event, and usually the point but not the position of maximum engagement. A view obstruction is often common to two drivers involved in a multiple accident. Other than these, they may have little or nothing in common as to cause or chain of events. Investigators and analysts must examine each separately for what its driver, its vehicle, and its part of the road contributes. The point of surprise and the point of no escape of the two units involved always occur at different places and usually at different times.

Sometimes there are more than two vehicles involved. The first or key event may be only the beginning of a fantastic series of mishaps, all of which make one very complicated multiple accident.

The most common multiple accident of this kind happens when a vehicle runs into another vehicle that has just had an accident. More than 50 cars have been known to pile up in one multiple accident before the hazard of those previously involved could be removed. Although these are counted as single accidents, there is actually a separate accident for each road user unit involved.

Sometimes the key event may be a considerable distance from the main cause of damage. A flying piece of metal may strike a bystander some distance off. Gasoline running down a gutter may start a fire a block away. A broken utility pole can bring a live wire against a fence and electrocute a cow half a mile off. All these are parts of complex accidents—each starting with a key event which fixes the time, place, and type, and each consisting of as many single accidents as there are transportation user units involved.

RECONSTRUCTION

By reconstruction we do not mean the repairing of damage or injuries done in the accident. We mean the process of trying to figure out afterward what happened. From information we can get following the accident, we can think back to what must have happened to produce such results. The bits of information can be fitted together to make a logical and sensible explanation of the chain of events including the direct cause and many of the immediate causes. This is like fitting together a jigsaw puzzle. Parts of the puzzle are nearly always missing, and we can only infer what the missing part of a picture was like; but if not too many parts are missing, this inference can be good enough for our purposes. In fact, circumstantial evidence of what happened is often sufficient to prove in court some events to which there was no witness.

The explanation developed in reconstructing an accident must fit all of the information we know to be fact. It may also prove that some information we have received is not fact. There must be a place in our completed picture for all of the pieces we know belong to it. The assembly of these pieces can tell us whether some pieces mixed in with the others just don't belong in the picture.

There is always a considerable danger in reconstructing an accident beyond the point where facts support us. People who are less familiar with accidents and accident investigation are more likely to make incorrect inferences concerning them than the expert. It is entirely possible that such hastily drawn conclusions can result in serious miscarriages of justice.

CONCLUSION

Only by close study of individual actions can we ever hope to learn enough about how and why accidents happen to guide us in our efforts to prevent them. This is not a casual job for the ordinary person, but has become a speized business requiring some knowledge of the fundamentals of accidents, what their parts are, and how they are named. It is especially important to realize that an accident is a chain of events, and that the cause is a combination of many circumstances often extending back over many years.

THE ASSESSMENT

AND STATISTICAL ANALYSIS

OF CAUSES

7. THE TECHNIQUE OF "DISCERNING"

by Mirra Komarovsky

[In *The Unemployed Man and His Family*, Mirra Komarovsky, by means of a series of intensive interviews, undertook to analyze the impact of the depression on social relationships within the family. One question of special interest to her involved the impact of unemployment upon the loss of family authority by the head of the household. In her description of "discerning," Dr. Komarovsky describes her procedure for assessing evidence in particular cases.—ED. NOTE.]

IN DISCERNING the causal relation between loss of authority and unemployment it must be made clear that we refer to the causal relation *in a particular case*. No generalization is attempted at this point as to how universally unemployment causes the change in question. Unemployment may be the cause of loss of authority in a particular case, but this in itself tells nothing of the relative tendency of unemployment to cause loss of authority. The case may be an exceptional one. Unemployment may be modified by numerous other factors to such an extent that it produces change under relatively exceptional conditions.

The procedure of discerning to be described below consists of the following steps:

1. Preliminary checking of the evidence to make it more specific and complete.
2. Checking the evidence for its consistency with other situations in the life of the respondent and, generally, with human reactions observed in similar situations.
3. Testing the possible alternative explanations of the change. The criteria in the third step are once again the relative consistency of one or another explanation with what is known of the life of the respondent and with general knowledge concerning human behavior in similar situations.

Before describing these various steps we shall present the *kinds of initial evidence* upon which discerning was based.

The initial statements of the respondents on changes during unemployment are of the following kinds:

a. *Statement of some sequence of events involving unemployment:* "Prior to unemployment the children used to go to my husband's church. Now they go with me to the Catholic Church." "My husband has been drinking since

---

he has been unemployed." "I used to enjoy sex relations with my husband. I don't any more."

The above statements describe a sequence of events without any statement as to their causal relation. The change may refer to activity or to a state of mind, but there is no link between unemployment and the change.

b. *An interpretation of a sequence concerning another person:* "My wife lost respect for me because I failed as a provider." "My husband nags since unemployment because he has nothing to do all day."

c. *The person's confessed experience that unemployment caused a change:* Whenever a person reports not only a change but a personal motivation of the change, we have this kind of evidence. "I lost my love for my husband because he turned out to be a failure." "Unemployment made me lose faith in myself."

If the woman says, "We don't talk to each other as often as we used to," we have merely a sequence of unemployment and the change. If she adds, "because I am too disgusted with him to bother talking to him," then we have her experience as to the relation between unemployment and the change.

Many initial statements of the family involve a combination of the various kinds of evidence. "My wife used to be patient and kind, but now she nags so much that I cannot stand her any more and try to stay out of the house as much as I can." Such a statement includes both a report of a sequence of events (unemployment, wife nags more), and a testimony of a personal causal experience (nagging, caused man to stay away from home).

The first step of discerning is to subject the initial statements to a preliminary checking. There are two possible sources of error. The changes indicated may not have taken place, and they may not have been due to unemployment. Although logically the procedure of discerning deals with the problem of the causal relation between unemployment and loss of authority or some other change, practically the two problems are interwoven and similar techniques are involved in the attempt to solve them.

The preliminary checking of the initial statements is achieved by a series of specifying questions to make the evidence more concrete and complete.

1. PRELIMINARY CHECKING TO MAKE THE EVIDENCE MORE SPECIFIC AND COMPLETE

One kind of specifying question attempts to supplement sequences of unemployment and some change with statements of *experienced interconnection between the two.* This can be done by asking the respondents as to possible motives by which unemployment and the change in question could be linked more strongly.

It has been established that a man goes to church more often. Does he know why he goes more often now? Is it in the hope of making useful contacts or as a substitute for more expensive leisure time activities or because of increased need for religious consolation?

Similarly questions might be directed to find out what feature in unemployment appears to the respondent as the cause of the change.

It has been established that a man reads fewer books since he became unemployed. What in the unemployment situation has been the decisive causal feature of this decrease? Lack of money to pay his dues? Having no longer any access to the factory library? Spending all his time on job hunting? Losing interest in books because of worry?

Another kind of specifying question *is directed at a more detailed statement* of the link between unemployment and the change.

If a man says, "I used to be boss in the family, but now no one pays any attention to me," he is asked questions as to intermediate steps of this process. How did he recognize the fact? When did he first feel it? What did he do about it? How did members of the family react to it? And so on.

Submitting the original statements of the respondent to the above-described questioning may in some cases serve completely to eliminate alleged causal relations. If the reported sequence constituted a perfunctory answer, the respondent may not withstand the barrage of questions. In other cases, if we succeed in transforming statements of sequence into statements of experience of a causal relation, we have a more satisfactory kind of evidence. The woman who said that her children since her husband's unemployment had been going to the Catholic Church may confess that prior to unemployment she had had to acquiesce to her husband's demands because otherwise he threatened to withdraw his support from the family. Now she no longer depends upon him for support and can do whatever she wants to. This is considered a more adequate kind of evidence because on the basis of our general observation of human behavior we can understand it, we can perceive how unemployment has led to the change.

The next check of the evidence for the causal relation between unemployment and the change is an attempt to discover whether the alleged condition is consistent with what we know of the life of the respondent.

2. TESTING THE CONSISTENCY OF THE EVIDENCE

Can the causal relation between unemployment and the change be true? If one factor is alleged to be the cause of some situation, then there must be an association between the two phenomena. If we find that one exists without the other, then the causal relation between them is not possible. Therefore, we look at the following situations as tests of the validity of the causal explanation offered by the informant.

a. *The alleged causal factor was present in a different situation in the informant's life without producing the action or attitude claimed to be a result of it.*

A wife testifies to a growth of conflict with her husband when she began going out evenings. "I can't stand his reading a book all evening without a word for me. I'd stay at home if he'd pay some attention to me." Upon analysis it may appear, however, that he always was fond of reading in the evening and never paid any more attention to her than at the time she made the statement. The fact is that, for one reason or another, she has refused to tolerate this situation since he has been unemployed.

A woman says that it is natural that unemployment would make her lose all respect for her husband, that a man who is a failure cannot be respected; yet there is evidence that her unemployed brother still has her respect and affection.

b. *The result has existed previously in the life of the informant even when the alleged causal factor was absent.*

The woman says that it is only unemployment that keeps the family together, that they are very unhappy, and if it were not for their poverty, they would break up the family. But the couple stayed together prior to unemployment when they could afford to maintain separate homes, although evidence shows that relations were not better then.

In addition to such logical tests, an attempt was made to consider whether the statements of the respondents were psychologically consistent with the total evidence of the case. A woman may deny that loss of earning ability has undermined her respect for her husband. This statement may be inconsistent with what is known about her values of life, her attitude towards her husband at the time of marriage, and her present behavior towards him.

There were cases in which it was not possible to get the respondent to state what the causal link was between unemployment and the change. A woman maintained that she did not know why she ceased to enjoy sex relations with her husband since unemployment. In this case and a few others, however, the causal link between the two phenomena seemed highly probable in spite of the fact that the respondent had not admitted it. Other information indicated that the failure of the husband as a provider was a sharp blow to the wife. She was disillusioned in the husband. His continuous presence at home revealed to her, as she said, that he had no personality. She blames him for unemployment and feels that a real man should be able to provide for his family. Our general experience with human reactions suggests that there might be a causal link between these attitudes and the decline in this woman's response to her husband in the sexual sphere.

The usefulness of the above tests lies in revealing inconsistencies. They can show which of the alleged causal relations between unemployment and the change are inconsistent. They do not offer conclusive proof of their validity. Thus the wife might testify to the increase in quarrels and attribute them to the man's increased presence at home and interference with her educational policies with the children. While, in terms of our tests, this explanation may be consistent, it is possible that the cause of the quarrels may be in a sphere which has nothing to do with unemployment, perhaps, and the wife may prefer to rationalize it in terms of the man's increased presence at home. This leads us to another section of discerning: testing alternative explanations.

3. TESTING ALTERNATIVE EXPLANATIONS

What other factors might have accounted for the change in question? The more we know about the phenomena we are studying, the more hypotheses we can evolve as to the possible alternative interpretations of observed changes.

The problem of alternative explanations is particularly important in the consideration of parental relations. Father-child relations undergo changes in the normal course of development. More than that, the changes that take place are in the direction of the emancipation of the child from the father's authority. Adolescence is likely to bring about increased conflict and a more or less conscious struggle of the child for self-determination. In other words, coincident with unemployment there has been going on a process of growth. How can we decide whether the loss of authority is due to unemployment or to the growth of the child? As a matter of fact, we can seldom be sure that change in authority would not have occurred had it not been for unemployment. All we can say is that unemployment has been, or has not been, a contributory factor. It is judged to be a contributory factor under three conditions:

a. If the conflict which precipitated loss of control was an aspect of unemployment.

b. If the father felt that unemployment undermined his power in dealing with the child.

c. If the child explicitly utilized unemployment in his struggle for emancipation.

Cases in which loss of authority is observed, but in which the conditions, (a), (b), and (c) do not exist, we consider not affected by unemployment. There were 4 cases in which growth of conflict and some loss of the father's control was observed, but the change was to all appearances completely unrelated to unemployment.

Certain other alternative hypotheses with regard to changes in parent-child relations may be stated as follows:

a. *How may a possible change in folkways affect the problem?* Since times have changed, children may perhaps demand greater freedom from regulation.

b. *Has aging of parents anything to do with the change being studied?* Perhaps they are less patient and more irritable with the younger children, which in turn causes conflict. All such problems should, if possible, be tested according to the directions indicated above.

Even if there are no older children for purposes of comparison, the informant should be asked whether the mere fact of the children's growing older may not offer a complete explanation of the change. Can he be sure that the disciplinary problems would not have arisen had there been no depression?

c. *How do differences in personalities of the children affect the problem?* It may be that the differences between the older and the younger children are the result, not of the depression, but of differences in personalities—such as the fact that the younger ones may be more stubborn or rebellious.

To summarize, we have assumed that unemployment caused a particular change when:

a. The informant has answered satisfactorily the specifying questions.

b. No inconsistency has been observed between the explanation in the light of other evidence in his life.

c. Apparently no other factors were present to explain the change.

The procedure of discerning will be briefly illustrated as it was applied to two cases. We shall illustrate only the reasoning involved in stages two and three, omitting the preliminary set of questions designed to get as concrete and complete a statement of changes as possible.

BRIEF ILLUSTRATIONS OF DISCERNING

CASE 1—Evidence of unemployment being the cause of loss of authority.

1. Statement of wife that she is dissatisfied with her husband because of his unemployment.

2. Statement of the husband that there are more marital conflicts since unemployment.

3. Statements of both that the conflicts consist in the wife's blaming her husband for hardships.

4. Change in the manner in which the wife treats the husband. The wife used to control her dissatisfactions with her husband. She is freer in expressing her dissatisfactions now.

On the basis of other evidence in the case it appears that the respondents are sincere and intelligent. Therefore we accept their testimony as to the increase in conflict.

Internal Consistency and Alternative Explanations. As to the second problem, "Is the conflict due to unemployment?" we accept the contents of the conflict as strong evidence of the causal link. They fight over his inability to find work. This, however, is no final proof. We know that some quarrels are frequently symbolic of underlying conflicts—that the apparent cause of the discussion is not the real one. It is possible that the other changes in the relations of the couple that have nothing to do with unemployment caused the growth of conflict, and that both of them prefer to rationalize this other conflict in terms of his inability to find work.

Suppose his mother came to live in the city, and the wife became very jealous of her, and resented the mother-son relations. Suppose that because of her upbringing she considers filial obligations as holy, and doesn't dare to say anything about it. She may show her irritation by picking on his unemployment, while under ordinary circumstances she would have absolved him from guilt.

If this other real conflict is a result of unemployment, we can, of course, still relate the phenomena to unemployment. But if we do not know what this other conflict may be, we cannot do so. What did we do to elicit the hidden conflicts? We went through the daily routine of life. If the other conflict has been a conscious one, we might have got it through our questioning; but if it was suppressed, it is doubtful that we would have uncovered it. For the conflict to have eluded us we must assume further that it was suppressed and done so by both respondents, which is a more remote possibility.

To summarize: We have decided that unemployment caused a change in this particular case because we had a reasonable explanation of the manner in which unemployment has caused it together with an absence of any hint of other explanations.

CASE 2—Evidence of unemployment being the cause of loss of authority.
1. The husband's experience that unemployment caused a general change in the wife's sentiments: "I don't get as much love since I am unemployed."
2. The wife's experience that changes in husband irritate her: "I am disgusted with the way he has changed since unemployment."
3. Statement of both husband and wife that the wife is going out more often without the husband because he is too sour and depressed to want to go out.
4. Testimony as to sequences of events, closer relations between wife and daughter since unemployment, changes in the behavior of the husband.

The above testimony was checked for agreement in the three interviews.

Internal Consistency and Alternative Explanations. There are two possible sources of error in the above testimony: (a) The alleged changes may not have occurred at all; (b) the change may have occurred for some other reason than unemployment. When the man says he does not get as much affection because of his unemployment, we cannot accept his statement uncritically. Perhaps he was never loved by the wife, and he is glad to attribute the cause to unemployment. Now he can blame his wife for being mercenary and say, "Love flies out the window when money goes." When the wife says that she is disgusted with her husband for his unemployment, it is possible that she also prefers to attribute to unemployment attitudes which have their source elsewhere. It is possible that she has always been dissatisfied with her husband.

On the other hand, it is possible that the changes have occurred but that their reason lies not in unemployment but elsewhere. The husband may say that the reason for his wife's change in sentiments is his unemployment. Perhaps he has become less adequate as a lover for various reasons, and the wife's change of sentiment is a reaction to it. It is also possible that while she says she is disgusted with him because of changes in his personality, the truth may lie elsewhere. Such are the possible sources of error.

We have accepted, however, the original statements because the total interviews contained material in support of them.

There is evidence that his personality changed as a result of unemployment. He describes the feelings of uselessness, restlessness, and humiliation. The daughter whose attitude towards her father is favorable confirms that he has changed for the worse. All three members of the family confirm the fact that the mother spends more time with the daughter, which means less time with the husband. She does more things together with the daughter, leaving the husband alone evening after evening. We thus infer that she has less time for her husband and less chance for affection and companionship.

Furthermore, the study of predepression marital relations shows that the wife never loved her husband, but appears to be the kind of woman who would restrain her feelings in the interests of economic security. In other words, it seems reasonable that she might withdraw her semblance of affection when she became economically free of her husband.

We have scrutinized the evidence for a possible cause of the observed changes other than unemployment but found no hint of other factors.

In summary, it may be said that it was decided to consider that the change in the wife's sentiments has actually taken place. The change was attributed to unemployment because we found reasonable connection with unemployment in the absence of any suggestion of alternative explanations.

In the study of marital relations, we found only one case in which loss of the husband's authority was apparently unrelated to unemployment. There were four cases in parental relations in which the loss of authority was attributed to other factors than unemployment.

In the T. family the only indication of loss of authority is the wife's statement:

"But I think lately I am sticking up for my rights a little more than before. I told Mr. T. what I thought of his throwing the children out of the house. He did it anyway, but I told him what I thought of it. I argue more with Mr. T. about his strictness with the children. Mr. T. thinks that I have changed. He told me just the other day that he thinks I have changed a good deal. I don't notice it. I don't even know what he has in mind. No, I don't think he means that I am sticking up for my rights. I don't know what he means."

But there is no indication that that change, whatever its significance, has anything to do with unemployment. Mrs. T. doesn't blame her husband in the slightest for his unemployment. She doesn't feel that his unemployment reduces his claims upon the family. There are indications that she still admires Mr. T. and is devoted to him. She insists that it is the final fight with the children that convinced her that Mr. T.'s policy with the children does not work well. It is possible that she was sure of it before, but the outcome of the final fight with the children gave her courage to express herself.

The possible source of error in this interpretation is the following: Mrs. T. may prefer to attribute to Mr. T.'s educational policy what, in reality, is due to unemployment. Perhaps it is Mr. T.'s unemployment that diminished her awe of him. She realized that he was not infallible. However, there just doesn't seem to be any indication of that. It was not possible to arouse any emotion in Mrs. T. with regard to unemployment and the depression, while tears appeared in her eyes when parental relations were discussed. The interview with Mr. T. confirmed the impression that unemployment is as yet not a painful problem in marital relations.

CONCLUSIVENESS OF DISCERNING

Discerning whether or not unemployment was the cause of changes was not equally conclusive in all cases. In a general way the conclusiveness depends upon two conditions: (a) The nature of the causal connection between unemployment and the change in the particular case; and (b) completeness of available evidence. We shall discuss them briefly:

1. *The nature of causal connection between unemployment and the change.*

a. Is unemployment a sudden break or is it gradual? Discerning is easier when unemployment is a sudden change. First, if unemployment came about gradually, the change is less dramatic, and it is harder for the informant to perceive changes that are due to it; and secondly, it is somewhat harder for the interviewer to check the explanation.

Let us take two situations: A prosperous family suddenly losing its wealth as compared with another family becoming gradually impoverished. It is clear that in the first case the family will have a more vivid picture of the change, and will be able to realize more clearly what changes have occurred as a result of the loss of wealth. The advantage for the interviewer will be a similar one. He will have a clear-cut comparison, and will be able to check more easily the statements of the members of the family.

b. Is the change gradual or sudden? If the change is gradual it is harder for the informant to perceive it, and to perceive its connection with unemployment. Furthermore, it is harder to interpret it because other factors had a chance to intervene. This change may be a joint product of unemployment and other factors.

c. How direct is the relation between unemployment and the change? The more immediate the relation, the easier it is to discern it. If the relation is intermediate, there are more sources of error both in the informant's perceiving the relation and in the interviewer's checking of it. If the woman says, "Since unemployment my husband has been mean to the children; they resent it and give me more trouble, and I hate him for it," there are more steps that must be checked than if she had said, "Since unemployment we quarrel over relief."

d. The degree to which a single individual was actively implied in the change. If the change constituted a conscious decision which an individual had to make himself, the discernibleness of unemployment as a cause of this decision might be greater than if it were something which happened to the individual.

2. *The completeness of available evidence.*

a. How intelligent is the informant in analyzing sequences? Does he leave the interviewer with the statement: Husband started to drink after unemployment; or, is he analytical enough to explain the motives and interpret experience?

b. Is the informant frank, or is he on guard? Does he answer in cultural stereotypes, or confess socially disapproved attitudes?

c. Is there danger of a bias, conscious or unconscious, either in the direction of stressing or denying that unemployment is a cause of the change?

d. Are there inconsistencies and contradictions within the interview, or between the interviews?

8. WHY FAMILIES MOVE

by Peter H. Rossi

IN CONTEMPORARY AMERICA every year about one out of every five families change their residences. Some of these moves span long distances and contribute to the growth or decline of different regions. Most of these moves, however, cover very short distances and involve shifts among neighborhoods within cities or among neighboring settlements in more open country.

Within our urban areas, the cumulative effect of these short distance moves is to produce the impression of a restless "milling about," somewhat resembling a large scale game of "musical chairs" in which large numbers of American families exchange housing every year.

What produces residential mobility? Why do families reject one dwelling and move to another? The research reported here represents an attempt to answer some of these questions through a study of the reasons given by households for leaving their previous homes.[1]

Residential mobility presents a "natural" opportunity for the employment of action analysis. Unlike many other types of changes—for example, opinion shifts—a change in residence has a fairly definite structure. The shift itself has a definite locus in time, involving a fairly uniform sequence of acts. The structural orderliness of residential shifts helps movers to reconstruct the sequence of events and feelings which made up the act of moving. In addition, changing residences is usually quite a serious matter to a family. The decision involves the commitment of a large proportion of the household income. Moving changes the time-space relationships of residence to job, to friends and relatives, and to services. Respondents find it easy to remember the considerations which went into their decisions to move.[2]

This is a previously unpublished paper.

The analysis presented in this section was applied to moves undertaken by a sample of Philadelphia households. All the moves studied were undertaken within five years of the time of interview (1950). The sample covered a wide variety of family types, of different socio-economic levels, who occupied a range of housing accommodations.

Some Interviewing Problems. The first objective of an action analysis is to obtain from the persons involved reliable accounts of the actions in question. In the present case, the field operation consists essentially of asking respondents why they have moved. Although this might seem to be a simple enough procedure, actually, it can be quite complicated. It is not possible to ask directly, "Why did you move?" A general "why" question usually produces a congeries of answers, each kind of answer corresponding to a different interpretation of the question made by the respondent. There are many ways to answer such a question: some respondents will answer in terms of the event which "triggered" the move; others will tell why they left their previous homes; still others will tell why they chose their new homes, and so on.

Perhaps the best way to illustrate the inadequacies of the "general why" question is to present what happens when such a question is asked. In Table 1, drawn from another study of residential mobility,[3] we present a list of answers to the question "Why did you happen to move?"

Table 1—Reasons Given In Answer to "Why Did You Happen To Move?"

A.	"To secure better quarters or live in a better location"	18%
B.	"To build or purchase a home"	16
C.	"More space required"	13
D.	"Rents too high or house too large"	12
E.	"House sold, repaired, renovated, occupied by owner"	10
F.	"House in need of repairs, burnt or torn down"	3
G.	"Closer to location where employed"	10
H.	"Marriage"	5

Some of the respondents answered the question as if it referred to the house *to* which they had moved (G). Others answered in terms of the homes *from* which they had moved (A, C, D, and partly F).

In order to present more sharply the range of different interpretations given to this question by the respondents, their responses have been rearranged below in Table 2 according to the respondents' interpretations of the question.

Most of the new general classifications (marked by Roman numerals in Table 2) correspond to different interpretations of the general "why" question. Some respondents assumed that the interviewer wanted to know what was wrong with the former home (I); others assumed that the interviewer wanted to know what was so attractive about the new home (II), and so on.

Category III (Decision Not Respondent's) includes all responses which indicated that the respondent did not make the decision to move himself but that he was forced out of his old home by events that were beyond his control.

Note that in Table 2, a new response has been added to each of the main categories; the proportion of respondents who did not answer in a particular frame of reference is indicated. Thus we find that 54% of the respondents did *not* refer to the characteristics of the old home, 74% did *not* refer to the new home, and so on.

The difficulty with the general "why" question rests primarily on the large numbers of respondents who do not employ a mode of response. It is not possible from Table 2 to discuss what were the things about the old places which impelled the respondents to move because more than half of the respondents make no reference to their former homes. The fact that a respondent answered in terms of his new home does not mean that he was perfectly satisfied with his old home. It usually means that he interpreted the question to refer to the new home. At best, it may mean that he thinks

Table 2—Answer Categories Classified by the Frame of Reference Employed by the Respondent

I:	Characteristics of the Former Home:*	
	A. Better quarters or better location (i.e., unsatisfactory former home)	18%
	C. More space required	13
	D. Rents too high or house too large	12
	F. (In part) House in need of repairs	3
	Not answered in terms of former home	54%
II:	Characteristics of New Home:	
	G. Closer to location where employed	10%
	B. To build or purchase home	16
	Not answered in terms of new home	74%
III:	Decision Is Not Respondent's	
	E. House sold, repaired, renovated, occupied by owner	10%
	F. (In part) House burnt or torn down	3
	No information as to decision maker	87%
IV:	Changes in Housing Needs	
	H. Marriage	5%
	No information about changes in needs	95%

* Note that the categories included under I are not mutually exclusive. "Better quarters" might mean quarters which are lower in rent, larger or smaller in size, and so on. Hence many of the cases included in this general omnibus category might have been more properly placed in some of the more specific categories.

that the attractions of his new home were more important than the characteristics of his former home. The same defect characterizes each of the main categories of Table 2. The information obtained from a general "why" question lacks the uni-dimensionality which makes a sensible analysis possible.

In order to make use of respondents' accounts of their actions, it is necessary to break down the action into less complex topics. The general "why" question therefore has to be broken down into a set of specific "whys" each directed at one of these less complex topics. Thus a research into residence shifts might take the categories of Table 2 as a guide and set up a group of specific "why" questions each directed at one or another of the four categories of that table. The information obtained by such a set of questions would be uniform for each respondent and permit a fuller analysis.

The difficulties encountered in the use of the general "why" question point up the necessity for having some sort of *a priori* frame of reference outlining the kinds of specific topics to be discussed with the respondents. Such frames of reference have been called "accounting schemes." The function of such schemes is to specify in advance what are the aspects of the actions in question which will be discussed with the respondent. The accounting scheme guides the construction of the questionnaire and sets the framework for the subsequent analysis.

Where do the elements of an accounting scheme[4] come from? In part the scheme derives from the explicit or implicit theoretical position taken by the researcher; and, in part it derives from the structure of the behavior under study.

The accounting scheme employed in this study was derived from two sources. Migration studies, although mostly concerned with the problem of long distance moves, provided the general categories of "pushes," "pulls," and "information channels." Exploratory interviews with families provided knowledge of the structure of moving which guided the construction of the questionnaire.

The emphasis in the accounting scheme is upon housing and its characteristics. Practical interest in those factors which could be manipulated guided the selection of housing as the primary focus.

An Accounting Scheme for Residential Mobility. The basic structure of the accounting scheme is that of the familiar migration model[5] consisting of "pushes," "pulls" and "information channels." The act of moving is considered by this model as composed of reasons for leaving the old home, contact with a set of information sources which present a range of alternative destinations, and reasons for choosing among the alternatives so presented. Each respondent is asked why he left his old home, how he came to know about his new home, and why he chose his new home from among the choices available to him.

In the presentation here,[6] we will consider only the "pushes" category in the full accounting scheme. We will be entirely concerned with how the respondents made the decision to leave their former homes.

An accounting scheme must always be fitted to the intrinsic structure of the action under study. The experiences of respondents in coming to their decisions to move are not uniform and it is necessary to fit the interviewing procedure to these differences in experience. To illustrate these differences, it is useful to consider what is the "typical" sequence of stages in a decision to move.

Stage 1: The household is satisfied with the old dwelling. There are no complaints held by the family about the home or its surrounding environment.
Stage 2: Dissatisfaction is aroused. Something occurs to generate complaints. The family begins to have a desire to move.
Stage 3: The desire to move crystallizes into definite plans for moving and the move itself occurs.

The experiences of households differ because *not all* households go through the full sequence, although every household, by virtue of the fact that it has moved, goes through at least Stage 3 and one other stage. The variations on the sequence are three in number, as follows:

The Typical Move: Stage 1, 2, and 3.
The Delayed Move: Stage 2 and 3 only. The family has always been dissatisfied with the home and there never was a period when the family was completely satisfied with the old home.
The Forced Move: Stage 1 and 3 only. The household never becomes dissatisfied with the old home. The decision to move is forced either by some event

beyond the family's control or is implied by some non-housing decision made by the family.

According to the combination of stages which a family experiences, different kinds of information are required to account for why the move was undertaken. The sequence laid out implies that the following data be obtained to account for a family's transition from one to another stage.

I: *Changes Causing Complaints to Arise:*
What brings about the transition between Stages 1 and 2? What makes a previously satisfied household become dissatisfied?
Changes might be classified along the following lines:
A. Changes in the Dwelling or its Environs:
e.g. apartment falling into disrepair, neighborhood deterioration, etc.
B. Changes in the Structure of the Family Producing Changes in Housing Needs:
e.g. change in family size, shifts in age and sex compositions, etc.
C. Changes in the Family's Values and Aspirations:
e.g. shifts in social status, shifts in housing values of family, etc.

II. *Complaints:*
What are the things about the dwelling or its surroundings with which the family is dissatisfied?
A. Dwelling Design Complaints:
e.g. amount of space, utilities, layout, etc.
B. Dwelling Environment Complaints:
e.g. social composition of neighborhood, physical structure of the neighborhood, etc.
C. Space-Time Relationships to Significant Locations:
e.g. access to employment, services, friends, etc.

III: *Barriers:*
Once dissatisfaction is present, what prevents the desire to move from being realized? Often families harbor complaints for long periods of time without attempting to move.
Barriers may be classified as follows:
A. Deficiencies in Resources:
e.g. insufficient income, etc.
B. Pre-occupation with other matters:
e.g. ill-health, conflicting demands on income, etc.
C. Lack of Knowledge Concerning Opportunities:
e.g. family may believe that no housing is available to it.
D. Adverse State of Housing Market:
e.g. no appropriate housing available to family.

IV: *Precipitants:*
There is usually some time period between the arousal of dissatisfaction and the move itself. What are the events which permit or facilitate the translation of a complaint into action?
Precipitants might be classified as follows:
A. Changes in Household Resources:
e.g. increase in income, etc.

B. Changes in Relative Importance of Housing:
   e.g. with a family's rise in social status, a new residence might appear to be a more pressing need.
C. Change in the Housing Market:
   e.g. more vacancies on the market.
D. Events Forcing a Move:
   e.g. destruction of dwelling unit, change in marital status, eviction, etc.

From the Typical Mover, who goes through all three stages, information can be obtained on all four points. We could find out what caused a complaint to arise, what were the complaints held by the household, what factors may have held up the move, once moving was decided upon, and, finally, what were the events which facilitated the move itself. From the other types, less information can be obtained.

The types of data obtainable from the three types of moves is summarized in the following scheme:

	Causes of Complaints	Complaints	Barriers	Precipitants
Typical Moves	Yes	Yes	Yes	Yes
Delayed Moves	No	Yes	Yes	Yes
Forced Moves	No	No	No	Yes

This scheme allows one to distinguish different types of movers according to the way in which they experienced moving. The importance of these distinctions lies in the guides they provide for the interviewing program. The scheme indicates from what kinds of movers different kinds of data are obtainable.

Thus the accounting scheme, when properly constructed and applied, will produce data in which there are no obvious gaps (as in Tables 1 or 2). Each family is asked about the aspects of moving which apply to its experience. The "no answers" which plague the interpretation of the reasons given to the general "why" question, will be reduced to a minimum.

The Assessment of Complaints. Although the accounting scheme produces a set of uniform data, it does not assess the data collected. If the important question is *which change* was important in bringing about a complaint or *which complaint* was important in bringing about a decision to move, it is necessary to employ additional analytical devices. To illustrate one approach to the assessment of reasons, we will confine ourselves to just one of the elements of the accounting scheme presented earlier and attempt to assess the relative importance of different kinds of complaints in bringing about the decision to move.

It is easy enough to find out from each household what its complaints were about its former home. It is much more difficult to assess the importance of such attitudes in bringing about the household's decision to move. Such an assessment probably cannot be done with complete accuracy or certainty. What can be accomplished is some sort of approximation to an ideal. In other words, the assessment procedures we will discuss here should not be expected to produce statements about *the causes* of moving, but only statements about the complaints which are *most likely* to have played an important role in the move.

The first step in making assessments concerning the relative importance of different complaint types is to find out whether or not a particular type of complaint was present in each case of moving. Obviously, before a complaint can play a role it must be acknowledged by the family. The "coverage" of a complaint—whether or not it is present in a move—defines the necessary but insufficient condition for the complaint's playing an important role.

A complaint's coverage, therefore, needs to be supplemented by some way of characterizing its "impact"—the degree to which it was instrumental in bringing about a move. There are many ways in which this "impact" may be judged. In this study, impact is defined as the respondent's own judgment of the importance of a complaint. Thus, a complaint about the landlord is considered to have played an important role in bringing about a decision to move, if the family involved rates that complaint as important.

Although impact and coverage are by definition related to each other, they are somewhat independent. A particular complaint type may have a high coverage and a low impact while another type may have a low coverage but a high impact. In other words, some complaints may be present in a very large number of cases yet be rated as important in only a few. Another complaint type may be present in but a few cases, yet be rated as important in almost every case where it is found to be present. Thus, each complaint type can be characterized according to its "effectiveness"—the extent to which, when present, the complaint is rated as important.

The goal of the assessment procedure is to judge each complaint type according to three measures:

Coverage:[7] The extent to which a complaint is present among movers. The coverage of a complaint type is the proportion of movers who register a complaint of that type against their former homes.

Impact:[7] The extent to which a complaint type is rated as important by movers. The "impact" of a complaint type is the proportion of movers who say that they moved primarily because of their dissatisfaction in that respect.

Effectiveness: The extent to which a complaint, when present, is regarded as having an impact. The effectiveness of a complaint type is the proportion of families rating that type as important of all families who register a complaint of that type. Expressed in another way—

$$\text{Effectiveness} = \frac{\text{Impact}}{\text{Coverage}}$$

The collection of coverage and impact data for each of the major complaints types was accomplished by the use of three types of questions. First, each respondent was asked what might be called a *"stimulus question."*

"What was it that made you think of moving out?"

The rationale behind this question was that it would start the respondent thinking of the things that prompted his initial desire to move.[8] The respondent was, of course, free to answer this question in any fashion he chose. If he mentioned a particular complaint type, however, this was an indication of the importance of the complaint in the genesis of his family's move.

The next item type, called *"exposure" questions,* were designed to obtain the coverage of different complaints. These questions asked in a straightforward manner whether or not the respondent was dissatisfied with some feature of his former home. For example, with regard to complaints about space in his old home, we asked:

"Did you have too much room, enough room, or too little room in your old place?"

Finally, after a series of exposure questions had alerted the respondent to the frame of reference of complaints, an *"assessment" question* was asked, as follows:

"Now, you've mentioned several reasons why you and your family moved from your former place. Which of these would you say were the most important reasons?"

The importance of the assessment question is fairly obvious. The respondent himself is asked to make a judgment about the impact of a particular complaint.

Let us consider first of all what the answers to these three questions look like for a particular type of complaint: the costs of the former dwelling unit. The proportions complaining about costs in answer to each of the three question types is shown in Table 3. Note that the questions have been arranged in a sequence according to their "diagnostic" ability in assessing the

Table 3—Complaints about Costs

		Proportion Registering Complaints
1.	Exposure question	26%—Coverage
2.	Stimulus question	18%
3.	Assessment question	12%—Impact
	100% equals	(273)*

* The moving decisions of 444 households were under study in this research. 39% of these moves were classified as Forced Moves and, hence, were not considered here. The 273 cases referred to in this article are moves voluntarily undertaken. See previous section for the reason for considering only voluntary moves.

"cause" of a move. Least diagnostic is, of course, the exposure question, in response to which 26% of the households registered complaints. Next in diagnostic ability is the "stimulus" question which obtained complaints from 18% of the households. Most important, diagnostically, is the assessment question. Here we find that 12% registered a complaint.

Similar distributions can be shown for each of the complaint categories which we shall study in detail.[9] More households are *exposed* to a complaint than consider that complaint a *stimulus* to their move, or than consider that complaint an important motive for their move. The existence of such uniformities lends some support to this particular use of the questions.

How shall we use these questions to classify the households according to whether or not a particular complaint was effective in bringing about the move? Certainly the clearest case is where the household explicitly states that a particular complaint was the most important thing in causing it to move. These are cases which come closest to the ideal of *primary complaints.*

Some respondents mention a particular complaint spontaneously in response to the "stimulus" question but do not mention that complaint as one of the important causes of moving. Apparently the complaint brought the notion of moving to mind, but it was not the important reason for the move. In these cases, we shall consider that the complaint played a *"contributory"* role.

Next, we have households which mention being exposed to a particular complaint but do not rate that complaint as being an important reason for their move, nor do they mention the complaint as a stimulus to the desire to move. These are cases where the complaint was *ineffective* in bringing about the move.

Finally, we have households which were not exposed to the complaint in question. These are households, along with the previous group mentioned, to whom a particular kind of complaint was *irrelevant* to their moving decision.[10]

Recapitulating the classification in outline form, the three questions allow us to separate respondents into four groups with respect to each complaint type.

Primary Complaint—"Impact": Respondent mentions a particular type of complaint as being an important reason for his move.

Contributory Complaint: Respondent does not rate the complaint as important but mentions that the complaint was the thing which started him thinking about moving.

Ineffective Complaint: Respondent acknowledges complaint but does not rate it as of any importance in the move.

No Complaint: Respondent was satisfied with the previous home in this regard.

It should be noted that it is necessary to have an exposure question in order to present the classification discussed above. The complaint types have to be anticipated in advance and built into the questionnaire.

Three complaint categories will be considered: complaints about space or room; complaints about neighborhoods; and complaints about costs (rent or maintenance). These are obviously broadly conceived categories. Under the concept of neighborhood there is included such diverse aspects of the surrounding environment as its social composition, features of land use in the neighborhood, and the neighborhood's location with regard to transportation and services. For many purposes, it will be more profitable to break these broad categories down into more specific components. For the purpose of illustrating analytical procedures, such broad classifications will suffice.

The Assessment Ratings. The ratings resulting from the application of the assessment device are shown in Table 4. The coverage of the three complaints types varies considerably. Almost two out of three families complained that their previous homes had too little or too much space. Three out of ten families complained that their previous homes were too costly. Another thirty per cent registered complaints about their old neighborhoods.

Table 4—Assessment Ratings

Complaint Types	RATINGS			
	Primary Complaints (Impact)	Contributory Complaints	Ineffective Complaints	Total Coverage
Space Complaints	45%	8%	11%	64%
Neighborhood Complaints	14%	8%	7%	29%
Costs Complaints	12%	7%	13%	32%

The impact ratings also show a large variation. Almost half (45%) of the families rated space complaints as primary.[11]

The impact ratings of the other two complaints types were considerably smaller. In 14% of the moves, complaints about the neighborhood were primary. The corresponding percentage for costs complaints was 12%.

Note that the assessment procedure is accomplished separately for each complaint type. In other words, the households are rated first according to the role space complaints played in their moves, then according to the role played by neighborhood complaints, and so on. It is possible for several complaints to play primary roles in one and the same case. The number of such cases, however, was very small.[12]

The impact of a complaint is in part a function of its coverage. The more complaints of a particular type there are, the more likely such complaints are to be mentioned as primary reasons for moving. The relative effectiveness of a complaint type therefore has to be judged apart from its coverage. Table 5 presents in index form a measure of the relative effectiveness of each complaint type. The index is defined as follows:

$$\text{Index of Effectiveness} = \frac{\text{Primary Complaints}}{\text{Coverage}}$$

Space complaints, with an index value of .70, turns out to have the greatest effectiveness of the three, followed by neighborhood complaints (.48) and costs complaints (.38).

Table 5—Effectiveness Ratings of Complaint Types

Complaint Types	Effectiveness Index
Space	.70
Neighborhood	.48
Costs	.38

The presentation of the results of the assessment analysis attempted in this study has been detailed enough to show its utility. The procedure enables the analyst to classify each move according to the complaints which have most likely played primary roles in bringing the move about. From this point on, the analysis would be occupied with showing how the impact of different complaint types varies under different conditions and with different types of households.

The Validity of Assessment. How much confidence can one place in the assessment ratings which have been presented here? Although a rigorous validation study has not been undertaken, the results of assessment can be shown to be consistent with other information obtained from the households studied.

For example, if the assessment of space complaints is to have any validity, we should expect to find that the impact of this complaint type varies with the amount of space within the households' former homes. A good index of available space is the number of rooms in the former home, considered in relation to the number of persons in the household. Table 6 classifies families according to both the composition of the household and the amount of room in the families' previous homes.

Objectively measured space pressure and the number of primary space complaints shows a positive relationship. For a given family size, the smaller the dwelling unit, the more likely the household is to cite space complaints as a primary reason why it left its former home. Similarly, for a given dwelling size, the smaller the household the less likely the family is to cite space complaints as having had an impact on its moving decision. However, the relationships described in this table are not very strong.

There is a plausible reason why space pressure and the assessment of space complaints do not show a particularly high relationship. In other data analyzed in this study it was shown that family size had to be considered along with the age of the family in interpreting the relationship of family size to mobility desires. Young, large households living in small dwellings were the most likely to want to move. It was these households which had most likely experienced a recent increase in family size. Perhaps it is *change* in the relationships between space and family size which generates the impact of space complaints and not just the amount of space alone.

This explanation is consistent with the findings shown in Table 7. Families are classified in this table into those which have recently experienced a change in their size and those families which have not gone through this experience recently. When changes in family size had recently occurred,

Table 6—Family Size, Dwelling Size and Space Assessment (Proportion of cases in which Space Complaints were rated as Primary)

Dwelling Unit	HOUSEHOLD SIZE		
	1-2 Persons	3 Persons	4 or more
1-2½ rooms	45%	52%	54%
100% equals	(42)	(21)	(13)
3-4 rooms		41%	60%
100% equals	} 41%	(24)	(40)
5 or more rooms	(68)	35%	35%
100% equals		(20)	(40)

90% of the families complained about the space within their former homes. When change was not experienced the corresponding percentage was only 51%. The impact of space complaints shows a similar difference: where changes in size had occurred, the impact of space complaints was 71%; where such changes had not occurred the impact was only 33%. Note, however, that the *effectiveness* of space complaints did not change substantially.

The amount of space available to the family in its old home is apparently not as important as the experience of shifts in the relationship between this space and the size of the family. A family living in a dwelling with a particular amount of space becomes accommodated to that space over time. When the family expands, the space is then experienced as inadequate.

Similar evidence can be marshalled for the validity of neighborhood complaints. As Table 8, below, shows, the complaints associated with discerned

Table 7—Space Complaints and Changes in Household Size*

Space Complaint Assessment	Change in Household Size	No Change in Household Size
Impact (Primary Complaints)	71%	33%
Contributory Complaints	9	6
Ineffective Complaints	10	12
Coverage (Total Cases with Complaints)	90%	51%
Index of Effectiveness	.78	.65
100% equals	(86)	(178)

* Households were classified according to the answers to the following question: "Were there any changes in the number of persons living with you?"

changes in either the neighborhood itself or in the neighborhood needs of the family had a greater impact on the family's moving decision.

The reader is left to judge for himself whether the evidence presented for the validity of the assessment procedure is enough to lend some support to

Table 8—Neighborhood Change and Neighborhood Complaints*

Neighborhood Complaints	Change Associated Complaints	Complaints Not Involving Change
Primary Complaints	71%	32%
Contributory Complaints	20	31
Ineffective Complaints	9	37
100% equals	(35)	(45)

* A complaint was classified as associated with a felt change in the neighborhood if the respondent spontaneously mentioned such a change in registering the complaint. An item asking directly whether a change had been perceived in the neighborhood was *not* asked (as was the case in the previous Table 7).

the use of techniques of this sort as research devices. Certainly considerable development of the technique seems indicated before complete reliance on this technique would seem justified. The items used in assessment are crudely formulated. It should be possible to construct items which would enable respondents to assess factors in their actions with greater refinement than just whether the factor was "important."

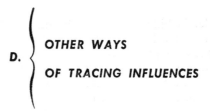

D. {
OTHER WAYS

OF TRACING INFLUENCES
}

9. THE ROLE OF THE COMMUNITY IN A LIFE HISTORY

by John Dollard

THE EARLY LIFE MATERIAL of a psychoanalytic life history may be an aid in picking out factors of relevance in community life. It reveals not only the processes familiar from studies on the societal level of perception but also other factors which cannot be sensed on this level. For example, the emotional forces bound by community life are seen near at hand through the telescope of the life history. A case in point would be the transfer, as in our subject, of a passive, dependent relationship from the parents to the leaders in the childhood playgroup. The intimidated child in the family set-up carries the marks of his intimidation over to his companions of the same age. Again, from the life history, one may see some of the functions of collective life which are not obvious if only the behavioristic cultural outlines are observed. Such a function is a special role of social arrangements in controlling aggressive behavior. The importance of intimacy, for instance, is more intelligible when one understands the degree to which it is assurance against doing harm to others or being injured by them. This kind of variable could not even be identified at the level of abstract community study, and yet everyone would agree that intimate relations are of importance in cementing communal solidarity.

With the conceptual instruments of the sociologist applied to carefully recorded psychoanalytic life history data, we may discover much of value to illustrate and illuminate societal life. It is true that some of this material, such as the size of the town, number of foreign born, etc., might have been gained and more sharply defined from existing census materials, but what the psychoanalytic study seems to provide is the identification of relationships which are not discerned by the census or discoverable in any other way than by intensive individual study.

The record from which these data are drawn was made on a male individual who was thirty years old at the time of the study. It represents data from the period when he was four to eight years old, i.e., between the years 1905 and 1909. The individual studied exhibited at the outset of the study serious deformations in his social relations, such as acute mistrust of other

Reprinted in part from "The Life History in Community Studies," *The American Sociological Review*, Vol. III, 1938, pp. 724-737, by permission of the author and the publisher. (Copyright, 1938, by The American Sociological Society.) Professor Dollard has kindly edited this article for inclusion in the present volume.

people, inability to work efficiently, and a low level of satisfaction in his married life. These problems and their solution will not be reported upon, but the attempt to solve them provided adequate motivation for the acquisition of a very detailed report of the person's life along its whole length.

The informant remembered his town as a long, narrow one, strung along the bank of a river. On one side were the shoe factories; on his side of the town was the business nucleus which was actually on the bank of the river with the residential area flung around it. He lived at the edge of town, and it was five minutes to open country from his house. He had a clear picture of the streaming throngs of workmen going across the bridge to the factories, and of the low mill buildings. On Saturdays, he recalled catching rides on the backs of farmers' wagons loaded with produce for the downtown stores.

This is obviously then a small industrial town in a rural area. Both parents came from farms in the area surrounding the town, which would suggest the possibility that the native born population is recruited for city life from this local area.

The informant's data provided immediate definition of the family form into which he came. He had the conventional recollections of being threatened with his father's authority for misdeeds at home. It was clear to informant that mother was dependent on father, and although she was the real boss in the house, she always pretended to defer to him and probably was at bottom afraid of him. There was no one around to dispute father's authority,—no grandfather, no uncle. Father did have a boss somewhere, but that did not mean much in the home.

The informant experienced a good deal of resentment toward both of his parents, but particularly toward his mother. She was busy with the other children, three of them, and the oldest son had to take his place in line. He craved for companionship with his father and that the father would take him as a real confidant, but this never happened; the father seemed too busy and too preoccupied with his own work. It seemed that he only came to his father's attention when disciplinary matters were involved. His mother was also busy. As a usual thing, there was no help in the house and beside childbearing there was the complete routine of family duties to be done. The mother seemed too harried and heckled by her life to spare love for the older children. The informant felt, therefore, very much alone and somewhat neglected in the family circle and, for this reason, welcomed with extreme eagerness his first playgroup contacts.

This partial rejection by his parents resulted in a considerable animosity toward them which could not be expressed, but toward the brothers and sisters who were in part the cause of the parental neglect he could and did feel extremely vindictive. They were relatively defenseless against him, and he showed a devious defiance toward his father by punishing his siblings.

The longing for tenderness from his parents accumulated on a particular Christmas in his fifth year. He had desperately expected some mark of preferment in the type of Christmas presents which he would receive. (He had exploded, of course, the Santa Claus legend by this time. This deceit on the part of his parents gave him some courage for the many deceits which he was practicing and later had to practice himself.) Christmas morning came, and the presents were just ordinary presents, not much better than those of the other children. This event ended the struggle for rapport with his father and mother. All right, then, it was every man for himself, and one got affection wherever one could get it and expected nothing more for nothing.

From the foregoing, we see the isolated, small family unit of the patriarchal type, with formal authority lodged in the father. There is no assertion that this family form was typical for the community. There must have been a type of family, however, which did its "duty" toward children, but was perhaps too busy to give its children the affectionate contacts which they needed. Possibly this family type develops strong and ruthless personalities in the most deprived children just because they must turn away from family sources of security at an early age.

Clear in the informant's account of his family was the imposition of the incest taboo. He remembered that occasion when he was still sleeping with his little sister, his next sibling. All he knew is that he felt something toward her, and that he was teasing her. He crawled over on top of her, though he did not exactly know what he wanted to do. She screamed and the mother came running. The sister "told" on him, though he tried to "shush" her. The mother threatened to tell the father when he came home, and a dreadful fear settled on the informant, but he did not know of what. Nothing seemed to have happened in fact, but the fear persisted, and with it persisted an animosity toward the sister. Undoubtedly this is the psychological correlate of the incest taboo. In this connection, the informant remembered, also, that when his father went away, he used to say, "Take care of your mother," and there seemed to be a warning lurking in his voice. He was warning his son to be obedient and docile toward his mother, but the informant took the words to mean something more.

The informant's feelings toward mother and sister were vague and confused, but he does remember strong, erotic wishes toward a maid who was in the house for a few weeks when he was six years old. On one occasion he got up his courage to approach the maid. She was standing at the telephone (certainly a mark of high working class status for this family) and the informant reached under her dress and grabbed her by the leg. She hit him a blow on the head which sent him spinning. She, too, apparently, was within the circle of the forbidden. He felt this blow on the head, in memory, many times later when he tried to make contact with women.

The informant learned another fact about the behavior of his family. He noticed that his parents would stop a quarrel if the maid were to appear. He learned that a family puts up an appearance of solidarity before the outside world whether it actually feels it or not and that in-family aggression is to be suppressed or concealed in the presence of "others." Impertinence toward his parents was reproved with special severity if outsiders learned about it because his parents "did not want to be made fools of by their own children." The informant was, of course, manifesting the mos which enjoins family solidarity.

The informant enumerated all of the people that he knew in his neighborhood group. It added up to about forty people. These people whom the informant knew all knew one another and were related to one another dynamically in important ways. He knew the parents of all his child friends, and their parents, in turn, knew his. He belonged, therefore, to a little "band" in Linton's[1] sense. Of course, it was not a band from the standpoint that there was common cooperative work but only from the standpoint of common occupancy of land and vital social relations. He noticed that there seemed to be a kind of informal policing of all the children by all of the parents as well as informal feeding and protection. It was a small, stable, neighborhood world into which our informant came.

The boys' group into which the informant was inducted at the age of six was a differentiated aspect of the neighborhood. If one did not belong to the group there were only the detested younger children to play with. However, one of the group leaders approached him and made him a proposal,—if our informant would agree to marry the leader's older sister when he grew up, he would be admitted to the group. The sister was very homely, but the informant felt that no price was too high to pay for this privilege, especially if payment was sufficiently deferred, so he consented to join. He was introduced to the hut behind the barn where you crawled in and told stories, allowed to compete with the older boys in walking the rails on the near-by railroad track and given much very specific sexual information. By age and emotional disposition our subject was always a "follower" in his playgroup. Placation of father and playgroup leader remained for many years a distinguishing psychic characteristic of this man.

No sex practices were carried on by the gang, but the subject was told, what he did not need to be told, that his father did something to his mother at night, and that this "something" made a baby in mother. He was rigorously warned never to let on to his parents that he had this information; he never did tell, and his father was so stupid when the boy was ten years older as to give him, very shyly, some of the information in a roundabout way which he had long had in concrete form. These data suggest the possibility that there is a definite "child level" of culture which is transmitted from one generation to the next, exclusive of the formal parental inculcation.

Another important aspect of the playgroup for the informant was that he was definitely weaned from close emotional dependency on his parents. The thoroughgoing band-control of child behavior by a unified group of parents was met by an opposed playgroup which validated many of the behavior tendencies disapproved by the adults. The playgroup performed a great service for this boy in thus mitigating the destructive effect of the high parental ideals of perfect behavior which were held up to him.

Although the neighborhood or band dominated his life quite completely at this age, he was not without knowledge that this neighborhood was limited in area. He knew, for instance, that there was a group of German boys in the same school where he went to first grade. There was fighting and stone throwing between his gang and this group. These boys talked a kind of gibberish at home and were said to eat nothing but sauerkraut and sausage. He knew the Poles also talked a funny language and lived on the other side of town. They were supposed to be dirty and very much less respectable than his own family. Once his gang went down to Polack-town and exchanged a shower of stones with the Polish boys. Polack girls were said to be easy to play with if you could once get at them.

We see above, of course, the familiar minority group picture which has shattered the solidarity of the native white American society and which differentiates a town like this one from a similar town in England. Where social groups of contrasting customs exist side by side, the impression of crushing absoluteness is gone from primary group life.

The informant's father did not drink, except for possibly a glass of beer at a family reunion. No liquor was kept in the house, but across the street was a saloon; there was much activity there, especially on Saturday night. The subject sometimes heard shouts and sounds of fighting from his bedroom. Some of the Polacks and "sausage-eaters" used to go to this saloon as well as the younger fellows just in from the farm. Now and then one of these fellows would try to pump the informant about the maid. He always resented these queries as invading the family privacy.

He was undoubtedly witnessing here a lower class recreational pattern which differed sharply from the conservative behavior of his parents and their immediate associates. The sight of this behavior was both appealing and terrifying, perhaps more the latter, but it did show at least that there were other modes of life than those so urgently recommended to him.

We have so far seen in our material the family form, band, and minority group phenomena; we might now note the establishment of a sharply differentiated male sex-role in our informant. He remembered, for instance, the time when his father had shamed him for playing with dolls, that his mother had told him "not to be a calf" and cry at disappointments, that little *boys* did not do this. His parents had forbidden him to attack his younger brothers and sister, but, on the other hand, he was not allowed to complain about challenges or assaults from other boys at school. Very strong also, was a wish to be like his father and to take the same confident and dominant attitude toward women which the latter did. He learned that he was not expected to be interested in cooking but that running errands was more suitable for a boy. He was quite outraged once when he had to wear a coat which was made over from a garment of his mother's; he had learned that it was improper to wear women's clothes even in a disguised form. One can see from the record the persistent sex-typing of character under the influence of his parents and colleagues.

He learned also of the dangers involved in stealing women. It came to him by a story which he heard from one of the older members of his playgroup. It was about a certain Bill Packer who came home and found another man with his wife, "doing it." Bill took out his jackknife on the spot and operated. The offender did not die, but he was not a man any more after that, and nobody did anything to Bill. Of course, this was only the case when you did something with another man's wife, but, the informant reasoned, even unmarried girls had brothers and fathers who might be possessive. His sex role was quite well consolidated by this event against premarital sex experience or adultery, and the taboo tended to spread to all girls, married or otherwise. It would seem an unintentional effect of our society to carry the mores against incest and adultery to objects other than the socially tabooed ones.

Due to the deprivations and dissatisfactions of childhood, there was aroused in our informant an intense desire to be grown up. Being grown up seemed the condition in which one could be independent of parental restriction and capable of building one's world on more satisfactory lines. His parents also described being grown up as a state when one had many more privileges.

Age-grading behavior is clearly delineated by the detailed life history which is adequately explored in its earlier phases. Protest against age-grading in childhood is undoubtedly one of the powerful emotional supports to social mobility in our society.

The informant's father was a plumber, and this gave the informant an unusual position in the band in which his family moved. He reported how surprised he was when one of his gang said to him, "Why, you're rich! You ought to be able to afford a bicycle because your father is a plumber." The speaker's father was a "hand" in the mills. The informant's father owned his house, had a telephone, had a bank account and was planning to "send the children on to school." The informant luxuriated in the high position of his father. He soon found out, however, that this status was likely to be a disadvantage in his playgroup, especially if he tried to utilize it outright. There was an aura about him, nevertheless; he valued it while he pretended to his playmates that it did not exist.

On the other hand, there was the case of Hanky Bisworth who went to the same school as our informant. His father was rich, really rich, and they lived in the biggest house in town. It was a great, dark red brick house and the informant always walked by it with a certain amount of awe. At home there was a good deal of conversation about the Bisworths, and his parents referred to them with extreme respect. Now he could see that merely being as good as his parents was not enough. There was something better to be than even these heroic figures.

Everyone will note in the foregoing how prestige levels are associated with wealth, because the Bisworth family made no other claim to eminence, and also how the informant perceived in a very simple sense how he stood on a status terrace with some below and others above him.

His mother was careful to tell him that she herself was an educated woman, that she had been two years in school after she finished her country school. Informant's mother felt superior to his father in this respect. The father had only a grade school education, and his father, in turn, could barely read and write. She justified many of her severe impositions on her children by stating that they were necessary to "get on" in the world. She also wholeheartedly conducted a domestic economy in the family which made it possible to save money and ultimately to realize her insistence on better opportunities for her children.

That the family was actually mobile is quite well shown by the fact that the informant was told about the different houses they had lived in. The house he was living in at age six was the best of the lot. It had more conveniences and a larger lawn, was farther removed from the annoyance of the railway tracks, and finally it was actually owned in full, whereas none of the others had been. He could see in sober fact that his family was getting on in the world and that he was to receive a projectile push from them.

He was himself required to make renunciations for his future schooling. He desperately wanted a bicycle, but it was decided by his parents that this was the type of item which the informant would have to do without in order that there might be a platform of capital for the later schooling. At the time, the boy was bitter over his disappointment and could have no conception of the compensating advantage of going to school, but the idea was so strong in his parents that he lived a very meager life so far as spending money was concerned during his entire childhood. The constant atmosphere of scrimping and saving, of everlasting worry about money, undoubtedly made the parents seem heavy and depressive to the informant. The future, in the sense of higher status, was too much present as a goal to allow for contemporary satisfactions.

All of the children of this family had occasion to thank their parents for these sacrifices when the compensations of higher status finally began to come in; all of the children secured college educations, and the mother and father are living an independent old age on their property. But the renunciations imposed in order to achieve higher status were in this case a real penalty and a penalty which had implications for the character formation of the subject.

The informant remembers both parents stating that they expected him to do better in life than they had done, and that they were going to aid him in getting better training so that he might thus be more secure against the hazards of life. Life was not represented to the informant as something to enjoy but rather as a mission in which he was to raise the family prestige.

Certainly we can see that from behind his memory comes discontent and rebellion and hatred against other people, both women and men. In a sense, the mobility pattern was passionately welcomed by this individual as an outlet and followed, one might almost say, with animosity. It is possible that the total frame of the family life, which imposed such privations on this subject, was determined by the powerful mobility tendencies which were present, especially on the mother's side. In the family struggle for social advancement, it is conceivable that too much pressure was exerted on this individual and too much renunciation expected of him.

The conception of differences of intelligence became quite clear to our subject through observing Art Bovis, the feebleminded boy. His blank, fat face, unintelligible muttering and ineffectual social responses were early observed and derided. It gave the informant a terrible pang to hear that this condition might have been associated with masturbation, and this news acted as an effective barrier in putting out of mind the genital sensations which the informant felt at times in childhood. At this time was established the conflict between intelligence and sexual impulse which is so common among those who expect to rise or have risen in status through their own talents. Indeed, one of our informant's difficulties in adult life was that when he was finally called upon in marriage to exercise a limited impulse-freedom he was out of practice and carried with him many strange and unsuitable internalized taboos.

The informant early learned that there were still other forces to which his parents submitted. One of these was God and his representative, the minister. At church he heard sermons that he did not understand very well, but he did learn that most of the things you wanted to do were sins, and that death was the one final punishment for these sins. There was also Hell and the everlasting vengefulness of a rejected and outraged God. The informant tended to associate everything that he feared as stern and severe with religion and to feel that the minister too demanded the deprivations which he experienced. There was, he knew in a vague way, other talk about the minister, talk of admiring him, of getting comfort from him, but this aspect of the religious institution made no appeal to our subject. One of our informant's first acts of adult rebellion was to renounce the religion of his childhood,—

with the aid, of course, of the permissive patterns which he found in college. If this hostile attitude toward religious symbols is held by many persons from the same social group as our informant, it may be seen as a permanent force for social change. Study of the life history may often show the concealed tensions which erupt in periods of social crisis.

A remark may be added on the question of the type of struggle which this man had with his environment. On the one hand, there is the struggle of very early childhood, which might be phrased as one between the organism and the unified family group. In this battle, of course, the individual is always beaten if he is socialized at all. There is a second type of conflict which this individual also exhibits and which is frequently noted by sociologists, viz., conflict in the mature person, i.e., within a developed personality which is faced by societal segments with opposing or confusing definitions of life. In the latter case, "choice" is offered, and it is apparently this choice which results in conflict. Both types are apparent in this case. My conclusion is that without the second type of conflict this individual would still have been neurotic, but his neurosis would have been smothered by the unified front opposed to him by society. His misery would have been laid to spirit-possession, the devil, or to biological defect.

10. THE FOCUSED INTERVIEW[1]

by Robert K. Merton and Patricia L. Kendall

FOR SEVERAL YEARS, the Bureau of Applied Social Research has conducted individual and group interviews in studies of the social and psychological effects of mass communications—radio, print, and film. A type of research interview grew out of this experience, which is perhaps characteristic enough to merit a distinctive label—the "focused interview."

In several respects the focused interview differs from other types of research interviews which might appear superficially similar. These characteristics may be set forth in broad outline as follows:

1. Persons interviewed are known to have been involved in *a particular concrete situation:* they have seen a film; heard a radio program; read a pamphlet, article, or book; or have participated in a psychological experiment or in an uncontrolled, but observed, social situation.

2. The hypothetically significant elements, patterns, and total structure of this situation have been previously analyzed by the investigator. Through this *content analysis* he has arrived at a set of hypotheses concerning the meaning and effects of determinate aspects of the situation.

3. On the basis of this analysis, the investigator has fashioned an *interview*

Reprinted in part from *The American Journal of Sociology*, Vol LI, 1946, pp. 541-557, by permission of the authors and the publisher. (Copyright, 1946, by The University of Chicago.)

guide, setting forth the major areas of inquiry and the hypotheses which locate the pertinence of data to be obtained in the interview.

4. The interview itself is focused on the *subjective experiences* of persons exposed to the pre-analyzed situation. The array of their reported responses to this situation enables the investigator

a) To test the validity of hypotheses derived from content analysis and social psychological theory, and

b) To ascertain unanticipated responses to the situation, thus giving rise to fresh hypotheses.

From this synopsis it will be seen that a distinctive prerequisite of the focused interview is a prior analysis of a situation in which subjects have been involved.

The interviewer who has previously analyzed the situation on which the interview focuses is in a peculiarly advantageous position to elicit details. In the usual depth interview, one can urge informants to reminisce on their experiences. In the focused interview, however, the interviewer can, when expedient, play a more active role; he can introduce more explicit verbal cues to the stimulus pattern or even *re-present* it, as we shall see. In either case this usually activates a concrete report of responses by informants.

USES OF THE FOCUSED INTERVIEW

The focused interview was initially developed to meet certain problems growing out of communications research and propaganda analysis. The outlines of such problems appear in detailed case studies by Dr. Herta Herzog, dealing with the gratification found by listeners in such radio programs as daytime serials and quiz competitions.[2] With the sharpening of objectives, research interest centered on the analysis of responses to particular pamphlets, radio programs, and motion pictures. During the war Dr. Herzog and the senior author of the present paper were assigned by several war agencies to study the psychological effects of specific morale-building devices. In the course of this work the focused interview was progressively developed to a relatively standardized form.

The primary, though not the exclusive, purpose of the focused interview was to provide some basis for *interpreting* statistically significant effects of mass communications. But, in general, *experimental studies of effects* might well profit by the use of focused interviews in research. The character of such applications can be briefly illustrated by examining the role of the focused interview at four distinct points:

1. Specifying the effective stimulus
2. Interpreting discrepancies between anticipated and actual effects
3. Interpreting discrepancies between prevailing effects and effects among subgroups—"deviant cases"
4. Interpreting processes involved in experimentally induced effects.

1. Experimental studies of effect face the problem of what might be called the *specification of the stimulus,* i.e., determining which x or pattern of x's in the total stimulus situation led to the observed effects. But, largely because of the practical difficulties which this entails, this requirement is often not satisfied in psychological or sociological experiments. Instead, a relatively undifferentiated complex of factors—such as "emotional appeals,"

"competitive incentives," and "political propaganda"—is regarded as "the" experimental variable. This would be comparable to the statement that 'living in the tropics is a cause of higher rates of malaria"; it is true but unspecific. However crude they may be at the outset, procedures must be devised to detect the causally significant aspects of the total stimulus situation. Thus Gosnell conducted an ingenious experiment on the "stimulation of voting," in which experimental groups of residents in twelve districts in Chicago were sent "individual nonpartisan appeals" to register and vote.[3] Roughly equivalent control groups did not receive this literature. It was found that the experimental groups responded by a significantly higher proportion of registration and voting. But what does this result demonstrate? To *what* did the experimental group respond? Was it the non-partisan character of the circulars, the explicit nature of the instructions which they contained, the particular symbols and appeals utilized in the notices, or what? In short, to use Gosnell's own phrasing, what were "the particular stimuli being tested"?

According to the ideal experimental design, such questions would, of course, be answered by a series of successive experiments, which test the effects of each pattern of putative causes. In practice not only does the use of this procedure in social experimentation involve prohibitive problems of cost, labor, and administration; it also assumes that the experimenter has been successful in detecting the pertinent aspects of the total stimulus pattern. The focused interview provides a useful near-substitute for such a series of experiments; for, despite great sacrifices in scientific exactitude, it enables the experimenter to arrive at plausible hypotheses concerning the significant items to which subjects responded. Through interviews focused on this problem, Gosnell, for example, could probably have clarified just what elements in his several types of "nonpartisan" materials proved effective for different segments of his experimental group.[4] Such a procedure provides an approximate solution for problems heretofore consigned to the realm of the unknown or the speculative.[5]

2. There is also the necessity for *interpreting* the effects which are found to occur. Quite frequently, for example, the experimenter will note a *discrepancy* between the observed effects and those anticipated on the basis of other findings or previously formulated theories. Or, again, he may find that one subgroup in his experimental population exhibits effects which differ in degree or direction from those observed among other parts of the population. Unless the research is to remain a compendium of unintegrated empirical findings, some effort must be made to interpret such "contradictory" results. But the difficulty here is that of selecting among the wide range of *post factum* interpretations of the deviant findings. The focused interview provides a tool for this purpose. For example:

Rosenthal's study of the effect of "pro-radical" motion-picture propaganda on the socioeconomic attitudes of college students provides an instance of *discrepancy between anticipated and actual effects*.[6] He found that a larger proportion of subjects agreed with the statement "radicals are enemies of society" *after* they had seen the film. As is usually the case when seemingly paradoxical results are obtained, this called forth an "explanation": "This negative effect of the propaganda was probably due to the many scenes of radical orators, marchers, and demonstrators."

Clearly *ad hoc* in nature, this "interpretation" is little more than speculation; but it is the type of speculation which the focused interview is particularly suited to examine, correct, and develop. Such interviews would have indicated how the audience actually responded to the "orators, marchers, and demonstrators"; the author's conjecture would have been recast into theoretical terms and either confirmed or refuted. (As we shall see, the focused interview has, in fact, been used to locate the source of such "boomerang effects" in film, radio, pamphlet, and cartoon propaganda.[7])

In a somewhat similar experiment, Peterson and Thurstone found an unexpectedly small change in attitudes among high-school students who had seen a pacifist film.[8] The investigators held it ". . . probable that the picture, 'Journey's End,' is too sophisticated in its propaganda for high school children."

Once again, the plausibility of a *post factum* interpretation would have been enhanced, and entirely different hypotheses would have been developed had they conducted a focused interview.[9] How did the children conceive the film? To what did they primarily respond? Answers to these and similar questions would yield the kind of data needed to interpret the unanticipated result.

3. We may turn again to Gosnell's study to illustrate the tendency toward *ad hoc* interpretations of *discrepancies between prevailing effects and effects among subgroups* ("deviant cases") and the place of focused interviews in avoiding them.

Gosnell found that, in general, a larger proportion of citizens registered or voted in response to a notice "of a hortatory character, containing a cartoon and several slogans" than in response to a "factual" notice, which merely called attention to voting regulations. But he found a series of "exceptions," which invited a medley of *ad hoc* hypotheses. In a predominantly German election district, the factual notice had a greater effect than the "cartoon notice"—a finding which at once led Gosnell to the supposition that "the word 'slacker' on the cartoon notice probably revived war memories and therefore failed to arouse interest in voting." In Czech and Italian districts the factual notices also proved more effective; but in these instances Gosnell advances quite another interpretation: "the information cards were more effective than the cartoon notices probably because they were printed in Czech [and Italian, respectively] whereas the cartoon notices were printed in English." And yet in a Polish district the factual notice, although printed in Polish, was slightly *less* effective than the cartoon notice.[10]

In short, lacking supplementary interviews focused on the problem of deviant group responses, the investigator found himself drawn into a series of extremely flexible interpretations instead of resting his analysis on pertinent interview data. This characteristic of the Gosnell experiment, properly assessed by Catlin as an exceptionally well-planned study, is, a fortiori, found in a host of social and psychological experiments.

4. Even brief introspective interviews as a supplement to experimentation have proved useful for discerning the *processes involved in experimentally induced effects*. Thus Zeigarnik, in her well-known experiment on memory and interrupted tasks, was confronted with the result that in some cases interrupted tasks were often forgotten, a finding at odds with her modal findings and her initial theory.[11] Interviews with subjects exhibiting this "discrepant" behavior revealed that the uncompleted tasks which had been forgotten were experienced as failures and, therefore, were subjectively "completed." She was thus able to incorporate this seeming contradiction into

her general theory. The value of such interpretative interviews is evidenced further in the fact that Zeigarnik's extended theory, derived from the interviews, inspired a series of additional experiments by Rosenzweig, who, in part, focused on the very hypotheses which emerged from her interview data.

Rosenzweig found experimentally that many subjects recalled a larger percentage of their successes in tasks assigned them than of their failures.[12] Interviews disclosed that this "objective experimental result" was bound up with the emotionalized symbolism which tasks assumed for different subjects. For example, one subject reported that a needed scholarship depended "upon her receiving a superior grade in the psychology course from which she had been recruited for this experiment. Throughout the test her mind dwelt upon the lecturer in this course: 'All I thought of during the experiment was that it was an intelligence test and that he [the lecturer] would see the results. I saw his name always before me.' "

Without such supplementary data, the hypothesis of repression which was introduced to interpret the results would have been wholly conjectural.

This brief review is perhaps sufficient to suggest the functions of the focused interview as an adjunct to experimental inquiry, as well as in studies of responses to concrete situations in everyday life.

OBJECTIVES AND PROCEDURES

A successful interview is not the automatic product of conforming to a fixed routine of mechanically applicable techniques. Nor is interviewing an elusive, private, and incommunicable art. There are recurrent situations and problems in the focused interview which can be met successfully by communicable and teachable procedures. We have found that the proficiency of all interviewers, even the less skilful, can be considerably heightened by training them to recognize type situations and to draw upon an array of flexible, though standardized, procedures for dealing with these situations.

In his search for "significant data," moreover, the interviewer must develop a capacity for continuously evaluating the interview as it is in process. By drawing upon a large number of interview transcripts, in which the interviewer's comments as well as the subjects' responses have been recorded, we have found it possible to establish a set of provisional criteria by which productive and unproductive interview materials can be distinguished. Briefly stated, they are:

1. *Nondirection:* * In the interview, guidance and direction by the interviewer should be at a minimum.

2. *Specificity:* Subjects' definition of the situation should find full and specific expression.

3. *Range:* The interview should maximize the range of evocative stimuli and responses reported by the subject.

4. *Depth and personal context:* The interview should bring out the affective and value-laden implications of the subjects' responses, to determine whether the experience had central or peripheral significance. It should elicit the relevant personal context, the idiosyncratic associations, beliefs, and ideas.

These criteria are interrelated; they are merely different dimensions of the same concrete body of interview materials. Every response can be

---

* Due to limitations of space, it has been necessary to omit the extensive discussion of "The Criterion of Nondirection," pp. 545-549 of the original article.—ED. NOTE.

classified according to each of these dimensions: it may be spontaneous or forced; diffuse and general or highly specific; profoundly self-revealing or superficial; etc. But it is useful to examine these criteria separately, so that they may provide the interviewer with guide-lines for appraising the flow of the interview and adapting his techniques accordingly.

For each of these objectives, there is an array of specific, effective procedures, although there are few which do not lend themselves to more than one purpose. We can do no more here than indicate the major function served by each technique and merely allude to its subsidiary uses. And since these procedures have been derived from clinical analysis of interview materials rather than through experimental test, they must be considered entirely provisional. Because, in the training of interviewers, it has been found instructive to indicate typical errors as well as effective procedures, that same policy has been adopted in this paper.

THE CRITERION OF SPECIFICITY

In the study of real life rather than, say, in nonsense-syllable experiments in rote memory, there is all the greater need for discovering the meaning attributed by subjects to elements, aspects, or patterns of the complex situation to which they have been exposed. Thus army trainees, in one such study, reported that "the scene of marching Nazi soldiers" in a documentary film led them to feel anxious about their ability to withstand the German army. This report does not satisfy the canon of specificity. Anxiety may have been provoked by the impression of matchless power symbolized by massed armies; by the "brutal expressions" on their faces to which the commentary referred; by the elaborate equipment of the enemy; by the extensive training seemingly implied by their maneuvers. Without further specification, there is no basis for selecting among the several possible interpretations.

In stressing specificity, we do not at all imply that subjects respond to each and every element of the total situation as a separate and isolated item. The situation may be experienced "as a whole" or as a complex of configurations. Individual patterns may be perceived as figures against a background. But we cannot rest with such facile formulations; we have yet to detect the "significant wholes" to which response has occurred, and it is toward the detection of these that the criterion of specificity directs the interviewer's attention. It is only in this way that we are led to findings which can be generalized and which provide a basis for predicting selective responses. Inquiry has shown that, as a significant whole, brief scenes in a motion picture, for example, have evoked different responses, quite apart from the fact that seeing-a-film-in-conjunction-with-two-thousand-others was *also* a "configurative experience." But without inquiring into specific meanings of significant details, we surrender all possibility of determining the effective stimuli patterns. Thus our emphasis on "specificity" does not express allegiance to an "atomistic," as contrasted with a "configurational," approach; it serves only to orient the interviewer toward searching out the significant configurations. The fact of selective response is well attested; we must determine what is differentially selected and generalize these data.

Procedures. We have found that specificity of reporting can be obtained through procedures in which the interviewer exercises a minimum of guidance.

It seems difficult, if not impossible, to recapture highly specific responses. Interviews on experiences of the immediate or remote past, of course, involve the problem of losses and distortions of memory. Extensive experimentation and clinical study have shown the importance of such lapses and modifications in recalled material.[13] The focused interview is, of course, subject to this same liability but not, perhaps, to the same extent as diffuse interviews; for there are certain procedures in the focused interview which facilitate the accurate report of the initial experience, which aid accounts of the "registration" of the experience rather than a distorted, condensed, elaborated, or defective report based on unaided recall.

Retrospective Introspection. These procedures are all designed to lead subjects to adopt a particular mental set—which may be called "retrospective introspection."

Mere retrospection, without introspection, usually produces accounts of what was remembered and does not relate these to significant responses. Introspection without retrospection, on the other hand, usually leads the informant to report his reactions after they have been reconsidered in the interval between the event and the interview, rather than his experience at the time he was exposed to the stimulus situation. To minimize this problem, procedures have been developed to expedite retrospective introspection by *re-presenting* the stimulus situation so far as possible.[14] They seek to approximate a condition in which subjects virtually *re-experience* the situation to aid their report of significant responses and to have these linked with pertinent aspects of it. Re-presentation also serves to insure that both interviewer and subject are referring to the same aspects of the original situation.

The most immediate means of re-presenting documentary material is to exhibit "stills" from a motion picture, to play back sections of a transcribed radio program, or to have parts of a pamphlet re-read. Although such devices do not fully reproduce the original situation, they markedly aid the subject in recapturing his original response in specific detail. Such re-presentations do have the defect of interrupting the smooth, continuous flow of the interview, at least for a moment. If they are used frequently, therefore, the interview is likely to deteriorate into a staccato series of distinct inquiries. The best procedure, then, is to combine occasional graphic re-presentations with more frequent verbal cues. But, except for the closing stages of the interview, such cues should be introduced only after subjects have spontaneously referred to the materials in point.

Each re-presentation, whether graphic or verbal, calls for reports of specific reaction. Otherwise, subjects are likely to take the re-presentation as an occasion for merely exhibiting their memory. Questions soliciting these reports take somewhat the following form:

Now that you think back, what were your reactions to that part of the film?

Whatever the exact wording of such questions, they have several features in common. The interviewer alludes to a retrospective frame of reference: "Now that you think back. . . ." He refers to introspection: "What were your reactions (or feelings, or ideas, etc.) . . . ?" And, finally, he uses the past tense: "What *were* your reactions . . . ?" This will lead the subject to concentrate on his original experience. Emphasis on such details as the components of this type of question may seem to be a flight into the trivial. Yet experience shows that omission of any of them lessens the productiveness of replies.

Explicit References to Stimulus Situation. To elicit specificity, the interviewer combines the technique of re-presentation with that of the unstructured question. A typical situation requiring further specification occurs when the subject's report of his responses has been *wholly unlinked* to the stimulus-situation. Repeatedly, we see the necessity for establishing such linkages, if observed "effects" are to be adequately interpreted. Thus tests in 1943 showed that documentary films concerning the Nazis increased the proportion of subjects in experimental groups who believed that Germany had a stronger army than the United States. Inasmuch as there was no explicit indication of this theme in the films, the "effect" could have been interpreted only conjecturally, had it not been for focused interviews. Subjects who expressed this opinion were prompted to indicate its source by questions of the following type:

Was there anything in the film that gave you that impression?

It soon became evident that scenes which presumably stressed the "regimentation" of the Nazis—e.g., their military training from an early age—were unexpectedly taken as proof of their exceptionally thorough training, as the following excerpts from interviews indicate:

It showed there that their men have more training. They start their men—when they are ready to go to school, they start their military training. By the time they get to our age, they are in there fighting, and they know as much as the man who has been in our service eight or nine years.
By the looks of them where they took the boys when they were eight and started training them then; they had them marching with drums and everything and they trained them for military service when they were very young. They are well trained when they are grown men.

Thus the search for specificity yielded a clue to the significant scenes from which these implications were drawn. The interpretation of the experimental effect rests on the weight of cumulative evidence drawn from interviews and not on mere conjecture.

This case serves to bring out the need for progressive specification. If the subject's report includes only a *general* allusion to one or another part of the film, it is necessary to determine the particular *aspects* of these scenes to which he responded. Otherwise, we lose access to the often *unanticipated symbolisms* and private meanings ascribed to the stimulus situation. A subject who referred to the "regimentation of the Nazis" exemplified in "mass scenes" is prompted to indicate the particular items which led to this symbolism.

What about those scenes gave you that impression?

It develops that "goose-step parades" and the *Sieg Heil!* chorus are taken as symbols of regimentation:

When it showed them goose-stepping out there; it numbed their mind. It's such a strain on their mind and body to do that. Just like a bunch of slaves, dogs—do what they're told.

It will be noted that these questions refer explicitly to the document or situation which is at the focus of the interview. We have found that, unless the interviewer refers to "scenes in this film," "parts of this radio program," or "sections of this pamphlet," the subjects are likely to shift toward an expression of generalized attitudes or opinion. Indispensable as such auxiliary data may be, they do not take the place of reports in which responses are linked to the test situation.

In general, specifying questions should be explicit enough to aid the subject in relating his responses to determinate aspects of the stimulus situation and yet general enough to avoid having the interviewer structure it. This twofold requirement is best met by unstructured questions, which contain explicit references to the stimulus material.

THE CRITERION OF RANGE

The criterion of range refers to the coverage of pertinent data in the interview. Since any given aspect of the stimulus situation may elicit different responses and since each response may derive from different aspects of the stimulus situation, it is necessary for the interviewer to uncover the range both of response and of evocative stimuli. Without implying any strict measure of range, we consider it adequate if the interview yields data which

a) Confirm or refute the occurrence of responses *anticipated* from the content analysis;

b) Indicate that ample opportunities have been provided for the report of *unanticipated* reactions; and

c) Suggest *interpretations* of findings derived from experiments or mass statistics.

Procedures. The tactics considered up to this point have been found useful at every stage of the interview. But the procedures primarily designed to extend range do depend, in some measure, on the changing horizons of the interview: on the coverage already obtained, on the extent to which subjects continue to comment spontaneously, and on the amount of time available. The interviewer must, therefore, be vigilant in detecting transitions from one stage of the interview to another, if he is to decide upon procedures appropriate for widening range at one point rather than at another. He will, above all, utilize these procedures when informants prove inarticulate.

The central tactical problem in extending range consists in effecting transitions from one area of discussion to another. In the early stages of the interview, such transitions follow easily from the intermittent use of general unstructured questions. But, as the interview develops, this type of question no longer elicits fresh materials. Subjects then require assistance in reporting on further foci of attention. From this point, the interviewer introduces new topics either through transitions suggested by subjects' remarks or, in the final stages, by the initiation of topics from the interview guide which have not yet been explored. The first of these procedures utilizes *transitional questions;* the second, *mutational questions.*

Subject Transitions. It is not enough to say that shifts to a new area of discussion should be initiated by the subject. The interviewer who is possessed of what Murray has called "double hearing" will soon infer from the context of such shifts that they have different functions for the informant and call for different tactics by the interviewer.

Of the several reasons for shifts engineered by the informant, at least three should be considered.

1. The topic under discussion may be peripheral to the subject's own interests and feelings, so that he turns to one which holds greater significance for him. In talking about the first topic, he manifests no affect but merely lack of interest. He has little to say from the outset and exhibits boredom, which gives way to heightened interest as he moves on to a new topic.

2. The informant may have talked at length about a given subject, and, having exhausted what he has to say, he moves the interview into a new area. His behavior then becomes very much the same as in the preceding instance.

3. He may seek to escape from a given area of discussion precisely because it is imbued with high affective significance for him, and he is not yet prepared to verbalize his feelings. This is betrayed by varying signs of resistance—prolonged pauses, self-corrections, tremor of voice, unfinished sentences, embarrassed silences, half-articulate utterances.

On the basis of such behavioral contexts, the interviewer provisionally diagnoses the meaning of the informant's transition and proceeds accordingly. If he places the transition in the third category, he makes a mental note to revert to this critical zone at a later stage of the interview. If, however, the transition is either of the first two types, he may safely abandon the topic unless it arises again spontaneously.

Interviewer Transitions. Generally preferable though it is to have the transitions effected by the subject, there will be occasions, nonetheless, when the interviewer will have to bring about a change in topic. When one topic is exhausted, when the informant does not spontaneously introduce another, and when unstructured questions no longer prove effective, the interviewer must introduce transitional questions if he is to tap the reservoir of response further. He may introduce a *cued* transition, or, as the interview progresses and he accumulates a series of items which require further discussion, he may effect a *reversional* transition.

In a *cued* transition, the interviewer so adapts a remark or an allusion by an informant as to ease him into consideration of a new topic. This procedure has the advantage of maintaining the flow of the interview.

Cued transitions may require the interviewer to exercise considerable ingenuity. In the following case, avowedly cited as an extreme, even bizarre, example, the informant was far afield from the radio program under discussion, but the interviewer ingeniously picked up a cue and refocused the interview on the program:

SUBJECT No. 1: The finest ingenuity in Germany that you ever saw. They are smart. But I think this: I don't think when this World War is over that we won't have another war. We will. We have had them since Cain killed Abel. As long as there are two human beings on this earth, there's going to be a war.

INTERVIEWER: *Talking about Cain,* he could be called something of a small-time gangster, couldn't he? Do you happen to remember anything about gangsters being brought out at any point in this program?

SUBJECT No. 1: Dillinger. That was where. . . .

(Here, although the interviewer's association was more than a little far fetched, it served its purpose in bringing the informant back to a consideration of the radio program. Had the interviewer simply changed the subject, he would have indicated that he thought the informant's remarks irrelevant, with a consequent strain on rapport. As it was, the cued transition led the informant to develop at length his structuring of a specific section of the program. When the time for the interview cannot be extended indefinitely, the cued transition enables the curbing of patent digressions, without prejudice to rapport.)

Reversional transitions are those effected by the interviewer to obtain further discussion of a topic previously abandoned, either because the subject had avoided it or, in a group interview, because someone had moved on to a new theme.

Whenever possible, the reversional question is cued, i.e., related to the topic under discussion. It can, for instance, take this form:

> That suggests something you mentioned previously about the scene in which . . . What were your feelings at that point in the picture?

When it does not seem possible to relate the reversional query to the present context, a "cold" reversion may be productive:

INTERVIEWER: A little while ago, you were talking about the scenes of bombed-out school houses, and you seemed to have more ideas on that. How did you feel when you saw that?

SUBJECT No. 2: I noticed a little girl lying under a culvert—it made me ready to go fight then. Because I have a daughter of my own, and I knew how I would feel if anything like that happened to her. . . .

This latter type of reversional query is used infrequently, however, and only in instances where it seems likely that the informant has "warmed up" to the interviewing situation sufficiently to be articulate about the topic he had avoided earlier.

Overdependence on the Interview Guide. As we have seen, misuses of the interview guide may endanger the nondirective character of the interview; they may also impose serious limitations on the range of material obtained.

The interviewer may confine himself to the areas of inquiry set forth in the guide and choke off comments which do not directly bear upon these areas. This may be termed the *fallacy of arresting comment*. Subjects' remarks which do not fall within these pre-established areas of interest may be prematurely and spuriously interpreted as "irrelevant," thus arresting what is at times the most useful type of interview material: the unanticipated response.

INTERVIEWER: Well, now what about the first part of the film? You remember, they had photographs of the German leaders and quotations from their speeches. . . .

SUBJECT No. 10: I remember Goering, he looked like a big pig. That is what that brought out to me, the fact that if he could control the land, he could control the people.

SUBJECT No. 7: He is quite an egotist in the picture.

INTERVIEWER: Did you get any impression about the German people from that?

(Here the interviewer introduces a section of the film for discussion. Before he has finished his remarks, an informant volunteers his impression. No. 7 then begins his interpretation of the section. Both remarks suggest that the informants have "something on their minds." Being more attentive to his interview guide than to the implications of the informants' remarks, the interviewer by-passes the hints which might have added further to the range of the interview. He then asks the question, from his guide, which he had probably intended to ask in the first place.)

Excessive dependence on the interview guide increases the danger of *confusing range with superficiality.* The interviewer who feels obligated to conform closely to the guide may suddenly discover, to his dismay, that he has covered only a small portion of the suggested areas of inquiry. This invites a rapid shift from topic to topic, with a question devoted to each. In some cases the interviewer seems scarcely to listen to the responses, for his questions are in no way related to previous comments. Comments elicited by this rapid fire of questions are often as superficial and unrevealing as those obtained through a fixed questionnaire. The quick "once-over" technique wastes time: it diverts respondents from their foci of attention, without any compensating increase in the interviewer's information concerning given areas of inquiry. In view of the shortcomings of rapid shifts in discussion, we suggest the working rule: *Do not introduce a given topic unless a sustained effort is made to explore it in some detail.*

THE CRITERION OF DEPTH

Depth, as a criterion, involves the elaboration of affective responses beyond limited reports of "positive" or "negative," "pleasant" or "unpleasant," reactions. The interviewer seeks to obtain a maximum of *self-revelatory comments concerning how the stimulus material was experienced.*

The depth of reports in an interview varies; not everything reported is on the same psychological level.[15] The depth of comments may be thought of as varying along a continuum. At the lower end of the scale are mere descriptive accounts of reactions which allow little more than a tabulation of "positive" or "negative" responses. At the upper end are those reports which set forth varied psychological dimensions of the experience. In these are expressed symbolisms, anxieties, fears, sentiments, as well as cognitive ideas. A main task of the interviewer, then, is *to diagnose the level of depth on which his subjects are operating at any given moment and to shift that level toward whichever end of the "depth-continuum" he finds appropriate to the given case.*

The criterion of maximizing depth—to the limited extent possible in a single focused interview—guides the interviewer toward searching out the *personal context* and the *saliency* of responses.

It is a central task of the focused interview to determine how the prior experiences and predispositions of respondents relate to their structuring of the stimulus situation.

Personal and social contexts provide the links between the stimulus material and the responses. It is through the discovery of such contexts that variations in the meaning ascribed to symbols and other content are understood; that the ways in which the stimulus material is imported into the experience world of subjects are determined; and that the self-betrayals and self-revelations which clarify the covert significance of a response are elicited. Thus, in the following excerpt, it becomes clear that social class provided the context for heightened identification with the British portrayed in a documentary film:

INTERVIEWER: In what way does this picture make you feel closer [to the British]?
SUBJECT No. 6: I don't come from such a well-to-do family as Mrs. Miniver's. Hers was a well-to-do family, and that picture didn't show anything of the poor families. But this one brought it closer to my class of people, and you realize we are all in it and everybody gets hurt and not just the higher class of people.

The criterion of depth also sensitizes the interviewer to variations in the saliency of responses. Some responses will be central and invested with affect, urgency, or intense feelings; others will be peripheral, of limited significance to the subject. The interviewer must elicit sufficiently detailed data to discriminate the casual expression of an opinion, which is mentioned only because the interview situation seems to call for it, from the strongly motivated response which reaches into central concerns of the informant. It appears that the atmosphere of an expressive interview allows greater opportunity for degrees of saliency to be detected than the self-ratings of intensity of belief which have lately been incorporated into questionnaires and attitude scales. But, unless the interviewer is deliberately seeking out depth responses, he may not obtain the data needed to distinguish the central from the peripheral response.

Procedures. In following up the comments of subjects, the interviewer may call for two types of elaboration. He may ask the subjects to describe *what* they observed in the stimulus situation, thus inviting fairly detached, though significantly selective, accounts of the content. Or he can ask them to report how they *felt* about the content. Both types of elaboration are useful; but, since the latter more often leads to depth responses, it is preferable in a fairly brief interview. Consequently, we sketch only those tactics which lead to the second type of elaboration.

Focus on Feelings. It has been found that subjects move rather directly toward a report of depth responses when the follow-up questions contain key words which refer explicitly to a *feeling context.* Focusing on a fairly recent, concrete experience, subjects usually become progressively interested in exploring its previously unverbalized dimensions, and, for the most part, no elaborate detour is needed to have them express their sentiments. But the context for such reporting must be established and maintained. Thus the interviewer should phrase a question in such terms as "How did you *feel* when . . . ?" rather than imply a mere mnemonic context by asking "What do you *remember* about . . . ?"

Illustrations are plentiful to show how such seemingly slight differences in phrasing lead respondents from an impersonal description of content to reports of their emotional responses to this content.

INTERVIEWER: Do you happen to remember the scenes showing Warsaw being bombed and shelled? What stood out about that part of the film?
SUBJECT No. 1: The way people didn't have any shelter; the way they were running around and getting bombed. . . .
(The interviewer's "What stood out?" has elicited only an abbreviated account of the film content. He might have proceeded to follow this line of thought— elaborations of the objective events, further details of the squadrons of bombers, and so on. But this would have been comparatively unproductive, since the interviewer is primarily concerned with what these scenes *meant* to the informant. Therefore, he shifts attention to the response level and at once elicits an elaborate report of feeling, which we reproduce in part.)

INTERVIEWER: How did you feel when you saw that?

SUBJECT NO. 1: I still can't get worked up over it yet [1942], because in this country you just can't realize what war is like over there. I'm talking for myself. I know I couldn't fight at the present time with the viciousness of one of those people. I could shoot a man before he'd shoot me, knowing he was going to shoot me. But I couldn't have the viciousness I know those people have. . . .

Restatement of Implied or Expressed Feelings. Once the feelings context has been established, further elaboration will be prompted by the occasional restating of the feelings implied or expressed in comments. This technique, extensively developed by Carl Rogers in his work on psychotherapeutic counseling, serves a twofold function. By so rephrasing emotionalized attitudes, the interviewer implicitly invites progressive elaboration by the informant. And, second, such reformulations enhance rapport, since the interviewer thus makes it clear that he fully "understands" and "follows" the informant, as he proceeds to express his feelings.[16]

Comparative Situations. In certain cases the interviewer can use the partially directive technique of suggesting meaningful comparisons between the test situation and parallel experiences which the subjects are known, or can be presumed, to have had. Such comparisons of concrete experiences aid the verbalization of affect. The suggested comparison is designed not so much to have subjects draw objective parallels (or contrasts) between the two experiences as to serve as a release for introspective and affective responses.

Witness the following excerpt from an interview with inductees, who had implied that they were viewing a documentary film of Nazi military training within the context of their own current experience:

INTERVIEWER: Do you suppose that we Americans train our men in the same way [i.e., comparison with Nazi training as shown in film]?

SUBJECT NO. 6: They train them more thoroughly.

SUBJECT NO. 2: The way we are rushed through our training over here, it doesn't seem possible.

SUBJECT NO. 1: That's what enters my mind about the training we are getting here. Of course, a lot of talk exists among the fellows that as soon as training is over, we're going into the fight. I don't know any more about it than they do. The training we're going to get right here is just our basic training and if we get shipped across, I can't see that we'd know anything about it except marching and doing a little left flank and right flank and a few other things like that. . . .

(The suggested comparison provided an apt opportunity for the subjects to go on to express their anxieties about going overseas unprepared for combat. The interviewer was then able to ascertain the specific scenes in the film which had further provoked these anxieties.)

It should be emphasized, however, that this procedure is effective only when the experience drawn on for comparison is known to be centrally significant to the subject and if the comparison flows from the interview. Otherwise, comparisons, far from facilitating depth responses, actually disrupt the continuity of the interview and impose an alien frame of reference upon the informant. In such instances the interviewer becomes a target for hostility: he is asked to define his terms, state the purpose behind his question, and the like.

Auxiliary Readings

A. THE STUDY OF BUYING AS A PARADIGM OF THE EMPIRICAL ANALYSIS OF ACTION

It is not easy to find auxiliary readings in this area. For division A, further consumer research studies would not provide new material. For the other divisions, most of the references are somewhat tangential; but the teacher should have no difficulty in making explicit their use of one or the other of the steps in the empirical analysis of action outlined above.

B. DEVELOPMENT AND USE OF ACCOUNTING SCHEMES

H. Krugman, "The Appeal of Communism to American Middle-Class Intellectuals and Trade Unionists," *Public Opinion Quarterly,* Vol. 16, No. 3, 1952.

> A number of case studies are summarized as to the role of prior experience, of social pressures, and of personal gratifications in holding Communists in their party. While no accounting scheme is stated, it is implicit in the report.

W. Healy, "The Causes of Crime," *The Individual Delinquent* (Boston: Little, Brown and Co., 1927), Chapter II.

> A general scheme is proposed to describe the "causal texture," which can account for a criminal act.

R. C. Angell, "Appendix on Method" *The Family Encounters the Depression* (New York: Scribner's Sons, 1936).

> Detailed case studies were conducted in order to trace the changes which the depression had brought about in a number of families. In a detailed methodological appendix, the author describes his various efforts to derive generalizations from his materials. The final and most productive combination of variables is similar to our accounting scheme, although no assessment *within* each case is attempted.

C. THE ASSESSMENT AND STATISTICAL ANALYSIS OF CAUSES

C. Burt, *The Young Delinquent* (New York: Appleton-Century, 1938).

> This is a study which uses two approaches. It compares statistically a set of young delinquents with a control group of non-delinquent boys for a variety of factors. In addition, it traces these factors in the life histories of the delinquent boys and assesses their causal role. It is therefore possible to compare the findings which result from these two procedures.

C. W. Mills, C. Senior, and R. K. Goldsen, *The Puerto Rican Journey* (New York: Harper & Bros., 1950) Chapter 3.

> Several hundred immigrants are interviewed as to their reasons for leaving Puerto Rico and coming to New York. The replies are classified according to such aspects as: Did he make his decision by himself or by following another person's lead; what attracted him to New York; how did he learn about these opportunities, etc. These are the categories of the scheme. They then tabulate these different categories against each other and thus show the use of an accounting scheme in the final statistical analysis.

"Cause of Death Coding," *Vital Statistics Instruction Manual,* Part II. Federal Security Agency, Public Health Service, National Office of Vital Statistics, Washington, D. C., Jan., 1951.

> How to assess and classify causes of death is an old problem of medical statistics closely related to the topic of this section. Continuous improvements are being made, the logic of which deserves careful study.

J. Watson, "Some Social and Psychological Situations Related to Change in Attitude," *Human Relations,* Vol. 3, 1950.

Through a mail questionnaire a number of people were located who recently had changed their attitudes toward ethnic minorities. They then were interviewed in detail as to the influences and situations which brought these changes about. A considerable number of generalizations are developed and supported by skilful statistical analysis of the interviews.

E. Ginzberg, S. W. Ginsburg, S. Axelrad and J. L. Herma, "The Problem of Occupational Choice," *American Journal of Orthopsychiatry,* Vol. 20, 1950, pp. 166-198.

Some decisions take a long period of time to crystallize and are, consequently, more difficult to study. Occupational choices are a typical example. The authors report their efforts to interpret a number of cases. They present a good account of the various systematic approaches they combine in their analysis.

Toward A Philosophy of The Social Sciences

So FAR, we have concentrated on the analysis of specific research operations. This final section provides samples of more general methodological discussions. They cannot be organized in any standard way, for they cover a very broad issue indeed: How can clear and creative thinking be applied to problems of the social sciences? Still, there are a number of basic issues which are always likely to come up in teaching as well as in scholarly work. Four of them have been selected in this section for closer attention. They are best described in connection with the special selections which we have chosen as examples.

A. *The location of problems.* Many an author is so involved in his problem that he never really states it clearly; all his effort is directed toward giving his answer. This might be justified for a man who makes an original contribution. But it is bad when the student comes and reiterates the answer without asking himself where the matter belongs in a broader context. The remedy is composed of several elements: we want to know what the general concern of the author is; how he came to pick the specific problem he is dealing with; what alternative formulations he either discarded or did not consider; what tacit assumptions he made himself or expected his reader to make.

The term "location of problems" seems to cover fairly well what we have in mind, and a very good example is our Selection (1), a condensation of a paper by Merton on the sociology of knowledge. All the studies in this area, he notes, are essentially concerned with one basic topic: How are cultural products related to the social context within which they are produced? But such a topic is so broad that it should be called a concern rather than a problem. Only after it has been specified at at least three points can it become a matter of concrete investigation. For one, the cultural products can vary greatly: science, literature, and so on. On the other hand, the "social base" can be understood in a variety of ways: we might think of class position, of ethnic affiliations, of forms of settlement, etc. Finally, the notion of "interrelations" may vary: one author may have causal connections in mind; another might rather think in terms of similarities or correspondences. Having outlined such a general scheme, Merton then locates various studies according to the specific choices the investigators make at the crucial points of the scheme. As a result, the student can decide whether two authors are really in disagreement or whether they are only discussing different aspects of the whole problem; he can spot omissions and over-generalizations.

On a more empirical level, Selection (2) develops "a paradigm for the study of leadership." A framework is developed for organizing the entire field of leadership study, including an examination of the nature of leader behavior and its causes and consequences. The authors, Morris and Seeman, were members of a team, which, at Ohio State University, had been working for many years on an extensive leadership project. It is very instructive to learn the role which such a paradigm plays in the coordination of research done by students with diversified backgrounds.

B. *Clarification of meaning.* In the general introduction to this Reader, the purpose of "explication" was mentioned. It is especially important in the social sciences, because the objects they are dealing with are less "firm" than the objects of the physicist; therefore, the range of possible meanings of concepts and their logical structure require especially careful analysis. Selection (3) provides a typical example. There are innumerable discussions dealing with whether "the whole is more than the sum of its parts." Nagel shows that practically every word in the sentence can have a variety of meanings; whether it applies to a specific problem, therefore, depends on how these terms are to be understood in a given context.

For further illustration, one specific type of concept has been singled out. The notion of "disposition" is central to the social sciences. Whether we talk about the attitude of a person or the resiliency of a group, we always refer to probable reactions to a large and not fully specified series of situations. In Selection (4), Kaplan discusses the logical structure of such disposition concepts. It is interesting to note that the logical problems here involved also appear in the natural sciences, although undoubtedly much less frequently than in the behavioral areas.

C. *The structure of arguments.* In any serious piece of scientific work, we do not deal just with a few terms which are linked together by a few simple propositions. We are confronted with long chains of thought directed toward a specific intellectual end. It can hardly be expected that a writer will spell out every little step in his argument. But it is up to the student to be able to reconstruct the formal aspects of a longer piece of a discourse. Only then can he be sure that he understands it, and only then might he be able to make his own contribution, be it critical or positive. We touch here on a subject which a social scientist will approach only with caution. After hundreds of years of development in their field, the mathematicians were certainly greatly helped when mathematical logic provided them with a more rigorous foundation. It is quite easy at this early stage of the social sciences for an over-supply of rigor to end up as a farce. But the student should be aware of the ways in which a systematic analysis of a chain of propositions proceeds. Only then can he decide at what points it is properly applied. In Selection (5) Zetterberg has provided an interesting—and as far as we know the first—example of a so-called axiomatic analysis of a set of social science propositions. He takes a series of statements dealing with the behavior of groups. It turns out that a part of the findings can be derived from the rest of them. There necessarily exists, however, a certain degree of arbitrariness in such a systematization. Which propositions should form a base, and which should be derived, depends on the confidence we have in our present knowledge and has an influence upon the further direction of empirical research.

In Selection (6) this general idea is applied to a specific problem. Davis goes back to the old idea of Malthus that the growth of population is likely to outrun the supply of food. He carefully spells out the variables involved in Malthus' original writing. If one tries to say specifically how Malthus thought these variables are related, it turns out that at many points he did not provide the necessary specifications. The controversies which have been carried on, therefore, have to be divided into two parts: those which try to clarify the original argument, and those which try to test the various elements empirically. This selection provides an interesting example of how an early statement of this kind would be formulated today, and how only in such a new form it can be related to, and be a guide to, empirical data.

D. *The nature of evidence.* The last selection has raised the question of how general methodology is related to the problem of empirical evidence. It seemed desirable, however, to highlight this matter by an especially sharp example. In Selection (7) Leites addresses himself to a series of writings by cultural anthropologists. The idea of a "national character" has, in recent years, captured the attention of a number of social scientists. Some of them maintain that the personality traits, the social relations, and the prevailing beliefs of the people exhibit an underlying unity, which in turn can be traced back to the kind of early childhood training practiced in the community. Leites shows the tremendous difficulties which one would encounter if he were to present evidence on these kinds of relationships. The tone of this discussion is a very good example of where the merits of such a methodological analysis lie. Leites is far from denying the value of the writings of the cultural anthropologists; they draw our attention to matters formerly not observed, and to the possibility of quite unexpected relationships. But by bringing out all the tacit assumptions, alternative hypotheses equally interesting come to light. And while no one would expect that within a few years all the necessary evidence will be forthcoming, the selection practically implies a whole research program from which special selections can be made more wisely than if the whole field had not been organized in this more systematic way.

The selections in this section can be very easily related to items in other parts of this Reader. Kaplan's analysis of disposition concepts could be considered a background paper for the discussion of index formation in Section I. Discussions on the nature of evidence are obvious generalizations of the more specific problems of how to use multivariate analysis to prove specific propositions (Section II). The statistical relations between group properties exemplified in Section IV reappear in Zetterberg's axiomatic analysis included here. The main utilization of the present section will therefore lie in relating it to the other parts of this Reader. Actually, there would have been good logical reason to start the Reader with these more general considerations. But the editors finally decided that it is more desirable first to give the student experience in the formal analysis of very specific research operations before he is "let loose" on more general discussions of methodology, which may so easily end up in diffuse "bull sessions." Even so, as has been mentioned in the introduction, we refrained from including selections which belong to the philosophy of science in its broadest sense. It is about at the point where our Reader ends that the teacher can properly direct the student to such literature as can be found in Feigl and Brodbeck's Reader* on the "philosophy of science," which has a special section (IV) devoted to the social sciences.

* H. Feigl and M. Brodbeck, *Readings in the Philosophy of Science* (New York: Appleton-Century-Crofts Co., 1954), pp. 663-756.

1. A PARADIGM FOR THE STUDY
OF THE SOCIOLOGY OF KNOWLEDGE

by Robert K. Merton

[The following selection is a condensation of "The Sociology of Knowledge," prepared with the permission of the author. The bases for the deletions made by the editors are explained in subsequent editorial notes.—ED. NOTE.]

THE LAST GENERATION has witnessed the emergence of a special field of sociological inquiry: the sociology of knowledge (*Wissenssoziologie*). The term "knowledge" must be interpreted very broadly indeed, since studies in this area have dealt with virtually the entire gamut of cultural products (ideas, ideologies, juristic and ethical beliefs, philosophy, science, technology). But whatever the conception of "knowledge," the central orientation of this discipline remains largely the same: it is primarily concerned with the relations between knowledge and other existential factors in the society or culture. General and even vague as this formulation of the central focus may be, a more specific statement will not serve to include the diverse approaches which have been developed.

Manifestly, then, the sociology of knowledge is concerned with problems which have had a long prehistory. So much is this the case, that this discipline has found its first historian, Ernst Gruenwald.[1] But our primary concern is not with the many antecedents of current theories. There are indeed few present-day observations which have not found previous expression in suggestive apercus. King Henry IV was being reminded that "Thy wish was father, Harry, to that thought" only a few years before Bacon was writing that "The human understanding is no dry light but receives an infusion from the will and affections; whence proceed sciences which may be called 'sciences as one would.' " And Nietzsche had set down a host of aphorisms on the ways in which "needs" determined the "perspectives" through which we interpret the world so that even sense perceptions are permeated with value-preferences. The prehistory of *Wissenssoziologie* only goes to support Whitehead's observation that "to come very near to a true theory, and to grasp its precise application, are two very different things, as the history of science teaches us. Everything of importance has been said before by somebody who did not discover it."

Reprinted in part from "The Sociology of Knowledge," *Twentieth Century Sociology*, G. Gurvitch and W. E. Moore, eds., pp. 366-405, by permission of the author and the publisher. (Copyright, 1945, by The Philosophical Library, Inc.)

To outline even the main currents of the sociology of knowledge in brief compass is to present none adequately and to do violence to all. The diversity of formulations—of a Marx or Scheler or Durkheim; the varying problems —from the social determination of categorial systems to that of class-bound political ideologies; the enormous differences in scope—from the all-encompassing categorizing of intellectual history to the social location of the thought of Negro scholars in the last decades; the various limits assigned to the discipline—from a comprehensive sociological epistemology to the empirical relations of particular social structures and ideas; the proliferation of concepts—ideas, belief-systems, positive knowledge, thought, systems of truth, superstructure, etc.; the diverse methods of validation—from plausible but undocumented imputations to meticulous historical and statistical analysis —in the light of all this, an effort to deal with both analytical apparatus and empirical studies in a few pages must sacrifice detail to scope.

To introduce a basis of comparability among the welter of studies which have appeared in this field, we must adopt some scheme of analysis. The following paradigm is intended as a step in this direction. It is, undoubtedly, a partial and, it is to be hoped, a temporary, classification which will soon disappear as it gives way to an improved and more exacting analytical model. But it does provide a basis for taking an inventory of extant findings in the field; for indicating contradictory, contrary and consistent results; setting forth the conceptual apparatus now in use; determining the nature of problems which have occupied workers in this field; assessing the character of the evidence which they have brought to bear upon these problems; ferreting out the characteristic lacunae and weaknesses in current types of interpretation. Full-fledged theory in the sociology of knowledge lends itself to classification in terms of the following paradigm.

PARADIGM FOR THE SOCIOLOGY OF KNOWLEDGE

1. *WHERE is the existential basis of mental productions located?*
   a. *social bases:* social position, class, generation, occupational role, mode of production, group structures (university, bureaucracy, academies, sect, political party), "historical situation," interests, society, ethnic affiliation, social mobility, power structure, social processes, (competition, conflict, etc.).
   b. *cultural bases:* values, ethos, "climate of opinion," Volksgeist, Zeitgeist, type of culture, culture mentality, Weltanschauungen, etc.
2. *WHAT mental productions are being sociologically analyzed?*
   a. *spheres of:* moral beliefs, ideologies, ideas, the categories of thought, philosophy, religious beliefs, social norms, positive science, technology, etc.
   b. *which aspects are analyzed:*
      their selection (foci of attention), level of abstraction, presuppositions (what is taken as "data" and what as "problematical"), conceptual content, models of verification, objectives of intellectual activity, etc.
3. *HOW are mental productions related to the existential basis?*
   a. *Causal or functional relations:* determination, cause, correspondence, necessary conditions, conditioning, functional interdependence, interaction, dependence, etc.
   b. *Symbolic or organismic or meaningful relations:*
      consistency, harmony, coherence, unity, congruence, compatibility (and antonyms); expression, realization, symbolic expression, *Strukturzusam-*

menhang, structural identities, inner connection, stylistic analogies, logi-comeaningful integration, identity of meaning, etc.

   c. *Ambiguous terms to designate relations:*

     correspondence, reflection, bound up with, in close connection with, etc.

4. *WHY? manifest and latent functions imputed to these existentially conditioned mental productions.*

   a. to maintain power, promote stability, orientation, exploitation, obscure actual social relationships, provide motivation, canalize behavior, divert criticism, deflect hostility, reassurance, control nature, coordinate social relationships, etc.

5. *WHEN do the imputed relations of the existential base and knowledge obtain?*

   a. historicist theories (confined to particular societies or cultures).

   b. general analytical theories.

There are, of course, additional categories for classifying and analyzing studies in the sociology of knowledge, which cannot be fully explored in this paper. Thus, the perennial problem of the implications of existential influences upon knowledge for the epistemological status of that knowledge has been, from the very outset, hotly debated. "Solutions" to this problem, which assume that a sociology of knowledge is necessarily a sociological theory of knowledge, range from the claim that the "genesis of thought has no necessary relation to its validity" to the extreme relativist position that truth is "merely" a function of a social or cultural basis, that it rests solely upon a social consensus and, consequently, that any culturally accepted theory of truth has a claim to validity equal to that of any other.

But the foregoing paradigm serves to organize the distinctive approaches and conclusions in this field sufficiently for our purposes.

The chief approaches to be considered here are those of Marx, Scheler, Mannheim, Durkheim and Sorokin. Current work in this area is largely oriented toward one or another of these theorists, either through a modified application of their conceptions or through counter-developments.*

The Existential Basis. A central point of agreement in all approaches to the sociology of knowledge is the thesis that thought has an existential basis insofar as it is not immanently determined and insofar as one or another of its aspects can be derived from extra-cognitive factors. But this is merely a formal consensus, which gives way to a wide variety of theories concerning the nature of the existential basis.

In this respect, as in others, Marxism is the storm-center of *Wissenssoziologie.* Without entering into the exegetic problem of closely identifying "Marxism"—we have only to recall Marx's *"je ne suis pas un marxiste"*— we can trace out its formulations primarily in the writings of Marx and Engels. Whatever other changes may have occurred in the development of their theory during the half-century of their work, they consistently held fast to the thesis that "relations of production" constitute the "real foundation" for the superstructure of ideas. "The mode of production in material life determines the general character of the social, political and intellectual

---

   * [The program of this paper is now clear. The writers just mentioned are to be discussed according to the main elements of the "paradigm." The editorial cuts were made in such a way that each writer is included, but not with regard to all of the points at which Professor Merton considered him. Thus, for example, the discussion of Marx is maintained under the heading of "existential basis," but largely eliminated under the heading of "mental productions." With Scheler the reverse decision was made. In this way the basic idea of such a "location" of writers could be preserved within the space limitations of this Reader. The specific cuts are indicated in subsequent editorial notes.—ED. NOTE.]

processes of life. It is not the consciousness of men that determines their existence, but on the contrary, their social existence determines their consciousness."[5] In seeking to functionalize ideas, *i.e.,* to relate the ideas of individuals to their sociological bases, Marx locates them within the class structure. He assumes, not so much that other influences are not at all operative, but that class is a primary determinant and, as such, the single most fruitful point of departure for analysis. This he makes explicit in his first preface to *Capital:* ". . . here individuals are dealt with *only in so far* as they are the personifications of economic categories, embodiments of particular class-relations and class-interests."[6] In abstracting from other variables and in regarding men in their economic and class roles, Marx hypothesizes that these roles are primary determinants and thus leaves as an open question *the extent to which they adequately account for thought and behavior in any given case.* In point of fact, one line of development of Marxism, from the early *German Ideology* to the latter writings of Engels, consists in a progressive definition (and delimitation) of the extent to which the relations of production do in fact condition knowledge and forms of thought.

However, both Marx and Engels, repeatedly and with increasing insistence, emphasized that ideologies of a given social stratum need not stem only from persons who are *objectively* located in that stratum. As early as the *Communist Manifesto,* Marx and Engels had indicated that as the ruling class approaches dissolution, "a small section . . . joins the revolutionary class . . . Just as therefore, at an earlier period, a section of the nobility went over to the bourgeoisie, so now a portion of the bourgeoisie goes over to the proletariat, and in particular, a portion of *the bourgeois ideologists,* who have *raised themselves* to the level of comprehending theoretically the historical movement as a whole."[7]

Ideologies are socially located by analyzing their perspectives and presuppositions and determining how problems are construed: from the standpoint of one or another class. Thought is not mechanistically located by merely establishing the class position of the thinker. It is attributed to that class for which it is "appropriate," to the class whose social situation with its class conflicts, aspirations, fears, restraints and objective possibilities within the given socio-historical context is being expressed. Marx's most explicit formulation holds:

> One must not form the narrow-minded idea that the petty bourgeoisie wants on principle to enforce an egoistic class interest. It believes, rather, that the *special* conditions of its emancipation are the *general* conditions through which alone modern society can be saved and the class struggle avoided. Just as little must one imagine that the democratic representatives are all shopkeepers or are full of enthusiasm for them. *So far as their education and their individual position are concerned,* they may be as widely separated from them as heaven from earth. What makes them representatives of the petty bourgeoisie is the fact that in their minds (im Kopfe) they do not exceed the limits which the latter do not exceed in their life activities, that they are consequently driven to the same problems and solutions in theory to which material interest and social position drive the latter in practice. *This is ueberhaupt the relationship of the political and literary representatives of a class to the class which they represent.*[8]

But if we cannot derive ideas from the objective class position of their exponents, this leaves a wide margin of indeterminacy. It then becomes a further problem to discover why some identify with and express the characteristic outlook of the class stratum in which they objectively find themselves whereas others adopt the presuppositions of a class stratum other than "their own." An empirical description of the fact is no adequate substitute for its theoretical explanation.

Mannheim derives from Marx primarily by extending his conception of existential bases. Given the *fact* of multiple group affiliation, the problem becomes one of determining *which* of these affiliations are decisive in fixing perspectives, models of thought, definition of the given, etc. Unlike "a dogmatic Marxism," he does not assume that class position is alone ultimately determinant. He finds, for example, that an organically integrated group conceives of history as a continuous movement toward the realization of its goals, whereas socially uprooted and loosely integrated groups espouse an historical intuition which stresses the fortuitous and imponderable. It is only through exploring the variety of group formations—generations, status groups, sects, occupational groups—and their characteristic modes of thought that there can be found an existential basis corresponding to the great variety of perspectives and knowledge which actually obtain.[9]

Though representing a different tradition, this is substantially the position taken by Durkheim. In an early study with Mauss of primitive forms of classification, he maintained that the genesis of the categories of thought is to be found in the group structure and relations and that they vary with changes in the social organization.[10] In seeking to account for the social origins of the categories, Durkheim postulates that individuals are more directly and inclusively oriented toward the groups in which they live than they are toward nature. The primarily significant experiences are mediated through social relationships, whice leave their impress on the character of thought and knowledge.[11] Thus, in his study of primitive forms of thought, he deals with the periodic recurrence of social activities (ceremonies, feasts, rites), the clan structure and the spatial configurations of group meetings as among the existential bases of thought. And, applying Durkheim's formulations to ancient Chinese thought, Granet attributes their typical conceptions of time and space to such bases as the feudal organization and the rhythmic alternation of concentrated and dispersed group life.[12]*

What Mental Productions Are Being Sociologically Analyzed? Even a cursory survey is enough to show that the term "knowledge" has been so broadly conceived as to refer to every type of assertion and every mode of thought ranging from folk belief to positive science. "Knowledge" has often come to be assimilated to the term "culture" so that not only the exact sciences but ethical convictions, epistemological postulates, material predications, synthetic judgments, political beliefs, the categories of thought, eschatological doxies, moral norms, ontological assumptions, and observations of empirical fact are more or less indiscriminately held to be "existentially conditioned."[13] The question is, of course, whether these

---

* [Eliminated from this section are the discussions of Scheler's and Sorokin's understanding of "existential bases." The following section begins with a critique of the Marxian notion of ideological superstructure which, in turn, has been omitted. The original paper also contains more examples from the Durkheim school than will be found in the next section.—ED. NOTE.]

diverse "ideas" stand in the same relationship to their sociological basis, or whether it is necessary to discriminate between spheres of knowledge precisely because this relationship differs for the various types of "ideas." For the most part, there has been a systematic ambiguity concerning this problem.

Scheler distinguishes a variety of forms of "knowledge." To begin with, there are the "relatively natural Weltanschauungen": that which is accepted as given, as neither requiring nor being capable of justification. These are, so to speak, the cultural axioms of groups; what Joseph Glanvill, some three hundred years ago, called a "climate of opinion." A primary task of the sociology of knowledge is to discover the laws of transformation of these *Weltanschauungen*. And since these are by no means necessarily valid, it follows that the sociology of knowledge is not concerned merely with tracing the existential bases of truth but also of "social illusion, superstition and socially conditioned errors and forms of deception."[14]

These *Weltanschauungen* constitute organic growth and develop only in large time-spans. They are scarcely affected by theories. Without adequate evidence, Scheler claims that they can be changed in any fundamental sense only through race-mixture or conceivably through the "mixture" of language and culture. Building upon these very slowly changing *Weltanschauungen* are the more "artifical" forms of knowledge which may be ordered in seven classes, according to degree of artificiality: 1. myth and legend; 2. knowledge implicit in the natural folk-language; 3. religious knowledge (ranging from the vague emotional intuition to the fixed dogma of a church); 4. the basic types of mystical knowledge; 5. philosophical-metaphysical knowledge; 6. positive knowledge of mathematics, the natural and cultural sciences; 7. technological knowledge.[15] The more artificial these types of knowledge, the more rapidly they change. It is evident, says Scheler, that religions change far more slowly than the various metaphysics, and the latter persist for much longer periods than the results of positive science, which change from hour to hour.

This hypothesis of rates of change bears some points of similarity to Alfred Weber's thesis that "civilization change" outruns "cultural" change and to the Ogburn hypothesis that "material" factors change more rapidly than the "non-material." Scheler's hypothesis shares the limitations of these others as well as several additional shortcomings. He nowhere indicates with any clarity what his principle of classification of types of knowledge—so-called "artificiality"—actually denotes. Why, for example, is "mystical knowledge" conceived as more "artificial" than religious dogmas? He does not at all consider what is entailed by saying that one type of knowledge "changes more rapidly" than another. Consider his curious equating of new scientific "results" with metaphysical systems; how does one compare the degree of change implied in neo-Kantian philosophy with, say, change in biological theory during the corresponding period? Scheler boldly asserts a seven-fold variation in rates of change and, of course, does not empirically confirm this elaborate claim. In view of the difficulties encountered in testing much simpler hypotheses, it is not at all clear what is gained by setting forth an elaborate hypothesis of this type.

Yet only certain aspects of this knowledge are held to be sociologically determined. On the basis of certain postulates, which need not be considered here, Scheler goes on to assert:

> The sociological character of all knowledge, of all forms of thought, intuition and cognition is unquestionable. Although the *content* and even less the objective validity of all knowledge is not determined by the *controlling perspectives of social interests,* nevertheless this is the case with the *selection* of the objects of knowledge. Moreover, the "forms" of the mental processes by means of which knowledge is acquired are always and necessarily co-determined sociologically, i.e. by the social structure.[16]

Since explanation consists in tracing the relatively new to the familiar and known and since society is "better known" than anything else, it is to be expected that the modes of thought and intuition and the classification of knowable things generally, are co-determined (*mitbedingt*) by the division and classification of groups which comprise the society.

Scheler indicates that different types of knowledge are bound up with particular forms of groups. The content of Plato's theory of ideas required the form and organization of the platonic academy; so, too, the organization of Protestant churches and sects was determined by the content of their beliefs which could exist only in this and no other type of social organization, as Troeltsch has shown. And, similarly, *Gemeinschaft* types of society have a traditionally defined fund of knowledge which is handed down as conclusive; they are not concerned with discovering or extending knowledge. The very effort to test the traditional knowledge, insofar as it implies doubt, is ruled out as virtually blasphemous. In such a group, the prevailing logic and mode of thought is that of an *"ars demonstrandi"* not an *"ars inveniendi."* Its methods are prevailingly ontological and dogmatic, not epistemologic and critical; its mode of thought is that of conceptual realism, not nominalistic as in the *Gesellschaft* type of organization; its system of categories, organismic and not mechanistic.[18]

Durkheim extend sociological inquiry into the social genesis of the categories of thought, basing his hypothesis on three types of presumptive evidence. (A) The fact of cultural variation in the categories and the rules of logic "prove that they depend upon factors that are historical and consequently social."[19] (B) Since concepts are imbedded in the very language the individual acquires (and this holds as well for the special terminology of the scientist) and since some of these conceptual terms refer to things which we, as individuals, have never experienced, it is clear that they are a product of the society.[20] And (C), the acceptance or rejection of concepts is not determined *merely* by their "objective" validity but also by their consistency with other prevailing beliefs.[21]

Yet Durkheim does not subscribe to a type of relativism in which there are merely competing criteria of validity. The social origin of the categories does not render them wholly arbitrary so far as their applicability to nature is concerned. They are, in varying degrees, adequate to their object. But since social structures vary (and with them, the categorical apparatus) there are inescapable "subjective" elements in the particular logical constructions current in a society. These subjective elements "must be progressively rooted out, if we are to approach reality more closely." And this occurs under determinate social conditions. With the extension of inter-cultural contacts, with the spread of inter-communication between persons drawn from different societies, with the enlargement of the society, the local frame of reference becomes disrupted. "Things can no longer be contained in the social moulds according to which they were primitively classified; they must be organized according to principles which are their own. So logical organization differentiates itself from the social organization and becomes autonomous. Genuinely human thought is not a primitive fact; it is the product of history. . . ."[22] Particularly, those conceptions which are subjected to scientifically methodical criticism come to have a greater objective adequacy. Objectivity is itself viewed as a social emergent.

Sorokin has cast into a distinctive idiom the fact of shifts of attention on the part of intellectual elites in different historical societies. In certain societies, religious conceptions and particular types of metaphysics are at the focus of attention, whereas in other societies, empirical science becomes the center of interest. But the several "systems of truth" coexist in each of these societies within given spheres; the Catholic church has not abandoned its "ideational" criteria even in this sensate age.

Insofar as Sorokin adopts the position of radically different and disparate criteria of truth, he must locate his own work within this context. It may be said, though an extensive discussion would be needed to document it, that he never resolves this problem. His various efforts to cope with a radically relativistic impasse differ considerably. Thus, at the very outset, he states that his constructions must be tested in the same way "as any scientific law. First of all the principle must by nature be logical; second, it must successfully meet the test of the 'relevant facts,' that is, it must fit and represent the facts."[23] In Sorokin's own terminology, he has thus adopted a scientific position characteristic of a "sensate system of truth." When he confronts his own epistemological position directly, however, he adopts an "integralist" conception of truth which seeks to assimilate empirical and logical criteria as well as a "supersensory, super-rational, metalogical act of 'intuition' or 'mystical experience.' "[24] He thus posits an integration of these diverse systems. In order to justify the "truth of faith"—the only item which would remove him from the ordinary criteria used in current scientific work—he indicates that "intuition" plays an important role as a *source* of scientific discovery. But does this meet the issue? The question is not one of the psychological *sources* of valid conclusions, but of the *criteria* and *methods of validation.* Which criteria would Sorokin adopt when "supersensory" intuitions are not consistent with empirical observation? In such cases, presumably, so far as we can judge from his work rather than his comments about his work, he accepts the facts and rejects the intuition. All this suggests that Sorokin is discussing under the generic label of "truth" quite distinct and not comparable types of judgments: just as the chemist's analysis of an oil painting is neither consistent nor inconsistent with its aesthetic evaluation, so Sorokin's "systems of truth" refer to quite different kinds of judgments. And, indeed, he is finally led to say as much, when he remarks that "each of the systems of truth, within its legitimate field of competency, gives us genuine cognition of the respective aspects of reality."[25] But whatever his private opinion of intuition he cannot draw it into his sociology as a *criterion* (rather than a source) of valid conclusions.

How Are Mental Productions Related to the Existential Basis? Though this problem is obviously the nucleus of every theory in the sociology of knowledge, it has often been treated by implication rather than directly. Yet each type of imputed relation between knowledge and society presupposes an entire theory of sociological method and social causation. The prevailing theories in this field have dealt with one or both of two major types of relation: causal or functional, and the symbolic or organismic or meaningful.[26]

Marx and Engels, of course, dealt solely with some kind of causal relation between the economic basis and ideas, variously terming this relation as "determination, correspondence, reflection, outgrowth, dependence," etc. In addition, there is an "interest" or "need" relation; when strata have (imputed) needs at a given stage of historical development, there is held to be a definite pressure for appropriate ideas and knowledge to develop. The inadequacies of these divers formulations have risen up to plague those who derive from the Marxist tradition in the present day.[27]

Since Marx held that thought is not a mere "reflection" of objective class position, as we have seen, this raises anew the problem of its imputation to a determinate basis. The prevailing Marxist hypotheses for coping with this problem involve a theory of history which is the ground for determining whether the ideology is "situationally adequate" for a given stratum in the society: this requires a hypothetical construction of what men *would think and perceive* if they were able to comprehend the historical situation adequately.[28] But such insight into the situation need not *actually* be widely current within given strata. This, then, leads to the further problem of "false consciousness," of how ideologies which are neither in conformity with the interests of a class nor situationally adequate come to prevail.

A partial empirical explanation of "false consciousness" implied in the *Manifesto* rests on the view that the bourgeoisie control the content of culture and thus diffuse doctrines and standards alien to the interests of the proletariat.[29] Or, in more general terms, "the ruling ideas of each age have ever been the ideas of its ruling class." But, this is only a partial account; at most it deals with the false consciousness of the subordinated class. It might, for example, partly explain the fact noted by Marx that even where the peasant proprietor "does belong to the proletariat by his position he does not believe that he does." It would not, however, be pertinent in seeking to account for the false consciousness of the ruling class itself.

Another, though not clearly formulated, theme which bears upon the problem of false consciousness runs throughout Marxist theory. This is the conception of ideology as being an *unwitting, unconscious* expression of "real motives," these being in turn construed in terms of the objective interests of social classes. Thus, there is repeated stress on the unwitting nature of ideologies:

> Ideology is a process accomplished by the so-called thinker consciously indeed but with a false consciousness. The real motives impelling him remain unknown to him, otherwise it would not be ideological process at all. Hence he imagines false or apparent motives.[30]

The ambiguity of the term "correspondence" to refer to the connection between the material basis and the idea can only be overlooked by the polemic enthusiast. Ideologies are construed as "distortions of the social situation";[31] as merely "expressive" of the material conditions;[32] and, whether "distorted" or not, as motivational support for carrying through real changes in the society.[33] It is at this last point, when "illusory" beliefs are conceded to provide motivation for action, that Marxism ascribes a measure of independence to ideologies in the historical process. They are no longer merely epiphenomenal. They enjoy a measure of autonomy. From this develops the notion of interacting factors in which the superstructure, though interdependent with the material basis, is also assumed to have some degree of independence. Engels explicitly recognized that earlier formulations were inadequate in at least two respects: (A) that both he and Marx had previously overemphasized the economic factor and understated the role of reciprocal interaction;[34] and (B) that they had "neglected" the formal side—the way in which these ideas develop.[35]

The Marx-Engels views on the connectives of ideas and economic substructure hold, then, that the economic structure constitutes the framework which limits the range of ideas which will prove socially effective; ideas which do not have pertinence for one or another of the conflicting classes may arise, but will be of little consequence. Economic conditions are necessary, but not sufficient, for the emergence and spread of ideas which express either the interests or outlook, or both, of distinct social strata. There is no strict determinism of ideas by economic conditions, but a definite predisposition. Knowing the economic conditions, we can predict the kinds of ideas which can exercise a controlling influence in a direction which can be effective. "Men make their own history, but they do not make it just as they please; they do not make it under circumstances chosen by themselves, but under circumstances directly found, given and transmitted from the past." And in the making of history, ideas and ideologies play a definite role: consider only the view of religion as "the opiate of the masses"; consider further the importance attached by Marx and Engels to making those in the proletariat "aware" of their "own interests." Since there is no fatality in the development of the total social structure, but only a development of economic conditions which make certain lines of change *possible* and probable, idea-systems may play a decisive role in the selection of one alternative which "corresponds" to the real balance of power rather than another alternative which runs counter to the existing power-situation and is therefore destined to be unstable, precarious and temporary. There is an ultimate compulsive which derives from economic development, but this compulsive does not operate with such detailed finality that no variation of ideas can occur at all.

The Marxist theory of history assumes that, *sooner or later,* idea-systems which are inconsistent with the actually prevailing and incipient power-structure will be rejected in favor of those which more nearly express the actual alignment of power. It is this view that Engels expresses in his metaphor of the "zig-zag course" of abstract ideology: ideologies may temporarily deviate from what is compatible with the current social relations of production, but they are ultimately brought back in line. For this reason, the Marxist analysis of ideology is always bound to be concerned with the "total" concrete historical situation, in order to account both for the temporary deviations and the later accommodation of ideas to the economic compulsives. But for this same reason, Marxist analyses are apt to have an excessive degree of "flexibility," almost to the point where *any* development can be "explained away" as a temporary aberration or deviation; where "anachronisms" and "lags" become labels for the explaining away of existing beliefs which do not correspond to theoretical expectations; where the concept of "accident" provides a ready means of "saving" the theory from facts which seem to challenge its validity.[36] Once a theory includes concepts such as "lags," "thrusts," "anachronisms," "accidents," "partial independence" and "ultimate dependence," it becomes so labile and so indistinct, that it can be reconciled with virtually any configuration of data. Here, as in several other theories in the sociology of knowledge, a decisive question must be raised in order to determine whether we have a genuine theory: how can the theory be invalidated? In any given historical situation, which data will contradict and invalidate the theory? Unless this can be answered directly, unless the theory involves statements which can be controverted by definite types of data, then it remains merely a pseudo-theory which will be compatible with any array of data.

Though Mannheim has gone far toward developing actual research procedures in the substantive sociology of knowledge, he has not appreciably clarified the connectives of thought and society.[37] As he indicates, once a given thought-structure has been analyzed, there arises the problem of imputing it to definite groups. This requires not only an empirical investigation of the groups or strata which prevalently think in these terms, but also an interpretation of why these groups, and not others, manifest this type of thought. This latter question implies a social psychology which Mannheim has not systematically developed.

The most serious shortcoming of Durkheim's analysis lies precisely in his uncritical acceptance of a naive theory of correspondence in which the categories of thought are held to "reflect" certain features of the group organization. Thus "there are societies in Australia and North America where space is conceived in the form of an immense circle, *because* the camp has a circular form . . . the social organization has been the model for the spatial organization and a reproduction of it."[38] In similar fashion, the general notion of time is derived from the specific units of time differentiated in social activities (ceremonies, feasts, rites).[39] The category of class and the modes of classification, which involve the notion of a hierarchy, are derived from social grouping and stratification. Those social categories are then "projected into our conception of the new world."[40] In summary, then, categories "express" the different aspects of the social order.[41] Durkheim's sociology of knowledge suffers from his avoidance of a social psychology.

The central relation between ideas and existential factors for Scheler is interaction. Ideas interact with existential factors which serve as selective agencies, releasing or checking the extent to which potential ideas find actual expression. Existential factors do not "create" or "determine" the content of ideas; they merely account for the *difference* between potentiality and actuality; they hinder, retard or quicken the actualization of potential ideas. In a figure reminiscent of Clerk Maxwell's hypothetical daemon, Scheler states: "in a definite fashion and order, existential factors open and close the sluice-gates to the flood of ideas."

Scheler operates as well with the concept of "structural identities" which refers to common presuppositions of knowledge or belief, on the one hand, and of social, economic or political structure on the other.[42] Thus, the rise of mechanistic thought in the sixteenth century, which came to dominate prior organismic thought is inseparable from the new individualism, the incipient dominance of the power-driven machine over the hand-tool, the incipient dissolution of *Gemeinschaft* into *Gesellschaft*, production for a commodity market, rise of the principle of competition in the ethos of western society, etc. The notion of scientific research as an endless process through which a store of knowledge can be accumulated for practical application as the occasion demands and the total divorce of this science from theology and philosophy was not possible without the rise of a new principle of infinite acquisition characteristic of modern capitalism.[43]

In discussing such structural identities, Scheler does not ascribe primacy either to the socio-economic sphere or to the sphere of knowledge. Rather, and this Scheler regards as one of the most significant propositions in the field, both are determined by the impulse-structure of the elite which is closely bound up with the prevailing ethos. Thus, modern technology is not merely the application of a pure science based on observation, logic and mathematics. It is far more the product of an orientation toward the control of nature which defined the purposes as well as the conceptual structure of scientific thought. This orientation is largely implicit and is not to be confused with the personal motives of scientists.

With the concept of structural identity, Scheler verges on the concept of cultural integration or *Sinnzusammenhang*. It corresponds to Sorokin's conception of a "meaningful cultural system" involving "the identity of the fundamental principles and values that permeate all its parts," which is distinguished from a "causal system" involving interdependence of parts.[44]

Having constructed his types of culture, Sorokin's survey of criteria of truth, ontology, metaphysics, scientific and technologic output, etc., finds a market tendency toward the meaningful integration of these with the prevailing culture.

Sorokin has boldly confronted the problem of how to determine the *extent* to which such integration occurs, recognizing, despite his vitriolic comments on the statisticians of our sensate age, that to deal with the "extent" or "degree" of integration necessarily implies some statistical measure. Accordingly, he developed numerical indexes of the various writings and authors in each period, classified these in their appropriate category, and thus assessed the comparative frequency (and influence) of the various systems of thought. Whatever the technical evaluation of the validity and reliability of these cultural statistics, he has directly acknowledged the problem overlooked by many investigators of "integrated culture" or *Sinnzusammenhaengen*, namely, the approximate degree or extent of such integration. Moreover, he plainly bases his empirical conclusions very largely upon these statistics.[45] And these conclusions again testify that his approach leads to a statement of the problem of connections between existential bases and knowledge, rather than to its solution. Thus, to take a case in point.

"Empiricism" is defined as the typical sensate system of truth. The last five centuries, and more particularly the last century represent "Sensate culture par excellence!"[46] Yet, even in this flood tide of sensate culture, Sorokin's statistical indices show only some 53% of influential writings in the field of "empiricism." And in the earlier centuries of this sensate culture,—from the late 16th to the mid-18th—the indices of empiricism are consistently lower than those for rationalism, (which is associated, presumably, with an idealistic rather than a sensate culture).[47] The object of these observations is not to raise the question whether Sorokin's conclusions coincide with his statistical data: it is not to ask why the 16th and 17th centuries are said to have a dominant "sensate system of truth" in view of these data. Rather, it is to indicate that even on Sorokin's own premises, overall characterizations of historical cultures constitute merely a first step, which must be followed by analyses of deviations from the "central tendencies" of the culture. Once the notion of *extent* of integration is introduced, the existence of types of knowledge which are not integrated with the dominant tendencies cannot be viewed merely as "congeries" or as "contingent." Their *social* bases must be ascertained in a fashion for which an emanationist theory does not provide.

A basic concept which serves to differentiate generalizations about the thought and knowledge of an entire society or culture is that of the "audience" or "public" or what Znaniecki calls "the social circle." Men of knowledge do not orient themselves exclusively toward their data nor toward the total society, but to special segments of that society with their special demands, criteria of validity, of "significant" knowledge, of pertinent problems, etc. It is through anticipation of these demands and expectations of particular audiences, which can be effectively located in the social structure, that men of knowledge organize their own work, define their data, seize upon problems. Hence, the more differentiated the society, the greater the range of such effective audiences, the greater the variation in the foci of scientific attention, of conceptual formulations and of procedures for certifying claims to knowledge. By linking each of these typologically defined audiences to their distinctive social position, it becomes possible to provide a *wissenssoziologische* account of variations and conflicts of thought within the society, a problem which is necessarily by-passed by any emanationist theory. Thus, the scientists in seventeenth century England and France who were organized in newly established scientific societies addressed themselves to audiences very different from those of the savants who remained exclusively in the traditional universities. The direction of their efforts, toward a "plain, sober, empirical" exploration of specific technical and scientific problems differed considerably from the speculative, unexperimental work of those in the universities. Searching out such variations in effective audiences, exploring their distinctive criteria of significant and valid knowledge,[48] relating these to their position within the society and examining the socio-psychological processes through which these operate to constrain certain modes of thought constitutes a procedure which promises to take research in the sociology of knowledge from the plane of general imputation to testable empirical inquiry.[49]

2. A GENERAL FRAMEWORK
FOR THE STUDY OF LEADERSHIP

by Richard T. Morris and Melvin Seeman[1]

THE DEMAND for effective leadership has been intensified in our society in recent years. Training and research programs developed during the war to improve the quality of military leadership have been continued and expanded. Industries have instituted programs to improve the effectiveness of supervisors, and in international as well as domestic affairs the call for leadership of high caliber has been abundantly expressed. Yet those who are leaders today or who train leaders must act on the basis of what remains largely a series of *ad hoc* maxims unsupported by either sound theory or empirical data.

Adequate research on this critical problem calls for the combined resources of the social sciences. For even the simplest definition of a leader, i.e., an individual influencing group effectiveness, indicates the need to study the attributes of groups—group morale, integration, and productivity—as well as the attributes of individuals—motivations, aspirations, and perceptions. We need, therefore, to explore in operational terms the meaning of interdisciplinary integration and to develop a theoretical framework incorporating the viewpoints and approaches of the several disciplines. This paper is largely concerned with the latter; it presents a framework for research on leadership.

A word about the operational nature of the interdisciplinary program from which this framework emerged may be helpful. Three major areas of integration have been feasible: *conceptual* integration, *approach* integration, and *technique* integration.

Conceptual integration, in the Ohio State Leadership Studies program, has not involved the development of an initial comprehensive theory which serves as a mold for individual research projects. It has, rather, come about largely through the exchange of new and useful ways of viewing from the standpoint of one discipline a concept which has become standard in another. Thus, the concept of "status" as traditionally used in sociology carries a new meaning when the statuses for which individuals strive are viewed, as they are in the psychology of motivation, as systems of punishment and reward.

Approach integration refers to the widening of research perspectives. Gains have come in studies of executive leadership, for example, from the sociological emphasis on the larger cultural context as a crucial interpretive factor. Similarly, the social psychologist's theories of social perception and the building of group norms have been useful to the economist who is con-

Reprinted from "The Problem of Leadership: An Interdisciplinary Approach," *American Journal of Sociology*, Vol. LVI, 1950, pp. 149-155, by permission of the authors and the publisher. (Copyright, 1950, by The University of Chicago.)

cerned with executive compensation or with an analysis of the differentially perceived economic goals of an organization.

Technique integration refers to the distinctive contributions of the several disciplines in research methodology. Perhaps the most important methodological difference demanding integration has been the empiricist versus the theorist approach to problem design: the former advocates relatively little a priori system (hypotheses, orientations, etc.), and the latter calls for a statement of a theoretical frame of research. Though these two viewpoints are not necessarily functions of the discipline from which the investigator comes, useful cross-pressure between them has been brought about in our program by the circumstance that the research men have been trained in various fields.

THE OVER-ALL FRAMEWORK

With this interdisciplinary thinking as background, individual staff members engaged in our study of leadership were left free to conceptualize and implement their own research projects; but it was deemed desirable to make explicit a general co-ordinating framework for the work as a whole.

The accompanying chart, which summarizes our conception of the study of leadership, was developed to serve this integrative function. It provides a rough map of the areas we are now studying, suggests duplications and lacunae both in problem and in methodology in the present studies, and helps to preserve a maximum of connection among the several studies as they are modified and expanded in the light of new data.

This chart, "A Paradigm for the Study of Leadership," is useful for ordering previous studies in the field as well as current studies. An analysis in terms of the chart framework, for example, of the studies reviewed by Stogdill[2] readily demonstrates the imbalance in kinds of variables, leader-designation procedures, and leadership definitions which have characterized many studies of leadership in the past. The chart may also be profitably used as a model for studies of other behavioral phenomena, such as criminal behavior, political behavior, and the like.

The whole design poses, as the major problem, the discovery of the relation of group and individual factors to differentials in leader behavior. These relations may be of several types. In the first place, they may be demonstrated to be *causal* in nature or to be simply *concomitant*. The causal type of relation may be either that group factors result from given behavior of the leader or that group factors determine the leader's behavior. Thus, for example, we may document the fact that given types of informal sociometric patterns among subordinates (*4D* in the chart) are the result of certain kinds of leader behavior (arrow *8-a*), that these sociometric patterns determine leader behavior (*6-a*), or simply that the given leader behavior and sociometric pattern coexist (*7-a*).

Though difficult to derive, it is the causal type of finding which is in one sense most crucial, since it bears directly upon the most critical hypothesis —usually assumed rather than tested—that the behavior of the "leader" does in fact make a difference in his group.

In addition to being viewed as causally or concomitantly related to leader behavior, the group and individual factors may be viewed as *conditioners* of relationships between given leader behavior and other factors (*9*). Thus,

Chart I—A Paradigm for the Study of Leadership

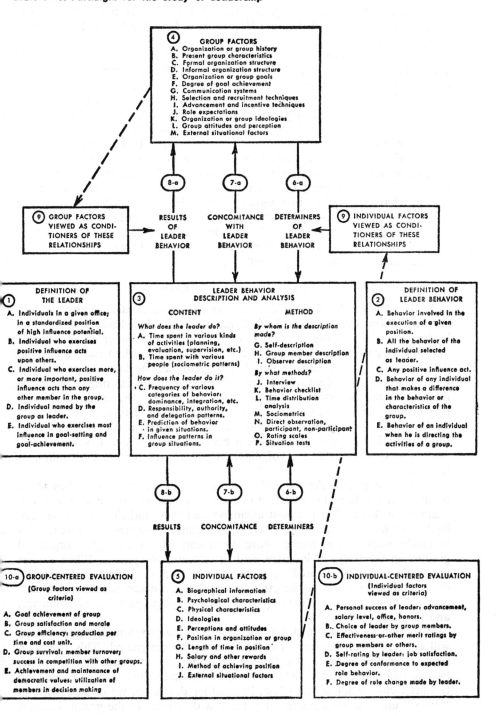

(4) **GROUP FACTORS**
A. Organization or group history
B. Present group characteristics
C. Formal organization structure
D. Informal organization structure
E. Organization or group goals
F. Degree of goal achievement
G. Communication systems
H. Selection and recruitment techniques
I. Advancement and incentive techniques
J. Role expectations
K. Organization or group ideologies
L. Group attitudes and perception
M. External situational factors

8-a   7-a   6-a

(9) **GROUP FACTORS VIEWED AS CONDITIONERS OF THESE RELATIONSHIPS**

RESULTS OF LEADER BEHAVIOR

CONCOMITANCE WITH LEADER BEHAVIOR

DETERMINERS OF LEADER BEHAVIOR

(9) **INDIVIDUAL FACTORS VIEWED AS CONDITIONERS OF THESE RELATIONSHIPS**

(1) **DEFINITION OF THE LEADER**

A. Individuals in a given office; in a standardized position of high influence potential.
B. Individual who exercises positive influence acts upon others.
C. Individual who exercises more, or more important, positive influence acts than any other member in the group.
D. Individual named by the group as leader.
E. Individual who exercises most influence in goal-setting and goal-achievement.

(3) **LEADER BEHAVIOR DESCRIPTION AND ANALYSIS**

CONTENT

What does the leader do?
A. Time spent in various kinds of activities (planning, evaluation, supervision, etc.)
B. Time spent with various people (sociometric patterns)

How does the leader do it?
C. Frequency of various categories of behavior: dominance, integration, etc.
D. Responsibility, authority, and delegation patterns.
E. Prediction of behavior in given situations.
F. Influence patterns in group situations.

METHOD

By whom is the description made?
G. Self-description
H. Group member description
I. Observer description

By what methods?
J. Interview
K. Behavior checklist
L. Time distribution analysis
M. Sociometrics
N. Direct observation, participant, non-participant
O. Rating scales
P. Situation tests

(2) **DEFINITION OF LEADER BEHAVIOR**

A. Behavior involved in the execution of a given position.
B. All the behavior of the individual selected as leader.
C. Any positive influence act.
D. Behavior of any individual that makes a difference in the behavior or characteristics of the group.
E. Behavior of an individual when he is directing the activities of a group.

8-b   7-b   6-b

RESULTS   CONCOMITANCE   DETERMINERS

(10-a) **GROUP-CENTERED EVALUATION**
(Group factors viewed as criteria)

A. Goal achievement of group
B. Group satisfaction and morale
C. Group efficiency: production per time and cost unit.
D. Group survival: member turnover; success in competition with other groups.
E. Achievement and maintenance of democratic values: utilization of members in decision making

(5) **INDIVIDUAL FACTORS**
A. Biographical information
B. Psychological characteristics
C. Physical characteristics
D. Ideologies
E. Perceptions and attitudes
F. Position in organization or group
G. Length of time in position
H. Salary and other rewards
I. Method of achieving position
J. External situational factors

(10-b) **INDIVIDUAL-CENTERED EVALUATION**
(Individual factors viewed as criteria)

A. Personal success of leader: advancement, salary level, office, honors.
B. Choice of leader by group members.
C. Effectiveness or other merit ratings by group members or others.
D. Self-rating by leader: job satisfaction.
E. Degree of conformance to expected role behavior.
F. Degree of role change made by leader.

the relation between a given mode of behavior in the leader, e.g., high dominance (*3C*), and a given group result, e.g., high group morale (*4B*), may be conditioned by such group or individual factors as the extent of by-passing of the formal structure (*4D*) or how long the leader has been in that position (*5G*).

Further, the group and individual factors may be viewed as *criteria* for the evaluation of leadership (*10-a* and *10-b*). The question of criteria for effectiveness is, of course, crucial and one on which little progress has been made. It is useful methodologically to state clearly in the chart that one may evaluate by using specified group effects (or concomitancies) of leader behavior as criteria or by using ratings of the individual leader.

One of the major points of the chart, in short, is that a given group or individual factor may be viewed in five ways in its relation to leader behavior: as result, concomitancy, determiner, conditioner, or criterion. The classification of a given variable as a group factor, individual factor, or leader behavior is a heuristic rather than an inherent categorical one. For example, though the communication system of the group finds its place here under the group factors (*4G*), it may also be examined as an aspect of leader behavior when we ask: How much and in what ways does the leader communicate with the group members?

THE PARADIGM IN DETAIL

1. *Who Is the Leader?*[3] This question has been classically answered in simple fashion: the leader is the individual who holds a leader's office. The leader of a business organization is the president; the leader of an army is the general; and so on. This is shown to be inadequate when more analytical definitions of "leader" are explored. For example, the leader may be designated as the individual who exercises more, or more important, influence than any other member; or the individual named by the group as leader; or the individual who exercises most influence in the setting or achievement of the goals of the group—to name but a few of the many definitions. As these and other definitions are used, it becomes necessary to develop greater awareness of the significance of different procedures for the designation of leaders.

To a large extent, the method used to date in the various studies made by the staff has been the selection of individuals in high office as persons to examine for leadership (without assuming that these individuals are, in fact, leaders in terms of the more operational definition suggested above). This is partly because the studies have been carried on in highly organized groups: in the navy, in industry, and in educational systems. When studies are made in less structured situations, it is especially important to employ other methods, such as sociometric choice, detailed observational techniques, analysis of reputational data, past-decision-making, patterns of influence, and the like.

It should not be assumed that the nature of the group under investigation will entirely determine how the leader is to be designated. This is also a function of the theory and definition of leadership involved. It is possible, by one definition, to designate as "leader" the individual in high office who has been chosen for study; while, by another definition, we cannot call him "leader" until he has demonstrably made a difference in the group, i.e., has exercised influence. The problem of designating the leader is of crucial concern in the study of leadership, especially in view of the fact that the office-holder as leader is a common stereotype in our culture. If this stereotype is uncritically carried over into research, it can severely restrict the applicability of leadership data to more general problems of social structure and social control.

2. *What Is Defined as Leader Behavior?* The individual designated as leader behaves in accordance with the demands of many roles in addition to that of leader. Clearly some of his behavior is to be considered as leader behavior and some is not. From one point of view it might be said that whatever the leader does in the execution of his position, or in the fulfilment of his expected role, is leader behavior per se. This distinction is operationally quite hard to draw—perhaps rigorous discipline of his children is expected in the leader and is evaluated by group members as an integral part of his leadership. It is also possible to extend the definition of leader behavior to include *all* the behavior of the individual selected as leader. Or, again, leader behavior may be defined as any behavior that makes a difference in the behavior of the group. In the latter case what is to be defined as leader behavior cannot be established a priori but can be operationally defined only after correlations have been established between what the designated individual does and the resultant group behavior. In any event, it seems essential, as methodologies of observation are worked out, to establish theoretically the limits of the phenomena to be observed.

3. *How Is Leader Behavior To Be Described and Analyzed?* Careful description of leader behavior has rarely been achieved in previous studies. The focus, for the most part, has been on either leader *evaluation* or on the *traits* of leaders, while the leader's behavior has been largely ignored. Thus, the typical study of traits has been concerned with such questions as: Do leaders, compared with nonleaders, exhibit higher I.Q.'s, greater personal security, etc.? In the evaluation studies, the investigations have again by-passed section 3 of the paradigm, examining, for example, the relation between the leader's effectiveness as rated by the group and the leader's emotional stability, scholarship, or extraversion.

The staff of the Ohio State Leadership Studies has made the description of leader behavior one of its chief responsibilities. Instruments designed to observe and analyze the behavior of leaders are being developed. We have found it useful to think in terms of the *what* and *how* of leader behavior: on what organizational functions does the leader spend his time,[4] and how does he perform these functions? Is he dominant? separated from the group?

Who shall describe the leader's behavior? The description may be made by the leader himself, by his subordinates, by his peers, by his superiors, or by the investigator, either as a participant observer or otherwise. The methods currently being used are listed in the chart: all may be applied to obtain descriptions of leader behavior from the entire range of personnel listed above. One of the instruments currently being analyzed (*3K*) contains one hundred and fifty items describing leader behavior in terms of nine categories (*3C*), calling for responses by the leader himself, his subordinates, and others.[5] This instrument can also be used to explore leadership ideologies (What should an ideal leader do?).

4-5. *What Group and Individual Factors Are Significant for Leader Be-*

havior? The category "group factors" refers to the characteristics of the group in which the individual designated as leader exercises the function of leader. These factors are distinguished from "individual factors" in that the latter refer to the characteristics of the individual designated as leader. The variables listed in these two sections of the chart are suggestive rather than exhaustive.[6]

In our own studies the effort has been made to sample broadly in these two areas, with each project centering upon a different type of group or individual factor as it relates to leadership. Four major types of variable have been focused upon for present study:

a) A job analysis and organizational structure approach, in which the central effort is upon describing *what* leaders actually do (*3A* and *3B*); and on how this is related to organizational structure, e.g., informal work patterns (*4D*), or echelon level (*4C*).

b) A communications and leader effectiveness approach, in which are examined, first, the relation of leader effectiveness to specific leader differences, e.g., the ability to estimate group opinion (*5E*); and, second, the relation among multiple criteria for effectiveness, e.g., high group morale (*10-aD*) and ratings by subordinates (*10-bC*).

c) A status factor approach, in which the emphasis is upon leadership as a status phenomenon, with major attention given to exploring the relation of the leader's and follower's behavior to status factors at work in the organization or community, e.g., the relation of leader behavior to commitments about or perceptions of status differences in society (*4C* and *5E*).

d) A group dimension approach, which seeks to explore situational differences in leader behavior, e.g., differences in leader operation associated with differences in group size, homogeneity, togetherness, etc. (*4B*).

The selection of these particular group and individual factors provides the opportunity to derive findings matching in scope the broadness of leadership itself as a problem—a problem in institutional theory, in social perception, in culture patterning, and in situational analysis.

6. *Why Does the Leader Behave as He Does?* We are interested here in discovering the group or individual factors which determine differences in leader behavior (*6-a, 6-b*). As such factors are found, we will be in a better position to test our findings by controlled experimentation in the selection, training, and evaluation of leaders. With regard to group factors, such research may be on the effect of an inadequate upward communication system upon the leader's behavior, the effect of group morale, or the effect of role expectations built up in the group by a previous leader. Research involving individual factors as determiners of leader behavior may include questions on the effect of frustration or of various kinds of incentives, ideologies, or attitudes on the leader's behavior.

7. *What Phenomena Are Concomitant with Given Kinds of Leader Behavior?* Though the ultimate effort is to isolate the crucial determining variables, all the studies listed in section 4-5 above are primarily, at the present time, studies not of causal but of concomitant relations. For example, the relation between high echelon level in an organization (*4C*) and given responsibility, authority, and delegation patterns (*3D*) cannot at present be stated in causal terms. To illustrate further: Seeman and Morris[7] found, in

a study of the relation of general-status attitudes to leadership ideology, that teachers who were committed to maintaining large status differences in a wide variety of social, political, and economic situations were those who wanted most direction, and clear "leader" rather than "member" behavior, from their "ideal superintendent." This suggests a concomitance between the status ideology of superintendents themselves and their behavior as described by subordinates. Seeking out such concomitancies is a vital preparatory step toward the establishment of causal patterns.

8. *What Are the Results of Leader Behavior?* Research here is concerned with the question: "What difference, if any, does the leader make?" It is presumably to such differences that the concept "leadership" refers. Any of the variables listed under group and individual factors may be viewed as products of leadership. One may ask whether, for example, a given supervisory pattern (*3A*) leads to the adoption of a given communication system in the group (*4G*).

The primary concern in describing results of the leader's behavior is with what we have called the "group factors." There are also, however, questions which center on the individual factors as results: Does dominance by the leader (*3C*) lead to given patterns of advancement for him in an organization (*5H*)?

9. *What Factors Serve as Conditioners?* Here the individual and group factors are viewed as conditioners of relationships between given leader behavior and other factors. Hemphill[8] found that the reported behavior of "superior" leaders differed significantly in terms of the size of the group in which they functioned. The differences were in the direction of greater tolerance for leader-centered direction in larger groups. These findings suggest that the size of the group is one important factor conditioning the relationship between leader behavior and his evaluation by subordinates. Similarly, the relation suggested in section 8 above between supervision pattern and the communication system in the group may hold only in groups of a given size or in groups having a given type of formal organization.

10. *How Are the Results of Leader Behavior Evaluated?* Studies of leadership which ignore the problem of evaluation can, of course, be made and may contribute important theoretical insights. Evaluation, however, takes on a special importance because of the strong pragmatic emphasis upon leadership in our culture. It is not enough to know what leadership is; the demand is for knowledge about *good* leadership in order to secure as much of it as possible as soon as possible.

Two kinds of criteria can be used: those which evaluate leadership in terms of the results for the group and those which focus simply upon the individual who is the leader. Any of the group or individual factors may presumably be used as bases for evaluation of leadership. Thus, the criteria of effectiveness may be increased cohesiveness of the group (*4B*), the extent to which it has achieved given goals (*4F*), or the leader's success in gaining promotion (*5H*).

Criteria for effectiveness may vary systematically with the individual making the evaluation: different people want different things of leadership; or with the situation: what is effective leadership in peace may not be effective leadership in war. Studies, therefore, which examine the relations among multiple criteria of effectiveness are of vital importance.

Concerted interdisciplinary attack on the problem of leadership in American society has been instituted along the lines suggested above. This program is yielding data and methodologies of broad scope and application, integrated in that they use the resources of the several social sciences and contribute to an organized view of the total leadership problem.

3. ON THE STATEMENT "THE WHOLE IS MORE THAN THE SUM OF ITS PARTS"

by Ernest Nagel

IN CONNECTION with the subject of reduction and emergence, it is helpful to discuss a familiar notion that is frequently associated with these themes. According to this notion there occurs in nature an important type of individual wholes (which may be physical, biological, psychological, or social) that are not simply "aggregates" of independent members, but are "organic unities"; and such wholes are often characterized by the familiar dictum that they possess an organization which makes each of them "more than the sum of its parts." Examples of wholes that are "organic," and which allegedly also illustrate this dictum, can be cited from many fields of inquiry. Since such alleged facts are sometimes taken as indications of limits to the possibility of reduction and to the scope of the methods of the physical sciences, it is instructive to consider them with some care. And in the course of examining them we shall be compelled to recognize distinctions that will be useful in the sequel.

The first point to note, however, is that words like "whole" and "sum" as commonly employed are usually vague, ambiguous, and even metaphorical; and until their senses are clarified, it is frequently impossible to assess the worth of statements containing them. Let us make this evident by an example. A quadrilateral encloses an area, and either one of its diameters divides it into two partial areas whose sum is equal to the area of the whole figure. In this and many analogous contexts the statement "The whole is equal to the sum of its parts" is usually said to be not only true, but *necessarily* true, so that its denial is commonly regarded as self-contradictory. On the other hand, some writers have maintained, on comparing the taste of sugar of lead with the taste of its chemical components, that in this case the whole is not equal to the sum of its parts. Now this assertion is intended to supply some information about the matters discussed; and it cannot be rejected without further ado as simply a logical absurdity. It is clear, therefore, that in this latter context the words "whole," "part," and "sum" (and perhaps "equal") are being employed in senses different from those associated with

Reprinted from "Wholes, Sums, and Organic Unities," *Philosophical Studies*, Vol. III, No. 2, 1952, pp. 17-26, by permission of the author and the publisher. (Published by the University of Minnesota Press.)

them in the previous context. We must therefore assume the task of distinguishing between a number of senses of these words that appear to play a role in various inquiries.

1. WHOLES AND PARTS

The words "whole" and "part" are normally used for correlative distinctions, so that x is said to be a whole in relation to something y which is a component or part of x in some sense or other. It will be convenient, therefore, to have before us a brief list of certain familiar "kinds" of wholes and corresponding parts.

a. The word "whole" is used to refer to something with a spatial extension, and anything is then called a "part" of such a whole which is spatially included in it. However, there are several special senses of "whole" and "part" which fall under this head. In the first place, they may refer to specifically spatial properties, so that the whole is then some length, area, or volume which contains as parts lengths, areas, or volumes. In this sense, neither wholes nor parts need be spatially continuous—thus, the United States and its territorial possessions are not a spatially continuous whole, which contains as one of its spatial parts the desert regions which are also not spatially continuous. In the second place, "whole" may refer to a non-spatial property or state of a spatially extended thing, and "part" designates an identical property of some spatial part of the thing. Thus, the electric charge on a body is said to have for its parts the electric charges on spatial parts of the body. In the third place, though sometimes only such spatial properties are counted as parts of a spatial whole which have the same spatial dimensions as the latter, at other times the usage is more liberal. Thus, the surface of a sphere is frequently said to be a part of the sphere, even if on other occasions only volumes in the sphere's interior are so designated.

b. The word "whole" refers to some temporal period, whose parts are temporal intervals in it. As in the case of spatial wholes and parts, temporal ones need not be continuous.

c. The word "whole" refers to any class, set, or aggregate of elements, and "part" may then designate either any proper subclass of the initial set or any element in the set. Thus, by a part of the whole consisting of all the books printed in the United States during a given year may be understood either all the novels printed that year, or some particular copy of a novel.

d. The word "whole" sometimes refers to a property of an object or process, and "part" to some analogous property which stands to the first in certain specified relations. Thus, a force in physics is commonly said to have for its parts or components other forces into which the first can be analyzed according to a familiar rule. Similarly, the physical brightness of a surface illuminated by two sources of light is sometimes said to have for one of its parts the brightness associated with one of the sources. In the present sense of the words, a part is not a spatial part of the whole.

e. The word "whole" may refer to a pattern of relations between certain specified kinds of objects or events, the pattern being capable of embodiment on various occasions and with various modifications. However, "part" may then designate different things in different contexts. It may refer to any one of the elements which are related in that pattern on some occasion of its embodiment. Thus, if a melody (say "Auld Lang Syne") is such a whole, one of its parts is then the first tone that is sounded when the melody is sung on a particular date. Or it may refer to a class of elements which occupy corresponding positions in the pattern in some specified mode of its embodiment. Thus, one of the parts of the melody will then be the class of first notes when "Auld Lang Syne" is sung in the key of G minor. Or the word "part" may refer to a subordinate pattern in the total one. In this case, a part of the melody will be the pattern of tones that occurs in its first four bars.

f. The word "whole" may refer to a process, one of its parts being another process that is some discriminated phase of the more inclusive one. Thus, the process of swallowing is part of the process of eating.

g. The word "whole" may refer to any concrete object, and "part" to any of its properties. In this sense, the character of being cylindrical in shape or being malleable is a part of a given piece of copper wire.

h. Finally, the word "whole" is often used to refer to any system whose spatial parts stand to each other in various relations of dynamical dependence. Many of the so-called organic unities appear to be systems of this type. However, in the present sense of "whole" a variety of things are customarily designated as its parts. Thus, a system consisting of a mixture of two gases inside a container is frequently, though not always in the same context, said to have for its parts one or more of the following: its spatially extended constituents, such as the two gases and the container; the properties or states of the system or of its spatial parts, such as the mass of the system or the specific heats of one of the gases; the processes which the system undergoes in reaching or maintaining thermodynamical equilibrium; and the spatial or dynamical organization to which its spatial parts are subject.

This list of senses of "whole" and "part," though by no means complete, will suffice to indicate the ambiguity of these words. But what is more important, it also suggests that since the word "sum" is used in a number of contexts in which these words occur, it suffers from an analogous ambiguity. Let us therefore examine several of its typical senses.

2. SENSES OF "SUM"

We shall not inquire whether the word "sum" actually is employed in connection with each of the senses of "whole" and "part" that have been distinguished, and if so just what meaning is to be associated with it. In point of fact, it is not easy to specify a clear sense for the word in many contexts in which people do use it. We shall accordingly confine ourselves to noting only a small number of the well-established uses of "sum," and to suggesting interpretations for it in a few contexts in which its meaning is unclear and its use misleading.

a. It is hardly surprising that the most carefully defined uses of "sum" and "addition" occur in mathematics and formal logic. But even in these contexts the word has a variety of special meanings, depending on what type of mathematical and logical "objects" are being added. Thus, there is a familiar operation of addition for the natural integers; and there are also identically named but really distinct operations for ratios, real numbers, complex numbers, matrices, classes, relations, and other "entities." It is not altogether evident why all these operations have the common name of "addition," though there are at least certain formal analogies between many of them—for example, most of them are commutative and associative. However, there are some important exceptions to the general rule implicit in this example, for the addition of *ordered* sets is not uniformly commutative, though it is associative. On the other hand, the sum of two entities is invariably some unique entity which is of the same type as the summands— thus, the sum of two integers is an integer, of two matrices a matrix, and so on. Moreover, though the word "part" is not always defined or used in connection with mathematical "objects," whenever both it and "sum" are employed they are so used that the statement "The whole is equal to the sum of its parts" is an analytic or necessary truth.

However, it is easy to construct an apparent counterinstance to this last claim. Let K^* be the *ordered* set of the integers, ordered in the following manner: first the odd integers in order of increasing magnitude, and then the even integers in that order. K^* may then be represented by this notation: $(1,3,5 . . ., 2,4,6 . . .)$. Next let K_1 be the class of odd integers and K_2 the class of even ones, neither class being an ordered set. Now let K be the class-sum of K_1 and K_2, so that K contains all the integers as members; K also is not an ordered class. But the membership of K is the same as that of K^*, although quite clearly K and K^* are not identical. Accordingly, so it might be argued, in this case the whole (namely K^*) is not equal to the sum (i.e., K) of its parts.

This example is instructive on three counts. It shows that it is possible to define in a precise manner the words "whole," "part," and "sum" so that "The whole is unequal to the sum of its parts" is not only not logically absurd, but is in fact logically true. There is therefore no a priori reason for dismissing such statements as inevitable nonsense; and the real issue is to determine, when such an assertion is made, in what sense if any the crucial words in it are being used in the given context. But the example also shows that though such a sentence may be true on one specified usage of "part" and "sum," it may be possible to assign other senses to these words so that the whole *is* equal to the sum of its parts in this redefined sense of the words. Indeed, it is not standard usage in mathematics to call either K_1 or K_2 a part of K^*. On the contrary, it is customary to count as a part of K^* only an *ordered* segment. Thus, let K_1^* be the ordered set of odd integers arranged according to increasing magnitude, and K_2^* the corresponding ordered set of even integers. K_1^* and K_2^* are then parts of K^*. (K^* has other parts as well, for example, the ordered segments indicated by the following: $(1,3,5,7)$, $(9,11 . . . 2,4)$, and $(6,8 . . .)$ Now form the *ordered sum* of K_1^* and K_2^*. But *this* sum yields the ordered set K^*, so that in the specified senses of "part" and "sum" the whole *is* equal to the sum of its parts. It is thus clear that when a given system has a special type of organization or structure, a *useful* definition of "addition," if such can be given, must take into account that mode of organization. There are any number of operations that could be selected for the label "summation," but not all of them are relevant or appropriate for advancing a given domain of inquiry.

Finally, the example suggests that though a system has a distinctive structure, it is not in principle impossible to specify that structure in terms of relations between its elementary constituents, and moreover in such a manner that the structure can be correctly characterized as a "sum" whose "parts" are themselves specified in terms of those elements and relations. As we shall see, many students deny, or appear to deny, this possibility in connection with certain kinds of organized systems (such as living things). The present example therefore shows that though we may not be able *as a matter of fact* to analyze certain highly complex "dynamic" (or "organic") unities in terms of some given theory concerning their ultimate constituents, such inability cannot be established as a matter of *inherent logical necessity*.

b. If we now turn to the positive sciences, we find that here too there are a large number of well-defined operations called "addition." The major distinction that needs to be drawn is between scalar and vector sums. Let us consider each in turn. Examples of the former are the addition of the numerosity of groups of things, of spatial properties (length, area, and volume), of temporal periods, of weights, of electrical resistance, electric charge, and thermal capacity. They illustrate the first three senses of "whole" and "part" which we distinguished above; and in each of them (and in many other cases that could be mentioned) "sum" is so specified that the whole is the sum of appropriately chosen parts.

On the other hand, there are many magnitudes for which no operation of addition is defined, or seems capable of being defined in any useful manner, such as density or elasticity; most of these cases fall under the last four of the above distinctions concerning "whole" and "part." Moreover, there are some properties for which addition is specified only under highly specialized circumstances; for example, the sum of the brightness of two sources of light is defined only when the light emitted is monochromatic. It makes no sense, therefore, to say that the density (or the shape) of a body is, or is not, the sum of the densities (or shapes) of its parts, simply because there are neither explicitly formulated rules nor ascertainable habits of procedure which associate a usage with the word "sum" in such a context.

The addition of vector properties, such as forces, velocities, and accelerations, conforms to the familiar rule of parallelogram composition. Thus, if a body is acted on by a force of 3 poundals in a direction due north, and also by a force of 4 poundals in a direction due east, the body will behave as if it were acted on by a single force of 5 poundals in a northeasterly direction. This single force is said to be the "sum" or "resultant" of the other two forces, which are called its "components"; and conversely, any force can be analyzed as the sum of an arbitrary number of components. This sense of "sum" is commonly associated with the fourth of the above distinctions concerning "whole" and "part"; and it is evident that here the sense of "sum" is quite different from the sense of the word in such contexts as "the sum of two lengths."

It has been argued by Bertrand Russell that a force cannot rightly be said to be the sum of its components. Thus, he declared:

Let there be three particles *A, B, C.* We may say that *B* and *C* both cause accelerations in *A*, and we compound these accelerations by the parallelogram law. But this composition is not truly addition, for the components are not *parts* of the resultant. The resultant is a new term, as simple as their components, and not by any means their sum. Thus the effects attributed to *B* and *C* are never produced, but a third term different from either is produced. This, we may say, is produced by *B* and *C* together, taken as a whole. But the effect which they produce as a whole can only be discovered by supposing each to produce a separate effect: if this were not supposed, it would be impossible to obtain the two accelerations whose resultant is the actual acceleration. Thus we seem to reach an antinomy: the whole has no effect except what results from the effects of the parts, but the effects of the parts are nonexistent.[1]

However, all that this argument shows is that by the component of a force (or of an acceleration) we do not mean anything like what we understand by a component or part of a length—the components of forces are not *spatial parts* of forces. It does not establish the claim that the addition of forces "is not truly addition"—unless, indeed, the word "addition" is being used so restrictively that no operation is to be so designated which does not involve a juxtaposition of spatial (or possibly temporal) parts of the whole said to be their sum. But in this latter event many other operations that are called "addition" in physics, such as the addition of electrical capacities, would also have to receive different labels. Moreover, no antinomy arises from the supposition that, on the one hand, the effect which each component force would produce were it to act alone does not exist, while on the other hand the actual effect produced by the joint action of the components is the resultant of their partial effects. For the supposition simply expresses what is the case, in a language conforming to the antecedent *definition* of the addition and resolution of forces.

The issue raised by Russell is thus terminological at best. His objection is nevertheless instructive. For it calls needed attention to the fact that when the matter is viewed abstractly, the "sum" of a given set of elements is simply an element that is *uniquely determined* by some *function* (in the mathematical sense) of the given set. This function may be assigned a relatively simple and familiar form in certain cases, and a more complex and strange form in others; and in any event, the question whether such a function is to be introduced into a given domain of inquiry, and if so what special form is to be assigned to it, cannot be settled a priori. But the heart of the matter is that when such a function is specified, and if a set of elements satisfy whatever conditions are prescribed by the function, it becomes possible to *deduce* from these premises a class of statements about some structural complex of those elements.[2]

c. We must now consider a use of "sum" that is associated with the fifth sense of "whole" and "part" distinguished above—a use that is also frequently associated with the dictum that the whole is more than, or at any rate not merely, the sum of its parts. Let us assume that the following statement is typical of such usage: "Although a melody may be produced by sounding a series of individual tones on a piano, the melody is not the sum of its individual notes." The obvious question that needs to be asked is: "In what sense is 'sum' being employed here?" It is evident that the statement can be informative only if there *is* such a thing as the sum of the individual tones of melody. For the statement can be established as true or false only if it is possible to compare such a sum with the whole that is the melody.

However, most people who are inclined to assert such a statement do not specify what that sum is supposed to be; and there is therefore a basis for the supposition that they either are not clear about what they mean, or do not mean anything whatever. In the latter case the most charitable view that can be taken of such pronouncements is to regard them as simply misleading expressions of the possibly valid claim that the notion of summation is *inapplicable* to the constituent tones of melodies. On the other hand, some writers apparently understand by "sum" in this context the *unordered class* of individual tones; and what they are therefore asserting is that this class is not the melody. But this is hardly news, though conceivably there may have been some persons who believed otherwise. In any event, there appears to be no meaning other than this one which is associated with any regularity with the phrase "sum of tones" or similar phrases. Accordingly, if the word "sum" is used in this sense in contexts in which the word "whole" refers to a pattern or configuration formed by elements standing to each other in certain relations, it is perfectly true though trivial to say that the whole is more than the sum of its parts.

As has already been noted, however, this fact does not preclude the possibility of *analyzing* such wholes into a set of elements related to one another in definite ways; nor does it exclude the possibility of assigning a different sense to "sum" so that a melody might then be construed as a sum of appropriately selected parts. It is evident that at least a partial analysis of a melody is effected when it is represented in the customary musical notation; and the analysis could obviously be made more complete and explicit, and even expressed with formal precision.[3]

But it is sometimes maintained in this connection that it is a fundamental mistake to regard the constituent tones of a melody as independent parts, out of which the melody can be reconstituted. On the contrary, it has been argued that what we "experience at each place in the melody is a *part* which is itself determined by the character of the whole. . . . The flesh and blood of a tone depends from the start upon its role in the melody; a *b* as leading tone to *c* is something radically different from the *b* as tonic."[4] And as we shall see, similar views have been advanced in connection with other cases and types of *Gestalts* and "organic" wholes.

Now it may be quite true that the *effect* produced by a given tone depends on its position in a context of other tones, just as the effect produced by a given pressure upon a body is in general contingent upon what other pressures are operative. But this supposed fact does not imply that a melody cannot rightly be viewed as a relational complex whose component tones are identifiable independently of their occurrence in that complex. For if the implication did hold, it would be impossible to describe how a melody is constituted out of individual tones, and therefore impossible to prescribe how it is to be played. Indeed, it would then be self-contradictory to say that "a *b* as leading to *c* is something radically different from the *b* as tonic." For the name "*b*" in the expression "*b* as leading to *c*" could then not refer to the same tone to which the name "*b*" refers in the expression "*b* as tonic"; and the presumable intent of the statement could then not be expressed. In short, the fact that in connection with wholes that are patterns or *Gestalts* of occurrences the word "sum" is either undefined, or defined in such a way that the whole is unequal to the sum of its parts, constitutes no inherently insuperable obstacle to analyzing such wholes into elements standing to each other in specified relations.

d. We must finally examine the use of "sum" in connection with wholes that are organized systems of dynamically interrelated parts. Let us assume as typical of such usage the statement "Although the mass of a body is

cqual to the sum of the masses of its spatial parts, a body also has properties which are not the sums of properties possessed by its parts." The
comments that have just been made about "sum" in connection with patterns of occurrences such as melodies can be extended to the present context
of usage of the word; and we shall not repeat them. In the present instance,
however, an additional interpretation of "sum" can be suggested which may
put into clearer light the content of such statements as the above.

When the behavior of a machine like a clock is sometimes said to be the
sum of the behaviors of its spatial parts, what is the presumptive content
of the assertion? It is reasonable to assume that the word "sum" does not
here signify an unordered class of elements—for neither the clock nor its
behavior is such a class. It is therefore plausible to construe the assertion
as maintaining that from the theory of mechanics, coupled with suitable
information about the actual arrangements of the parts of the machine, it
is possible to deduce statements about the consequent properties and behaviors of the entire system. Accordingly, it seems also plausible to construe
in a similar fashion statements such as that of J. S. Mill: "The different
actions of a chemical compound will never be found to be the sums of actions
of its separate parts."[5] More explicitly, this statement can be understood to
assert that from some assumed theory concerning the constituents of chemical compounds, even when it is conjoined with appropriate data on the
organization of these constituents within the compounds, it is not in fact
possible to deduce statements about many of the properties of these compounds.

If we adopt this suggestion, we obtain an interpretation for "sum" that is
particularly appropriate for the use of the word in contexts in which the
wholes under discussion are organized systems of interdependent parts. Let
T be a theory that is in general able to explain the occurrence and modes
of interdependence of a set of properties P_1, P_2 . . . P_k. More specifically,
suppose it is known that when one or more individuals belonging to a set K
of individuals occur in an environment E_1 and stand to each other in some
relation belonging to a class of Relations R_1, the theory T can explain the behavior of such a system with respect to its manifesting some or all of the
properties P. Now assume that some or all of the individuals belonging to
K form a relational complex R_2 not belonging to R_1 in an environment E_2
which may be different from E_1, and that the system exhibits certain modes
of behavior which are formulated in a set of laws L. Two cases may then be
distinguished: from T, together with statements concerning the organization
of the individuals in R_2, it is possible to deduce the laws L; or secondly, not
all the laws L can be so deduced. In the first case, the behavior of the system R_2 may be said to be the "sum" of the behaviors of its component
individuals; in the second case, the behavior of R_2 is *not* such a sum. It is
evident that in a currently accepted sense of "reducible," the conditions for
the reducibility of L to T are satisfied in the first case; in the second case,
however, although one of these conditions may be satisfied, the other is not.

If this interpretation of "sum" is adopted for the indicated contexts of
its usage, it follows that the distinction between wholes which are sums of
their parts and those which are not is *relative to some assumed theory T* in
terms of which the analysis of a system is undertaken. Thus, as we have seen,
the kinetic theory of matter as developed during the nineteenth century was

able to explain certain thermal properties of gases, including certain relations between the specific heats of gases. However, that theory was unable to account for these relations between specific heats when the state of aggregation of molecules is that of a solid rather than a gas. On the other hand, modern quantum theory is capable of explaining the facts concerning the specific heats of solids, and presumably also all other thermal properties of solids. Accordingly, although relative to classical kinetic theory the thermal properties of solids are not sums of the properties of their parts, relative to quantum theory those properties are such sums.

4. DEFINITION AND SPECIFICATION OF MEANING [1]

by Abraham Kaplan

THE PROCESS by which a term is introduced into discourse or by which the meaning of a term already in use is more exactly specified, may be called *specification of meaning*. This process is ordinarily explicated by the concept of definition—a logical equivalence between the term defined and an expression whose meaning has already been specified. That this procedure is not always a satisfactory treatment of specification of meaning was pointed out by Carnap in his "Testability and Meaning," where he developed the concept of "conditioned definitions" or reduction sentences.[2] This concept was elaborated primarily to meet the paradox of material implication when it enters into definitions of the ordinary sort. But there are more general considerations pointing to the inadequacy of definition as a treatment of specification of meaning.

Definitions construe science and its language not as processes of inquiry and communication, but only as the outcome of these processes at some particular stage. In fact specification of meaning is processive; it is hypothetical and provisional, and undergoes modification as inquiry proceeds. The concept of definition does not in itself provide a logical account of this modification. Moreover, "the" process of inquiry is an abstraction from particular inquiries, so that a given concept has various meanings in different contexts—meanings not related to one another as logical equivalents, but empirically coinciding to a greater or lesser degree.[3] It follows that one can not speak of "the" meaning of a concept as it actually functions in inquiry. But just such a determinate reference is assigned to it in the definitional representation of the language of science. Every concept is purported to be defined in one particular way and no other.

Reprinted from *The Journal of Philosophy*, Vol. XLIII, No. 11 (May 23, 1946), pp. 281-288, by permission of the author and the publisher. (Published by the Journal of Philosophy, Inc.)

So long as the representation is in abstract and general terms, the procedure seems to be satisfactory. But serious problems arise when the attempt is made to give the representation specific content from some particular field of inquiry. The formulation of a definition for any empirical concept satisfactory to all investigators employing the concept is notoriously difficult. And this difficulty, it is here suggested, is due, not to a psychology of captiousness, but to the logical requirements of the varying contexts in which the concept functions.

Let us take a single example, the biological concept of species. J. S. Huxley, in a book on problems of systematization and classification in biology, observes:

> There is no single criterion of species. Morphological differences; failure to interbreed; infertility of offspring; ecological, geographical, or genetical distinctness —all these must be taken into account, but none of them singly is decisive. . . . A combination of criteria is needed, together with some sort of flair. With the aid of these, it is remarkable how the variety of organic life falls apart into biologically discontinuous groups.[4]

Another biologist writes in the same volume:

> As a definition of species . . . I would suggest something on the following lines, and analogous definitions could be constructed for other categories. "A species is a group of individuals which, in the sum total of their attributes, resemble each other to a degree usually accepted as specific, the exact degree being ultimately determined by the more or less arbitrary judgment of taxonomists." Admittedly this definition, based as it is on resemblance in total attributes, is a very vague one, but any attempt to define a species more precisely in terms of particular attributes breaks down.[5]

Clearly, the function of the concept does not depend on its having been *defined,* if there has been a specification of its meaning in some other form than a definition. The argument that the fact that no satisfactory definition of "species" can be found shows only how "hopelessly vague" the concept is, but not that meanings can be specified otherwise than by definition, loses force when confronted with the multitude of important concepts in other fields of inquiry which have proved equally impossible to define once for all. To reply that inquiry in these fields is not "genuinely scientific" simply side-steps the problem, of course. Inquiry *is* going on in these areas; and how it proceeds with undefined concepts is surely a matter to be explicated.

It may be said that the use of definitions in the rational reconstruction of the language of science does not involve a denial that all terms of empirical reference are vague to a greater or lesser degree, but only constitutes an idealization of what is actually found. The question being raised, however, is, Of what is definition an idealization? What are the processes of specification of meaning which approximate the logical character of definition? And how is this approximation made closer?[6]

No attempt is made here to answer these questions, i.e., to develop an explicatum for "specification of meaning" which would clarify the matters not explicated by the concept of definition. Let us call such an explicatum a *theory of specification,* "definition" thus being only a special form of specification. The following paragraphs do not constitute a theory of specification, but are intended only to suggest some matters which might be taken account of in such a theory.

Whenever a term is introduced into a context of inquiry—whether *de novo* or extended from some other context—situations (pertaining to the new context) are described in which the term may be applied. Any such description may be called an *indicator* for the term. But the term is not in general logically equivalent to any or all of its indicators; they assign to the application of the term under the described conditions, not a logical certainty, but only a specified weight.[7] Thus, failure to interbreed is an indicator for distinctness of species; but that two animals do in fact interbreed does not logically entail that they belong to the same species, but only adds some weight to the assumption.

Such weights are not specified quantitatively, but they are ordered, at least with regard to other indicators for the same term. The weight which an indicator assigns to the application of a term is often called the *reliability* of the indicator. In the example, infertility of offspring is a more reliable indicator of distinct species than differences in phenotypic characteristics; geographical distinctness is perhaps less reliable, and so on. In general, one indicator may be said to be more or less reliable than another for the same term, even though it be impossible to compare the reliability of indicators for different terms. (Without such "internal" comparisons, it would be impossible to improve the reliability of indication, as is in fact constantly being done.) Thus, just as semantical rules of the familiar sort specify the meaning of a sentence by giving the conditions under which the sentence would be true, the indicators specify a more or less indefinite meaning by giving conditions under which the term is likely to apply. (We shall consider below how the meaning is made less indefinite.)

There may, of course, be negative indicators specifying situations to which the term is likely not to apply. In general, the negation of a positive indicator is a negative indicator but of different weight than the positive. A test may be highly sensitive to the presence of a particular property, but may sometimes react even in its absence; it would then be a highly reliable negative indicator, but not as good a positive indicator. Or, to take an example of the converse, two animals that closely resemble one another phenotypically (as do, say, two dachshunds) may reliably be presumed to belong to the same species; but that two animals belong to *distinct* species is less reliably indicated by phenotypical *differences*.

A set of indicators may therefore be exhaustive but nevertheless incomplete if their reliabilities are less than maximal. P may assign to the application of the term T a weight $w,$ and *not-P* to the application of *not-T* a weight v; some meaning is thereby specified for T for all cases (every situation is either P or *not-P*). But the set is incomplete in so far as w or v or both could be made higher by other indicators.[8] Thus, to delimit a particular species one could specify maximal differences in a number of bodily characteristics—size and shape of head, legs, tail; color and markings; length of hair; etc., etc. If the differences in these characters exceed the specified maximum, the animals compared are to be classed in distinct species, and if not, they are not. Such a delimitation is, logically, complete—it can be applied in all cases. But the specification of meaning is incomplete in that further indicators can increase the reliability of a classification made on this basis alone.

The specification of indicators for a term is not in itself sufficient for the use of the term. The indicators describe situations to which the term probably applies, but given a sentence in which the term occurs, we can not *deduce* characteristics of the situation described: a *reverse* weight for these indicators must be separately specified. Such reverse specifications may be called *references* of the term. Thus, a proposition about species can be interpreted as making reference to morphological differences, to genetic or geographical distinctness, to phenotypic differences, and so on. All these references are involved in varying weights (degrees of relevance). The weights of the references will obviously differ in different contexts of inquiry, and need not correspond to the weights of the indicators. For a particular problem, P may be the most reliable indicator of T, but some other property Q may have a higher weight as a reference of the hypotheses concerning T formulated to solve the problem. In Darwin's investigation of the distribution of species, geographical distinctness had perhaps a high weight as an indicator, but the reference of "species" in the resultant hypotheses was more to genetic and morphological distinctness.

The weight of a reference depends, not just on the weight of the corresponding indicator, but on the weights of the entire set of indicators. A particular indicator may be more reliable than others but occur less frequently or under more limited conditions, so that its weight as a reference will be correspondingly less as compared with other references.[9] The set of references and the set of indicators thus coincide, but the corresponding weights in general differ from one another. It is this difference, indeed, which requires the distinction between indicators and references. The distinction can not be made in the case of definition because logical equivalence is symmetrical. The specification of a meaning consists, therefore, of weighted indicators and references both.

The references can not be *substituted* for the term whose meaning is specified, any more than could the term for its indicators. The transition from a proposition containing the term to one containing only its references is not, as in the case of definition, an immediate deduction, but one in which the premise gives the conclusion only some weight or other. But the term is useful even though (perhaps one should say *because*) it can not be eliminated with strictness and certitude. It provides a linkage among its set of indicators (or references) as a whole.[10] It embodies, in fact, a propositional content: that the members of this set are positive   related with one another. The term is applied and refers to a var   situations which do not necessarily all exhibit some single common character, but a number of distinct characters empirically related to one another. From this standpoint, the term "species"—to pursue the example—is not eliminable from the language of biology.[11] Its introduction does not constitute merely a convenient shorthand for more cumbersome locutions, but marks an advance in biological theory—that the various characteristics serving as indicators and references of the concept have an empirically significant relatedness: problems of biology can be formulated and solved in terms of this relatedness.

Specification of meaning is thus hypothetical throughout, the hypothetical element lying not so much in whether a particular specification will accord with a given usage, but in whether it will accord with linkages in the phenomena to be comprised in the meaning. For while the weight of any single indicator can be fixed by stipulation, that for a set can not be so stipulated. It is fixed by the empirical relations holding among the separate indicators. For instance, if infertility of offspring is stipulated as an indicator of high weight for distinctness of species, and certain morphological differences have a high positive correlation with such infertility, this correlation fixes a lower limit to the weight of morphology as an indicator of distinct species. Similarly, the weight of a compound indicator—for instance, infrequent *and* sterile offspring—depends not only on the weights of its components, but also on the empirical relations between these components. If the components are not independent, the compound indicator may have only a slightly higher weight, if at all, than either singly.

Specification of meaning thus has both a conventional and an empirical aspect; the situation is like that of the delicately balanced constructions by Calder, in which the artist is free to add or remove weights wherever he pleases, but must make compensating changes to maintain the balance. The specification results from a decision as to meaning, but, as Reichenbach has emphasized, a particular decision may entail others as a consequence of empirical interconnections.

Thus the specification at any stage is a provisional one, both as to the indicators included, and the weights associated with them. We begin with indicators by which the initial partial extension of the term is selected, and in terms of which the initial context of application can be confirmed. As the context of application grows, the specified meaning grows—and changes— with it. The stipulation of new indicators affects the weights of the old ones, while they in turn limit the range of choice in the stipulation. The adequacy of a particular indicator is not judged by its accordance with a pre-deter- mined concept; the new and old indicators are appraised conjointly.

The fact that a particular concept is sometimes "defined" in one way and sometimes another can also be formulated in these terms. It is not ordinarily *defined* at all, but its meaning is specified by a set of indicators. In differ- ent contexts, different indicators are stipulated to have a certain weight, the weight of the others being empirically limited in relation to these. Those stipulated thus have a logical status akin to a definiens; their relation to the term whose meaning is specified is a matter of decision, and not subject to disconfirmation. The point being made is that this status is functional and contextual. It is not being denied that there is any difference between prop- ositions of a logical and of an empirical purport, but only that the distinction can be applied in abstraction from the way in which the proposition is used in specific contexts of inquiry.[12]

An explicatum of specification of meaning along the lines discussed would thus take the acknowledged vagueness of all terms directly into account. The designation of a term would not in general be represented as a well- defined area, but as an open set of regions overlapping to a greater or lesser degree, each indicator determining one such region. The meaning of this term would correspond neither to the logical sum nor product of these regions, but to the pattern as a whole. The designatum, to paraphrase Claude Bernard's famous dictum about disease, is not an entity but a complex of symptoms. It is made clear, not by a precise definition, but by a specifica- tion of the characteristic syndrome.

The "sameness" of a concept employed in different contexts of inquiry (or communication) would thus be explicated, not by the constancy of a single reference, but by the pattern of its references. It is like the "same face" in the members of a family; the familial resemblance is constituted, not by similarity in some one feature, but in the general cast of features. Every term designates in this sense a "family of meanings."[13] The inevitable vagueness of the term results from this dispersion of its reference.

This dispersion is reduced, and the meaning of the term brought into sharper focus, as the reliability of the indicators is improved and the degree of their overlapping increased. This degree of overlapping may be called the *congruence* of the indicator set. At each stage the attempt is to specify the meaning in a way which will maximize both reliability and congruence. The addition of more and more reliable indicators may necessitate rejection of some old ones to preserve congruence; indicators which lower congruence may nevertheless be adopted to increase reliability. In a limiting case, indicators are subdivided into two or more groups, each of higher congruence and reliability than the original set. We say that the term was ambiguous, and specify distinct meanings.

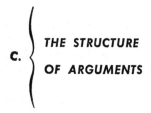

5. ON AXIOMATIC THEORIES IN SOCIOLOGY

by Hans Zetterberg

[In his monograph *On Theory and Verification in Sociology,* Zetterberg undertook to specify the form and elements constituting a sociological theory. One
of his major concerns involves the development of a formal procedure for the
analysis of what he terms a "middle-range" or "miniature" theory. In the selection
which follows, he discusses and illustrates certain advantages to be derived from
the use of such a miniature theory—ED. NOTE.]

THE MOST SATISFACTORY structure of a theory is perhaps the one that is
called axiomatic. If we were to formulate an axiomatic theory—or deductive-
type theory, as it is also called—we would proceed in roughly the following
way.[1]

1. We will list a series of primitive terms or *basic concepts.* These are
definitions which we, strictly speaking, will introduce as undefined. However, by circumlocutions and examples, we may convey what we intend them
to mean. There is nothing mystically "fundamental" or "basic" about these
concepts—they only represent an assumption of an agreement that we may
use certain words in certain ways.

2. We will define the *derived concepts* of our theory by means of these
concepts. The derived concepts are obtained through combinations of the
basic concepts. Granted the basic concepts we accordingly can say that the
derived concepts are precise. If we illustrate them with examples, we should
remember that these examples do not add or subtract anything from the
definitions. The basic concepts and the derived concepts form the 'nominal definitions' of the theory.

3. We will formulate the *hypotheses* of the theory. These hypotheses must
not contain any other concepts than the nominal definitions. We will formulate these hypotheses as we usually do in science. Thus they should be chosen
so that they do not contradict what we know is true, and, we will cite scientific research supporting these hypotheses, or in the absence of the latter,
we will cite informal observations in favor of them.

4. We will select from among the hypotheses formulated a certain number to be the *postulates* of our theory. The postulates should be chosen so
that all other hypotheses, the *theorems,* should be capable of derivation from
these postulates. Specifically, the postulates should be chosen so that they

Reprinted from *On Theory and Verification in Sociology,* pp. 16-28, by permission of the
author and the publisher. (Copyright, 1954, by The Tressler Press.)

become consistent and independent. In other words, no postulate should contradict any other, and no postulate should follow from any other postulate as a theorem.[2] If we prefer a very high degree of precision we may also specify the rules we are permitted to use when we make these derivations. At present, we may, however, as far as sociology is concerned, be quite satisfied with the use of the derivation rules implied in ordinary language. Sometimes sociological hypotheses are written as mathematical functions; then the laws of mathematics constitute the appropriate derivation rules.

Then, if we would like to further verify the theory, we would select a certain number of propositions to be tested empirically. We would select them so that our postulates can be derived from these propositions. If the empirical test is favorable and no mistake has been made in the derivation, we can claim empirical validity for the whole theory.

This kind of theory construction is unfortunately rather unknown in sociology[3] and a few words to justify the choice of this form of theory are appropriate at this point.

We are going to claim five advantages of the axiomatic theory for sociological research. In this context we will only illustrate these advantages by fictitious examples.

The *first* virtue we claim for this kind of theory is that *the concepts and postulates of an axiomatic theory offer the most parsimonious summary of anticipated or actual research findings.* This point might be clarified by an example.

Let us suppose that we have studied a number of groups with respect to: (a) the number of members in the group; (b) the solidarity of the group; (c) the degree of uniformity of behavior around group norms; (d) the degree of deviation from group norms; (e) the division of labor in the groups; and, (f) the extent to which persons are rejected or pushed out of the group when they violate group norms. These six variables, we assume, are found to be interrelated in the following way:

1. The greater the division of labor, the more the uniformity.
2. The greater the solidarity, the greater the number of members.
3. The greater the number of members, the less the deviation.
4. The more the uniformity, the less the rejection of deviates.
5. The greater the division of labor, the greater the solidarity.
6. The greater the number of members, the less the rejection of deviates.
7. The greater the solidarity, the more the uniformity.
8. The greater the number of members, the greater the division of labor.
9. The greater the division of labor, the less the deviation.
10. The less the deviation, the less the rejection of deviates.
11. The greater the solidarity, the less the rejection of deviates.
12. The greater the number of members, the more the uniformity.
13. The greater the division of labor, the less the rejection of deviates.
14. The greater the solidarity, the less the rejection of deviates.

Summarizing these findings according to the model of the axiomatic theory we can proceed like this:
Introduce as basic concepts:

behavior	group	solidarity	rejection
member	norm	division of labor	

Formulate as derived concepts:

uniformity: the proportion of members whose behavior is the norm of the group.
deviation: the proportion of members whose behavior is not the norm of the group.
deviate: member whose behavior is not the norm of the group.

Select as postulates, for example, findings (5), (7), (8), and (14):

I. The greater the division of labor, the greater the solidarity.
II. The greater the solidarity, the more the uniformity.
III. The greater the number of members, the greater the division of labor.
IV. The greater the solidarity, the less the rejection of deviates.

It is easily realized that from these four postulates all fourteen findings can be derived as they are combined with each other and with the nominal definitions. We find that what is emerging is a distorted version of Durkheim's theory of division of labor[4] in a considerably more elegant form than the mere listing of the fourteen findings.

In passing we may note a couple of interesting features in this kind of theory. Firstly, we may observe that the four propositions we have chosen as postulates are not the only ones from which all the others can be derived. For example, findings (1), (2), (3), (4) could also have qualified as postulates. We have chosen numbers (5), (7), (8), and (14) simply because they resemble most closely Durkheim's formulation. In other words, there is no inherent difference between postulates and theorems.[5] The postulates are in no respect more "basic," "granted," or "self-evident" than the theorems. Secondly, we may stop to think of what defines the "parsimony" of the theory. Usually it is felt that it is desirable to have so few basic (undefined) concepts as possible and so few postulates as possible. This is the reason why we introduced "uniformity," "deviation," and "deviate" in terms of the undefined "norm." This made uniformity and deviation mutually dependent and any proposition about uniformity was also a proposition about deviation. If this had not been done, the number of postulates would have been eight. In the present case there is accordingly no conflict between parsimony in terms of few basic concepts and parsimony in terms of few postulates. When such a conflict occurs it is probably wisest to choose the formulation that gives the greatest parsimony in terms of basic concepts.

We have shown how the use of this theoretical model helps us to summarize our hypotheses and research findings. Let us now turn our attention to the problem of how this model adds to the verification of our hypotheses.

The *second* virtue we claim for this kind of theory is that *the axiomatic theory has the highest plausibility per amount of supporting empirical data.* Let us illustrate this by using the theory we have formulated above.

Suppose we have fourteen researchers who do not know of one another and who independent of each other verify one of the fourteen hypotheses we have listed above. On the basis of their investigations they assign a certain probability that the hypotheses are true. Let us, for the sake of argument, assume that they all regarded this probability to be .95. Suppose further that we have a more theoretically oriented sociologist who formulates our theory and tests the same fourteen hypotheses now derived from the theory. Suppose that he performed exactly the same tests as his four-teen colleagues and obtained in each test a probability of .95 that the single hypotheses were correct. However, when the latter now talks of one of the hypotheses he can claim that its probability is far beyond .95.

The reason for this claimed gain in probability is that the scientist work-ing with theory—although he performs the same test as the scientist without a theory—also verifies several implications of his hypothesis. His procedure is practically identical with replications of a statistical test. The evidence from the latter tests reflects on the hypotheses as additional support accord-ing to a well known law of probability calculus.

This virtue of the axiomatic theory can be used also in another way. Sup-pose our theoretically oriented researcher is satisfied with a probability of .95. To obtain this he may verify only a selection of hypotheses—for exam-ple, the first five or six in our list. If he establishes them with a probability of .95 he can claim that his whole theory has about the same probability. Through the use of his theory he, hence, has saved a great deal of experi-mental work.

Just how much probability is transferred when a deduction from an already verified postulate is tested is a matter of some debate. Most writers in the field seem to hold the view that a deduction carries the same probability as the propo-sition from which it is deduced. We have no reason to enter the discussion. In our opinion, however, it is at present desirable that we in sociological research do not claim too much from the transfer of probability since our deductions are not too precise so long as our concepts are defined in normal prose and the deduction rules of ordinary language are used.

As a *third* virtue we claim that *the axiomatic theory locates strategic re-search problems*. When a set of hypotheses is written up in the shape of an axiomatic theory we can at any stage of the verification enterprise figure out what parts of the theory are verified and what parts are not verified. This property of the axiomatic theory can be used to locate the research problem the solution of which will contribute the most towards the verification of the theory.

Let us again assume that we are interested in verifying the theory out-lined above. Now it is often the case in science that we know of no way to test the postulates directly. We therefore test the postulates by testing their implications. It is in such a case that the third virtue of the axiomatic theory is important.

By way of an example, let us assume that we want to test the postulate that increased division of labor results in increased solidarity. Since we, supposedly, do not know of any direct way to test this hypothesis, we in-stead test hypotheses of the theory which are more easy to test. Suppose that these hypotheses are: 'large membership leads to less rejection of devi-ates,' and 'large membership leads to greater division of labor.' If these hypotheses are accepted, we are faced with the problem of determining the next step in verification of the postulate.

The following summary may help us to solve the problem:

We want to test by implication: Division of labor leads to solidarity.
We have tested: Large membership leads to less rejection of devi-
                                ates.

Large membership leads to greater division of labor.

We, hence, need to test: Solidarity leads to less rejection of deviates.

We conclude, then, that we have to test the latter hypothesis in order to give plausibility to the postulate that division of labor leads to solidarity. In the present case we could solve the problem by mere inspection. In more complicated cases it may be profitable to resort to mathematics or to the calculus methods developed in symbolic logic in order to find out how to test a seemingly "untestable" hypothesis by testing its implications.

The general procedure to figure out what parts of a theory are verified at certain stages appears from the above illustration. We, then, start from the propositions we have verified and try to deduce the postulates from them. By the same procedure we may also decide what propositions are most worthwhile to take up for empirical verification in the next step of the empirical labor.

The three virtues we have discussed up to this point have assumed that the tests of the hypotheses involved were successful. The next advantage of the axiomatic theory is important on the many occasions when our hypotheses fail to "come out" when checked against observation.

The *fourth* virtue we claim for the theory we advocate is that *the axiomatic theory provides a limited area in which we can locate the source of the failure of a hypothesis to meet the empirical test.*

Suppose that we are interested in the verification of our theory of the division of labor through the test of the hypotheses:

1. The greater the division of labor, the more the uniformity.
2. The greater the number of members, the less the deviation.
3. The greater the solidarity, the greater the number of members.
4. The less the deviation, the less the rejection of deviates.

From these hypotheses the four postulates of our theory can be derived. Suppose, however, that the last one fails the empirical test. Apparently, something must be wrong about the postulates. There are now possibilities of locating the source of this failure. One of the simplest ways is to derive the postulates from the hypotheses tested. Any postulate that requires the false hypotheses for its derivation is suspect:

We first derive Postulate III.

According to hypothesis (2), we have:

The greater the number of members, the less the deviation.

Combined with our definitions of deviation and uniformity, this becomes:

The greater the number of members, the more the uniformity.

Now, according to hypothesis (1), we have:

The greater the division of labor, the more the uniformity.

Combine this with the previous proposition and we obtain:

The greater the number of members, the greater the division of labor.

Which is Postulate III.

Postulate III, hence, can be derived from hypotheses (1) and (2). Since they were among those accepted on the basis of empirical tests we also accept Postulate III. We go on to derive Postulate I.

We have shown that from (1) and (2) comes:

The greater the number of members, the greater the division of labor.

But (3) states:

The greater the solidarity, the greater the number of members

Hence,

The greater the division of labor, the greater the solidarity.

Which is Postulate I.

We find that Postulate I can be derived from hypotheses (1), (2), and (3). Since all these hypotheses were accepted on the basis of empirical tests we also accept Postulate I.

We continue deriving Postulate II.

From the derivation of Postulate III, we remember that we obtained from hypothesis (2):

The greater the number of members, the more the uniformity.

Hypothesis (3) then states:

The greater the solidarity, the greater the number of members.

Combining these two we obtain:

The greater the solidarity, the more the uniformity.

Which is Postulate II.

Postulate II accordingly can be derived from hypotheses (2) and (3). Since we accepted these hypotheses as empirical evidence, we also accept Postulate II.

Finally, let us derive Postulate IV.

Hypothesis (2) states:

The greater the number of members, the less the deviation.

Hypothesis (4) states:

The less the deviation, the less the rejection of deviates.

Combining (2) and (4), we obtain:

The greater the number of members, the less the rejection of deviates.

We conclude that to derive Postulate IV we need hypotheses (2), (3), and (4). Now hypothesis (4) was found to be empirically untenable. Hence, we cannot accept Postulate IV either.

Our analysis located the error to Postulate IV which we should accordingly abandon. The remainder of the theory would still be tenable. The axiomatic theory, by virtue of its specified assumptions, made it easily possible to locate the error. Common sense reasoning and less strict scientific theories adds and subtracts assumptions more arbitrarily in the course of a discussion. Then we often do not know where to find the erroneous assumption after an empirical test has failed because we lack a statement of the assumptions of the theory.

Finally, as a *fifth* virtue we claim that *the axiomatic theory makes it easy to distinguish between propositions that are definitions and propositions that are hypotheses.*

This very plain virtue derives itself from the fact that the theorist using the axiomatic theory is required to specify his basic and derived concepts and his hypotheses in separate sections of the theory.[6] In the first place this virtue facilitates the communication about the theory and causes the reader to avoid misunderstandings about what is to be tested in the theory. Clarence C. Schrag makes this point in a review of *Toward a General Theory of Action:*

> Much of the difficulty encountered in reading the text is due to the failure of the authors to make a distinction between (1) statements which define terms, and (2) statements which specify an expected or empirically verifiable relationship between things that are independently defined. If, for example, the statement that 'behavior is motivated' is a hypothesis, then a test of it would require that certain 'motives' be defined independently of certain 'behaviors,' and that the kind and degree of association between these two sets of phenomena be stated and empirically verified. If, on the other hand, the statement is a definition, then it requires that categories of motivations be specified in such a way that all possible behaviors would clearly and reliably fall into one or another of these categories. In the present instance the issue is not settled at any place in the text, and the reader is forced to make his own decision as to how the statements were intended. This, of course, does not facilitate clear and efficient communication.[7]

Such misunderstandings are very unlikely to occur when axiomatic theories are used.

However, the question of what is a definition and what is a hypothesis might be a much more settled question. Consider, for example, many ideal type constructs used in sociology. Suppose we make a typology of groups like this:

Mechanical groups marked by: 1) low division of labor; 2) low solidarity; 3) small membership; and 4) strong rejection of deviates from group norms.
Organic groups marked by: 1) high division of labor; 2) high solidarity; 3) large membership; and 4) little rejection of deviates.

These two divisions *may* be just nominal definitions but they are likely to be treated as something more. Soon the sociologist will be caught saying that, "this group is more organic than that group." He will imply that groups can be put on a continuum being more and more organic. In doing so, however, he has accepted more or less unconsciously the theory we earlier spelled out about a positive relationship between high division of labor, high solidarity, many members and little rejection of deviates. His types of groups are not *nominal* definitions, they are *'real* definitions,' that is, they imply that genuine hypotheses are empirically true.[8] Real 'definitions' require testing before they can be accepted, but the sociologist theorizing along conventional lines is unlikely to be aware of the fact that they are real 'definitions,' so he will accept them without testing. By writing his theory in axiomatic form he stands a better chance to avoid these lapses.

Viewed in this way the many typologies and "ideal types" in sociology are found to be a rich source of more or less untested but important hypotheses.[9] We often use Cooley's term "primary group" implying the hypothesis that the more 'face-to-face contacts' there are in a group the greater is its 'we-feeling.' Our language habits in talking about the long array of society typologies from August Comte's "theological society" versus "positivistic society" to Redfield's "folk society" versus "secular society" can be analyzed in the same way for hidden hypotheses to be singled out and tested one by one. The personality typologies, finally, both from psychology—for example, Freud's oral and anal characters—and from sociology—for example, Riesman's inner-directed and other-directed personality—can be analyzed in the same way. Since the use of real 'definitions' seems so widespread in sociology, the analysis is particularly desirable there. Otherwise, sociology will include a number of untested, and perhaps questionable assumptions.

To these five virtues of the axiomatic theory could be added others. The ones mentioned, however, seem to be the most relevant for sociology. They carry, in our opinion, such weight and appeal that there is little reason to discourage attempts toward axiomatic theories in sociology.

It is plain that the first requirement of a theorem in an axiomatic theory is that it is non-contradictable by already available data. These data provide us with a pool of post factum hypotheses which are most valuable when we want to formulate an axiomatic theory. Our plea for axiomatic theories should, therefore, not be misunderstood to the extent that we look down upon previous research and want to cut ourselves off from the tradition of our science. The contrary is the case; without this tradition and its results our efforts toward this kind of theory construction would be pure guesswork.

6. MALTHUS AND THE THEORY OF POPULATION

by Kingsley Davis

THROUGHOUT the learned world there is currently a revival of interest in Malthus. This revival does not turn on precisely the same kind of issue that concerned him—the question of the perfectibility of mankind. The present age is too beset with cataclysmic international problems to spend much energy arguing that question. The main debate today concerns our ability to support a rapidly growing population at a rising standard of living, and Malthusian theory presumably bears on that problem. The reason for the present concern with the question, and hence for the revival of interest in Malthus, is seemingly threefold:

Reprinted in part from a speech delivered before The District of Columbia Sociological Society on Oct. 18, 1951, by permission of the author.

First, with better international statistics, there has been an increasing awareness of the extremely fast growth of the world's total population.

Second, there has been a widening realization that, because of the growing population and the ever more voracious appetite of industry, certain of the earth's resources are being exhausted and many of them wasted.

Third, those countries thought in the 1930's to be approaching a fixed population—most of the urban-industrial countries—have experienced during the subsequent decade an unexpected rise in the crude birth rate.

Thus the conditions are ripe today not only for directing attention to the problem that Malthus discussed—the problem of overpopulation—but for viewing it as even more critical than he and his friends viewed it. Contemplation of the current extraordinary rate of population growth raises the question of what will stop it. The progressive depletion of our resources through waste and exploitation suggests one possibility—the eventual inability to support more people. Since Malthus devoted much attention to the checks to population, and since among these checks he gave prominence to the lack of subsistence, it is natural that we look to him for a possible explanation of what may actually stop the present unequal trend.

We see, then, that there are good reasons for using Malthus as a point of departure in the discussion of population theory. These are the reasons that made his work influential in his day and make it influential now. But they have little to do with whether his views are right or wrong. There are two groups today who need correction: those who praise Malthus because they believe his theories are valid, and those who dispraise him because they believe his views are unimportant. Both, in my opinion, are wrong. Malthus' theories are not now and never were empirically valid, but they nevertheless were theoretically significant and, as a consequence, they hold a secure place in intellectual history. His mistakes are stimulating and relevant to the discussions of our day. His views have continued to be a center of controversy, and that controversy itself is enlightening.

It is precisely the question of logical adequacy and empirical validity that we wish to explore in Malthus' theory. I shall state what seem to be the main elements in a scientific theory and then discuss the Malthusian system in terms of these. In doing this, I shall allude only to the seventh edition of the *Essay*.[1] It has been pointed out by Gonnard that although the *Essay* in its later editions is a long book, the theoretical exposition of the Malthusian system occupies only the first two chapters, or less than 3 per cent of the total work.[2]

The Nature of a Scientific Theory. It may be taken as axiomatic that sheer empirical generalizations, or observed relationships, do not themselves constitute a science. People know that sexual intercourse is necessary for pregnancy, that the menses cease with pregnancy, and that on the average more boys are born than girls. Such knowledge, however, does not constitute science, because it does not embrace in one system the causes and conditions that connect these more readily observed phenomena. We give the name of science only to a body of abstract and logically interrelated principles which have a wide but never a perfect application in actual situations. The most highly developed systems of theory—e.g. atomic theory or Mendelian genetics—are precisely those most remote from immediate experience, but they have the advantage of being verifiable in a wide range of experimentally controlled situations. A science therefore arises only as it develops a systematic body of abstract and empirically tested theory.

But a "theory" embraces several different elements. Because of their importance in appraising Malthusian thought, attention should be called to the following four:

1. A frame of reference.
2. A set of deductive propositions. (These concern the relationships between variables defined in the frame of reference.)
3. A set of empirical propositions verified by disciplined observation.
4. Crude empirical propositions based only on commonsense observation.

The third element must be sharply distinguished from the fourth one, the "rough empirical generalizations" based on immediate experience and commonsense. The observation that the menses cease with pregnancy is inadequate as it stands, because it fails to account for the exceptional cases.

The Malthusian Frame of Reference. The frame of reference is the least understood part of scientific theory. Yet its role is seen when one realizes that, since sensory impressions are infinitely variegated, all human thought involves a *selection*. The mind at any one time can attend only to certain aspects of things. Whereas in everyday life those aspects are selected which seem essential to practical decisions, in science the selection, more explicit and systematic, is for the purpose of extending knowledge. A science can hardly arrive at a system of propositions unless it has clearly stated *what* these propositions are about. That "what" implies that in nature there are causal systems which hang together to a degree and can be profitably studied in abstraction from other systems. Any particular science therefore deals with "a body of phenomena sufficiently extensive, complex and diversified so that the results of their study are significant and not merely truistic, and sufficiently limited and simplified so that the problems involved are manageable and the investigator does not get lost in the maze."[3] Unless relationships within the frame of reference prove verifiable, its elements will be meaningless together and the alleged science will be spurious.

As "the most general framework of categories in terms of which empirical scientific work 'makes sense,' " the frame of reference has certain functions. In the first place, it provides a systematic criterion of relevance. In the second place, by providing a set of interrelated categories in terms of which an empirical system is to be described, it supplies a test of descriptive adequacy. A phenomenon, to be fully described within the system, must have its values specified with reference to a limited number of essential categories. By showing up instances where certain of the specifications are missing, the frame of reference helps us to locate the important gaps in available knowledge.[4]

The frame of reference, of course, does not itself explain anything. It merely provides the categories in terms of which an explanation will be given. It specifies the kinds of constants and variables, but the specific values or quantities of these is a matter of empirical determination. The frame of reference is thus mainly a matter of purposive definition. The definitions must be logically consistent with one another and yet they must, as part of an empirical science, refer to independent aspects of sensory experience.

Returning now to Malthus, we find that he seems at times to be trying unconsciously to work out a conceptual framework. But it is characteristic of him, and of his time, that he confuses the several elements of scientific theory. He is often doing one thing when he thinks he is doing another. To avoid such confusion and to clear up ambiguities, one must disentangle the different elements as far as possible.

The problems Malthus sets for himself are two: (1) What factors determine the rate of increase and hence the level of human numbers? (2) What are the consequences of these factors and of the numbers reached? These questions seem straightforward, but until they are put in terms of a framework they mean little. For instance, what *kinds* of determinants are envisaged, and what kinds of consequences? Malthus states that he is concerned with population in relation to "the progress of mankind towards happiness." This phraseology has a moral sound, suggesting that he may be concerned with what *ought* to be as well as what is. It is the type of problem that soon gets an author entwined in ethical rather than scientific reasoning. In fact, the first major criticism of Malthus' frame of reference is that it mixes moralistic and scientific aims almost inextricably, as closer scrutiny demonstrates.

As the accompanying diagram of his frame of reference shows, Malthus reasons in terms of two classes of phenomena—first, the capacity of human populations to grow; second, the checks which limit this capacity. He is committed to consider in his system anything which falls under these headings. The concepts resemble those in other fields of systematic inquiry, for a "capacity" is clearly a theoretical construct: it does not ever have to be realized perfectly in practice to be related nevertheless to what occurs in the actual world.

Having these two basic categories, we should expect next a sub-classification of all the types of phenomena which may be assumed to bear on them. Thus we should expect a careful definition of what is meant by the capacity for population growth and a set of inferences from this definition as to the factors which, if they were present, would maximize it. We should expect the same to be done with the checks. Malthus does do something like this for the checks, but with respect to the growth capacity he is content to attribute it to an instinct which man shares with the animals. If this instinct alone were operating, without any checks, "the increase of the human species would be evidently much greater than any increase which has been hitherto known." But he does not clarify the concept of instinct; he does not analyze the mechanisms of reproduction; and, as a consequence, he overlooks some implications that bear on the other side of his equation, the checks. The human and animal motivation, on the instinctual level, is primarily for sexual intercourse. Reproduction comes as a mechanical aftermath which, in the case of human beings, can be avoided. By saying that man is "impelled to the increase of his species" by a "powerful instinct," Malthus overlooks an opportunity to clarify his concept of growth capacity in such a way as to draw implications for his conception of the checks.

The checks to population, we are told, may be classified under two headings, the preventive and the positive. The preventive checks, when voluntary, are peculiar to man, for they arise out of his ability to foresee future events and to take measures to change them. From this we would deduce that anything influencing human beings to reduce their fertility below what it would otherwise be (in modern terms, below their fecundity) is a preventive check. The *positive* checks, on the other hand, "include every cause . . . which in any degree contributes to shorten the natural duration of human life."

Although the terms "preventive" and "positive" would not now be used, this clear division between factors affecting fertility and those affecting mortality would form part of a modern demographic frame of reference. Malthus, however, is not content to let well enough alone. Having given us a dichotomous classification of the checks, he immediately gives us a triplicate classification which cuts across this one. He says, "On examining those obstacles to the increase of population which I have classed under the heads of preventive and positive checks, it will appear that they are all re-

Malthus' Frame of Reference

CAPACITY for Population Growth	CHECKS to Population Growth											
	Preventive Checks						Positive Checks					
	Voluntary or Rational Limitations on Births						All Causes of Mortality					
Instinct	MORAL RESTRAINT			VICE			VICE			MISERY		
of	Means of Subsistence			Means of Subsistence			Means of Subsistence			Means of Subsistence		
Reproduction	Land	Arts	Social Organization	Land	Arts	Social Organization	Land	Arts	Social Organization	Land	Arts	Social Organization

solvable into moral restraint, vice, and misery." To a modern ear these terms seem loaded with moralistic connotations. The only reason Malthus introduced them, so far as I can see, is that he wished to bring moral considerations into his conceptual scheme—a view substantiated by the definitions he gives to the terms.

Moral restraint, he tells us, is postponement of marriage accompanied by abstention from irregular gratifications. It is a wholly preventive check. Vice, on the other hand, is both preventive and positive. It is preventive when it includes "promiscuous intercourse, unnatural passions, violations of the marriage bed, and improper arts to conceal the consequences of irregular connections"—anything, that is, which lessens fertility and at the same time is considered immoral. Vice is positive when it includes those causes of mortality "which we obviously bring on ourselves." Finally, misery is wholly in the positive class of checks. It embraces those causes of mortality "which appear to arise unavoidably from the laws of nature," together with certain consequences of vice.

From the standpoint of a scientific frame of reference, the tripartite classification of factors into moral restraint, vice, and misery is a curious one.

What is moral and what is vice varies from one culture to another, since it depends not on the facts but on the values or attitudes that one has. In eighteenth-century India, for example, and among many in that country today, postponement of marriage is not viewed as "moral restraint" but as immoral. Again, misery is a subjective term. Death can arise from a cause that brings no misery at all—e.g. from an overdose of sleeping pills—and a very long life can be achieved by people who suffer great misery. Furthermore, there is no particular logical connection between this subjective classification and the preventive-positive dichotomy. The one cannot be inferred from the other nor systematically related to it. The conclusion is hard to escape that Malthus put this classification on the checks into his scheme because he was confusing moralistic and scientific reasoning. If one is interested solely in the factors governing population growth, the question of whether these factors are moral or immoral, miserable or unmiserable, is extraneous.

The consequences of Malthus' moralistic bent can be seen when we turn to other aspects of his thought—namely, the deductive and inductive propositions about the relations between the various factors. Before doing this, however, I should like to mention one more element in his frame of reference—the means of subsistence.

The place of the means-of-subsistence category in Malthus' scheme cannot be understood apart from his two basic dichotomies, that of reproductive capacity versus the checks on the one hand, and that of preventive versus positive checks on the other. As the diagram previously referred to shows, the means of subsistence is a check, but it is both a preventive and a positive check. Lack of subsistence may cause people to die from starvation or malnutrition, and it (or the fear of it) may cause them to limit births by either moral restraint or vice. In a sense, the means of subsistence is a sort of master-check behind all the other checks. By reason of its importance to him, its ambiguity is unfortunate. At times it seems to refer to the physical requirements for human beings to remain alive. At other times it refers to the assorted requirements for the maintenance of a given standard of living. This ambiguity is, like his moralism, one of the chief weaknesses of his frame of reference.

Subsistence seems to be determined in Malthus' view by three main classes of causes, viz., the supply and quality of land, the industry and social organization of the people, and the state of the arts.

We now have before us the principal categories in the Malthusian frame of reference. They can be seen at a glance in the chart already given. Like most other things in science, a frame of reference must be evaluated mainly in terms of how it works, which cannot be determined until the propositions made within the framework are examined for both logical rigor and empirical truth. Prior to such analysis, however, one can ask whether or not a frame of reference contains clear definitions, offers a convenient and flexible classification of factors, and seems to make provision for all the main determinants within the field. On all of these points Malthus is open to criticism. He seemingly comes out best with respect to completeness, because almost anything having to do with population can somehow be squeezed into his categories; but this is due partially to ambiguity and the stretching of meanings rather than to genuine comprehensiveness. This is especially true with reference to the neglected reproductive side. Perhaps his most ambiguous concept is "means of subsistence," which, as our table shows, is also given such undue prominence that rigidity results. Another source of ambiguity and rigidity is his confusion of two universes of discourse—the moral and the scientific. A frame of reference should be neutral with respect to the quantitative and causal relations of the things it defines and classifies. It should allow for the maximum possibilities in order to offer the investigator who uses it the best chance of describing actual reality. If it biases the possibilities, it operates as a limitation on what the investigator can find and causes him to overlook or misinterpret causal relationships. In our table, the row of categories (moral restraint, vice, and misery) might well be replaced by two rows, one classifying the actual mechanical and physical factors in fertility and mortality—such as contraception, abortion, infanticide, disease, violence, etc.—and the other classifying the moral attitudes, customs, and social institutions affecting these same factors. Far from being Malthus' own moral preconceptions, the latter would be general categories into which the moral preconceptions of *any* population, no matter how bizarre or repugnant to us, could be fitted. In this way the mores of a people would be the *objects,* not the *assumptions,* of study. An act which an observer feels is immoral may have more influence on population than one he feels is moral, but unless he is on his guard he tends unconsciously to reason that since it *should* have less importance it will in fact have less importance. We shall see that Malthus' moral preconceptions, embedded in his frame of reference, were the chief reason why his theory of population failed as a predictive instrument.

Malthusian Theory as a Deductive System. The definitions in a frame of reference, if it is of any use, can be utilized to form propositions which follow from those definitions. Such propositions are of the type, "If *p* then *q.*" Their truth is quite independent of whether or not the premise *p* actually holds in fact or whether *q* ever occurs in nature. Instead, their truth depends entirely on the validity of the logical processes by which *q* is inferred from *p,* and this in the last analysis is a matter of the definition of *q* and *p* and of any conditions, say *M* and *V,* involved in their relationship.[5]

Since the logical interrelations between concepts are all derivable from the definitions of the concepts, it follows that pure theory is always tautalogical. Tautalogical does not, however, mean "self-evident" on first acquaintance. "Because the proposition 2 x 2 = 4 is to most people probably obvious or 'self-evident,' while the proposition 17 x 37 = 629 is probably not, this does not imply that they are of different logical type."[6] Tautalogical or circular reasoning is an essential element in all science because it is an important tool of discovery. As mathematics demonstrates, the logical interrelations between propositions may be anything but self-evident. They often require painstaking work and special symbols to find. When worked out they enable us to establish important and often unsuspected interconnections between empirical propositions. "It is often difficult, if not impossible, to determine the [empirical] truth of a proposition directly, but relatively easy to establish the truth of another proposition from which the one at issue can be derived."[7] Indeed, the most valuable propositions of science are of this indirectly established kind. Without propositions of pure theory we could never get off the ground, so to speak, and thus could never erect a superstructure of science.

In modern demography the relations between mortality, fertility, and the age structure have been worked out mathematically as propositions of pure theory. They hold universally because they are logically deduced from the assumptions. This work has given rise to a number of mathematical and statistical tools of wide applicability in empirical investigations. For example, the concepts of the life table, the gross and net reproduction rates, the stable population and the true rate of natural increase have been deductively elaborated, with the result that modern demography has analytical tools hardly dreamed of in Malthus' day.[8]

One of the chief weaknesses of Malthus is that he did not clearly distinguish between propositions of pure theory and those of empirical reference. Not only did he jump at once into deductive propositions without much logical analysis behind him, but he sometimes assumed these to be descriptive of nature itself. For instance, he has three propositions that are worth careful scrutiny from this standpoint: (1) Man's capacity to reproduce is greater than his capacity to increase the means of subsistence. (2) The ultimate check to population lies in the food supply. (3) The preventive and positive checks vary inversely. At times these propositions are announced as if they were axioms, at other times they are construed as describing a readily observable state of affairs. Their exact logical status is thus hard to specify, and this difficulty is made worse by the fact that they are stated differently in different contexts. In the present section, however, we shall treat them as deductive propositions.

(1) Although Malthus tries to give empirical proof of the first proposition, to the effect that the reproductive capacity is greater than the subsistence capacity, he is actually talking about a relationship between two *capacities* neither of which has ever expressed itself fully in practice. He admits, on the one hand, that "in no state that we have yet known has the power of population been left to exert itself with perfect freedom"; and, on the other, that after tens of thousands of years of existence on the earth, there are still broad areas, like the United States, where subsistence is highly abundant. In other words, the proposition is purely theoretical; it says nothing about any actual state of affairs. Yet, if he offers no empirical proof of it (as we shall see more clearly in a moment), he offers no logical proof of it either. Its role in his system is therefore that of an axiom.

(2) The second proposition, to the effect that the ultimate check lies in the food supply, is a corollary of the first if by "subsistence" (in the first proposition) he means simply food. We have already seen that he is ambiguous on this point; but skipping that, we find him saying that *if* population increases continually, as it has the capacity to do *when unchecked,* and *if* the food supply is limited by the finite extent of the world's land, then, theoretically, the *ultimate* check will be lack of subsistence. Independently of the empirical situation, this proposition is logically questionable in terms of his frame of reference. Reference to our table of categories will show that between the means-of-subsistence row and the preventive-and-positive row he has inserted the categories of moral restraint, vice, and misery. Although these categories suffer the difficulties previously mentioned, they nevertheless show that there is nothing in the frame of reference to prevent the deduction that moral restraint and vice, or birth control and disease, are the ultimate checks on population. In other words, he has in his frame of reference elements which do not force one logically to accept the assump-

tion that the capacity to reproduce will be realized except in so far as it is limited by the food supply. He is of course operating in the belief that moral restraint, vice, and misery are activated "ultimately" or "primarily" by the lack of food, but this is a gratuitous assumption within the system and is therefore at best axiomatic.

(3) The third proposition stating an inverse correlation between the preventive and positive checks can be derived by deduction from the first one. If the capacity to reproduce is greater than the capacity to produce subsistence, then obviously either reproduction must be lowered or else the checks due to lack of subsistence will operate. Malthus has, however, treated even the preventive checks as due to lack of subsistence. The preventive and positive checks are therefore simply two ways in which the scarcity of food manifests itself. Since they are the only two ways, and since, according to the second proposition, the food supply is the ultimate limit, necessarily if one way is not effective the other must compensate for it. The third proposition is thus seen to stem from the second one more directly than from the first, although the ambiguity of "subsistence" makes it impossible to follow the line of reasoning with perfect confidence.

The belief that the want of food is the ultimate check contains an ambiguity beyond that found in "subsistence." Malthus says:

"The ultimate check to population appears then to be a want of food, arising necessarily from the different ratios according to which population and food increase. But this ultimate check is never the immediate check, except in cases of actual famine."

But what does "ultimate" mean? Does it mean later in time? Evidently no. It appears to mean that the want of food is the independent variable, all other checks being dependent on it. Any other check is therefore like the pressure of air when a door is closed: one may feel the pressure without being touched by the door. To derive the primacy of the food supply from the finite character of the world's land is not conclusive, because other things may equally be assumed to be finite—such as the lack of living space apart from subsistence, resources for other wants than the need for food, and the ability of men to get along peacefully with one another. There is no logical ground why one or several of these should not be the ultimate limit. One could say, "Suppose the means of subsistence to be completely adequate, then men would *ultimately* either die of disease and warfare until population growth ceased or, because they could not have the things they want by virtue of decreasing resources other than those connected with food, they would limit their fertility until growth ceased."

It thus appears that Malthus did not state his deductive propositions with a sufficient degree of generality. Given the two assumptions—the infinite capacity to reproduce and the finite character of the world—population growth will be checked, but the specific way in which it will be checked is an empirical question. Deductively, it may be checked by other elements in Malthus' own framework than the want of food—that is by *any kind of scarcity* which weakens either the ability to keep alive or the desire and ability to reproduce. That most goods are scarce relative to the needs and desires of men can hardly be denied, because a "good" is such in view of its difficulty of attainment. Thus scarcity of almost any kind, depending on conditions, may, in the terms of Malthus' frame of reference, affect the growth of population. The scarcity of money for education may lead people to want fewer children. The scarcity of doctors may cause disease to be more rife than otherwise. The scarcity of employment may cause postponement of marriage or use of contraception. There is no a priori ground for saying that because food is a necessary condition of existence, its scarcity is the "ultimate" check to population.

Empirical Propositions and Crude Generalizations. By definition, any proposition is a statement which is either true or false. But the method of demonstrating truth and falsity differs as between deductive and inductive propositions. A deductive proposition can be shown to be logically valid or invalid, regardless of whether its premises hold in fact. An inductive proposition, on the other hand, states that such and such is true in fact and therefore has to run the gamut of empirical test.

The ideal test of an empirical proposition is an experiment, for in the experiment all variables except those explicitly involved in the proposition are ruled out. Unfortunately, common language does not differentiate between the two kinds of propositions. The expression, "if *p,* then *q,*" means either kind; but in a deductive sense it means that *q* can be logically inferred from *p,* whereas in an inductive sense it means that *p* is invariably connected with *q.*[9] Now we know in actual fact that very seldom is any one thing *invariably* connected with something else. What we really find is that a thing is usually or often connected with something else. This is because in nature any one relationship is affected by many different kinds of variables. Ordinary observation does not allow us to eliminate all the variables that are of no concern to us. Laboratory experiment is the nearest approximation to such control, but even there we must talk of probabilities rather than certainties. In the less controlled situations in which even scientific observations must usually take place, we have to be content with rather crude generalizations. It is the constant aim of science, however, to refine these generalizations by getting increased experimental, statistical, and logical control of the factors involved. As long as our generalizations remain at a crude level, an exception does not necessarily disprove them. But the exception does force us to look more closely at the factors we may not have controlled, and thus plays a role in the refinement of knowledge. Furthermore, crude generalizations can be related to a general system of theory by speculation, even though they cannot be related to it by precise verification. Crude propositions are therefore not to be dismissed lightly, although no science can be composed exclusively of them. A science generally begins with a body of unrealistic and perhaps metaphysical theory on the one side and a set of crude generalizations on the other. It progresses by refining both sides and bringing them into integral connection, for both sides are necessary.

Malthus failed to support his empirical propositions with experimental evidence not only because good statistics were lacking but also because his theoretical structure was not rigorous enough to make genuine testing possible. His *Essay* is replete with anecdotal examples which neither verify nor disprove his ideas. Nevertheless, his crude generalizations are worthy of careful attention.

Since he did not always distinguish between a proposition of pure theory and one of empirical reference, we are forced to discuss again some of the same ideas already mentioned. He tried to offer factual proof, for instance, that population tends to grow faster than subsistence, that population is limited by the food supply, that the preventive and positive checks vary inversely. In addition, he seemed to believe that the postponement of marriage is the only preventive check of any great importance. These ideas are so central to his system that they have been called "assumptions," and so they are; but they are assumptions that he believed to be factually true.

With respect to the capacity for population growth, the evidence of America is given. Because of abundant subsistence in a rich new territory with few people, the population, we are told, goes on doubling itself every 25 years. A population therefore has the capacity to grow at least this fast and possibly faster. On the subsistence side, evidence is more difficult to find. It is admitted that some improvement can be made, but in general, as common experience will show, a rapid increase in crops is out of the question, especially since the supply of land is limited anyway. This argument is interesting because, clearly, "subsistence" is being used in the narrow sense of agricultural products and because, equally clearly, hypothetical reasoning is being confused with actual evidence. The argument says, in effect, that a population can double every 25 years, because there are actual cases on record; but that subsistence cannot increase that fast because there are no cases on record. Such reasoning is patently absurd. Since, as Malthus himself states, a population is limited by its food supply, it cannot increase faster than its necessary food increases. Therefore, if in the United States the population has been doubling every 25 years, and if, as he says, the standard of living has not declined, then it must inevitably be that the means of subsistence have been doubling every 25 years too. The evidence for the one is just as good as the evidence for the other.[10] The defenders of Malthus will say he meant that ultimately, or in the long run, the means of subsistence cannot increase that fast. Perhaps he did, but an empirical argument cannot rest on "ultimately" or on an indeterminate "long-run." Malthus measures the capacity of a population to grow by certain facts; he is bound to measure the capacity of subsistence to grow by the same facts. He has actually compared two non-comparable things—a demonstrated capacity with a theoretical incapacity. Instead, the comparison should be either in empirical or in theoretical terms. In theoretical terms there is good ground for saying that neither population nor subsistence can continue to increase forever, but that the "capacity" of either, granted the most favorable conditions in everything else, is one of extremely rapid increase. Moreover, as Malthus acknowledges repeatedly, the product from the land is a function not of land alone but of the arts applied to it. There is no ascertainable limit on what science and technology can do. The imaginative critic of Malthus is quick to point out that, given a sufficient development of technology, contact can be established with the planets and other heavenly bodies—and these, for all we know, are infinite in number. Such thoughts, however, have nothing to do with empirical knowledge, which is our concern at the moment.

That Malthus does regard his axiom as factually true is shown by the footnote at the end of Chapter II:

"I believe that there are some instances where population does not keep up to the level of the means of subsistence. But these are extreme cases; and, generally speaking, it might be said that, Population **always** increases where the means of subsistence increase."

Yet his own evidence does not support him. At times he interprets "means of subsistence" as the actual food on hand,[11] but admits at other times that population growth is checked *before* it reaches the limit of food. "A man who is locked in a room," he says, "may fairly be said to be confined by the walls of it, though he may never touch them."[12] One intervening variable is the standard of living. Obviously people do not use all their resources merely for food, because they have other desires, for comforts, luxuries, etc. Furthermore, Malthus admits that the standard of living is indefinitely expandible. In fact, in his last chapter he recommends that a taste for luxuries be spread among the general population, because then people will postpone marriage in order to enjoy these luxuries and there will be less population pressure.[13] He also acknowledges that men postpone marriage because of the effect of a large family on their rank in society and on their children's rank. It is, as he realizes, the better-circumstances class which limits its fertility—i.e., the class which has the most means of subsistence and is therefore farthest from absolute want. In view of these admissions, "the constant tendency in all animated life to increase beyond the nourishment prepared for it" does not necessarily apply to man. It is merely a deduction which would be true *if* certain other checks to population were not present; but in fact these checks are always present. Malthus therefore is suffering from the ambiguity of failing to distinguish between a purely theoretical and an empirical proposition. It is impossible to determine what he "really meant to say," because, as a result of this basic confusion, he did not have any more clarity in his intentions than in his expressed ideas.

When Malthus states that "population is necessarily limited by the means of subsistence," he is on perfectly safe ground, because the statement is true by definition. "Subsistence" is defined as that which is necessary for life to be maintained. But it does not follow from this truism that "population always increases where the means of subsistence increase." Warmth is necessary for comfort, but comfort does not always increase when heat increases. We must conclude, then, that such a proposition is true only under certain conditions and that the attempt to treat it as true regardless of the conditions is a mistake. One may turn the matter around and ask why the means of subsistence (i.e., food) should increase beyond the needs of a population? This happens only as a result of a mistaken view of the market demand on the part of producers or as a result of the ceremonial and other non-organic use of food. We should not therefore expect the food supply to outrun the population, although it should not be deduced from this fact that the population is always as big as the *potential* food supply.

If Malthus had given more weight to the other variables in his frame of reference, treating them as parts of an equilibrium, instead of trying to view means of subsistence as a single determinant of everything else, he would have been on better empirical ground. Today, for example, a densely settled peasant-agricultural country finds it difficult to industrialize because its surplus population is a drain on its agricultural economy and this, in turn, makes capital accumulation and the build-up of heavy industry very difficult. The density itself inhibits the technological and social changes that would make a greater density possible. This is true in India, China, and

Egypt, and demonstrates that the means of subsistence is itself dependent on both population and technology.[14]

Although he admitted the existence of other checks than lack of subsistence, Malthus always came back to the food supply as the "ultimate" limit. His ambiguity, already mentioned, allowed him illegitimately to squeeze by criticisms of his theory. If a critic pointed out that population was actually checked by people's desire to live well and to have their children live well, he would reply that this was really due to a lack of subsistence, because, though they were not actually hungry or anywhere near it, they nevertheless *feared* hunger and thus postponed marriage. It is thus impossible to disprove Malthus' principle by an appeal to the facts, because he switches the meaning of his "principle" as forensic necessity requires. Yet the structure of his whole argument is weakened by this procedure. It is now well known, even if it was not then, that many places are scarcely populated, not because food is scarce but because disease is rampant—e.g., tsetse-fly areas of Africa ravaged by sleeping sickness and parts of India ravaged by malaria. In turn, many regions are sparsely populated because the people deliberately limit their marital fertility—e.g., Australia and New Zealand—and in these cases it is fantastic to twist words so as to maintain that they do so because they fear a want of food. The effort to prove that lack of subsistence is nearly always a major check is consequently a principal source of empirical distortion in Malthusianism, justly criticised by contemporary and later critics.

Even when food is a factor limiting population increase, one must inquire into the factors lying behind its scarcity. It may be want of land, want of technology, or want of trade. The Indians of North America had just as much land as the subsequent European colonists—indeed, it was the same land; and yet the production of food was enormously greater after the colonists came. Empirically speaking, then, we find that want of technology is, if anything, a more important limitation on population than want of land. The emphasis on lack of food led Malthus to underrate the importance of technological developments already started in his day and to ignore the possibility of a rapid population growth *with* a concomitant rise in the level of living, a trend that has actually occurred.

Malthus believed that the positive checks were more powerful than the preventive, and that, among the preventive checks, only the postponement of marriage was of practical significance. The reader will recall that he defined postponement of marriage as "moral restraint" and all other preventive checks as "vice." He then unconsciously made the assumption, very common in human reasoning, that what one feels is ethically bad cannot be empirically predominant. Postponement of marriage thereby became for him the only check which could lower fertility enough to escape the direct pressure of lack of subsistence.

Since in his view the "sex instinct" was so powerful and premarital virtue so prevalent that most classes could not long postpone marriage, he did not think that even this acceptable preventive check could be very effective in ameliorating population pressure. He thus did not predict the sharp and unprecedented drop in the birth rate of industrial peoples which began about 50 years after his death. Had his theory been less moralistic, he might have predicted this occurrence. He could have kept his assumption of a strong sex drive, his assumption of a high reproductive capacity, and yet predicted a declining fertility based on scientific contraception *within* wedlock and arising from the same incentives which he mentions for postponing marriage.[15] Obviously, the same motives for restricting offspring will be more effective if the means is simply a device to prevent conception than if it is the inconvenience and pain of long years of celibate continence. But this he could not see.[16]

Thus one of Malthus' great empirical mistakes is traceable to a weakness of his conceptual framework, the confusion of moral evaluation with scientific analysis. As a result of it, he did not recognize the seeds of a new epoch in the facts around him. His was not a scientifically adequate theory for his own time.

7. PSYCHO-CULTURAL HYPOTHESES
ABOUT POLITICAL ACTS

by Nathan Leites

DURING RECENT YEARS there has been a noticeable rise in the production of, and interest in, a relatively new kind of analysis of political behavior. Anthropologists had become increasingly concerned with describing and explaining the entire way of life of the non-literate societies they were studying. Some of them came to believe that cultural anthropology should return to home, *i.e.,* that the methods of observation and recording, and also the theories which they had developed on so-called primitive material should be applied to our own society and other large and complex groups. At the same time, psychologists and psychiatrists had become increasingly interested in describing and explaining the entire way of life, subjective and behavioral, of the individuals they were studying. They tended to be particularly interested, on the one hand, in the broad varieties of human nature ("character types" and "defense mechanisms") and, on the other, in the unique structure of each case. But some of them came to be interested in ascertaining the psychological regularities, if any, in large groups. The confluence of these two developments in the human sciences led to the emergence of what we may call psycho-cultural analyses of social events.[1]

As in many other instances of intellectual change, this development provoked both intensely friendly and hostile reactions. While those involved in the discussion tended to be either "for" or "against" the kind of analysis in question, there was often insufficient clarity and agreement about what the specific points of contention were. In view of this situation, I propose to examine with some explicitness a number of the general aspects of the psycho-cultural analysis of political acts. I shall do so by recalling particular representative statements without trying to be systematic or exhaustive.

One set of relevant propositions are concerned with how culturally typical political acts are related to the past life experiences of those who perform them. They thus correspond, in the formulation of Heinz Hartmann and Ernst Kris, to the "genetic propositions" in psychoanalysis which indicate "how any condition . . . has grown out of an individual's past."[2] One major general hypothesis in this area runs as follows: if children adopt a certain reaction in certain emotionally important—usually, but not always, familial

Reprinted from *World Politics*, Vol. I, 1948, pp. 102-119, by permission of the author and the publisher. (Copyright, 1948, by the Princeton University Press.)

—situations, they are later on apt to adopt a similar reaction in structurally analogous political situations.[3]

According to Clyde and Florence Kluckhohn,[4] there is a relationship between the American orientation on "effort and optimism"—presumably an important one in American political behavior—and the following fact: the mother in America offers her love to the child on condition of his fulfilling certain performance standards which the child has a good chance of reaching.[5] According to Ruth Benedict "the will to achieve . . . has little place with Rumanians" whose view of the universe attributes a dominant role to "luck." These adult feelings and behaviors—of obvious political relevance —are related to the fact "that the Rumanian child did not have to earn as a youngest child his mother's unconditional pleasure in him; with the birth of a next child it was . . . lost . . .; his mother punished him according to her own mood of the moment. Rewards, either from the mother or from other persons, were not given for specific approved acts or for achievements . . . even to 'think' praise was supposed to cast the evil eye. The child did not know what he could do to earn approval."[6]

Statements of this kind raise many questions, such as the following:

(1) If one wants to be very "precise," it is necessary to indicate more specifically under what conditions we will choose to say that the "will to achieve" (or the "orientation on effort") have "little" or "much" place in the life of an individual and of a culture. In both cases we are presumably dealing with continua: the intra-individual continuum ranging from "no" to "total" orientation on effort; the inter-individual continuum ranging from the complete absence of "highly" effort-oriented individuals in a culture to a situation in which all members of a culture are so oriented. When we speak of "high" ("low") in either case, we introduce "arbitrary" cuts in these continua. That is, we decide to say that a society is "highly" effort-oriented if more than a specified number of its members (we may add, members in such and such positions of influence) are "highly" effort-oriented; and we may decide to say that an individual is "highly" effort-oriented if more than a specified number of his acts of certain emotional weight are undertaken with some sense of strain and are intended to produce ulterior results. This, of course, leads to further definitions of "act," "emotional weight," "sense of strain," "intended" (consciously and/or unconsciously?), and so forth. All these definitional operations are required if and only if one wants to make the proposition involved capable of full empirical proof or disproof. The "practical" difficulties one encounters are not different from those one meets in making any proposition "operational" which refers at least in part to "subjective" events.

(2) Suppose we had evolved all the definitions which may be required— i.e., suppose we had translated our hypothesis from "theoretical" into "empirical" language—we would then come up against the next obstacle: the appropriate observations have been not at all or only insufficiently made and recorded. The "translation" I spoke of would furnish a statement of the required evidence. Its very statement would make it plain that the available evidence falls far short of it.[7]

In the current discussion of the kind of statements I am concerned with in this paper one can frequently discern an objection against the utterance (particularly in printed form) of statements for which only quite insufficient evidence is available in proper records. (I am talking here not about the researcher's degee of subjective certainty about how the records would look if they existed, but only about whether they exist.) The answer to the question—which statements should or should not be "admitted" as members of the class of "scientific" statements?—is presumably a decision rather than a factual (true or false) statement. This decision need not be the same in the following two cases.

(a) statements for which available evidence is low, and which are presented without an explicit indication of this;

(b) similar statements which do explicitly indicate the gap between required and available evidence.

Presumably many human scientists object to (a) without objecting (with the same intensity) to (b). Many object to the kind of hypotheses dealt with in this paper because they regard them as falling within class (a). Do we really know scientifically that the Rumanian degree of effort-orientation is significantly lower than the American one?[8]

In part, a failure of communication seems to occur here. My guess is that most of the statements involved are meant by those who advance them as statements of class (b). Possibly those who propose them are rather sure about the outcome of an adequate collection of comparative data concerning Rumanian and American effort-orientation (and may therefore not want to spend too much time on collecting them). But they agree, I think, that, while their points are based on already collected data, sufficient data have not yet been collected. In other words, they advance their statements as hypotheses, often with a high expectation-of-full-verification feeling about them. It may be that the expressions of this feeling prevent many critics from perceiving that everybody agrees on the lack of full evidence.

Both critics and advocates of current psycho-cultural hypotheses about social behavior might, I propose, accept the current usefulness of publicly communicating "mere" hypotheses. Such a communication may foster their fuller disproval, or proof, and promote the invention of other hypotheses, with similar consequences. We are at present still hampered by a lack of explanatory hypotheses about social behavior.

(3) Suppose the difficulties mentioned under (2) had also been resolved: *i.e.*, suppose we had fully established the asserted Rumanian-American differences in (a) child-training patterns (b) adult behaviors. What about the relationship between them? The transition from "correlation" to "causation"[9] implies a "universal proposition" of the logical form "if a, then b." What is the particular universal proposition implied in our instances? In the present style of psycho-cultural analysis this premise is often not stated explicitly —another instance of the elliptic mode of expression already discussed under (2). It is some such sentence as this (I am simplifying it for the purposes of this discussion): if a child is rewarded for efforts undertaken he is (*caeteris paribus*) more likely to show high effort-orientation as an adult than if he is not so rewarded. (This would be a member of the class of statements affirming the transfer of patterns of feeling and behavior "learned" in early intimate relations to adult social relations.)

Hence, the degree of confirmation of a "psycho-cultural" statement such as the one I choose as an example will depend in part on the degree of confirmation of the implied universal proposition. This will usually be one from "dynamic psychology." Frequently, of course, this premise itself is not yet fully proved. However, here again explicitness about what the premises are and what their present scientific status is would fulfill one version of the requirements of "science." In addition the present status and rate of progress of dynamic psychology are viewed by a number of specialists in a rather favorable light.

According to Geoffrey Gorer[10] and Ruth Benedict[11] Japanese adults issue complicated and heavily sanctioned prescriptions to the child as to how and where he may or may not move around the house (in American terms, they behave as if most of the house were composed of radiators and as if they were set upon punishing the child for having touched hot radiators). This childhood experience has, it is asserted, an adult sequel which has been of considerable military significance in the late war: Japanese are much disoriented if they find themselves without preparation in an unknown environment; hence the intense striving to "learn" new environments one goes into. Available Rorschach performances indicate that "unforeseen situations, which cannot be handled by rote, are frightening."[12]

A statement of this kind raises the three issues already discussed with the aid of our previous example, and others (which were equally present though not discussed) such as these:

(4) It is not implied that the peculiar Japanese treatment of early locomotion is the sole cause of adult Japanese preferences for situations believed to be thoroughly known.[13] Other childhood experiences—such as certain aspects of sphincter training—probably contribute to the same adult trait.

The type of communication failure mentioned under (2) operates here too. Critics of a particular psycho-cultural hypothesis frequently assume that the condition-factor focussed upon is asserted to be the *sole* cause of the phenomenon. Usually this will not have been meant by the researcher who put the hypothesis forward, though he may not have stated this qualification explicitly. It is a frequent fallacy in the human sciences to believe that, if somebody at a certain moment talks about the importance of factor A, he is running down the importance of factors B, C. . . .[14]

(5) It is not implied that only intimate ("psychological") childhood events determine adult behavior to the exclusion of various wider ("economic," "political," "social," etc.) aspects of the adult environment. On the contrary, the presumption is that any adult act is related to (a) the predisposition of the individual—which in its turn is connected with his previous experiences from birth (at least) to the present moment; (b) the (human and non-human) environment which contains "stimuli" evoking the act involved.[15]

One may expect an adult's reaction to any given social environment to vary with his predisposition. The close and comparative examination of any given act-in-situation will show that other persons (groups) have responded differently to a similar situation, revealing another of the many potentialities of "human nature." The differences in response can often be related to differences in predisposition rather than to nuances in the current environments which almost always leaves "choices" open. If two culturally contrasting groups are faced with overwhelming odds, one may tend recurrently to submit, the other to fight it out. We may find a link between such propensities and the ways in which parents expected their children to behave in fights with other children.

While predispositions are "important," it is equally true that we may expect the reactions of a number of adults with similar predispositions to vary according to the situations in which they find themselves. Thus, it is entirely compatible with the hypothesis stated above to assume that adult Japanese preferences for known routines are (also) related to the tradition and presence of a socio-political order rewarding (on the whole) compliance with very specific and differentiated rules applying to one's status.

(6) While psycho-cultural analysis of adult political behavior thus does not imply that "childhood" is "all-important," it does—as already conveyed by the examples quoted—affirm that it is "important." In doing so, it can —apart from the specific evidence of an increasing number of particular propositions—refer to the following general points:[16]

(a) Acts called political begin to occur (in Western culture at least) late in childhood or even later.

(b) It is a fundamental truism much confirmed by 20th century research that act patterns arising as "late" as that in life are very apt to be noticeably influenced by what happened earlier. Thus, the intimate (and to the adult often "trivial") experiences of the child with the few persons who begin his socialization are apt to influence (mostly unconsciously) the adult when he is concerned with local, regional, national, and world politics.

(7) While patterns of child training are regarded as important in the explanation of political behavior, it is not implied that these patterns in their turn are uninfluenced by such behavior.[17] On the contrary, it is assumed that the behavior of adults towards children is influenced not only by the adults' childhood[18] but also by their current life experiences; and these include politics, or politically determined events (in our culture, increasingly so). Thus the stimulation of competition among siblings by parents may derive in part from the competitive acts of the parents outside the family. In the previously mentioned instance, Japanese parents may model their imposition of rules within the home on their own subjection to political rules outside the home. Also, while Japanese parents "exaggerate the dangers of the house [*i.e.*, the danger of the child's spontaneous movements damaging the house], it is true that Japanese houses are so constructed that "when children can walk they can do a lot of mischief."[19]

It is common knowledge that in recent Anglo-American inter-personal relations on various civilian and military levels Americans not infrequently exhibited a type of behavior which Britons called "boasting," while Britons frequently impressed Americans as being "arrogant." Many political scientists with appropriate experiences in the late war would probable agree that this was a politically relevant situation. According to Gregory Bateson[20] and Margaret Mead[21] this is related to certain differences in childhood experiences in the two cultures: "In Britain . . . Father . . . exhibits to his children: he is the model for their future behavior. Father does the talking . . . before a very quiet and submissive audience, in accordance with the . . . ethical disapproval of overuse of strength. He underplays his strength, understates his position, speaks with a slight appearance of hesitation in his manner, but with the cool assurance of one who knows. . . . At the American breakfast table, it is not Father but Junior who talks, exhibits his successes and skills, and demands parental spectatorship and applause with an insistence that can be clamoring and assertive because . . . he is speaking from weakness to strength." In adulthood "an American spoke . . . as he had learned to speak when he was small . . . a Briton spoke . . . as he had heard his father and other elders speak . . ."[22]

This statement raises the issues (1) through (7) discussed above, and also some others (equally applicable to our previous examples):

(8) It is not implied that all Britons (Americans) exhibit adult understatement (overstatement) to the same high, or to any high, degree at all periods. Nor is it implied that all Americans (Britons) have been equally vocal (silent) at their early breakfast tables (which stand, of course, in Bateson-Mead's language for a large number of childhood situations). It is implied that these are "typical" patterns; the existence of "idiosyncrasies" is not denied, nor their possibly vast consequences.[23] We are confronted here with one of those statements which may need greater precision in the fashion discussed under (1). I shall not repeat that discussion, but only add some specific points.

(a) When current psycho-cultural hypotheses imply (or state explicitly) that a certain act is "typical" in a certain culture at a certain time, they do not imply (nor do they deny) that this act is equally typical at other times. Psycho-cultural analysis does not "deny history." On the contrary, it is particularly apt to take account of history as it focusses on the causal role of life experiences rather than of hereditary endowment.[24] Presumably Junior talks more and louder at breakfast tables today in this country than, say, three generations ago. Psycho-cultural analysis is interested in whether this is so, why, and what of it.

(b) When it is asserted that a certain behavior is "typical" in a given culture at a given time, it is not implied that it is equally frequent and emphasized in all sub-groups of this culture. (I am not interested in making the definition of "culture" more precise at this point.[25] I am using the term in a sense which allows us to talk about "American culture," "British culture," "French culture," "Great Russian culture.") It is entirely compatible with psycho-cultural analysis to assume considerable differences, in child training patterns and adult experiences, between various "social classes," regions, ideological groups, or any number of other sets of persons who are all members of a given culture.[26] As the pertinent data are at present largely uncollected (cf. [2] above), it is impossible to say how large these intracultural differences are in any given case; presumably cultures vary widely in their degree of internal homogeneity. Some researchers have been impressed by the plausibility of the guess that the various Western national cultures have a higher degree of internal homogeneity than was assumed in previous decades under the influence, e.g., of Marxist hypotheses. Sometimes these researchers have been misunderstood to imply that such an assumption—it is no more than that at the present moment—is, as it were, an axiom of psycho-cultural analysis. It is, of course, just a special (though a major) hypothesis to be "processed" like any other hypothesis. It is in this fashion that one might interpret a point of Ruth Benedict's.[27] One's property, she suggests, is felt as very close to the core of one's self in Dutch culture, "whether the individual belongs to court circles or can only say in

the words of a proverbial expression: 'If it's only a penny a year, lay it by.' "
On the other hand, one's property is felt as remote from the core of the
self in Rumanian culture: "An upper class person may be . . . a pensioner
of a wealthy man without loss of status or self-confidence; his property, he
says, is not 'himself.' And the poor peasant argues that, being poor, it is
futile for him to lay anything by . . ."[28]

(c) When it is asserted that certain behaviors are "typical" in a certain
culture, it is not denied that certain subgroups of this culture may show
substantial similarities with corresponding subgroups in other cultures. One
may choose to use the term "national character" to refer to similarities between members of a sub-group of Western culture called a nation. One may
also use the term "class character" to refer to similarities between members
of a subgroup of Western culture called a class. Thus certain aspects of the
life of a *petit bourgeois* in Tours may be referred to in a "national (French)
character" proposition; and others (or sometimes the same?) in a "class
(lower middle) character" proposition. The question has often been asked:
do people have more in common with other members of their nation or with
the members of some trans-national group, e.g., class? To this one may
reply that (1) "more in common" has not yet been well defined, operationally; (2) the pertinent data have not been collected; (3) if they were,
the answer would presumably be different in different cases; (4) this question does not seem urgent if we want to decide on the next steps in research.

(d) When it is asserted that a certain behavior is "typical" in a certain
culture, it is not implied that there is no other culture in which it is, at the
same or some other time, equally "typical." What has hitherto turned out
to be rather unique is the syndrome of each culture (the ensemble of its
regularities), but not each element of this syndrome. The conscious aver-
sion against hitting the fellow who has already fallen down may be typical
in both British and American culture; but it is in each of these cultures
related to other distinctive reactions towards violence.

As stated above, the propositions hitherto examined were largely concerned with the continuation of certain childhood patterns in adult political
activities. There are of course many other and more complex interrelations
between early private life and later public life. I shall mention some, with
the aim of illustrating current work rather than of being systematic and
complete.[29] Take the following two points.

According to Geoffrey Gorer, in contemporary America "custom and
votes, other things being equal, go to the man who most adequately demonstrates friendly interest." He relates this to the fact that Americans are "insatiable" in their demands for "the signs of friendship, of love." This in turn
is related to the fact that "any occasion on which they are withheld raises the
. . . doubt that maybe one is not loveable."[30] And this doubt goes back to
the "conditional" character of parental love already mentioned above.

As to destructiveness,[31] according to Geoffrey Gorer,[32] Burmese admire
intensely "successful daring and ingenuity" in exploits of violence (p. 61);
the dacoit (outlaw) who specializes in such acts is highly esteemed. The
aims for which violence is being used are less stressed: "the Burmese dacoit
is to be admired for his violence as such"; various violent Burmese movements had "no program" (p. 43); "two Burmese policemen . . . quarrelled
about the merits of two . . . *danseuses* . . . the crowd, relishing the absurdity

of the thing, backed up the quarrel with such energy . . . that . . . a ward in the infirmary was filled."[33] Further, "the use of violence for long-term ends (such as railroad sabotage to produce a bottleneck twelve months hence) would probably seem nonsensical and repulsive to the Burmese" (p. 60). Violence tends to be accompanied by looting. There is a tendency to use violence also in situations "with no hopes of success." Violence tends to be set off with little premeditation: ". . . accidentally, usually in a crowd, a spark will set off a fight which will sweep like a forest fire through the people present" (p. 41); ". . . folk tales and plays are full of situations in which a character feels a sudden desire to commit some unlawful act . . . and immediately proceeds to commit the act" (p. 38); Burmese quite consciously entertain "the belief that temptation is irresistible" (p. 38). There is a pattern of "running amok." "Drunken Burmese are said to become aggressive" (p. 52). In addition, "Burmese violence is easier to start than stop" (p. 60). As a counterpart to these traits "there are practically no professional criminals" (p. 39). In the case of adult outbursts of criminality "no explanation is apparently given or required" (p. 38).

This adult handling of violence is related to various experiences of the Burmese child. "The preponderant relationship in childhood is between the boy and his mother" (p. 31). There is evidence for "the Burmese woman's unwillingness to bear children" (p. 29). "The nursing situation is unemotional . . . the mother talking or transacting her other business while the infant suckles" (p. 29). During the first years of life the Burmese mother, "firm and business-like" (p. 33), gives her child "good-humored, cool, rather impersonal efficient succorance" (p. 32). "Most of the time baby does not get much attention . . . most of the time he will be left alone . . . near to mother" (p. 32). After a long nursing period, the child is weaned, usually at the birth of the next sibling: "The child is apparently just pushed away, perhaps with some verbal admonitions . . . A period of crying and babyish behavior is expected from the weaned baby . . . nothing is done about this; the child is just left to recover" (p. 30). Similarly, as to the frequent temper tantrums of the male child, set off by maternal refusal to accede to the boy's demands: "The mother does nothing in the face of these temper tantrums, waiting for the child to recover its equanimity without action or consoling word . . . the boy will be allowed to kick and scream until he exhausts himself" (p. 32). However, "there are no situations in which it is permissible to answer back at or interrupt . . . [the] parents, much less show any overt aggression" (p. 34).

While, thus, the Burmese mother usually exhibits little affection towards her young child, she will sometimes become "intensely . . . affectionate, playing with the child, tickling it . . . nuzzling it . . . Very often in these bursts of loving the mother will massage the baby all over with oil . . . even playing with the baby's genitals" (p. 32). At other times "she will tease the child . . . 'making him cry and lose control' " (p. 32). The mother acts as her "whim" suggests it. Transitions between these various rather contrasting behaviors are apt to be sudden and quick; the length of each spell short, irregular, unpredictable.

What are the relationships between these various aspects of Burmese child training and the adult Burmese handling of violence? They are probably manifold and require for their elucidation—in the fashion discussed under (3)—a number of special propositions of dynamic psychology. Space, and the purpose of this paper, preclude a full statement of this matter.

First, the previously illustrated pattern of continuing early reactions is present here too: some aspects of Burmese adult violence may be continuations of early temper tantrum behavior. As temper tantrums made no impression on mother, adult tantrums may be gone through "with no hopes of success."

Second, another type of relationship involved here is as follows: adults are apt to react in wider relations in ways in which adults had acted towards them when they were children, in intimate relations. The Burmese mother does not explain the deprivations she inflicts on her child. The Burmese man does not explain acts of violence.

Third, the following relation seems to be involved: adult (political) behavior may in part act out infantile strivings which had been interfered with, or not sufficiently gratified.

The insatiable love demand of the American child may thus be striving for satisfaction when it is desired that "the smallest purchase should be accompanied by a smile . . . [and that] the weightiest business or political conference . . . [should] start with those greetings and anecdotes which demonstrate that the conferers like one another."[34]

The Burmese mother[35] presumably arouses intense rage towards her in her child in a variety of ways. She also promotes intense repression, by the child, of his own rage by her impassivity (invulnerability) and by prohibiting overt aggression against herself (both of these behaviors also contribute to the intensity of the child's rage). At the same time her erratic and (to the child) unloving behavior hampers the development of strong powers of reason and conscience in the child. (The "weak" role of the Burmese father in the family works in the same direction.) Hence, the Burmese adult is able to go through with acts of destructiveness not so much when reason and conscience can be brought to approve them as when these restraints can be put out of action: in a crowd, in a fugue state, under alcohol. The connection between the seizure of somebody else's property (in kleptomania or looting) and rage about unsatisfied early love-demands is well established. The "close shave" reduces anxiety about retaliation (I made it) and alleviates guilt (I exposed myself).

A fourth type of relationship can be illustrated by the following point. According to Erik Homburger Erikson[36] one of the major aspects of the image of Hitler in Nazi Germany was that of "an adolescent who never gave in." This is related to idiosyncratic aspects of Hitler's life and fantasy; and to typical aspects of life and fantasy in German middle class youth in the first half of the 20th century.

In *Mein Kampf*, "Hitler spends a considerable and heated portion of his first chapter in the description of how 'no power on earth could make an official' out of him . . . This was his father's greatest wish . . ." (p. 477). He did not become a *Beamter*.

In his *Sturm und Drang* phase "the German boy would rather have died than be made aware of the fact that . . . [his rebellion] would . . . lead to exhaustion. The identification with the father which had been . . . established in childhood would come to the fore. In intricate ways *Fate* would

. . . make a *Buerger* out of the boy—a 'mere citizen' with an eternally bad conscience . . ." (p. 480).

This represents a type of proposition related to that discussed just before: somebody else's (here a leader's) adult political behavior may in part act out strivings of the self which had been interfered with, or not sufficiently gratified; and this may foster positive reactions towards that other person.

To state a fifth type of relationship, Rudolph M. Loewenstein's discussion of anti-semitism[37] suggests the following sequence (in the terminology of psychoanalysis): the power-relations between the diaspora Jews and their human environment may have reinforced those aspects of Jewish child-training which in their turn induced a Jewish "compulsive character . . . based on . . . the repression of aggressive impulses" (p. 345). The "contemporary German compulsive character . . . based on 'sphincter morals' [*i.e.,* the repression of 'anal' rather than 'sadistic' strivings]" (p. 345) used the Jews as targets for the re-projection, and subsequent destruction, of its superego: "Jews have represented for the Nazis . . . those who repress aggression and, like Christ, suffer for the faults of others. They are the incarnation of the tendency of their own superego to repress aggression" (p. 346).

This represents a type of proposition related to that discussed just before. In contrast to the preceding proposition it is concerned with intercultural rather than intracultural relations; and with the basis of negative rather than positive interpersonal reactions.

The propositions discussed hitherto were all, as indicated above, concerned with relationships between the present and an ostensibly remote and irrelevant past. Besides such "genetic" statements there are "dynamic" ones which, in the words of Heinz Hartmann and Ernst Kris[38] "are concerned with the interaction . . . of forces within the individual and with their reaction to the external world, at any given time or during brief time spans" (p. 11).

Thus, Geoffrey Gorer[39] and Ruth Benedict[40] recall the polarized reactions, in pre-occupation Japan, towards the Emperor (against whom no negative reactions were expressed) and other members of the political elite (against whom such reactions were easily, frequently and intensely expressed). They also recall the Japanese propensity to consider as hostile towards the Emperor behaviors which were ostensibly either slips (*e.g.,* in the ceremonial readings of Imperial rescripts) or unrelated to the Emperor (*e.g.,* a railway man temporarily and without consequences misplaces a signal while the Imperial train is somewhere within the wider area). As to polarized reactions to the political elite apart from the Emperor, these authors mention the coexistence of "fanatic discipline" and gross insubordination towards military authorities.

This entire pattern of submission-revolt is related to the presence of intense, and intensely warded off, hostilities towards authority figures, dealt with by the mechanisms (among others) known in the language of psychoanalysis as reaction-formation (going to the opposite of an objectionable striving) and decomposition of ambivalence (splitting up the mixed feelings towards a given object between at least two).

A special set of "dynamic" propositions in psycho-cultural analysis indicates those interrelations between culturally typical acts which are in themselves culturally typical. An instance of this was the proposition just mentioned that the Japanese "choice" between available "psychological mechanisms" prefers (though, of course, not exclusively) reaction formation and decomposition of ambivalence.

Another instance would be the previously implied proposition that the Japanese "choice" between available life aspects stresses the continuum submission-revolt (Japanese acts cluster towards both ends of this continuum).[41]

Available "genetic" propositions in psycho-cultural analysis—which formed the bulk of the examples in this paper—almost always deal with the conditions of one or a few culturally typical acts. Similarly, available "dynamic" propositions deal with the interrelations within a very limited set of acts which is usually much smaller than the list of variables we are interested in. (While we may have some hypotheses about the interrelations between Japanese reactions to the Emperor and to the "rascals around the throne," we may not have any hypotheses about the interrelations between these reactions and those, say, of an employer towards his employees.) The advance of psycho-cultural research may furnish more genetic explanations of more complicated dynamically explained syndromes.

Auxiliary Readings

A. THE LOCATION OF PROBLEMS

E. Hilgard, *Theories of Learning* (Ginn & Co., 1942), pp. 11-23

The author develops a set of six topics to which a complete theory of learning addresses itself. He then reviews the ideas of a number of writers to show which of these topics they single out for discussion and what their specific positions are.

R. M. MacIver, "Modes of the Question Why," *Social Causation* (New York: Ginn & Co., 1942), Chapter I, Section II.

Authors who try to explain something can interpret their task in six different ways: they can look for invariant laws, for organic functions, for motives, for regularities as a result of many interactions, for logical necessities, and for norms. These six modes are clearly distinguished; they are used subsequently to locate a large number of empirical studies.

P. F. Lazarsfeld, "Remarks on Administrative and Critical Communications Research," *Studies in Philosophy and Social Science,* Vol. XI, 1941, pp. 2-16.

Studies of the effects of mass media are quite different according to whether the interest focuses on intended "campaign effects" or unintended social consequences. Most academic research is concerned with the former. Certain formal aspects of the latter are brought out by using as examples various essays on mass media written by Horkheimer and his associates.

B. THE CLARIFICATION OF MEANING

H. A. Simon, "Comments on the Theory of Organizations," *The American Political Science Review,* Vol. XLVI, No. 4, 1952.

Distinguishes between groups, organizations, and institutions. The paper shows how these terms so frequently used by social scientists are best circumscribed by comparing them to each other. The notion of level of analysis plays a role here.

H. Blumer, "What Is Wrong with Social Theory?" *American Sociological Review,* Vol. 19, 1954, pp. 3-10.

The argument is made that many concepts in social research have mainly the purpose of sensitizing the reader to observations which he would otherwise miss.

G. Allport, "Attitudes," in *Handbook of Social Psychology,* C. A. Murchison, ed. (Worcester: Clark University Press, 1935), and C. Kluckhohn, "Values," in *Toward a General Theory of Action,* T. Parsons and E. A. Shils, eds. (Cambridge: Harvard University Press, 1951), Part IV, Chapter II.

These two papers, published fifteen years apart, deal with very much the same material and have very much the same organization. They both give the history of the major concept and its relation to related concepts like motives, opinions, etc. The student will do well to read the two papers concurrently, focusing on the point where they both compare attitudes and values.

T. Abel, "The Operation Called *Verstehen,*" *American Journal of Sociology,* Vol. 54, 1948-49, pp. 211-218.

The meaning of a much misused term is analyzed in the light of concrete research procedures.

C. THE STRUCTURE OF ARGUMENTS

R. K. Merton, "Manifest and Latent Functions," *Social Theory and Social Structure* (Glencoe, Ill.: The Free Press, 1949), pp. 21-81.

The most systematic attempt at codification of functional analysis in sociology. Includes a discussion of vocabularies of functional analysis, prevailing postulates, and logic of procedures, seeking to make explicit certain underlying assumptions. Attention is directed particularly toward the paradigm for functional analysis on pages 50-54 which presents, in compact form, the central concepts and problems in this area of concern.

E. Kris, "The Nature of Psychoanalytic Propositions and Their Validation," *Freedom and Experience,* S. Hook and M. Konvitz, etd. (Ithaca: Cornell Univ. Press, 1947), pp. 239-259.

A discussion of the possibility of validating psychoanalytic propositions by such methods as: predicting future behavior, predicting a reaction by presenting a stimulus ("interpretation"), "predicting the past," i.e., an interpretation of past behavior awaiting subsequent verification, and experimental procedures in the laboratory. It is pointed out that some psychoanalytic propositions are not subject to verification, and some attention is given to falsification of propositions.

D. THE NATURE OF EVIDENCE

G. Lindzey, "Thematic Apperception Test: Interpretive Assumptions and Related Empirical Evidence," *Psychological Bulletin,* Vol. 49, No. 1, 1952, pp. 1-21.

Projective tests assume that the motives of respondents are revealed in the way they interpret unstructured material. This paper analyzes the implications which must be accepted if projective tests are to be used as evidence of underlying motives. It is probably the most sophisticated analysis of this kind, but could not be included in the Reader because space prohibited inclusion of all the bibliographical material which is woven into it.

S. E. Morison, "Were the Settlers of Massachusetts Bay Puritans?" *The Builders of the Bay Colony* (Boston & New York: Houghton-Mifflin Co., 1930), Appendix 2, pp. 339-344.

The controversies and available evidence regarding the question of whether the Pilgrims came for religious or economic motives are reviewed. The author refers facetiously to the idea that one might have used questionnaires for the sake of the future historian. His own analysis, however, shows how good an idea that would have been.

R. Bower, "Opinion Research and Historical Interpretation of Elections," *Public Opinion Quarterly,* Vol. 12, 1948, pp. 455-464.

In writings on American history, the outcome of elections is often explained with great confidence. On the other hand, since we now have more detailed statistical data on elections, the difficulty of really proving these interpretations has become more and more evident. Specific examples are cited and discussed.

Notes

[*The footnotes which follow are reproduced in the identical form in which they appeared in the original articles; the variations in form are due to the different styles of journals and authors.*

*We wish to explain the format employed in the main body of the text. In order to save space, the following basic principle was adopted: In those articles containing only major headings, the headings were presented as italicized side run-ins. Where two levels of heading appeared, the major headings were presented in centered small capitals and the minor headings in italicized side run-ins. At some points, however, this procedure was modified slightly in order to make the material more readable.—*ED. NOTE.]

SECTION I

Concepts and Indices

1. TYPES OF INTEGRATION
AND THEIR MEASUREMENT
by Werner S. Landecker

1. The writer is indebted to Professor Robert C. Angell for helpful suggestions.

2. For a detailed analysis of the concept "cultural integration" in a broader sense see John P. Gillin, *The Ways of Man* (New York: Appleton-Century-Crofts, Inc., 1948), chap. xxiv; see also David F. Aberle, "Shared Values in Complex Societies," *American Sociological Review*, XV (1950), 495 ff.

3. Ralph Linton, *The Study of Man* (New York: D. Appleton-Century Co., 1936), p. 282.

4. Emile Durkheim, *The Elementary Forms of the Religious Life* (London: George Allen & Unwin, 1926), p. 12.

5. Research in the study of conflict among norms which apply to the same social role and which apply to persons who combine several roles with one another provides a fruitful point of departure for the mechanics of index construction (see Samuel A. Stouffer, "An Analysis of Conflicting Social Norms," *American Sociological Review*, XIV [1949], 707 ff.; and Mirra Komarovsky, "Cultural Contradictions and Sex Roles," *American Journal of Sociology*, LII [1946], 184 ff.; see also Paul Wallin, "Cultural Contradictions and Sex Roles: A Repeat Study," *American Sociological Review*, XV [1950], 288 ff.).

6. Robert C. Angell, *The Integration of American Society* (New York: McGraw-Hill Book Co., 1941), p. 22. For a similar view see Talcott Parsons, *Essays in Sociological Theory, Pure and Applied* (Glencoe, Ill.: Free Press, 1949), p. 50.

7. Robert C. Angell, "The Social Integration of Selected American Cities," *American Journal of Sociology*, XLVII (1941-42), 575 ff.; "The Social Integration of American Cities of More than 100,000 Population," *American Sociological Review*, XII (1947), 335 ff.

8. Emile Durkheim, *Le Suicide* (Paris: Felix Alcan, 1897).

9. Charles H. Cooley, *Human Nature and the Social Order* (rev. ed.; New York: Charles Scribner's Sons, 1922), pp. 256-60.

10. Norman Cameron, "The Paranoid Pseudo-community," *American Journal of Sociology*, XLIX (1943), 32 ff.

11. Theodore M. Newcomb, "Autistic Hostility and Social Reality," *Human Relations*, I, No. 1 (1947), 69 ff.; see also H. Warren Dunham, "Social Psychiatry," *American Sociological Review*, XIII (1948), 183 ff.

12. Olen Leonard and C. P. Loomis, *The Culture of a Contemporary Rural Community: El Cerrito, New Mexico* ("Rural Life Studies," No. 1 [Washington: U. S. Department of Agriculture, Bureau of Agricultural Economics, November, 1941]), pp. 38-48.

13. Frank L. Sweetzer, Jr., "A New Emphasis for Neighborhood Research," *American Sociological Review*, VII (1942), 525 ff.

14. F. Stuart Chapin, "Social Participation

and Social Intelligence," *American Socio-logical Review*, IV (1939), 157 ff.

15. See Stuart A. Queen, "Social Partici-pation in Relation to Social Disorganization," *American Sociological Review*, XIV (1949), 251 ff.

16. *Op. cit.*

17. "Sociometry of Morale," *American Sociological Review*, IV (1939), 799 ff.

18. *Op. cit.*

19. *Ibid.* and the evidence reviewed there.

20. See Amos H. Hawley, "Dispersion vs. Segregation: Apropos of a Solution of Race Problems," *Papers of the Michigan Academy of Science, Arts, and Letters*, XXX (1944), 667 ff. Hawley stresses the influence of spa-tial segregation on the inferior status of minorities.

21. Julius Jahn, Calvin F. Schmid, and Clarence Schrag, "The Measurement of Eco-logical Segregation," *American Sociological Review*, XII (1947), 293 ff.; and Richard A. Hornseth, "'A Note on 'The Measurement of Ecological Segregation' by Julius Jahn, Calvin F. Schmid, and Clarence Schrag," *American Sociological Review*, XII (1947), 603 ff.

22. For a survey see Robin M. Williams, Jr., *The Reduction of Intergroup Tensions: A Survey of Research on Problems of Ethnic, Racial, and Religious Group Relations* (So-cial Science Research Council Bull. No. 57 [New York: Social Science Research Coun-cil, 1947], pp. 112 ff.

23. Hawley's term is "ecological organiza-tion" (See Amos H. Hawley, *Human Ecol-ogy* [New York: Ronald Press Co., 1950], chap. x).

24. R. D. McKenzie, *Readings in Human Ecology* (rev. ed., Ann Arbor, Mich.: George Wahr, 1934), p. 333.

25. Don J. Bogue, *The Structure of the Metropolitan Community: A Study in Domi-nance and Subdominance* ("Contributions of the Institute for Human Adjustment, Social Science Research Project" [Ann Arbor: Uni-versity of Michigan, 1949]).

26. Emile Durkheim, *The Division of La-bor in Society*, trans. George Simpson (New York: Macmillan, 1933), pp. 148 ff.

2. THE RATIONALE OF THE

CURRENT LABOR FORCE MEASUREMENT

by A. J. Jaffe and Charles D. Stewart

1. See Bruce Waybur and Russ Nixon, "A Report on the National Unemployment Es-timates of the Bureau of the Census as Pub-lished in the Monthly Report on the Labor Force." See also Russ Nixon, "Correction of Census Bureau Estimates of Unemploy-ment," *Review of Economics and Statistics*, XXXII, 1, Feb. 1950.

2. See Charles D. Stewart, "The Definition of Unemployment," *Review of Economics and Statistics*, XXXII, 1, Feb. 1950.

3. The employed category includes all per-sons in the civilian, noninstitutional population 14 years of age and over who during the specified week are reported as: (1) *at work* on a private or government job, including the self-employed and unpaid family workers, and (2) *with a job but not at work* because of vacation, illness, attending to personal af-fairs, labor dispute, bad weather, or tempor-ary layoffs with definite instructions to re-

turn to work within 30 days, or definite ar-rangements made to go to work at some future date—the so-called "inactive employed." See also footnote 7 in this chapter.

4. It should be noted that the value of home-produced foodstuffs consumed by the farm household is included in income data on an imputed basis. A market economy is an implicit assumption: Such foodstuffs would otherwise be obtained through the market. Thus the residual subsistence strata in the economy are brought within national income accounting, and so in fact are workers who may be subsistence farmers. But this is pos-sible, or rational, only where the market dominates the economic structure.

5. See footnote 3.

6. An illustration of this is the highly criti-cal report, referred to in footnote 1, pub-lished by the United Electrical, Radio, and Machine Workers of America (CIO), which presents a substantially different current un-employment series based upon recombina-tion and "adjustments" of the official census series.

7. Note that "seeking work" takes priority in classification over "with a job but not at work." Hence persons reporting that they are looking for work will be classified as *unem-ployed* if, although they have a job to which they can return, they are not at work during the enumeration week. On the other hand, a person at work is classified as *employed* even if seeking another job.

8. Labor input in a national product con-text has not been seriously urged as an exclu-sive basis for defining employment in the United States, although there are suggestions that seem to imply this. Considerable effort has been made in census enumeration in re-cent years to improve the *at work* series as a measure of labor input. The effect of this, largely, has been to increase the number of persons who are discovered to be contrib-uting to the national product. The more in-tensive probing of respondents to obtain more complete enumeration of persons at work has generally involved individuals whose ma-jor activity is other than work (e.g., students or homemakers) rather than persons actively seeking work.

9. How a worker laid off because of a strike elsewhere than at his own place of employment is classified depends upon the definiteness of his instruction to return to work, if any, or upon his own reaction to the situation—i.e., whether he actively seeks other employment.

10. A temporary layoff is defined as one where the employer has given an employee a definite instruction to return to work with-in a period no longer than 30 days from day of layoff. If no specific instruction is given, even though the layoff may be expected to be relatively short, or if the specified period is more than 30 days, the layoff is regarded as an indefinite one, and the respondent is automatically classified as *unemployed.*

11. This may be the result of lack of ef-fective demand in an economic sense or lack of effective organization of the labor market in an institutional sense—i.e., there may be a job available in which he has not been placed.

12. A person on temporary layoff who is reported as seeking work is, of course, clas-sified as unemployed. The census questions are asked in such a fashion, if carefully fol-lowed by enumerators, to afford a reasonable

possibility that respondents will report looking for work.

13. It may be noted that estimates of the number of persons counted as employed but on temporary layoff are published monthly and thus are available for analysis. In May 1950 the number was given as 110,000.

14. This type of criticism generally takes the form that, if prospective job takers are to be counted as employed, their counterparts —all persons who are to be laid off—ought to be counted currently as unemployed. If this is not simply *reductio ad absurdum*, the principal grounds for the position is that, once the time reference for the balancing of job applicants and job openings is allowed to become somewhat indefinite—that is, other than the current week—it is no longer possible to adhere rigidly to the current week time reference generally.

15. Bruce Waybur and Russ Nixon, *op. cit.*, p. 3.

16. "Unemployed persons include those who did not work at all during the survey week and were looking for work. Also included as unemployed are persons who would have been looking for work except that (*a*) they were temporarily ill, (*b*) they expected to return to a job from which they had been laid off for an indefinite period, or (*c*) they believed no work was available in their line of work or in the community."

17. One of the important criticisms of the current labor force statistics in the United States is that a dearth of jobs at prevailing wage rates has the effect (in part) of reducing the numbers in the potential labor supply who report themselves as job seekers. The reverse effect is also much commented upon: When the primary wage earner is unemployed in a depression period, the unemployed total may be swollen by secondary family workers. These two statements are not necessarily inconsistent; those who despair of finding jobs, such as the aged, may withdraw from the labor force, while others who are more hopeful of obtaining employment, such as younger persons, may enter the labor force.

18. Unemployment compensation claimants exceeded total unemployment as reported by the Monthly Report on the Labor Force for thirteen months, despite the fact that unemployment compensation covers only part of American industry. Special tests verified the explanation given in the text above.

19. The present schedule is not so well designed as the schedule before July 1945 to probe for these groups. In the schedule questions in effect before July 1945, a specific question was asked as to reason for not looking, the purpose of which was to probe directly to discover these groups of the inactive unemployed. The present schedule, which probes more closely to discover employment status than the old schedule, is admittedly less effective on this point. On the present schedule, the information is elicited (if at all) in response to the direct question whether the individual was looking for work.

20. Thus they are distinguished from potential workers who are not looking for work because (all things considered) they do not choose to do so. Whether the current labor force statistics are deficient because, in this respect, inclusion in the labor force rests on subjective decisions rather than considerations of economic need, etc., has been referred to above.

3. OBJECTIVE INDICATORS

OF SUBJECTIVE VARIABLES

by Stuart A. Rice

1. This is alleged to have been common among recruits who took the army alpha psychological tests by several of the number to whom I have talked. In class-room experiments I have found it a possible source of error against which it was necessary to guard.

2. George E. G. Catlin, *The Science and Method of Politics* (New York: Alfred A. Knopf, 1927).

3. *Columbia University Studies in History, Economics and Public Law,* Whole Number 253, New York, 1924. The material which follows is taken from pp. 174-177, with the permission of the editors of the Studies.

4. According to campaign literature of the last-named organization. A leading Democratic Party politician in Nebraska has recently described the alignment to me as having been almost wholly spontaneous in character.

5. All election figures in this chapter are taken from the *Nebraska Blue Book*, 1922.

6. Conservatives and progressives may both have split their votes, but in equal numbers so that they balance.

4. A REVIEW OF INDICATORS

USED IN "THE AMERICAN SOLDIER"

by Patricia L. Kendall

1. This difference is too large to be accounted for by the educational superiority of the selectees, even though there are educational differences in the preferences expressed.

2. From the point of view of survey techniques this finding is an important one. It indicates that, contrary to the expectations of many critics of public opinion research, respondents do not answer all questions simply by projecting their own attitudes or opinions. If this were the case, if the answers merely reflected the soldiers' own feelings about promotion and status, there would be no such difference in the proportions agreeing with the statements.

5. THE CONCEPT OF PROPERTY-SPACE

IN SOCIAL RESEARCH

by Allen H. Barton

1. This has special characteristics which are used in latent-structure analysis, but this will not be discussed here. A dichotomous system is also equivalent to a binary number system, or an "off/on" system of information, as used in computing machines and in communication theory.

2. Many concrete examples can be found in Ch. VI in Hans Zeisel, *Say It With Figures* (New York: Harper, 1947).

3. Glencoe, Illinois: The Free Press, 1951.

4. The use of this typology is discussed in Robert K. Merton, "Patterns of Influence: A Study of Interpersonal Influence and of Communication Behavior in a Local Community," in Paul F. Lazarsfeld and Frank N. Stanton (ed.), *Communications Research*

1948-1949 (New York: Harper, 1949).

5. Kingsley Davis, *Human Society* (New York: Macmillan, 1949), Chapter III.

6. Discussed in Paul F. Lazarsfeld, "Some Remarks on the Typological Procedure in Social Research," *Zeitschrift für Sozialforschung*, Vol. VI, 1937.

7. Actually each of these threefold classifications was based on a reduction of a fourfold table produced by two dichotomous questions. This example is discussed in greater detail in Paul F. Lazarsfeld and Allen H. Barton, "Qualitative Measurement in the Social Sciences," in D. Lerner and H. Lasswell, *The Policy Sciences* (Stanford: Stanford University Press, 1951).

6. A MULTI-DIMENSIONAL CLASSIFICATION

OF ATROCITY STORIES

by Philip E. Jacob

1. Harold Lasswell, *Propaganda Technique in the World War*, p. 205.

7. THE COMPUTATION OF INDEXES

OF MORAL INTEGRATION

by Robert C. Angell

[1. See the author's "The Social Integration of Selected American Cities," *American Journal of Sociology*, Vol. XLVII, Jan. 1942, pp. 575-592; "The Social Integration of American Cities of More Than 100,000 Population," *American Sociological Review*, Vol. 12, 1947, pp. 335-342; and "Moral Integration and Interpersonal Integration in American Cities," *American Sociological Review*, Vol. 14, 1949, pp. 245-251.]

9. A COMPARISON OF THREE MEASURES

OF SOCIOECONOMIC STATUS

by George A. Lundberg and Pearl Friedman

1. F. S. Chapin, *The Measurement of Social Status* (University of Minnesota Press, 1933). Reprinted with revisions, 1936.

2. L. Guttman, "A Revision of Chapin's Social Status Scale," *American Sociological Review*, VII (1942), 362-369.

3. W. H. Sewell, *The Construction and Standardization of a Scale for the Measurement of the Socio-Economic Status of Oklahoma Farm Families*. Oklahoma Agricultural and Mechanical College, Technical Bulletin No. 9 (Stillwater, Oklahoma, 1940). See also W. H. Sewell, "The Development of a Sociometric Scale," *Sociometry*, V (1942), 279-297.

4. Manning's *Bennington, Shaftsbury and Arlington Directory* (Volume 28, H. A. Manning & Company, March, 1942).

5. L. Guttman, *op. cit.*, p. 366.

6. The average scores of farm and village homes on the two scales in our sample were as follows:

TABLE V—Chapin and Sewell Averages
for Farm and for Village
Homes

	CHAPIN		SEWELL	
	Farm	Village	Farm	Village
	N =	N =	N =	N =
	126	105	126	105
Mean	101	112	180	190
Median	96	111	181	191
Mode	74	106	174	189

The mean score for village homes on both scales is about 10 points higher than for farm homes. The distributions are not otherwise significantly different.

7. *The Logic of Modern Physics* (Macmillan, 1932), p. 30.

10. THE INTERCHANGEABILITY OF

SOCIO-ECONOMIC INDICES

by Hortense Horwitz and Elias Smith

1. P. F. Lazarsfeld, "Interchangeability of Indices in the Measurement of Economic Influences," *Journal of Applied Psychology*, 23, 1939, 33-45.

2. This question was found to have been asked in both Survey No. 112 and Survey No. 120, and is therefore counted as two of the three highest ranking questions. Both times, then, this question turned out to be sensitive to social stratification.

11. A BASELINE FOR MEASUREMENT

OF PERCENTAGE CHANGE

by Carl I. Hovland, Arthur A. Lumsdaine

and Fred D. Sheffield

1. The above formula applies for responses that are increased by the film. If the film decreases a particular response and it is desired to express this negative effect, the analagous formula is $\frac{P_2 - P_1}{P_1}$. This will give an effect with a negative sign and which measures the decrease as the proportion of maximum decrease possible.

12. SOME GENERAL PRINCIPLES OF

QUESTIONNAIRE CLASSIFICATION

by Paul F. Lazarsfeld and Allen H. Barton

1. For a discussion of general versus concrete categories in content analysis, see Bernard Berelson, *Content Analysis in Communication Research* (1952).

2. Samuel A. Stouffer, *et al.*, *The American Soldier* (*Studies in Social Psychology in World War II*, Vols. I and II [1949]).

3. *Ibid.*, II, 107. The chapter from which this and the following list were drawn was written by Robin M. Williams, Jr., and M. Brewster Smith.

4. *Ibid.*, p. 77.

5. *Ibid.* This list is adapted from p. 107.

6. *Ibid.*, pp. 112-18.

7. This list is adapted from chapter i, "How to Tabulate Reasons."

8. Unpublished research on "Psychological and Sociological Implications of Economic Planning," carried out by the Sociological Institute, University of Oslo, under the direction of Allen H. Barton.

9. This example and the following are taken from F. J. Roethlisberger and W. J. Dickson, *Management and the Worker: An Account of a Research Program Conducted by the Western Electric Company, Hawthorne Works, Chicago* (1939), pp. 248-68.

13. THE EFFECT OF MILITARY RANK ON

VARIOUS TYPES OF ATTITUDES

by Hans Speier

1. See my review of Mannheim's *Ideology and Utopia* in *The American Journal of Sociology*, July 1937, pp. 155-166 and "The Social Determination of Ideas," in *Social Research*, May 1938, pp. 182-205.

2. Table I has been computed from a large number of surveys undertaken by the Research Branch and reported in *The American Soldier*. Each item refers to a particular percentage between the opinions of officers and men in checking a specific response to a question. Only one of various possible responses was selected for inclusion in Table I. For example, in the case of items No. 1-5, the question asked by the Research Branch was worded, "In your opinion what should be done with men who crack up in action, that is, men who get shell-shocked, blow their tops, go haywire?" The Research Branch reported the percentage distribution of four responses, namely, "Most of them" (1) "should be treated as sick men," (2) "should be treated as cowards and punished," (3) "should be treated some other way," and (4) "no answer." The opinions of officers and enlisted men of five separate divisions can be compared for each of the four responses. In the table only the percentages of officers and men giving the first response have been included. Answers in response to other multiple choices have been reported in a similarly selective way. This procedure appears justified, since we are not interested in the distribution of different possible responses to the same question, but in the frequency differences of the same response as given by officers and enlisted men, i.e., the two groups whose "perspectivism" we want to examine. Moreover, in a few cases, for example item No. 46, the Research Branch itself gives the figures for only one of the possible answers.

In Items No. 10 and and 11, two answers reported by the Research Branch have been combined into one ("all" agree and "most" agree). The wording of the question is not always reproduced verbatim but can be checked at the page referred to in column 2 of Table I.

The differences between the percentages of responses given by enlisted men and officers are reported as *absolute* and *relative* differences. In item No. 2, 67 per cent of the officers and 72 per cent of the men checked the answer "should be treated as sick men"; the absolute difference is therefore +5, the ratio being 1.2. The ratio has been computed in *all* cases by putting the larger percentage in the denominator regardless of whether the percentage of officers or that of enlisted men was larger. Otherwise the average for each class of opinions would not reflect the average *size* of the difference. Absolute differences are listed with a minus sign, however, whenever the percentage of enlisted men was smaller than that of officers. Thus the *direction* of each individual difference can be examined in the Table. In computing the average absolute differences for each class of opinions, all differences have again been treated as positive values.

SECTION II

Multivariate Analysis

2. OPINION FORMATION IN A

CRISIS SITUATION

by S. M. Lipset

1. On the background and history of the controversy, see George R. Stewart, *The Year of the Oath*, New York: Doubleday, 1950.

2. This study was originally undertaken as a class project in a course in research methods. The number of students who contributed to it are too numerous to be mentioned here. I would, however, like to express my thanks to them. Mr. Morgan Yamanaka, who served as the assistant in this course, aided greatly in both the collection of data and the analysis. Funds for analysis were obtained from the University of California, Institute of Social Sciences.

3. The six questions were agree-disagree statements concerning the Taft-Hartley Law, socialized medicine, government breakup of large corporations, government ownership of public utilities, belief that most strikes are unnecessary, and belief that the British Labor Government deserved to be reelected. A conservative answer was given a score of 2, a liberal answer 0, and don't know a score of 1. A perfect conservative score, therefore, would be 12, while an extreme liberal score would be 0.

4. Lazarsfeld, Paul F. and Robert K. Merton, "Mass Communication, Popular Taste and Organized Social Action" *Communication of Ideas*, Lyman Bryson, ed., New York: 1948, pp. 95-118.

5. Adorno, T. W., *et al.*, *The Authoritarian Personality*, New York: Harper, 1950, p. 216.

6. Father's occupation, as such, did not differentiate opinions on the issues. The children of professionals and of farmers were most conservative, although it is hard to see why they should have been more conservative than the children of business proprietors or executives. The lack of consistent differences related to father's occupation does not necessarily mean that socio-economic status was unrelated to these issues, since the occupational categories which were employed did not actually differentiate between high and low non-working class status.

7. This hypothesis is similar to that advanced by Theodore Newcomb in his study of the political attitudes and behaviors of "upper-class" girls at Bennington College.

Newcomb found that students integrated into the campus community tended to adopt the attitudes of the faculty, while those who retained strong home ties, or were unintegrated for other reasons tended to retain the conservative attitudes of their families. See Newcomb's discussion in terms of reference group concepts in Muzafer Sherif, *An Outline of Social Psychology* (New York: Harper, 1948), pp. 139-155.

8. The same pattern appears in response to the question, "How many unions in the United States do you think are controlled by the Communist Party?" Less than a third of the pro-oath group, as compared with half the anti-oath group, believed that less than ten of the roughly 150 national unions are controlled by the Communist Party. The pro-oath group believed many unions were controlled by Communists.

9. Krech, David and Richard S. Crutchfield, *Theory and Problems of Social Psychology,* New York: McGraw-Hill, 1948, p. 190; emphasis theirs.

10. *Ibid.*, p. 188.

11. See Daniel M. Wilner and Franklin Fearing, "The Structure of Opinion: A 'Loyalty Oath' Poll," *The Public Opinion Quarterly,* Vol. 15, No. 4 (Winter, 1950-51), for report on student opinion at U.C.L.A.

3. WHO WERE THE MOST CRITICAL OF THE

ARMY'S PROMOTION OPPORTUNITIES?

by Samuel A. Stouffer

and Leland C. DeVinney

1. Table of Organization. This specified the number of grades authorized for the organization.

2. In view of the possibility that some of the apparent difference between the less educated and better educated conceivably could be attributable to an artifact—namely, a slightly greater tendency of the less educated than the better educated to check the first and extreme category in a list of responses-- it is worth noting that when comparisons are made in Chart II after combining the responses of "very good chance" and "fairly good chance," the conclusion is essentially unaltered. The less educated still were more favorable than the better educated in 18 out of 24 comparisons, with 6 reversals. Because of the extremely skewed nature of the overall distribution of responses, 80 per cent of the entire sample checking either "very good" or "fairly good," comparisons on the basis of the "very good" category alone are preferable, as long as the educational response bias is not more serious. An educational response bias would not likely apply, of course, to other comparisons, for example between rank groups, as education is at least broadly controlled in these comparisons.

3. Assuming, as a null hypothesis, that a positive difference was equally as likely as a negative difference and calling ties failures, the likelihood of getting 12 or more successes by chance, in 16 comparisons, would be less than .04. The likelihood of getting 13 or more successes would be .01 (using the point binomial distribution).

4. Based on the proportions answering "very satisfied" to the question on job satisfaction. If the "satisfied" are added to the "very satisfied," Air Forces exceed Ground Forces in 15 out of 16 comparisons, Air Forces exceed Service Forces in 14 out of 16, and Service Forces exceed Ground Forces in 14 out of 16. There were no ties.

5. Again based on those answering "very satisfied." If the "satisfied" are added, the men of higher rank are more likely to express satisfaction in 28 out of 30 comparisons.

4. THE INTERPLAY OF DEMOGRAPHIC AND

PSYCHOLOGICAL VARIABLES IN THE

ANALYSIS OF VOTING SURVEYS

by Edward A. Suchman and Herbert Menzel

1 See Bernard Berelson, *et al, Voting: A Study of Opinion Formation in a Presidential Campaign.* (Chicago: University of Chicago Press, 1954.)

2. Or have led in the past. See item 7 below.

3. However, these are not necessarily the only two processes at work. E.g., the patronage system may be of such a nature that strictly economic or power reasons make it hard for many people to break with a political machine once they have thrown their lot in with it.

4. However, there is evidence in the Elmira study suggesting that the perpetuating power of these social and psychological processes is gradually slipping as time goes on. The evidence is only suggestive, because it is based on a comparison of the present votes of old and young individuals, rather than on a comparison of past and present votes. The association of Catholicism with Democratic vote and of Protestantism with Republican vote is considerably stronger among old than among young voters; this finding parallels the historical trend toward less influence of religious denomination upon vote, which might be explained by the upward social mobility of Catholics, referred to above.

But when attention is focused specifically on those to whom the "relevant factors" apply least—middle-class Catholics and working class Protestants — we find an even stronger drop in the association between religion and vote. This suggests that the motivated conformity and the screening of communications through the selective social environment are becoming less powerful within these religious groups. The younger people are more likely to vote with the class pressure:

PER CENT REPUBLICAN OF TWO-PARTY INTENTIONS IN AUGUST

	BUSINESS & WHITE COLLAR		UNIONIZED WORKERS	
	Young	*Old*	*Young*	*Old*
Catholics	42	28	30	31
Protestants	77	77	51	64

6. FAITH IN PEOPLE AND

SUCCESS-ORIENTATION

by Morris Rosenberg

1. Robert S. and Helen M. Lynd, *Middletown in Transition* (New York: Harcourt, Brace and Co., 1937), p. 404.
2. *Ibid.*, p. 406.
3. Robert K. Merton, "Social Structure and Anomie," in *Social Theory and Social Structure* (Glencoe, Ill.: The Free Press, 1949), p. 132.
4. Robin M. Williams, Jr., *American Society* (New York: A. A. Knopf, 1951), p. 390.
5. John F. Cuber and Robert A. Harper, *Problems of American Society: Values in Conflict* (New York: Holt, 1948), pp. 356-358.
6. Gunnar Myrdal, *An American Dilemma* (New York: Harpers, 1944), p. 210.
7. Erich Fromm, *Escape from Freedom* (New York: Rinehart, 1941), Ch. VII, part 2, *passim*.
8. Karen Horney, *The Neurotic Personality of Our Time* (New York: Norton, 1937), Ch. 15.
9. Margaret Mead, *And Keep Your Powder Dry* (New York: Morrow, 1943), *passim*.
10. Karen Horney, *Our Inner Conflicts* (New York: Norton, 1945), Ch. 4.
11. *Op. cit.*, p. 393.

8. THE TWO PURPOSES OF DEVIANT

CASE ANALYSIS

by Patricia L. Kendall and Katherine M. Wolf

1. In unpublished lectures on social research delivered in the Department of Sociology, Columbia University.
2. This function has been recognized, and briefly commented on by other social scientists. See, for example, Paul Horst, *The Prediction of Personal Adjustment*, Social Science Research Council, Bulletin 48 (New York: Social Science Research Council, 1941), pp. 117-118; and Milton Gordon, "Sociological Law and the Deviant Case," *Sociometry*, X (1947), especially p. 257.
3. Although detailed interviews are most frequently used, there is no specific technique for studying deviant cases. Such analysis can be achieved by virtually all of the methods of social research.
4. See Hadley Cantril, Hazel Gaudet, and Herta Herzog, *The Invasion from Mars* (Princeton: Princeton University Press, 1940), pp. 76-79. The Princeton Office of Radio Research was the predecessor of the Bureau of Applied Social Research of Columbia University.
5. Another reason will be discussed below when we consider the second function of deviant case analysis.
6. Mirra Komarovsky, *The Unemployed Man and His Family* (New York: The Dryden Press, Inc., 1940). See especially pp. 57-58.
7. See Robert K. Merton, *Mass Persuasion* (New York: Harper & Brothers, 1946), pp. 125-130.
8. The adequacy of deviant case analyses is checked in subsequent studies where the newly uncovered or newly refined variables are incorporated into the predictive scheme, and new cases examined to see whether errors in prediction have been decreased.
9. See Cantril, Gaudet, and Herzog, *op. cit.*, p. 80.

9. DEFINITIONS OF A SITUATION

by Robert K. Merton, with the assistance of

Marjorie Fiske and Alberta Curtis

1. Compare Malinowski's account of "the type of situation in which we find magic." "Man, engaged in a series of practical activities, *comes to a gap;* the hunter is disappointed in his quarry, the sailor misses propitious winds, the canoe-builder has to deal with some material of which he is never certain that it will stand the strain, or the healthy person suddenly feels his strength failing. What does man do naturally under such conditions, setting aside all magic, belief and ritual? Forsaken by his knowledge, baffled by his past experience and by his technical skill, *he realises his impotence. Yet his desire grips him only the more strongly; his anxiety, his fears and hopes, induce a tension in his organism which drives him to some sort of activity.* Whether he be savage or civilised, whether in possession of magic or entirely ignorant of its existence, *passive inaction*, the only thing dictated by reason, *is the last thing in which he can acquiesce.* His nervous system and his whole organism drive him to some *substitute activity.*" B. Malinowski, "Magic, Science and Religion," in *Science, Religion and Reality* (ed. by Joseph Needham) (New York: The Macmillan Company, 1925, p. 73). (Italics inserted.)
2. "The function of magic is to ritualise man's optimism, to enhance his faith in the victory of hope over fear." *Ibid.*, p. 83.

10. THE PREDICTION OF PERSONAL

ADJUSTMENT AND INDIVIDUAL CASES

by Paul Horst

1. Burgess, E. W. and Cottrell, Leonard S., Jr., *Predicting Success or Failure in Marriage.* New York: Prentice-Hall, Inc., 1939, pp. 310-311. Burgess and Cottrell studied cases in which marital adjustment was incorrectly predicted, and concluded that personality factors had not been sufficiently utilized in making the predictions.

11. THE INFLUENCE OF THE NORTHERN

ENVIRONMENT ON THE INTELLIGENCE

TEST SCORES OF NEGROES

by Otto Klineberg

1. J. Peterson and L. H. Lanier, "Studies in the Comparative Abilities of Whites and Negroes," *Mental Measurement Monographs*, 1929, No. 5.
2. *Ibid.*, pp. 17-18.

12. EFFECT OF INCOME CHANGES

ON THE RATE OF SAVING

by George Katona

1. J. M. Keynes, *The General Theory of Employment, Interest, and Money* (New York, 1936), pp. 96 and 97.

2. There may have been different degrees of accepting the thesis. The relationship is considered a "fact" by one author, a "tendency" by a second, and is described by a third as something which "may be assumed" to hold true, as can be seen from three references found in one single issue of the *American Economic Review* (June, 1947): ". . . is due . . . to the fact that consumption increases in slightly lesser proportion than income" (M. Kalecki, p. 395). "In the short run, the response of consumers to rising income tends to be delayed" (D. McC. Wright, p. 450). "For those whose income was increasing, a low (marginal) propensity to consume may be assumed" (J. K. Galbraith, p. 292).

3. Reports of the surveys have appeared in the *Federal Reserve Bulletin*. Concerning the 1947 survey, see the June, July, and August 1947 issues, and concerning the 1948 survey, the June, July, August, and September 1948 issues. These reports contain a discussion of the sample, the survey methods, and the reliability of findings, in addition to presenting findings. The data presented in this article have, however, not been published previously. The author of this article was in direct charge of the surveys. He wishes to acknowledge his great indebtedness to his collaborators, both in the Survey Research Center and the Division of Research and Statistics of the Federal Reserve Board. They are, however, not responsible for conclusions drawn from survey material in this article.

4. No information is available concerning the first question because the survey questions about amounts saved concerned one year only. In other words, at the beginning of 1948, for instance, questions were asked concerning income and amounts saved in 1947 and income in 1946 but not concerning amounts saved in 1946. The last question was omitted because of the length and complexity of the measurement of amounts saved which prohibited the repetition of that inquiry for a second year during the same interview. The samples of the consecutive annual surveys consisted of different respondents so that they cannot be used jointly to derive information on changes in amounts saved by the same individuals.

5. This is in essence the Keynesian hypothesis expressed by Keynes as follows: "A man's habitual standard of life usually has the first claim on his income, and he is apt to save the difference which discovers itself between his actual income and the expense of his habitual standard; or, if he does adjust his expenditure to changes in his income he will over short periods do so imperfectly." (*Op. cit.*, p. 97.)

6. Both hypotheses are based on the assumption that expenditures and not amounts saved represent people's primary concern. Empirical studies showed that it is much more usual for people to meet their expenses first and save what is left than to consider saving as the first charge on their income.

7. The two groups, spending units headed by young people and by war veterans, are of course composed of the same people in most cases.

8. These propositions are elaborated and the relation between psychology and economics is discussed in the following papers of the author: "Psychological Analysis of Business Decisions and Expectations," *American Economic Review*, XXXVI (1946), pp. 44-62, and "Contribution of Psychological Data to Economic Analysis," *Journal of American Statistical Association*, XLII (1947), pp. 449-59.

9. It is possible that this omission would not detract much from the validity of this study because pre-1945 income levels may have played only a small role in people's understanding of postwar income changes. At certain times, however, for instance during a depression, the previous income level may be of great immediate significance.

10. The findings just enumerated and the breakdown of the relation between income changes and purchases of durable goods by income classes are not presented in tabular form in this article. Different forms of dissaving are analyzed in an article of the author entitled "Analysis of Dissaving," *Amer. Econ. Rev.*, Vol. 39, 1949.

11. One other possible factor, price expectation, was studied in the Surveys of Consumer Finances. It was found that in 1946 and 1947 price expectations apparently did **not** influence the purchase of durable goods.

13. "FRIENDS AND NEIGHBORS"—

THE APPEAL OF LOCALISM

IN VOTING BEHAVIOR

by V. O. Key

1. The friends-and-neighbors spirit colors the following letter to the editor of the *Birmingham News* (February 9, 1947): "It seems that some persons don't know Mr. Folsom, our governor, well enough to wait and see how he will do. . . .

"I happened to be born on one side of the road and Jim Folsom on the other side. My father and Jim's father were old pals. I lived in sight of five Folsom families, Jessie, Frank, Thomas, Mrs. Millie and Marion Folsom, Jim's father. The first school teacher I went to was Miss Ola Folsom (deceased). I want to say to the citizens of Alabama and elsewhere that there is no better community in Alabama than is the Folsom community about 16 miles northeast of Elba.

"I have worked in the fields with the Folsoms. There are no better managers than the Folsoms. There are no better neighbors than the Folsoms. (No, I am not related to them.)

"When I saw Jim's picture and that he was in the race for governor, I put one of his large pictures up in my shop and began speaking my knowledge of the Folsoms and won him many friends, of which some were business men. . . . I just knew there was a man from a good family seeking a place where he could serve many people the best way."

SECTION III

The Analysis of Change Through Time

1. THE IMPACT OF THE HARVEST
ON POPULATION CHANGE
by Dorothy S. Thomas

1. *Emigrationsutredningen, Betänkande* (Stockholm, 1913), pp. 74-75.
2. This conclusion is based on period averages. It is highly probable that the harvest failures of the late 1860's were an important cause of observed declines in marriage and birth rates.
3. Sundbärg estimates the average per capita consumption of brandy (50% alcohol) at 40 liters in the 1820's. (*Emigrationsutredningen, Betänkande,* Stockholm, 1913, p. 87.) In 1855, home distilling was prohibited, and in the following decades consumption averaged around 10 liters per inhabitant up to the 'eighties when a further decrease set in. Present per capita consumption is about 4 liters. (*Statistisk Årsbok for Sverige,* 1936.) It is probable that deaths from alcoholism varied positively with prosperity and were, therefore, a disturbing factor in the observed correlation of all deaths with the harvest index. See D. S. Thomas, *Social Aspects of the Business Cycle* (London, 1926), pp. 131-132.
4. Not all emigrants, of course, sought America as a destination. On the basis of reported destinations the percentage of emigrants migrating to the United States varied from 67% to 88% by decades from the 1850's to 1901-10. The only other numerically important destinations were Norway and Denmark, which drew from 9% to 23% of the total (*Emigrationsutredningen, Bilaga* XX, Stockholm, 1911, p. 55). It would have been desirable to use data on emigrants to America rather than a net emigration, but the latter, as corrected by Sundbärg, is the only series of requisite reliability for showing annual variations. Sundbärg summarizes the status of statistics of emigrants as follows:
Abstracts from passport journals were sent in [to the Central Statistical Bureau] for the years 1851-55 and 1856-60. These notations . . . left much to be desired, [but] . . . even they were discontinued in 1860. . . . For some years thereafter emigration statistics were at a low point. . . . [In 1865 an attempt was made to summarize the data for the missing years from the parish registers and the pastors were required to send in yearly reports thereafter.] These reports [from the pastors] . . . are, up to the present, the main source of our emigration statistics. . . . Concerning their value . . . they are of equal reliability with the other excellent Swedish population statistics regarding details [of age, sex, civil status, etc.], but their *completeness* leaves much to be desired, and varies for the different periods. For the 1850's, the incompleteness is greatest. . . . For 1885-1893 they are almost complete. . . . That their incompleteness again increased, approximately from 1893, depends on the fact that emigration status no longer carried exemption from military service; . . . Because of this regulation, considerable unlawful emigration began. (*Emigrationsutredningen, Bilaga* IV, pp. 250-252.)
5. Life histories of emigrants (published in *Emigrationsutredningen*) are replete with complaints about these aspects of Swedish life. It is, however, impossible to determine the extent which they reflect American ideologies assimilated *after* emigration to the United States.

2. SOCIAL OPTIMISM AND PESSIMISM
IN AMERICAN PROTESTANTISM
by Thomas Hamilton

1. W. M. Horton, *Contemporary Continental Theology*, pp. 98-99.
2. For all classifications the mean difference between the means described is social optimism, — 5 1/9; social pessimism, + 1 7/45.

3. PUBLIC OPINION AND
THE LEGISLATIVE PROCESS
by Frank V. Cantwell

1. Hadley Cantril, *Gauging Public Opinion* (Princeton, 1944), p. 226.

4. THE EFFECTS OF RADIO
UPON NEWSPAPER CIRCULATION
by Samuel A. Stouffer

1. An individual study of each city was made at the office of the Audit Bureau of Circulations in Chicago. All cities which changed the boundaries of their retail trading zone in the time period considered were omitted, as also were cities with one or more non-ABC papers. *Editor and Publisher* tables on this must be disregarded entirely, because so many cities altered the boundaries of their zones and *Editor and Publisher* ignores this change.
2. See footnote 1.
3. This table, compiled from data in *Editor and Publisher*, includes newspapers that are not members of the Audit Bureau of Circulations. The publisher's estimates of circulation in such cases are not always dependable, but failure to include such newspapers results in a much more serious bias. For classification by city size, 1930 census figures are used.

5. THE PROCESS OF OPINION

AND ATTITUDE FORMATION

by Paul F. Lazarsfeld, Bernard Berelson

and Hazel Gaudet

1. Hans Zeisel, *Say It with Figures* (New York, Harper and Bros., 1947), Chapter X.
2. Paul F. Lazarsfeld, Elihu Katz, *et al.*, *Personal Influence.* (Glencoe, Ill.: The Free Press, 1954.) In press.

6. SOME APPLICATIONS OF THE PANEL

METHOD TO THE STUDY OF CHANGE

by Charles Y. Glock

1. The present analysis is restricted to the relationship between attitude and behavior patterns exhibited by the same people at different times. Another important aspect of a panel study is the possibility of asking people who have recently changed their attitudes or behavior the reasons why they changed. No analysis of reasons is included in the present paper.
2. This example is taken from an unpublished study sponsored by the American Jewish Committee with the assistance of the Bureau of Applied Social Research, Columbia University.
3. Level of anti-Semitism was determined through answers to four questions: (*a*) It would be a good idea if more business firms refused to hire Jews. (*b*) Most Jews in this country are Communists. (*c*) Although there are plenty of exceptions, most Jews are dirty. (*d*) In general Jews should not be allowed to hold high political office. Agreement with any of these items was considered evidence of anti-Semitism. Agreement with three or four was considered a high level of anti-Semitism, agreement with two a medium level, and agreement with none or one a low level.
4. It could also be, of course, that the film "boomeranged" for some respondents, leading to exactly the opposite effect from that intended by the producers.
5. The American Association for the United Nations, the United Nations Association of Cincinnati, Ohio, and the Stephen H. Wilder Foundation of Cincinnati.
6. This example is taken from an unpublished study conducted jointly by the National Opinion Research Center and the Bureau of Applied Social Research.
7. The level of interest was based on the number of items in which the respondent expressed keen interest in answer to the following question: "We'd like to know how much interest the public takes in a number of questions. For example, do you yourself take a keen interest, only a mild interest, or practically none at all in news about (*a*) Our trade with other countries, (*b*) Our relations with Russia, (*c*) The United Nations, (*d*) The control of the atomic bomb." Individuals reporting keen interest in three or four items were classified as having high interest; keen interest in two items represented medium interest; and keen interest in none or one item represented low interest.

8. Index of exposure: respondents were classified as exposed if they indicated that they had done any one or more of the following: (*a*) Heard short radio mention of the United Nations between programs. (*b*) Seen any signs or posters about the UN. (*c*) Read any pamphlets or leaflets on the UN. (*d*) Been to any meetings where the UN was talked about or discussed. (*e*) Heard anything about the UN in church. (*f*) Seen or heard the slogan, "Peace begins with the UN; the UN begins with you."
9. This study, now in the process of analysis, was a joint endeavor of Chicago, Columbia, and Cornell Universities, as well as International Public Opinion Research, Elmo Roper, and General Motors.
10. This table is taken from a manuscript prepared by Norman Kaplan of Cornell University.
11. Refinements of the techniques reported here are underway and will be reported on elsewhere in the near future.
12. The example reported on here is taken from Samuel Stouffer *et al*, *The American Soldier*, Vol. I, p. 265, Chart XI.
13. Conformity scores were based on the answers to the following questions:
(*a*) How much of your training or duty time is used in doing things that do not seem important to you? Conforming response: "None of it."
(*b*) In general, how well do you think the Army is run? Conforming response: "It is run very well."
(*c*) In general, how serious an offense do you think it is for a soldier to be AWOL? Conforming response: "Very serious."
(*d*) Do you feel that the Army is trying to control you and other soldiers more strictly and in more ways than it needs to? Conforming response: "No."
(*e*) Do you usually feel that what you are doing in the Army is worth while or not? Conforming response: "I usually feel it is worth while."
(*f*) How important is to you personally to make good as a soldier? Conforming response: "It is very important."
Those giving a conforming response to 5 or 6 items were rated as giving a relatively high score; a conforming response to 3 or 4 items was rated as a medium score; and a conforming response to none, one or two items was rated as a relatively low score.
14. See Theodore Newcomb, *Personality and Social Change*, Dryden, 1943, especially p. 29.
15. This example is taken from Patricia L. Kendall, *Conflict and Mood—Factors Affecting the Stability of Responses* (Glencoe, Ill.: The Free Press, 1954).
16. Determination of mood (good or bad) was made by dichotomizing response patterns obtained in connection with four barometers.
(*a*) First of all, we would like to know whether you are in pretty good spirits or pretty bad spirits today.
(*b*) Next, we'd like to know how irritable you feel today. For example, would you be annoyed if something relatively unimportant went wrong.
(*c*) And how about your feelings of optimism and pessimism? At the present time do you have the feeling that things are going pretty well or pretty poorly.
(*d*) Finally, we know that people vary from day to day in their feelings of physical

well-being. On some days, they are listless and tired; and on other days they are full of pep and feel like conquering the world. How do you feel in this respect today?

17. Criterion questons:

(a) Suppose that you had a lunch date with a very close friend who was late and kept you waiting for a long time. Unaggressive response: "Just wait calmly until it seemed clear that my friend would not show up."

(b) Suppose you and a friend were standing in line waiting to get into a movie and noticed that a couple had sneaked in ahead of you. Unaggressive response: "Just ignore the couple and continue to wait in line."

(c) Suppose that you were in a crowded subway and were continuously jostled by a woman carrying a lot of bundles. Unaggressive response: "Move to another part of the subway."

7. FACTORS INFLUENCING CHANGE

OF OCCUPATIONAL CHOICE

by Morris Rosenberg

1. See Eli Ginzberg, Sol W. Ginsburg, Sidney Axelrad, and John L. Herma, *Occupational Choice* (New York: Columbia Univ. Press, 1951).

2. The question dealing with occupational values was phrased in the following way:

"When they reported their requirements for an IDEAL JOB OR PROFESSION, students said it would have to satisfy certain requirements. Some of these requirements are listed below.

As you read the list, consider to what extent a job or career would have to satisfy each of these requirements before you could consider it IDEAL.

Indicate your opinion by writing:

H (high) next to the requirements you consider highly important

M (medium) next to the requirements you consider of medium importance

L (low) next to the requirements you consider of little or no importance, irrelevant, or even distasteful to you.

INDICATE   *The ideal job for me would*
H, M, L   *have to . . .*
....A. "Provide an opportunity to use my special abilities or aptitudes."
....B. "Provide me with a chance to earn a good deal of money."
....C. "Permit me to be creative and original."
....D. "Give me social status and prestige."
....E. "Give me an opportunity to work with people rather than things."
....F. "Enable me to look forward to a stable, secure future."
....G. "Leave me relatively free of supervision by others."
....H. "Give me a chance to exercise leadership."
....I. "Provide me with adventure."
....J. "Give me an opportunity to be helpful to others."

Now GO BACK and look at the requirements you rated "high." Rank them in the order of importance to you by writing next to each H

1 for the most important

2 for the next in importance

and so on, for all the H's on your list. Do *not* rank the M's and L's."

8. THE PREDICTION OF SOLDIERS' RETURN

TO PRE-WAR EMPLOYMENT

by John A. Clausen

1. Walter J. Couper, "The Reemployment Rights of Veterans," *Annals of the American Academy of Political and Social Science*, Vol. 238 (March 1945), p. 112.

2. The questions asked on these topics were as follows:

After the war, do you think you could get work with the company or person you worked for before you came into the Army, if you wanted to? (Check one)

....Yes, I'm almost sure I could

....Yes, I think so, but I'm not sure

....No, I probably couldn't

....I'm sure I could not

....I worked for myself before I came into the Army

....I was not working before I came into the Army

Do you think you *actually will* go back to work for the same employer (company, person, etc.) you worked for before you came into the Army? (Check one)

....Yes, I'm quite sure I will

....I may, but I'm not sure

....No, I don't think I will

....I worked for myself before I came into the Army

....I was not working before I came into the Army

3. Information and Education Division Report No. B-129, *Post-War Occupational Plans of Soldiers*, March 1, 1945, p. 18.

4. An alternative method of prediction, which did not eliminate men who were not employed immediately prior to induction, yielded an estimate of 47 per cent return for December separatees.

5. The self-reporting of governmental employment is known to contain a large element of error because of misconceptions held by many soldiers as to the scope of such employment. Thus many classified work in plants with war contracts as federal employment.

6. Because of the small number of cases involved when comparing employees of large and small companies, matching length of preservice employment and plans to return, the significance of the differences between matched pairs were tested by the use of the statistical signs test after eliminating all pairs in which either member contained less than twenty cases. In six out of six pairs included, the rate of return was highest for employees of larger companies.

7. See, for example, the report of the Standard Oil Company of New Jersey in the pamphlet "A Generation of Industrial Peace" (1946), p. 5.

9. THE PREDICTION OF ADJUSTMENT

IN MARRIAGE

by Ernest W. Burgess and

Leonard S. Cottrell, Jr.

1. Due to the fact that most of our schedules were anonymous, we were not able to contact very many of the subjects for subsequent study.

2. These were eleven "agreement" questions.

3. For computing this coefficient the distribution of ratings was split into two groups so as to include the ratings of "happy" and "very happy" in one group and all other ratings in another. The adjustment scores were split into two groups at the median of the distribution.

4. As would be expected we found that wide differences in educational achievement were associated with low adjustment scores.

10. GENERALIZING THE PROBLEM

OF PREDICTION

by Leo A. Goodman

1. See, for example, Paul Horst, et al., *The Prediction of Personal Adjustment*, New York: Social Science Research Council, 1941; Lloyd E. Ohlin and Otis Dudley Duncan, "The Efficiency of Prediction in Criminology," *American Journal of Sociology*, Vol. LIV (March, 1949), pp. 441-52; and Albert J. Reiss, Jr., "The Accuracy, Efficiency, and Validity of a Prediction Instrument," *American Journal of Sociology*, Vol. LVI (March, 1951), pp. 552-561.

2. Abraham Wald, *Statistical Decision Functions*, New York; John Wiley and Sons, Inc., 1950, pp. ix, 179.

3. R. Clay Sprowles, "Statistical Decision by the Method of Minimum Risk: An Application," *Journal of the American Statistical Association*, Vol. 45 (1950), pp. 238-48.

4. L. J. Savage, "The Theory of Statistical Decision," *Journal of the American Statistical Association*, Vol. 46 (1951), pp. 55-67.

SECTION IV

Formal Aspects of Research on Human Groups

1. THE RELATION BETWEEN INDIVIDUAL

AND GROUP CHARACTERISTICS IN

"THE AMERICAN SOLDIER"

by Patricia L. Kendall and Paul F. Lazarsfeld

1. The number of times a soldier has had malaria would be a summation over time, which is excluded from the present discussion.

2. For the sake of completeness we should also reflect a moment on the index used in the second row. It is based on an index of psychoneurotic symptoms which the Research Branch had developed. This was originally, again, a kind of continuous variable where soldiers could vary over a wide range of scores. But, for a variety of reasons, this variable was reconverted on the individual level into a dichotomous attribute: soldiers were divided according to whether their score was above or below the critical level. Out of this dichotomy, then, on the group level, a continuous rate was formed as in the case of malaria. This double conversion, however, is rare and will not be considered further.

3. It should be helpful for the reader to think of a variety of other areas where these five types would obviously apply. A good example can be taken from ecology. The home of an individual man can be in good or bad repair; the census tract can be characterized by the proportion of houses in good repair. (Type I) The census tract can also be characterized by the average rent paid. (Type II) The census tract can be either homogeneous or heterogeneous in regard to rent. (Type

III) The tracts can also be classified according to the proportion of shopping which people do within the tract. (Type IV) Finally, the tract can be characterized by the playground areas to be found there. (Type V) All five items together might be combined into a broader index of "area wealth" of the kind Thorndike has developed for the "goodness of life of cities."

4. In II, 426, Chart I, a psychoneurotic test is validated against the incidence of actual commitments to psychoneurotic wards. This is done in the following way. A cross-sectional sample of soldiers was divided into 12 groups according to age and education. The same was done for a group of hospital inmates. This then defines 12 abstract age-education groups, each of which serves as a unit in the correlation analysis. The two variables which are related are (a) the relative incidence of psychoneurosis and (b) the proportion in the cross-section receiving critical scores on the psychoneurotic test. A high correlation exists. Here the interesting idea is that the two sets of data characterizing each "unit" are taken from different samples.

5. A similar example can be found in connection with the study of four divisions considered above. On a unit basis, the table from which we quoted gives a positive correlation between a psychoneurotic rate and average duration in combat. A table on p. 451 of the same chapter (II, Chap. IX) shows a corresponding association between time in combat and psychoneurotic score based on personal data.

6. A second comparison is made in Chart X between ground forces, service forces and

Air Corps, leading to substantially the same results.

7. At several points of the text (*e.g.*, II, 40 and 249), the whole topic is mentioned in the following way. Variations *between* units may have to be interpreted differently than variations *within* units. It can easily be seen that this and our formulation of the problem are equivalent.

8. Again, comparisons with other fields should be helpful. Workers in England are more likely to vote for the Labour Party than white-collar people. But a worker in a white-collar district is less likely to vote Labour than a worker in a workingman's district. In the same way, the crime rate of Negroes in Negro sections of a city seems to be lower than the crime rate of Negroes in mixed areas.

2. TYPES OF GROUP CHARACTERISTICS

by Raymond B. Cattell

1. J. K. Hemphill and C. M. Westie, "The measurement of group dimensions," *Jour. of Psych.*, 1950, 29, 325-342.
2. R. B. Cattell and L. G. Wispe, "The dimensions of syntality in small groups." *J. Soc. Psych.*, 1948, 28, 57-78.
3. The 16 Personality Factor Questionnaire, Champaign, Illinois, Institute for Personality and Ability Testing, 313 West Avondale Street, 1949.
4. J. K. Hemphill, "Situational Factors in Leadership," Bureau of Educ. Res., Columbus, Ohio, Monograph No. 31, Ohio State University, 1949.
5. L. Festinger, K. Back, S. Schachter, H. H. Kelley, and J. Thibaut, *Theory and Experiment in Social Communication*. Res. Cent. for Group Dynam., Michigan University, 1950.
6. L. Carter, W. Haythorn, and M. Howell, "A further investigation of the criteria of leadership." *J. abnorm. soc. Psychol.*, 1950, 45, 350-358.
7. *Ibid.*
8. S. Asch, "Effects of group pressure upon the modification and distortion of judgments," *Groups, Leadership and Men*, H. Guetzkow, ed., (Pittsburgh: Carnegie Press, 1951), pp. 177-190.

4. STATISTICAL RELATIONS AMONG

COMMUNITY CHARACTERISTICS

by George P. Murdock

1. J. H. Steward, "The Economic and Social Basis of Primitive Bands," *Essays in Anthropology Presented to A. L. Kroeber* (Berkeley, 1936), pp. 331-50.
2. R. Linton, *The Study of Man* (New York, 1936), pp. 209-30.
3. G. P. Murdock, C. S. Ford, A. E. Hudson, R. Kennedy, L. W. Simmons, and J. W. M. Whiting, "Outline of Cultural Materials," *Yale Anthropological Studies*, II (1945), 29.
4. E. M. Weyer, *The Eskimos* (New

Haven, 1932), pp. 141-4. Cf. also, J. H. Steward, "The Economic and Social Basis of Primitive Bands," *Essays in Anthropology Presented to A. L. Kroeber* (Berkeley, 1936), pp. 332-3.
5. R. Linton, *The Study of Man* (New York, 1936), p. 218.
6. W. H. Goodenough, "Basic Economy and the Community" (unpublished article, 1941). This study, undertaken in the files of the Cross-Cultural Survey at the suggestion of Professor W. F. Ogburn, covered 40 tribes for which reliable population data were available.
7. An independent estimate by Steward also arrives at 50 persons as the average population of a band and finds, in addition, that the area exploited by a band averages approximately 100 square miles. See J. H. Steward, "The Economic and Social Basis of Primitive Bands," *Essays in Anthropology Presented to A. L. Kroeber* (Berkeley, 1936), p. 333.
8. Cf. J. H. Steward, "The Economic and Social Basis of Primitive Bands," *Essays in Anthropology Presented to A. L. Kroeber* (Berkeley, 1936), pp. 332-3.
9. F. G. Speck, "The Family Hunting Band as the Basis of Algonkian Social Organization," *American Anthropologist*, n.s., XVII (1914), 289-305; "Family Hunting Territories and Social Life of Various Algonkian Bands of the Ottawa Valley," *Memoirs of the Canada Department of Mines Geological Survey*, LXX (1915), 1-10; "Kinship Terms and the Family Band among the Northeastern Algonkian," *American Anthropologist*, n.s., XX (1918), 143-61; "Mistassini Hunting Territories in the Labrador Peninsula," *American Anthropologist*, n.s., XXV (1923), 452-71; "Family Hunting Territories of the Lake St. John Montagnais," *Anthropos*, XXII (1927), 387-403; *Penobscot Man* (Philadelphia, 1940), pp. 203-12.
10. Cf. W. G. Sumner, *Folkways* (Boston, 1906), p. 12.
11. Cf. the New England "town meeting" in our own society.
12. W. L. Warner and P. S. Lunt, *The Social Life of a Modern Community* (New Haven, 1941).
13. J. H. Steward, "The Economic and Social Basis of Primitive Bands," *Essays in Anthropology Presented to A. L. Kroeber* (Berkeley, 1936), p. 331.
14. *Ibid.*, p. 334.
15. *Ibid.*, p. 338.
16. R. Linton, *The Study of Man* (New York, 1936), p. 229.
17. H. M. Miner, *St. Denis* (Chicago, 1939), pp. 58-60, 68-9.

5. COMMUNICATION PATTERNS IN

TASK-ORIENTED GROUPS

by Alex Bavelas

1. For the purpose of this discussion, if individual p is linked to individual q it will mean that p may communicate to q, and that q may communicate to p—that is, the link is symmetrical.
2. We assume subjects with perfect knowl-

edge of poker-hand ratings.

3. This is not intended to exclude the possibility that in certain patterns "morale" effects will materially affect the speed with which an individual might perform.

4. Unpublished; manuscript in preparation.

5. For a detailed account of this experiment, see Harold J. Leavitt, "Some Effects of Certain Communication Patterns on Group Performance" (Ph.D. dissertation, Massachusetts Institute of Technology, 1949).

6. In this quotation, pattern letters used in Figure 9 have been substituted for the letters used in Leavitt's report.

7. He could see all six symbols on his box of six switches.

6. THE MEASUREMENT OF

GROUP DIMENSIONS

by John K. Hemphill and Charles M. Westie

1. These scales have been developed as part of a 10-year research program on leadership conducted by the Ohio State Leadership Studies. The research staff includes C. L. Shartle, Director; Alvin E. Coons, Melvin Seeman, Ralph Stogdill, Associate Directors; John Hemphill, Research Associate; Donald T. Campbell, Research Consultant; Charles M. Westie and Richard T. Morris, Research Assistants.

2. M. Smith, "Social situation, social behavior, social group," *Psychol. Rev.*, 1945, Vol. 52, 224-229.

3. For a discussion of the analysis of behavior at a molar as contrasted with a molecular level see E. C. Tolman, *Purposive Behavior in Animals and Men*. New York: Century, 1932, and C. L. Hull, *Principles of Behavior*. New York: Norton, 1943.

4. The term viscidity is used here to refer to a specifically defined concept of group unity. Many other terms are in current use which refer to similar concepts; for example, cohesion, solidarity, "we" feeling, togetherness, group morale, etc. It is hoped that the use of this new term will help to avoid confusion with these other terms.

5. These questionnaires were used by the senior author in an exploratory study of the relation of group characteristics to the behavior of leaders. A report of this study is available as a monograph, *Situational Factors in Leadership*, (Columbus: Ohio State University, Bureau of Educational Research, Monograph 31, 1949).

6. The judges included a clinical psychologist, an industrial psychologist, a social psychologist, a sociologist, and an advanced graduate student in sociology.

7. The index of "homogeneity of placement" was computed using the following formula:

$$I_i = \frac{N \sum\limits_{j=1}^{n} X_{ij} - \sum\limits_{i=1}^{N} \sum\limits_{j=1}^{n} X_{ij}}{2\,[2n\,(N-1)] + \sum\limits_{i=1}^{N} \sum\limits_{j=1}^{n} X_{ij} - N \sum\limits_{j=1}^{n} X_{ij}}$$

where: j = any judge
i = any dimension in the system
n = number of judges
N = number of dimensions
X = Score assigned to item placement as follows:
Definitely applies = + 1
Undecided = 0
Definitely does not apply = — 1

8. The index of "homogeneity of placement" differs in two ways from certain other techniques for examining item content. First, it is based on "expert" judgment of probable response to the items, not on actual item response data. Second, unlike indices such as "internal consistency," "homogeneity," or "unidimensionality" all of which refer to relationship among items, the index of "homogeneity of placement" involves both relationships among items (as reflected by judge agreement that certain items apply to the same dimension) and independence of relationship of the item to other dimensions making up the same general heuristic system.

9. The value of I selected as the cut-off score for the retention of an item was .50.

10. Jeanne S. Chall, Research Associate, Bureau of Educational Research, The Ohio State University.

11. F. M. Lord, "Alignment chart for calculating the four-fold point correlation coefficient," *Psychometrika*, 1944, Vol. 9, 41-42.

12. L. Chesire, M. Saffir, and L. L. Thurstone, *Computing diagrams for the tetrachoric correlation coefficient*. Chicago: Univ. Chicago Bookstore, 1933.

13. C. C. Peters and W. R. Van Voorhis, *Statistical Procedures and their Mathematical Bases*. New York: McGraw-Hill, 1940.

7. THE FOLK-URBAN CONTINUUM

by Horace Miner

1. *Life in a Mexican Village: Tepoztlán Restudied*, Urbana: University of Illinois Press, 1951.

2. *Tepoztlán, A Mexican Village*, Chicago: University of Chicago Press, 1930.

3. *A Village That Chose Progress, Chan Kom Revisited*, Chicago: University of Chicago Press, 1950.

4. Dr. Allen Spitzer, San Francisco College for Women, is director of the American part of the project, of which the Universidad Nacional del Sureste, in Yucatan, is co-sponsor. *Human Organization*, 10 (Fall, 1951), p. 41.

5. Robert Bierstedt, "Sociological Theory: Work in Progress," *American Sociological Review*, 17 (February, 1952), p. 81.

6. Robert Redfield, "The Folk Society," *The American Journal of Sociology*, 52 (January, 1947), p. 294.

7. *Ibid.*, p. 295.

8. *Ibid.*, p. 293.

9. *Loc. cit.*

10. *The Folk Culture of Yucatan*, Chicago: University of Chicago Press, 1941, p. 344.

11. *Ibid.*, p. 369.

12. *Loc. cit.*

13. "Culture and Civilization in Guate-

malan Societies," *The Scientific Monthly*, 48 (May, 1939), p. 467.

14. *The Folk Culture of Yucatan*, p. 369.

15. "World View and Social Relations in Guatemala," *American Anthropologist*, 43 (January-March, 1941), p. 37.

16. *St. Denis, A French-Canadian Parish*, Chicago: University of Chicago Press, 1939.

17. *The Primitive City of Timbuctoo*, Princeton: Princeton University Press, 1953.

18. *The Folk Culture of Yucatan*, p. 360.

19. Quotations extracted from *Life in a Mexican Village*, pp. 432-440.

20. *Ibid.*, p. 129.

21. *Ibid.*, p. 130.

22. *Ibid.*, p. 131.

23. *Ibid.*, p. 93.

24. *Ibid.*, p. 148-49.

25. *Ibid.*, p. 157.

26. "The Folk Society," p. 306.

27. *The Folk Culture of Yucatan*, p. 364-369.

28. *Ibid.*, p. 344.

29. Ralph Beals, in his review of Lewis' work, comments, "Even if we cannot define the significant variables satisfactorily, it seems hard to avoid recognition of important differences between urban and non-urban culture and behavior." *American Sociological Review*, 16 (December, 1951), p. 896.

30. *The Folk Culture of Yucatan*, p. 343.

31. *Anthropology*, New York: Harcourt, Brace and Co., 1948, pp. 280-86.

32. *The Folk Culture of Yucatan*, p. 364; "The Folk Society," p. 308.

33. "World View and Social Relations in Guatemala," pp. 29-30.

34. "Culture and Civilization in Guatemalan Societies," *The Scientific Monthly*, (May, 1939), p. 467.

35. *The Folk Culture of Yucatan*, p. 346.

36. Review of *The Folk Culture of Yucatan*, *American Anthropologist*, 45 (January-March, 1943), pp. 133-136.

37. *Man and His Works*, New York: Alfred A. Knopf, 1948, pp. 604-07.

38. See, for example, Amos Hawley, *Human Ecology*, New York: The Ronald Press Co., 1950, Chapter 11.

8. SOME UNIFORMITIES OF BEHAVIOR
IN SMALL SOCIAL SYSTEMS

by Robert F. Bales

1. For a technical description of the method, see Robert F. Bales, *Interaction Process Analysis, A Method for the Study of Small Groups* (Cambridge, Mass.: Addison-Wesley Press, 1950). The present article is largely composed of selected portions of previously published articles. I am personally much indebted to present and former students, some of whom are indicated as co-authors:

Robert F. Bales, "A Set of Categories for the Analysis of Small Group Interaction," *American Sociological Review*, April 1950, XV, No. 2, 257-263.

Robert F. Bales and Fred L. Strodtbeck, "Phases in Group Problem Solving," *Journal of Abnormal and Social Psychology* (in press).

Robert F. Bales, Fred L. Strodtbeck, Theodore M. Mills and Mary Roseborough, "Channels of Communication in Small Groups."

American Sociological Review, August 1951, XVI, No. 4, 461-468.

Robert F. Bales, "Some Statistical Problems of Small Group Research." *Journal of the American Statistical Association*, September 1951, XLVI, No. 255, 311-322.

2. Barbara Norfleet, "Interpersonal Relations and Group Productivity," *Journal of Social Issues*, 1948, IV, No. 2, 66-69.

3. Bernard M. Bass, "An Analysis of Leaderless Group Discussion," *Journal of Applied Psychology*, 1949, 33, 527-533.

4. Fred L. Strodtbeck, "Husband-Wife Interaction over Revealed Differences," *American Sociological Review*, 1951, XVI, No. 4, 468-473.

5. Joseph B. Koller, "Notes On 'Channels of Communication in Small Groups,' " *American Sociological Review*, 1951, 16, No. 6, 842-843.

9. MATRIX ANALYSIS OF GROUP STRUCTURES

by Leon Festinger, Stanley Schachter,
and Kurt Back

1. Northway, M. L., "A Method for Depicting Social Relationships Obtained by Sociometric Testing," *Sociometry*, Vol. 3, pp. 144-150, 1940.

2. Cook, L. A., "An Experimental Sociographic Study of a Stratified 10th Grade Class," *American Sociological Review*. Vol. 10, pp. 250-261, 1945.

3. Forsyth, E., and Katz, L., "A Matrix Approach to the Analysis of Sociometric Data: Preliminary Report," *Sociometry*, Vol. 9, pp. 340-347, 1946.

4. The application of matrix multiplication to the analysis of sociometric patterns was developed together with Mr. Albert Perry and Mr. Duncan Luce of the Massachusetts Institute of Technology.

10. THE OPERATION OF GROUP STANDARDS

by Leon Festinger, Stanley Schachter,
and Kurt Back

1. M. Sherif, *The psychology of social norms*. New York: Harper, 1936.

2. K. Lewin, *et al. Level of aspiration*. In J. McV. Hunt (Ed.) *Personality and the behavior disorders*. Vol. I, New York: Ronald, 1944.

3. T. Newcomb, *Personality and social change*. New York: Dryden Press, 1943.

4. The significance of the differences in this and the following tables was computed by taking the means for each court and comparing the distributions of these means. This was done because the effects of group standards made the group, not the individual, the unit of sampling. This difference is significant at the 7% level of confidence for choices given. Significance is at the 17% level of confidence for choices received.

5. Significant at the 2% level of confidence.

6. For all comparisons this is significant, at least at the 3% level of confidence.

7. Not statistically significant.

The Empirical Analysis of Action

2. DO PEOPLE KNOW WHY THEY BUY?

by Elias Smith and Edward A. Suchman

1. See Stanton, Frank, "A Two Way Check on the Sales Influence of a Specific Radio Program," *Journal of Applied Psychology,* Vol. XXIV, 1940, p. 665 ff.

2. These telephone interviews were made by Market Research Corporation of America.

3. A matching procedure would meet this objection.

4. The subjects for this interview study were chosen at random from the upper left-hand box of table 1 and a second similar one; this box contains Philco owner-Boake Carter listeners found in the telephone survey. However, in the interviewing it was necessary to eliminate those individuals who had bought their Philcos before ever listening to Boake Carter. It was also necessary to eliminate those respondents who upon being interviewed turned out to be only occasional listeners to Boake Carter.

5. Paul F. Lazarsfeld, "The Use of Detailed Interviews in Market Research," *The Journal of Marketing,* July, 1937.

6. The reason for this correlation being higher after the change of time than before does not make any difference for the purpose of this study. The most probable interpretation which comes to mind is that the more loyal Boake Carter listeners are more likely to adjust their own schedules to the new time of the broadcast; since they are more loyal to the program they might easily be influenced by it. So after the change of time we find a higher correlation between listening and ownership. However that may be, for our present purpose the only information needed is the very fact that we have here two samples, with one showing a higher correlation than the other. Incidentally, it is from these two samples that our 155 cases were selected for personal interview. See footnote 4.

7. This expectation would be justified only if none of the spurious factors mentioned at the beginning of this paper entered into those two correlations. Fortunately this seems to be the case. By including telephone subscribers only, we eliminate the lower economic half of the population, which, it is well known, listens much less to commentators. For the telephone subscribers there appeared no significant difference in Boake Carter listening or in Philco ownership when special tabulations for different economic groups were made. Furthermore, twenty-three Philco owners who started to listen to Boake Carter after buying the Philco were interviewed as to whether ownership made them more inclined to listen when the program came on; no trace of such a direct relationship (listening influenced positively by ownership) could be found.

8. For this test the interviews taken in the first sample consisted of 78 cases and, in the second sample, of 77 cases. The difference is statistically reliable.

3. EVALUATING THE EFFECTIVENESS OF ADVERTISING BY DIRECT INTERVIEWS

by Paul F. Lazarsfeld

1. This discussion, which is designed to lead to psychological problems, omits the question of statistical reliability.

2. G. U. Yule and M. G. Kendall. *An Introduction to the Theory of Statistics.* London: J. B. Lippincott Co., twelfth revised edition, 1937. Pp. 34 ff.

3. Other examples of this interviewing technique can be found in two earlier papers by the writer, "The Art of Asking Why," *National Marketing Review,* Summer 1935, 1 (1):1-13, and "The Use of Detailed Interviews in Market Research," *Journal of Marketing,* 1937, July:3-8. In these papers, however, the technique of specifying questions was recommended only as useful, and was not linked up with an analysis of the concept of "reason," itself.

4. See the report of a study done by Cornelius DuBois, Continuity Study, *Tide Magazine,* 1940, 14 (21, November 1):13.

5. *See* Frank Stanton, A Two-Way Check on the Sales Influence of a Specific Radio Program. *Journal of Applied Psychology,* 1940, 23 (6, December):665-672.

6.

$$\left(\frac{277}{393} - \frac{135}{437}\right)393 = 158$$

7. As the study was not originally devised for the purpose for which it is being used here, the following tabulation of reasons was decided upon. Those people were considered most strongly influenced by location of the store who, as reason for not buying at the store, only mentioned its inconvenient location (33 per cent). Fifteen per cent said inconvenience and poor opinion of the store kept them from buying there. As there were no further data available, half the people were counted as influenced by inconvenient location. In a study more pointed to the problem of reasons, it would have been necessary to continue the interview and find out whether they bought at other stores more inconveniently located, whether they had less good opinion about other stores where they still bought, and so on, using the technique elaborated in Section 2.

8. It is revealing to study in great detail the "deviate cases" in this table. One-fourth of the respondents do not voice any criticism in the attitude test but still give bad opinion of the store as their reason for not buying. This is easily explained by the fact that our simple scale worked only with six criticisms, whereas they by no means exhaust all possible objections which might be raised. An inspection of the cases in the first line of Table IV shows indeed that those women refer in their reasons to other items than the one about which they have explicitly been

asked in the attitude questions. At the other end, there are 22 per cent of the people who have more than three criticisms but who do not give bad opinion as the reason for their not buying. These people, upon closer scrutiny, appear to be those for whom inconvenient location is also so dominant a reason that they would not buy at the store even if they did have a good opinion of it. Therefore, even if they have a bad opinion and do not buy there, the two factors are not causally connected.

9. See E. Smith and E. A. Suchman. Do People Know Why They Buy? *Journal of Applied Psychology,* 1940, 24 (6, December):673-684.

8. WHY FAMILIES MOVE

by Peter H. Rossi

1. This section is abstracted from a study of residential mobility conducted jointly by Columbia University's *Bureau of Applied Social Research* and *Institute for Urban Land Use and Housing Studies* under contract to the *Housing and Home Finance Agency.* The action analysis presented here is one of the several approaches employed in the study of residential mobility. A full report on the research will be published by The Free Press, Glencoe, Illinois.

2. An indication of the ease of recall and its reliability was the way in which accounts of the moving decision obtained from different members of the same household usually varied in only minor ways from each other.

3. Adapted from a nation-wide survey of housing satisfactions and dissatisfactions: Melville C. Branch, *Urban Planning and Public Opinion,* Bureau of Urban Research, Princeton, 1942. The reasons presented in Table 1 are abridged from a longer table presented in that publication.

4. Much of what is called "theory" in the behavioral sciences can be looked upon as accounting schemes which specify what data categories (concepts) are necessary to explain certain types of phenomena.

5. See C. Wright Mills, Clarence Senior, and Rose K. Goldsen, *The Puerto Rican Journey* (New York: Harpers, 1950).

6. The full analysis which considers "pulls" and information channels as well, is presented in the report to be published by The Free Press, Glencoe, Illinois.

7. The terms "coverage" and "impact" are borrowed from the field of communications research, where they have similar meanings. The assessment procedure employed here was first applied to a study of brand shifting undertaken by Paul F. Lazarsfeld and his associates.

8. This question followed another question directed at bringing the respondent back to the point at which the desire to move first entered his mind: "When did you first think of moving out of your former place?"

9. See footnote 10, below, for one complaint category for which such a distribution was not obtained and the reasons for the deviation from expectations.

10. Actually, there are eight possible response combinations to the three questions employed, and the classification given here is a reduction of these patterns according to a particular scheme. The full response patterns are as follows (a plus sign indicates that a respondent has mentioned a particular complaint in answer to the question indicated by the column heading):

TYPE COMBINATION	EXPOSURE ITEM	STIMULUS ITEM	ASSESSMENT ITEM	COMPLAINTS ABOUT LANDLORDS (*Previous Renters Only*)
A	+	+	+	6
B	+	|	+	0
C	|	+	+	[8]
D	|	|	+	[5]
E	+	+	|	5
F	|	+	|	[22]
G	+	|	|	8
H	|	|	|	143
				Total [197]

According to the classification scheme used, response combinations A, B, C, and D have been classified as "primary complaints," E and F as "contributory complaints," G as "ineffective complaints" and H as "no complaints."

It can be seen that certain of the response patterns are "contradictory." For example, patterns C, D and F represent cases where the respondent does not acknowledge exposure to a complaint but rates that complaint as of some degree of effectiveness. If the classification is to make sense, the number of such cases should be very small. Errors of measurement arising out of interviewing and processing inevitably lead to a few such "contradictory" cases. In the tables presented in the text the number of such cases is very small.

But what happens when the number of such cases is relatively large? In the last column of the table in this footnote the distribution of previous renters with regard to complaints about their landlords is shown. The contradictory cases are represented by the bracketed numbers in this table. Most of them seem to be caused by an unfortunate misunderstanding of our exposure question, "Did you get along with your previous landlord?" The respondent interpreted the question to mean disputes of an interpersonal nature. As one respondent put it, "We got along alright, but he never wanted to fix up the place or give us enough heat." The intended meaning of the exposure question was to cover any aspect of the dwelling unit which was customarily the landlord's obligation to provide. An unfortunate question wording necessitated dropping the analysis of complaints about landlord from the presentation in this selection.

The experience with landlord complaints points up the necessity for clearly specifying what exposure questions are meant to cover. The respondents' view of a particular stimulus may not coincide with the investigator's definition and the incongruence between the two may often, as in the case above, vitiate the research efforts.

11. This result is consistent with other findings, obtained by other methods, of this study. One of the primary sources of mobility is the lack of congruence between the households' needs in the way of dwelling space and the way in which the housing occupied by the households is fulfilling these needs.

12. For example, in only 19 cases were both space complaints and neighborhood complaints rated as primary or contributory.

9. THE ROLE OF THE COMMUNITY

IN A LIFE HISTORY

by John Dollard

1. Ralph Linton, *The Study of Man*, 210-211, New York, 1936.

10. THE FOCUSED INTERVIEW

by Robert K. Merton and Patricia L. Kendall

1. We are indebted to Dr. Samuel A. Stouffer and Dr. Carl I. Hovland for permission to draw upon materials for the Research Branch, Information and Education Division, Army Service Forces. To Miss Marjorie Fiske and Miss Eva Hofberg, colleagues in the Bureau of Applied Social Research, Columbia University, we are grateful for assistance in the preparation of material.

2. "What Do We Really Know about Day Time Serial Listeners?" in Paul F. Lazarsfeld and Frank N. Stanton (eds.), *Radio Research, 1942-43* (New York: Duell, Sloan & Pearce, 1944).

3. Harold F. Gosnell, *Getting Out the Vote: An Experiment in the Stimulation of Voting* (Chicago: University of Chicago Press, 1927).

4. Significantly enough, Gosnell did interview citizens in several election districts who received notices. However, he apparently did not focus the interviews in such fashion as to enable him to determine the significant phases of the total stimulus pattern; see his summary remark that "interviews . . . brought out the fact that [the notices] had been read with interest and that they had aroused considerable curiosity." And note his speculation that "part of the effect [of the mail canvass] may have been due to the novelty of the appeal" (*op. cit.*, pp. 29, 71). Properly oriented focused interviews would have enabled him to detect the points of "interest," the ineffectual aspects of the notices, and differences in response of different types of citizens.

5. The same problem arises in a more complicated and difficult form when the experimental situation is not a limited event but an elaborate complex of experiences. Thus Chapin studied the gains in social participation which can be attributed "to the effects of living in the [public] housing project." As he recognized, "improved housing" is an unanalyzed "experimental" situation: managerial policies, increased leisure, architectural provision for group meetings, and a host of other items are varying elements of the program of "improved housing" (see F. S. Chapin, "An Experiment on the Social Effects of Good Housing," *American Sociological Review*, V [1940], 868-79).

6. Solomon P. Rosenthal, "Change of Socioeconomic Attitudes under Radical Motion Picture Propaganda," *Archives of Psychology*, No. 166, 1934.

7. Paul F. Lazarsfeld and Robert K. Merton, "Studies in Radio and Film Propaganda," *Transactions of the New York Academy of Sciences, Series II*, VI (1943), 58-79; Robert K. Merton and Patricia Kendall, "The Boomerang Effect—Problems of the Health and Welfare Publicist," *Channels* (National Publicity Council), Vol. XXI (1944); and Paul F. Lazarsfeld and Patricia Kendall, "The Listener Talks Back," in *Radio in Health Education* (prepared under the auspices of the New York Academy of Medicine) (New York: Columbia University Press, 1945).

8. Ruth C. Peterson and L. L. Thurstone, *Motion Pictures and the Social Attitudes of Children* (New York: Macmillan Co., 1933).

9. On the problems of *post factum* interpretations see R. K. Merton, "Sociological Theory," *American Journal of Sociology*, L (1945), esp. 467-69.

10. *Op. cit.*, pp. 60, 64, 65, 67.

11. B. Zeigarnik, "Das Behalten erledigter und unerledigter Handlungen," *Psychologische Forschung*, IX (1927), 1-85.

12. Saul Rosenzweig, "The Experimental Study of Repression," in H. A. Murray, *Exploration in Personality* (Oxford University Press, 1938), pp. 472-90.

13. See the survey by David Rapaport, *Emotions and Memory* (Baltimore: Williams & Wilkins Co., 1942).

14. A mechanical device, the Lazarsfeld-Stanton Program Analyzer, has been developed to serve much the same purpose with certain kinds of test materials (for a detailed description of the Analyzer and its operation see Tore Hallonquist and Edward A. Suchman, "Listening to the Listener," in Lazarsfeld and Stanton [eds.], *op. cit.*).

15. F. J. Roethlisberger and W. J. Dickson, *Management and the Worker* (Cambridge: Harvard University Press, 1938), pp. 276-78.

16. Carl Rogers, *Counseling and Psychotherapy*, and "The Non-directive Method for Social Research," *American Journal of Sociology*, L (1945), 179-83.

Toward a Philosophy of the Social Sciences

1. A PARADIGM FOR THE STUDY OF

THE SOCIOLOGY OF KNOWLEDGE

by Robert K. Merton

1. Nothing will be said of this prehistory in this paper. Ernst Gruenwald provides a sketch of the early developments, at least from the so-called era of Enlightenment in *Das Problem der Soziologie des Wissens*, (Wien-Leipzig: Wilhelm Braumueller, 1934). For a recent survey, see H. Otto Dahlke, "The Sociology of Knowledge," H. E. Barnes, Howard and F. B. Becker, eds., *Contemporary Social Theory*, (New York: Appleton-Century, 1940), pp. 64-89.

2. See Karl Mannheim, *Ideology and Utopia*, (New York: Harcourt, Brace, 1936), pp. 5-12; 45; P. A. Sorokin, *Social and Cultural Dynamics*, (New York: American Book Co., 1937), II, pp. 412-413.

3. Freud had observed this tendency to seek out the "origins" rather than to test the validity of statements which seem palpably absurd to us. Thus, suppose someone maintains that the center of the earth is made of jam. "The result of our intellectual objection will be a *diversion of our interests; instead of their being directed on to the investigation itself*, as to whether the interior of the earth is really made of jam or not, *we shall wonder what kind of man it must be who can get such an idea into his head. . . .*" Sigmund Freud, *New Introductory Lectures*, (New York: W. W. Norton, 1933), p. 49. On the social level, a radical difference of outlook of various social groups leads not only to *ad hominem* attacks, but also to "functionalized explanations."

4. The concept of *pertinence* was assumed by the Marxist harbingers of *Wissenssozologie*. "The theoretical conclusions of the Communists are in no way based on ideas or principles that have been invented, or discovered, by this or that would-be universal reformer. *They merely express, in general terms, the actual relations* springing from an existing class struggle, from a historical movement going on under our very eyes. . . ." Karl Marx and Friedrich Engels, *The Communist Manifesto*, in *Karl Marx, Selected Works*, (Moscow: Cooperative Publishing Society, 1935), I, p. 219.

5. Karl Marx, *A Contribution to the Critique of Political Economy* (Chicago: C. H. Kerr, 1904), pp. 11-12.

6. Karl Marx *Capital* (Chicago: C. H. Kerr, 1906), I, p. 15; *cf.* Marx and Engels, *The German Ideology* (New York: International Publishers, 1939) p. 76; *cf.* Max Weber, *Gesammelte Aufsaetze zur Wissenschaftslehre* (Tuebingen: J. C. B. Mohr, 1922), p. 205.

7. Marx and Engels, *The Communist Manifesto*, in *Karl Marx, Selected Works*, I, p. 216.

8. Karl Marx, *Der Achtzehnte Brumaire des Louis Bonaparte* (Hamburg: 1885), p. 36 (italics inserted).

9. Karl Mannheim, *Ideology and Utopia* (New York: Harcourt Brace, 1936), pp. 247-8. In view of the recent extensive discussions of Mannheim's work, it will not be treated at length in this essay. For the writer's appraisal, see R. K. Merton, "Karl Mannheim and the Sociology of Knowledge," Chapter IX of *Social Theory and Social Structure*, (Glencoe, Ill.: The Free Press, 1949).

10. Emile Durkheim and Marcel Mauss, "De quelques formes primitives de classification," *L'Annee Sociologique*, 6: 1-72, 1901-02. ". . . even ideas as abstract as those of time and space are, at each moment of their history, in close relation with the corresponding social organization." As Marcel Granet has indicated, this paper contains some pages on Chinese thought which have been held by specialists to mark a new era in the field of sinological studies.

11. Emile Durkheim, *The Elementary Forms of the Religious Life* (Glencoe: The Free Press, 1947), pp. 443-4; see also Hans Kelsen, *Society and Nature* (University of Chicago Press, 1943), p. 30.

12. Marcel Granet, *La pensee chinoise* (Paris: La Renaissance du Livre, 1934), *e.g.* pp. 84-104.

13. *Cf.* Merton, *op. cit.*, 133-135, Kurt H. Wolff, "The Sociology of Knowledge: Emphasis on an Empirical Attitude," *Philosophy of Science*, 10: 104-123, 1943; Talcott Parsons, "The Role of Ideas in Social Action," *Essays in Sociological Theory*. Chapter VI.

14. Max Scheler, "Probleme einer Soziologie des Wissens," *Die Wissensformen und die Gesellschaft* (Leipzig: Der Neve-Geist Verlag, 1926), pp. 59-61.

15. *Ibid.*, p. 62.

16. *Ibid.*, p. 55.

17. See the same assumption of Durkheim, cited in fn. 11 of this paper.

18. Scheler, *Die Wissensformen . . .*, pp. 22-23; compare a similar characterization of "sacred schools" of thought by Florian Znaniecki, *The Social Role of the Man of Knowledge* (New York: Columbia University Press, 1940), Chap. 3.

19. Durkheim, *Elementary Forms . . .*, 12, 18, 439.

20. *Ibid.*, pp. 433-435.

21. *Ibid.*, p. 438.

22. *Ibid.*, pp. 444-445; 437.

23. Sorokin, *Social and Cultural Dynamics*, I, p. 36; *cf.* II, pp. 11-12n.

24. *Ibid.*, IV, Chap. 16, *Sociocultural Causality . . .*, Chap. 5.

25. *Sociocultural Causality . . .*, pp. 230-1n.

26. The distinctions between these have long been considered in European sociological thought. The most elaborate discussion in this country is that of Sorokin, *Social and Cultural Dynamics*, e.g. I, Chapters 1-2.

27. *Cf.* the comments of Hans Speier, "The Social Determination of Ideas," *Social Research*, 5: 182-205, 1938; C. Wright Mills, "Language, Logic and Culture," *American Sociological Review* 4: 670-680, 1939.

28. *Cf.* the formulation of Mannheim, *Ideology and Utopia*, pp. 175 ff; Georg Lu-

kács, *Geschichte und Klassenbewusstsein* (Berlin: 1923), pp. 61 ff; Arthur Child, "The Problem of Imputation in the Sociology of Knowledge," *Ethics*, 51: 200-219, 1941.

29. Marx and Engels, *The German Ideology*, p. 39. "In so far as they rule as a class and determine the extent and compass of an epoch, it is self-evident that they do this in their whole range, hence among other things rule also as thinkers, as producers of ideas, and regulate the production and distribution of the ideas of their age . . ."

30. Engels' letter to Mehring, 14 July 1893, in *Marx, Selected Works*, I, pp. 388-9; *cf.* Marx, *Der Achtzehnte Brumaire*, p. 33; *Critique of Political Economy*, p. 12.

31. Marx, *Der Achtzehnte Brumaire*, p. 39, where the democratic Montagnards indulge in self-deception.

32. Engels, *Socialism: Utopian and Scientific*, pp. 26-27. *Cf.* Engels, *Feuerbach*, pp. 122-23. "The failure to exterminate the Protestant heresy *corresponded* to the invincibility of the rising bourgeoisie. . . . Here Calvinism proved itself to be the true religious disguise of the interests of the bourgeoisie of that time. . . ."

33. Marx grants motivational significance to the "illusions" of the burgeoning bourgeoisie, *Der Achtzehnte Brumaire*, p. 8.

34. Engels, letter to Joseph Bloch, 21 September 1890, in *Marx, Selected Works*, I, p. 383.

35. Engels, letter to Mehring, 14 July 1893, *ibid.*, I, 390.

36. *Cf.* Max Weber, *Gesammelte Aufsaetze zur Wissenschaftslehre*, pp. 166-170.

37. This aspect of Mannheim's work cannot be treated in detail here; *cf.* Merton, "Karl Mannheim and the Sociology of Knowledge," *loc. cit.*, pp. 135-139; also Mills, "Language, Logic and Culture," *loc. cit.*

38. Durkheim, *Elementary Forms . . .*, pp. 11-12.

39. *Ibid.*, pp. 10-11.

40. *Ibid.*, p .148.

41. *Ibid.*, p. 440.

42. *Ibid.*, p. 56.

43. *Ibid.*, p. 25; *cf.* pp. 482-84.

44. Sorokin, *Social and Cultural Dynamics*, IV, Chap. 1: I, Chap. 1.

45. Despite the basic place of these statistics in his empirical findings, Sorokin adopts a curiously ambivalent attitude toward them, an attitude similar to the attitude toward experiment imputed to Newton: a device to make his prior conclusions "intelligible and to convince the vulgar."Note Sorokin's approval of Park's remark that his statistics are merely a concession to the prevailing sensate mentality and that "if they want 'em, let 'em have 'em." Sorokin, *Sociocultural Causality, Space, Time*, p. 95n. Sorokin's ambivalence arises from his effort to integrate quite disparate "systems of truth."

46. Sorokin, *Social and Cultural Dynamics*, II, p. 51.

47. *Ibid.*, II, p. 30.

48. The Rickert-Weber concept of "Wertbeziehung" (relevance to value) is but a first step in this direction; there remains the further task of differentiating the various sets of values and relating these to distinctive groups or strata within the society.

49. This is perhaps the most distinctive variation in the sociology of knowledge now developing in American sociological circles, and may almost be viewed as an American acculturation of European approaches. This development characteristically derives from the social psychology of G. H. Mead. Its pertinence in this connection is being indicated by C. W. Mills, Gerard de Gre and others. See Znaniecki's conception of the "social circle," *op. cit.*

2. A GENERAL FRAMEWORK FOR

THE STUDY OF LEADERSHIP

by Richard T. Morris and Melvin Seeman

1. This paper was co-operatively produced by the Ohio State Leadership Studies, whose staff includes, in addition to the authors: executive director, Carroll L. Shartle, Personnel Research Board; associate directors, Alvin E. Coons, department of economics, and Ralph M. Stogdill, department of psychology; research associate, John K. Hemphill, department of psychology; research consultant, Donald T. Campbell, department of psychology; research assistant, Charles M. Westie, department of sociology.

2. Ralph M. Stogdill, "Personal Factors Associated with Leadership: A Survey of the Literature," *Journal of Psychology*, XXV (1948), 37-71.

3. The number of each of the ten questions in this section corresponds to a number in the chart. Thus, "I. *Who is the leader?*" corresponds to box 1 in the chart, "Definition of the Leader."

4. Ralph M. Stogdill and Carroll L. Shartle have described some of the methods already developed for this type of analysis; *cf.* their "Methods for Determining Patterns of Leadership Behavior in Relation to Organization Structure and Objectives," *Journal of Applied Psychology*, XXXII (1948), 286-91; and Shartle, "Leadership and Executive Performance," *Personnel*, XXV (1949), 370-80.

5. A mimeographed staff report on this instrument indicates that the original one hundred and fifty items, classified into nine categories of leader behavior (including domination, organization, initiation, etc.) can be reduced by factor analysis to three major components: goal-attainment behavior, maintenance of membership character, and member-interaction facilitation.

6. "External situational factors" are listed in two places (*4M* and *5J*), though it would be possible to make a separate box for them. Reference here is made to such factors, external to the group or individual per se, as conditions of war, extreme heat, etc. They are included under group and individual factors on the assumption that their bearing on leader behavior is mediated through whatever effect they may have on these factors.

7. These findings are contained in a mimeographed staff report entitled "The Status Correlates of Leader Behavior."

8. John K. Hemphill, "Group Factors in Leadership. I: Relations between the Size of the Group and the Behavior of Superior Leaders," *Journal of Social Psychology* (forthcoming).

3. ON THE STATEMENT "THE WHOLE IS MORE THAN THE SUM OF ITS PARTS"

by Ernest Nagel

1. Bertrand Russell, *The Principles of Mathematics* (Cambridge: Cambridge University Press, 1903), p. 477.
2. An issue similar to the one raised by Russell has been raised in connection with the addition of velocities in relativity theory. Let A, B, C be three bodies, so that the velocity of A with respect to B is V_{AB}, that of B with respect to C is V_{BC} (where the direction of V_{BC} is parallel to the direction of V_{AB}), and of A with respect to C is V_{AC}. Then, according to classical mechanics, $V_{AC} = V_{AB} + V_{BC}$. But according to the special relativity theory,

$$V_{ac} = \frac{V_{ab} + V_{bc}}{1 + \frac{V_{ab} \cdot V_{bc}}{c^2}}$$

where c is the velocity of light. It has been argued that in the latter we are not "really adding" velocities. However, this objection can be disposed of in essentially the same manner as Russell's argument.
3. For an interesting sketch of a generalized formal analysis of Gestalts such as melodies, cf. Kurt Grelling and Paul Oppenheim, "Der Gestaltbegriff in Lichte der neuen Logik," *Erkenntnis*, 7:211-25 (1938).
4. Max Wertheimer, "Gestalt Theory," in Willis D. Ellis, *A Source Book of Gestalt Psychology* (New York: Harcourt Brace, 1950), p. 5.
5. J. S. Mill, *A System of Logic* (London, 1879), Bk. III, Chap. VI, Sec. 2, Vol. I, p. 432.

4. DEFINITION AND SPECIFICATION OF MEANING

by Abraham Kaplan

1. The material in this paper originated in the course of discussions with Prof. H. D. Lasswell.
2. *Philosophy of Science*, Vol. 3 (1936), pp. 419-471, and Vol. 4 (1937), pp. 1-40.
3. The problem of what makes it "the same concept" in all these cases will be considered below.
4. *The New Systematics*, ed. by J. S. Huxley, Oxford, 1940, p. 11.
5. J. S. Gilmour, "Taxonomy and Philosophy," *ibid.*, pp. 468-469. It is interesting that considerations of biological concepts led Bergson to criticize the application to them of what he called "static definitions," which "automatically settle" in any particular case questions of classification. The group, he urges, "must not be defined by the possession of certain characters, but by its tendency to emphasize them" (*Creative Evolution*, Chap. 2). The present considerations, however, do not rest on any special features either of the subject matter or of the concepts of biology. Equally striking examples could be found in other fields of inquiry.
6. The problem to be solved with regard to idealization is analogous to that for which, in the case of geometry, Whitehead developed his theory of extensive abstraction. The application of "ideal" points and lines to experiential objects is explicated in terms of properties of regions which are not themselves "ideal."
7. The term "weight" is used here in the sense of degree of confirmation; whether in a theory of specification it would be explicated in terms of statistical probability or of purely logical concepts would depend, presumably, on its explication as applied to confirmation of hypotheses. Reduction sentences, on this basis, would also be only special types of indicators, since the conditions they specify give the application of the term maximal weight. What is being suggested here, in short, is that indicators be formulated in terms of some type of probable implication.
8. Since reduction sentences correspond to maximal weights, they are complete when exhaustive. Hence bilateral reduction sentences, as exhaustive pairs are called, can be replaced by definitions if their initial condition is universally satisfied.
9. The situation is thus similar to that dealt with in Bayes' theorem, and might perhaps turn out to be explicable in those terms.
10. Something of this sort, perhaps, is intended by Kurt Lewin and others in speaking of "intermediate constructs." On the present account, all concepts are intermediate constructs; this involves a regress, but not a vicious one.
11. This is not to say, of course, that biology will never be able to do without the term, but only that its *present* functions do not allow for its elimination.
12. The question, for instance, whether "f equals m.a" is a definition of force or an empirical law of motion obviously makes no sense without further data as to its occurrence. What is suggested here is that the rational reconstruction of the language of science take account of its occurrence in both forms rather than choosing only the one or the other.
13. The term is Wittgenstein's; whether its present use is one intended by him is of course another question. Compare also William Empson's notion of a "body of meaning, continuous in several dimensions," as developed in his *Seven Types of Ambiguity*.

5. ON AXIOMATIC THEORIES IN SOCIOLOGY

by Hans Zetterberg

1. Cf., for example, C. West Churchman, *Elements of Logic and Formal Science*, Chicago, J. B. Lippincott Company, 1940, p. 134.
2. The choice of the term 'postulate' is perhaps an unfortunate one. It gives the idea that we are dealing with an assumption that does not have to be empirically tested. This, of course, is not the intention. 'Postulate' is here used in the same sense as we know it from Hull who, in his theory of learning, accounts for what he knows about learning in a limited number of hypotheses, the postulates. See Clark L. Hull, *Principles of Behavior*, New York, D. Appleton-Century Co., 1943.

3. Cf., however, a similar approach in Arnold M. Rose, "A Deductive Ideal-Type Method," *The American Journal of Sociology*, Vol. LVI (1950), pp. 35-42.

4. Emile Durkheim, *De la division du travail social*, Paris, Felic Alcan, 1893, (English edition available from The Free Press, Glencoe). It should perhaps be stressed that nothing in this chapter is intended as a review or criticism of this classical work.

5. Cf., for example, Alfred Tarski, *Introduction to Logic and to the Methodology of Deductive Sciences* (translated by Olaf Helmer), New York, Oxford University Press, 1941, pp. 130-132.

6. See pp. 16-17.

7. Clarence C. Schrag, Review of Talcott Parsons and Edward Shils (editors), *Toward a General Theory of Action*, Cambridge, Harvard University Press, 1951, in the *American Sociological Review*, Vol. XVII (1952), pp. 247-249. We believe that Parsons and his associates did once and for all settle the question (see p. 12). However, as a principle the point is well made in this quotation.

8. Morris R. Cohen and Ernest Nagel, *An Introduction to Logic and Scientific Method*, London, Routledge & Kegan Paul, 1934, pp. 230 ff.

9. About other aspects of ideal types in research, see, for example, Howard Becker, "Constructive Typology" in H. Elmer Barnes, Howard Becker, and Frances Becker (editors), *Contemporary Social Theory*, New York, D. Appleton-Century, 1940, pp. 17-46.

6. MALTHUS AND THE

THEORY OF POPULATION

by Kingsley Davis

1. T. R. Malthus, *An Essay on Population*, 2 vols. (London: J. M. Dent, Everyman's Library, 1914).

2. Rene Gonnard, *Histoire des Doctrines de la Population* (Paris: Nouvelle Librairie Nationale, 1923), p. 264.

3. Talcott Parsons, *Essays in Sociological Theory* (Glencoe, Illinois: Free Press, 1949), p. 18.

4. *Ibid.*, p. 19.

5. T. W. Hutchison, *The Significance and Basic Postulates of Economic Theory* (London: Macmillan, 1938), pp. 23-27.

6. *Ibid.*, p. 28.

7. Morris R. Cohen and Ernest Nagel, *An Introduction to Logic and Scientific Method* (New York: Harcourt, Brace, 1934), pp. 22, 207.

8. See Alfred J. Lotka, "Analyse demographique avec application particuliere a l'espece humaine," *Exposes de biometrie et de statistique biologique*, XII (Paris: Hermann, 1939); Robt. R. Kuczynski, *The Balance of Births and Deaths* (New York: Macmillan, 1928), *The Measurement of Population Growth* (New York: Oxford University Press, 1936), and *Fertility and Reproduction* (New York: Falcon Press, 1932); David Glass, *Population Policies and Movements in Europe* (Oxford: Clarendon Press, 1940), Appendix and the bibliography of Lotka's writings on p. 467; Louis I. Dublin, Alfred J. Lotka, and Mortimer Spiegelman, *Length of Life* (New York: Ronald Press, 1949), Chaps.

9, 12, 14-15. For a critique of the misconceived application of pure theory to empirical prediction, see John Hajnal, "The Analysis of Birth Statistics in the Light of the Recent International Recovery of the Birth-Rate," *Population Studies*, Vol. I (September 1947), pp. 137-164.

9. Hutchison, *op. cit.*, pp. 23-27.

10. This is a point brought out by Edwin Cannan, *Wealth* (London: King, 1928), p. 47.

11. James Bonar, *Malthus and his Work* (New York: Macmillan, 1924), pp. 90, 98.

12. Quoted by Harold Wright, *Population* (New York: Harcourt, Brace, 1923), p. 32.

13. In this matter it is surprising that Malthus makes no reference to William Bell, who, in his Dissertation (Cambridge: J. Bentham, 1761), maintained that the principal check to population increase lay in the demand for unnecessary luxuries.

14. See D. Ghosh, *Pressure of Population and Economic Efficiency in India* (New Delhi: Indian Council of World Affairs, 1946), Parts II-III. Kingsley Davis, *The Population of India and Pakistan* (Princeton: Princeton University Press, 1951), Chaps. 21-23; and "Population and the Further Spread of Industrial Society," *Proceedings of the American Philosophical Society*, Vol. 95, No. 1, February 1951.

15. By labeling as "vice" all other means than postponement of marriage, Malthus tacitly assumed that any use of these other means could not be due to the same motives that would prompt people to use "moral restraint." The main motive he speaks of is the desire to have few enough children to be able to support and rear them properly without endangering the family's position in the social scale. Since this is a "good" motive, it could not use "vice" as its means, so that the other preventive checks would have to be due to vicious motives.

16. Francis Place (1771-1854) was one of the first to inject the issue of birth control into the Malthusian debate. "It was in the course of arbitrating the Malthus-Godwin controversy that Place came to reject the Malthusian remedy of moral restraint . . . and to propose in its stead the regulation of population and of the size of the family by the employment of contraceptive measures. The doctrine, which he was not the first to suggest, but of which he became the first systematic expositor, was to initiate what has since become perhaps the most significant social reform movement of modern times." His *Illustrations and Proofs of the Principle of Population* appeared in 1822. Edited by Norman Himes, it was reprinted in 1930 (London: Allen and Unwin). The introduction by Himes, pp. 7-63, is extremely instructive, as is also his Appendix A, "Note on Malthus' Attitude Toward Birth Control," pp. 283-298.

7. PSYCHO-CULTURAL HYPOTHESES

ABOUT POLITICAL ACTS

by Nathan Leites

1. [Even today the great body of literature on national character traits is largely impressionistic. What distinguishes the analyses with

which Mr. Leites is concerned from the works of say W. Dibelius or P.Cohen-Portheim on English national character is the statement of "psychological regularities in large groups" on the basis of observations systematically made and recorded by trained social scientists. Behavioral regularities in the membership of national groups are obviously of prime significance for the study of world politics.—Editor of *World Politics*.]

2. Heinz Hartmann and Ernest Kris, "The Genetic Approach in Psychoanalysis," *The Psychoanalytic Study of the Child*, New York, 1945, I, 11.

3. This is obviously an incomplete hypothesis. Clearly it is not always true (see below), and clearly it is sometimes true. (Hence, stated without qualifications, it is false.) The question is: Under what particular conditions are adults apt to continue (in a way) certain early patterns? This is the type of question which is now beginning to become central (cf. footnote 2 below). The same considerations are applicable to the further types of psycho-cultural hypotheses to be mentioned below.

4. Clyde and Florence R. Kluckhohn, "American Culture: Generalized Orientations and Class Patterns," *Conference of Philosophy, Science and Religion*, New York, 1946, pp. 106-28.

5. This point was also conveyed by Margaret Mead, *And Keep Your Powder Dry*, New York, 1943.

6. *Rumanian Culture and Behavior*, New York, 1943, p. 54. Distributed by the Institute for Intercultural Studies.

7. Cf. Paul Kecskemeti and Nathan Leites, "Some Psychological Hypotheses on Nazi Germany," *Journal of Social Psychology*, XXVI (1947), 143.

8. Propositions about national differences are of course subject to the suspicion of being derivatives from "stereotypes" which in their turn may be connected with "nationalist" reactions.

9. I am not referring to affirmations about a single cause. Cf. points (4) and (5) below.

10. Geoffrey Gorer, "Themes in Japanese Culture," *Transactions of the New York Academy of Sciences*, New York, 1943, V, 106-24.

11. Ruth Benedict, *The Chrysanthemum and the Sword: Patterns of Japanese Culture*, Boston, 1946.

12. *Ibid.*, p. 292.

13. Frequently, similar cultural results are produced by various combinations of various factors.

14. Most disagreements about "degrees of importance" of various factors are at present undecidable in this research area, as the term "degree of importance" itself usually does not receive a sufficiently precise definition.

15. This point has been formulated with particular clarity and force by Harold D. Lasswell, *The Analysis of Political Behavior: An Empirical Approach*, London, 1948, pp. 195-234.

16. Cf. Harold D. Lasswell, *Psychopathology and Politics*, Chicago, 1930.

17. Psycho-cultural analysis in the late 1930's and 1940's has largely taken child training patterns as given, and focussed on the investigation of their consequences. It is to be expected that the 1950's will drop this limitation, and attempt to develop a richer set of prop-

ositions about culture change (including zero change).

18. This is not a logically circular, but factual "feedback" system. Cf. Gregory Bateson, "Morale and National Character," in Goodwin Watson, ed., *Civilian Morale*, Boston, 1942, pp. 71-91.

19. Ruth Benedict, *The Chrysanthemum and the Sword*, p. 260. This leads to the further question: What factors have determined the choice of such a fragile house structure? Presumably they were not all "environmental." Little systematic speculation (and less research) has as yet been done on questions of this kind, as implied in footnote 17, above.

20. Bateson, *loc. cit.*

21. Margaret Mead, *op. cit.*, and in "The Application of Anthropological Techniques to Cross-National Communication." *Transactions of the New York Academy of Sciences*, Series II, IX (1947), No. 4, pp. 133-52.

22. Margaret Mead, "The Application of Anthropological Techniques to Cross-National Communication," pp. 136-138. In the American case, there is adult continuation of certain childhood behavior patterns; in the British, an assumption of the adult role which one had first perceived (but not adopted) in childhood. What are the conditions making for invariance in the one case, and change in the other? (That is, what are the conditions making for the choice of different "psychological mechanisms"?) Psycho-dynamics and psycho-cultural analysis have during the last fifteen years enriched our inventory of "solutions" which human beings find in given situations. The 1950's will presumably more systematically attempt to enrich knowledge about the conditions fostering or hampering the adoption of any given solution.

23. Cf. Clyde Kluckhohn and William H. Kelly, "The Concept of Culture," in Ralph Linton, ed., *The Science of Man in the World Crisis*, New York, 1946, pp. 87-88.

24. When a probably inexpedient term like "national character" is used by the researchers here discussed, it carries no connotations of national biological peculiarities. Thus Geoffrey Gorer, *loc. cit.* states: ". . . I have assumed . . . that the genetic peculiarities of the Japanese do not involve any . . . psychological differences from other groups of human beings."

25. Cf. Clyde Kluckhohn and William H. Kelly, *loc. cit.*

26. It is highly likely that such differences "cog into each other," e.g., that each "promotes" the other. That is, it is unlikely that they are "mutually irrelevant." Cf. Bateson, *loc. cit.*

27. Ruth Benedict, "The Study of Cultural Patterns in European Nations," *Transactions of the New York Academy of Sciences*, Series II, VIII (1946), No. 8, pp. 274-79.

28. *Ibid.*, pp. 277-78. Presumably the position of a culture on this variable has politically relevant consequences, e.g., as to reactions to politically induced property loss. A somewhat fuller explanation of the political impact of, e.g., the agrarian changes in Rumania after the first war may be thus obtained.

29. A complete and systematic typology would presumably be isomorphic with one of relationships established in dynamic psychology.

30. *The American People: A Study in National Character*, New York, 1948, pp. 133-134.

590

31. Cf. Talcott Parsons, "Certain Primary Sources and Patterns of Aggression in the Social Structure of the Western World," *Psychiatry*, X (1947), No. 2, 167-82.

32. Geoffrey Gorer, *Burmese Personality*, New York, 1945. Distributed by the Institute for Intercultural Studies.

33. *Ibid.*, quoting Sir James G. Scott, p. 42.

34. Geoffrey Gorer, *The American People*, p. 133.

35. I am now adding some specific hypotheses about the interrelations between Burmese childhood and adulthood to Mr. Gorer's points.

36. "Hitler's Imagery and German Youth," *Psychiatry*, V (1942), No. 4, 475-93.

37. "The Historical and Cultural Roots of Anti-Semitism," in *Psychoanalysis and the Social Sciences*, Geza Roheim, ed., New York, 1947, pp. 313-56.

38. Hartmann and Kris, *loc. cit.*

39. "Themes in Japanese Culture," *Transactions of the New York Academy of Sciences*, New York, 1943, V, 106-24.

40. *The Chrysanthemum and the Sword*, *loc. cit.*

41. Cf. Bateson's, *loc. cit.*, formulation: "We shall not describe varieties of character . . . in terms of . . . [their] position on a continuum between extreme dominance and extreme submissiveness, but we shall instead try to use . . . some such continua as 'degree of interest in . . . dominance-submission.'"